Money and Beauty

Bankers, Botticelli and the Bonfire of the Vanities

edited by
Ludovica Sebregondi
and *Tim Parks*

gamm
GIUNTI

Fondazione
Palazzo
Strozzi

Under the High Patronage
of the President of the Italian
Republic

Money and Beauty.
Bankers, Botticelli and the Bonfire of the Vanities
Florence, Palazzo Strozzi
17 September 2011
22 January 2012

With the sponsorship of
Ministero per i Beni e le Attività Culturali

Promoted and organised by

FONDAZIONE PALAZZO STROZZI

MINISTERO PER I BENI E LE ATTIVITÀ CULTURALI

SSPSAE PMCF

with

COMUNE DI FIRENZE

PROVINCIA DI FIRENZE

Camera di Commercio Firenze

APPS Associazione Partners Palazzo Strozzi

and

REGIONE TOSCANA

From an idea of
James M. Bradburne

Curated by
Ludovica Sebregondi
Tim Parks

Historical consultant
Franco Franceschi

Scholarly advisory board
Cristina Acidini
Alessandro Cecchi
Dora Liscia Bemporad
Franco Franceschi
Robert Mundell
Beatrice Paolozzi Strozzi
Jacob Rothschild
Gerhard Wolf

Exhibition realised by
Fondazione Palazzo Strozzi

Installation design
Luigi Cupellini
with the collaboration of
Carlo Pellegrini

Graphic design for communication and exhibition
RovaiWeber design

Exhibition installation
Galli Allestimenti
Atlas e Livelux Light Designers
Stampa in Stampa
Alessandro Terzo
Franco Bianchi

Accompanying texts in the exhibition
Ludovica Sebregondi
Tim Parks

Translation of accompanying texts
Konrad Eisenbichler
Manuela Faimali
Xue Cheng
Mila Alieva

Communication and promotion
Susanna Holm
Sigma CSC

Press office
Antonella Fiori
(national press)
Sue Bond Public Relation
(international press)

Website
Netribe

Interactive game "Follow Your Florins"
From an idea of
James Bradburne
Illustrations
Giuseppe Palumbo
Game development and texts
Tim Parks
Multimedia applications
Netribe
Onde
Technologies coordination
Matteo Lotti Margotti
Technologies
Datalogic
Cosmos Network
Research
Benedetta Scarpelli

Family itinerary
Texts
James M. Bradburne
Translation
Lara Fantoni
Illustrations
Elisabet Ribera-RovaiWeber design

Programming for families, youth and adults
Fondazione Palazzo Strozzi

Groups and schools programs
Sigma CSC

Exhibition reservation office
Sigma CSC

Exhibition and ticketing personnel
TML Service

Ticketing
Vivaticket by Charta

Audio guides
START

Main Sponsor

BANCA CR FIRENZE

Sponsor

eni cultura dell'energia energia della cultura

FERROVIE DELLO STATO ITALIANE · FIRENZE CONTAGIOSA BELLEZZA FIRENZETURISMO.IT · ataf · AdF Aeroporto di Firenze · SAT Aeroporto Galileo Galilei Pisa · coop UNICOOP FIRENZE · FIRENZE PARCHEGGI

State Indemnity
Ministero per i Beni e le Attività Culturali
Direzione Generale per la valorizzazione del patrimonio culturale
Mario Resca
Servizio I - Valorizzazione del patrimonio culturale, programmazione e bilancio
Manuel Roberto Guido
Ufficio Garanzia di Stato
Antonio Piscitelli
Marcello Tagliente
Angelina Travaglini
Istituto Superiore per la Conservazione ed il Restauro
Marìca Mercalli
Gabriella Prisco
Maria Concetta Laurenti
Ministero dell'Economia e delle Finanze
Dipartimento Ragioneria dello Stato, Ispettorato Generale del Bilancio - Ufficio XI
Rosario Stella
Collaboratori
Sebastiano Verdesca
Paola Pollastri

Insurance
AON Artscope
Lloyd's

Transportation
Arterìa

Preventive conservation and climate control
Opificio delle Pietre Dure, Preventive conservation and climate control department
Roberto Boddi, Director
Sandra Cassi, Assistant
Inspection of the conservational status of the works and State Indemnity
Opificio delle Pietre Dure
Easel painting department
Marco Ciatti, Director
Chiara Rossi Scarzanella, Technical Director
Condition reports
Francesca Ciani Passeri, Luisa Gusmeroli, Alessandra Ramat, Isabella Sicoli
Bronze and metal department
Maria Donata Mazzoni, Director
Condition reports
Stefania Agnoletti, Annalena Brini

Head of security
Ulderigo Frusi

Electrical systems assistance and maintenance
Simone Bagnoli

Alarm systems assistance and maintenance
Professional Security srl

Conditioning systems assistance and maintenance
R.S. di Rossi Sergio & C. srl

Lenders
Antwerp, MAS - Museum Aan de Stroom
Arezzo, Soprintendenza BAPSAE di Arezzo - Museo Statale d'arte Medievale e Moderna
Bruges, Musea Brugge, Groeningemuseum
Empoli, Museo della Collegiata di Sant'Andrea
Ferrara, Pinacoteca Nazionale
Florence, Archivio di Stato
Florence, Banca CR S.p.a.
Florence, Basilica di Santa Maria Novella*
Florence, Biblioteca Medicea Laurenziana
Florence, Biblioteca Nazionale Centrale
Florence, Biblioteca Riccardiana
Florence, Galleria e Museo di Palazzo Mozzi Bardini
Florence, Collezione Liana e Carlo Carnevali
Florence, Gabinetto Disegni e Stampe degli Uffizi
Florence, Galleria degli Uffizi
Florence, Galleria dell'Accademia
Florence, Galleria e Museo di Palazzo Mozzi Bardini
Florence, MUDI - Museo degli Innocenti
Florence, Museo Archeologico Nazionale
Florence, Museo dell'Opera di Santa Croce*
Florence, Museo di Palazzo Davanzati
Florence, Museo di San Marco
Florence, Museo Nazionale del Bargello
Florence, Collezione Mario e Luigi Bellini
Florence, Museo Stibbert
Florence, Palazzo Pitti, Galleria Palatina
Florence, Palazzo Pitti, Museo degli Argenti
Florence, Provincia di Firenze
Florence, Soprintendenza per i Beni Archeologici della Toscana
Florence, Soprintendenza PSAE e per il Polo Museale della città di Firenze
Florence, Università degli Studi di Firenze
Forlì, Pinacoteca civica, Musei San Domenico
London, The National Gallery
London, Victoria and Albert Museum
Lucca, Museo Nazionale di Villa Guinigi
Milan, Museo Poldi Pezzoli
Nuremberg, Germanisches Nationalmuseum
Paris, Bibliothèque nationale de France
Perugia, Galleria Nazionale dell'Umbria
Prato, Diocesi di Prato - Musei Diocesani
Prato, Fondazione Casa Pia dei Ceppi
Prato, Ministero per i Beni e le Attività Culturali - Archivio di Stato
Prato, Museo del Tessuto, Collezione Comune - Cariprato
St. Bonaventure, NY, St. Bonaventure University, The Regina A. Quick Center for the Arts
Rome, Biblioteca Casanatense
Rotterdam, Museum Boijmans Van Beuningen
Turin, Galleria Sabauda
Vatican City, Musei Vaticani
Venice, Fondazione Musei Civici di Venezia, Museo Correr
*Fondo Edifici di Culto, Ministero dell'Interno - Dipartimento per le Libertà Civili e l'Immigrazione - Direzione Centrale per l'Amministrazione del Fondo Edifici di Culto

We are also grateful to the private lenders.

Restorations
Coo.be.c., Spoleto, Perugia (cat. no. 8.13)
Lucia Biondi, Florence with the collaboration of Roberto Buda and Maurizio Spatafora (cat. no. 1.13); with the collaboration of Federica Corsini (cat. no. 5.5)
Marisa Caparra, Bologna (cat. no. 7.24, frame)
Rossella Lari, Florence (cat. no. 6.8)
Simone Martini, Florence (cat. no. 4.7)
Restauri Dipinti Studio 4 s.r.l., Florence (cat. no. 7.10, reflectography IR)
Lisa Venerosi Pesciolini and Luca Romanelli, Florence (cat. no. 4.13)
Laboratorio di restauro Lisa Venerosi Pesciolini with Iolanda Larenza, Florence (cat. no. 2.2)
Silvia Verdianelli, Pelago, Florence (cat. no. 6.10)

Acknowledgements
This initiative has been made possible by the contribution of countless people, whom the Fondazione Palazzo Strozzi, the Scholarly advisory board and the curators would like to thank. We are especially grateful to the museum directors, public and private lenders, and all those who have personally been involved in the loans of the works on display.
Tim Parks offers his warmest thanks to James Bradburne whose constant encouragement made everything possible.
Ludovica Sebregondi is especially grateful to Vanna Arrighi, Giacomo Bei, Giuseppe Biscione, don Ulisse Bresciani, Elena Capretti, Stefano Casciu, Viola Cattaneo, Domenico De Martino, Maria Raffaella De Gramatica, Konrad Eisenbichler, Stefano Filipponi, Federico Fiorentini, Fabrizio Lanza Tomasi, Piero Marchi, Piero Mioli, Giuliana Montanari, Elisabetta Nardinocchi, Claudio Paolini, Gabriele Rossi Rognoni, Mario Ruffini, Stephen Tobin, Andrea Vanni Desideri, Lisa Venerosi Pesciolini, Giulia Zanasi. Thanks to all friends, colleagues and collaborators of the Fondazione Palazzo Strozzi, for having contributed to the preparation of the exhibition, which was both careful and meticulous, and only realised thanks to their professional support. The curators would like to thank Casa Editrice Giunti, especially Claudio Pescio and Ilaria Ferraris, Sara Draghi and Stefano Rovai, for the elegant design of the exhibition catalogue.
Thanks to Franco Franceschi who follow the development of the exhibition with invaluable advice, suggestion and factual correction, with the attention of a scholar and the flexibility of a friend.
An affectionate and heartfelt thanks to Luigi Cupellini for having know how to translate the concept of money and beauty into built form, with his usual intelligent narrative sensibility which reveals itself room after room.

Special thanks to Miel de Botton and to Walter and Lucille Rubin.

We are also grateful to Wanni di Filippo - Il Bisonte for the suitcase for the family activities "*The Banker's Change Purse*"; Lorenzo Villoresi for the perfumes in the "*The Banker's Change Purse*"; Arrigo Berni, Maria Sebregondi and Roberto Di Puma for the Moleskine notebooks; Niccolò Manetti for the alimentary gold; Datalogic for the interactive technology in the exhibition; Paolo Penko for the Florins; Francesca D'Anselmo, Giulia Giuffrida and Ilaria Del Giudice of Saatchi & Saatchi Rome for the "*Eyes wide open*" campaign; Andrea Falcone and Floor Robert for the Kamishibai.

SAATCHI & SAATCHI

Warm thanks to Querciabella for the generous contribution.

Querciabella

We also would like to thank Save the Queen for the uniforms of the Palazzo Strozzi Staff.

Catalogue
Giunti Editore

Edited by
Ludovica Sebregondi
Tim Parks

Editorial manager
Claudio Pescio

Editor
Ilaria Ferraris

Contribution by
Cristina Acidini, Lorella Alderighi, Vanna Arrighi, Giuseppe Biscione, Mirella Branca, Elena Capretti, Michele Cassandro, Benedetta Chiesi, Ilaria Ciseri, Stefano Dall'Aglio, Andrea Di Lorenzo, Simona Di Marco, Willy Durinx, Franco Franceschi, Geert Geysen, Francesco Guidi Bruscoli, Nicole Hegener, Philine Helas, Giovanna Lazzi, Dora Liscia Bemporad, Maria Pia Mannini, Marino Marini, Chiara Marcheschi, Donatella Mascalchi, Silvia Mascalchi, Eleonora Mazzocchi, Lorenza Melli, Beatrice Paolozzi Strozzi, Daniela Parenti, Tim Parks, Francesca Petrucci, Nicoletta Pons, Luciana Prati, Ludovica Sebregondi, Romano Silva, Sergio Tognetti

Design
RovaiWeber Design

Editorial collaboration
Elena Capretti, Sara Draghi, Manuela Faimali

Translation
Catherine Frost

Iconographical research
Cristina Reggioli

Technical coordination
Alessio Conticini

Technical supervision of images
Nicola Dini

Lorenzo Bini Smaghi
Chairman Fondazione Palazzo Strozzi

Florence was not only the cradle of Western culture, it was also the birthplace of the modern financial system. Here in the various city states protected by the Tuscan hills, innovative merchants began to experiment with the techniques of wealth creation that have come to shape the modern world. The word risk is derived from a Tuscan term, *rischio*, which allowed bankers to name an amount to cover their costs that would not be defined as interest on a loan, which of course they could not exact from their fellow Christians without the taint of the sin of usury. The great Tuscan banking families—the Bardi, the Peruzzi, and of course later, the Medici, created lasting monuments to their financial ingenuity, not only by amassing vast fortunes, but by translating those fortunes into the works of art that have become a part of the world's cultural heritage.

Although the idea for the exhibition was originally proposed in the summer of 2006, just months after the birth of the Fondazione Palazzo Strozzi, the events of recent years, including the near collapse of the banking system in 2008—due in part to innovative and perhaps overly risky financial instruments—make an exhibition on the birth of banking and financial speculation particularly timely. *Money and Beauty. Bankers, Botticelli and the Bonfire of the Vanities* is an exceptional exhibition. It is not an exhibition about Botticelli, although the exhibition closes with several of his paintings and looks at Savonarola's influence on his work. It is something even more interesting, an exhibition about the birth of modern banking. Nor is this merely an historical exhibition, focused on Florence's past glories. The lack of understanding of how money is made and the rewards given to those who make it are as relevant today as they were in the days of Savonarola. The exhibition is also exceptional in having two clear, transparently declared curatorial voices—that of Tim Parks, the Booker-nominated English novelist and author of *Medici Money*, and that of Ludovica Sebregondi, one of Italy's leading specialists in Renaissance religious art and the author of the *Iconography of Girolamo Savonarola. 1495-1998*. Their voices take visitors through the exhibition like a Renaissance motet, sometimes in harmony, sometimes in counterpoint, sometimes striking a dissonant note when they differ in their interpretation of the same object.

In addition to all the professionals who helped bring *Money and Beauty* to Florence, the Fondazione Palazzo Strozzi would like to thank the public and private collections which generously loaned important works to the exhibition. Our thanks once again go to the Banca CR Firenze, the exhibition's main sponsor, who as always generously contributed to the Fondazione's projects. We would like to thank the Founders of the Fondazione Palazzo Strozzi; the Province of Florence, the City of Florence, the Florentine Chamber of Commerce, and the Association of Private Partners of the Palazzo Strozzi, on whom the Fondazione depends in so many ways. We would like to thank all the exhibition's public and private sponsors, including the Regione Toscana, all of whom strongly supported the exhibition from the outset. Finally we would like to thank the entire Fondazione Palazzo Strozzi team—its Board of Trustees, its International Advisory Board, its Director and its staff—for having worked so hard to create an exhibition celebrating the invention of the globalised economy we now all inhabit.

Aureliano Benedetti
President Banca CR Firenze

Latest in a long line of successful events, the Fondazione Palazzo Strozzi presents the exhibition *Money and Beauty. Bankers, Botticelli and the Bonfire of Vanities,* which will be open to the public from September 17th through to January 22nd. Once again a rare versatility of ideas and an unusual capacity to arouse public interest in cultural initiatives of the highest quality make this the kind of venture in which the Banca CR Firenze is proud to have taken part.

Through the masterpieces of Botticelli, Filippo Lippi, Fra Angelico and Antonio del Pollaiolo, the exhibition documents the rise of the first Florentine bankers at the dawn of the Renaissance and the meshing of their financial and political power with civil society; a splendid period of cultural exchange and commercial development that would be interrupted by the new climate of severity introduced by Savonarola's sermons. Reaching beyond the purely artistic, this exhibition displays Florence at the peak of its political and economic supremacy.

The Banca CR Firenze has always been strongly committed to promoting culture through its support for initiatives of broad and generous scope and events that attract visitors to Florence from all over Italy and the world.

In contributing once again to promoting and showcasing Florence, we hope that the city will maintain its role at the centre of international attention as a cultural model to be emulated the world over.

Cristina Acidini

Soprintendente per il Patrimonio Storico, Artistico ed Etnoantropologico e per il Polo Museale della città di Firenze and, ad interim, *of the Opificio delle Pietre Dure*

In representing the Florence Museums and the territorial protection of Florence's artistic heritage, it has been my great pleasure to follow every stage of the planning of this exhibition, within the Board of Administration of the Fondazione Palazzo Strozzi.

It is an exhibition that presents the Renaissance, in Florence and elsewhere, under an innovative profile. While in-depth studies on the complex relationships linking money to power, religion and culture belong to a specialized bibliography—dealing mainly with architecture, the arts, and book collecting—the communicational potential of a great exhibition has until now been denied them.

At last, through a group of exceptionally well-chosen masterpieces, the curators Ludovica Sebregondi and Tim Parks are offering visitors full immersion in the many-faceted scenario of 14th-15th-century Florence, where excellence reached unparalleled heights in a unique conjunction of circumstances: vast wealth acquired and spent, magnanimous public commissions, splendid private patronage, the flourishing of the arts and a wave of reform sweeping through Christianity.

The leading actors are well known: the names of Lorenzo the Magnificent, Girolamo Savonarola and Sandro Botticelli evoke images in dramatic chiaroscuro, where the glowing splendour of gold florins and brightly coloured paintings mingles with the ominous sparks of bonfires. But in this exhibition other players too emerge, other logics are revealed. And everything pertaining to money, from the mint to the Money Changers' Guild, from trading to banking, resumes its rightful place in the guild system that deeply permeated the society of the day.

From this journey backward in time we return not only enchanted and informed, but also provided with new critical tools, directly proposed by the past to help us interpret the present.

Contents

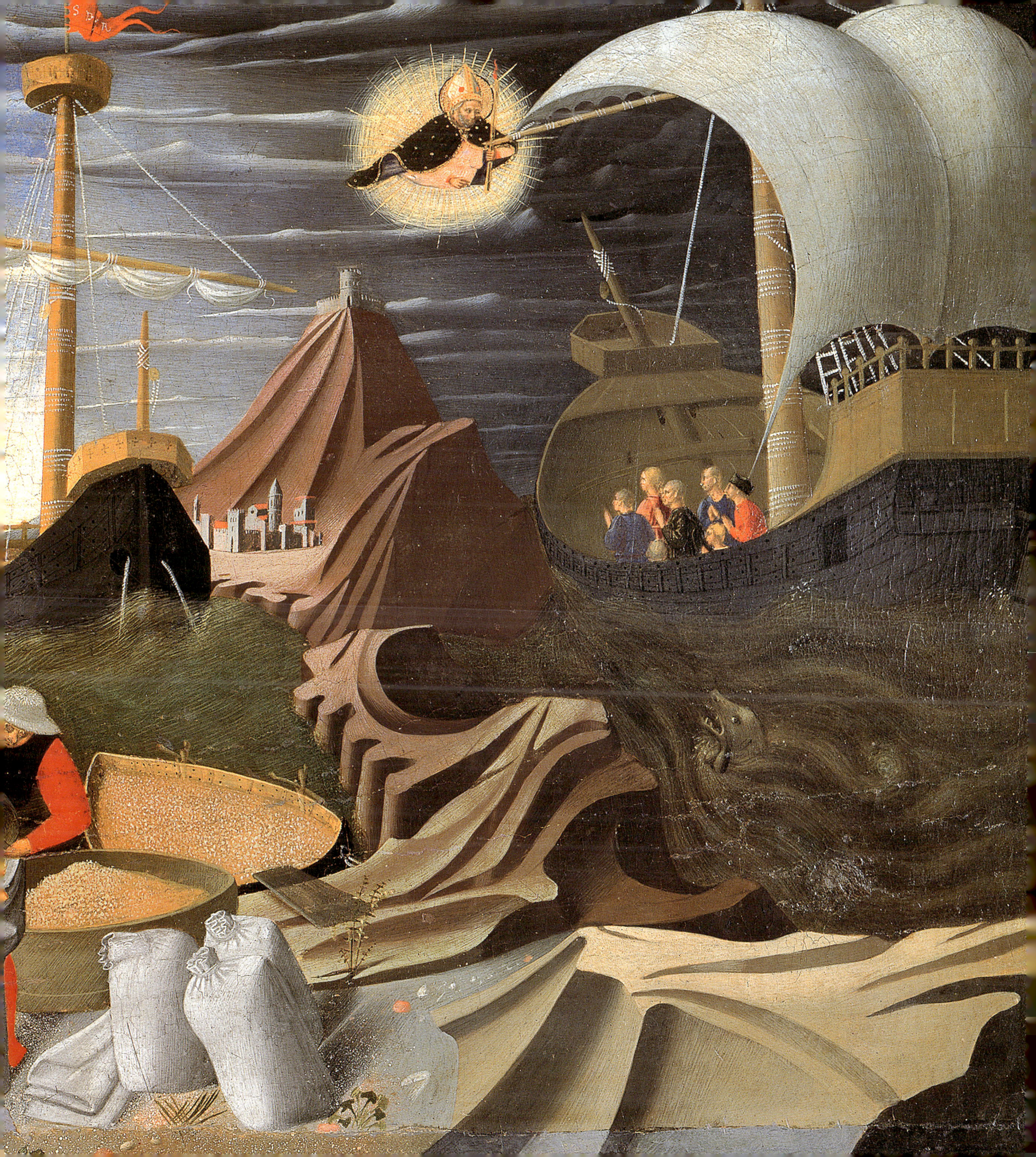

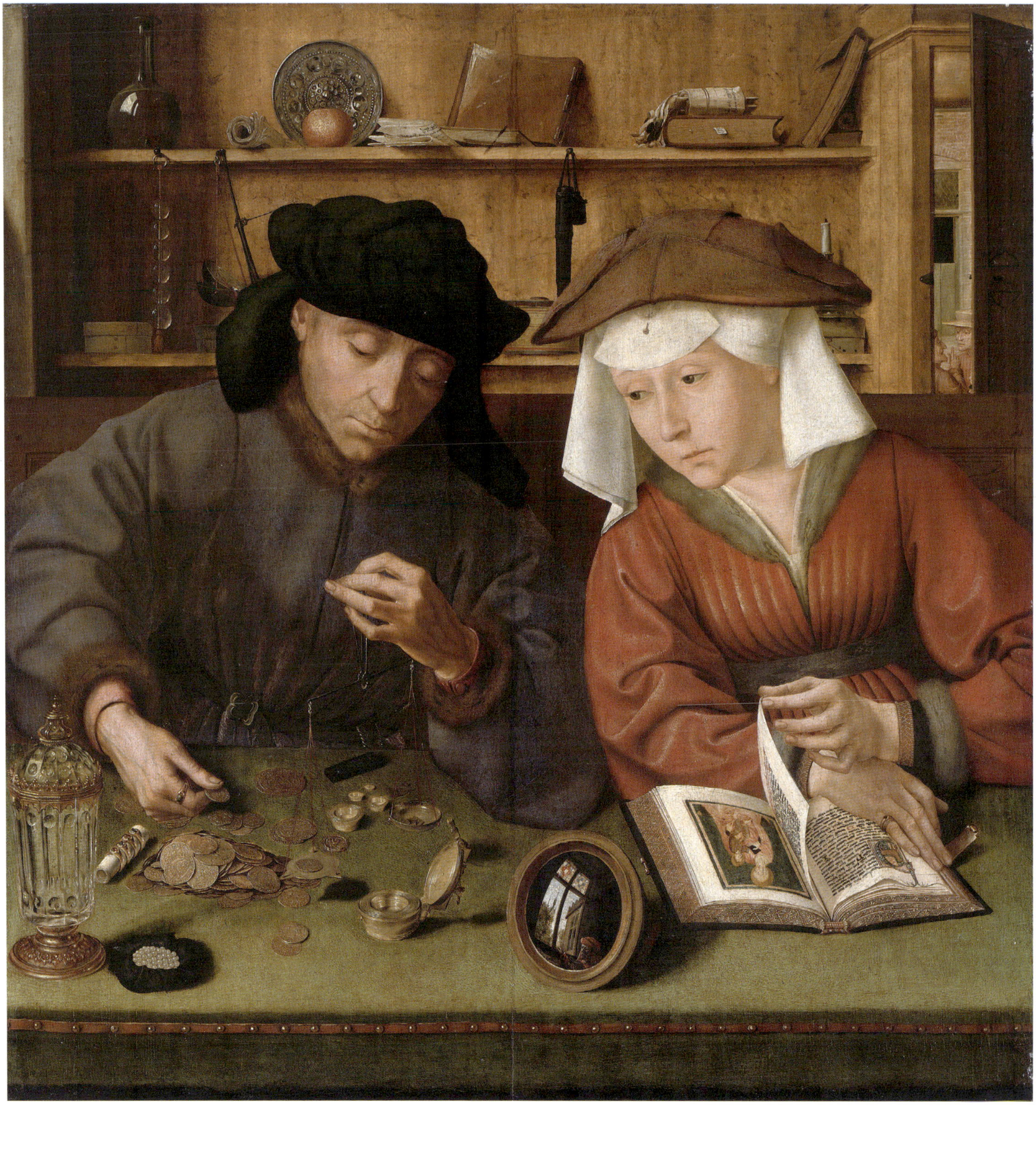

Ludovica Sebregondi

Money and Beauty, the Economy and Art: in Praise of Opposites

Opposites, perhaps, but not necessarily enemies, Money and Beauty are categories. Money, pertaining to having, takes concrete shape in coins. Beauty, a form of being, finds expression in a vast range of artistic creations. Apparently far apart, Money and Beauty are linked by invisible ties. An exhibition provides the ideal context for bringing them together, and Florence is the fitting place for illustrating that dualism; in the city's busy, fertile culture, the modern banking system and the Renaissance developed in parallel. Money and Beauty, economics and art.

Bruges presents many analogies. Both commerce and finance—dominated by foreign banks, mainly Italian—flourished within its walls; it became the birthplace of modern painting in its northern version. Tuscany and Flanders were not only great poles of economic renewal but also places where the urge to represent space in realistic detail took concrete shape, albeit in very different ways. The Flemish artists depicted reality empirically, with diffused light as the unifying element. In Italy, along with the search for verisimilitude, the revival of classical antiquity and the study of mathematical and scientific rules as guides to artistic vision were

1. Quentin Metsys
The Money Changer and his Wife
Paris, Musée du Louvre

fundamental. In this regard, a surprising relationship can be seen between the invention of perspective in painting and double-entry bookkeeping in accounting.[1]

The mercantile tradition had ancient, distant roots. In the 13th and early 14th centuries, goods and money were traded at the fairs held in Champagne. Since markets moved from one town to another, the operators travelled with them, setting up benches spread with luxurious carpets to display their wares. As seen in numerous paintings and woodcuts, the cloth-covered bench became a symbol of the merchant-bankers' activity. Moreover, the word *banco* (bench) is the origin of our modern term "bank," a word adopted in many languages. The term "bankrupt" comes from the custom of breaking the bench of an insolvent banker. Even today the terminology of the credit system—*Konto*, *Skonto*, *Giro* in German, for example (but not only German)—still has Italian roots.

Although many financial operators came from Genoa, Asti, Venice and Florence, the Italian bankers came to be known as *Lombards*, a term still recognizable today in *Lombardsatz* (interest rate), one of the words in which these historical roots live on.[2] But one word in particular reveals the importance of the Florentine commercial system, and that is *florin*, the gold coin symbol of the "City of the Flower," whose name eventually seduced all of Europe. How important this word was is shown by the numerous forms it took in the many languages that adopted it: *florin* in English, *Florin* in German, *florijn* in Dutch (until the introduction of the Euro) *forint* in Hungarian.

As banking developed and standardized, the Florentine banks established branch offices abroad, manned by personnel sent out from the mother company. Business was now done indoors, in a room dominated by a great counter—placed in full light as required by the laws protecting clients—and furnished with benches. The bank had now become an information centre, a meeting point for merchants, a workplace for employees, members of their families, accountants and apprentices sent out to distant lands in early adolescence. But little by little, the characteristic ring of coins flung onto the counter (with the ever-present precision balance to ensure they had not been "clipped") was supplanted by writing materials and sheets of paper for letters of exchange, correspondence, letters written in code (with a well-hidden deciphering system), ledgers, secret account books, and the abacus, ancestor of the computer, for calculating. Always at hand were treatises on arithmetic, useful for solving calculating problems, or texts on commerce, used to compute interest rates rapidly. Moreover, strongboxes, coffers, keys, padlocks, pockets and bags designed to enclose, lock, safeguard, transport, or conceal, were indispensable tools of the trade for operators in the fields of finance and commerce.[3]

The negative connotations of money were rooted in the distant past, and even Sophocles had declared, "There is nothing worse than money in human society." The same theme was reiterated, around 1230, in the *Carmina Burana*, Song 11, *Money is Lord of all*:

"Loved and sweet as honey, on earth today is only money.
Money loved by sovereigns, who seem in fact its minions,
Money loved by the devout, who fear being left without,
Money by priest praised higher, than even by the friar,
Money over monk prevails, likewise sister in her veils,
Money gives good counsel, to those sitting on the Council,
Money leads to peace, but war too if it please
Money brings to blows or pulls the rich down low,
Money in a trice can raise a beggar high."[4]

The negative view expressed by the Church ("you cannot serve God and mammon," Matthew, 6:24) led to the condemnation of the usurer who was guilty of selling the interval of time between the moment money was lent and the moment it was recovered with interest. But time is God's alone and selling it a heinous sin. However, as hard work and trade gradually built up large fortunes, wealth began to assume positive values, even in the eyes of some churchmen. Related to this rise of a mercantile social class, and as if in reaction to it, new forms of religious expression emerged, such as the mendicant orders, *in primis* the brotherhood founded by Francis, son of the wealthy Bernardone, who in the early 13th century took the Lady Poverty as his ideal.[5]

Negative views of money were extended to images of wealth (first in the Catholic world, later by the Lutherans, though not the Calvinists), since wealth was seen as bringing with it immorality, greed and degeneration. No such stigma attached, however, where wealth was transformed into Beauty, a quality entirely lacking in money as such. Jewellery, fine clothing and works of art, while displaying their owners' wealth, were not surrounded by the same aura of reprobation as money, whose provenance, being unclear, aroused some suspicion as to how it had been earned and what it had been used for. In 14th and 15th century Florence, there was a sharp rise in the demand for art for use in private homes, works commissioned by a mainly mercantile wealthy class that sought prestige through patronage of the arts in a society still open to upward mobility. Furniture, wall-hangings and precious objects, often bought for weddings and births, were kept in the master bedroom, sanctuary of devotional and secular images, beds of course, strongboxes, furnishings and painted trays.[6] Not only the most prominent families such as the Medici, but the entire mercantile world commissioned works of art; and in this way money broke free from its ties with sin and vulgarity.

It was within this context that towards the end of the century the city was shaken by a crisis precipitated by Savonarola. Invited to Florence by Lorenzo the Magnificent to take charge of the Convent of San Marco, this vehement friar and preacher, became his fiercest enemy, going so far as to brand Lorenzo a tyrant. Bent on reform that would ensure justice for all, Savonarola dreamed of a free city governed by the people, with all classes of citizens represented, as was the case in Venice. For public meetings, a Great Council Hall was built in Palazzo Vecchio, symbol of the "democratic" regime inspired by Savonarola; but to implement his vision of a city obedient to the will of God, total austerity was required, and Savonarola imposed the strictest of rules, which were rejected by some sectors of the population.

2. Marinus van Reymerswaele
Two Tax Collectors
c. 1540
London, The National Gallery

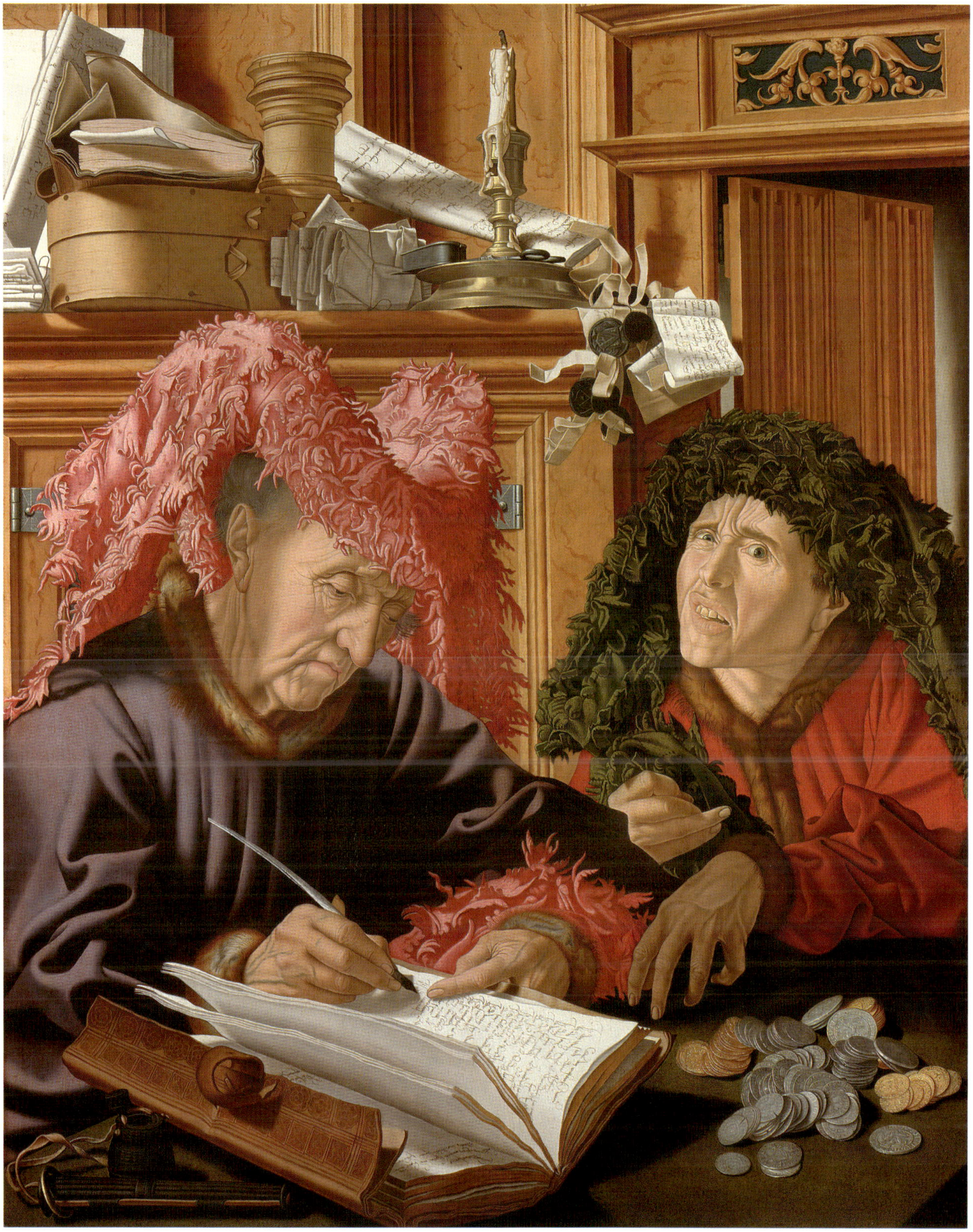

Florence's various factions formed two opposing camps. The Arrabbiati, members of the upper class who had been damaged by the new political system, the Palleschi or Bigi, that is the Medicean faction and the Compagnacci, opponents of Savonarola's moral reforms, all joined forces against the Frateschi or Piagnoni (literally, "moaners") as they were known because of their constant complaints over the depravity they saw around them. Savonarola's ideas were attractive to the lower classes in particular, but many others found his fanaticism intolerable. The Friar railed endlessly against Pope Alexander VI Borgia and his depraved customs. Excommunicated, he nevertheless continued to preach. Florence supported him at first, but when threatened with interdiction people began to worry not just about the religious implications (something that had not bothered them in the past) but also the political and above all economic repercussions, which they found alarming. During the second "bonfire of the vanities," on Carnival Tuesday of 1498, riots broke out, fomented by the Compagnacci.

The bonfires Savonarola instigated were nothing new. Books, paintings and other luxury items have been burned in this way from ancient times up to the present day, and not only by the Church. The destructive force of fire has always been projected onto enemies, and even more so onto the books that express their thinking.[7] Hence Fra Girolamo's initiative was part of a long tradition; but while the exploits of his forerunners (Bernardino da Siena, Giovanni da Capistrano and others) have been mostly forgotten, Savonarola's bonfires have led to his entire life's work being judged. Not that one doesn't regret the many works of art that were destroyed. Vasari reports that Savonarola's vehement sermons denouncing immoral images led Fra Bartolomeo—emulated by Lorenzo di Credi and others—to throw his drawings "of nudes" into the flames. However, opposition was growing; if some were ready to accept the wilful destruction of works of art, it was met with "dismay by many."

Obviously, this was only one of the issues behind the struggle, all the same, the attempt to moralize public life by force, dramatically manifested in the bonfires, took on a symbolism that led directly to clashes between opposing factions. Brewing beneath the surface was a malaise that would erupt in the following months, when the monastery of San Marco was attacked and Fra Girolamo led away to prison. On May 23, 1498, in the same public square where only the previous February the so-called "triumph" had been raised to burn the vanities, a scaffold was now erected where Savonarola and two of his followers were hanged and then burned. While the ambitions of the Piagnoni and the views of their adversaries were totally irreconcilable on the political and moral level, it must be acknowledged that both of these factions contributed significantly to the genesis of Florentine Renaissance culture.

1. Esch 2002, p. 23.

2. Stammerjohann, Seymer 2007, pp. 50–1.

3. Barlucchi 1997.

4. *Money is Lord of all*, Song 11, *Carmina Burana c.* 1230. Translated by Tim Parks.

5. Petrocchi 1995, p. 485.

6. See *Virtù d'Amore* 2010.

7. On the subject of destroyed books, from the "Sumerian tablets to the War in Iraq," see Báez 2007.

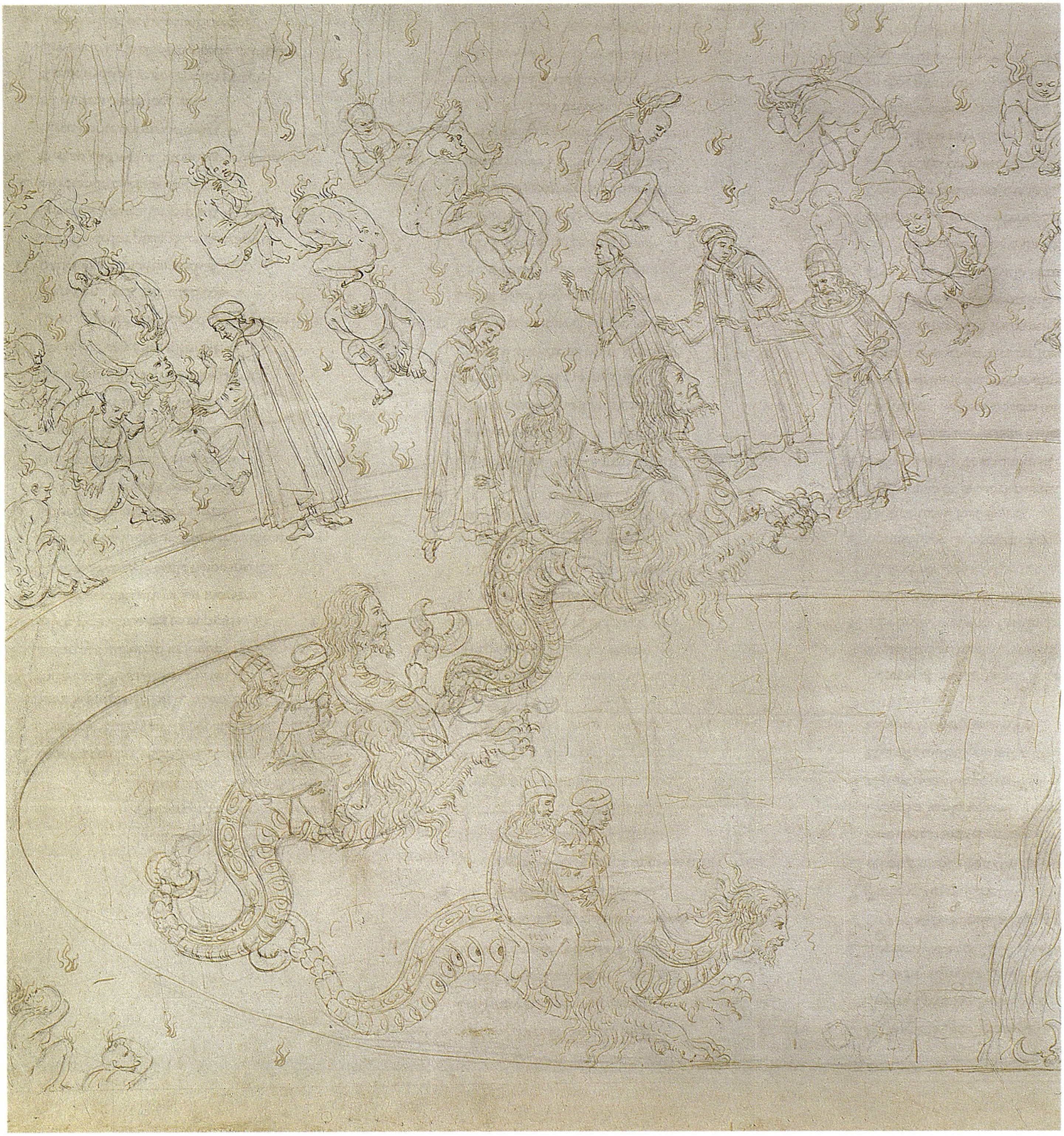

Tim Parks

The Vanities before the Bonfire: Buying Beauty in Renaissance Florence

Astonished by the sheer wealth of the Palazzo Medici as it was in 1459, "the decorative tapestries, the chests of inestimable craftsmanship and value, the masterful sculptures, the infinitely varied patterns and silverwork," Galeazzo Sforza concluded that "money alone"[1] could not compete with what his guests had achieved. Yet everything that the Duke of Milan's son was looking at—including works by Donatello, the Beato Angelico and Fra Lippi—had all had been bought with money, everything depended on the financial clout of a major bank.

The same could be said of much of the great painting, sculpture and architecture of Renaissance Florence. We like to think of art as free from the "contamination" of lucre. We read Ezra Pound's famous lines "With usura/Hath no man a painted paradise on his church wall"[2]—and we nod our heads in agreement. We feel it's good to keep merely countable value—the product and its price tag—well away from those inspired creations that transcend mere accumulation, turning our minds to higher things.

But Pound was wrong. Not only was much of Renaissance art paid for by Italy's bankers but a great deal of it actually came out of the aspirations and tensions that galvanized their

1. Sandro Botticelli
The Usurers (*Inferno*, Canto XVII)
c. 1490
drawing
Berlin, Kupferstichkabinett, Hamilton ms. 201

lives. As Galeazzo Sforza sensed, the Medici and many other banking families hadn't just put money into their *palazzi*, but much else as well. Our ambition in setting up this exhibition is to affirm the link between art and its patrons, introducing visitors to the dynamic world of Florentine finance and suggesting how its intense and troubled relationships with Church and State throughout the 14th and 15th centuries both influenced and were reflected by the great works of art that the city's bankers commissioned.

Florence was not the home of the modern bank. In the 13th century Genoa, Siena and Lucca had all been more important financial centres. However, by the end of the 14th century, both for the number of its banks and the extension of their subsidiary agencies across Europe, Florence was dominant. In the absence of paper money, one of the great problems merchants faced at the time was the movement of money from one country, or even one town to another, either to pay for goods they wished to purchase or to bring home the income from goods sold. Italian banks had largely resolved this problem with the invention of the "letter of exchange," a document that allowed for money to be paid into a bank in, say, Florence and then paid out by that bank's agent in Geneva, or Naples, or Bruges, or Venice, without any coin being physically moved. But this financial instrument only worked if a bank had an extended network of agencies. Florence's winning card had been the readiness of its merchants and bankers—and more often than not the merchants were bankers—both individually and as a team, to create a web of commerce and credit that stretched northwards to London, east as far as Constantinople, west to Barcelona, south to Naples and Cyprus. The city became the hub and motor of international finance.

But the generation of wealth is not without its anxieties. If the invention of money made it possible to store wealth, dividing and distributing it as we wished, there was the embarrassing corollary that every good and service now had to be ascribed a unit value that allowed the most heterogeneous phenomena to be compared. A barrel of wine costs twenty *soldi*, a prayer for a deceased loved one ten, a prostitute fifteen, a doctor's visit one florin. Then a mule costs fifty florins and a slave sixty and a church altar piece ninety.

This creates uneasiness. Is a prayer worth less than a prostitute? We feel things should not be put on a level in this way. This uneasiness was stronger in a society that still thought of itself as a hierarchical commonwealth underwritten by God. "Money puts the peasant in high estate" complains one 14th century Italian poet, and "even opens, if you want, the doors of paradise."[3] This wasn't right. It challenged the status quo. It challenged Christian metaphysics.

One way these anxieties were quietened in late medieval Florence was with the use of two separate currencies. Minted for the first time in 1252, the gold florin, albeit no larger than a modern English penny or American nickel, packed a big punch. It was solid gold after all. It could buy twenty yards of red linen. Or pay a master cook to prepare a banquet for a hundred guests. As a result it was used mostly, though by no means exclusively, by the wealthy classes. For smaller purchases, or workers' wages, there was the *picciolo*, a quite different currency, minted in silver. To convert one into the other you needed to know the current relative values of gold and silver. You needed a bank.

If someone from the poorer classes did accumulate some florins there were the so-called sumptuary laws to tell him what he could, or rather couldn't do with them. Only a man of a certain class could wear a red cloak. Only a lady of a certain degree could have buttons on her sleeves. Lavish spending on dinners or funeral processions was for the privileged alone. So a society excited by money and commerce introduced rules to limit the social mobility that might result, a town specialised in the production of high quality wools and silks tried to keep a lid on the desire for fine clothes.

Then as today, it was bankers who bore the brunt of collective concern about the power of money. Having "accumulated quite a bit on his conscience," Vespasiano da Bisticci wrote of Cosimo de' Medici, "as most men do... who want to be ahead of the rest," he sought an audience with his bank's most important client, Pope Eugenius, to ask how God might "have mercy on him, and preserve him in the enjoyment of his temporal goods."[4] How can we keep our cash and be considered good? This is ever the banker's dilemma.

Invest ten thousand florins in the restoration Convent of San Marco, was the Pope's reply.

What sin might Cosimo have committed that demanded such huge restitution? Arrested in 1433 he had been accused, at least according to Machiavelli's version of events, of plotting "to make himself great," to raise himself above his social position, and threatened with execution. But more likely what he was thinking of now was the sin of "usury," of lending money at an interest. The two crimes were not unconnected. Officially the Church banned usury because the Bible enjoined us to make our living by the sweat of our brow; work was part of God's plan for us and usury wasn't work. But of course, it is access to credit that can free a man from his station and upset the status quo.

Florentine banks accepted deposits from private citizens, dukes and cardinals, paying in return an annual interest contractually described as a discretionary gift and hence not officially usury. They invented complicated games with letters of exchange so that what legally speaking was a mere movement of money from one place and currency to another actually became a profitable interest-bearing loan. The theologians analysed each new financial instrument for possible sin. Worried for their immortal souls, the bankers distributed considerable sums to charity.

Doubtless the impulse behind many commissions of religious art was similarly penitential. But pouring money into the church also allowed bankers to exhibit their wealth and taste publically and even to influence the ethos of the institution that constantly scrutinised the morality of their practises. When it came to commissioning paintings, bankers preferred the rich Magi with their celebrated gifts to sinners roasting in hell. And all the better if they themselves could creep into the sacred space in their smart clothes, kneeling at the feet of the Madonna perhaps. The Church became more comfortable. This kind of

2. Marinus van Reymerswaele
The Money Lenders
1542
Munich, Bayerische Stadtgemäldesammlung

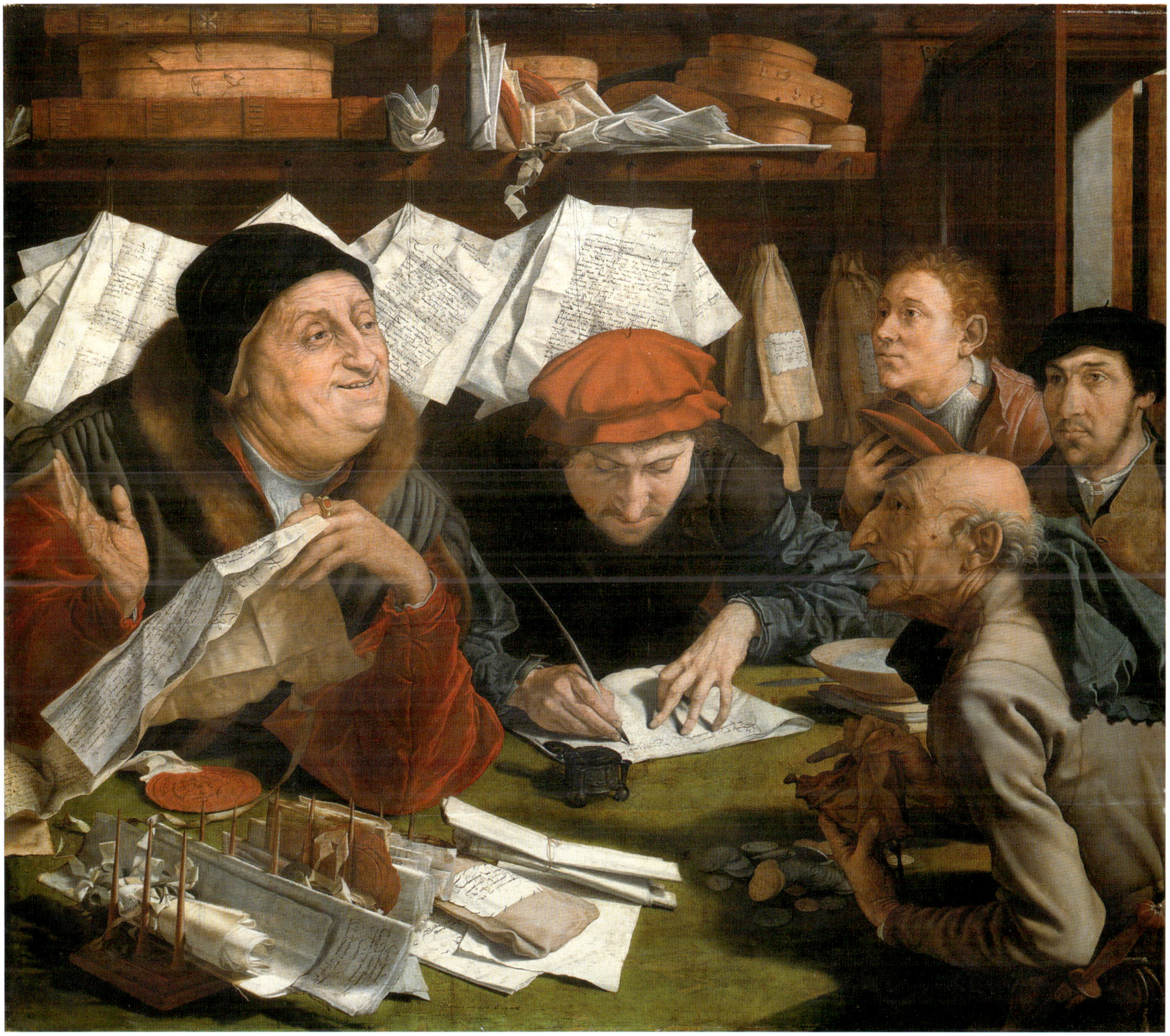

patronage was more interesting than giving to the poor.

Cosimo agreed to restore San Marco but on condition that the lax and libertine Silvestrines who ran the convent be replaced by the severe Dominicans. He wanted his money accepted by an order that renounced all ownership of private wealth, men whose prayers would really count. To achieve his goals he brought in a painter of the calibre and piety of Fra Angelico, who "never painted a crucifix without tears running down his cheeks."[5] All the same, some priests were not happy to see God's house "frivolously adorned with superfluous sculptures and paintings."[6] On one fresco in a dormitory corridor where the only viewers would be monks, a scroll reads "I invoke God's curse and mine on the introduction of possessions into this order."[7]

Throughout the 14th and 15th centuries there was a see-sawing tension between Florence's pious vision of itself as a city of God, the New Jerusalem even, and its vocation for luxury goods and international finance. Caught in the midst of this, the bankers sought to have their cake and eat it, to enjoy their fortunes and occupy key places in church. When in 1491 the fiery Savonarola became Prior of San Marco, preaching implacably against the arrogance of wealth and organizing in 1497 his bonfires of the vanities—including many works of art—the creative compromise between church and finance that had characterized the preceding decades went up in smoke.

This exhibition seeks to put the Florentine art of the period in relation to the bankers who commissioned so much of it and the complex world they moved in. We have chosen to focus on the work of Botticelli because more than any other painter his career reflects the shifts and tensions between secular and sacred, as he moves from the sumptuous earlier works that show the Madonna dressed in Florentine finery, shining with gold leaf, through the great mythical paintings that conjure up the Neo-Platonism of Lorenzo the Magnificent's time, to the more austere and emotionally charged devotional images of the 1490s that suggest the artist's receptiveness to Savonorola's preaching.

1. Hatfield, 'Some Unknown Descriptions' 1970, pp. 232–49.

2. Pound 1996, p. 229

3. Niccolò de' Rossi, *Denari fano l'omo comparere*, in *Rimatori* 1969, pp. 689–90.

4. Vespasiano da Bisticci (*c*. 1480-98), ed. Greco 1970-6, II, 1976, p. 177.

5. Vasari 1568, ed. Bettarini, Barocchi 1966-97, III, 1971, p. 277.

6. Kent 2000, p. 174.

7. Ivi, pp. 150-1.

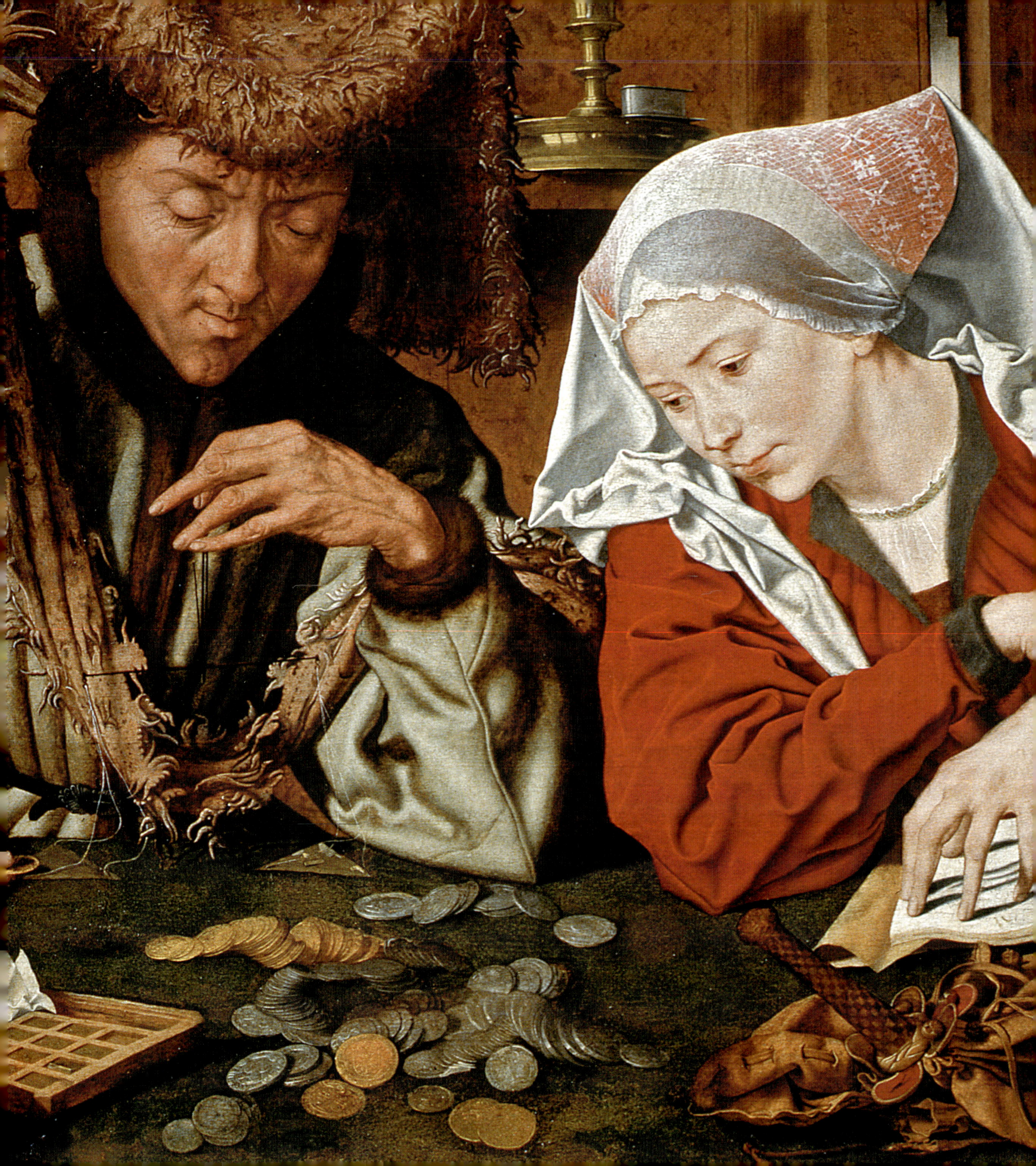

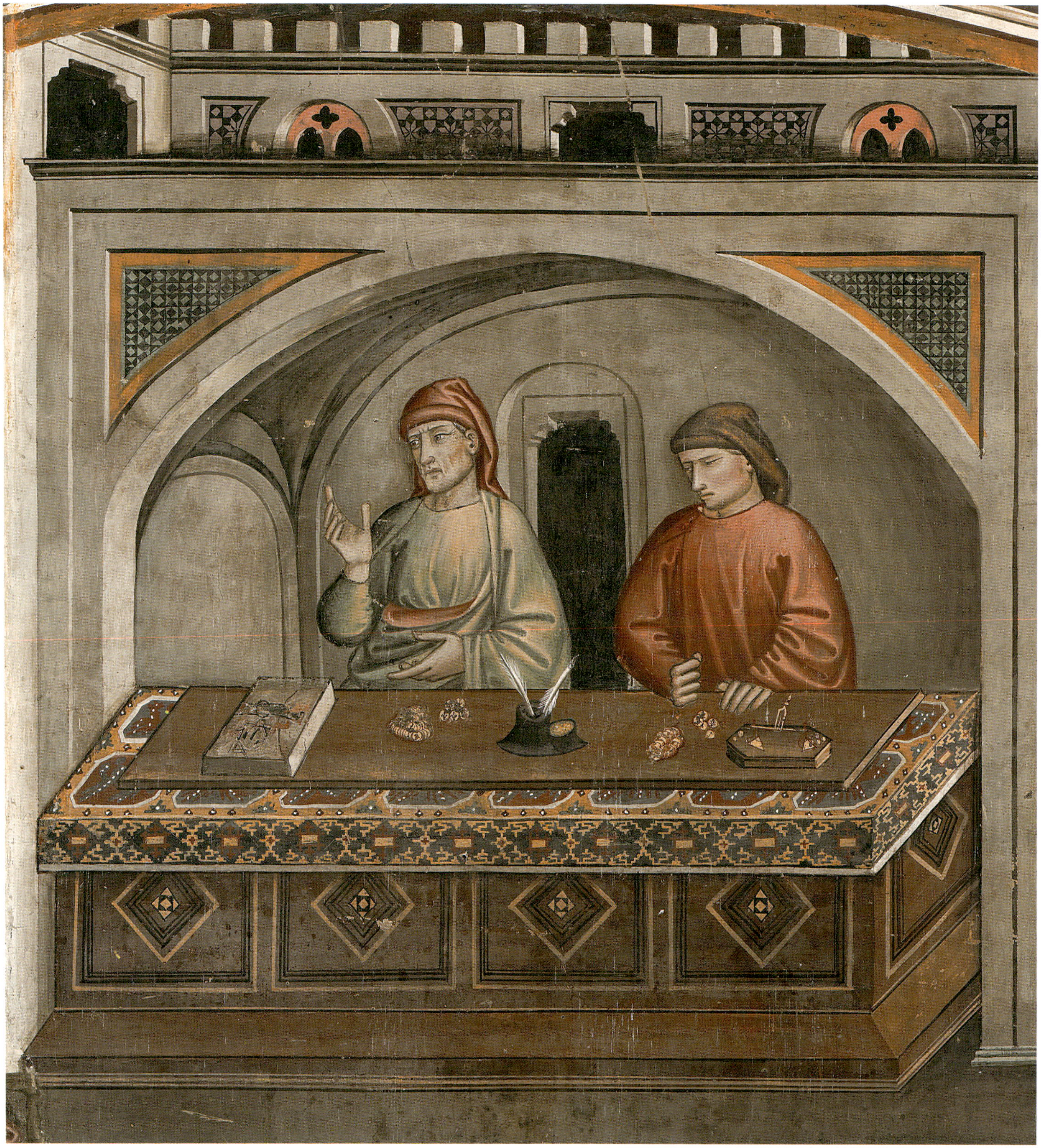

The Merchant-Bankers of 15th-Century Florence

Franco Franceschi

The population of 15th-century Florence was considerably smaller than it had been in the time of Dante and Giotto and the number of businesses had likewise declined. Nevertheless, Florence remained a nodal point in the European economy and a city where great fortunes were amassed. According to historians, the Florentine entrepreneurs in the Renaissance century par excellence were just as successful as the Bardi, Peruzzi and Acciaioli families had been with their "super-companies" in the 13th and 14th centuries.[1] However, the impressive case study of the Medici firms may have led to overestimating the importance of the banking sector in accumulating this wealth.

Although it is entirely legitimate to describe Cosimo de' Medici, Giovanni Rucellai, Filippo Strozzi and Franceschino de' Pazzi as "bankers," this label does not fully depict the nature of their activity. In late medieval and Renaissance society in fact—and Florence was no exception—"business and banking went hand-in-hand."[2] Even the term *bancherius* did not necessarily distinguish a financial operator from a *mercator*, since both of these categories could engage in trade as well as currency exchange and money lending.[3]

The term "bank" is equally ambiguous. It originally indicated the *tavola*, or bench, where money-lending and currency exchange operations were carried out, then came to designate the firm that owned it. After the studies of Raymond De Roover, it has become customary to distinguish between *a minuto* banks and *grossi* banks. The former operated mainly in the local sphere, exchanging currency and granting loans against a pledge of jewels or other valuables. The latter, instead, offered banking and financial services on an international scale,[4] ranging from extending credit to individuals, governments and local authorities to transferring money over long distances, from debit and credit operations in the European fairs to managing the financial affairs of popes and sovereigns.

This distinction, however, is not as sharp as might appear at first sight. On the one hand, the Florentine *a minuto* banks served other important functions as well (such as accepting

1. Niccolò di Pietro Gerini
Stories of St. Matthew
c. 1395
Prato, Church of San Francesco, Migliorati Chapel

interest-bearing term deposits, financing businesses, opening current accounts that allowed for overdrafts, and making money more available through bank payment orders and transfer accounts);[5] on the other, the *grossi* banks were always ready to invest in local businesses. Francesco Datini followed this strategy, albeit only for a short time,[6] and likewise Giovanni Serristori and his nephew Antonio di Salvestro,[7] the Cambini brothers[8] and even the Medici, whose bank always had a branch in Florence.[9] To operate on the local level a bank did not have to establish a specific, independent firm, but—as shown by the documentation on the Cambini Bank—just keep separate account books for local operations.

The data available for the Cambini Bank demonstrate that local banking, though less profitable than international trade and finance, satisfied other demands, such as extending the clientele and procuring money for investment.[10] Abundant liquidity, in fact, allowed the city's mercantile-banking elite, among other things, to finance the public debt with short—or very short—term loans to the State. From December 1430 to August 1432, for instance, the Florentine government borrowed over 560,000 florins. Half of this amount was lent by only four banks: the Medici, Pazzi, Lamberteschi and Strozzi. This practice, which earned the lenders a minimum interest of 12% a year with peaks of 30%, was intensified over the course of the 15th century.[11]

Apart from differences in scale, however, the greatest ambiguity in the current terminology concerns the company profile. Rarely, in fact, were the *grossi* banks purely banking enterprises, but, in a policy of diversifying investments and risks common to all the other entrepreneurs of the time, they engaged in a broad range of activities—trade, banking, finance, insurance and even manufacturing. The Medici Bank itself was a system of firms operating in such fields as manufacturing wool and silk fabrics and trading in a vast range of articles, including luxury goods: woollen cloth and silk fabrics, furs, jewels, silverware, tapestries, paintings, books, spices and even olive oil, citrus fruit, almonds, alum, iron and horses.[12] Equally diversified, as shown by the budget drawn up in 1431, was the activity of the bank directed by Antonio Serristori. It not only furnished such services as mercantile and financial brokerage but also extended credit in various forms to individuals, financed the floating debt of the Florentine State, functioned as an *a minuto* bank, formed partnerships with firms operating in Florence and abroad, traded in English wool and Florentine furnishing fabrics, Spanish grain, paper from Colle Valdelsa, alum from Asia Minor and soap from Gaeta.

Some thirty years later Antonio's sons were to open a silk-works and another workshop that produced gold yarn for weaving gold-embroidered furnishing fabrics.[13] The *grossi* banks were, in fact, multipurpose enterprises owned by "merchant-bankers" who sometimes operated as entrepreneurs in the production sector as well.

This wealth of interests, reflecting an economy that continued to integrate business, banking and manufacturing, probably to an extent unknown to any other Italian city, also reflected the organization of the guilds. While the Arte del Cambio, the bankers' guild, has often been called the fortress of the great 15th-century bankers, this was generally the case only for local banks, since the guild had no jurisdiction over merchant-bankers operating exclusively on the international level. The owners of the major international firms were instead often enrolled in the Arte di Calimala, the Arte della Lana, the Arte della Seta or in several of these guilds at the same time.[14] This does not mean, of course, that the different fields of activity were equally important. Raymond De Roover considered the Medici Bank to be a firm specialized

2. Niccolò Miretto or Stefano da Ferrara
The Banker (*Sign of Virgo*)
1425–40
Padua, Palazzo della Ragione

3. Andrea Orcagna and Jacopo di Cione
The Calling of St. Matthew (from the pillar of the Arte del Cambio in Orsanmichele) *c.* 1367–8
Florence, Galleria degli Uffizi

in banking operations; Giovanni Cassandro has shown that the Della Casa-Guadagni firm, active in Geneva from 1450 to 1464, did most of its business in letters of exchange and not mercantile trading;[15] while more recently Sergio Tognetti, although deeming exaggerated the claim that the Florentine businessman of the 15th century was "essentially a great financier and international foreign exchange dealer," has noted that investing in these fields was a growing trend.[16]

From the economic perspective, the Florentine Quattrocento was an epoch of change, stemming in part from the profound upheavals of the previous century. The severe demographic downturn resulting from the plague of 1348 and the waves of epidemics that followed led to drastic reduction in the overall volume of manufactured goods, in trading and in banking, along with shrinkage in the average size of enterprises and disappearance of the old "super-companies." On the other hand, the increase in per capita income of the survivors, a phenomenon common not only to Florence but to Europe as a whole, triggered a number of convergent processes: the development of long-distance trading of numerous inexpensive articles to satisfy the greater capacity for consumption of the lower and middle classes, favoured by revolutionary changes in the cost of maritime shipping; the parallel growth of a demand for luxury goods, especially silk fabrics and art objects, coming mainly from the secular and ecclesiastical elites of Europe and the Middle East; the progressive extension and complexity of the banking system, where cross-border financial transfer was assuming ever greater importance.[17]

These profound changes challenged Florentine businessmen with new problems, which they managed to solve brilliantly thanks to the support of a more decisive economic policy and the advantages deriving to Florence when it acquired the Port of Pisa in 1421 and established a regular "State" mar-

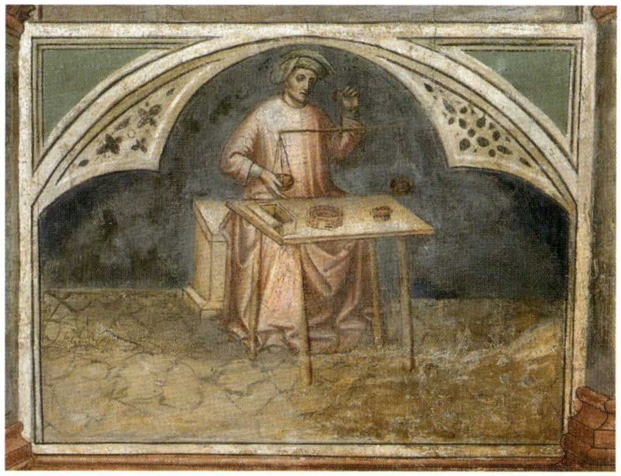

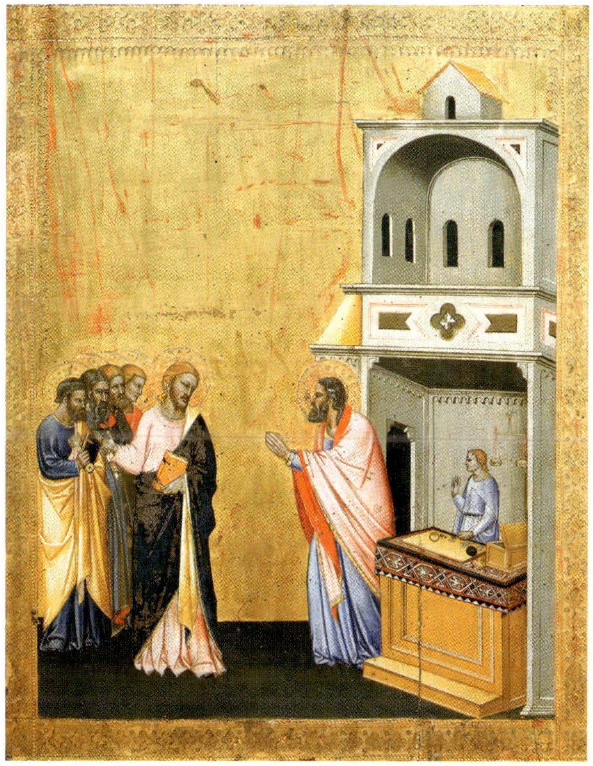

itime shipping service that remained in operation for much of the 15th century.[18] To the decline in the Florentine production of luxury fabrics, caused mainly by the growing difficulty of procuring English wool and the competition of new centres of production in England, Flanders, Catalonia and Languedoc, the textile manufacturers responded by turning to Italian or Iberian wool and favouring a type of cloth of medium quality and cost, called *Garbo*.[19] An equally creative response, when recession in the wool industry hit its lowest point, was the launching of a new product destined to meet with enormous success, namely silk furnishing fabrics, until then produced only in Lucca, Genoa, Venice and Bologna. According to estimates that are approximate but nevertheless based on documents of the time, the production of the Florentine silk fabrics, worth 233,000 florins in 1436-7, had risen to 400,000 by 1490. Gold-beaters' shops, linked to the production of silk fabrics, also began to flourish. Many of these enterprises were owned by such great merchant-banker families as the Gondi, the Portinari, and the Ridolfi, joined in the late 15th-early 16th century by the Strozzi, Capponi and Salviati.[20] In the 15th century, the availability of up-to-date sample collections of fabrics led to another profitable development, consisting of a great expansion in economic relations with the Near East. Although based on trading the new textile products manufactured in the city for the local alum, dyes and silks, this expansion was only possible thanks to the Florentine government's skilful management of relations with the region even after the capture of Constantinople by the Turks (1453) and the founding of the Ottoman Empire.[21]

In Europe the great Florentine enterprises remained present in all of the major business and banking centres, from London, Bruges and Geneva to Lyon, Paris and Avignon, from Genoa and Venice to Rome, Naples and Milan, from Barcelona and Valencia to Majorca, Seville and Lisbon. In some of these cities, the Florentines actually strengthened their interests. In Italy this was true especially of Rome, once again the papal seat at the conclusion of the Avignon "captivity" and the Great Schism (1416). In Rome the Florentines became even more powerful, both in the papal administrative and financial systems and in the gigantic economic and financial organism represented by the Roman Catholic Church. Over the course of the century, the director of the branch of the Medici Bank "at the court of Rome" frequently held the position of Prefect of the Apostolic Chamber, serving as a real official of the ecclesiastical administration in the capacity of financial agent. At other times this advantageous position was held by Florentine merchant-bankers from the Spini, Bardi, Della Casa, Martelli, and Spinelli families. But the entire administrative system of the Church, on every level, was permeated with Florentine depositaries and treasurers, who exploited their positions to dominate both banking and trading, the importation of luxury articles in particular.[22]

Another city of strategic interest was Naples, not only a capital and great centre of consumption but also a natural market for some of the Kingdom's productions, such as silk from Calabria. From as early as the time of the Angevins, Naples had attracted a colony of Florentine traders. And even when the continental South passed under the dominion of the Aragons, the Florentines did not abandon Naples, despite the political antagonism of the Iberian sovereigns to the Medici dynasty and the support lent by King Alfonse the Magnanimous (1442-58) to the Catalonian merchants. During the reign of Ferrante I (1458-94) conditions for Florentine entrepreneurs were even better. The Strozzi Bank, whose services as agent for the administrative and financial organs of the State constituted one of its core activities, rose to the apex

4. Domenico Ghirlandaio
Portrait of Francesco Sassetti with his Son Teodoro I
c. 1487 (?)
New York, The Metropolitan Museum of Art,
Jules Bache Collection

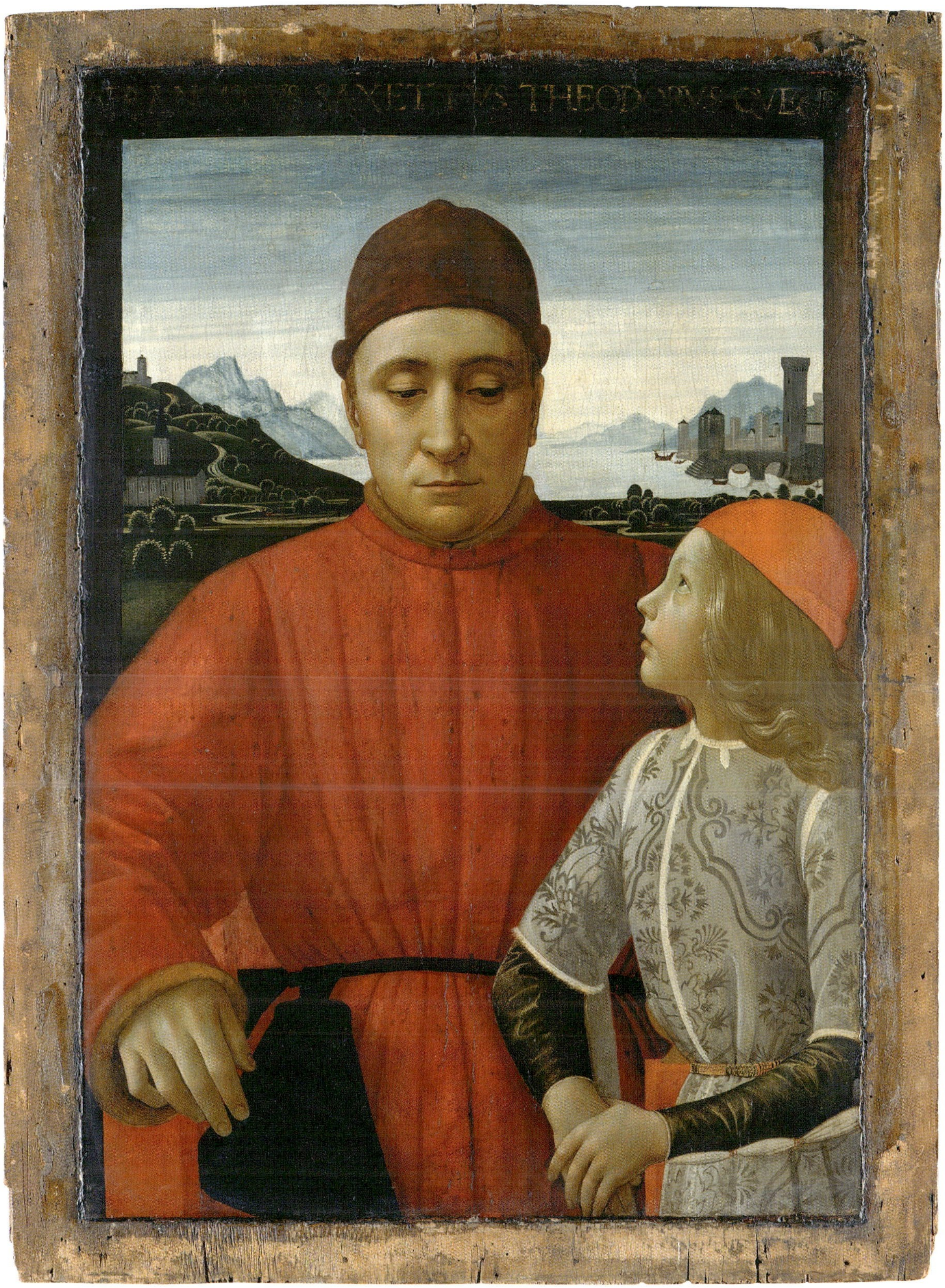

of a mercantile-banking system that included other Florentine firms (the Medici, Ginori, and Tommasi-Arrighi) as well as local and Catalonian companies. A number of mercantile-banking fortunes amassed over the course of the 15th century had their origins in Naples, first among them the empires of Filippo Strozzi and Giuliano Gondi, two of the foremost builders of Renaissance palaces.[23] In Southern Italy the Florentine businessmen also established profitable relations with the towns of Abruzzo, which became important markets for procuring wool, silk and saffron.[24]

In Mediterranean Europe the Florentine merchant-bankers were present in numbers on the Iberian peninsula, where they imported finished products coming from all over Italy and purchased foodstuffs and raw materials for the city's workshops.[25] With the new opportunities provided by the development of Atlantic trade this area, Portugal in particular, assumed growing importance in the Florentine economic system. In Portugal the Florentines traded mainly in slaves, leather, silk, coral and fish. And when Giovanni Salviati introduced the cultivation of sugarcane to the Island of Madeira, a flourishing line of trade was developed. Some of the Florentine firms financed voyages of discovery to Africa, and later to India and Indonesia. Among them was the Cambini Bank, which furnished Henry the Navigator (1394-1460), and the Portuguese Navy in general, with geographical maps commissioned in Florence expressly for this purpose. Their pre-eminent position favoured the penetration of Florentines into the nerve centres of the administration, as exemplified by Francesco Corbinelli who, in the early years of the 16th century, was appointed director of the royal treasury in the Region of Goa on behalf of the Portuguese crown. A similar position was held by Piero Strozzi in Coromandel, on the east coast of India.[26]

North of the Alps, the major centre for the banking and business of the Florentine merchant-bankers, at least up to the late 1460s, was Geneva with its fairs. Here, under the company name of Giovanni Benci and Francesco Sassetti, the Medici Bank started operating in 1420, and here such Florentine firms as the Della Casa-Guadagni accumulated most of their wealth. But Geneva was also a flourishing market for luxury goods as well as for gold and silver in coins or bullion. For Florence it was the chief market for selling its silk furnishing fabrics, and some of the firms operating in Geneva were direct branches of the silk manufacturers' enterprises.[27] It's worth noting that, in the mercantile accounting books, we sometimes find entries on silk goods supplied to the Florentine shops with a clause postponing payment until such time as the mules returning from Geneva had delivered to the manufacturers, in the form of cash or letters of exchange, the profit deriving from sale of the fabric.[28]

Geneva went into decline after 1463 when King Louis XI, intent on developing a rival centre of economy in France, persuaded foreign merchants to move their businesses to Lyon by granting them highly attractive concessions. The Florentines responded at once, and their migration was largely responsible for the success of the new trading centre. By the end of the year the first Florentine bank had already arrived in the city on the Rhone. In 1466 it was joined by the Medici, and soon after by the firms of the Pazzi, Nasi, Falconieri, Bardi, Capponi, Buondelmonti, Martelli, Frescobaldi and many others.

In Lyon, as had been the case in Geneva, the scene was dominated by luxury articles, primarily the Italian velvet, satin and damask fabrics that in the mid-16th century still accounted for nearly 50% of all the products traded at fairs, which were also the major clearing-houses for international payments. In Lyon, any transaction made anywhere in Europe "could ar-

5. Andrea del Verrocchio
Portrait of Cosimo the Elder
c. 1464
Berlin, Staatliche Museen zu Berlin

rive at its financial conclusion," as would be demonstrated by the operations for financing the voyage of Giovanni da Verrazzano to America, documented in one of the Gondi account books.[29]

The profits earned by the great merchant-bankers were impressive. Between 1397 and 1420 the overall profit recorded by the Medici Bank amounted to 151,820 florins, between 1420 and 1435 it rose to 186,382, while in the following fifteen-year period it reached a peak of 290,791 florins. Over the span of forty-three years the Medicean holding company thus earned a profit of some 629,000 florins, of which 440,000—an average of 10,000 florins a year!—went to members of the family and the rest to the other partners.[30] In the four years from 1485-9 the Capponi brothers made a profit of 19,324 florins.[31] Profits expressed as a percentage of invested capital were equally positive. Between 1455 and 1459 the Rome branch of the Cambini Bank produced an annual profit of over 30%.[32] Between 1485 and 1492, the earnings of the company owned by Antonio and Carlo Martelli in Lyon were only a little lower—26.25%—while Bernardo Bardi, active on the French market at this same time, recorded an annual profit of around 18% for four years.[33] The significance of these figures becomes fully apparent when comparing them with others from the same period. Rarely did the annual profit generated by the Florentine textile manufactories exceed 10%, the interest on term deposits ranged around 8%, while profit deriving

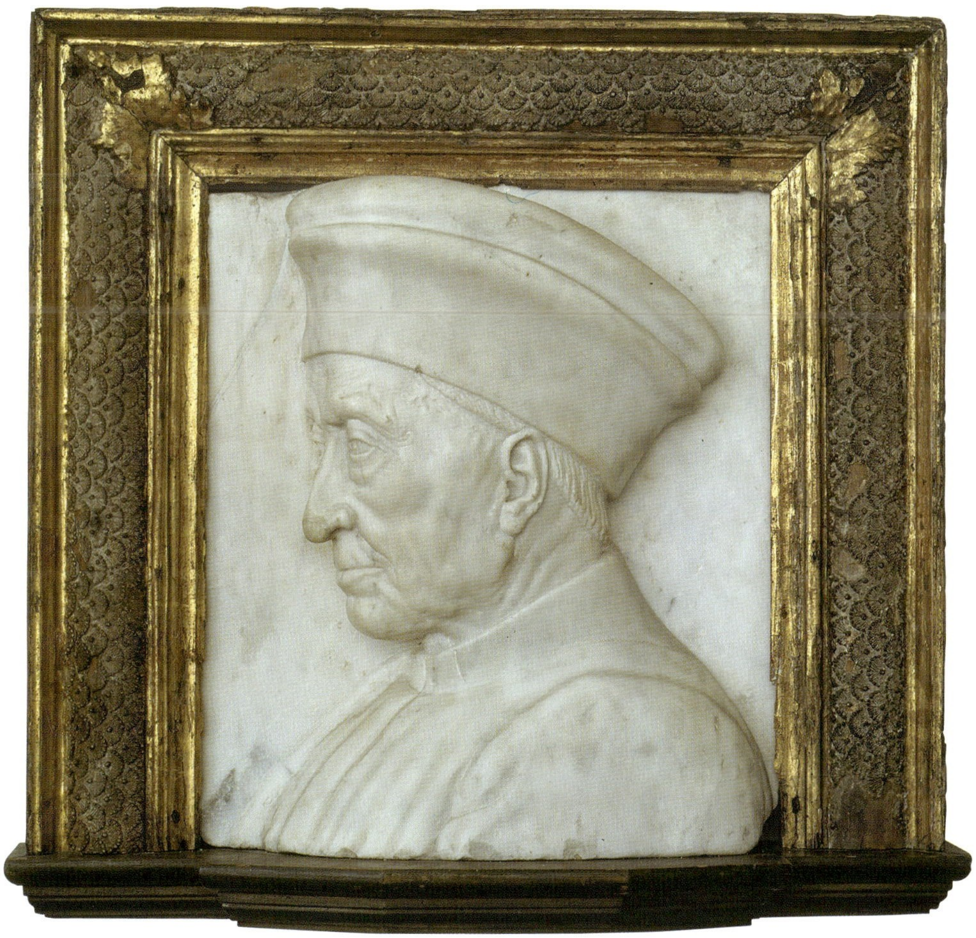

from ownership of land and buildings was about one point lower. Certainly, there were continuing fluctuations depending on market conditions and differences pertaining to the various sectors of investment, as is well illustrated by the two firms owned by Filippo Strozzi in Naples, the bank proper and the commercial enterprise. Between 1478 and 1484 the profit of the former fluctuated between 5 and 42% with an average of 18%, that of the latter between 7.5 and 29%, averaging around 15%. Hence banking ensured a higher return on capital than mercantile activity, but was also subject to severe fluctuation in profit; in other words, it involved greater risk.[34]

In the world of the merchant-bankers danger was the order of the day. Even the most dynamic economies were frequently exposed to the devastating impact of war, famine, and epidemics, determining the sudden downturn or disappearance of markets that had been highly lucrative only a short time ago. Thanks to the relatively open society of 15th-century Florence, personal and family fortunes could be rapidly amassed, as the rise of such families as the Serristori, Nasi, Della Casa and Cambini demonstrates, but could just as rapidly decline or be wiped out by their worst enemy: bankruptcy. Richard Goldthwaite has recently reported data on this subject coming from 15th-century chronicles: six bankruptcies in 1425, more in the years 1464–5, seven in 1474 and one in 1502.[35] Different sources report other episodes, including the collapse of the broad network of international companies owned by the Alberti in the 1430s, the downfall of the Pazzi companies after the conspiracy of 1478, the bankruptcy of the Cambini in 1481 and of course the liquidation of the Medici enterprises in 1494. This concentration of adverse events starting from the 1460s led De Roover to state that "the last decades of the 15th century […] saw a long and deep depression" and that "the demise of the Medici Bank coincided with the collapse of the entire Florentine banking system."[36] De Roover supported his thesis with data, taken from the archives of the Arte del Cambio and from chronicles, on the reduction in the number of banks in the city, which dropped from 72 in 1422 to 33 in 1470 and to only 8 in 1516.[37]

Today, although debate on the dynamics of the late 14th-century Florentine economy is still open, few would endorse the idea of severe recession in the mercantile-banking sector. In evaluating the behaviour of this sector, the data on the number of banks operating in Florence are not a reliable indicator, since not all of the firms engaged in international business had branches in the city; and in any case, a more recent study of the Arte del Cambio documentation shows that between 1460 and the end of the century the number of Florentine banks remained around 35-40, with no striking changes.[38]

Aside from these considerations, to determine the scope and dimensions of Florentine mercantile-banking activity, we must go outside the city itself and examine the nodal points in the "economy of great spaces,"[39] where Florentine entrepreneurs were still a vital presence, starting with Lyon. On this subject Federigo Melis has termed "impressive" the list of companies operating on the French market in the second half of the 15th century and well into the 16th.[40] Bruno Dini, in turn, has found in the records of only three early 16th century account books references to twenty-three Florentine banks then present at the Lyon fairs, and has hypothesized that many more existed.[41]

Undoubtedly, the liquidation in 1494 of such a colossus as the Medici Bank, with its network of partnerships, branches, and correspondents all over Europe, cast a deep shadow over a time already shaken by the death of Lorenzo the Magnificent and struggling to reinvent a new political order and government after the expulsion of Piero de' Medici. From the strictly financial viewpoint, however, neither the demise of the Medici holding company nor the exile of the family that had ruled Florence for sixty years seem to have had any major consequences. A century and a half before, both the Bardi and the Peruzzi had been destroyed, but this time no bank was sucked down with them and the overall functioning of the system was never smoother.[42] Little affected by the bankruptcy of the merchant-bankers, the city continued to benefit from the vast wealth these men had amassed.[43] It was a flow of money that did not trigger, as in the 13th century, a burst of demographic and economic growth; rather it fed a privileged class's demand for magnificence leading to the creation of works of art that are still amazing the world five hundred years on.

1. The reference is to the super-companies studied by Hunt 1994.
2. Goldthwaite 2009, p. 205.
3. Guidi Bruscoli 2007, p. 546.
4. De Roover 1963, ed. 1970, pp. 19–23.
5. See Goldthwaite 1985, pp. 17–31; Tognetti 1997.
6. Melis 1962, pp. 212–6.
7. Tognetti 2003, pp. 41–4 and 62–4.
8. Tognetti 1997.
9. De Roover 1963, ed. 1970, pp. 323–43.
10. Goldthwaite 2009, p. 417; Tognetti 1997.
11. See Molho 1971, pp. 166, 172–5, 180–1; Conti 1984, pp. 71–8; Goldthwaite 1996; Molho 2006, pp. 85–6.
12. De Roover 1963, ed. 1970, pp. 203–11.
13. Tognetti 2003, pp. 77–89 and 106–12.
14. Goldthwaite 2009, p. 429.
15. Cassandro 1976, pp. 99 and ff.
16. Tognetti 1999, pp. 327–31, quotation p. 328.
17. See Franceschi 2004, pp. 129–31.
18. Franceschi 1994, pp. 106–8.
19. See Hoshino 1980, pp. 231–44; Franceschi 1993, pp. 30–1.
20. Dini, 'L'industria' 1995, p. 82; Dini, 'La ricchezza' 2001, p. 29.
21. Hoshino, 'Il commercio' 2001; Dini, 'Mercati' 2001, pp. 121–2
22. See De Roover 1963, ed. 1970, pp. 284–7; Esch 1981, pp. 30–50; Palermo 2000.
23. Del Treppo 1986; Goldthwaite 2009, pp. 136–41.
24. See Hoshino 1988, pp. 71 ff.
25. Melis, 'Industria' 1984, pp. 165–9; Dini, 'L'economia' 1995, pp. 199–200.
26. See Goldthwaite 1980, ed. 1984, pp. 65–6; Melis, 'Industria' 1984 pp. 166–7; Spallanzani 1997, pp. 12–3.
27. Cassandro 1990, especially pp. 29–34.
28. Tognetti 2001, p. 474.
29. Dini, 'L'economia' 1995, pp. 198–9.
30. De Roover 1963, ed. 1970, pp. 68–71, 80–1, 101–2.
31. Goldthwaite 1968, p. 201.
32. Tognetti 1999, pp. 193–4.
33. Dini, 'L'economia' 1995, p. 204.
34. Del Treppo 1985, p. 577 and Tab. 2 p. 592.
35. Goldthwaite 2009, p. 455.
36. De Roover 1963, ed. 1970, pp. 541 and 543.
37. Ivi, pp. 22, 543.
38. See Goldthwaite 1985, p. 43.
39. The definition, now famous, is by Federigo Melis: Melis, 'Industria' 1984, p. 126.
40. Ivi, p. 176.
41. Dini, 'L'economia' 1995, p. 203.
42. Goldthwaite 2009, pp. 455–7.
43. Ivi, p. 457.

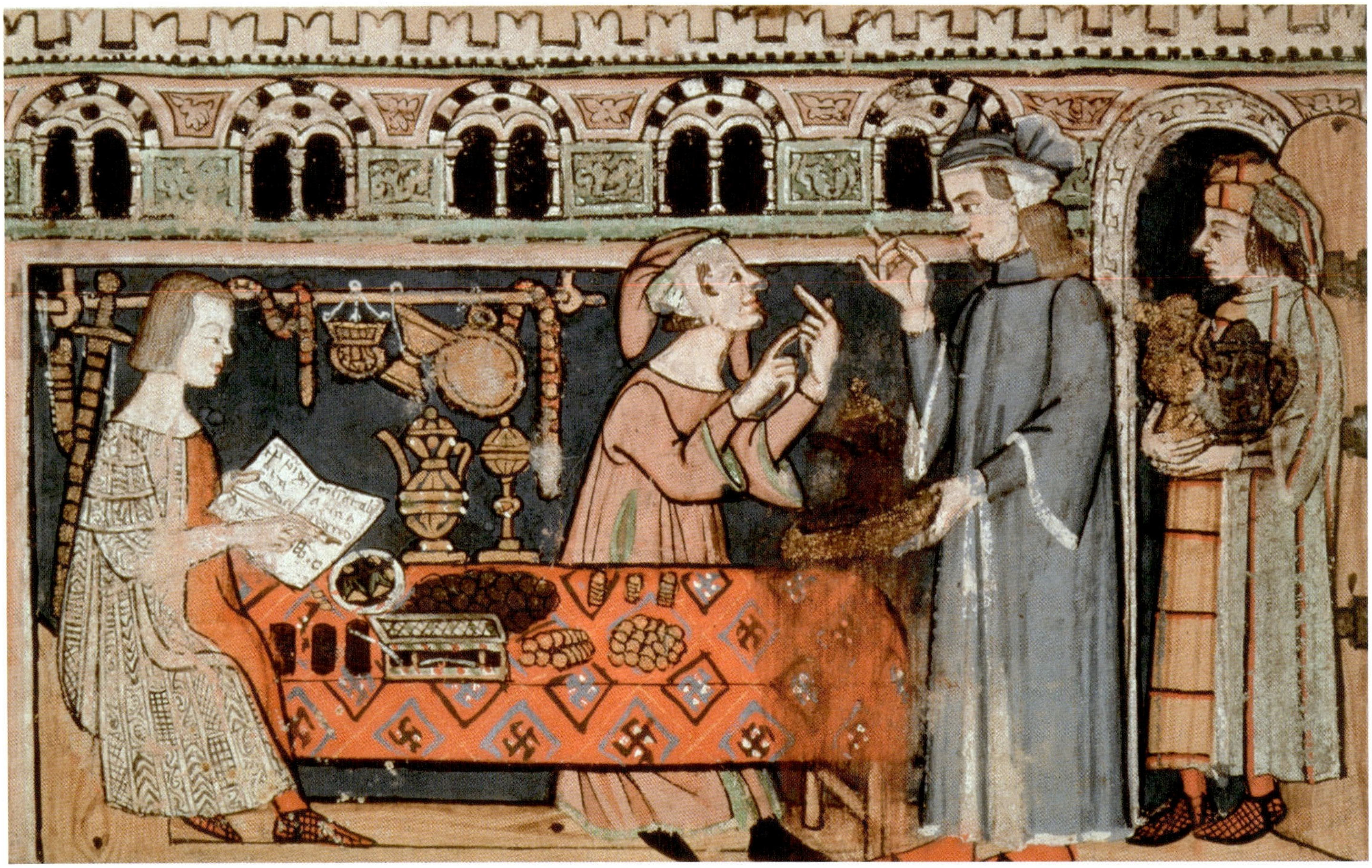

The Problem of Usury and the Jews in Renaissance Florence

Michele Cassandro

Money, interest, usury; since the dawn of a monetary economy, these three words have been closely intertwined. Very early in history the need arose to obtain money, for one reason or another, from someone willing and able to lend it. Money loaned by one subject to another, when returned, inevitably called for the payment of an additional sum; in other words, interest, or usury, as it had always been termed. Numerous mentions of this practice appear in the Holy Scriptures, both the Old Testament and the New, where the term "usury" indicated the interest, either great or small, added to any sum of money loaned.[1] This soon gave rise to heated debate, first philosophical and then more technical, involving ethics and economics, on whether *fenus*, that is, interest, could legitimately be charged.[2] And even earlier Aristotle, some of whose writings deal exclusively with economics, came out firmly against the practise. That money alone could produce other money was deemed unnatural and hence unlawful by the great philosopher.[3]

Following Aristotle's verdict and its interpretation by the Scholastics, and borrowing from both the Holy Scriptures and the Greek and Latin Fathers of the Church, who had been influenced by Aristotle, the accent began to be placed on Christian ethical and moral principles. Human activities, including financial transactions, came to be judged in the light of those values. Inevitably, some acts, contracts and transactions deemed contrary to the unwritten moral principles that had penetrated deep into the conscience of society were condemned. Very early, moreover, canon law branded the practice of usury illicit. An exhaustive study of this subject was made by Thomas Aquinas, the great theologian and leader of the Scholastics. In his monumental *Summa Theologica* and other minor works[4] he examined the most controversial operations and contracts, whose full legitimacy had fallen under suspicion.

Thomas Aquinas, after reviewing and discussing the concepts of just price and joint assessment in sales contracts, of consequential damage and lost profit in connection with loans, arrived at the point of justifying a certain minimum recompense on money loaned. Generally speaking, any trans-

1. *Allegory of Usury*
London, British Library, ms. Add. 7695, fol. 7v

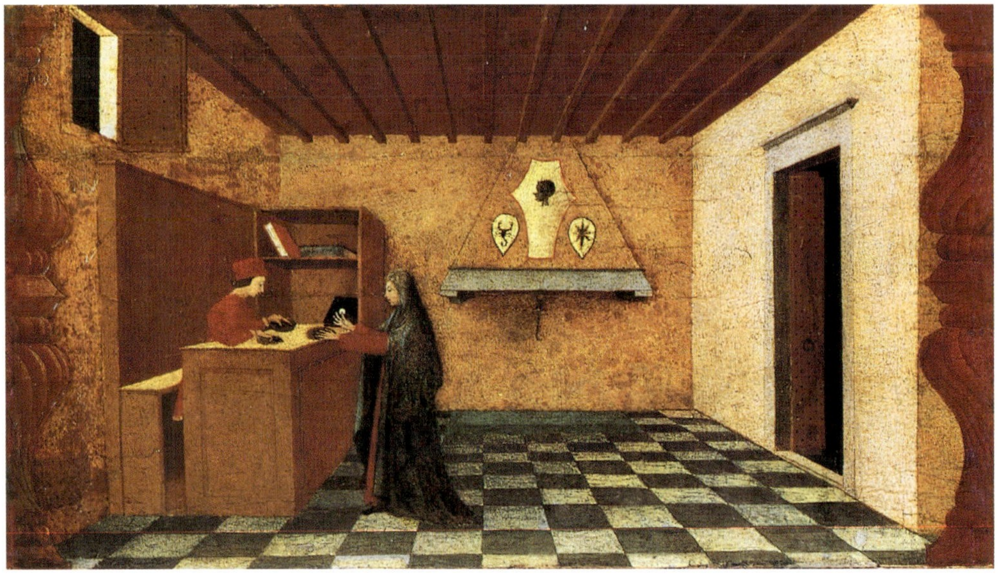

action stipulated between two persons had to safeguard the rights of each and become a common good for both parties. Referring specifically to loans, Aquinas stated that the added amount, even if small, served to protect the interests of the lender by ensuring he would suffer no consequential damage or loss of profit resulting from unavailability of the money for the duration of the loan. At the beginning of Aquinas' analysis, this possibility was contemplated in the case of failure to pay back the loan by the established due date. It was in fact an admission that, although within narrowly restricted limits, charging a minimum percentage of interest was permissible. As the debate went on, only "*graves et immoderatae usurae*" came to be considered illicit. Applying high interest rates, then, was decidedly condemned. And although the term "usury" was adopted throughout the Middle Ages, the banning of credit transactions referred specifically to cases—and they were the majority—involving a medium-high rate of interest. Furthermore the debate, on both the theological and juridical sides, focussed mainly on operations that appeared fictitious, designed to conceal loans and interest. These included, for example, sales contracts scheduled to conclude after a certain time, with a surcharge to be paid at the end; and some insurance contracts, formally valid but actually fictitious, where the premium stipulated was in reality interest and the sum

2. Paolo Uccello
Selling the Consecrated Host to a Jew,
first scene of predella *The Miracle of the Profaned Host*
1467–9
Urbino, Galleria Nazionale delle Marche

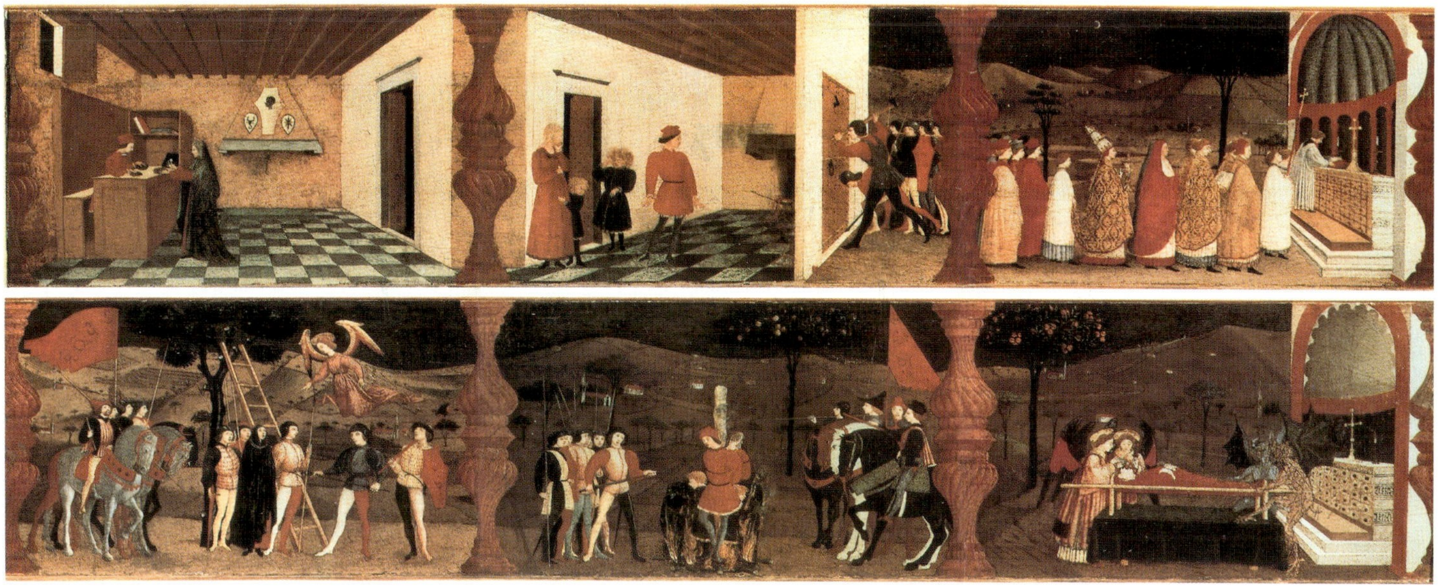

insured was really a loan. Or lastly—and this was the favourite expedient—presenting a transaction as foreign exchange rather than a loan, where the difference in the previously established exchange rate actually represented the interest on a loan granted by the subject who issued the letter of exchange. Hence the person receiving it was really the beneficiary of a loan and not of a foreign exchange transaction.[5]

These stratagems were all motivated by the need to respect, both formally and in substance, the canon laws forbidding usury. In the field of loan contracts, this resulted in a split along parallel lines between appearing and being, between theoretical concept and concrete action, which gave rise to an infinite number of treatises dealing with exchange rates, insurance and all the circulating assets suspected of being loans with interest. The debate continued without a pause throughout the Middle Ages and into the Renaissance, with many variations on the theme. On the one hand, all of the stratagems used to conceal loans granted at rates constituting usury were progressively invented, studied and described; and on the other, further expedients were sought to evade the canonical condemnation of usury. Obviously, the age-old question, unanswerable in practical life, as to the legitimacy of charging interest, led to officially acknowledging the role of the Jews as money lenders. Only they, in principle, could

3. Paolo Uccello
The Miracle of the Profaned Host
1467–9
Urbino, Galleria Nazionale delle Marche

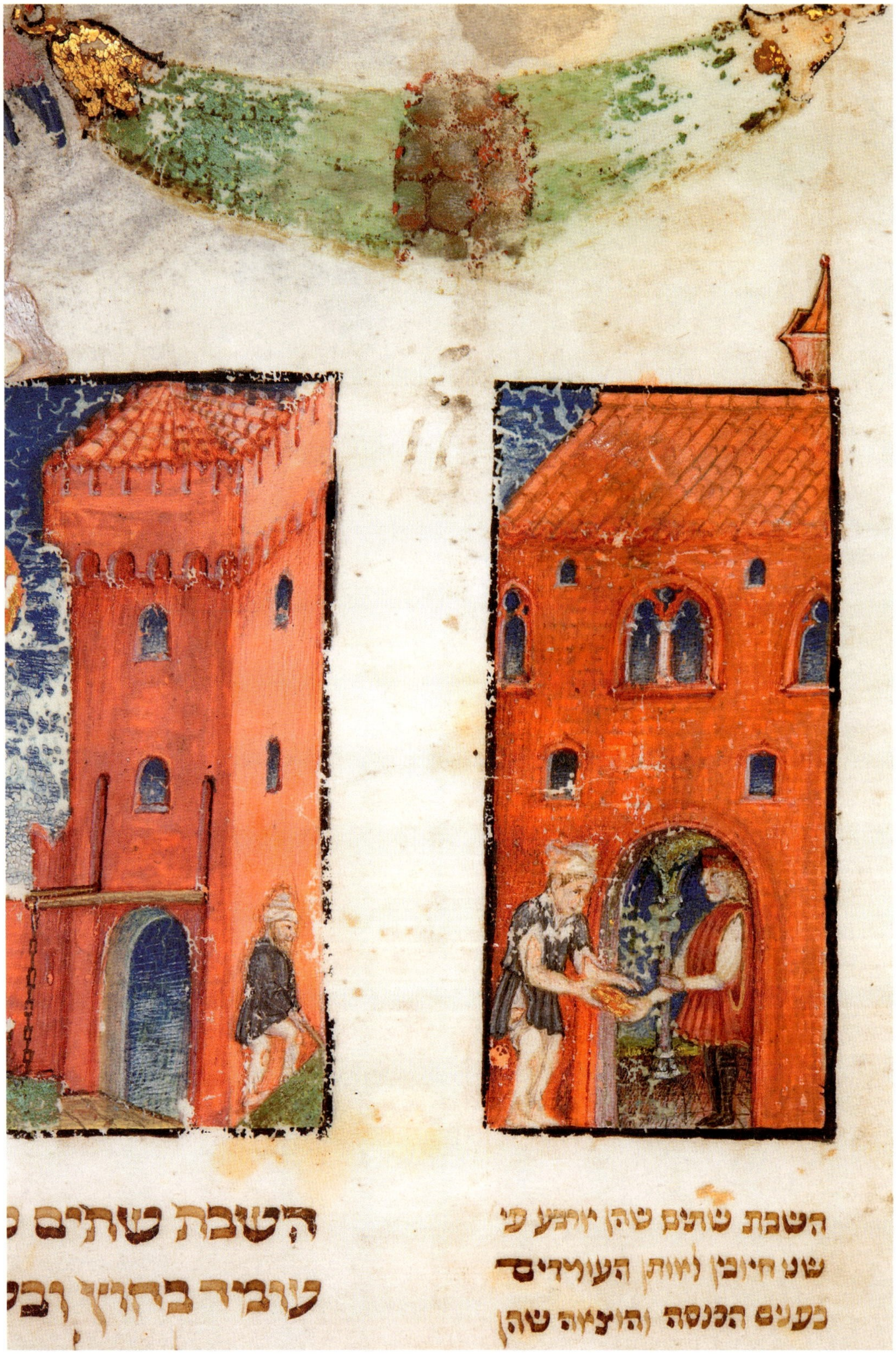
השבת שתים
עומד בחוץ
השבת שתים שהן ארבע פי
שני חיובין לאות העומדים
בפנים הכנסה והוצאה שהן

be authorized to practice usury since, not belonging to the Christian world, they were not subject to its laws. And in the Holy Scriptures, most notably some passages from the Old Testament, Jewish tradition seemed to legitimize the practice of taking interest on loans granted to foreigners, those of another faith.[6]

In the late Middle Ages the legitimacy of "usury," that is, lending money with interest, was questioned with renewed fervour in Florence, where it had traditionally been practiced by Christian money lenders, subject to the scruples of conscience but not to any express prohibition. Censorious voices were raised and possible restrictive measures were considered; but even when first introduced, these restrictions were not obeyed. At times a sort of compensation was offered with the payment of substantial amounts as penalty. Then in 1394, Christians were officially barred from lending money at interest. Although the idea of replacing them with Jewish money lenders[7] soon arose, this was actually to happen only much later. A clear distinction may be drawn between two historical periods. In the first, the beginning of the late Middle Ages, Jewish money lenders were present only in the *contado*, the small or medium-sized localities of the Florentine State. During the second period instead, starting only in 1430, the Jews, some of whom were probably already living in the city at the time, were authorized to open loan banks in Florence. Jewish money-lending was officially recognized in 1437 when Abramo di Dattilo di San Miniato was granted permission to open three banks, collaborating with other partners in a kind of banking consortium, and two years later the banks had become four in number. The city's authorities took this radical step in the hope of definitively halting the spread of usury practiced by Christian money lenders, something they had never managed to do before. After 1437 then, the Jewish community in Florence increased substantially, in keeping with the growing number of banks opened in the following years. This situation attracted still further arrivals, a tendency observed elsewhere in similar conditions.

The banks owned by the Florentine Jews, situated at the heart of the city, bore names related to the sites they occupied. In the early days, from 1437 to 1441, four Jewish banks were opened: Santa Trinita, occupying premises in Palazzo Spini Feroni still to be seen today, directed by the first Jew granted permission to open a bank, the previously mentioned Abramo di Dattilo di San Miniato; the so-called "della Vacca" bank, directed by Dattilo di Consiglio da Tivoli with other partners;[8] the Soldani bank,[9] directed by Jacob da Perugia and Jacob da Toscanella and later by Vitale da Rimini; and lastly the Ricci bank,[10] directed by Salomone di Bonaventura da Terracina. This personage, who represented the third generation of a family from Lazio that had settled in Tuscany, was the well-known owner of an important loan bank in Prato[11] and a partner in the banks of Monte San Savino and Pisa.[12] To open the loan bank in Florence he had been obliged to disburse the large sum of 800 florins, equivalent to the amount charged him as annual fee for operating the bank in Prato.

The Florentine venture of Salomone di Bonaventura was not a happy one. Accused years later of having illicitly managed the de' Ricci loan bank, since it was formally owned by his sons although still minors, he was inflicted by the Potestà of Florence, Niccolò Porcinari, with a colossal penalty of 20,000 florins.[13] This penalty, applied on rather spurious grounds, put the bank in such deep trouble that it was finally forced to declare bankruptcy.

Subsequently, after alternating fortunes and hard-won confirmation of permission to continue in the banking field, two more banks were founded: that of the Borghese family,

4. *Residence of Jewish money lenders*
Parma, Biblioteca Palatina, ms. Parm. 3273, fol. LV

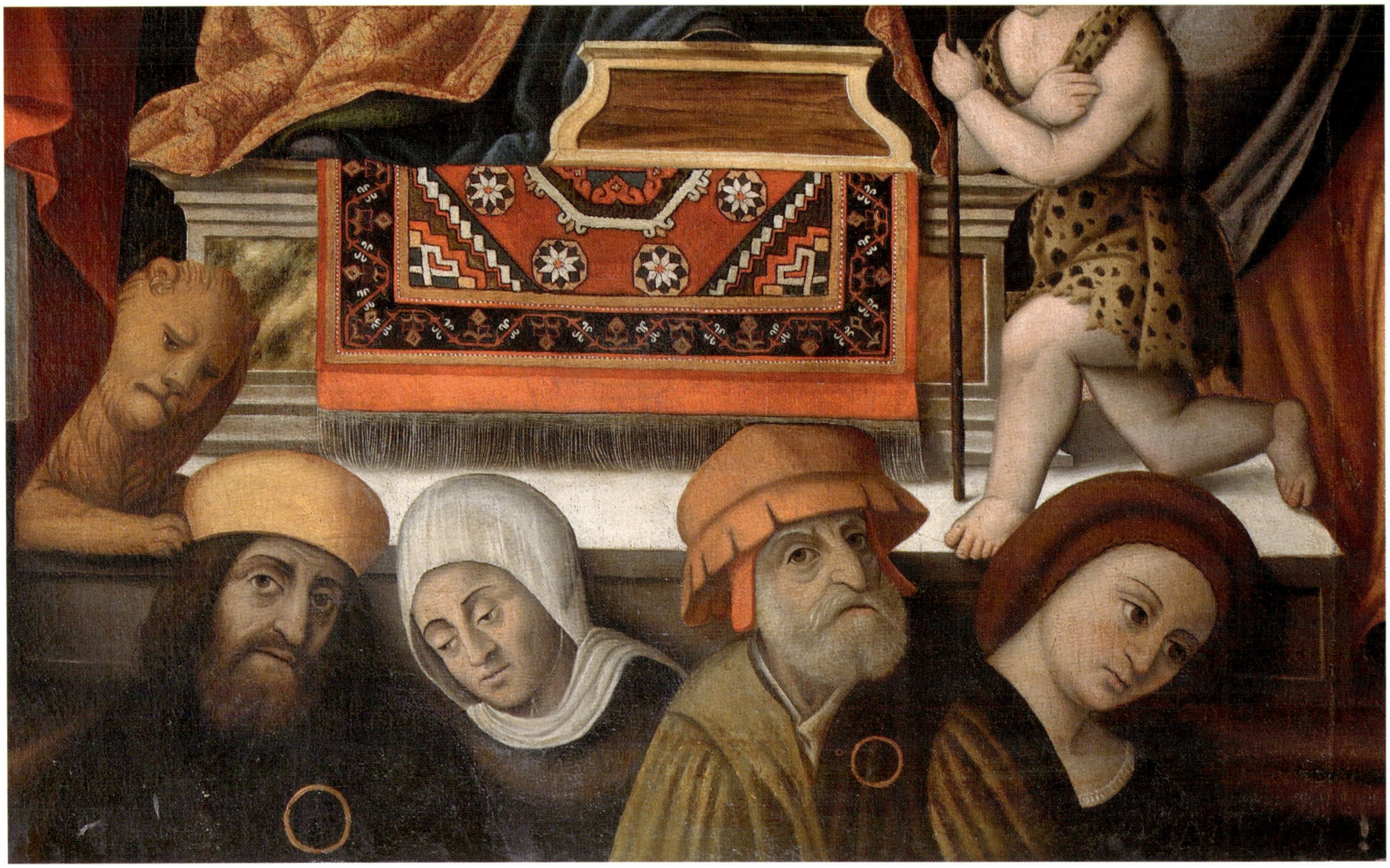

5. School of Mantegna
Members of the Norsa family, Jewish bankers, detail from the *Virgin and Child with Saints*
first decades of the 16th century
Mantua, Church of Sant'Andrea

who took over the Ricci bank after its bankruptcy,[14] and that of the Quattro Pavoni.[15] The licensing fee, originally amounting to 600 florins, rose to no less than 1200 florins with the renovation of the banks in the 1480s. These were truly exorbitant amounts, proving once more that the second reason for allowing Jewish banks to open, in addition to replacing Christian usurers with Jewish ones, was to procure conspicuous sums for the city's treasury. The conditions set for the operation of the Florentine Jews' banks were basically the same as elsewhere, disciplined by precise clauses that stipulated a mean interest rate of 20% a year. At the most favourable moment, the time of greatest acceptance of the Jewish banks, the interest rates rose as high as 30%. The lives and businesses of the Jews in Florence were marked by controversial incidents deriving from basic intolerance dating back to the ancient accusation of deicide hurled at the Jews, viewed as enemies of the Christian faith, but now intensified by having labelled them usurers. Over the nearly century-long span of their activity as bankers in Florence the Jews experienced, albeit with profound, contradictory fluctuations in their status and living conditions, moments of extreme tension alternating with periods of serene tranquillity.

After the misadventure of Salomone di Bonaventura, artfully schemed by the Florentine authorities, another equally grave episode involved Vitale di Dattilo da Montalcino, who, along with his brothers Guglielmo and Consiglio, had been authorized to lend money against pledges. Accused, whether rightly or wrongly is unknown, of having continued to practice money-lending beyond his term of authorization, he was obliged to pay an enormous penalty, no less than 22,000 florins, to avoid ending up in prison.[16] One of the persistent afflictions that plagued the Florentine Jews was the obligation to wear a distinctive badge, usually a yellow wheel. This very

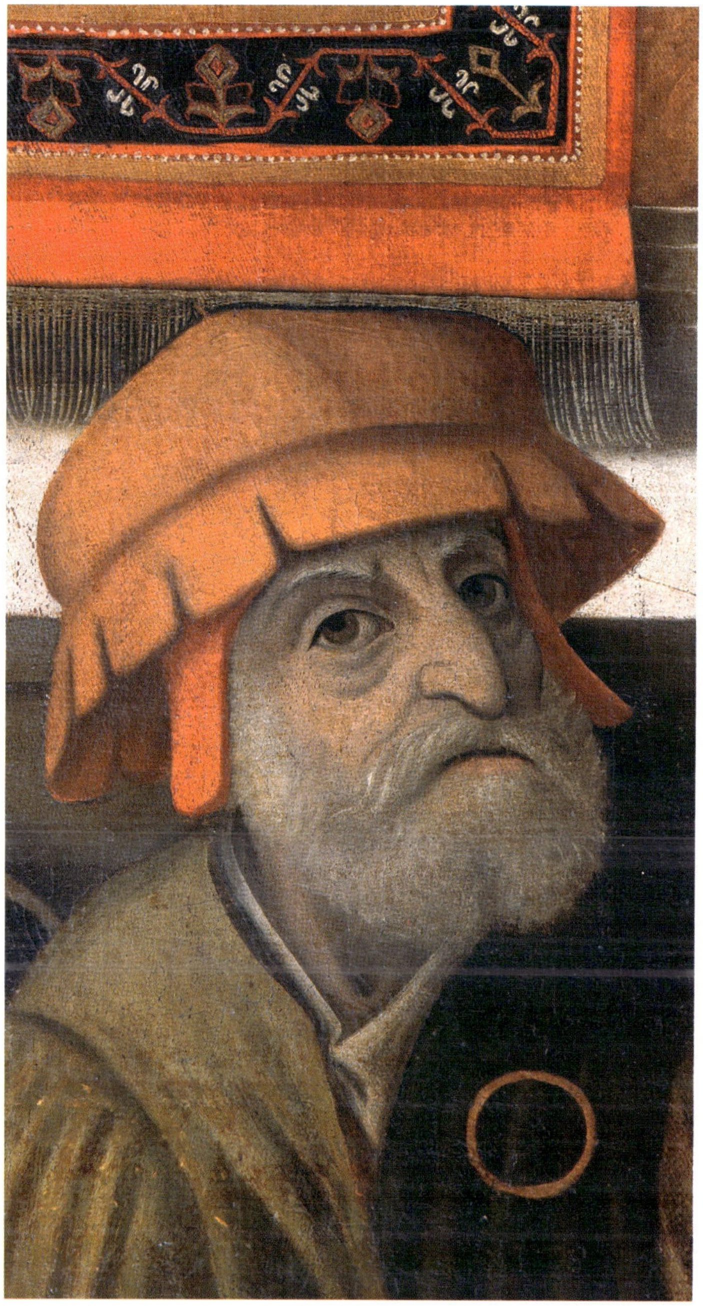

widespread imposition on Jews met with fierce resistance, especially because the badge, by immediately identifying a Jew, could expose him to violence. The Jews who loaned money against pledges generally managed to obtain for themselves, and sometimes their families, exemption from wearing the detested badge. For the Florentine Jews the situation wavered between granting and denying exemption.[17] This problem, like all the others affecting their lives and banking business, was influenced by the attitude and politics of the Commune of Florence, depending on who headed the government of the Republic.

With the coming to power of the Medici, conditions improved for the Florentine Jews. We have reports of friendly and almost intimate relations, albeit with due respect, among members of the Florentine Jewish community and the Medici family.[18] By contrast, after the restrictive measures of the 1450s and 1460s limiting the number of Jews residing in the city to seventy persons[19] and the reintroduction of the badge in 1463, there had even been a movement, accompanied by a show of public hostility, to close the Jewish banks. At this time there had begun to flourish, urged on by the exhortations of the Minor Friars and then the Dominicans, the pawnshops known as Monti di Pietà,[20] charity institutions, at least according to the original idea, designed to extend loans guaranteed by pledges practically free of charge.

The mendicant orders preached in Tuscany too, Florence in particular, with regular sermons, starting in the late 1480s, by Bernardino da Feltre,[21] the great promoter of the Monti di Pietà, who planned to open one in Florence as well. But at this point the Medici policy, generally pro-Jewish, intervened once again to suppress the uprisings against the Jews that often broke out after a sermon by Bernardino. The Medici government enacted protective measures to ensure that no episodes of intolerance or violence would occur again, going so far as to exile the Franciscan friar from the city.[22] For the Florentine Jews the last years of Lorenzo the Magnificent's Signoria were peaceful and serene, and during this period all the concessions for loan banks were renewed under the same terms. This may be considered the golden age of Jewish banking in Florence, thanks to the protection of the Medici. Even the hotly debated issue of opening a Monte di Pietà pawnshop reached a truce. But after the fall of the Signoria in 1494, the problem of eliminating Jewish usury and founding a Monte di Pietà arose again. This plan was vigorously promoted by Girolamo Savonarola, who had assumed political control of the city when the Medici abandoned it.[23] The Monte entered operation in 1496, interrupting the long duration of Jewish banking. But the Jews remained in Florence and, having returned to political favour with the restoration of Medici power in 1512, resumed their role as money lenders starting in 1514.

There was now of course the rivalry of the Monte di Pietà to contend with, but since the Jewish bankers' role was equally necessary, the conditions for renewing permission to open banks were less burdensome. The annual tax in particular was much lower. Two Jewish banks were opened in 1518. They were managed by the Rieti family, destined to play an increasingly important role in Tuscany and to become leaders of the Jewish community in Florence, and later in Siena.[24] The city government continued to contract heavy debts with the Jewish banks, deducting the amounts it owed from the licensing fee of 600 florins paid annually by the banks. In 1527 the Medici were driven out for a second time. The definitive demise of the Jewish banks and the progressive expulsion of

6. Francesco Rosselli
The Preaching of Fra Marco da Montegallo
late 15th century
Florence, Gabinetto Disegni e Stampe degli Uffizi,
Stampe sciolte 239 B.

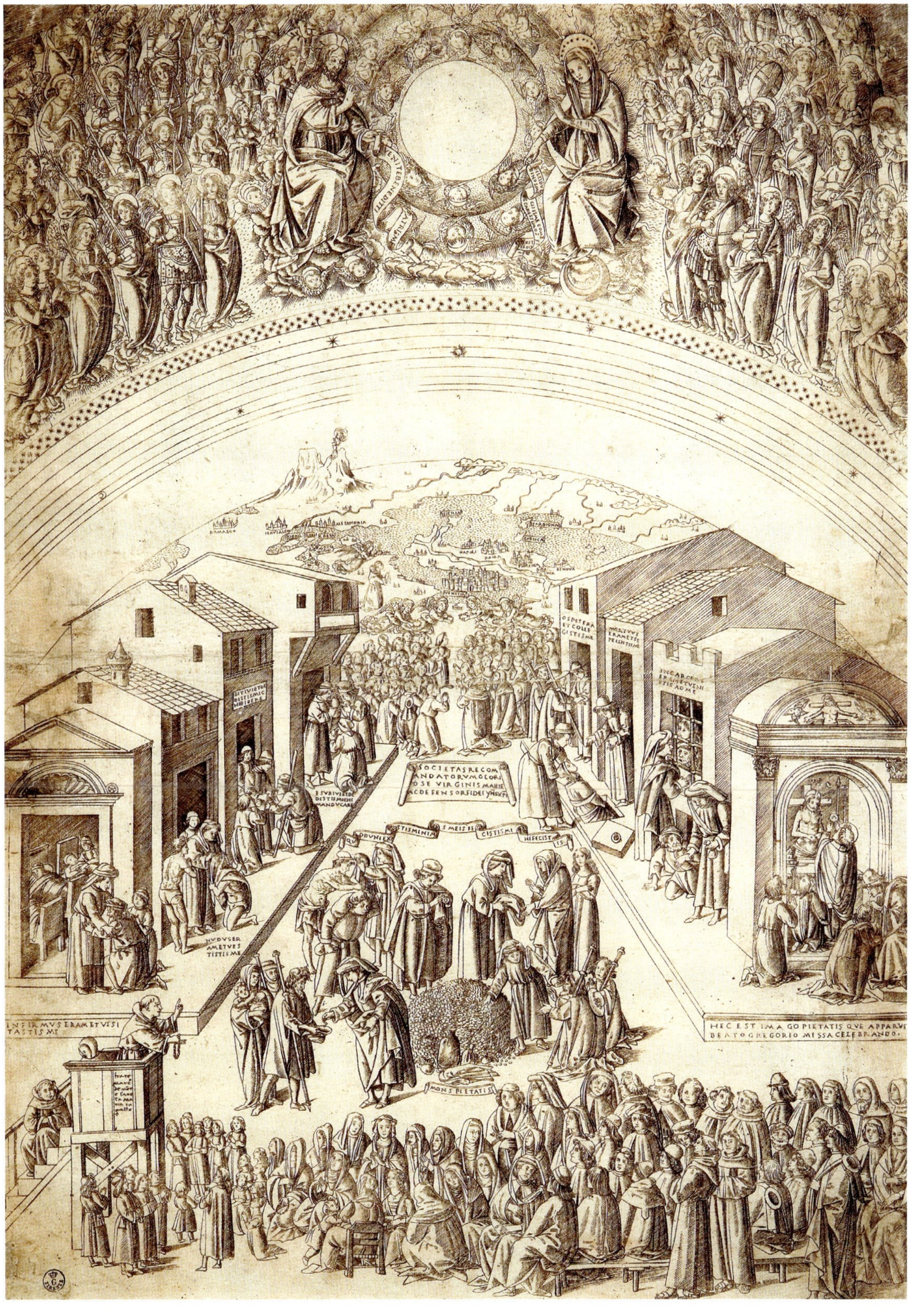
SOCIETAS RECOM
ANDATORVM GLORI
OSE VIRGINIS MARIE
AC DEFENSOR FIDEI YHS XPI
INFIRMVS ERAM ET VISI
TASTIS ME
HEC EST IMAGO PIETATIS QVE APPARVI
BEATO GREGORIO MISSA CELEBRANDO.
MONS PIETATIS

55

the Jews gave rise to a diaspora, involving even such eminent families as the Da Pisa and Da Rieti. With the return of the Medici, the Jews who had remained in Florence then benefited by a new political situation, although their traditional loan banks were opened or confirmed only in the territory, and no longer in the city of Florence. At this time their interests turned toward the field of commerce, thanks to the concessions granted them by Cosimo I.

Then the Jews' position was threatened again by the introduction of the ghetto, in Florence in 1570, in Siena in 1571. After the war with Siena and the unification of the two States under the name of Grand Duchy, in fact, the policy of restriction and confinement imposed by the Church starting with the Papal Bull of Paul IV was extended to Tuscany.[25] But by now the activity of the Jewish bankers in Florence had long ceased, never again to return. Usury, while still branded as iniquitous apart from the official role of the Monte di Pietà, was to be directly or indirectly practiced, more or less unofficially when not actually clandestinely, by Christian operators.

1. This is clearly evident, for example, in the famous passage from *Deuteronomy* (23:19-20), which states: "*Non foenerabis fratri tuo ad usuram pecuniam, nec fruges, nec quamlibet aliam rem, sed alieno. Fratri tuo absque usura id quo indiget commodabis.*" And again in *Leviticus* (25:35-37): "*Pecuniam tuam non dabis ei ad usuram.*" For a discussion of the significance of the passage from *Deuteronomy* and its consequences, see the classic work of Benjamin Nelson (Nelson 1949).

2. In the Latin patristic tradition, the totally negative nature of taking interest, a practice that caused the death of the soul, is strikingly expressed: "*Fenus pecuniae funus est animae.*"

3. The Latin expression that succinctly translates Aristotle's view is: "*Pecunia pecuniam parere non potest.*"

4. Among the other works of Thomas Aquinas dealing marginally or directly with problems of life and financial activity, especially pertinent are: the *Summa contra Gentiles*, the *Commento all'Etica nicomachea*, the *De Regimine principum* and the reply to a letter from the Duchess of Brabante, entitled *De Regimine Judareorum ad Ducissam Brabantiae*. In general, on the overall contribution of the Scholastics to the question of usury, see the ample, classic study of John T. Noonan (Noonan 1957). For an in-depth synthesis of ethical thought on economic and financial issues from antiquity to the Renaissance, the work of Gino Barbieri (Barbieri 1963) is fundamental.

5. See, on this subject, especially the profound analysis of Raymond de Roover (1953).

6. Compare in this regard the above-mentioned passage from *Deuteronomy* (see note 1), which emphatically states that usury should be reserved to foreigners. The whole question of the origin and foundations of Jewish money-lending is dealt with in Cassandro 2008, pp. 39–48, which also takes into consideration the ample debate on this subject held in the last few years.

7. See Cassuto 1918, pp. 13–5. It appears evident here how attempts to enforce the prohibition were opposed by strong resistance and by the interests of the Florentine money lenders, going so far as to issue, in 1406, a provision contrary to the decisions taken years before, since it prohibited Jewish money-lending.

8. The bank known as "della Vacca" may have been situated in what is now Via dei Pecori, between Piazza dell'Olio and Via Brunelleschi (Cassuto 1918, p. 125).

9. It was situated in the so-called Canto de' Soldani, near the Church of San Remigio (Cassuto 1918, pp. 124–5).

10. This bank was situated in Canto de' Ricci in one of the family's houses, probably on the Corso (Cassuto 1918, p. 125).

11. See Cassandro 1991, pp. 444–5.

12. See Cassuto 1918, p. 126, no. 1.

13. On this topic, see the article by Antonio Panella (Panella 1909) and the ample commentary by Umberto Cassuto (Cassuto 1918, pp. 127–30), who, contrary to the author's opinion, does not consider the Potestà's sentence to be illegal, even though clearly determined by the desire to obtain a large sum of money to cover the enormous expenses of the Republic in severe financial trouble, due also to the extraordinary expense incurred in buying Borgo San Sepolcro from the Pope.

14. The Borghese bank, according to the in-depth study of Cassuto, was named for the site it occupied, in the ancient Chiasso del Borghese, more or less the area now occupied by Via degli Anselmi (Cassuto 1918, pp. 132–3).

15. The location of this bank too has been identified by Cassuto, who has proposed the part of Oltrarno situated between Via dello Sprone and Via Toscanella (Cassuto 1918, p. 137). On the Quattro Pavoni loan bank, see the recent study by Flavia Careri, centred on the account book of Isacco da San Miniato (Careri 2001).

16. Cassuto 1918, pp. 138–9.

17. See on this subject again Cassuto, who points out the alternating provisions, often contradictory, on exemption from or obligation to wear an identifying badge, even for Jewish bankers (Cassuto 1918, pp. 37–41).

18. Cassandro 1977, p. 431 note 17 and pp. 445–7, containing two letters from Jacob di Consiglio to Giovanni di Cosimo de' Medici, dated 1461 and 1463 respectively.

19. Cassuto 1918, p. 47.

20. On the Monti di Pietà, ample historiography has existed for years, tracing the spread of this institution all over the Italian territory. For examples of some cases of different provenance, of their relations with public banks and of the debate on these institutions, see some articles included in the proceeds of a conference held at Genoa several years ago (*Banchi pubblici* 1991).

21. On the figure of Bernardino da Feltre, on his preaching, and on the publication and content of his Sermons, various studies of different kinds have confronted the analysis from different angles: Casolini 1939; Bernardino da Feltre (1493), ed. 1940; Barbieri 1963; Muzzarelli 1978. See also entry 3.7 in this catalogue.

22. Cassuto 1918, pp. 56–9.

23. The entire episode has been thoroughly described in the study of Marino Ciardini with the ample reproduction of documents (Ciardini 1907).

24. Simonsohn 1972.

25. This is the famous Papal Bull *Cum nimis absurdum* of 1555, which sanctioned the institution of the ghetto in Rome.

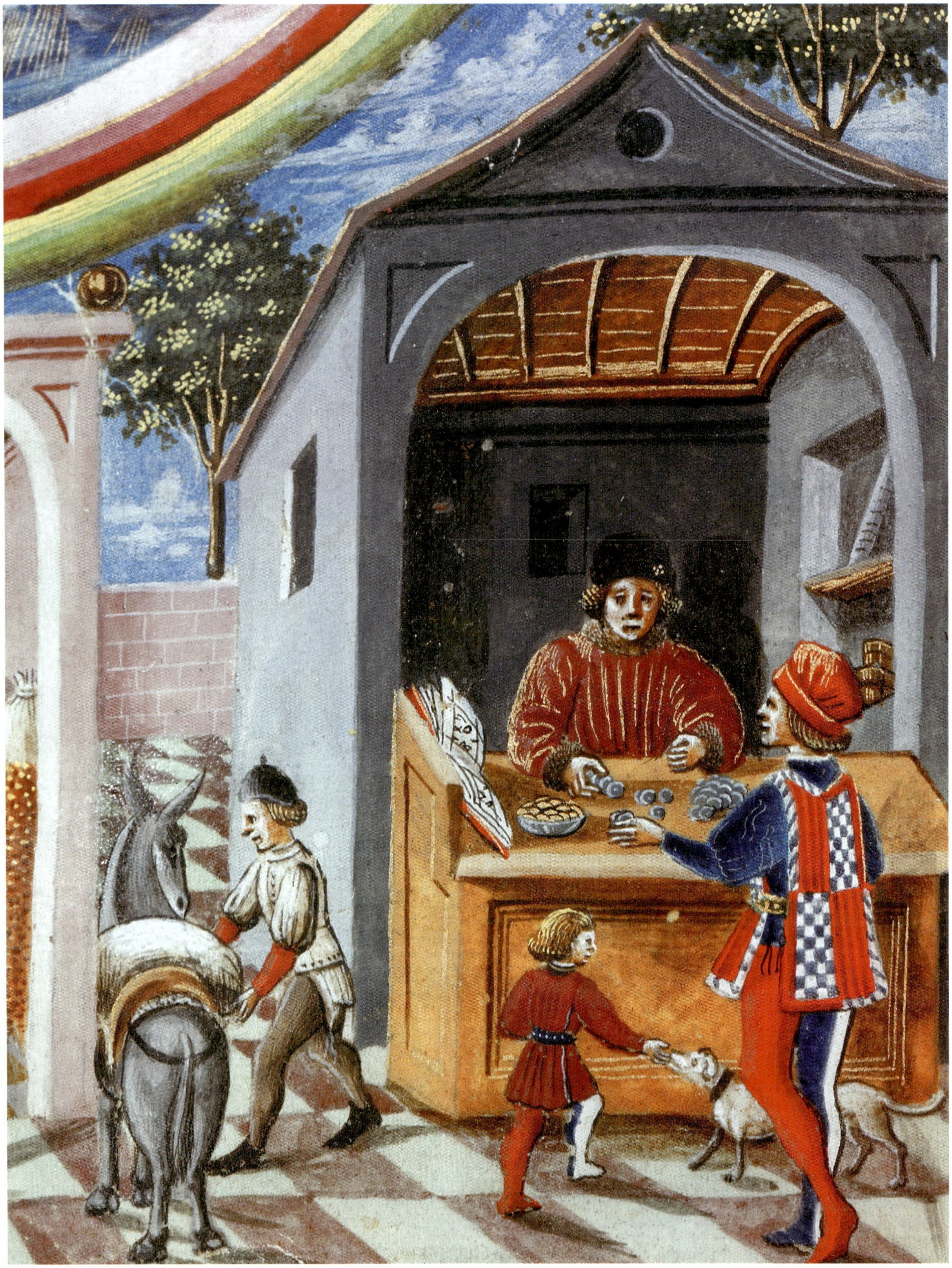

Banks, Letters of Exchange and International Business

Francesco Guidi Bruscoli

"And so Franciescho di Marcho intends to lose his reputation as the greatest merchant in Florence to become a money changer, since a man who doesn't make usury contracts is a nobody." When in 1398 the great merchant of Prato Francesco di Marco Datini decided to open a local banking concern, his assistant Domenico di Cambio warned him that this could damage his reputation, as he had "heard said by a number of persons."[1] Not that Datini had been immune to the accusation of practicing usury before, with his network of enterprises scattered all over Europe, operating in Avignon, Florence, Genoa, Pisa, Catalonia and elsewhere. But opening a bank would make things all too obvious. The great merchant-bankers, in fact, wore an aura of respectability that placed them far above other operators in the banking sector. Lending vast sums of money to great sovereigns, including the Pope, they combined banking transactions with the business of international trade, and sometimes with entrepreneurial ventures, mainly in the field of textile manufacturing. Local bankers, instead, were accorded much less prestige, being equated with money changers or—worse still—pawnbrokers, only operating on a larger scale.[2]

The merchant-bankers were active in numerous fields where business and finance were closely interwoven, finance being a derivate of mercantile activity. In the mid-15th century the illustrious merchant from Ragusa, Benedetto Cotrugli, summed up the situation with a metaphor, describing foreign exchange as "a staple and condiment of all things mercantile, so that, just as a man cannot be formed without various foods, trade cannot exist without exchange."[3]

Throughout the late Middle Ages, one of the constant features of the Florentine economy was a credit balance. The global value of the goods exported by Florence was consistently higher than that of the products it imported. Considering the alarming risks involved in transporting coins and precious metals, the gap in the balance of trade was filled by sending "paper" money. This was not of course the modern banknote—introduced centuries later—but instruments of various kinds, by far the most important being the letter

1. Cristoforo De Predis, attributed to
The Money Changer's Bench, in *De Sphaera*
second half of the 15th century
Modena, Biblioteca Estense Universitaria,
Cod. Lat. 209, fol. 6v

of exchange, true symbol of the network of economic and financial relations that was binding the markets of late medieval Europe ever closer.

One of the early roots of this international financial network was the collection of "Peter's pence," the offerings flowing to the Church of Rome from every corner of Christianity. Even prior to the 13th century, financial operators in Florence and other Italian cities were involved in transferring these tithes to the papal court. Occasionally they managed to exploit the momentary availability of funds to carry out commercial operations as well. In England, for instance, the great monasteries that owed money to the Pope possessed only limited funds, but abundant wool. In this case, banking and trade converged to perfection, since the raw material was transported to the South and sold at a profit to the industrious Florentine wool-workers, the income then being used to pay the tithe in Rome.

When tithes came from areas beyond the Italian-dominated trading network, or from places which had no produce for which there was a demand, these assets (in goods or cash) would be sent to one of the great European economic-financial centres, whence the money could be transferred to Italy, often through a letter of exchange. In north-central and north-eastern Europe, this function was served by Bruges, one of the largest commercial and financial marketplaces on the continent in the 14th and 15th centuries. As early as the first third of the 14th century, thanks to the capability and scope of such great Florentine merchant-bankers as the Bardi, Peruzzi and Acciaioli (the only operators able to organize such a system), the Apostolic Chamber had money coming from the remotest corners of Christendom via the Flemish city, and could even request advance payment of sums that were guaranteed by the future inflow of tithes: "The system had arrived at a state of virtual perfection."[4]

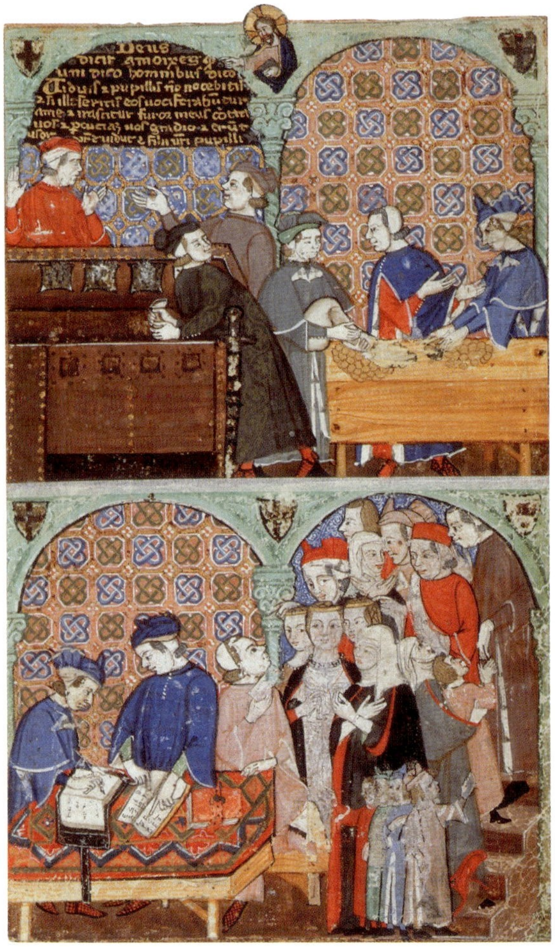

2. Cybo, Monk of Hyères
Two scenes of banking in Genoa in the *Treatise on Vices*
c. 1375–1400
London, British Library, ms Add. 27695, fol. 8

Hence the letter of exchange originally served the purpose of allowing international transfer of funds. Exactly when this instrument was created is not known. In the surviving documentation it is mentioned for the first time near the end of the 13th century.[5] In its standard form, a letter of exchange presumed the existence of two cities belonging to different monetary areas, and four operators (two in each city). In place A, the *giver* assigned a sum of money to the *payee* so that, at an established date, an equivalent sum would be paid, in place B (and in the currency of that place), by the *drawee* to the *beneficiary*. The payee consigned the letter of exchange to the giver, so that he could send it the beneficiary; at the same time he wrote to the drawee, informing him of the transaction in course. Obviously, the payee and the drawee were bankers bound by ties of custom and trust. At the specified due date, the beneficiary went to the drawee to collect the amount due him, at an exchange rate established when the letter was issued. At first the order to pay was included in a business letter, but in the 14th century a clearly defined form was established, written on a little strip of paper. No stage of the transaction called for certification by a notary.

The letter of exchange was thus a mean for transferring money; but it could also serve another purpose, one that contributed significantly to its great success. It could, in fact, be used to extend credit.[6] The problem in granting loans was, as we know, remuneration. The anti-usury laws tried to keep money from producing money, as it did when a loan was burdened by interest. In the fast-growing economy spurred on by a revolution in trade, however, it was unthinkable not to recur to credit, and not to remunerate it.

Consequently, the merchant-bankers employed various instruments—including the letter of exchange—to "conceal" the interest charged. In effect, the credit transaction took place through an exchange and a re-exchange, accomplished by sending two letters: the first from place A to place B and the second, compiled after expiry of the first, in the

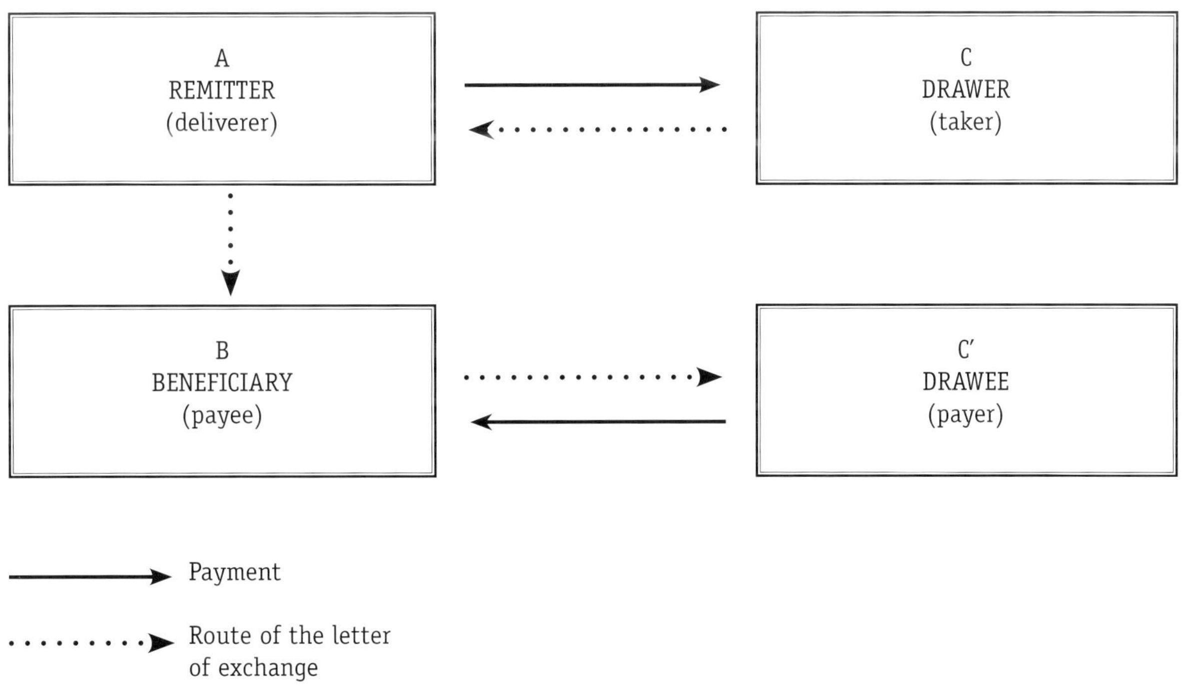

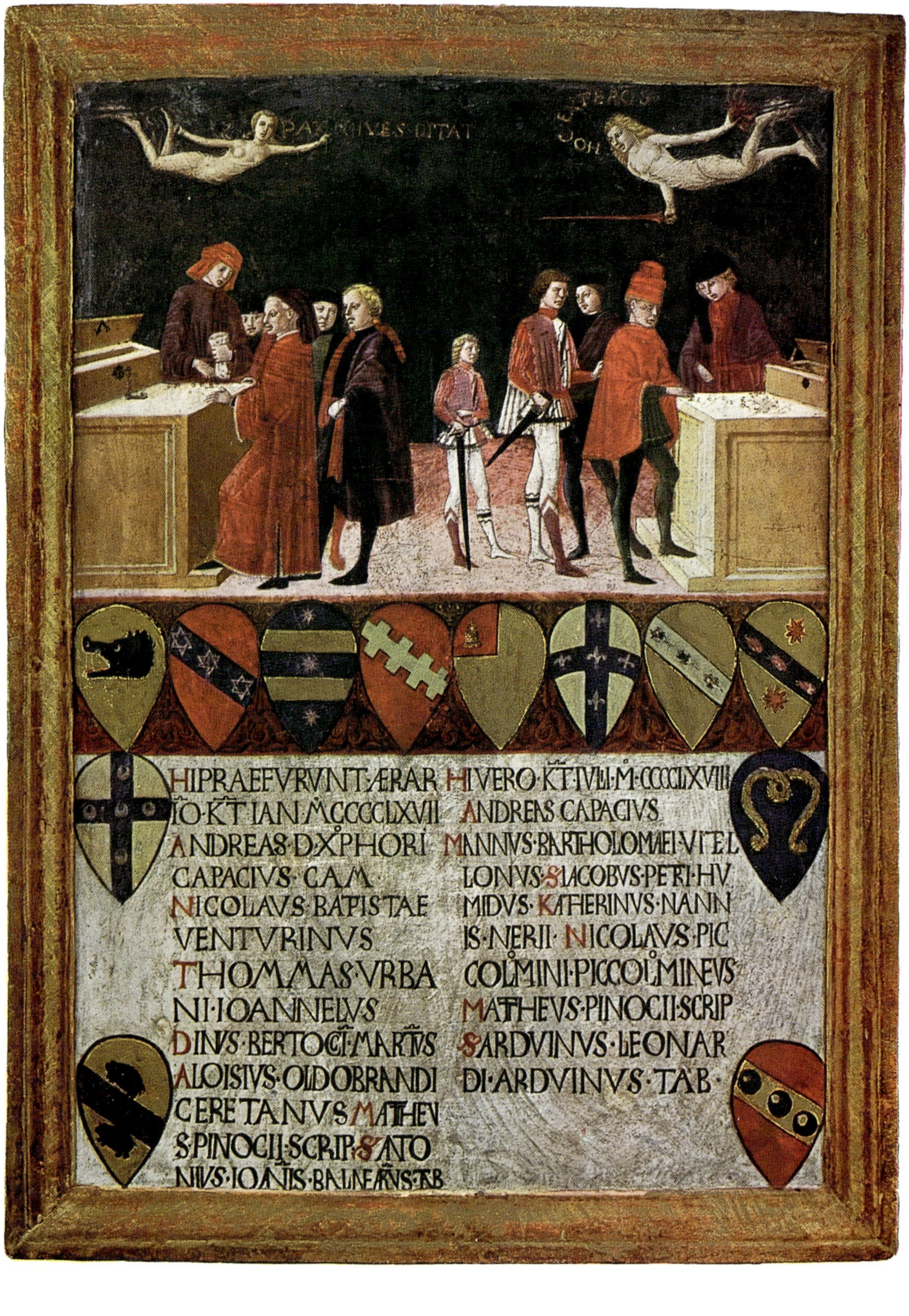
HI PRAEFVRVNT ÆRAR
IO·KT IAN·M·CCCCLXVII
ANDREAS·D·XPHORI
CAPACIVS·CAM
NICOLAVS·BATISTAE
VENTVRINVS
THOMMAS·VRBA
NI·IOANNELVS
DINVS·BERTOCCI·MARTVS
ALOISIVS·OLDOBRANDI
CERETANVS·MATHEV
S·PINOCII·SCRIP·S·ATO
NIVS·IOANIS·BALNEARNS·TAB
HI VERO·KT·IVLII·M·CCCCLXVIII
ANDREAS CAPACIVS
MANNVS·BARTHOLOMAEI·VITEL
LONVS·S·IACOBVS·PETRI·HV
MIDVS·KATHERINVS·NANN
IS·NERII·NICOLAVS·PIC
COLOMINI·PICCOLOMINEVS
MATHEVS·PINOCII·SCRIP
S·ARDVINVS·LEONAR
DI·ARDVINVS·TAB·

opposite direction. The giver, who had paid the money in place A, received, at the due date of the second letter, a sum that was generally greater than the original amount, for reasons I shall discuss. In this case we speak of a *dry exchange*, because the first letter was not really liquidated, and in fact the roles of drawee and beneficiary were frequently assumed by a single merchant-banker, who served only to prepare and send the second letter (his role in this transaction being that of giver-payee). At a further stage, this "fiction" too was abolished; or rather, a more blatant fiction was introduced, since it was the letter itself to become fictitious, being neither written nor sent but appearing only in the accounting records of the operators involved.

In effect, the currency exchange rates in the different marketplaces were exploited for the purpose of earning profit. Since the rates were variable, it could be legitimately claimed that any resulting profit was aleatory and as such could not be considered remuneration for money, but rather compensation for risk. Clearly, the difference is a subtle point, so finedrawn that centuries of debate led to granting more or less restrictive exceptions.

It is astonishing that in times when information was conveyed through the slow (and occasionally unpredictable) postal service, the merchant-bankers almost always managed to earn profit on international transactions that might take as long as six months to arrive at conclusion. Numerous uncertainties and extraneous factors (not least among them war) could interfere in the meantime, altering exchange rates and thus changing the context in which the agreement was made. It was crucially important to have a wide-ranging, trustworthy information network, and it is no coincidence that having "ink-stained hands" was a distinctive trait of the medieval merchant.[7] But the real key to the operation lay in the dif-

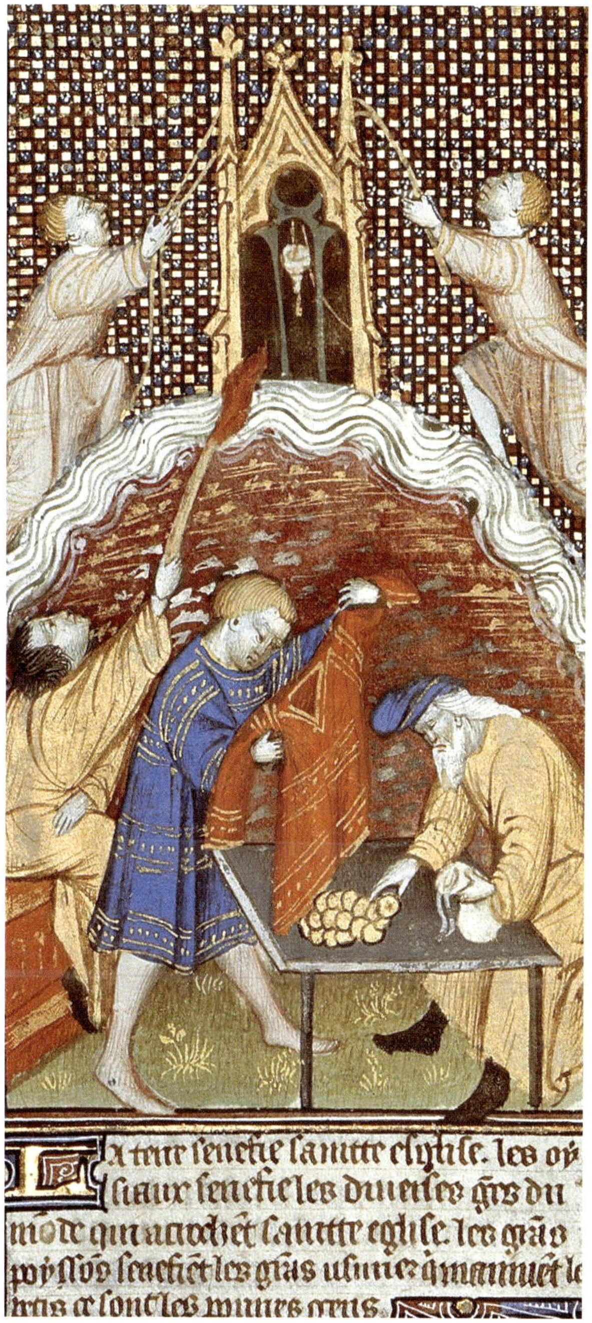

3. Benvenuto di Giovanni
The Finances of the Commune in Times of Peace
(when the Bankers are paid)
and in Times of War (the Mercenaries)
1468
Siena, Archivio di Stato, Tavoletta di Biccherna 35

4. *Pawnbroker* from the *Heures du Duc de Rohan*
c. 1425–8
Paris, Bibliothèque nationale de France, Mss. fr 9471

ferent quotations of the *pecunia presens* and the *pecunia absens*; which is to say, a coin (the florin, for instance) was worth more in the place where the letter of exchange was issued (Florence) than in the place where it was then liquidated in foreign currency. The same thing, basically, is still true today.

Over the course of a year fluctuations determined a greater or lesser difference between the two values. Sometimes fluctuation in exchange rates was predictable, since it was linked to seasonal trading, that is, to the departure—which would take place at a certain time of year—or return—somewhat less predictable—of the convoys of galleys and sailing ships that connected the great mercantile centres. For this reason, Venice emerged as an exchange centre of primary importance. It was the port of departure for regular convoys (called *mude*) headed both east and west, and a centre for the collection of vast amounts of silver coming from the mines of east-central Europe and destined mainly to the Near East.

Moments of *larghezza* (abundance) and *strettezza* (scarcity) of money, and hence its varying cost, were common occurrences. Since exchanging currency at the right moment obviously ensured maximum profits, attempts were made to reduce uncertainty to a minimum; but unforeseen events could still make exchange transactions risky, causing losses. Basically, as has been said, it was just this risk that "saved" the merchant-bankers from the tirades of the Church. Where there was no certainty of gaining profit, nor of how much, condemnation was less harsh.

Even so, the subject was a slippery one. One of the aspects that could be evaluated was intention. As Bernardo Davanzati wrote in the late 16th century, "The greed for [...] profit has transformed foreign exchange into an art. They send money to be exchanged, not because they need to have it elsewhere, but to get it back with profit; and they take it, not to bring their money back from somewhere else, but to use that of others for some time with interest."[8] For years, such accusations had been laid against the Italians in foreign markets, where the favour of the sovereign often contrasted with the rancour of local merchants, who felt outdone and ignored. In 1421–3, for example, the mayor of Barcelona praised the *ars mercantilis* for being able to transport goods from places where they abounded to others where they were scarce. In his opinion, however, the Italians had distorted this ability by inventing fictitious contracts of exchange and re-exchange ("*cum per ipsorum subtilia et prava ingenia deserendo utilitatem* [...] *intendunt ad contractus ymaginarios cambiorum, recambiorum, assecuramentorum et aliorum similium*").[9] In 1436, to give another example, a slanderous pamphlet was published in England, *Libelle of Englyshe Polycye*, declaring that the Italians took advantage of their dominant position on the international money market to profiteer.[10]

Even in its simplest form, the letter of exchange served a credit function, lasting from when the money was paid in place A to when the letter was liquidated in place B. In later developments, as has been seen, this function became predominant and was a major stimulus to the development of international exchange. Among other things, the payee himself could use the money received to extend credit on his own. In doing so, he provided one of the functions typical of banks (gathering savings and channelling them into investment) while simultaneously incrementing the resources available for the system.

The Tuscan archives, those of Florence in particular, contain a mass of commercial documents from the late Middle Ages to be found nowhere else in Italy. Regrettably, it is often

5. Assistants of Sano di Pietro
Paying the Employees of the Commune
c. 1430–46
Siena, Archivio di Stato,
Tavoletta di Biccherna 92

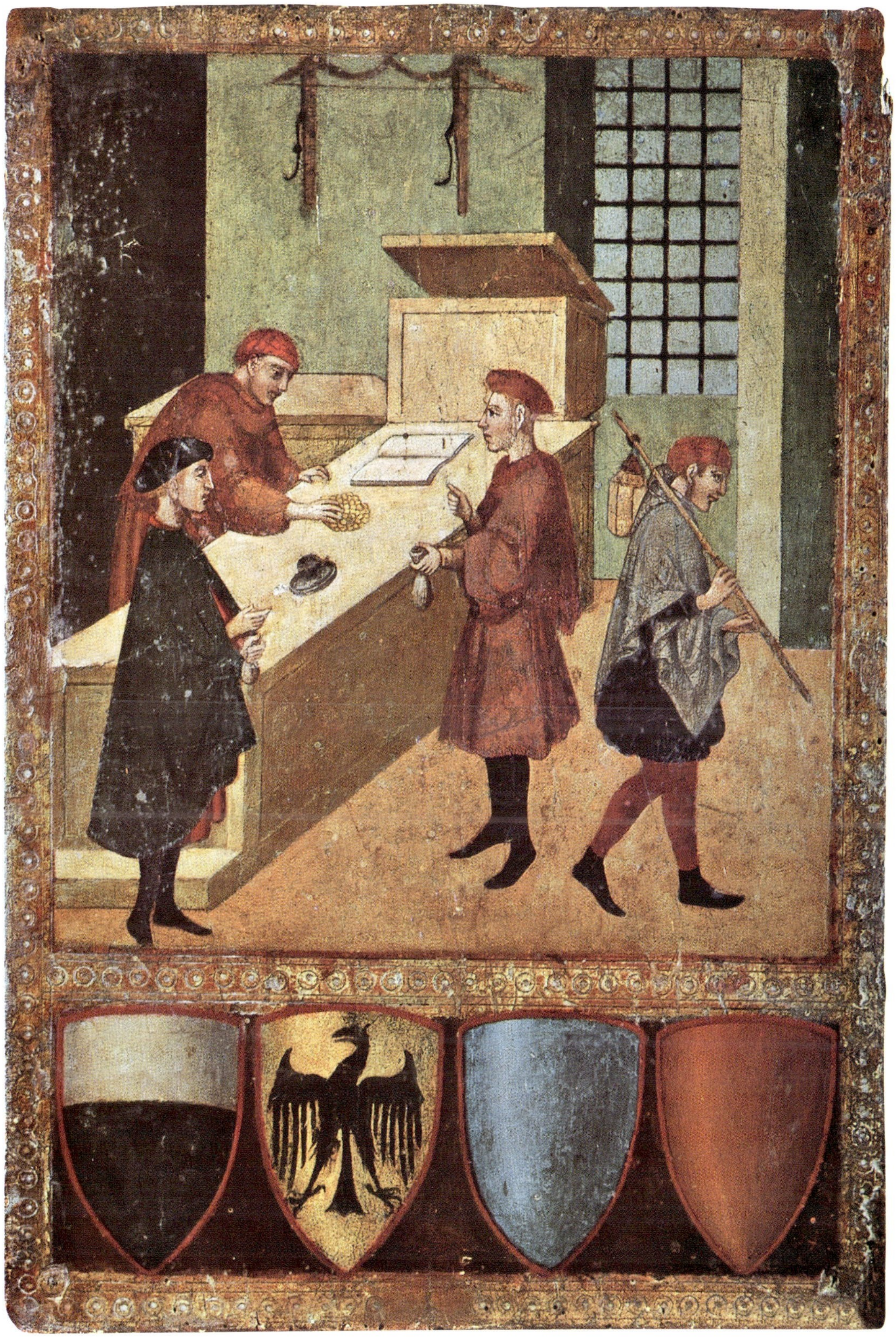

hard to understand, either from the accounting records or the letters of exchange themselves, the reasons behind these exchange transactions. But whether it concealed the granting of a loan or served to effect an international monetary transfer, the letter of exchange had highly advantageous features. It was convertible into money at the due date, was renewable (through repetition of the exchange/re-exchange transaction) and its remuneration, although uncertain, was sufficiently predictable.[11] Consequently, it was used on a vast scale, adapting perfectly to the mechanism of the great trade fairs (first in Geneva, then in Lyon), which provided for clearance and delayed payment. Later on, it was to play a leading role at the fairs—now purely financial—held by the Genoese in various European cities.

Advanced banking techniques, such as the refined and sometimes extremely complex role of the letter of exchange, were not the only reasons for the Italian merchant-bankers' success.[12] It is a fact, however, that the Italians were the leaders of European economy in the Renaissance. They established close ties with the sovereigns of various countries, lending them money in exchange for profitable trading licences. Sometimes disasters occurred (as in the notorious 14th-century bankruptcies of the Bardi and Peruzzi firms, caused mainly by losing the enormous sums they had lent to Edward III, King of England when he defaulted on the debt) but despite the risks they continued to invest and extend their network.

Luxury goods and ordinary merchandise, business letters and letters of exchange travelled over this network, in a system that functioned thanks to the existence of an abstract but crucially important element: trust. Without trust, in fact, it was unthinkable that large sums could be liquidated merely upon the presentation of a little strip of paper. The handwriting, of course, could be a sign of recognition proving the authenticity of a letter. As the Davanzati firm in Venice wrote to the Datini company in Pisa in 1384, "Be advised [...] of what hand you should recognize, in which the order to do what we wish will be sent, and in the same way you should tell us in what hand will be written any mandate for us to do something."[13]

There could be "social sanctions" too. The Florence mercantile communities abroad were numerically rather small, ensuring a mutual control that could lead to expulsion from the business network, if not worse. In case of dispute, the verdict of the Merchants' Court could always be invoked. In some letters we find complaints about the behaviour of fellow countrymen or warnings of their untrustworthiness. But on the whole, everyone knew that the system operated better in the absence of friction, and peaceful coexistence for all was better than fierce competition in the long term.

The largest European companies had a more or less extensive network of branch offices in the main European centres where they engaged in both trade and foreign exchange. Handling credit and deposits in the local sphere was quite limited at first, so these operators cannot be called bankers in the modern sense of the term. But when credit transactions linked to letters of exchange began to be offered on a vast scale, even to persons in no way connected to the commercial system, concrete steps were taken in this direction.[14]

However modern this banking activity became it nevertheless lay under the perpetual threat—more moral than legal—of being considered usury. Although in their everyday work the merchant-bankers "clothed" usury in more presentable robes, they knew at bottom that their activity bordered on the morally illicit. Hence they unfailingly devolved a certain percentage of their profit "to God's poor" and made donations—in life but even more in death—to churches and other religious institutions, though this was not always enough to still the nagging voice of conscience.

1. Luca Del Sera, Datini's partner for many years, commenting on the same subject, claimed the superiority of commerce over banking: "I see most of the money changers moving toward trade and abandoning banking, because they find more profit and also because it is more pleasing to God." Both letters are published by Melis 1962, p. 213.

2. For two examples of local Florentine banks see Goldthwaite 1985 and Tognetti 1997.

3. Cotrugli (*ante* 1469), ed. Tucci 1990, p. 165.

4. Renouard 1965 (quotation p. 110).

5. Bruno Dini notes a letter dated March 24, 1291, with a remittance enclosed, sent by the Cerchi firm from Florence to their agents in England (Dini 1982, p. 104). But the earliest original, independent letter of exchange extant is probably the one sent by the Gallerani-Fini from London to the Papal Court in Rome on October 5, 1305 (now in Gand, published by Cella 2009, pp. 290–1). Genoese notarial records show, however, examples of exchange contracts dating from the late twelfth century (De Roover 1953, pp. 25–9).

6. On connections between the prohibition of usury and the success of the letter of exchange, see De Roover 1963, ed. 1970, pp. 157–202. Other scholars tend to belittle this connection, claiming that there was no need to complicate things, since interest could also be concealed—more simply—by declaring higher sums than those actually lent or by applying fines for delayed payment which had in reality been agreed upon beforehand (Munro 1982, p. 195).

7. On the importance of this information see Guidi Bruscoli 2011.

8. Davanzati (1581), ed. 1988, p. 70.

9. Del Treppo 1968, p. 208.

10. *The Libelle* (1436), ed. Warner 1926, pp. 23–4.

11. Mueller 1997, pp. 353–4.

12. On the banking techniques of the late Middle Ages and the link between these techniques and the success of the Italian merchant-bankers see Guidi Bruscoli 2007.

13. ASPo, *Datini*, 548, Manetto Davanzati and company and Francesco Datini and company, Venice-Pisa, 4 October 1384 (548.2/403198); published, in English, by Mueller 1997, p. 271.

14. Goldthwaite 1987, pp. 6–7; Goldthwaite 2009, pp. 219–21.

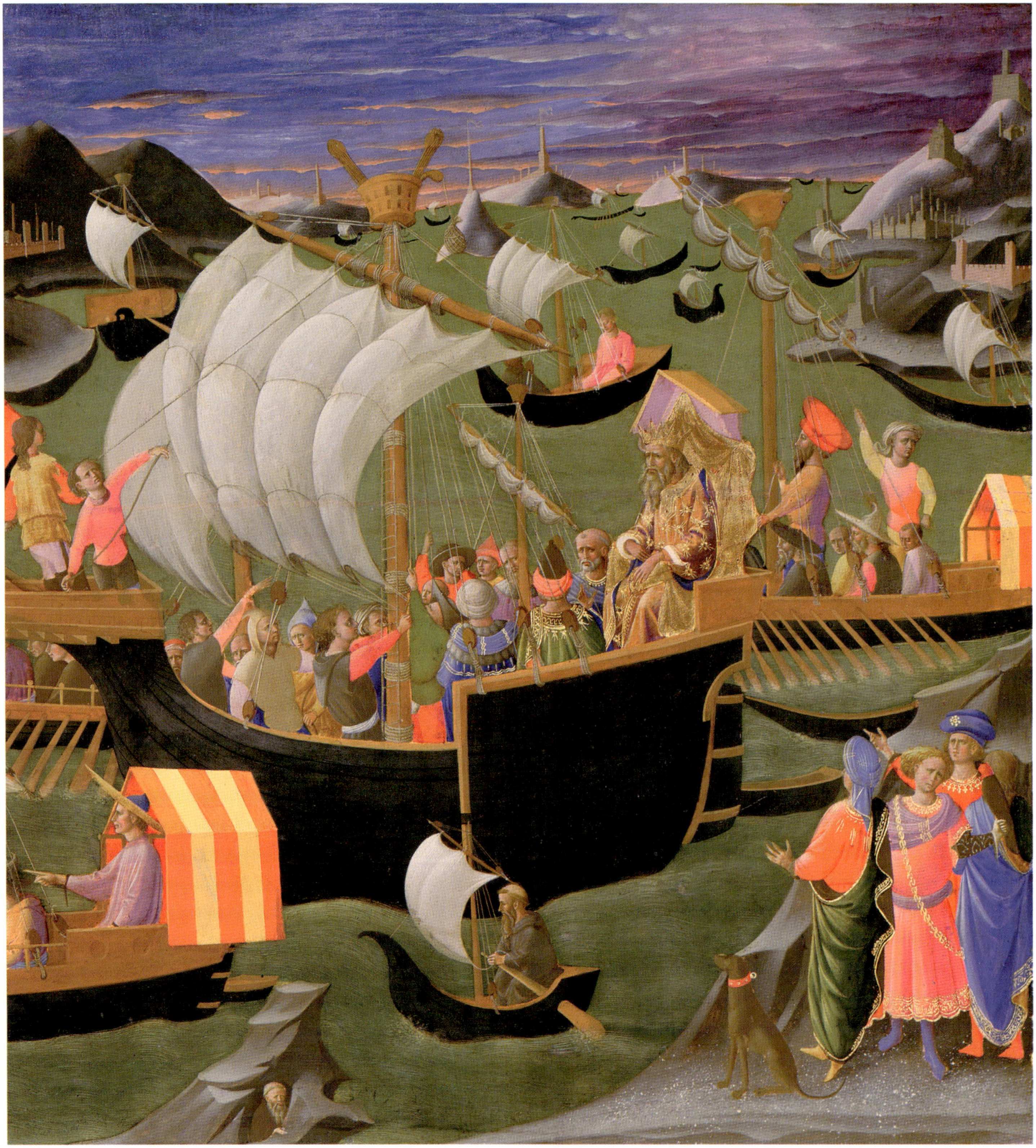

Transport and Commercial Communications in 14th-15th-Century Florence

Sergio Tognetti

The revolution in trade and the appearance of a new figure—the businessman—in the society of late medieval Europe are inextricably linked to a remarkable moment when new horizons were opening out, transport and communications were improving, and countries and economies in different stages of development were gradually integrating. In Venice, Genoa and Pisa, leaders in this exceptional economic transformation, the rising mercantile class acquired its wealth in the following ways: by purchasing raw materials and finished products to be sold on markets often very far from their places of origin; by concentrating on goods destined to a medium-upper, if not decidedly upper-class clientele; and by avoiding sectorial specialization, their commercial, financial, and insurance activities all being carried out within the same company. In other words, the greatest profits could be earned by operating in long-distance trade, investing in goods valuable enough to compensate for the costs of transport and targeting a clientele of aristocratic laymen and ecclesiastics.

Obviously, such commercial and financial activity had a strong speculative element involving high risks. Moreover, it required capital, a stable company structure, and coordination between enterprises and political institutions. In Venice, the cradle of maritime trade par excellence, the task of creating an institutional structure to back up mercantile activity was largely assumed by the State, which was governed by a nobility of mercantile extraction. This was done by building an arsenal, by instituting a maritime trade policy regulated by the Senate and enforced by public officials and, above all, by launching an aggressive foreign policy aimed at establishing a maritime empire, stretching from the hinterland of the Veneto to the Bosporus, passing though Istria, the Dalmatian cities, and the Greek islands in the Ionian Sea, with some ports of call in the Peloponnese, Crete and Negroponte. In Genoa, where the private sector had always been more important than the public, the great mercantile-shipbuilding families of the aristocracy played a decisive role by bringing together the interests of dozens of families of navigators, shipbuilders

1. Pesellino (Francesco di Stefano)
The Journey of the Magi: Melchior Crossing the Red Sea
c. 1446–7
Williamstown,
Sterling & Francine Clark Art Institute

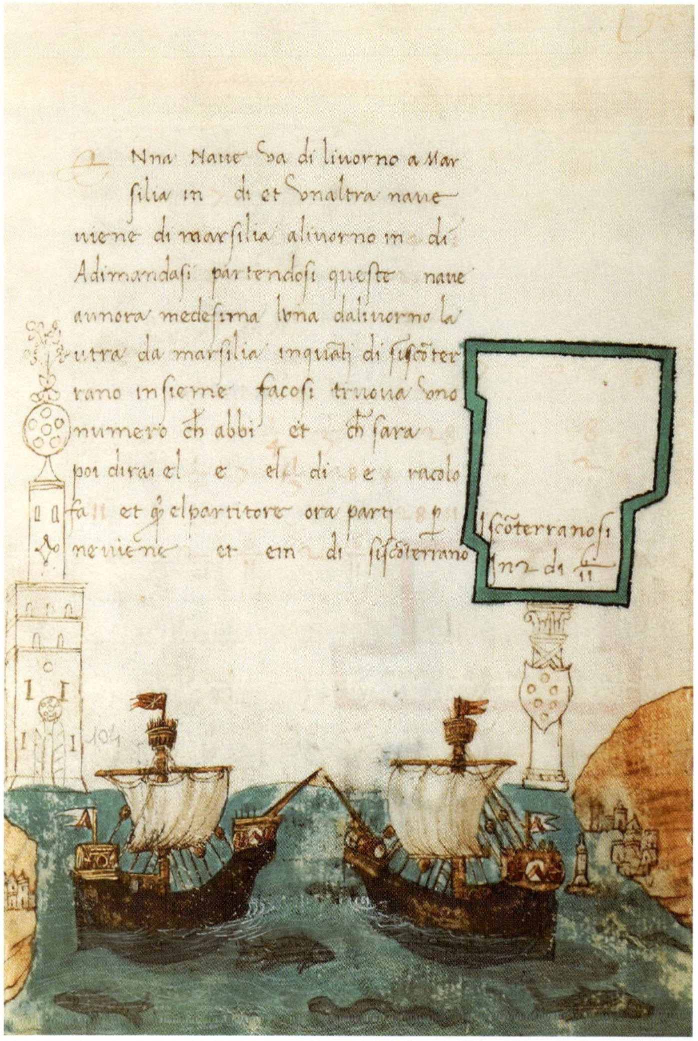

and small and medium-size businessmen, while the high levels of emigration led to the formation of far flung but structured Genoese communities, boasting representative consuls, warehouses, churches, barbers, doctors and notaries, from London to Seville, Tunisia to Constantinople, and Barcelona to Caffa in the far-away Crimea, extreme European outpost of Western Christianity in the midst of peoples of Turkish-Mongolian extraction.[1]

Florence, like other land-locked Italian cities, developed later than Genoa, Pisa and Venice. In the early 13th century, a foreign observer would have deemed Pisa the most important business centre in Tuscany. But by the time of Dante the situation had been reversed, and in the 15th century, after the conquest of Pistoia (1371), Arezzo (1384), Pisa (1406), and the acquisition of the port of Livorno (1421), Florentine hegemony was total. In the port cities, the rhythm of the economy was set by the seasonal departures and arrivals of convoys and lone ships. Here companies were formed specifically for this or that ship's journey, lasting as long as weather and fortune determined, then dissolved as soon as the ship had returned to its port of departure.

For Florence, having no such source of income deriving from the sea, it was harder to enter the complex mechanisms of international commerce. To solve this problem the Florentine merchants, emulating similar institutions set up in Siena and Lucca, formed well-organized companies for the long-term management of commercial and financial operations. These companies were family-based (the forerunners of today's co-partnerships), made up of a certain number of partners, often kinsmen, whose capital could not be withdrawn before the expiration of the partnership agreement, and employees of various levels to work in the parent company as well as its foreign branches.

2. *Calculating the duration of voyages by sea*
in Filippo Calandri, *Treatise on Arithmetic*
late 15th century
Florence, Biblioteca Riccardiana, ms. 2669, fol. 104

3. Benozzo Gozzoli
Goods transported on muleback
detail of the *Cavalcade of the Magi*
1459–63
Florence, Palazzo Medici Riccardi, Chapel of the Magi

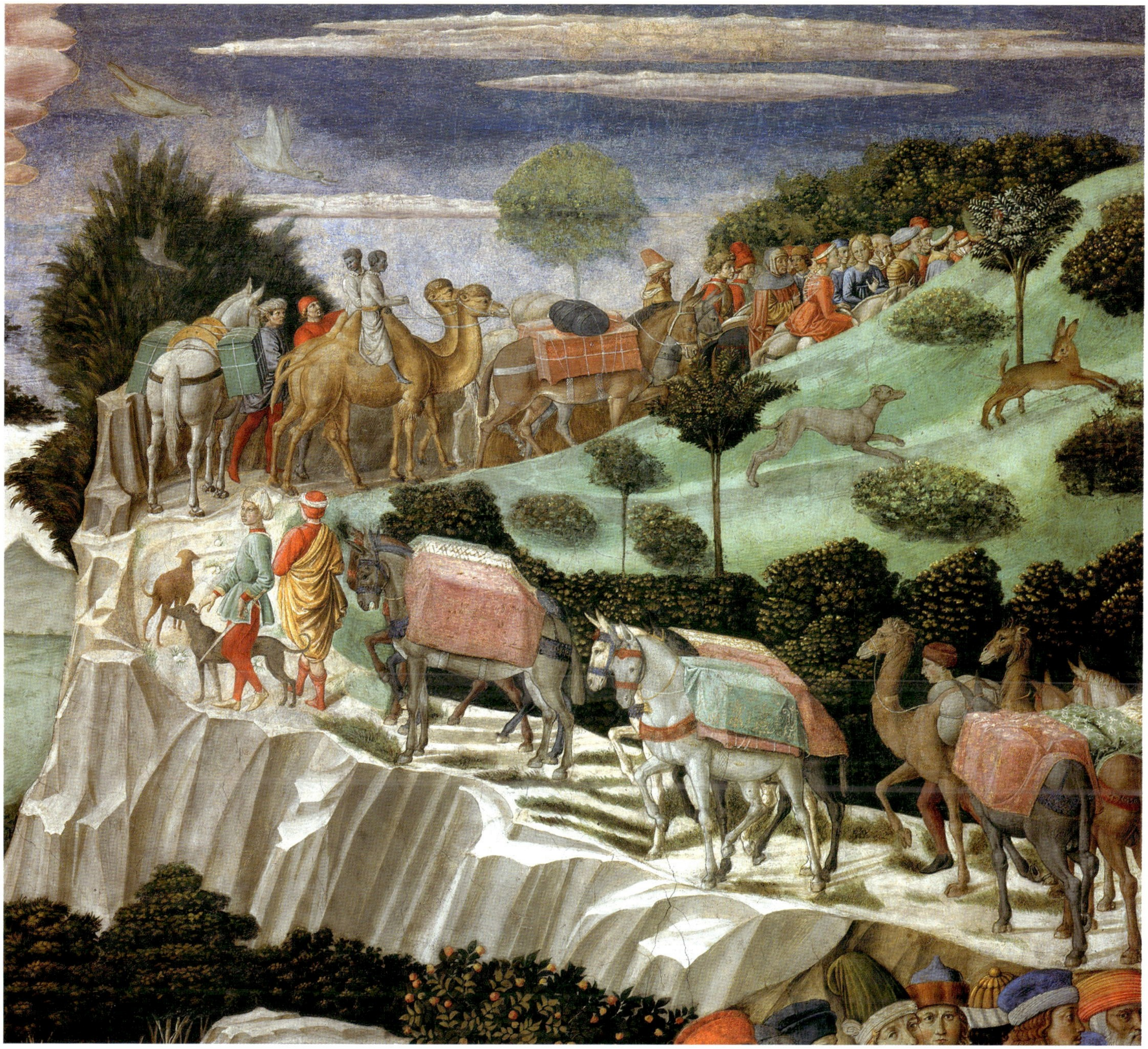

72

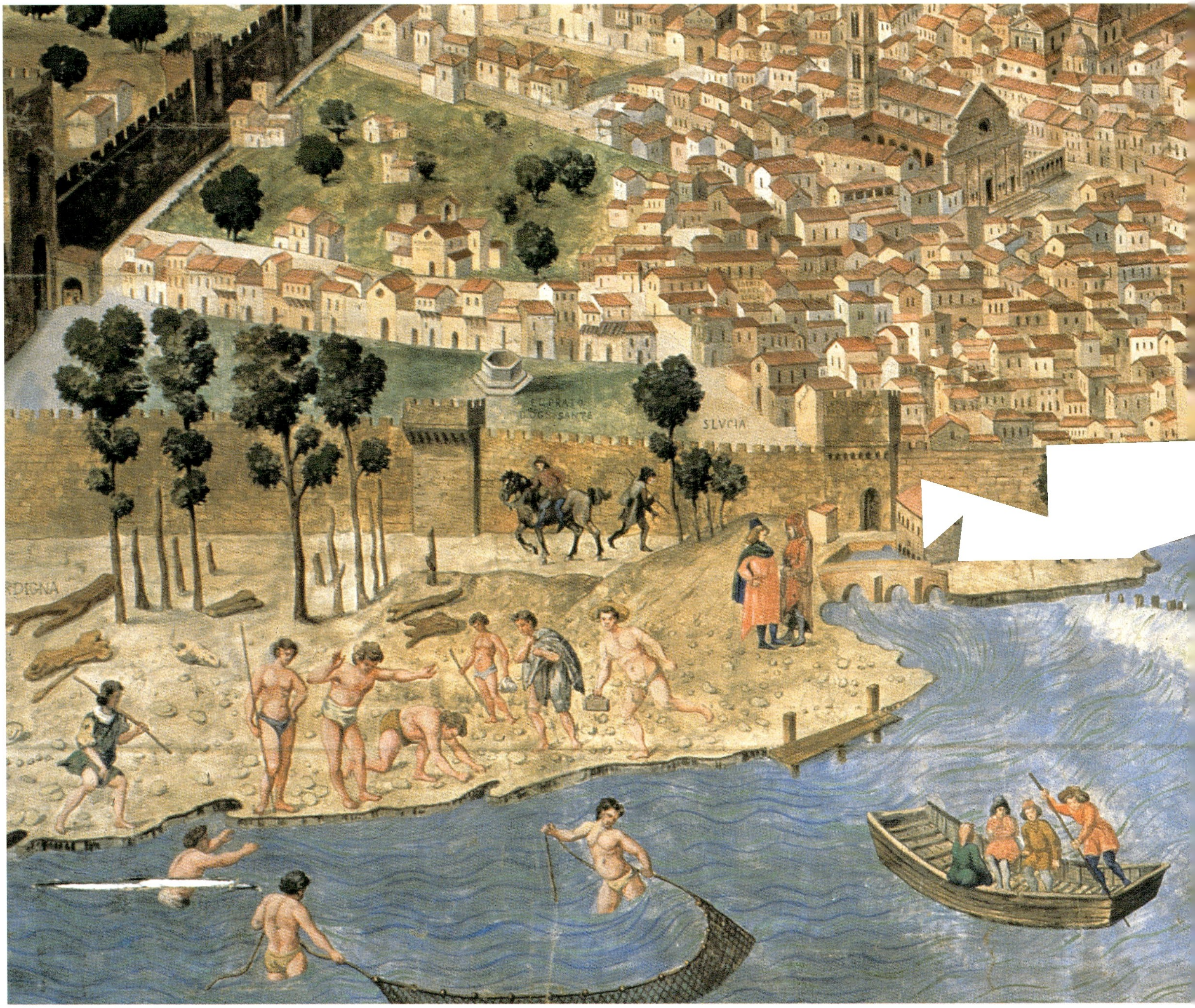

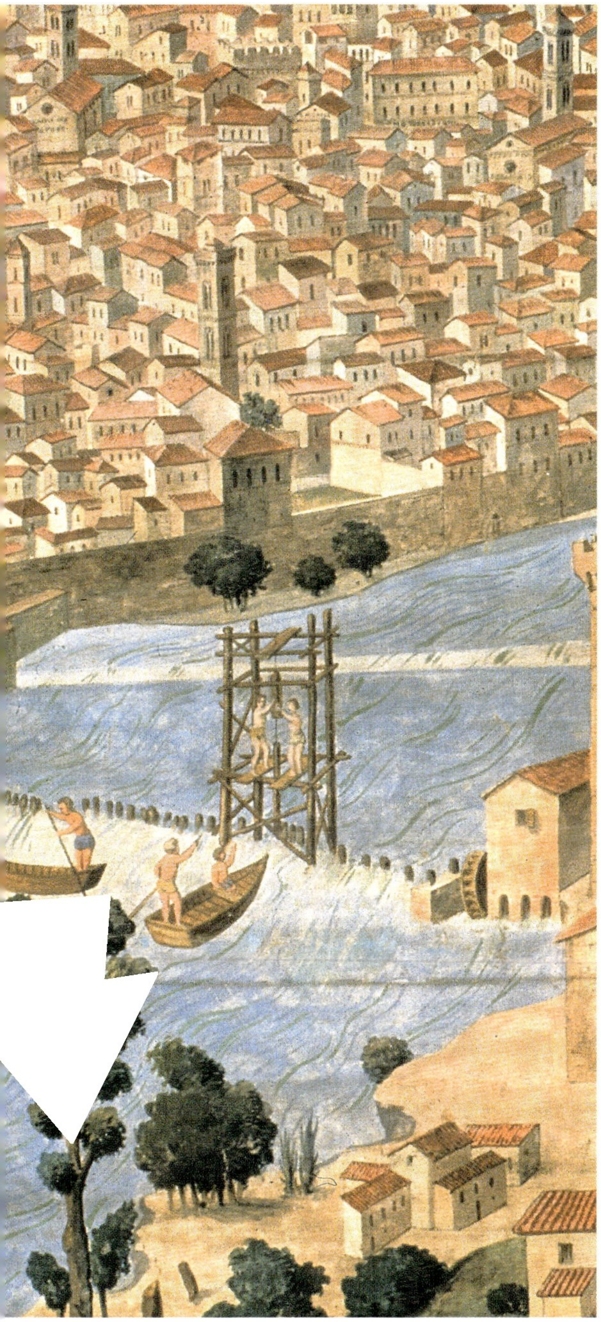

Such a company could not operate without the meticulous selection and training of personnel, the adoption of increasingly complex systems for recording the accounts of its numerous businesses, and the systematic exchange of information among the various branches through intense commercial correspondence.[2] Thanks to the customary period of training abroad and the skills acquired operating such enterprises, the Florentines eventually surpassed the other Italian merchant-bankers in technical capability; and at times, their cultural interests went beyond the mere practice of business, to the extent that in the early 15th century we find one Catalan writer declaring that, "They are for the most part great philosophers."[3]

In the last two centuries of the Middle Ages, major changes took place not only in the Florentine companies' geographical sphere of operation, but also in the terrestrial, fluvial and maritime routes and the choice of carriers used for transport. One constant that runs through the whole economic history of Florence from Dante to Machiavelli and Guicciardini is the slow integration between the international trade network and the city's manufacturing sector, centred on the production of fine woollen and silk textiles for exportation.[4] In the early 14th century, transport over land (supplemented by brief tracts of maritime or fluvial transport) predominated. The primary destinations were the markets of Northern France (the fairs of Champagne and Paris), Bruges and the other Flemish cities and then, across the English Channel, London. The main route was the Via Francigena, the early medieval road that led from Rome to Paris and then on to the northern coast, passing through Viterbo, Siena, Lucca, Piacenza, Asti, Torino, the Val di Susa, Savoy, and the cities of Burgundy and Champagne. There was also an alternative route, used by pilgrims and merchants of every kind that went through

4. *"Navalestro," or Ferryman, on the Arno*
detail of the *Pianta della Catena*
coloured copy, 19th century
Florence, Museo di Firenze com'era

Piacenza, Pavia, Vercelli, Aosta, the Gran San Bernard Pass and the region of Vaud, traversed by pilgrims and merchants.

For transporting spices and other Oriental products, the companies of nearby Pisa could be contacted directly, and likewise those of Genoa or Venice. The export markets were situated mainly on the Italian Peninsula or in its immediate vicinity, most notably the Papal Curia (in Rome up to 1309, and then at Avignon) and Anjouin Naples. The favourite means of transport was the pack mule, as seen in a famous detail in the fresco of *Good Government* painted by Ambrogio Lorenzetti in the Palazzo Pubblico of Siena. On the European plains north of the Alps, two- or four-wheeled wagons, drawn by horses, were also used. Complementary to overland travel was fluvial transport, along the Po, the Rhone, the Saône, the Loire, the Seine and the Rhine; as well as transport by cargo ship, connecting the ports of Provence with Genoa and/or Porto Pisano.

In the second half of the 14th century, when the Kingdom of France was devastated by the Hundred Years' War, the exportation of high-quality English wool was sharply reduced as a result of protectionist measures instituted by the crown. At the same time, the young but growing silk industry was calling for a more aggressive attitude toward procuring raw materials. Consequently, the Florentine trading companies diverted men and means toward previously neglected areas. The most striking example can be seen in the great mercantile emporiums of Eastern Spain: Barcelona, Valencia, and Majorca. There the Florentines found good quality wools to feed the Tuscan workshops, primarily those set up in Prato by Francesco Datini. In the late 14th century, in addition to the workshops of his native town, Datini's business empire included mercantile-banking firms in Florence, Pisa, Genoa, Avignon, Barcelona, Valencia and Majorca; he also did busi-

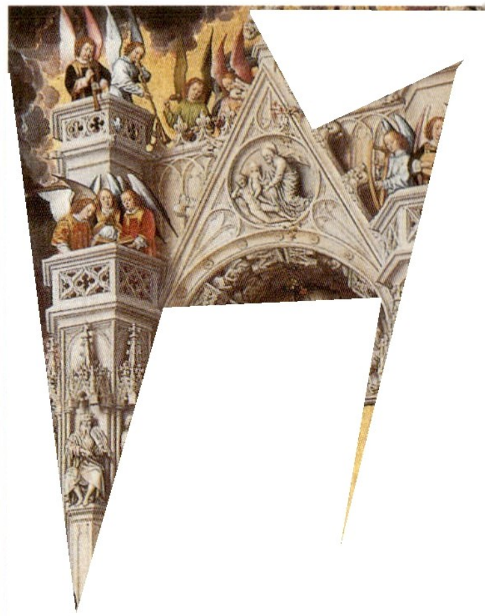

5. Hans Memling
The Last Judgement Triptych
1467–71
Danzig, Muzeum Narodowe

The triptych, commissioned by Agnolo Tani in Bruges and sent to Florence by sea, was seized by pirates and brought to Danzig.

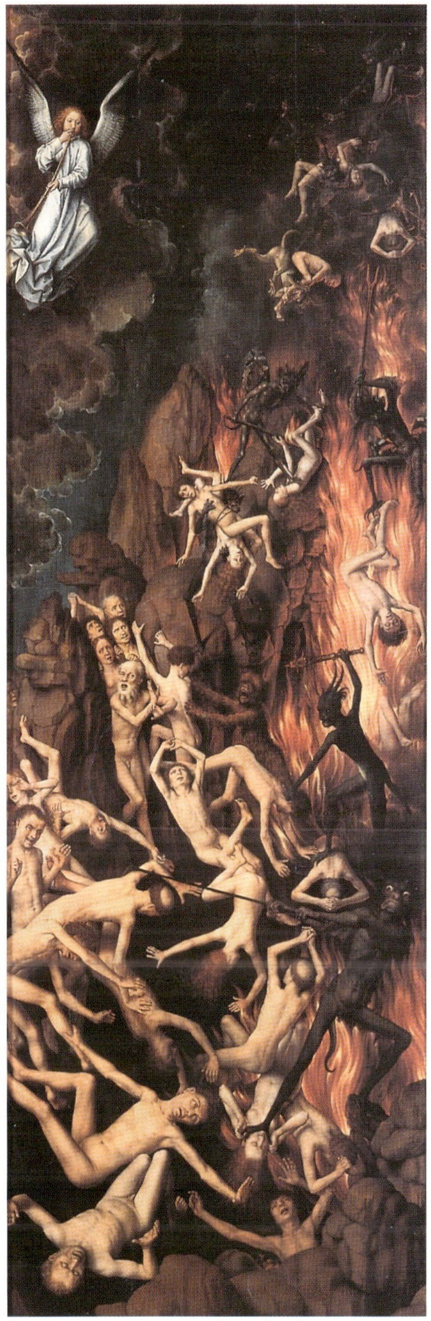

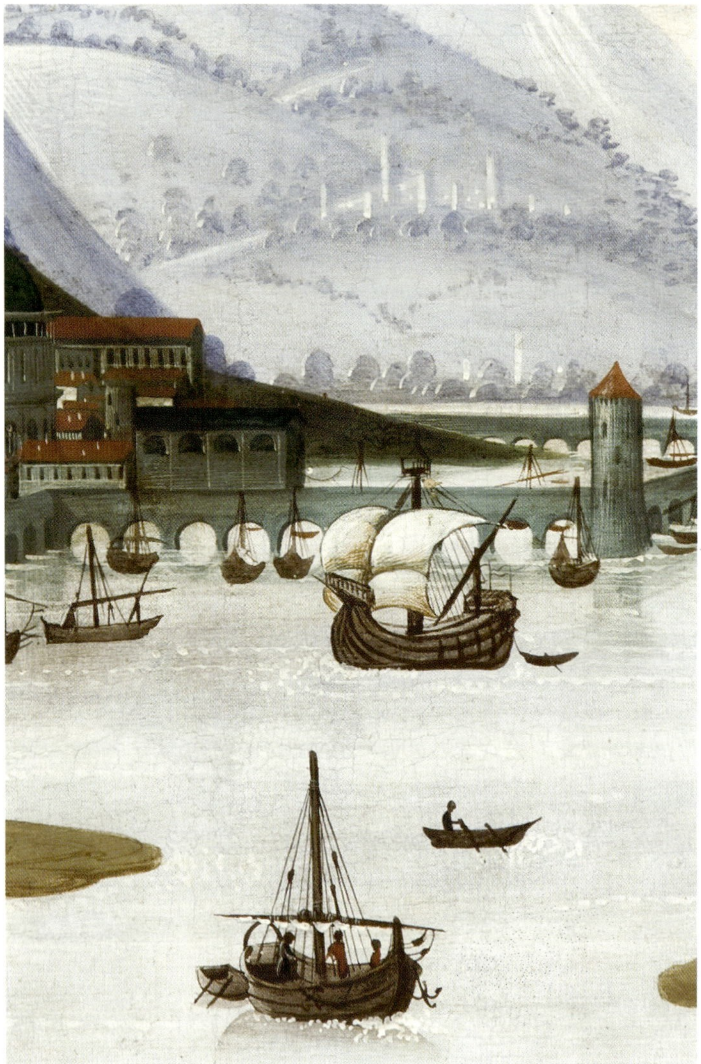

ness with many Tuscan companies and others scattered over half of Europe (from London to Palermo, Bruges to Milan, Paris to Venice, and Malaga to Bologna).[5] Further south, in Castilian Andalusia and the Islamic Kingdom of Granada, the silk industry found raw materials to supplement those from Sicily, Calabria and Persia (the Persian silk being imported through Venice). With the opening of new trade relations, special endeavours were made to organize and integrate the new markets.

Maritime transport was by far the most economic, since ships departing from northern ports bound for Tuscany could carry cargoes to and from the ports of the Iberian Peninsula, and the coasts of Provence and Liguria or those of the central-southern Tyrrhenian Sea. In the late 15th century, for trading to either the Mediterranean or the Atlantic ports, maritime transport was widely used. The Florentines used Genoese and Catalan mercantile fleets for the most part, as well as Provencal and Venetian ships, Pisa's fleet being by this time only a memory. Studies on port traffic in the Livorno-Porto Pisano Basin during the years prior to the Florentine conquest show that, when it came to ships of a certain size and capacity, the most important Tuscan port was monopolized by foreign craft.[6] Among these, the Genoese predominated not so much numerically as for their greater tonnage. Unlike the galley ship, a typically narrow, elongated craft with mixed propulsion, used mainly for transporting merchandise of high unit value that was easy to stow, such as spices, perfumes, precious metals and jewels, the Genoese cargo ships were rounded in shape, with foredecks, poop decks and high sides. Not needing rowers, they made do with small crews and had large, capacious holds suitable for shipping such bulky merchandise as wool, cotton, salt, leather and hides, grain and timber at low cost.[7]

6. Domenico Ghirlandaio,
Bartolomeo di Giovanni, David Ghirlandaio
Port
detail of the *Adoration of the Magi*
1488–9
Florence, MUDI - Museo degli Innocenti

In the second half of the 14th century, this cooperation between foreign ships and Florentine entrepreneurs produced major innovations in the field of maritime commercial institutions. First among them was the insurance sector, with the introduction of a private deed written in the vernacular that established the premium to be collected beforehand by the insurer, which was calculated as a percentage of the value of the cargo insured; it was a model that centuries later Lloyds of London made standard practice all over the world. Insurance rates fluctuated in relation to the routes taken and the kinds of ships involved. Premiums could range from 1% on Venetian convoys escorted by armed galleys to 12% for ships with rounded hulls travelling alone through dangerous waters threatened by pirates or hostile warships.[8]

In the 15th century, maritime insurance became a widespread practice. The directors of the various branches of the Medici Bank, for instance, were obliged to insure all freight that had not been embarked on galleys sailing in a convoy, while the accounting records of the Cambini Bank (from the 1450s through the 1470s) show that a pregnant woman slave was deemed merchandise at special risk, so that her life was usually insured from the moment she embarked on ship.[9]

The other and equally important innovation introduced in the late 14th century concerned the method of calculating the cost of freightage. Basically, costs were no longer calculated in relation to the physical space occupied on a ship, but to the monetary value of the goods transported. Rates of this kind allowed bulky goods to be transported without the previous added cost, facilitating the circulation of merchandise otherwise relegated to local or regional trading circuits. The ship's owner lost nothing, since the lower returns on bulk goods were amply compensated by the mark-up on the more expensive items.[10]

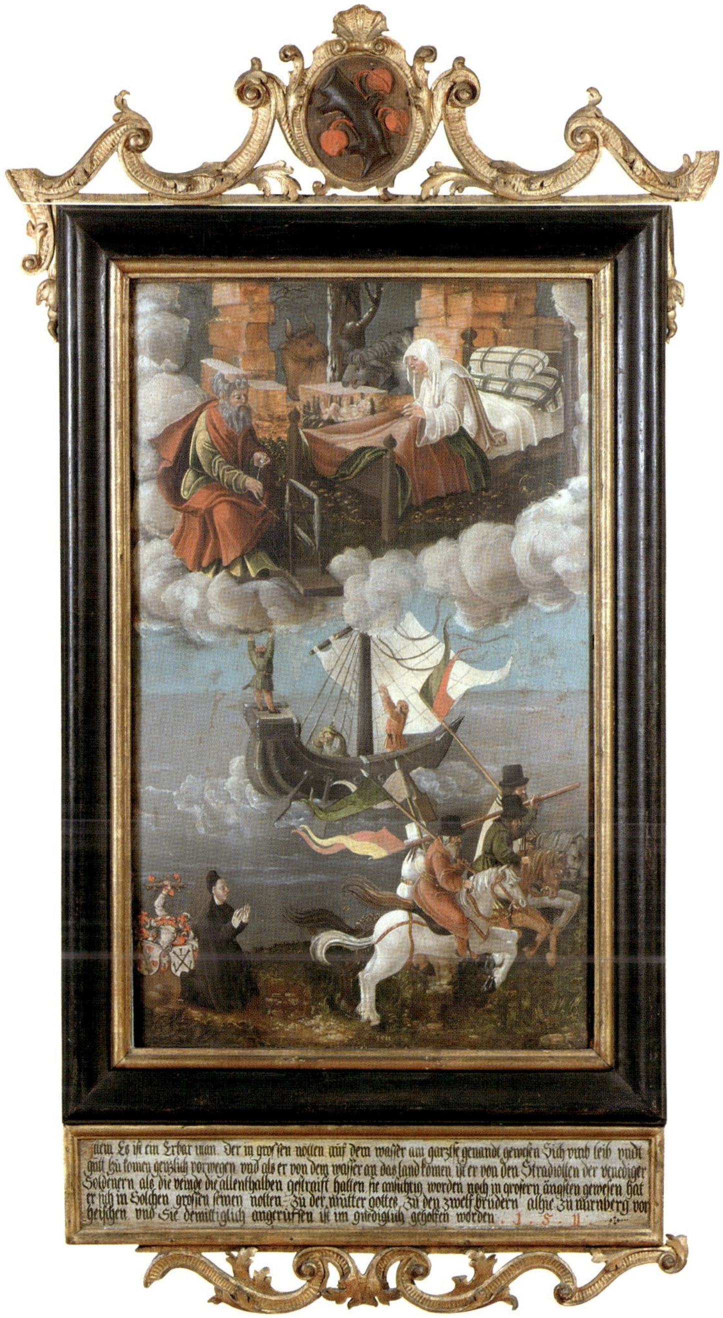

7. Paul Lautensack the Elder
A Merchant's Risks and Hazards, ex voto
1511
Nuremberg, Germanisches Nationalmuseum

In the 1420s, the transport system gravitating around the Florentine mercantile entrepreneurs entered a new stage. Having acquired Pisa and its port, the Florentine Republic decided to adopt a marine policy on the Venetian model, instituting a fleet regulated and coordinated by the State, and made up of "full-bellied" mercantile galleys sold by the Sea Consuls at public auctions held under the Loggia dei Priori. The itineraries included routes to Flanders and England, passing through the ports of Provence, Catalonia, Andalusia and Lisbon; to the Maghreb, Andalusia and the entire western Mediterranean; to Catalonian ports, Provence and the entire Tyrrhenian Sea; to Constantinople passing through Naples, Palermo, Messina, Modone and the Negroponte; and, finally, to Alexandria, Egypt, stopping off at the southern Tyrrhenian ports and at Crete, Rhodes, Cyprus and Beirut. With this system in place alongside the traditional recourse to foreign fleets, more ships became available; however, around 1480 the system was abandoned due to high costs and an overly rigid bureaucracy.[11]

While from the institutional and managerial viewpoint the influence of the Venetian model is obvious, studies conducted on the practical utilization of State galleys have shown that the goods transported continued to be mostly raw materials for the textile industry and finished products from the Florentine workshops. It is true, for instance, that ships sailing toward the northern seas were filled with dried fruit and nuts, rice, olive oil and other Mediterranean products in the Iberian ports, used by the Florentines to pay the English for their shipments of wool without having to bring with them money in cash or precious metals. The galleys that arrived in Constantinople and the eastern Mediterranean ports, seeking to bring back not so much spices as silk or cotton, took growing quantities of finished textiles to these ports. The Ottoman city of Constantinople, having now become capital of the Turkish empire, was considered a sort of "stomach for Florentine cloth." Regardless of the ultimate failure of the galley system, it did allow the Florentine merchants to become familiar with the world of navigation, an important training experience when we think that it was a Florentine who would later give his name to the new world discovered by Christopher Columbus.

The 15th century, however, also marks a revival in overland transport. In continental Europe this coincided with the conclusion of the long-lasting hostilities between France and England; and in Central-Southern Italy, with the definitive return of the papacy to Rome (1417) and the end of the interminable civil wars that had ravaged the Kingdom of Naples since the Aragonese conquest in the 1440s. In the mid-15th century, most of the costly silk furnishing fabrics produced by the Florentine silk-works were sent to the markets by means of carrier companies using dozens of pack mules. Of one of these firms, owned by the Florentine shipper Battista di Taccino di Bizzino and specialized in transporting fabrics, two account books for the years 1452–67 entitled *mandate di mercanzie* (goods shipped) have survived.[12] The Florentines' favourite clients were found in Naples, Rome and above all Geneva, where the largest mercantile and financial fairs in Western Europe were held. From Geneva, ruled by the Dukes of Savoy at the time, Italian fabrics (including those of Florence) were shipped to French and German markets.

Starting in the 1460s, the French King Louis XI offered tax breaks to attract foreign merchants (Italian in particular) away from Geneva and toward Lyon, where international fairs were now being held on an even larger scale. Hence by the end of the 15th century Lyon had become almost a second home for Florentine bankers and silk merchants.[13]

An exemplary case of the new horizons opened out by the Florentine entrepreneurs can be seen in the relations established in the 15th century between Florence and Lisbon, the rising star of maritime trade across the Atlantic. Thanks to the survival of a detailed company archive kept at the Istituto degli Innocenti in Florence,[14] we not only have an in-depth knowledge of mercantile trade and financial relations between Tuscany and Portugal, but are also informed by numerous account books of a very particular commerce, having to do with the world of culture. Literary and religious manuscripts, juridical codices, reading glasses and magnifying lenses were shipped (along with the finest fabrics) from the Cambini Bank to its Florentine correspondents in the Lisbon branch to satisfy the demands of a clientele gravitating around the court of the Portuguese Avis dynasty and the various bishoprics in the kingdom. Other Portuguese prelates and university students can be seen embarking at Lisbon bound for Livorno, whence they set out along the road to the *Studia* of Bologna, Siena or Perugia, not without having first settled their current accounts in Florence by cashing letters of exchange and ordering money transfers to other Italian centres. Participating in this flow of Portuguese trade to Florence in the 15th century was Don Jaume, a member of the royal house and the only cardinal in Portugal. Dying in the home of the Cambini Bank's majority partner, he left a large sum to be used to build his chapel in the left nave of the Basilica of San Miniato al Monte. The Bishop of Faro in Algarve, Alfonso Alvaro, spent years supervising the work of constructing the sumptuous funerary monument, entrusting it to the hands of such fine artists as Antonio and Bernardo Rossellino, Luca della Robbia, and Antonio and Piero del Pollaiolo.

1. Tangheroni 1996; Spufford 2005.

2. Sapori 1955–67; De Roover 1963, ed. 1970; Melis 1991; Goldthwaite 2009, first part.

3. Del Treppo 1968, ed. 1972, p. 306.

4. Hoshino 1980 and Id., 'Industria' 2001; Dini, 'Saggi' 1995 and Id. 'Manifattura' 2001; *Arti fiorentine* 1998–2003, I-III, 1998–2000; Tognetti 2002.

5. Melis 1962; *Francesco di Marco Datini* 2010.

6. Tognetti 2010.

7. Heers 1984.

8. Melis 1975.

9. De Roover 1963, ed. 1970, pp. 216–8; Tognetti 2005.

10. Melis, 'I trasporti' 1984.

11. Mallett 1967.

12. Hoshino 1980, pp. 244–5, 248–9, 285.

13. Dini 2006.

14. Tognetti 1999.

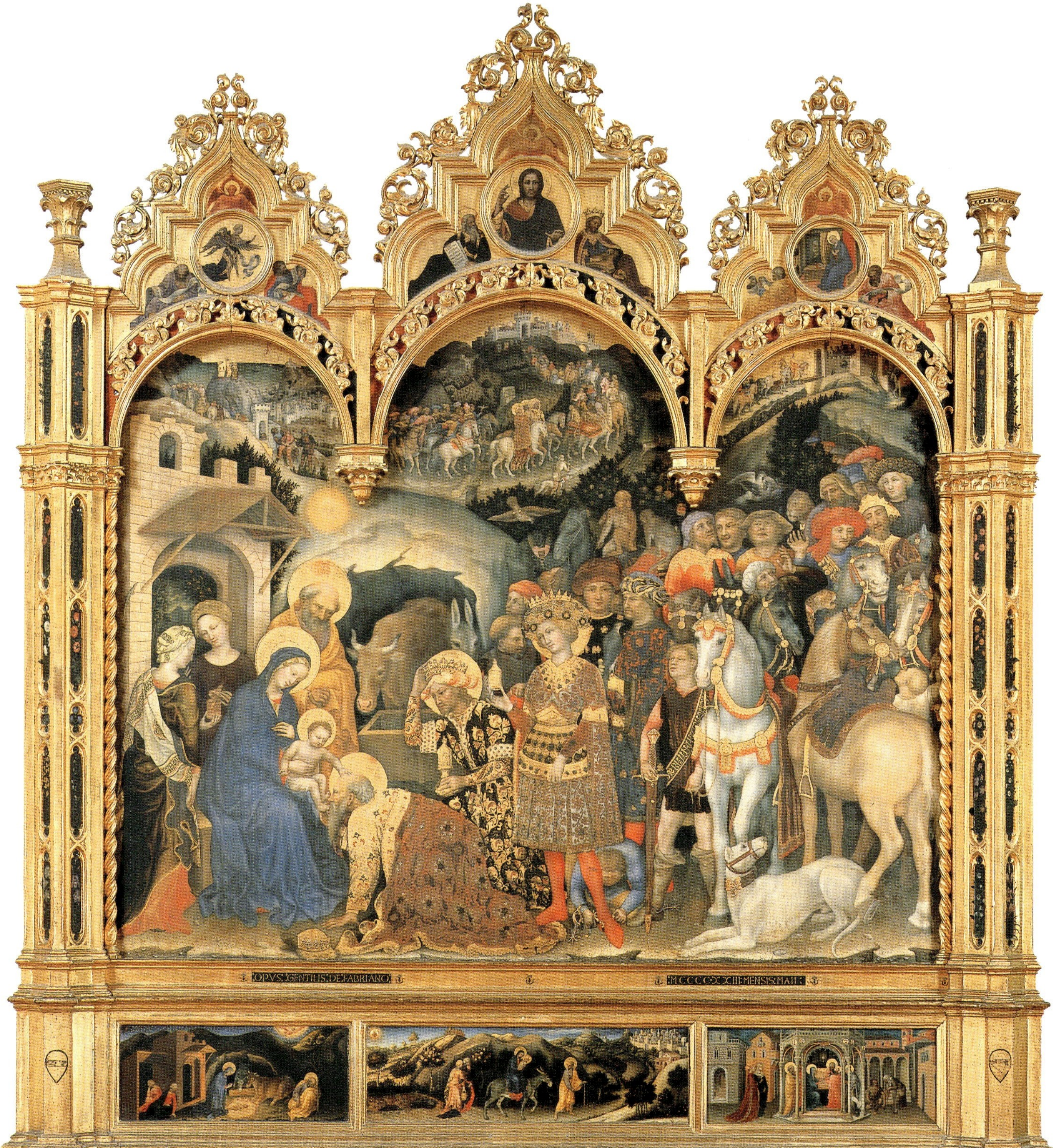
OPVS GENTILIS DE FABRIANO
MCCCCXXIII MENSIS MAII

Hierarchy, Privilege and Luxury in the Florentine Sumptuary Laws

Dora Liscia Bemporad

When in 1456 legislators explained that the sumptuary provisions had been issued "to give honest form to the clothing of women and to ensure that, in those and other ornaments, they did not incur extravagant expenditures, for the conservation and good example of the city," he stressed only some of the aspects, frequently noted by scholars, that led to the issuing of these laws. The whole question needs to be examined in context, considering that the laws were in force for nearly four centuries, a span of time that saw profound changes in society, great political upheavals, and important developments in inter-cultural relationships. Moreover, a great many foreigners were living in Italy at the time, making it impossible to analyze the sumptuary laws from a single viewpoint. In Tuscany, for instance, each city passed its own provisions, all severe and prohibitive. While in many cases these laws were identical to those of Florence, in others they differed according to local customs and usage.

The reasons that gave rise to the sumptuary laws were many and at certain times some may have been more important than others, but clearly, all of them were accommodated within a set of laws designed to establish rules for civil life, and in particular the behaviour of women. The laws aimed to keep family wealth from being drained away in ruinous expenditure; to curb any public display of riches; to ban clothing deemed licentious; and lastly, to fix the identity of the various classes of citizens, something that would have been impossible had people been free to choose how they dressed. One of the basic principles of Renaissance society, heir to an even more restrictive Middle Ages, was that the different social levels should not mingle. Each class had to remain perfectly identifiable, above all through its dress. This point, however, never explicitly stated in the statutes, should be studied in parallel to the preceding ones, in a general historical context.

The Florentine Republic never hesitated to censure the public ostentation of wealth. Palla Strozzi, for example, was severely criticized when in 1423 he displayed the sumptuously beautiful *Adoration of the Magi* by Gentile da Fabriano

1. Gentile da Fabriano
Adoration of the Magi
1423–4
Florence, Galleria degli Uffizi

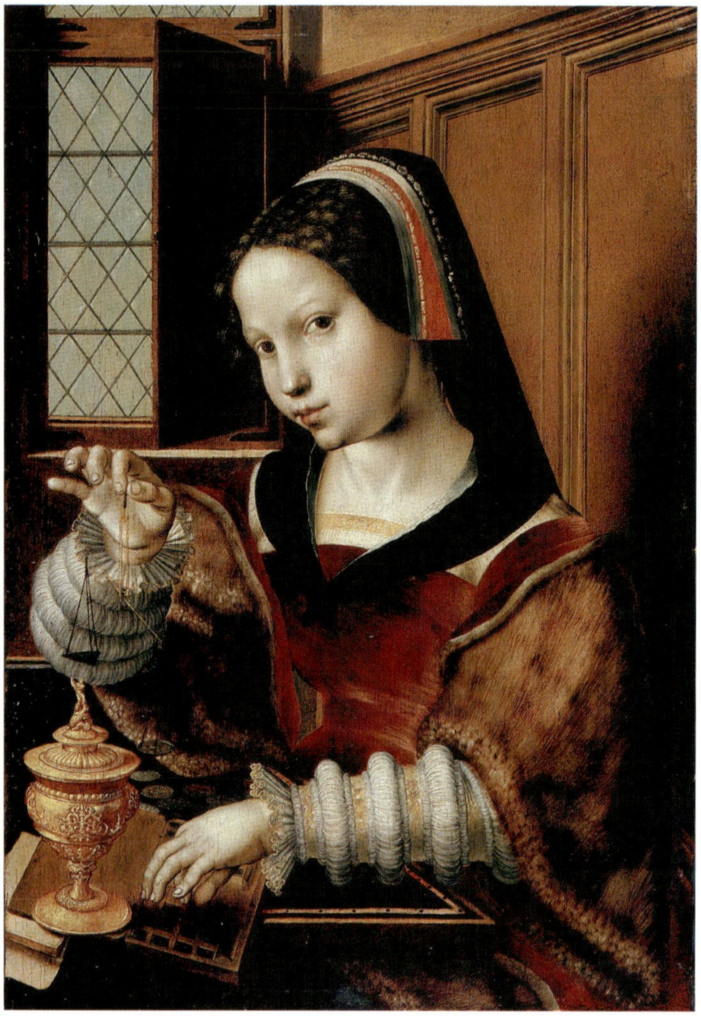

in his private chapel in the church of Santa Trinita.[1] The representation of this religious scene lit up the dim chapel, gleaming bright with a profusion of fine-spun gold threads covering brocaded gowns, jewels, crowns, and horses' trappings. Strozzi's ostentation was in sharp contrast to the prudent caution of his rival Cosimo de' Medici, who revealed the power of his wealth only within the walls of his palace on Via Larga, a severe, fortress-like residence situated far from the centre of city government. The interior, however, embellished by Cosimo, by Piero and by Lorenzo, was "surrounded, overloaded, with the splendour of a wealth that, although not flaunted but on the contrary half-concealed, is so lavish as to be almost cumbersome."[2] Filarete in his *Treatise on Architecture*, composed between 1460 and 1464, maintained that in 15th-century society, the man of "quality" reflected his status not only in his residence but also in his dress, and habits in the broadest sense. This concept was reiterated later in Baldassarre Castiglione's *Cortegiano.*[3] Masculine sobriety was always seen in contrast to women's unbridled desire for luxury, justifying the fact that laws and restrictions were aimed only at feminine dress and ornaments.[4] Although *cavalieri*, *dottori* and their womenfolk were not subjected to the same restrictions as other citizens, any excessive display of luxury in public was frowned upon as inappropriate and even indecorous.[5]

Dante, in the XV Canto of the *Paradiso* (98-102) denounced the present-day freedom of customs as compared to the time when "Florence, within her ancient boundary/Abode in quiet, temperate and chaste/No golden chain she had, nor coronal/Nor ladies shod with sandal shoon, nor girdle/That caught the eye more than the person did." This is one of the reasons why Villani enthusiastically greeted the issuing of the first sumptuary law in April 1330. The six male foreigners, who were hired on regular salaries to roam the city searching for law-breakers

2. Jan Sanders van Hemessen
Woman Weighing Gold
c. 1530–5
Berlin, Gemäldegalerie

were not always able to decide whether the new fashions violated the sumptuary laws or not. Hence they welcomed anonymous denunciations from people who were sometimes only too happy to have a chance to get at an old enemy.

The sumptuary law of 1388 tried to achieve some clarity by forbidding tailors to cut garments in new styles, in the hope of restraining the pace of change that made it so hard to interpret new fashions in the light of the law.[6] The first fully formulated sumptuary law was issued in the statute of 1415, which regulated all *ornamenta mulierum*. Even more than in the past, the law tried to ban innovative fashions among the rising middle classes, whose members tended to emulate their betters in amassing wealth as well as in displaying it.

In 1427 the *Officiales super ornamentis mulierum* was established. It was a magistrature composed of eight male Florentines, thought to be more familiar with the local fashions; but it proved very hard to find men willing to assume this duty. Accordingly, the Conservatori di Leggi, responsible for prosecuting crimes of corruption, were assigned the task of enforcing the sumptuary laws in 1459. This further duty was unwelcome due to the poor remuneration and the difficulty of applying rigid regulations to such an ambiguous area as women's fashion.[7] The styles, in fact, evolved too rapidly for the all-male officials to keep up with them and amendments had to be issued constantly.[8] It was virtually impossible to ensure respect for the law, even though the severity of the provisions should have made them feared and hence effective.[9]

The misogyny of the Church and the preachers who spoke for it played a major role in the issuing of sumptuary laws. The entire 15th century shows the influence of such figures as the Blessed Giovanni Dominci with his *Regola del governo di cura familiare* [Rules governing the family] written in the vernacular, St. Bernardino da Siena with his sermons on the transi-

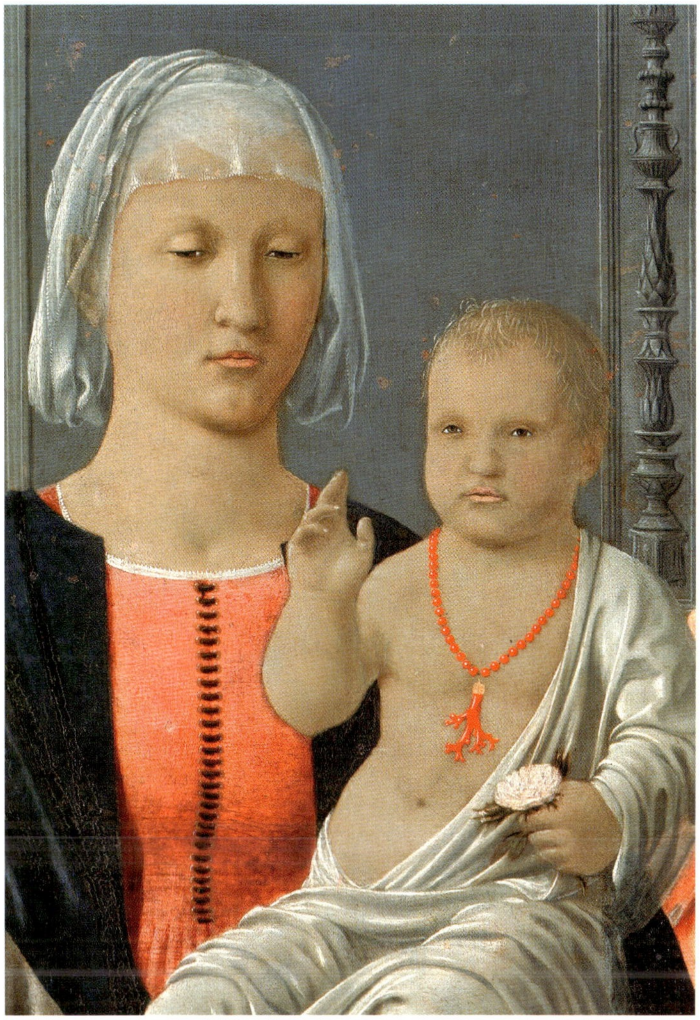

3. Piero della Francesca
Madonna of Senigallia
detail
c. 1470
Urbino, Galleria Nazionale delle Marche

ence of worldly goods, and Fra Girolamo Savonarola with his bonfires of the vanities and fiery sermons. Their presence and their words, entering the debate over banning luxury, sank deep into the conscience of the people. The Church, even in its institutional structures, upheld one of the most contradictory aspects of the Renaissance, heir to the medieval tradition of woman's dual nature as both diabolic being and heavenly mother, an attitude that reached its greatest intensity with the proclamation of the Dogma of the Immaculate Conception by Pope Sixtus IV (1477–87).[10]

San Bernardino, one of the most fervent opponents of luxury goods for women, thundered against the ostentation of wealth and extravagant styles, branding them a sign of moral decadence suggested by the devil. He criticised the belts women wore and the long trains on their gowns, declaring that this fashion made them look like animals with tails. The proclamation of 1464 outlaws any "train more than a yard long, on either the gowns or the mantles of women in mourning," specifying how to take the measurement[11] and states that women can "have three belts and no more, for any reason, also that the metal, silver and gold on them cannot weigh more than a *libra* in all; and those weighing over a *libra* must, within a month from the issuing of this proclamation, be officially registered."[12]

Woman as a demonic being with beastly appetites is a recurrent theme, expressed in the laws that governed prostitution. Prostitutes were allowed to wear the reviled trains, which became symbols of their depravation. But preachers were only parroting the stereotype that saw women as capable only of spending money others had earned, brainless, thoughtless creatures to be kept subject to their husbands, who in turn were threatened with severe penalties if they failed to curb their wives' extravagance.[13] The *pater familiae* displayed his

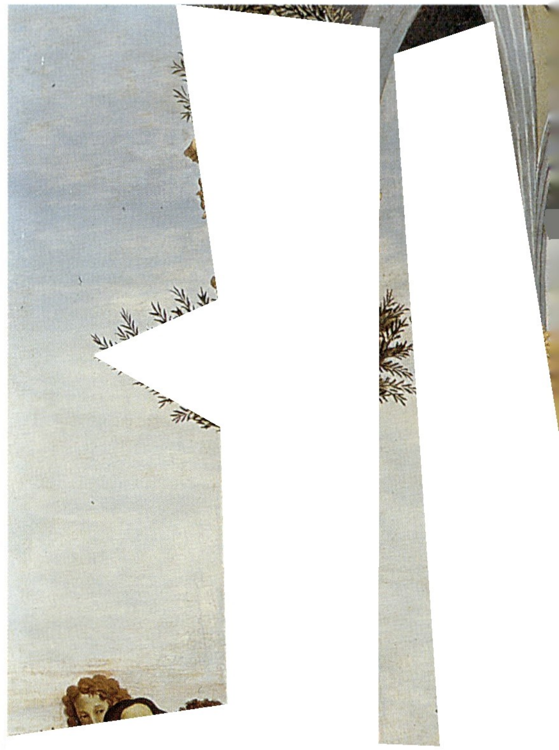

4. Assistants of Sandro Botticelli
Wedding Banquet,
panel from the *Story of Nastagio degli Onesti*
1483
Private Collection

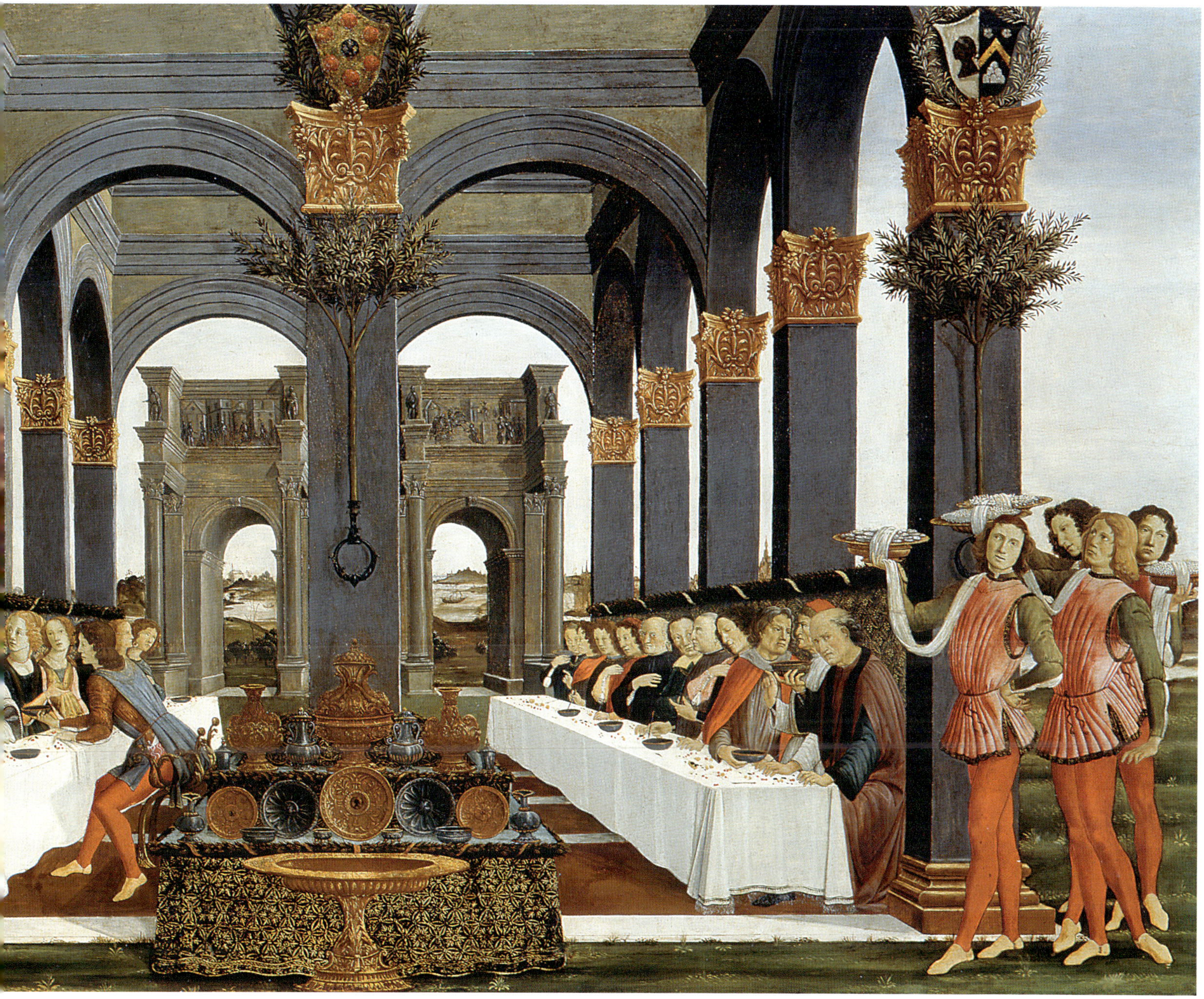

status in society through the behaviour of the women who lived under his roof. These resolutions were taken both because women had no money of their own, and because their disobedience was indicative of weakness in the family helmsman who was to steer the ship on a straight course. The slings and arrows of the moralizers, in fact, were hurled not only at wasteful expenditure and flaunted wealth, but also at women who revealed too much of their bodies, behaviour then blamed on the men who should have kept them in line. Soon the width and depth of necklines "from cleavage to throat," the transparency of veils draped over bare shoulders, and the length of sleeves were also being measured.[14]

Leon Battista Alberti, in the four books *Della Famiglia* written between 1433 and 1441, had already condemned behaviour not complying with the more or less explicitly formulated rules, urging modesty and restraint in luxuries. Reiterating these concepts in the *De Iciarchia* of 1464, he speaks of the decadent dress habits of Florentines, something he had observed and criticized on a visit to Florence four years earlier. To the man of the house, "a male and first prince of his family," he assigned the specific duty of demanding honest behaviour from all members of the family, just as a prince does with his subjects.[15]

In examining the phenomenon of the sumptuary laws, a sense of family unity is one of the themes to be kept in mind, since it was the cohesion and compactness of the core that provided each member with security, which was not simply financial. The patrimony of each family, then, was the foundation stone of its wealth as well as the basis for its strength in dealing with other groups in the society around it. Weddings, often public exhibitions of opulence, were particularly targeted by the legislators, who saw them as occasions for squandering vast amounts in futile ostentation.[16] In the earlier provisions of 1356 the lawmakers' intention was clear in the very title: "Provisions against superfluous ornaments for women and excessive costs *de 'moglazzi e de' morti* (of weddings and funerals)."[17] Basically, the sumptuary laws served to establish a balance between the citizens and the State, in an appar-

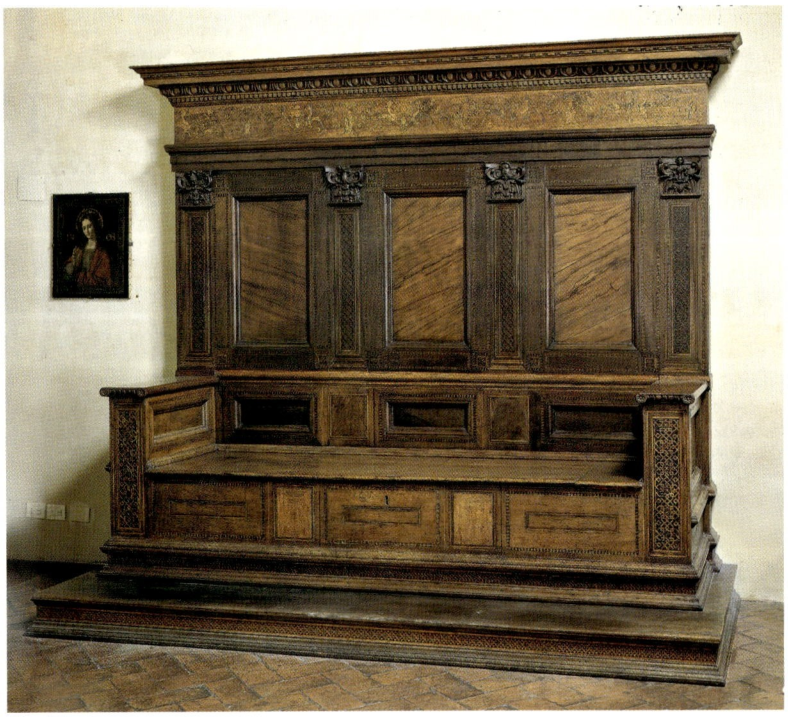

ent levelling aimed not merely at exterior appearance, as has often been thought, but also at power relations between the sexes, among individuals, and with their rulers. This harmonious balance was broken with the rise in Florentine society of a number of richer families who used their personal influence to undermine the system.[18]

The marriage game played out within a limited circle of families created networks of alliance. These unions, often arranged without even asking the consent of the couple involved, were so important as to become occasions for display, events where it was necessary and by no means unseemly for a family to flaunt its wealth. The laws restraining luxury were thus evaded with the complicity of the persons specifically responsible for having them observed. This is one of the reasons why, unlike the situation in the 14th century, restrictions on weddings and wedding dresses ceased to exist or became so bland that it was hard indeed to distinguish between prohibitions and concessions.[19] This was because the laws conflicted with the need, which became ever more urgent as political and financial power in the city was concentrated in the hands of just a few families, to weave matrimonial ties binding these families in a blood relationship. Weddings became a tool of power, serving the same public function as civil and religious ceremonies, as exemplified by the pomp and ceremony surrounding the wedding of Lorenzo de' Medici and Clarice Orsini. This event involved the whole city for three days, until the bride "went to hear Mass at San Lorenzo with one of the wedding gifts in her hand," "a little book of Our Lady, marvellous, written in letters of gold on ultramarine blue paper, with a binding of crystal and chased silver."[20]

The reason why the law was more lenient with young girls than with married women becomes clear. The concessions granted them were extended for three years after the wedding, poor recompense indeed for the burdensome restrictions they would have to endure for the rest of their lives.[21] "As for unmarried girls, no prohibition is specified in these provisions, except that they may not wear any gold or silver brocade beyond what is permitted to married women."[22] It even became customary for husbands to offer their wives a sort of counter-dowry, a trousseau of gowns, jewels and even money, worth more than the dowry brought by the bride, especially if the groom's social status was lower than hers.[23] The greater the inequality in rank between the spouses, the more splendid were the ceremonies, banquets, festivities and decoration. The sumptuary laws thus aimed from the start to restrain lavish expenditure for weddings only in some social classes, focusing particularly on the magnificence of the gifts, the abundance and quality of the garments, the dishes served, and the number of guests. But as has often been noted, the more something is prohibited, the more desirable it becomes, indicating the power to break the law without fear of punishment.[24]

The lawmakers themselves realized how hard it was to limit the number of gowns and specify the permissible fabrics, embroidery, furs, ornaments and jewels, without negatively affecting the city's economy. When in fact monetary fines were imposed on tailors, goldsmiths, embroiderers, furriers and anyone who contributed to making the clothing and jewels listed in the regulations, a sharp downturn occurred in the manufacturing system that had largely contributed to the power of Florence.[25] The solution to this dilemma was found in imposing taxes on clothing, rather than banning it, and then "marking" the clothing.

Exemptions for children were made for very different reasons. The belief that the miraculous protective power of some materials and certain "signs" could protect children

5. Florentine workshop
Lettuccio (Day bed)
late 15th century
Florence, Museo Horne

from illness and death was more powerful than any strictness lawmakers could impose, thus inducing them to contemplate a broad range of exceptions: "Children, both male and female, up to the age of three, are allowed to wear around the neck a little chain with gold or silver or a Lamb of God, a cross, branch of coral or dog's tooth or similar with a silver ring, as is the custom, without pearls or jewels of any kind."[26] Included in brides' dowries, which usually listed clothing, household linens and personal lingerie, were objects linked to procreation as well as bunches of coral to protect a mother from the dangers of childbirth and safeguard her vulnerable newborn.[27] The only household goods included were the basin and ewer used for daily ablutions.

The same attitude of rich simplicity informed the laws on furniture and interior decoration. In the home sobriety was essential and only on certain occasions were luxurious hangings and tapestries temporarily displayed. Aside from fabrics, a subject to which we will return, furniture was subject to severe rules as regards the wood and structure. It consisted of cabinets, chests and chairs so sober as to be called *salvatici* (wild, rude) while the more luxurious pieces, the *sfoggiati*, were adorned with embellishments authorized by the payment of a supplementary tax.[28] How important these laws were in governing the life of the city is clearly shown by the persistence in Italian of some terms whose original meaning has been lost. To go "beyond the *foggia*," the style imposed, has become synonymous with ostentation.

The same system for evading the law was applied to such luxury goods as jewels and fabrics. In 1433 it was decided that, instead of banning the possession of jewels, it would be better to take advantage of the weaker sex's obstinate pursuit of beauty by levying a tax on all the clothing and ornaments they purchased.[29] Furthermore, women who insisted on wearing jewels would have to bring their husbands a large dowry, a condition that limited the number of those authorized to do so. These measures were designed to contribute to the common good of all citizens. Garments that were "marked," that is, not complying with the prescribed measurements and rules, could be worn for three years from the day of the proclamation and afterwards, within the limits set by law.[30]

The repeated prohibitions issued one after another show that the lawmakers' stated intention of halting the dissipation of wealth and public ostentation of luxury was regularly ignored. There were other implications too, some profound, others more frivolous (or only apparently so), such as the need to adapt the laws to rapidly evolving fashions and changes in society.[31] In any case, these regulations are a precious source of information, giving insight into the needs of a society in which the public sphere dominated the private, creating conflicting attitudes that persisted throughout the 15th century. Even the feast day of St. John the Baptist, held in honour of Florence's patron saint, one of the annual festivities involving everyone without distinction, became a contest among those who participated in religious and civil life with pageantry, decorations, and scenic effects that turned the whole city into an enormous stage. The streets and houses were adorned with brightly coloured tapestries and hangings, far from the grey-and-white image handed down to us by 19th-century historiographic tradition.[32]

An extraordinary example can be seen in the 15th-century array of decorative hangings that entirely covered the interior of the Badia Fiorentina. The great hangings, up to sixteen *braccia* in height, made of red velvet brocade gleaming against a bright yellow background, were woven in one of the most spectacular textile patterns of all time, both for size and complexity. The long branches of the *griccia*, a pattern over a metre high, consisting of a wavy branch interrupted by an ogive with a golden pomegranate at its centre, symbol of abundance and fecundity, climbed up the walls in a triumph of splendour. Other hangings and banners bedecked the city, forming a theatrical stage-set that served as backdrop to the processions and horse races. Although very few of these decorations have survived, we have many paintings that record them, illustrating in minute detail the fabrics that transformed the grey walls of austere palaces into lush gardens.

The silk fabrics of the 15th century seemed to invite the lawmakers to set strict limits to their excessive use. Gold yarn, frequently used as backing to relief patterns on velvet, highlighted in turn by curlicues of precious metal, consisted of fine gold or silver foil wound around a core of silk or leather (giving rise to the term *orpello*—tinsel—still in use today). Use of gold yarn required serious financial investment, especially when one considers that it was discarded and burned when frayed or out of fashion. Fabrics, even more than jewels, which to judge by the paintings were not particularly ostentatious in the 15th century, were the chief outward sign of the wearer's wealth.

The behaviour of Florentine society involved strong contrasts: on the one hand, public displays of opulence; and on the other, modest behaviour within the family and the home, at least until the Signoria became a poorly masked oligarchy. Not only was parsimony strictly observed, it was thought unseemly that others might gossip about a family's wealth. "And thus it was that while the plate in private homes was all made of brass, except for four or six pieces in silver, the strongboxes were filled to overflowing with silver and gold coins."[33]

Statutes and provisions describe in iportat minute detail fabrics that were banned because the costly materials and the long, intricate manufacturing processes raised their prices to

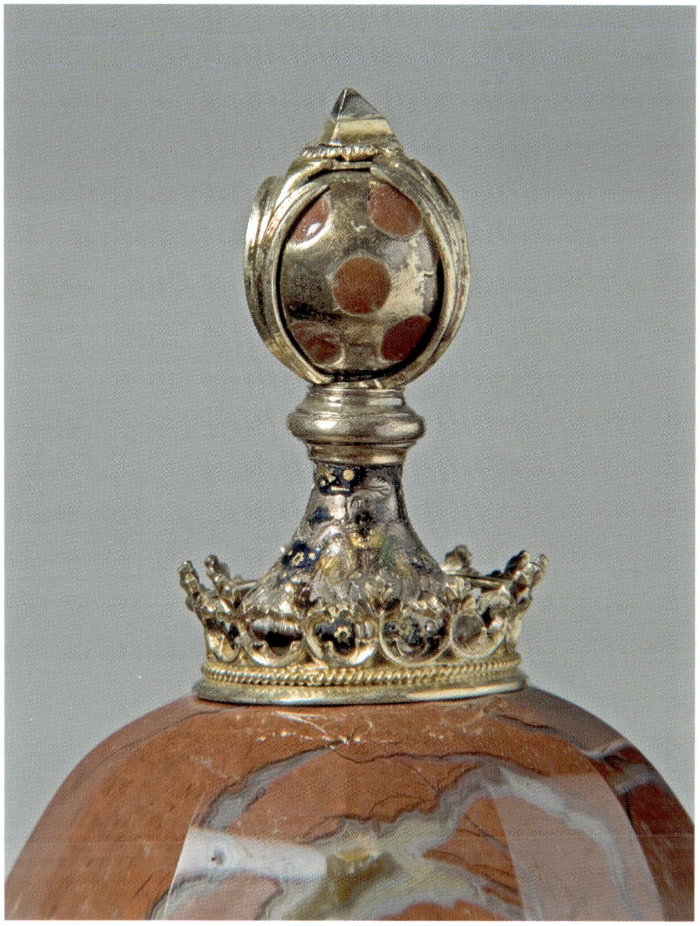

6. Florentine workshop
Jasper vase with two handles
c. 1460
Florence, Museo degli Argenti
(detail of crown with diamond ring)

prohibitive levels. Setting up a weaving loom was a time-consuming process, sometimes lasting for months, so that fashions in woven fabrics over the course of the Middle Ages and Renaissance persisted much longer than in the centuries to follow. It is no coincidence that the statutes explicitly banned any fabric "entirely or partially figured."[34] Included in this category were heraldic fabrics, which, being made for the members of a single family or its retainers, could not be amortized by high levels of production, like those produced for the rest of the population or for churches.

Parallel to the long list of garments that made up Renaissance clothing is the equal if not greater number of ornaments constituting the jewellery of women in wealthy families. It was hard for anyone to get his bearings among the quantity of new articles dictated by the developing fashions, and even more so for the small group of outsiders whom the earliest sumptuary laws appointed to police the community. Difficulties interpreting the regulations made it impossible to enforce them, no matter how detailed and precise they were, with the result that new laws were constantly being issued. The terminology employed in these descriptions is extremely interesting, and has hardly been studied as yet.

Frequently, prostitutes were not required to observe these severe laws. Interesting in this regard, although not pertaining to the period examined here, is the sumptuary law of 1562, where prostitutes were granted extraordinary freedom in clothing and ornaments on the grounds that, being "by nature" brazen and rebellious, they would be more liable to disobey a law the more it was coercive.[35] They were usually authorized to wear costume jewellery which was totally forbidden to "virtuous" women: ornaments "of gold or silver, or gilded or silver-plated, or made of pearls or any kind of precious stones, or of other metals differing from the aforesaid."[36] On occasions when they left the brothel district, prostitutes were obliged to wear distinctive signs (often a yellow sleeve, veil, or strip of fabric), so that they would not be confused with other women. Their ostentatious dress became a tool of the trade to attract clients, and was even sometimes considered an expedient to combat the rising tide of sodomy with more wholesome appetites.[37]

The list of ornaments banned to women included not only the usual jewels but also the decorations that, created to serve a specific function, were soon transformed into ostentatious luxuries. Buttons, for example, were one of the items most often prohibited. It was repeatedly stated that only buttons having matching buttonholes were permitted. Buttons sewn onto garments merely as embellishment were forbidden. Noteworthy is the wealth of terms used to identify the various types of ornamentation having similar functions but different appearance, long-lasting in fashion but often subject to the changing styles of the day. Their use, more than their form, hindered the interpretation of items subject to incessant innovation. Even jewels could have a different appearance when worn with new fashions. Jewels, by their very nature, remained unchanged for much longer periods of time, both for the expense incurred in purchasing them and because in this area changes were accepted rather more slowly.

The sumptuary laws tended to govern not so much the form and quality of ornaments as how they were displayed in dress. Hence we find, precisely listed, how many rings could be worn on a hand, how many chains around the neck, how many hair-clasps, how many buttons, in a crescendo of details that document the inane efforts of the lawmakers to keep up with the inventions of women, and their ability to evade the controls.[38]

1. For the painting as an iconographic source see Cappi Bentivegna 1962.

2. Del Lungo 1926, p. 206.

3. Frick 2002, p. 179.

4. Polidori Calamandrei 1924, p. 20.

5. For an overview of the sumptuary laws and their significance not only in Florence, see Levi Pisetzky 1964–9, II, 1964, pp. 468–73; Levi Pisetzky 1978, pp. 30–6; Lightbown 1992, pp. 79–89; Peri 2006, pp. 367–434.

6. Polidori Calamandrei 1924, p. 22.

7. Frick 2002, pp. 179–200.

8. The Florentine laws were issued at a growing pace. After the 14th-century statutes (Lastri 1821, pp. 83–94) those of 1415, the laws of 1439 (*Deliberazione* [1439], ed. Morelli 1881), of 1456 (Pellegrini 1898), of 1459 (Municchi 1909), of 1464 and of 1472 (*Due provvisioni* [1464–72], ed. Mazzi 1908), in 1500 (Sanesi 1893). For the archival characteristics and coding of the laws and statues, see Biscione 2009.

9. Muzzarelli 2007, pp. 399–400.

10. Mazzi 1991, p. 85.

11. *Due provvisioni* (1464–72), ed. Mazzi 1908, p. 4.

12. *Due provvisioni* (1464–72), ed. Mazzi 1908, p. 5.

13. Lightbown 1992, p. 79; Debby 2001, p. 137.

14. *Due provvisioni* (1464–72), ed. Mazzi 1908, p. 7.

15. Baron 1988, p. 287.

16. Polidori Calamandrei 1924, p. 22.

17. *Legge suntuaria* (1355), ed. Fanfani 1851, p. 5.

18. See also Burke 1972.

19. For more detailed information on the policy behind the sumptuary laws, see also Hughes 2002.

20. Del Lungo 1926, pp. 205–6.

21. Polidori Calamandrei 1924, p. 28; Herald 1981, pp. 151–2.

22. *Due provvisioni* (1464–72), ed. Mazzi 1908, p. 7.

23. Klapish-Zuber 1988, pp. 160–3.

24. Muzzarelli 2007, p. 401.

25. Del Lungo 1926, p. 91; *Due provvisioni* (1464–72), ed. Mazzi 1908, p. 8.

26. *Due provvisioni* (1464–72), ed. Mazzi 1908, p. 11.

27. Klapish-Zuber 1988, p. 202.

28. Schiaparelli 1908, pp. 231–41.

29. Debby 2001, p. 138.

30. *Due provvisioni* (1464–72), ed. Mazzi 1908, p. 8.

31. Guidotti 1984, p. 627.

32. Schiaparelli 1908, pp. 195–230.

33. Lastri 1831, p. 58.

34. Lastri 1821, p. 87.

35. Carnesecchi 1902, p. 9.

36. Del Lungo 1926, p. 86; see also *Due provvisioni* (1464–72), ed. Mazzi 1908, p. 10.

37. Levi Pisetzky 1964–9, II, p. 471.

38. *Due provvisioni* (1464–72), ed. Mazzi 1908, p. 10.

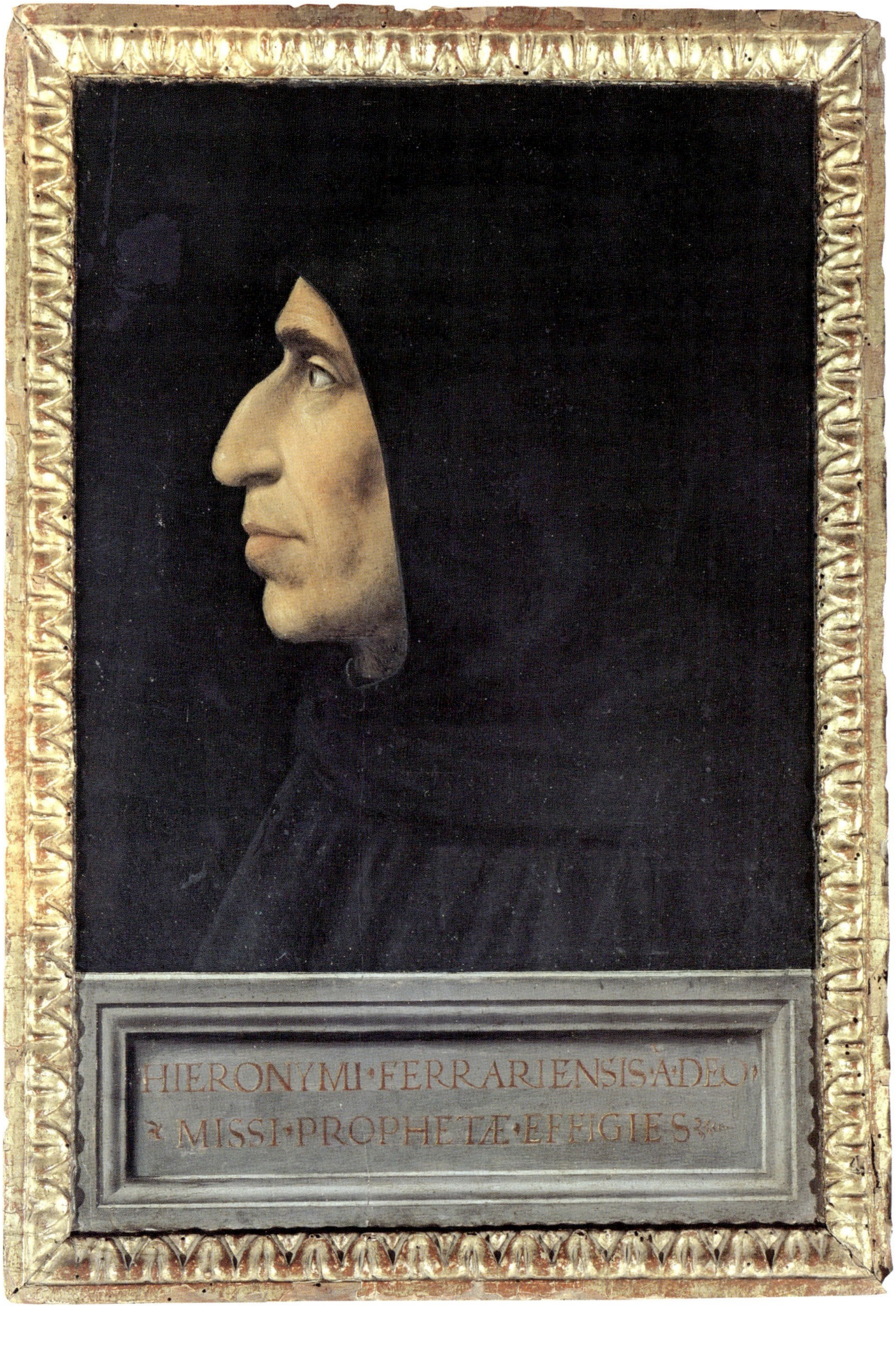
HIERONYMI·FERRARIENSIS·A·DEO
MISSI·PROPHETÆ·EFFIGIES

Girolamo Savonarola and his Dream of Reform: Art, Money and the Bonfire of Vanities

Stefano Dall'Aglio

The bonfire that, on May 23, 1498, enveloped the lifeless body of the Dominican Friar Girolamo Savonarola was only the last of the blazes that illuminated his decline. A little over a month before, on April 7, the dreams of his devoted followers—the so-called *Piagnoni*—had been shattered by the failure of an "experiment with fire" that Fra Girolamo had done his utmost to avoid. Invited to undergo an impossible trial—passing unharmed through fire to prove the truth of the Friar's doctrine—Savonarola's followers failed to show the Florentines the miracle they flocked to see. The collapse in consensus was so immediate that within a day of that failure Savonarola was thrown into a prison he would leave only for the gallows. Two other bonfires, not long before, had pointed toward the inevitable end of Savonarola's life. These were the two impressive bonfires of the vanities with which the Friar had tried to express his ideas of reform through an event of great symbolic and dramatic significance.[1]

Many years had passed since, on September 21, 1452, Girolamo Savonarola was born in Ferrara. The turning point of his life came when, at the age of only twenty-two and unbeknown to his parents he abandoned his home town for the Monastery of San Domenico in Bologna. Leaving behind the physician's career planned for him, he became a "doctor of the soul," as a Dominican friar and preacher. In 1490 he moved to Florence and, renowned for his austere life and his rousing sermons,[2] in a few months he became Prior of the Monastery of San Marco. In the mind and the words of Savonarola, themes began to take shape, ideas that would emerge repeatedly over the years to come, expressed with growing emphasis and self-confidence. From preaching he soon moved on to prophesying, assisted by a series of events that appeared to come as confirmation of his predictions. "*Ecce gladius domini super terram cito et velociter*," he had thundered from the pulpit on April 8, 1492,[3] and a few hours later Lorenzo the Magnificent, the man who most symbolized Florence, died in his Villa di Careggi. "Soon there will come one from the mountains who, like Cyrus [...] will take the city and its fortresses,"[4] was the friar's next prediction,

1. Fra Bartolomeo
Portrait of Fra Girolamo Savonarola
post 1498
Florence, Museo di San Marco

and soon afterward Charles VIII, King of France, crossed the Alps and invaded Italy at the head of a considerable army, arriving unhindered at the gates of Florence.

Regardless of what these predictions were based on, it is hardly surprising that many Florentines were convinced that Savonarola was a true prophet inspired by God. The role of unrivalled authority he held after the expulsion of the Medici in 1494 was only a logical consequence of the popular veneration arising out of that very particular sequence of events. It is also unsurprising that the institutional upheaval that opened the way to eighteen years of republican government was triggered by the teachings of the passionate Dominican friar. Suddenly Fra Girolamo's impressive ideas for reform, hitherto limited to the faithful who sat below his pulpit, found an unexpected outlet for their concrete and rapid implementation. In his sermons, the change from apocalyptic tones to prophetic utterances of a typically millenarian variety suggests that the friar's pessimistic expectations of an imminent end of the world had been replaced by an optimistic vision of a new era of glory, prosperity and wealth, above all for Florence.[5]

The Tuscan city that had welcomed the young friar years ago was assigned a place of unrivalled pre-eminence in his prophetic vision, to the point of becoming the "city of the elect" and "the new Jerusalem" whence the proclaimed reform would spread throughout the world. "He preached that the Church must be renewed, but first it must be beaten by a great whip and purged,"[6] one biographer of the time reported, but his reform project was actually much broader and not limited to the clergy alone.

Society as a whole, each individual, would have to undergo radical change, involving every social class without distinction, in the public as well as the private sphere. Among the many facets of such an all-pervasive reform project, the financial and artistic spheres played a fundamental role, something that has not always been sufficiently recognized. Thus the bonfires of the vanities lit at Carnival-time in 1497 and 1498 were only the dramatic outcome of ideas that had long been present in Savonarola's mind and sermons.

The question of money was so important for Savonarola that he confronted it in the first sermon of the so-called Haggeus series that began in November 1494, when Charles VIII was at the gates of the city, and continued throughout the frenetic days of the Medici's expulsion and the founding of the Republic. Combating usury was an integral part of the Dominican project for financial reform as articulated by Savonarola from the pulpit of the Cathedral. In this sermon, the rejection of any profit deriving from interest-bearing loans was coupled with a renunciation of superfluous luxuries; it was a first hint of the purifying flames that would be lit two years later in February 1497:

> "O merchants, abandon your practice of usury, give back what has been illicitly taken and the property of others, for if not you will lose everything. O you who delight in excess, give it to the poor, since it is not yours, bring it to the Compagnia di San Martino, where it will be distributed to the humble poor, who often die of hunger, while you have so much more than you need [...] O you whose houses are filled with vanities and images and shameful things and evil books and the *Morgante* and other poems against the faith, bring them to me, to be burned as sacrifice to God. And you, mother, who adorn, your daughters with so many vanities and luxurious ornaments and wigs, bring them all here to us to send them up in flames, so that, when the

wrath of God shall descend, these things will not be found in your homes."[7]

But while the bonfire of "images and shameful things" would be a while in coming, the usury reform was a priority. This was one of the key points in Savonarola's broad project for social and moral renewal, attentive as it was to the needs of the lower classes, whose members were obviously the primary victims of the interest demanded by money lenders. These money lenders were for the most part Jews, many of whom had settled in Tuscany after having been driven out of the Iberian Peninsula in 1492. The provision issued by the Florentine authorities on December 26-28, 1495 was not limited to instituting a Monte di Pietà, a pawnshop where the poor could get money without having to pay interest, but also dealt with the question of the Jewish presence in Florence. A hasty, unwise decision decreed their expulsion from the Florentine State, to take place within a year from the issuing of the provision.

The problems, however, were far from solved and Savonarola's sermons over the following months show the preacher's concern for a provision that could not be enforced without concrete action. "You know that you have officially instituted a Monte di Pietà to drive the Jews from your land," stated Fra Girolamo in March 1496, "and this goal should be pursued."[8] Obviously, the new Monte di Pietà needed substantial financial backing in order to survive and provide the needy with the necessary assistance. On this subject, Savonarola's concern emerged in his next sermons, in which he exhorted Florentines to finance the new institution—"now whoever has money should lend it to this Monte"—to march in processions praying that Divine favour descend on it and to issue further laws that would punish usurers even more harshly.[9]

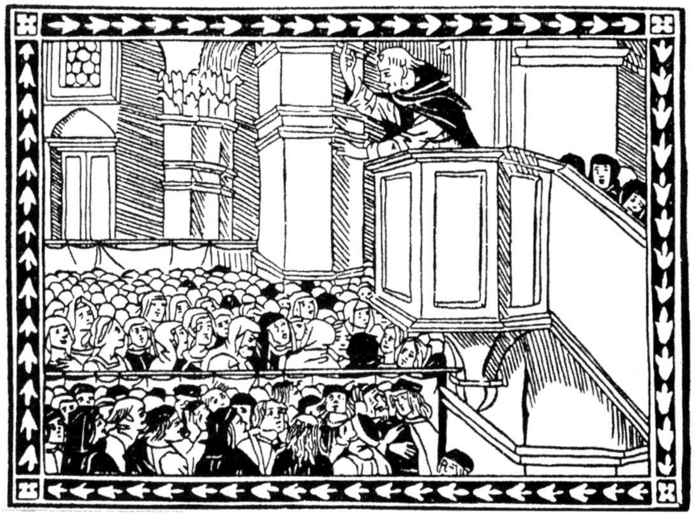

2. Anonymous Florentine engraver
Savonarola Preaching in the Florence Cathedral
1 September 1495
in Girolamo Savonarola, *Compendio di Revelatione*, Florence, Lorenzo Morgiani and Giovanni di Magonza, September 1, 1495, fol. 1r

But a temporary downturn had struck the Florentine economy.[10] Although the Monte di Pietà had been founded to replace the Jews, the authorities realized that their presence was still indispensable and decided to reconsider the situation. In November 1496, slightly before the deadline imposed on the Jews for leaving the city, a new provision was issued. With a hint of blackmail, it allowed the Jews to remain in Florence for another three years on condition that they would lend the Monte di Pietà six thousand florins. Paradoxically, while being obliged to refill the coffers of the State, the Jews were also forbidden to lend money and another discriminatory provision forced them to wear yellow badges for immediate recognition. The passage of time was to weaken a provision that enjoyed popular support but ran counter to the financial interests of the State. The decree expelling the Jews was never enforced, and the issue disappeared almost entirely from Savonarola's busy agenda.[11]

Although the Jews were not expelled, the introduction of the Monte di Pietà in Florence did achieve its practical purpose and also overcame the historic aversion of Savonarola's Dominican brothers to an institution traditionally linked to Franciscan spirituality. The friar's hostility to the Jews on this occasion was inspired not so much by ideological prejudice[12] as by the nature of his moral reform in the area of finance. Thus tirades against usury continued to appear in his writings, but without further reference now to the Jews,[13] while other measures to alleviate the financial problems of the poor were called for and enacted. These included fiscal innovations that taxed the wealthy more heavily, to the advantage of the lower classes, and the setting up of a network of social assistance whose most active institution was the Buonuomini di San Martino.[14]

But Savonarola's reform programme had only just begun, and the relentless moralizing crusade against corrupt customs was one of its salient features up to the very last days of his life. The ceaseless admonitions addressed to Pope Alexander VI and the corrupt clergy as a whole could not, in fact, be separated from the insistent tirade against "vice" and superfluous luxury expressed in the friar's sermons in increasingly emphatic tones. The raids conducted by the so-called *fanciulli*, young men who terrorized prostitutes and gamblers, continued to be one of the most conspicuous aspects,[15] but even more effective were the laws issued by the Great Council handing out ever more severe penalties for homosexuals and gamblers. "Once again they issued other laws in Council to keep the city purged and free of gambling and swearing and all vices; the laws stipulated that each individual should live decently," observed one of the friar's most convinced apologists some years later, with evident self-satisfaction.[16]

It was in this atmosphere of growing religious fervour that the idea of a bonfire of the vanities arose. There was nothing new about this, there had been other bonfires in 15th-century Italy. But Savonarola hoped to win over the Florentines with this spectacular visual renunciation of superfluous luxury and lascivious objects. The contemporary historian Iacopo Nardi left a precise list of what would be tossed in the flames: "A marvellous multitude of shameful sculptures and paintings, as well as dead hair and ornamental headdresses for women, Middle Eastern articles, cosmetics, orange blossom water, musk, perfumes of various kinds and similar vanities, and nearby little tables and chessboards, beautiful and expensive, playing cards and dice, harps, lutes, zithers and similar musical instruments, the works of Boccaccio and the *Morganti*, as well as an extraordinary number of books of enchantments, magic and superstitions."[17]

Regardless of what Savonarola considered "shameful sculptures and paintings," it was a long personal battle, close-

3. Hippolyte Flandrin
Savonarola Preaching at San Miniato
1840
Lyon, Musée des Beaux-Arts

ly linked to the preacher's concept of art. The same ideal *simplicitas* that pervaded every aspect of Fra Girolamo's life held true for art as well. "Ask the painters which is more pleasing, a figure that is artificially forced or one that is effortlessly natural. They will say that the natural one is certainly better and more pleasing," the friar had theorized from the pulpit. "In like manner, to the true Christian, outer simplicity is more pleasing than pomp and superfluous luxury."[18] Savonarola believed that art should imitate nature and reflect the early-Christian spirit of simplicity. "Obviously, simple works are more pleasing and acceptable to us than artful ones," he had declared in the *De simplicitate christianae vitae*, which contains the essence of his thought on the subject.[19] For Savonarola, the inspiring principle of the frescoes in churches should be no different from the spirit underlying all other spheres of human activity: "Only good masters should paint in the churches, and they should paint things that are honest," admonished Fra Girolamo in another of his sermons.[20]

Savonarola's criticisms were not, of course, aimed exclusively at works of art, but also at the elaborately decorated exteriors of churches. He may even have hoped that a new monastery would be built, in keeping with his ideal model, bare and devoid of decoration, "so that everything gives off the fragrance of devotion and simplicity."[21] On this point he was attacked by more than one adversary, replying that ornamentation was for the glory of God.[22]

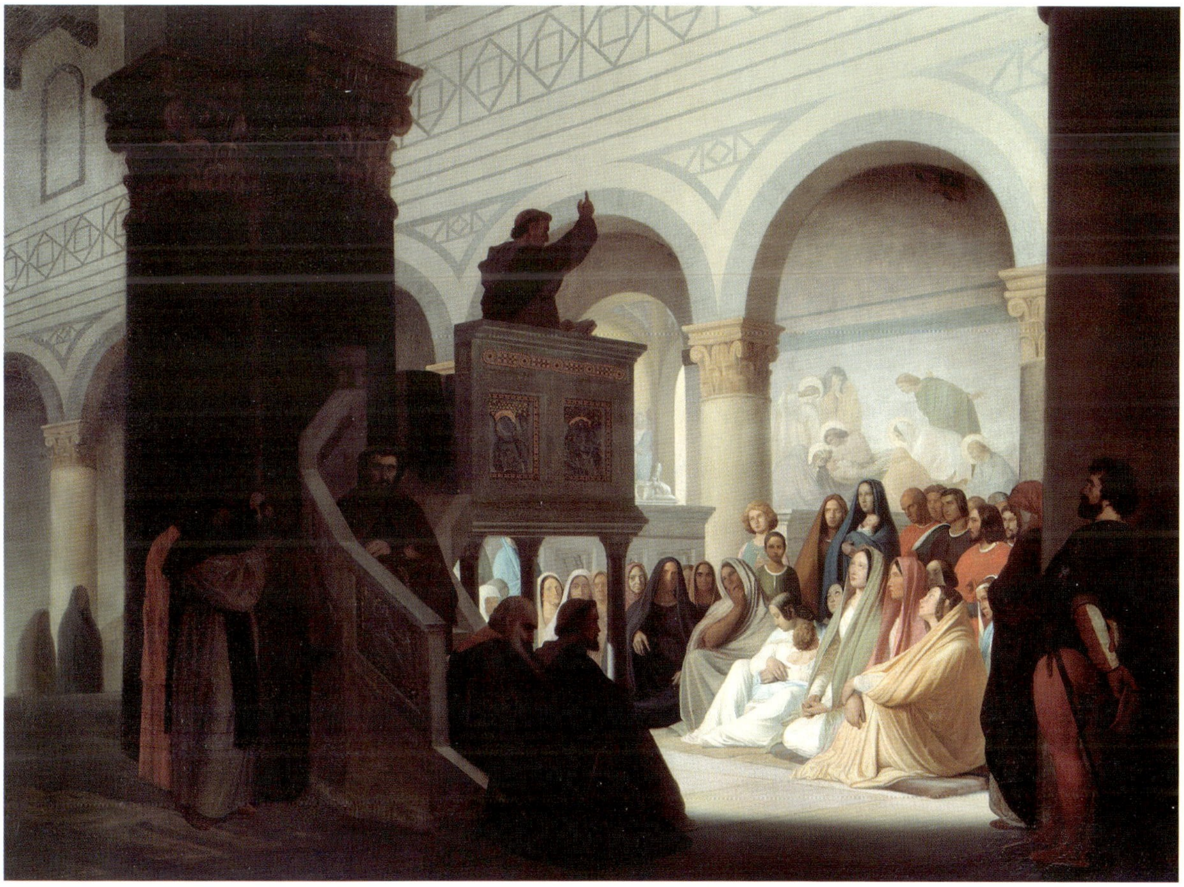

Clearly, however, in Savonarola's purifying vision, God would be glorified not by luxury goods, but by their renunciation. Moved by the same spirit, hundreds of people flocked to Piazza della Signoria on February 7, 1497, the last day of Carnival. This gathering marked the climax of the profound change the friar had imposed on this secular festival, transforming it into a religious ceremony. And while in the Carnival of 1496 his followers had limited themselves to a procession—far indeed from the traditionally rowdy festivities held under Lorenzo the Magnificent—the following year Fra Girolamo decided that the time was ripe to go further. In January 1497 the election of an ultra-Piagnona Signoria led by the faithful Francesco Valori underlined the success of Savonarola's followers. At the peak of their power, they now created the political conditions for organizing a Shrove Tuesday that would remain in the memory of the Florentines for centuries to come.

As recalled by one of the most renowned 16th-century biographers, the propaganda behind the celebrations planned by the friar had a precise ideological intention: "All this they did to extirpate the abusive, perverse customs of Carnival, since during those days it was customary to go around masked, and to give banquets where license and drunkenness held sway."[23] The break with this tradition was sealed when, as the flames soared upward, a hymn was sung "composed in horror of Carnival, and with honour and praise to Jesus Christ King of Florence."[24] The hymn was probably the *Canzona che fa uno fiorentino a Carnasciale* [Song sung by a Florentine at Carnival], a dialogue in verse between a devout Piagnone and Carnival itself, obviously perturbed by a ceremony that sanctioned its death sentence.[25]

The collection of sinful objects destined to the fire had begun already several months before, but the most open "search" took place on the day of the bonfire itself. Wearing white gowns, with garlands on their heads and carrying red crosses, Savonarola's young men crossed the city in procession, caught up in feverish excitement, going from door to door to collect lascivious objects to be burned. As proof of the link between the ceremony of the bonfire of vanities and

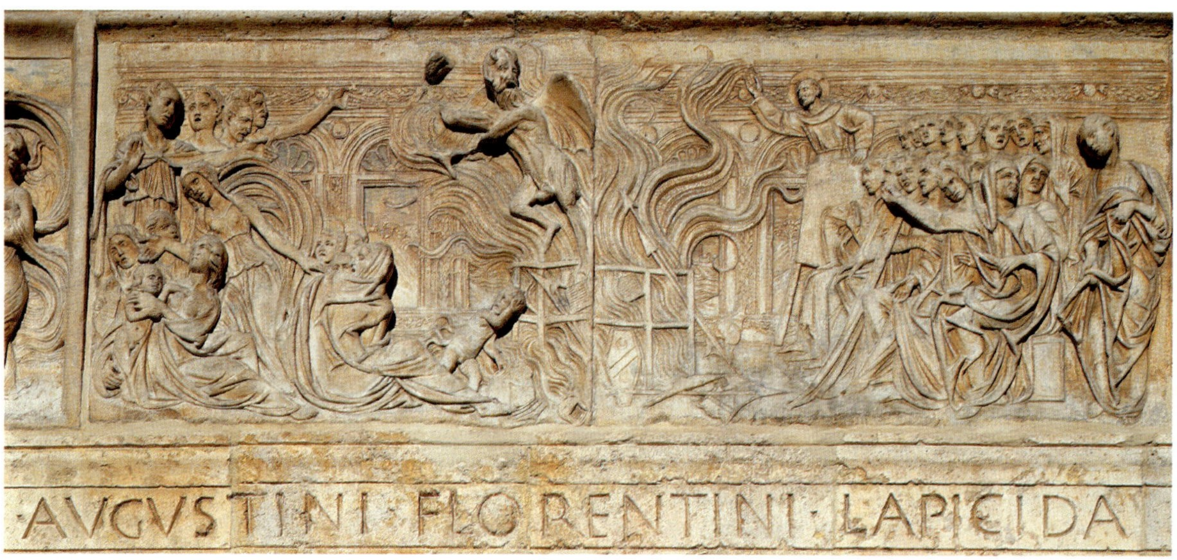

the project for helping the poor by opening a Monte di Pietà, the young men also collected money for both purposes. The fact that the burning of vanities and the provisions against usury were two faces of the same coin was admitted years later by one of Savonarola's most fanatical supporters, intent on enumerating the friar's praiseworthy actions to a sceptical listener:

> "And you must still remember the paintings and other shameful things that he had burned in the public square [...] as well as the many alms he had collected for the poor and the Monte della Pietà, so that Jews would not remain in Florence to practice usury."[26]

The enormous heap of sticks and straw in the shape of a pyramid some fifteen metres high, surmounted by an image of Satan, was deliberately piled up in Piazza della Signoria, symbolic centre of the city and its institutions. The ceremony unfolded in a carefully planned choreography. Representatives of the various quarters lit the fire to burn the sinful objects, while hymns and psalms accompanied the fascinating spectacle of flames reducing human vanities to ashes.[27]

Like all of Savonarola's actions, the ceremony was certain to arouse conflicting reactions. The astute chronicler Piero Parenti observed that "almost all the populace" participated, while noting that "only the friar's followers praised it as something well done and commendable, while the others criticized it severely."[28] The debate was to continue, especially in regard to the real or presumed mass destruction of works of art perpetrated on that occasion. This aspect, apparently of little concern to Savonarola's contemporaries—almost never being mentioned in pamphlets of the time—would later inflame a debate that still continues today.[29]

Basically, Fra Girolamo's attitude toward art was not much different from his opinion of Carnival. Far from opposing the festival in itself, Savonarola aimed to Christianize it, to bring it back within the fold of a reform project intolerant of worldly or pagan activities. Indeed the bonfire is the best possible example of the friar's severe reforming spirit. The episode penetrated so deeply into the collective unconscious as to cause one renowned American sociologist to state that "Savonarola's most famous act was the bonfire of the vanities."[30]

Not content with the success of February 7, 1497, the friar launched another attack on the following day, calling for the collection of other objects to be burned.[31] But the bonfire lit for the next Carnival, on February 27, 1498, was not to meet with the same success. With the Pope pronouncing him excommunicated and the Signoria turning hostile, there were signs of Savonarola's imminent and inevitable downfall. Less than three months later, with the bonfire of vanities forgotten, another fire would summon Florentines to gather in an equally crowded and emotionally charged Piazza della Signoria. This was the fire that burned Savonarola, condemned as a heretic and schismatic, and two of his most faithful followers. Together with their ashes, the friar's dream of reform vanished in the waters of the Arno.

1. On the subject of fire as *leitmotiv* of Savonarola's last year of life, see also Prosperi 2009.

2. The principal biographies of Savonarola are still Villari 1930; Schnitzer 1931 and Ridolfi 1997, which are however by now dated and reveal an approach overly favourable to the friar, to which may be added Cordero 2009, of radically opposed position, and Martines 2008. Pending publication is a new, important biography by Donald Weinstein.

3. Savonarola (1495), ed. Romano 1969–74, I, p. 56.

4. Agostino di Duccio
Bernardino da Siena Preparing a Bonfire of the Vanities
1457–61
Perugia, Oratorio di San Bernardino

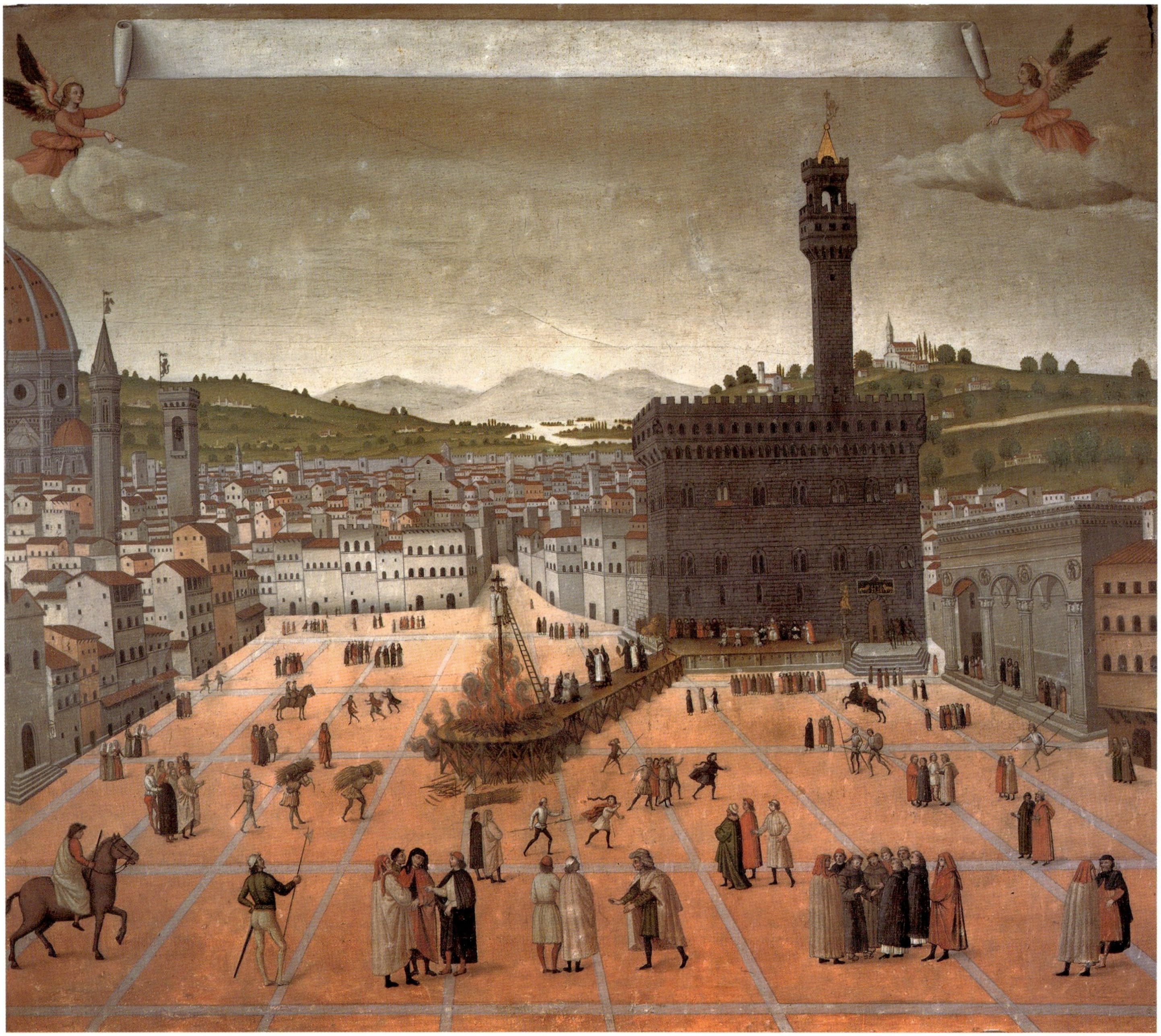

4. These are Savonarola's words reported by the contemporary biographer Placido Cinozzi (Cinozzi [*ante* 1503], ed. Villari, Casanova 1898, p. 17) and clearly inspired by the passage found in Savonarola (1495), ed. Crucitti 1974, pp. 14–5.

5. On this transformation, first delineated by Weinstein 1958, see above all Weinstein 1976.

6. This passage is in Pico (c.1530), ed. Castagnola 1998, p. 17.

7. Savonarola (1494), ed. Firpo 1965, pp. 19–20.

8. Savonarola (1496), ed. Ghiglieri 1971, II, p. 106.

9. The quotation is in Savonarola (1496), ed. Ghiglieri 1971, II, p. 433, but see also ivi, III, p. 71.

10. On this point, see Ciappelli 2009, pp. 203–10.

11. On provisions concerning usury, the Jews and the Monte di Pietà in Florence during the period 1495–6, refer to: Ciardini 1907, pp. 94–106; Cassuto 1918, pp. 66–76; Salter 1936; Menning 1992; Polizzotto 1994, pp. 36–7; Luzzati, Galasso 1996. More generally, on the development of the Monte di Pietà in Florence in the 15th–16th century, see Goldthwaite 2009, pp. 470–6.

12. On Savonarola's non-prejudicially hostile attitude toward the Jews, see the letter to the Signoria of Lucca dated May 18, 1493, in Savonarola (1475–98), ed. Ridolfi *et al.* 1984, pp. 39–41.

13. See for example Weinstein 1998, pp. 32–3.

14. See at least Polizzotto 1994, pp. 31–5.

15. On Savonarola's *fanciulli*, I will only refer to Terreaux-Scotto 1997, Niccoli 1997, Polizzotto 1998.

16. See Violi (*c.* 1545), ed. Garfagnini 1986, pp. 59–60.

17. Nardi (*ante* 1563), ed. Gelli 1858, I, p. 92.

18. Savonarola (1496), ed. Romano 1962, I, p. 143.

19. Savonarola (1496), ed. Ricci 1959, p. 192.

20. Savonarola (1496–97), ed. Ridolfi 1955, I, p. 354. On Savonarola's conception of art, refer to Steinberg 1977 and Assonitis, 'Art and Savonarolism' 2003.

21. The quotation is taken from *La vita* (c.1527), ed. Ginori Conti 1937, pp. 51–2. On this point see also Assonitis, 'Art and Savonarolan Reform' 2003, pp. 227–30, but also keep in mind Polizzotto 2009, p. 183.

22. See at least Catarino 1548, c. 40r–v.

23. *La vita* (c.1527), ed. Ginori Conti 1937, p. 123.

24. Parenti (*ante* 1519), ed. Matucci 1994–2005, II, p. 76.

25. See *Canzona* (1497), ed. 1864, pp. 1–21. On the transformation of Carnival in Florence during the Savonarola period, see Ciappelli 1996 and Ciappelli 1997.

26. Luschino (1523), ed. Dall'Aglio 2002, p. 87.

27. In addition to the works previous cited, on Savonarola's bonfires of vanities see also Ciappelli 1999 and Valeri 2010.

28. Parenti (*ante* 1519), ed. Matucci 1994–2005, II, p. 76.

29. On the historiographic debate on the bonfires, see. Ciappelli 1999, pp. 262–7.

30. Sennett 2006, p. 291.

31. See the passage found in Savonarola (1496–7), ed. Ridolfi 1955, I, p. 138.

5. Francesco Rosselli, attributed to
The Execution of Savonarola
post 1498
Florence, Museo di San Marco

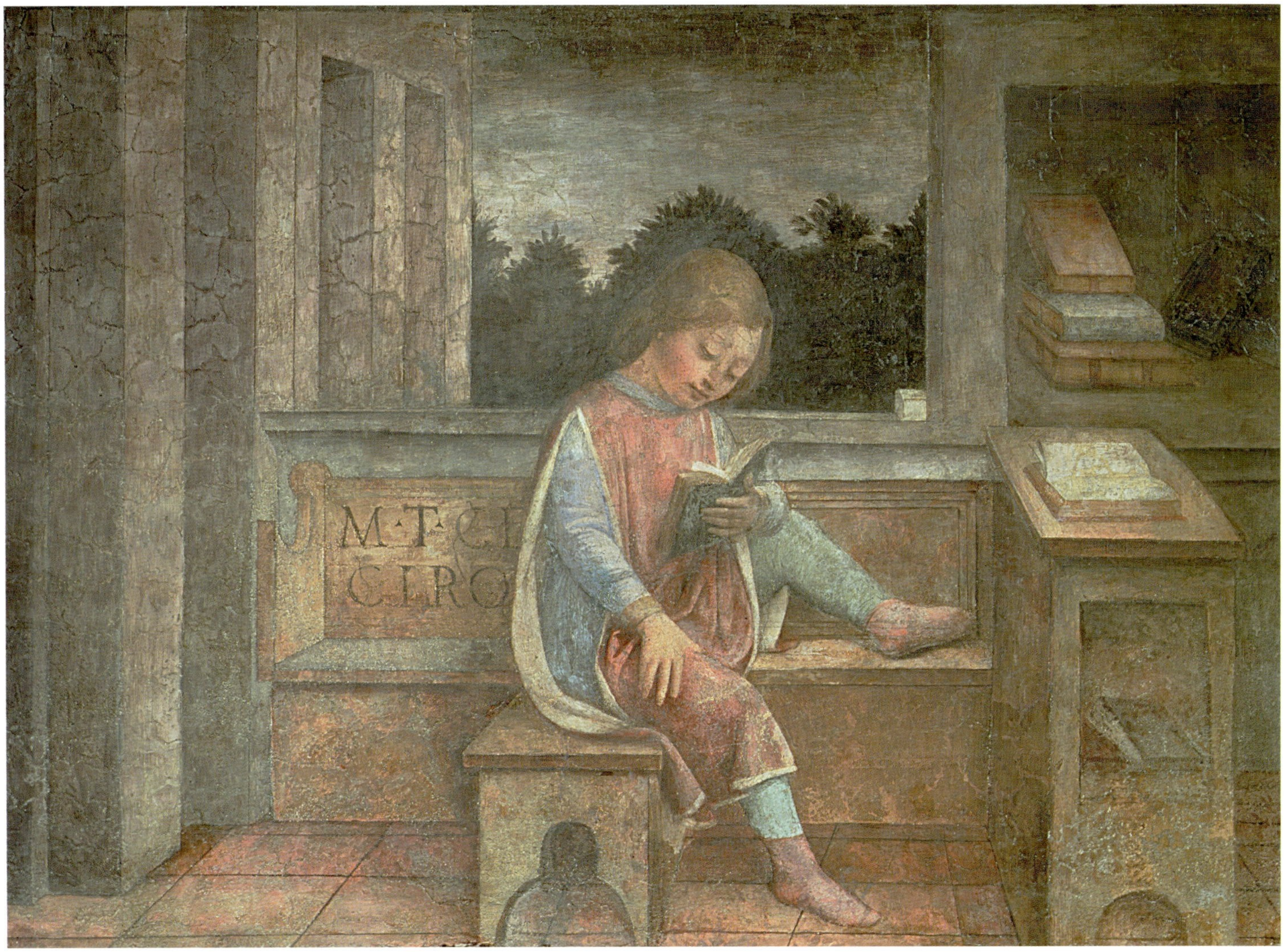

Cosimo, Piero and Lorenzo. From Money to Maestri

Cristina Acidini

Relations between art and money have always been and always will be close, multi-faceted, and inextricably linked to the powers that are founded on money and make use of it. Florence, dominated by merchant-bankers in the splendid era of the 14th and 15th centuries, experienced, developed and benefited from this relationship to the highest degree. The exceptional case of this city is admirably exemplified, if not fully explored, in this exhibition. The immense bibliography on the public and private commissioning of art in the Gothic Era and the Renaissance (continuing with Baroque and arriving—from Neo-classicism on—at the threshold of modern times) offers a broad survey of this subject, assigning well-deserved supremacy to the Medici family in its various branches. *God and Money: Florence and the Medici in the Renaissance* is the title of a book of essays by Richard Fremantle, whose subject is obviously close to our own.[1] Religion and wealth, Florence and the Medici, the Renaissance: the title and subtitle list all of the ingredients of a mixture about to burst into flame, in cultural terms. Burning on for centuries, this flame generated the artistic flourishing of a city that was actually quite small and—on the European chessboard of fast-growing powers—insignificant, yet able to leave an indelible imprint on western civilization.

The commitment of Florence's wealthy merchant-banker families, most notably the Medici, to patronising the arts, commissioning architectural projects and forming "cultural" collections in the broadest sense of the term, has furnished material for endless studies, too many to mention here, even briefly. We will only open a few windows, then, on a scenario studded with episodes (ranging from the territorial to the micro-dimensional scale of the gemstone), only glance briefly at scenes from an enthralling drama—money earned by business and finance invested in "culture"—that we can only hope may one day be staged again by comparable actors. Three episodes, each concerning a Medici from the main branch of the family, beginning with Cosimo and continuing with Piero and Lorenzo, may be taken as emblematic.

---

1. Vincenzo Foppa, attributed to
Boy Reading Cicero (or *The Young Cicero Reading*)
fragment of wall decoration (transferred onto canvas) in the
Milan branch of the Medici Bank.
1462–4
London, Wallace Collection

"Bibliothecas extruxit superbissimas" [2]
Cosimo and his Education

Few men, in the span of recorded history, have believed in the value of education imparted through culture—philosophical, literary and scientific—as passionately and consistently as Cosimo di Giovanni di Bicci, honoured by the posthumous title of *Pater Patriae* and known, in the 16th century, as The Elder. Of his century, only Pope Nicholas V and Federico da Montefeltro, Duke of Urbino, were driven by such an avid love of books, by such a vision of the library as the tool of civilization. Research on Cosimo shows how numerous and fruitful were his voyages along the routes of knowledge, entrusted to the written word in codices, whether splendid illuminated manuscripts or the humble products of copyists used only for reading. Starting as a young man, he formed a vast, illustrious book collection, including ancient volumes. He took this collection with him on some of his journeys, and later it accompanied him in exile.

When Cosimo contrived to bring the Great Council of the Eastern and Western Churches from Ferrara to Florence in 1439, the Orthodox delegates brought with them numerous Greek books. Their arrival marked the beginning of renewed studies on the ancient Hellenic texts and the birth of Humanism imbued with Neo-Platonic philosophy. With the founding of the Platonic Academy at the Villa of Careggi, lent to Cosimo for an experiment in reviving the ancient Academy of Athens, the heritage of books left in Florence after the Council began to bear priceless fruit in translations and new texts.

Cosimo and books: an association that—aided and abetted by the versatile talent of his favourite architect Michelozzo di Bartolomeo—was to lead to the foundation and enlargement of numerous libraries, in Florence and elsewhere. Exiled to Venice for a short time (1433–4), Cosimo had donated to the Benedictine Monastery of San Giorgio Maggiore the *Libraria Nova*, or new library; an entire building, according to Giorgio Vasari (which may have been a remodelled older structure), complete with benches and furnishings and filled with books.[3] Returning to his native city, Cosimo addressed his munificence and Michelozzo's talent to the libraries of Bosco ai Frati, Santissima Annunziata, and San Bartolomeo a Monteoliveto. Grandest of all was the library in the Dominican Monastery of San Marco. Variously dated between 1438 and 1442–4, it was designed and built in a synthesis of rigorous perspective and architectural levity that made it a three-naved temple of the intellect. Here diffused light reflected from walls painted—as shown by samples taken under the white plaster—in the light green colour used for *scriptoria* to intensify the scholars' concentration, made this place a haven for reading and meditation.[4] And here were brought the codices from Niccolò Niccoli's magnificent library, which were later to form one of the basic cores of the Libreria Medicea Laurenziana in San Lorenzo.

Cosimo's passionate belief that books are the foundation stone and tools par excellence of knowledge is mirrored figuratively in one of the most enchanting, mysterious images of 15th-century painting, which unfortunately migrated long ago from its birthplace, the Milan branch of the Medici Bank. Called *The Young Cicero Reading*, it is a fragment of wall decoration attributed to Vincenzo Foppa, now at the Wallace Collection in London.[5]

In this bright, pleasant composition, an elegantly dressed boy, seated under a loggia overlooking a flourishing garden between the side wings of a building, is intent on reading a book. Other books, already or still to be read, can be seen in a bookcase and on the shelves of a nearby "reading desk." On the parapet appear the letters "M.T. CI/CERO," trans-

2. Florence, Biblioteca di San Marco

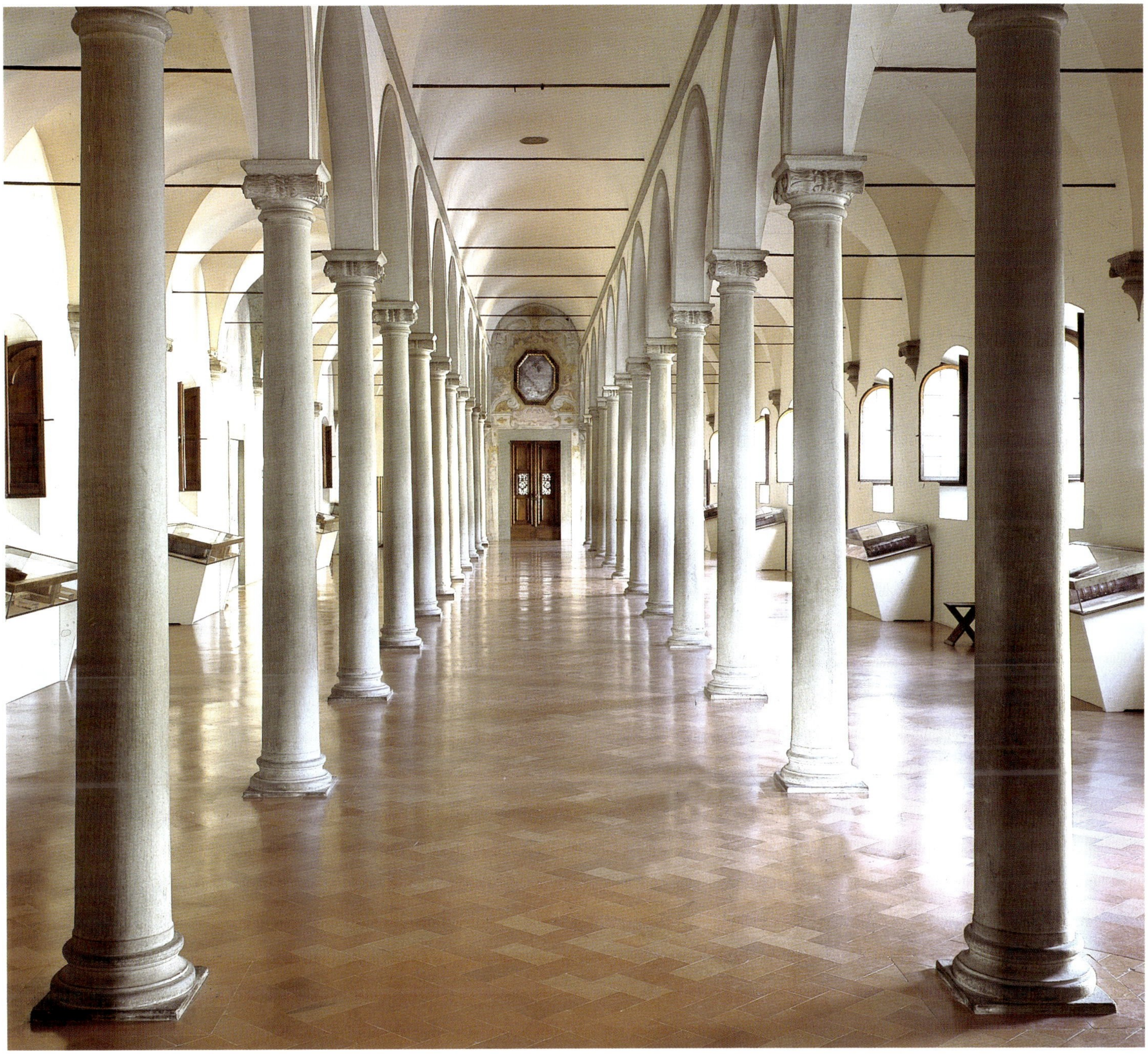

formed by restoration into the disconcerting and erroneous "M.T. CE/CIRO." This scene, detached from the Bank building by the restorer Bertini, presumably around 1863, was the only visible fragment of the extensive, diversified decoration that had adorned the porticoed courtyard of irregular rectangular shape.[6]

Examination of the various sources and descriptions—starting with the written testimony of Antonio Averlino, known as Filarete, a Florentine architect and sculptor active also in Milan and Rome[7]—shows the intention of glorifying the person and family of Francesco Sforza, who in 1455 had granted Cosimo de' Medici use of the land and existing houses over which to build his bank. The Medici too were celebrated through portraits, heraldic devices and coats of arms. Personifications and *exempla* illustrated the good principles of virtuous conduct and worldly knowledge: the labours of Hercules, the story of Susannah and of the Emperor Trajan, and the cardinal virtues. The atrium must have been decorated, at the initiative of Pigello Portinari, with images of Ptolemy and astrologers, the fixed stars, the planets and the signs of the zodiac.

To bring the unique, surprising theme of *The Young Cicero Reading* into the scheme, Ellis Waterhouse hypothesizes the existence of another series of images depicting the Liberal Arts, where this scene would have represented Rhetoric.[8] It was Waterhouse who definitively identified the subject, which was, and still is, sometimes interpreted as *A Boy Reading Cicero*. After a first tentative reference to the Leonardesque or Bramantine schools of Lombard art, the scene was definitively attributed to Vincenzo Foppa. This artist, having come to Milan in 1462–3 at the service of Francesco Sforza, painted the loggia of the Bank in 1463–4 under the guidance of the Medici agent Pigello Portinari, who soon afterward commissioned Foppa to decorate his own family chapel in Sant'Eustorgio.

Unfortunately, it is hard to evaluate the stylistic traits in this painting. Since it cannot be lent, according to the Wallace Collection statute (and was not even shown, in fact, at the 2002 monographic exhibition in Brescia),[9] it is never visible from nearby. Extensively restored, the wall painting shows similarities to Foppa's paintings of the time, such as—a comparison suggested in the catalogue of the aforesaid exhibition—the *Madonna and Child with an Angel* in the Galleria degli Uffizi (1479–80).[10] It differs in some respects however, such as the absence of the effect of the heavier contours and silvery grey dusting on the surface noted in the past by Roberto Longhi. These absences, however, may depend on the technique of wall painting, or even on impoverishment of the layer of plaster.

Hence no other consideration on the painting technique can be made. Furthermore, this is the only secular painting attributed to Foppa, making it hard to find iconographic comparisons; nor does the young reader's "casual attitude," with one foot resting on the bench, justly noted by the critics, seem fully compatible with Foppa's eloquently quotidian narrative vein, as exemplified by *The Miracle at Narni* in the Portinari Chapel. Ideal companions for the young Cicero might be found, instead, in the numerous workshop boys, adolescents and young men shown engaging in the most diverse activities in the memorable drawings of the contemporary Florentine goldsmith and engraver Maso Finiguerra. Reading or drawing, playing musical instruments or sculpting, meditating or sleeping, caught in the repose or tension of everyday situations, their bodies become interpreters, far removed from the noble models of culture but immersed instead in the vibrant contemporary realm of naturalism.[11]

Since, moreover—whether or not following Michelozzo's

design, something Patetta doubts[12]—the Bank seems to have been built and decorated by local workmen, as demonstrated by the stone portal now in the Museo del Castello Sforzesco,[13] it is probable that the cycle of frescoes would also have been entrusted to Lombard painters, or at least to artists working in Milan.

What interests us here, however, is the concordance of the theme with the personality and interests of Cosimo de' Medici, who indirectly commissioned the pictorial decoration as well as the architectural remodelling of the Bank. Dale Kent, in her monograph devoted to Cosimo (for which she drew on the studies carried out and coordinated in the 1980s and 1990s by Francis Ames-Lewis, and on an earlier pioneering article by Matthias Winner),[14] has not failed to underscore the connection between Cosimo and books. His personal library, in fact, rivalled those of the literates and philosophers, in an atmosphere of friendship and competition between merchant banker and humanists, masterfully evoked by Roberto Rossellini in the three episodes of the televised mini-series called *The Age of Cosimo de' Medici* (1973).

Cosimo's biographers report his exhortations to cultivate knowledge from early youth, through good literature (as reflected in the marginal notes written in his own hand beside selected passages), in the conviction that culture acquired at an early age is a resource, a talent to be invested for future progress in life. Since, from *Plutarch's Lives* on, Cicero had always been presented as a model student and a prodigiously fast reader at school, there could be no better *exemplum* to illustrate the educational principles upheld by Cosimo, who moreover identified with Cicero, as noted by Winner, in some respects. Although we cannot know the true weight of Cosimo's personal preferences in the Lombard decorative scheme, followed *in loco* by the Portinari, and although the date gener-

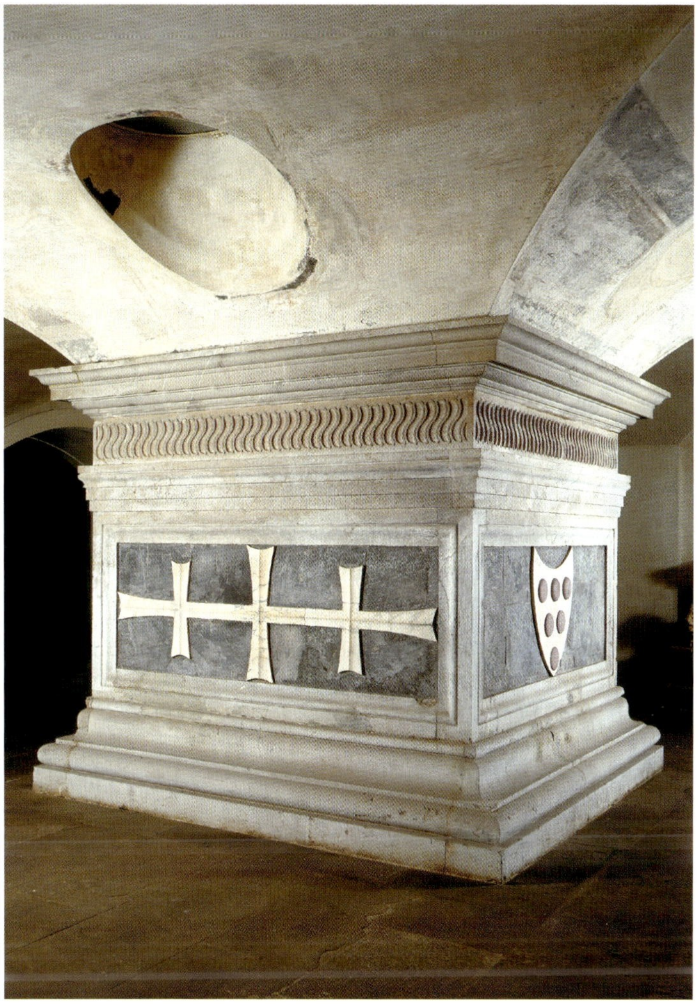

4. Andrea del Verrocchio (?)
Tomb of Cosimo de' Medici
1472
Florence, Basilica di San Lorenzo

ally accepted for the painting brings us to his very last years and months of life, the guiding idea for this remarkable artistic episode can only have come from him, from his moral and philosophical world, from his consolidated certainties and reiterated admonitions.

The image of a boy destined to a great future, intent on educating himself by reading, inserted in the decorative scheme of a bank, was a brilliant expression of the relationship between culture and art on the one hand, and money (to be invested) on the other. Only such a very great man as Cosimo de' Medici could have conceived of this idea. And it may well serve as fruitful inspiration for those who, engaged in either the former or the latter activity, take steps to create occasions where these two worlds converge.

"The brocade and other things will be made then
with patterns, and soon"
The splendours, private and public, of Piero the Gouty

These words are taken from one of the letters from Benozzo Gozzoli to Piero de' Medici when the artist was decorating the chapel dedicated to the Nativity and the arrival of the Magi in the Medici's new palace on Via Larga (1459), and Piero had been delegated by his father, Cosimo, to supervise the undertaking.[15] In the letter, dated September 11, 1459, the painter promises to devote the necessary attention to an especially precious fabric, as he presumably will to every other display of sumptuous magnificence. The fabrics embroidered in gold and silver, the gowns and banners, the headdresses and crowns, the belts and spurs, the horses' trappings embellished with gold and pearl decorations, all adorning the Magi and the procession of their followers, transformed the chapel into the fabulous, courtly evocation of a religious scene. Piero was to appear at the head of the procession behind the young Mago Gaspar on the east wall of the chapel, and Benozzo diligently painted the colourful sleeve of his green-and-gold brocade mantle, decorated with a large pomegranate motif.

Such attention on Piero's part is hardly surprising. He was required in this, as in other works commissioned by himself or his family, to ensure that the importance of the Medicean investment, whether inspired by fervent piety or civil magnificence, or both at once, would be obvious to observers of all classes and cultural levels; but even more, his initiatives expressed his own love of refined forms and costly materials.

As compared to his father, omnipresent in Florence with highly visible construction and restoration projects not to mention equally important projects elsewhere (the list begins with Milan, but could continue with Volterra and other cities), Piero tended to concentrate on fewer building initiatives, but more thoughtfully designed and more exquisitely decorated. While Cosimo could be cited by the humanist Giovanni Pontano in his *De magnificentia* (1498) as an exemplary patron of the arts, builder at his own expense of edifices for public use and the glory of Florence, Piero's commissions were more inclined toward the private field.

In the Medici dynasty, this father-son relationship seems to anticipate by over a hundred years the rapport between Cosimo, Duke of Florence, and his elder son Francesco, in the mid-16th century. Cosimo engaged in multifarious projects, not always on the monumental scale, in the city as well as its territory, while at the same time assiduously collecting art. Francesco kept within the very private dimension of "his" places of scientific experimentation, artistic creation and the collection of artefacts and curiosities related to his unflagging investigation of the wonders of nature and art. The Casino di San Marco, the Studiolo adjacent to the Hall of the Five Hundred in Palazzo Vecchio, the villa and park of Pratolino, the Grotta

3. Benozzo Gozzoli
Portrait of Piero de' Medici
detail of the *Cavalcade of the Magi: The procession of the "Youthful Magus"*
1459–63
Florence, Palazzo Medici Riccardi, Chapel of the Magi

Grande in Boboli, the Tribune in the Uffizi to a great extent absorbed his attention and resources. And Piero appears as forerunner to the "Prince of the Studiolo" when we project him into his favourite scenario, the *studietto*, his small study in Palazzo Medici. In the grandiose edifice designed and built by Michelozzo for Cosimo (who had refused, according to Vasari, an even more grandiose project designed by Brunelleschi), Piero arranged a smallish room—about 4 x 5.50 metres—as a refuge for long sessions of solitary meditation[16] and his connoisseur's delight in books,[17] antiquities and art.

The *studietto* or *scrittoio* was described with admiration by the anonymous author of the *Terze rime* in 1459; by Antonio Averlino, known as Filarete, a friend of Piero's and one of the finest artists and intellectuals in his circle; and then by Giorgio Vasari. It had a barrel-vaulted ceiling and was decorated with twelve glazed terracotta tondos by Luca della Robbia entitled *Work in the Fields*, accompanied by precise astronomical annotations (London, Victoria and Albert Museum).[18] This exquisite series, one of Luca's rare ventures into two-dimensional painting rather than painted sculpture, hailed the cyclic passage of Time through the months of the year, illustrated by scenes of farm work. It was an ancient theme, but linked here to the return of Time, a subject so dear to the Medici that it found permanent expression in the family symbols bearing the device of the *ouroboros* and the reflowering branch, and in the motto *Le tems revient*.[19]

In the basically monochrome painting of the tondos, the most delicate chiaroscuro effects are obtained using the whole range of blues, from midnight to pure white, with the precious gold insert of a radiant planet in opposition to a white sickle moon for each month of the year. Through this haunting blueness dart slender, lively figures, amid trees and objects defined by quick, nervous strokes. Even the glazed terracotta floor had come from the Della Robbia workshop.[20]

The anonymous author of the *Terze rime*—a poetic description of the palace on the occasion of the ceremonial events of 1459—mentions still further embellishments of the *scrittoio*, "all decorated in intarsia and painting," probably referring

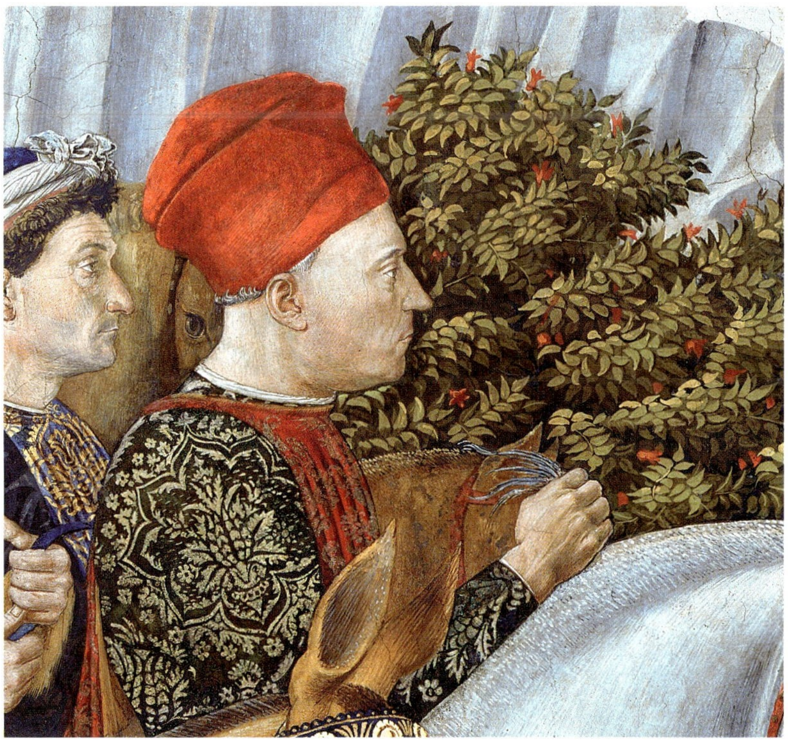

to cabinets with inlaid doors surmounted by frescoes on the walls.[21] On the shelves stood codices, inventoried in 1456 and then in 1464 according to the Florentine calendar (1465 in the ordinary style); not many, since space was limited, but vivacious and luxurious, with elegant, refined bindings in multicoloured leather and velvet as described by the inventories, and by Filarete, who compared them to "a heap of gold."[22]

The palace was the first home of the Medicean treasure, whose variety of categories and superb quality were to serve as guide to its expansion by Piero's sons, Lorenzo and Giuliano, both known as the Magnificent. The contemporary inventories of the Medicean collection list bronze statuettes, both ancient and modern (in 1465 Filarete donated a small replica of the Campidoglio *Marcus Aurelius*, thought at the time to represent Commodus Antoninus and placed in the Lateran, a lofty symbol of Imperial Rome), rare oriental porcelains, medals, coins, vases of semiprecious stone and rock crystal. Introduced by Cosimo, there was also a case containing twenty-one gemstones in 1456, a number that had risen to thirty by 1465. Although negligible compared to the eight hundred and twenty engraved gemstones owned by Cardinal Pietro Barbo, the future Pope Paul II, the Medici collection already included pieces that were to become famous and inspire artists. Among these was the cameo in sardonyx onyx or *niccolo* portraying *Icarus, Dedalus, Pasiphae and Artemis*, perhaps made in a workshop of Asia Minor in the first half of the 1st century B.C. (Naples, Museo Archeologico); the great onyx sardonyx cameo depicting *The Contest of Poseidon and Athena for the City of Athens*, by Aspasios or his assistants, dating from around the middle of the 1st century B.C. (Naples); and the *Entry into the Arc*, an onyx cameo dating from the 13th century, believed to have come from the court of Frederick II (London, British Museum). Of all the collections, furnishings, and works of art acquired by the Medici in the 15th century, each with its own degree of artistic quality and value, by far the most representative—and thus deserving of further study—are the gems and semiprecious stones, which include some of the most costly objects collected by the family.[23] An expensive and aristocratic passion, the engraved gemstones displayed to the admiration of selected visitors and connoisseurs had remote ancestors in the courts of Roman emperors and, more recently, those of Roger II, Frederick II, and Jean the Duke of Berry. Hence this collection was a tool of social prestige and vehicle of fame spreading far beyond the city's walls.

In Florence as elsewhere, the presence of these fabulous gems, combining rare, costly materials, superb craftsmanship, remote antiquity and an illustrious provenance, real or presumed, aroused a fervour of imitation and re-interpretation among the artists of the time, who saw in them—and were guided by the humanists to see—sources of fascinating images and elegant stylistic traits to be revived. As for the monetary value of the collection, which increased rapidly in just three years, it's worth noting that in Piero's inventory of 1465 the *Icarus* was estimated at 100 florins, and in the inventory compiled on the occasion of Lorenzo the Magnificent's death in 1492, 400 florins; the *Poseidon* rose in value from 180 to 800 florins; and the *Entry* from 300 to 2,000.

The extent to which the glyptic collection was a status symbol is demonstrated by the Medici's decision to use these gemstones as the basis for the imagery in the tondos by an unknown follower of Donatello that adorned the frieze along the stringcourse in the courtyard of the palace on Via Larga.

As for the vase collection, in Piero's time there was a rock crystal goblet bearing the heraldic arms of the Duke of Milan (perhaps received as a gift), vases made of jasper and, a true *unicum*, a rock crystal glass with a gold lid and enamels and

5. Royal workshop of Alexandria, Egypt
Farnese Cup
middle of the 2nd century B.C.
Naples, Museo Archeologico Nazionale

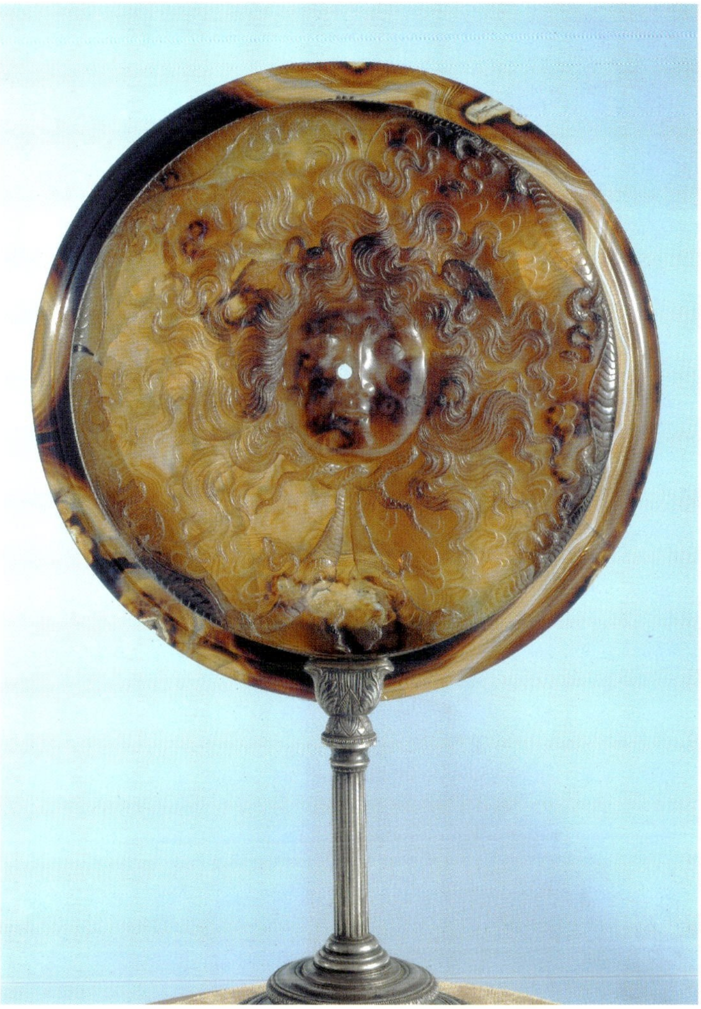

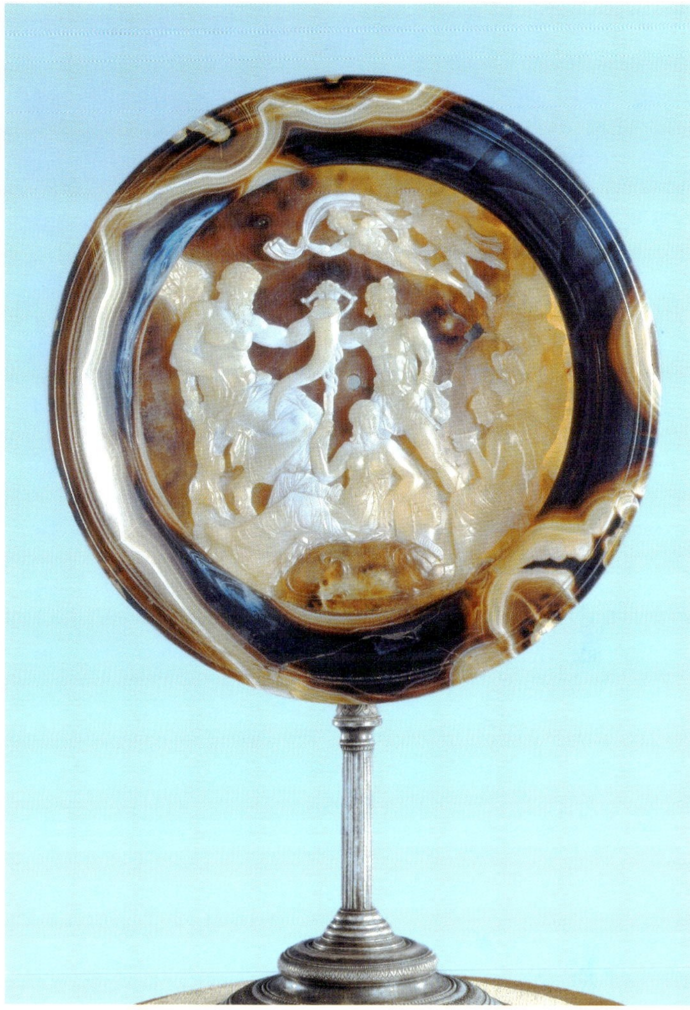

gemstones produced in Burgundy, which is now in the Museo delle Cappelle Medicee. Piero's most important artistic initiatives were to be found within the walls of the family palace—Donatello's *Judith*, Verrocchio's *David*—and in the Basilica of San Lorenzo, the dynasty's true church; perhaps the marble lavabo in the left-hand recess of the Old Sacristy, certainly the floor-level funerary memorial to his father Cosimo (1464–7) in which Verrocchio commemorates the deceased not by his own image but by the proportioned majesty of the geometric layout, the costly marble work, the elaborate bronze grids and the heraldic eloquence of the coats of arms. As Cosimo himself requested, his tomb, occupying the great pillar supporting the central nave, fits in with the decorated flooring in the crypt.

Although Piero commissioned fewer public works than his father, they reached supreme peaks of art in the highly decorated chapels he ordered to be built from 1448 on. The chapel in the Santissima Annunziata was commissioned to glorify the miraculous image of the Madonna; the chapel in San Miniato al Monte to safeguard the similarly miraculous Crucifix of St. Giovanni Gualberto. To give a real splendour to these buildings, carved marble with inserts of precious enamels, mosaic-work and gold were used in the first (accompanied by the inscription "Piero di Cosimo de Medici had this built, and Pagno di Lapo da Fiesole made it in MCCCCIIL. The marble cost 4000 florins"), and glazed terracotta with marble inserts in the second. Small when compared to the basilicas they were housed in, these chapels displayed a refined architectural style inspired by antiquity, for whose design Gabriele Morolli has proposed Leon Battista Alberti, rather than, as has been traditionally thought, Michelozzo.[24] Piero, whom the King of France had honoured in 1465 by granting an azure ball with gold lilies to be added to his coat of arms, and owner of the *Reliquiario del libretto* of illustrious French provenance, appears as a demanding and refined patron of the arts eager to distance himself from the merchant-banker founder of the family's fortunes, preferring instead to emulate the great nobles of France and Burgundy.

"The chalcedony bowl"
Lorenzo the Magnificent and the price of regal status

In the Egyptian city of Alexandria, at the height of the Ptolemaic dynasty, between the 2nd and 1st centuries B.C., one of the finest cameos of the ancient world was created, a cup made of sardonyx agate with a diameter of nearly twenty centimetres, engraved in relief both inside and out.[25] On the outside appears the monstrous Gorgon—Medusa's head—with its thick, waving hair of snakes, on the inside a scene from Graeco-Egyptian mythology in which eight figures, beside the Sphinx, are acting out an allegory celebrating the prosperity of Egypt. The cameo is known as the *Farnese Cup*, although this name was given it only in 1537, more than one thousand five hundred years after it was created.

In this vast span of time, the Cup entered and departed from many public and private collections, following a pendular route between Europe and Asia that has been patiently traced by historians, although some stages in its journey are still doubtful. Having entered the State treasury of Rome when the Ptolemaic dynasty came to an end (30 B.C.), it went on to Constantinople, which was sacked in 1204 during the IV Crusade. At this point it is thought to have migrated westward again, being purchased in 1239 by Emperor Frederick II of Swabia. His treasure was dispersed after his death (1250) and all trace of the cameo was lost until around 1430, when the Persian painter Mohammed al-Khayyam saw it at the court of Herat or Samarkand and made a drawing of the scene on the inside.[26] But prior to 1458 the cup had returned to the

6. Sandro Botticelli
Birth of Venus
1484–5
Florence, Galleria degli Uffizi

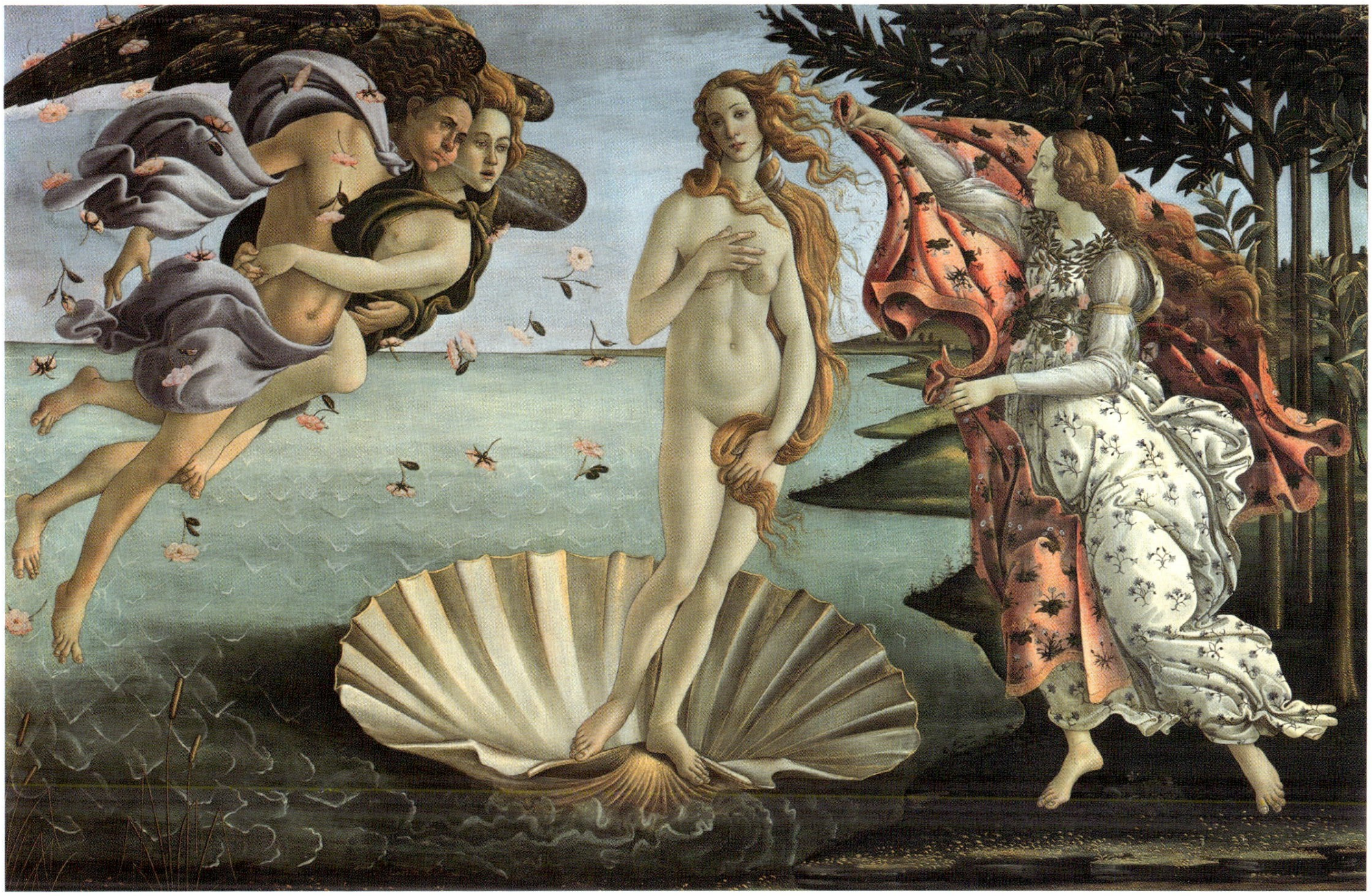

Mediterranean area, being purchased by Alfonso of Aragon, King of Naples. This gave rise to an anecdote reported by the Florentine man of letters Agnolo Poliziano, undoubtedly to please the Medici: "King Alfonso having bought from a merchant the chalcedony bowl now being used by Lorenzo de' Medici, at the price of a thousand ducats, said that he had been unable either to sell it or give it away."[27]

It next appeared in the inventory compiled in 1465 at the death of the arch-powerful cardinal and patriarch of Aquileia, Ludovico Trevisan, known as Scarampi Mezzarota, where it was unmistakeably described as "A bowl of chalcedony and sardonyx with figures engraved in it, having a diameter of about 1/3 *braccia* with a medusa on the bottom of said bowl, which is kept in a black case."[28] How the object came into the possession of Scarampi is unknown, but it may have been through his friendship with King Alfonso, to whom he is said to have lost 8,000 ducats in one night of gambling.

The piece was acquired, along with the rest of the Scarampi heritage, by Pope Paul II Barbo, an ardent collector of gemstones who had owned over eight hundred of them while still a cardinal. At his death in 1471 it was put up for sale by his successor Sixtus IV, who, to convert his predecessor's magnificent collection into money, entrusted it to the Medici-Tornabuoni Bank in Rome. And it is here that the path of this priceless ancient cameo crossed that of the Medici, at a time when the family was headed by Lorenzo, the twenty-two-year-old eldest son, after the death of his grandfather Cosimo (1464) and father Piero (1469). In 1471 Lorenzo, visiting Rome to pay his respects to the new Pope, managed to obtain the piece—assessed at a price of 10,000 ducats—as partial coverage of an old debt owed the Medici by the papacy.[29] The cup was not his only acquisition on that occasion. Through the Bank, Lorenzo also acquired from the Barbo legacy the chalcedony gemstone depicting *Diomedes and the Palladium* (now lost), which had been bought from the humanist Niccolò Niccoli for 5 florins and resold to Scarampi for 200 ducats. Years later, in 1487, Lorenzo had an agent in Venice buy from the famous jeweller Domenico di Piero another magnificent piece that had come from the Scarampi-Barbo collection: the carnelian then attributed to either Polycletus or Pyrgoteles, and now to Dioskourides, depicting *Apollo, Marsyas and Olympus*. This gem had been in Florence in the third decade of the century where, mounted in a setting by Ghiberti, it had become famous under the name of "Nero's Seal." Acquired by the Florentine Signoria, it was probably donated to Scarampi, who had led the papal troops to victory, beside the Florentines, over the Milanese in the Battle of Anghiari (1440).

Since early youth then, the eldest son of the merchant-banker dynasty that openly ruled Florence, investing in grandiose projects, both public and private, had shown his aristocratic, and quite probably regal inclinations by acquiring the most costly of all antiques, made famous by their passage through illustrious hands. In this refined collector's passion he was joined by his younger brother Giuliano, destined to die young in the Pazzi Conspiracy of 1478.[30]

It is uncertain how much was known at the time of the astounding genealogy of the Ptolemaic Cup's owners, ranging from the Kings of Egypt to the Roman Emperors of the West and East, to Emperor Frederick II and then to a king, a cardinal, and a pope. But even the 15th-century transfers of ownership of the piece entering Lorenzo's collection placed the young sons of the Medici family among the ranks of the ultra-exclusive community of engraved gemstone collectors, who spent fortunes to acquire them in quantity and quality; because, as Pontano remarked, "It's not enough to have a few very rare gemstones, unless they are also many and varied."[31]

After the death of Lorenzo, his most famous gems met the same fate as his other treasures. Safeguarded in Via Larga by his son Piero, after the latter's exile in 1494 some pieces, including "Nero's Seal" and the *Farnese Cup*, were confiscated by the Signoria and immediately donated to the Tornabuoni, as compensation for their investments in salvaging the Roman branch of the Bank. Subsequently, along with the vases and other precious objects, they returned to Florence and to Medici ownership, inherited by Margaret of Austria after the death of her husband Duke Alessandro de' Medici in 1534, and brought by her as part of her dowry when she married Ottavio Farnese in 1537. From Florence to Parma, from Parma to Naples, following the Farnese-Bourbon dynasty, the gemstones of the Medicean treasure arrived at the place where they are still found today, the Archaeological Museum of Naples.

Their sojourn in Florence, lasting only some seventy years, was thus a brief episode in their more than millenarian history. But for the first two decades especially, from the *studietto* set up by Piero di Cosimo and inherited by Lorenzo (and by Giuliano, for his brief lifetime), those ancient masterpieces imbued with mysterious elegance irradiated pervasive inspiration, arousing echoes in the philosophy and literature of Humanism, and above all, stirring artists to re-elaborate their iconography and motifs in singular, erudite images. Lorenzo delighted in showing his glyptic collection to his favourite artists, both friends of his own age such as Sandro Botticelli, and young talents to be cultivated and protected, such as Michelangelo. Both of these supreme artists, and others as well, were allowed to nourish their creativity directly from the artefacts of the ancient world splendidly present, albeit on a small scale, in those treasures. It is obvious, for instance, how carefully the *Farnese Cup* was studied by Botticelli, who took from the Medusa's head the motif of hair waving in fluid curves, using it most notably in the *Birth of Venus*, and borrowed from the Nilotic scene, for the same painting, the couple flying through the air.

The iconographies and formal solutions of these gemstones were broadly disseminated, not only by direct observation but also through drawings, casts and plaques taken from the originals, spreading their fame far beyond the walls of the Medicean *scrittoio*.

The Laurentian gems share their rarity and value with the vases made of semiprecious stones, further testimonials to the collector's inexhaustible quest for splendour ennobled by an aura of antiquity: fabulous pieces of Imperial Roman, Fatimid or Sassanid origin, in rock crystal, sardonyx, amethyst, jasper and chalcedony, most of them set in mountings by Florentine goldsmiths. According to the inventory compiled in 1492, there were no less than thirty-two vases in the collection when Lorenzo died.

Both gemstones and vases bear the still mysterious *ex gemmis* inscription: "LAV·R·MED," in which the "R" separated from the first syllable of the Christian name has always aroused questions as to its meaning. While *Rex* would be the most obvious explanation, more elaborate reflections have been made by Anna Lenzuni, suggesting Horace's formula "*Rex paterque*," addressed to his patron Maecenas; and by Laurie Fusco on the ambiguity of the initial "R," common to both *Rex* and *Respublica*.[32] The doubt remains, nor can there be any definitive answer in the absence of sources and documents. But certainly, in relating this invasively repetitive *ex gemmis* to the world of symbolic signs used by Lorenzo the Magnificent to denote his most cherished belongings, we can offer some further considerations. We might note, for instance, among the personal devices marking his illuminated manuscripts (existing in great number in the Biblioteca Medicea Laurenziana) the image of the six beehives (called *fiali* in the ancient documents, another word for honeycomb) with bees (*pecchie*) swarming around them. Many Latin authors, based mainly on Aristotle, had praised bees as example of a clean, sensible, monarchical, loyal, industrious community, expert at architecture and capable of maintaining perfect social relations. The beehive was taken as a model of society, honey as the symbol of eloquence, and the search for pollen, or rather for honey (believed to be rained down from heaven onto flowers by the dew, and collected directly from them) as a paradigm of thoughtful intellectual selection. Inserted in the decorations of manuscripts, bees showed the reader's virtuous intent of distilling from the texts the best of knowledge. No less significant was the monarchical message implicit in the evocation of a community of tireless, industrious insects, rotating around the regal authority of the King Bee.[33]

The insistent presence of symbols cryptically alluding to the sovereignty of the Laurentian universe authorizes us to conjecture that Lorenzo, *primus inter pares* on the Florentine public scene, in the privacy of his study felt himself a king surrounded by his treasure of jewels and books. Thirty years later the exiled Niccolò Machiavelli was to describe his own metamorphosis in the presence of the ancient authors: "I enter my study; and within the door, I exchange my daily garment, full of mud and mire, for royal and curial robes; and having thus dressed decently, I enter the ancient courts of the men of old."[34] In similar manner, the son and grandson of merchant bankers may have tried, through contact with objects recognised by ancient powers, surviving from remote and splendid eras and bought at exorbitant prices, to feel some continuity with the sovereigns of the past, his true, magnificent predecessors.

Financial troubles, an inept son, religious and political upheaval, and lastly his untimely death would blight, if indeed it had ever blossomed, the belated flower of that fragile monarchical dream. But the "R" engraved in the hard, durable material remains, enigmatic and discreet, to keep alive the doubt and the memory.

Money or Maestri? In conclusion, a dilemma

Lorenzo de' Medici was well acquainted with the busy world of the Florentine workshops, where he was on friendly terms not only with great artists but also with minor craftsmen such as the metal worker Niccolò Grosso known as Caparra, and the painter Graffione, an eccentric pupil of Alesso Baldovinetti. As regards the latter, Giorgio Vasari reports: "They say that the magnificent Lorenzo de' Medici, in reasoning one day with Graffione, who had a strange mind, told him, 'I want to have all of the interior angles of the dome decorated with mosaic and stucco-work.' To which Graffione replied, 'You don't have the maestri to do it', and Lorenzo answered, 'We have enough money, though.' Graffione immediately objected, 'Eh, Lorenzo, it's not money that makes maestri, but maestri that make money'."[35]

Whether or not this anecdote is true we will never know. But most certainly, with its pithy, earthy folksiness, it raises a crucial question. Can money invested in training and supporting artists and commissioning works of art improve the conditions for artistic creation? Or are inventive capacity and technical mastery beyond being produced by money, while nevertheless offering a source of income to those who possess such qualities, with economic repercussions for a range of related enterprises and businesses?

Without attempting to solve this ancient dilemma, we will express the sincere hope that money will continue to be invested in maestri, and that the maestri will in turn make money.

1. Fremantle 1992, still in publication in Florence in the edition translated in 2008.

2. Fra' Mariano da Firenze, cited in Barletti, Boddi 1998, p. 306.

3. Vasari 1568, ed. Bettarini-Barocchi 1966–97, III, 1971, p. 231.

4. *La biblioteca di Michelozzo* 2000.

5. E. Caldara, in *Vincenzo Foppa* 2003, p. 143, no. 27.

6. The planimetries in Patetta 1998, pp. 238–9, figs. 1–2. See also, on this subject, Paoletti 1994.

7. Filarete [*c.* 1464], ed. Finoli, Grassi 1972, pp. 683–704.

8. Waterhouse 1950.

9. *Vincenzo Foppa* 2003.

10. Romano 2003, p. 37 note 41.

11. Melli 1995, pp. 34–6.

12. Patetta 1998, pp. 238–9.

13. *La scultura* 2010, pp. 145–6, 223 (no. XIV.4).

14. Kent 2000, ed. 2005; Ames-Lewis 1984; Winner 1970.

15. Letter from Benozzo Gozzoli to Piero de' Medici (Florence, September 11, 1459), in: Gaye 1839-40, I, 1839, p. 192; Padoa Rizzo 1993, p. 362; Ahl 1996, p. 277, Doc. 10c. See also: Acidini Luchinat, 'La Cappella dei Magi' 1993, p. 15.

16. Gnocchi 1988, pp. 53–6.

17. Ames-Lewis 1984.

18. *Terze rime in lode di Cosimo de' Medici* [1459], in Hatfield, 'Some Unknown Descriptions' 1970, p. 248 (fol. 30r, vv. 3-15); Filarete [*c.* 1464], ed. Finoli, Grassi 1972, II, pp. 696–7; Vasari 1568, ed. Bettarini-Barocchi 1966–97, II, 1967, pp. 53–4.

19. Horowitz 2003. On the Medici devices, especially those linked to the theme of Time returning: Cox-Rearick 1984; P. Ventrone in *Le tems revient* 1992, pp. 167–8; Ricciardi 2001, pp. 80–7 (with bibliography); Koch 2010.

20. On the glazed terracotta tiling produced by Luca della Robbia for the Studiolo of Piero de' Medici, see in particular: Lethaby 1906; Pope-Hennessy 1964, I, pp. 104–12, nos. 82–3; Del Bravo 1985, pp. 46–8; Liebenwein 1988, pp. 55–9; Bulgarelli, Ceriana 2009, p. 140; Gentilini 2009, pp. 154–5.

21. *Terze rime in lode di Cosimo de' Medici* [1459], in Hatfield 'Some Unknown Descriptions' 1970, p. 248 (fol. 30r, v. 6).

22. Filarete [c.1464], ed. Finoli, Grassi 1972, II, p. 686.

23. For the Medicean collection of gems in the 15th century, see the catalogue of the recent exhibition *Pregio e bellezza* 2010 and in it the article by Riccardo Gennaioli (2010), with bibliography.

24. Morolli 1998; Morolli 2006.

25. U. Pannuti, in *Il Tesoro* 1973–4, I, 1973, pp. 69–72, no. 43.

26. M.A. Di Pede, in *Pregio e bellezza* 2010, pp. 108–9, no. 23.

27. *Angelo Polizianos Tagebuch* 1929, p. 78, no. 163. This anecdote was linked to the *Farnese Cup* for the first time by the writer: Acidini Luchinat, 'La "santa antichità"' 1991, p. 146 note 21.

28. Bagemihl 1993, p. 562.

29. For the most recent review of information on the *Farnese Cup* see the catalogue *Pregio e bellezza* 2010, in particular the above-mentioned entry no. 23 on p. 108.

30. Fusco, Corti 2006, p. 5.

31. Pontano 1498, ed. Tateo 1999, pp. 239–40.

32. Acidini Luchinat, 'Library' 1993, p. 120; Fusco, Corti 2006, pp. 149–55; Gennaioli 2010, p. 25.

33. That the dominant bee is not a king (according to a belief dating back to Aristotle) but a queen, would become known only in 1669, with the publishing of the *Historia Insectorum Generalis* by Jan Swammerdam.

34. Letter from Niccolò Machiavelli to Francesco Vettori (Florence, December 10, 1513), in Machiavelli (1497–1513), ed. Gaeta 1961, p. 340.

35. Vasari 1568, ed. Bettarini-Barocchi 1966–97, III, 1971, pp. 317–8.

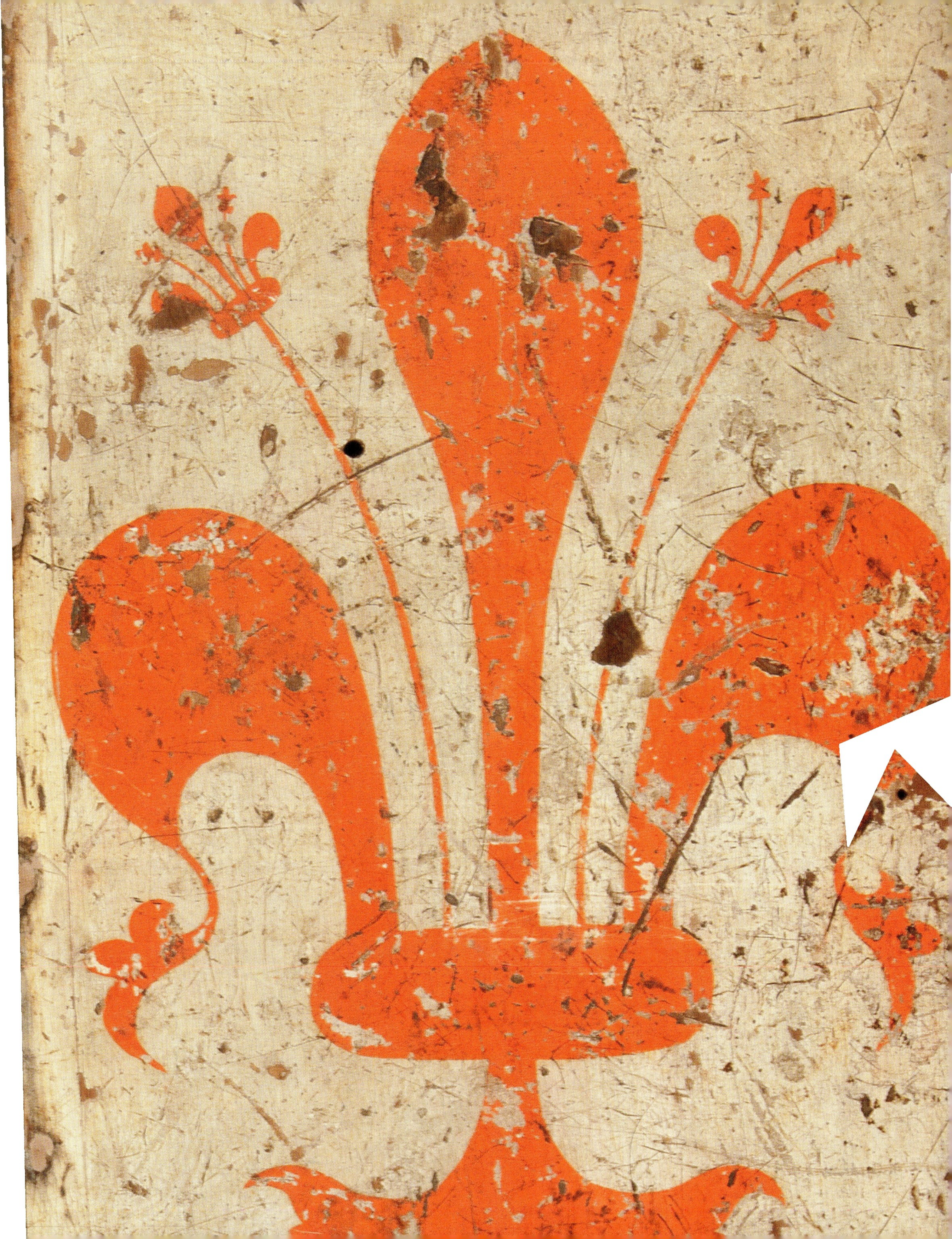

Section 1
The Florin: Florence’s Ambassador to the World

The problem was how to do business. A unit of exchange was needed that really was worth something. There was no question of paper money or a notional value fixed by a central bank, as we have today. Coin must be worth what it bought, in itself. It must be silver or gold.
In the mid 13th century there was a confusion of currencies. The Florentines were using the worn out silver coinage of a declining Holy Roman Empire that was now worth so little it had to be supplemented with more valuable coins from Lucca and Siena. In 1252 Florence began minting the golden florin.
It would be hard to exaggerate the seriousness of the venture. Only pure twenty-four carat gold was used. Each coin would weigh exactly 3.53 grams; that is, ninety florins would weigh exactly one pound. Records would be kept of all dates of issue and changes of design. Supervisors and quality-control inspectors were appointed by different trade guilds and would hold their positions only briefly to prevent them from becoming too friendly with the mint workers. Filing coins or counterfeiting cheap versions with inferior gold was severely punished.
The florin was small, the size of an American nickel or the Euro's five-cent piece. But today those 3.53 grams of gold would cost you $150 or 110 Euro to buy. So this was not petty cash. In fact, for everyday expenses in Florence people would go on using silver. The new coin was for serious trade. The florin was made to travel. And the message it took around the world was that the Florentines could be trusted, their gold was good; you could do business with them.
There was no duke's head on the coin, no king, or Pope, or emperor. Florence was a republic. By the late 13th century they had banned their old aristocracy from any role in government. So the coin showed a lily on one side, emblem of the town (the name of the coin, *fiorino*, comes from *fiore*, flower), and on the other St. John the Baptist, the city's patron saint, forerunner of Christ. Thus piety, beauty, local identity and rock-solid commercial value were elegantly fused together, in gold.
The city's neighbors were impressed. Europe was impressed. Very soon the florin would be the preferred coin for business between the Italian republics and its many trading partners from Cyprus to London, Barcelona to Constantinople. And since the Florentines had proved so expert at minting and monitoring their currency, they soon found themselves being invited to help others do the same. In 1278 a Florentine was given the job of minting gold and silver coins in Naples. In 1279 Boniface Galgani took over quality control at the Royal mint in England. Other Florentines took key positions in mints in Paris, Dublin and Lübeck while others still were involved with precious metal mines supplying mints in Bohemia, Hungary, Poland and Slovakia.
The development was important. The key to banking success in the late Middle Ages was a bank's ability to pay and receive monies in as many trading centres as possible, so that their merchant clients need not move coin from one country to another. And of course, with interest-bearing loans forbidden, banks were generating much of their income from such transfer operations.
The presence of Florentines who were experts in finance in so many European cities facilitated the city's development of an international banking network.
What's more, these men were on good terms with the local rulers, well placed to negotiate loans for kings and dukes who found it hard to collect enough taxes; in fact such loans were often repaid by allowing the Florentine lender the right to collect taxes or customs duties on behalf of the government, or alternatively by exempting them from paying duties when they bought and exported, for example, wool from England. In the early 14th century the Frescobaldi, Bardi, and Peruzzi firms all had rights to collect taxes in England, while a century later the Medici would lend money to the English King in order to obtain the right to export wool to feed the two factories they owned in Florence.
The glittering little florin that rested so lightly on the tip of a finger was largely responsible for all this.

Tim Parks

1.1.
Statutes of the Florentine mint
1314–1461
parchment codex, bound in studded half-leather and wooden panels; 22 fols., old-style numbering, fols. 6r, 21 and 22 left blank; 2 parchment flyleaves. The codex is formed of three notebooks written at different times and bound together later; minute chancery in various hands, with rubricated first letters and titles
29 x 21 cm
Florence, Archivio di Stato, Ufficiali della Moneta, later Maestri di Zecca, 1

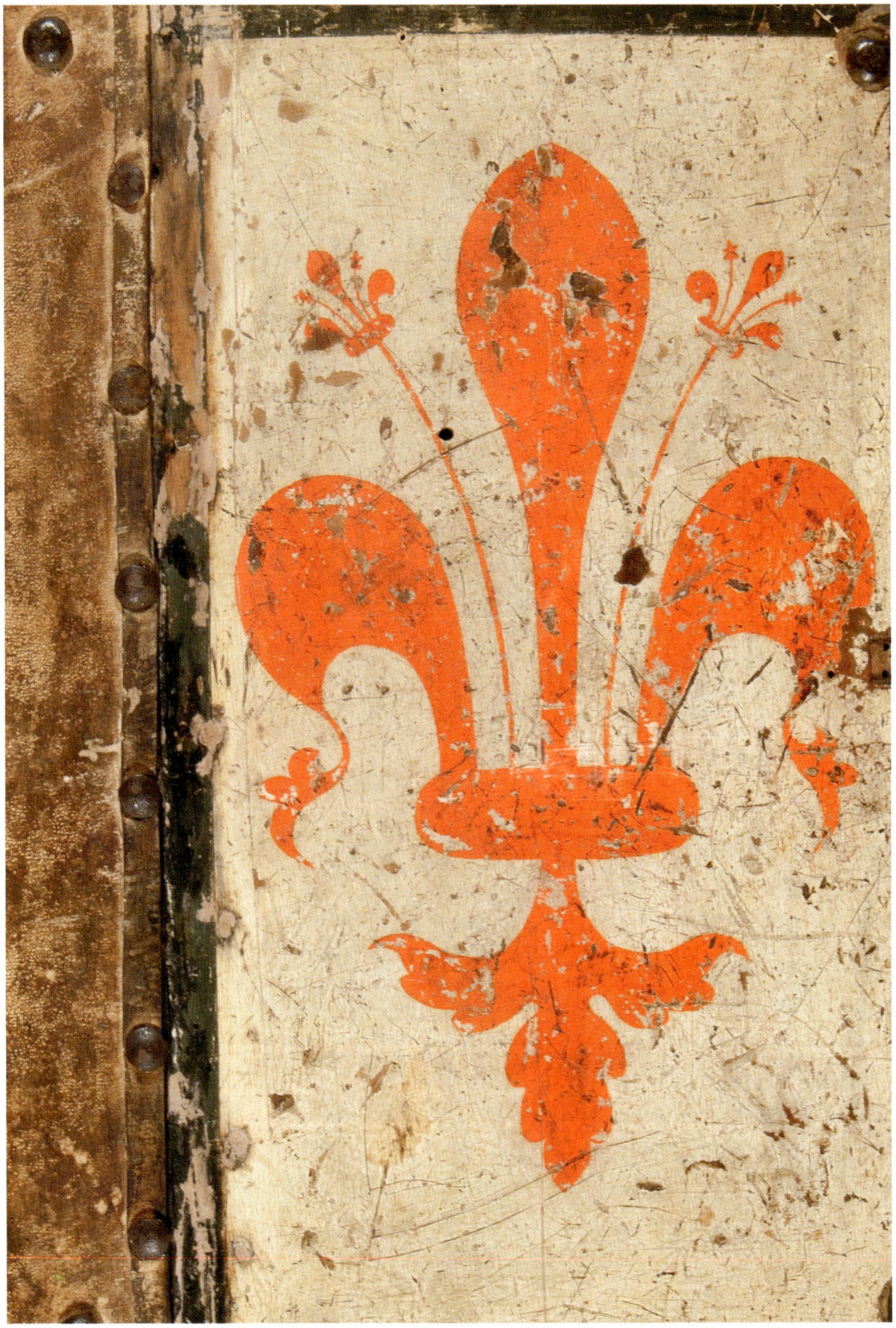

This register contains the Statutes of the Minters, officials assigned to manage the coinage of money, later called Mint Masters. Records of their activity start from 1252, the year when the first gold florin was struck. From then on, Florence had a bimetallic monetary system and the two types of coins, gold and silver, were managed separately. At first the mint officials were responsible for inspecting the minting dies and verifying the regular weight and correct coinage of their production. Other duties added later included supervising the circulation of money and judging monetary offences (most notably, counterfeiting).

This codex contains the oldest surviving regulations on minting, dating from the early 14th century, compiled in dual form. The first version, in Latin, is incomplete, insofar as it lacks the last six rubrics found in the second, with the additions of December 18, 1314, which constitute the *ante quem* of the original

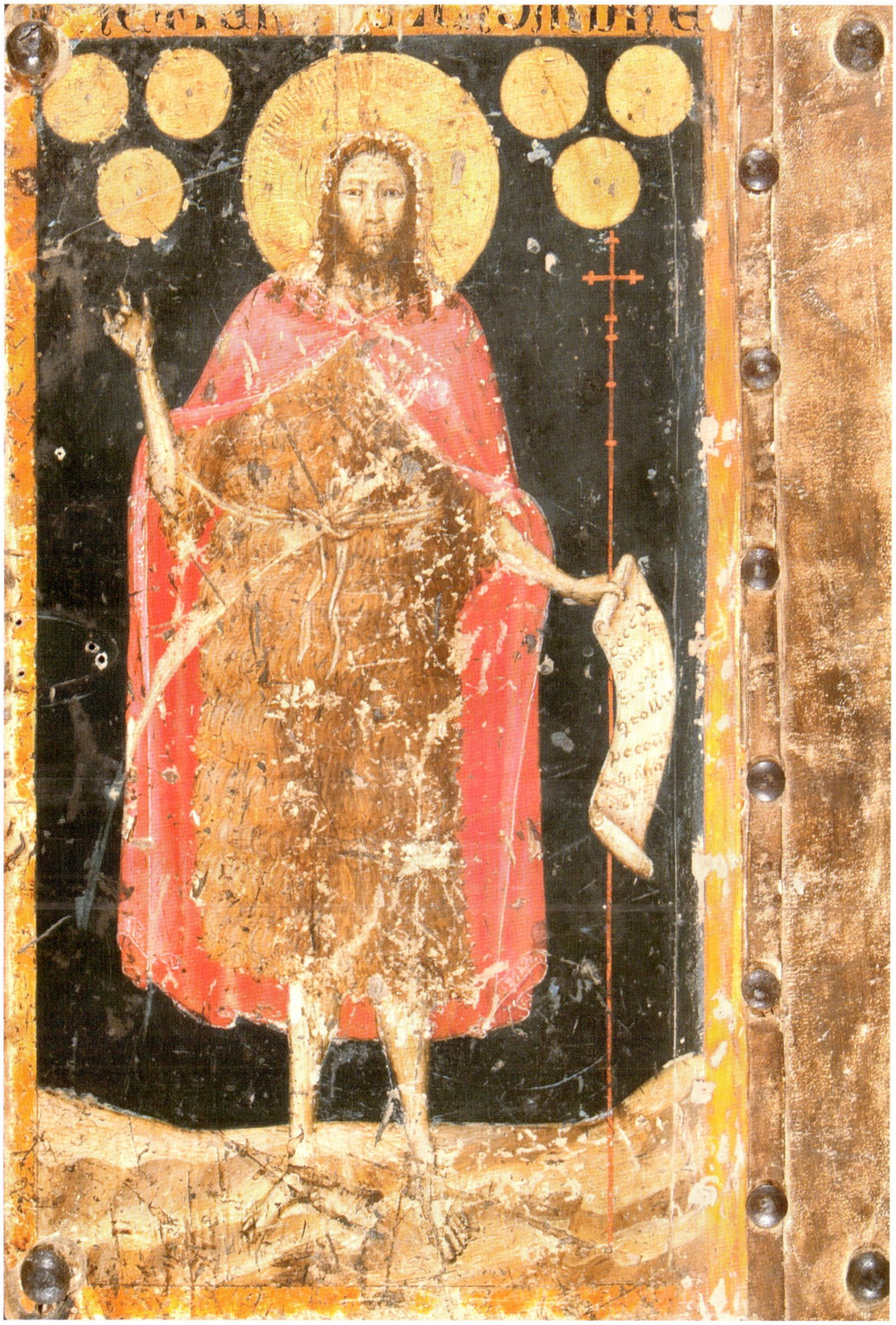

version, whose precise dating cannot be established.

The second version, in the vernacular, is an almost literal translation of the first and is divided into 36 rubrics. The codex is completed by lists of Mint Masters, added at the end of the Statutes, reports on elections of officials, sentences handed down by them, etc., up to 1461.

The codex, setting forth the rules to be followed by minters, was crucially important for every step in the process of coining money. The minters did not form a true guild, recognized in the Florentine political and guild system, but a professional association directed by a provost and a group of councillors, who served terms of six months. Their organization was however directly inspired by the city's twenty-one guilds, in the ample space devoted to designating positions within the association as well as in the rules calling for solidarity among its members (as demonstrated by the prescription "*To assist companions having impediments*", fol. 9v).

The codex's wooden cover is imprinted on both sides with the iconography of the first gold florins: on the front, the lily of Florence; and on the back, St. John the Baptist, the city's Patron Saint, holding a scroll depicting the *Agnus Dei*, the Lamb of God, surrounded by six golden disks (presumably coins) and surmounted by the inscription, now almost illegible, "*Monetieri del chomune*" (minters to the Commune).

Vanna Arrighi

Bibliography: *Constitutum* (1314–1407), ed. Ginori Conti 1939; Bernocchi 1976, pp. 14-24.

1.2
"Fiorinaio"
1317–1834
parchment register, bound in leather and wooden boards, with metal studs and fasteners; 235 fols., miscellaneous numbering, fols. 44, 69, 79, 220-33 left blank; minute chancery in the different hands of the notaries who served the Mint Officials
47.5 x 35 cm
Florence, Archivio di Stato, Ufficiali della moneta, later Maestri di zecca, 79, fol. 14r

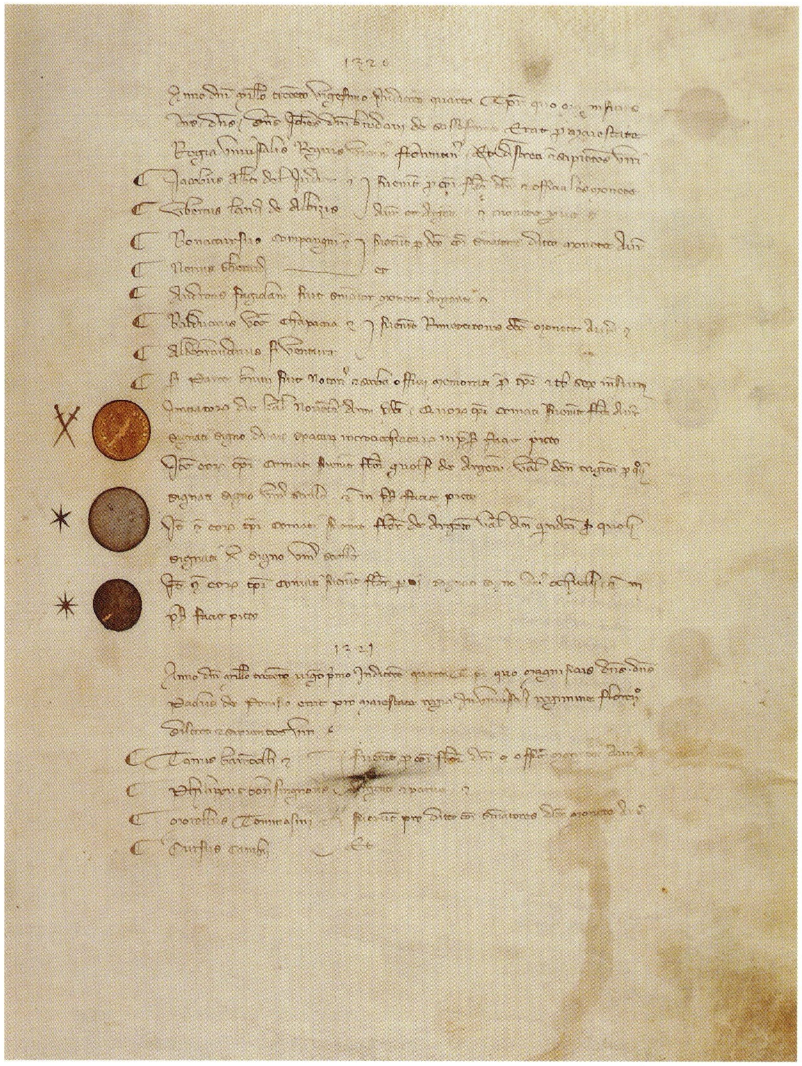

The *Fiorinaio* is a register containing copies of the various coins struck in Florence from the 13th to the 19th century, arranged in chronological order and interspersed by reports on appointments of the officials responsible for coinage, and rules governing their activity. These officials, called Signori della Moneta up to 1373 and Ufficiali della Zecca afterwards, were entitled to choose the symbols and decoration imprinted on the coins struck during their term of office.

The register was begun in the month of March 1317 by Ser Salvi Dini, at the time notary to the mint officials. On the first pages he transcribed earlier information and documents, dating back to1252, the year when the first gold florin was struck, and then continued to record current entries up to 1321 (fol. 11v). After this date the register was kept by others until 1834.

Before the 16th century, two officials were responsible for coining money, one designated by the Arte di Calimala (also called Arte dei Mercanti or Mercatanti, the international merchant's guild), the other by the Arte del Cambio. The former was responsible for imprinting the so-called "sign," or mark, on gold florins, while the latter did the same for silver alloy coins. They usually held their position for six months, although longer or shorter terms are documented. At first the coins were usually imprinted with imaginary designs but after 1375 it became customary to imprint the family coat of arms.

The two main officials were assisted by a staff of *sentenziatori* (judges), also called assayers, approvers or revisers, responsible for quality controls of various kinds (weight, engraving, quality of the alloy); appraisers and repairers, who corrected any defects; and skilled labourers (smelters, engravers, incisors) who actually manufactured the coins.

Minting was done mainly at the initiative of private individuals, notably merchants and bankers, who, in need of cash, delivered gold and silver—in the form of metal bullion or foreign coins—to the mint, to have it melted down and cast in florins. When the coined money was consigned to its owner, the officials detracted a percentage destined in part to the city treasury and in part to the mint. In very rare cases, the Florentine government requested the coinage of money.

In republican times the mint was situated near Palazzo della Signoria, first in rented quarters, then, from 1363, in premises purchased especially for it. This register includes (fol. 70) the purchasing contract for a building in Via dei Forbiciai, that was to house the mint.

Vanna Arrighi

Bibliography: Bernocchi 1974.

The history of Florentine currency begins a little before the middle of the 13th century. Until then Florence had no mint of its own, using the coinage of Lucca first and then of Pisa. This is unsurprising, considering that both cities were wealthier and more powerful than Florence at the time.

Over the course of the twelfth century, Europe's economy had developed significantly, and the monetary system introduced by Charlemagne and still used all over the Western World was becoming increasingly inadequate. The coinage was exclusively silver, based on the lira (or pound)—purely a money-of-account, in the ratio of 1/240—and the *soldo*, an equally abstract currency, worth 12 *denari*.

In contrast to the revival of trade and business, the *denaro* had become increasingly debased. In the words of Carlo Maria Cipolla, it was "reduced to miserable size and appearance; an ugly, thin little disk, of low-alloy metal, easily lost and even broken" (Cipolla 1982, p. 116). In the late 12th-early 13th centuries, Genoa and Venice had responded to the new economic needs by issuing the silver grosso, which was immediately welcomed in Middle Eastern markets and soon coined by foreign mints as well.

While Western Europe and Northern Italy remained linked to a monometallic silver-based monetary system, Southern Italy, always close to the Arab and Byzantine sphere, continued to strike gold coins, first the tarì (a fraction of the Arab dinàr) and then the augustal, introduced by Frederick II in 1231, having a weight of 5.28 g., a purity of 20.5 carats and a minting die of obvious classical inspiration.

In the next twenty years the need for a universally accepted gold coin as basis for trade was urgently felt in the rest of Italy too. It would be a marked improvement over the old silver coins, differing from one another in weight and fineness. In 1252, only a few months apart, the gold genovino was struck in Genoa and the florin in Florence (1.3). The florin was destined to outrank all other currencies. In the words of Vettori, "For its validity and beauty [the florin] rose so high in esteem as to extinguish all other gold coinage then in circulation; and giving its name to all the others [...] became virtually the common currency of Christianity, being struck by the greatest Kings and Princes in every province" (Vettori 1738, p. 1). Gold florins were, in fact, soon being issued by almost all the mints in the Western World, in imitation of the Florentine prototype but never equalling its outstanding formal qualities and 24-carat purity.

In November 1252, when the first gold florin was struck, the mint had only recently come into being, around the time when the city became a Free Commune, independent of the Margravate of Tuscany, in 1237. One of the first coins to be struck was the old silver florin, worth 12 *denari* (cat. 1.4), from which the gold florin derived its iconography.

The first known documents mentioning the mint date from the late 13th century, and become more frequent in the next century. Up to 1363 the coins were produced in a building situated in Piazza della Signoria, beside the entrance to Palazzo Comunale. But in that year construction began on the Loggia dei Lanzi, and to make room for it the building and its tower were demolished. The mint was confined to the adjacent premises, later encapsulated in the Uffizi, where it remained for years. A surviving element, the architrave of a door opening onto Piazzale della Galleria, can still be seen today. Carved at the centre of the architrave is the lily of the Republic, flanked by the symbols of the Arte del Cambio, the Arte dei Mercatanti, the Popolo di Firenze and the Capitani di Parte Guelfa, that is, all of the official bodies responsible for issuing and controlling currency.

The organisation of the mint, with its institutes, magistrates and staff, remained virtually unchanged for nearly three centuries, from its origins to the end of the republican era (1533). It was not managed directly by the Signoria, but its activity and profits were conditioned by the gold and silver sent in bulk to be coined by private individuals, mainly bankers and merchants. The officials of the mint served for terms of office limited to six months, to discourage close relationships with the permanent staff.

The mint's activity was controlled by two of the major guilds, the Arte di Calimala and the Arte del Cambio, which chose two of their members by lot every six months to direct the mint. The Arte di Calimala elected a Mint Master for Gold, the Arte del Cambio a Mint Master for Silver and Mistura (low-alloy coins). The chief magistratures of the city government were consulted only in exceptional cases, such as the issuing of a new coin. The Commune was responsible, however for establishing production costs, which differed for the various coins. These costs, detracted from the coined money returned to the clients, were appropriated in part by the Commune and in part by the mint, which became economically independent thanks to this income, sufficient to cover production costs and the salaries of its staff.

The Mint Masters (who had become four by the end of the republican era, two for gold and two for silver and alloy) received salaries during their terms of office, as did the notary, elected every six months by the seven Arti Maggiori. His duties included checking and recording in the *Libro del Camerario* all of the administrative procedures (receipts, reports, deliveries, etc.) and submitting them at the end of his term to the approval of the Custodian of Deeds in the city government. As can be seen, the organisation of the mint was complex and strict. In 1316, at the suggestion of the historian Giovanni Villani—Mint Master for Silver at the time—a new tool of recording was introduced, the *Libro della Zecca*, now in the Florence State Archive (cat. 1.2), which is the chief source for studies on Florentine money (the so-called *Fiorinaio*, published for the first time by Ignazio Orsini in 1760).

As regards strictly technical aspects, the mint's staff included two or three assayers, who verified the alloy, weight and minting dies of all the coins. Elected for terms of six months, they had to be certified goldsmiths, under the age of sixty. During their term of office, they and all members of their families were barred from participating in the minting process. The cutters of the minting dies, who cut the tools used to strike the coins, were instead highly skilled labourers who occupied their positions for years. Many of their names are recorded in the *Libro della Zecca*.

The mint's other permanent staff included cashiers (first one, then two); a governor of the treasury with his assistant; a custodian, and various skilled labourers, such as refiners for gold and smelters for silver and *mistura* (the copper or tin alloy used for small-denomination coins); the labourers who prepared metal blanks of the correct weight for each coin; the straighteners, who conferred a regular shape on each blank; and lastly the minters, who imprinted the blanks with the mint dies of the various coins. Starting in 1372, only the sons and descendents of minters could aspire to this trade, which became a heredity calling.

From 1284, the Commune of Florence, to protect its coinage from counterfeiting, instituted the Ufficio del Saggio, which assayed the weight of the gold florins (established as 96 per pound). The Assay-master and his assistants belonged to the goldsmiths' guild, the Arte degli Orafi. They were elected by secret vote by representatives of the Commune and the guilds. Occupying their own offices, not a part of the mint, they were at the disposal of anyone bringing them coins to be verified.

The sealed moneybags that gave rise to the term "sealed florins" were not filled with full-weight florins (weighing 3.53 g and containing 72 grains of refined gold), but with coins that had been clipped or consumed by wear, whose value had to be officially re-established. For this reason they were sealed in bags with legal indication of their value. These coins could become sealed florins on condition that their gold content was not less than 70 ½ grains. If this condition was not respected, they were marked and sequestered. The invention of "sealed" florins served to keep the standard within certain tolerance limits, in other words, not to remove from circulation coins that had undergone a minor reduction in value, to avoid limiting excessively the number of gold coins on the market. A law issued in 1294 specified that the value of the sealed florin expressed in *soldi* di piccioli was about 2% less than that of the full-weight gold florin. In the following decades this difference increased, arriving at 8%. Sealed florins were issued only until the 1420s. While they disappeared as actual coins, however, sealed florins continued to be used as money-of-account at least up to 1471. In that year the sealed florin was declared null and its function as money-of-account was supplanted by the fiorino largo, or "wide florin;" yet it continued to live on. We find it, in fact, still utilized to calculate the amount of taxes or dowries, and in the account books of wool and silk manufacturers down to the end of the Republican period (see Goldthwaite, Mandich 1994, pp. 31–3, 52–4, 58–60, 124 and Goldthwaite 2009, pp. 52–4).

The mint and the Florence city government collaborated closely on such major decisions as the introduction of new coins or protective measures to be enacted against the exportation of gold and the circulation of foreign currencies, as well as sanctions against counterfeiters. A special council, composed of the Gonfaloniere of Justice, the Podestà, the Captain of the People, the Priors of the Guilds, the representatives of the various quarters, and the Mint Masters, issued specific provisions, effective immediately, concerning coinage.

From the time of its origin in 1252, the gold florin had to be protected against endless attempts at counterfeiting, imitations and frauds, due to the unanimous prestige it had enjoyed immediately, and its lifelong supremacy over other currencies.

Thanks to its universal fame and status, the florin remained unchanged in appearance for nearly three centuries (cat. 1.3, 1.10). Its weight and very pure alloy also remained virtually unchanged. From its first issue on, the florin always displayed the "flower," symbol of Florence, on the obverse and the city's Patron Saint, John the Baptist, standing and bestowing blessings, on the reverse. On the front appeared the inscription "FLORENTIA;" on the back, "S. IOHANNES B."

The significance of this iconography is explained by Vincenzo Borghini:

> "They put on it the lily, calling it by its common name, and that of the City, 'Flower'; and so both the City and its name were represented […] From elsewhere they took the image of St. John the Baptist, as was customary in other cities of the time, each of which took the image of the Saint they revered most […] or had chosen as Patron […]. Our city […] had for its advocate and protector, and as he is called by our great Poet, its first patron, Mars the Avenger. In the light of the new Faith they exchanged him for the Baptist, dedicating the first Temple to him and on that occasion imprinting his image on their coins" (Borghini 1585, ed. 1755, pp. 200–3).

The coinage of Florence was to remain strictly faithful to these formal characteristics over the nearly three centuries of the city's history as a republic.

The Florentine's pride in their currency, and a kind of superstitious aversion for innovations, defeated the rare attempts to introduce radical changes. This is demonstrated by the failure of a silver grosso, worth twenty *denari*, coined in 1316 and suspended in 1318, where the lily had been replaced by a cross (cat. 1.6); and a picciolo, struck in 1325 and suspended in 1327, without the traditional *fioretti* that made it immediately recognizable and, most important, distinguished it from the French fleur-de-lis.

Unlike the oldest florins (cat. 1.3) devoid of any symbol in the field, the newer ones soon began to display small abstract marks (perhaps as protection against imitations); and then symbols chosen by the various Mint Masters who succeeded one another every six months. In the second half of the 14th century these abstract symbols began to disappear, replaced by the heraldic arms or emblems of the Mint Masters, commonly found on fifteenth-century florins (cat. 1.11).

As for the distinction between "narrow florins" and "wide florins," frequently appearing in the documents of the time, it consisted only of a slight increase in the diameter of the coin, starting from 1422, made chiefly to adapt the florin to the size of the Venetian gold ducat, its rival in the markets of the East. The weight and "title" remained unchanged.

Silver and low-alloy coins (cat. 1.4, 1.5, 1.6, 1.7, 1.9, 1.11, 1.12), produced mainly for domestic use, were more varied in aspect due to the adaptations in value that, by causing the alloy and weight to be altered, required changes in the minting dies. Basically however, they too continued to display the iconography of the florin. Despite their formal evolution, all of them, throughout the republican era, continued to bear the image of St. John the Baptist on the reverse. The saint was shown standing, as on the so-called popolino, the grosso worth two *soldi* issued in 1306 (cat. 1.5); or half-length, as on the old silver florin, coined in the mid-thirteenth century (cat. 1.6) and the picciolo, a low-alloy coin dating from 1323 (cat. 1.7); or enthroned, preaching or bestowing blessings, as in the guelfo del fiore from the early 14th century and the silver grosso from the early 15th (cat. 1.9); or lastly, in the act of baptizing Christ, as in the silver carlino worth ten *soldi*, from the early 16th century; and on the obverse, always that special Florentine lily, which adorned the city's gonfalon, and which, as states Borghini,

> "is not the fragile white flower commonly called Giglio today, not at all like ours, which it resembles in no way, but the flower of a minor species of Giaggiolo, which is divided into three leaves of a sort [...] and has sometimes been called, correctly or not, *Iride Illirica*, and is found on Montemorello, where it grows wild in great abundance" (Borghini 1585, ed. 1755, pp. 210–1).

It is significant that the demise of the florin coincided with the end of the Florentine Republic and its mercantile supremacy. Already in the early 16th century, before the siege concluding with the establishment of the Medicean Principality, the production of florins was on the decline. At the same time, there was a growing interest among merchants and bankers in the gold scudo of the French type, a coin now being struck by all the major powers. This was the coin destined to become the new gold currency of Florence.

Beatrice Paolozzi Strozzi

Bibliography: Borghini 1585, ed. 1755; Orsini 1760; Vettori 1738; Bernocchi 1975; Bernocchi 1976; Cipolla 1982; Paolozzi Strozzi 1984; Toderi, Vannel 2005.

1.3
Gold florin
1252–1303
Obverse: "+ FLOR ENTI · A"
The Florentine lily, with pointed tip and two flowers
Reverse: "S IOHA NNES:B:"
St. John the Baptist standing, full-figure, with a beaded halo, cloth tunic and leather mantle fastened at the breast with a full button; his right hand is raised in blessing, and his left, holding a staff with a cross, rests on his shoulder; the orb is full; rimless gold; Ø 2.03 cm; weight 3.4 g
Florence, Museo Nazionale del Bargello, inv. 117 Monete

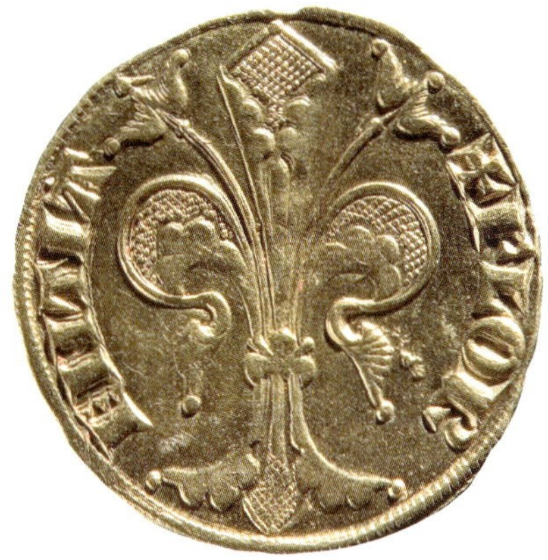

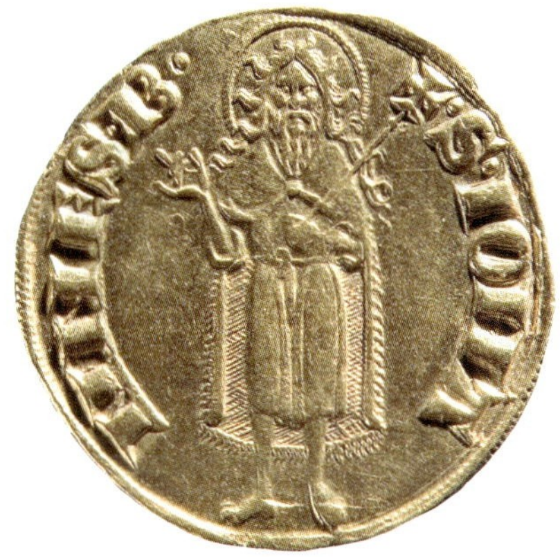

The dating of thirteenth-century gold florins is extremely difficult, since registration in the *Libro della Zecca* had not begun, and the earliest florins showed minor variations between one issue and another. According to the catalogue published by Mario Bernocchi (1975 and 1976), still the most complete repertory of Florentine mintage in the republican era, the first four series of gold florins were struck in Florence during the same time span, from 1252 to 1303. In the third series, from which this example is taken, the saint's halo is beaded (not plain, as in the first series) and there are various other small distinguishing marks.

The new gold coin imitated and refined the iconography of the slightly old silver florin (cat. 1.4) with the lily, the symbol of the city, on one side, and its patron saint on the other. Its weight was calculated so that a gold florin would be worth twenty silver florins, a value also known as a *lira* (or pound, an abstract money-of-account).

Vincenzo Borghini described all the advantages of this system, introduced by the Florentines, "who, without having to change anything in the silver coinage, found it most convenient, introducing no change whatsoever in new monies, no new accounting methods, no changes at all in trading methods; and in a word leaving, or should we say, keeping things in the very same state in which they had found them. Except that, upon arriving at the number of XX [old silver florins] which had previously made up a Lira, it could now be called, if so desired, a gold Florin" (Borghini 1585, ed. 1755, p. 223). Over the course of time, however, due to the debasement of silver coins (grossi) and low-alloy coins, the value of the gold florin (which always kept its 24-carat purity) increased notably, so that the ratio of 1 to 20 pertaining in 1252 had become 1 to 150 by the time of the last issue of florins, in 1533.

Beatrice Paolozzi Strozzi

Bibliography: Bernocchi 1975, no. 359; Bernocchi 1976, Pl. III; Paolozzi Strozzi 1984, p. 25, no. 8; Toderi, Vannel 2005, p. 12, no. 117.

1.4
Old florin, worth 12 denari
1250/1252–60
Obverse: "+ FLORENTIA ·"
The Florentine lily with two flowers; beaded rim
Reverse: "+ IOHANNES·B·"
St. John the Baptist viewed half-length, wearing a plain halo, his right hand raised in blessing, his left holding a rod with a cross, resting against his shoulder; beaded rim
silver; Ø 1.96 cm; weight 1.75 g
Florence, Museo Nazionale del Bargello, inv. 1 Monete

The old florin, worth twelve *denari*, was one of the first coins issued by the mint. Probably already in circulation in 1250, it continued to be struck until 1260. Although only slightly earlier than the gold florin (1252), it is the oldest Florentine coin of which any examples have survived. Based on comparison between the coins we have, the issues can be classified in three different series, distinguished by minor formal variations. For instance, in the case of the earliest gold florins (see 1.3), the oldest series, from which this example is taken, the halo of St. John the Baptist is plain, not beaded. As compared to the gold florin, struck very shortly afterward, this coin is much cruder and old-fashioned, resembling similar coins produced by other mints, both in Italy and abroad. It was in part the aesthetic improvement in the florin that led to its widespread acceptance throughout the Western World, assuring Florence an economic supremacy in the second half of the 13th century that it was never again to equal.

Beatrice Paolozzi Strozzi

Bibliography: Bernocchi 1975, II, no. 4; Bernocchi 1976, Pl. XXXII; Paolozzi Strozzi 1984, p. 22, no. 1; Toderi, Vannel 2005, p. 3, no. 3.

1.5
Grosso (popolino), worth two soldi *(24* denari*)*
1306
Obverse: "+ FLORENTIA"
The Florentine lily with two flowers, rimless
Reverse: "+ S.IOHANNES. B"
St. John the Baptist standing, full-length, with beaded halo; in his right hand he holds a long rod with a cross, terminating at his feet. His left hand is raised in blessing; at his sides are two small trees. At upper right, a five-pointed star, symbol of the Mint Masters for silver in 1306 Nerio di Guidingo, Piero di Borgo and Vanni di Puccio
silver; Ø 1.98 cm; weight 1.77 g
Florence, Museo Nazionale del Bargello, inv. 12 Monete

Documentary sources show that this coin, called the popolino, was already being struck in 1296, but no examples of that first issue have survived; nor do we know for how long it was produced since there are no records covering the period 1296 to 1306. In that year, a scarcity of silver coins, indispensable for local trade and everyday domestic use, led to the coining of new grossi and a popolini worth two *soldi*. Unlike the coins struck ten years before, a slightly poorer alloy was used, no longer containing 11 troy ounces and 15 *denari* of silver, but 11 troy ounces and 12 *denari*. The alloy then remained unchanged for grossi for centuries, as explained by Borghini: "This was the alloy that, as far as I can see, around the year MCCC or not much later, was stabilized at eleven and a half troy ounces of fine silver per pound, supplementing the half ounce with

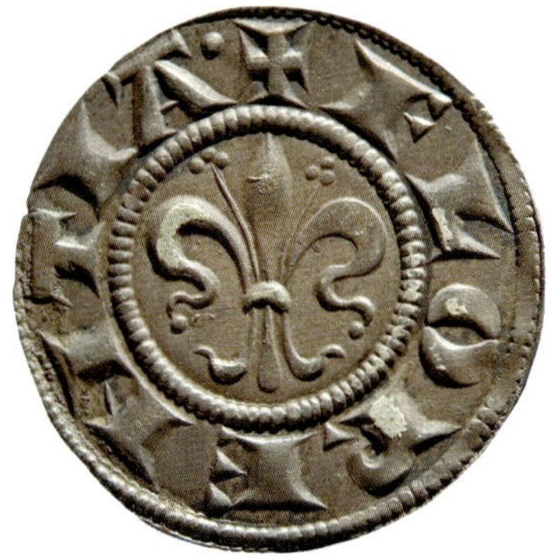

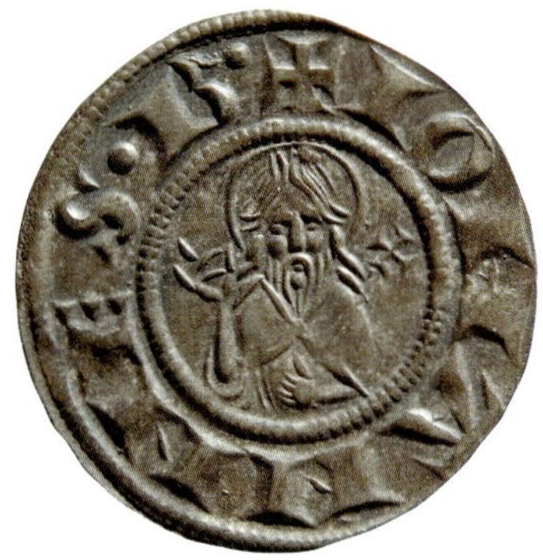

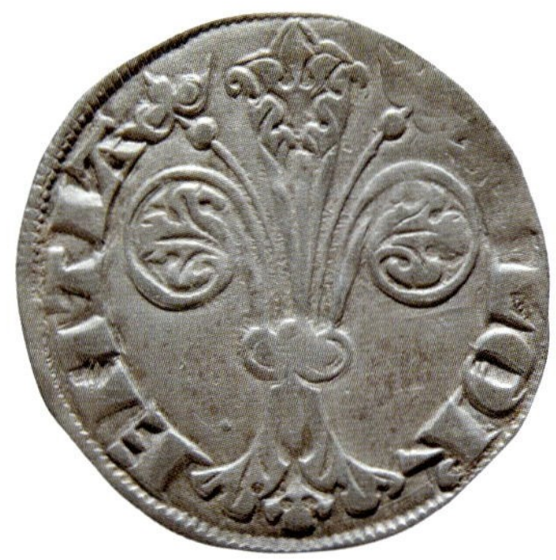

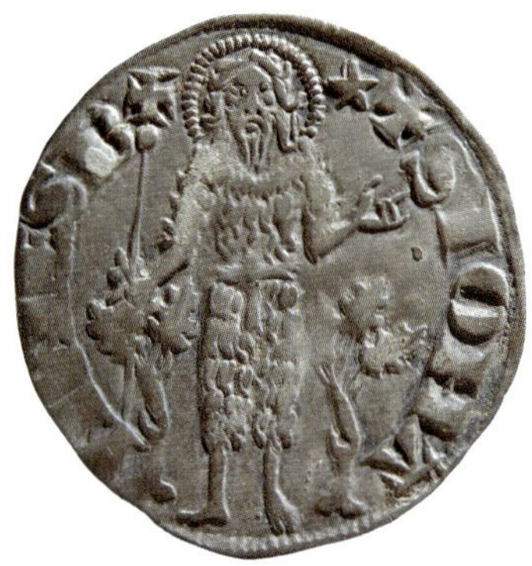

copper or some other metal; this can be called the common alloy, since this ratio has been followed by the best mints for many years. The first coins to be struck in this alloy were the *soldi*, also called grossi, whose proper name is popolini; as a result it seems that this silver has always been called, and is still called, popolini" (Borghini 1585, ed. 1755, pp. 195–6).

Beatrice Paolozzi Strozzi

1.6
Grosso, worth twenty denari
second semester 1316
Obverse: "(five-petal rosette) + F LOR ENT IA (five-petal rosette)"
Plain cross, dividing the coin into four sectors, in each of which is imprinted a small lily; beaded rim
Reverse: "S·IOHANNES·B·"
St. John the Baptist, knee-length figure, with beaded halo and hair shirt; his right hand is raised in blessing, his left holds a rod with a cross, leaning against his shoulder
silver; Ø 2.0 cm; weight 1.44 g
Florence, Museo Nazionale del Bargello, inv. 29 Monete

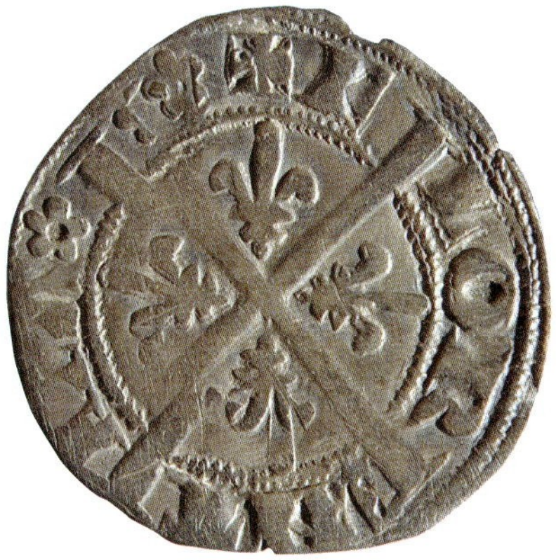

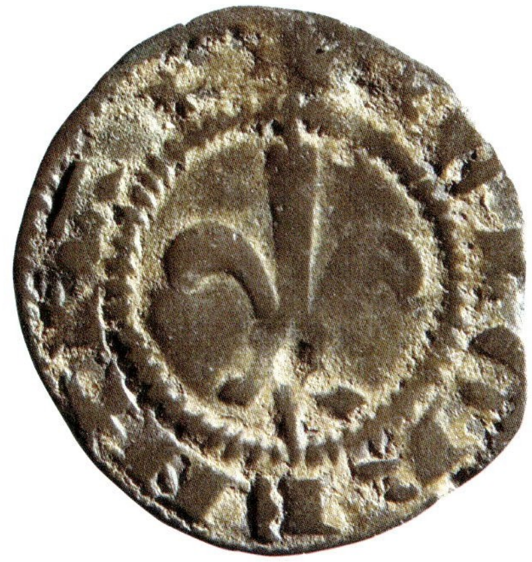

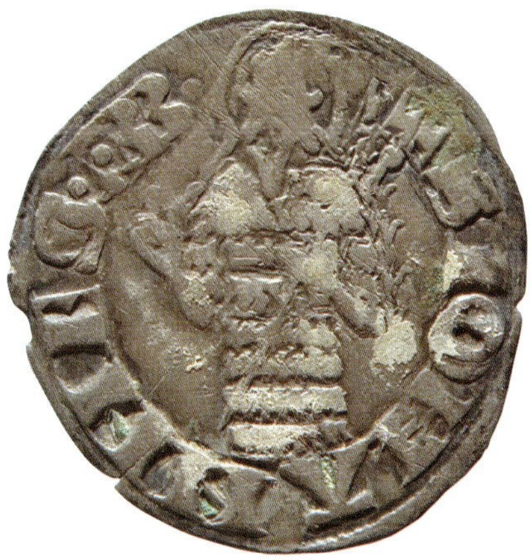

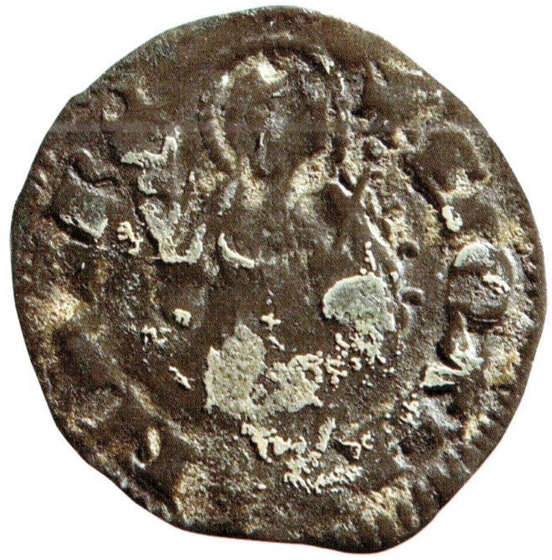

Very little information on this coin exists. It was identified by the description given in the *Libro della Zecca*. We know that it was struck only from the second semester of 1316 to the first semester of 1318. Villani states the reasons for such a brief life span: "They made a coin that was worth twenty danari. But since people did not like it, they then made the good guelfo coin, worth thirty *denari*" (Villani [*ante* 1348], ed. Moutier 1823, IV, book IX, p. 84; Bernocchi 1976, p. 172). Villani—the most famous historian of the Florentine fourteenth century—was the Mint Master for silver during this second semester of 1316, when the new coin was issued. As previously noted, it was he who instituted the *Libro della Zecca*, the most important source for the history of Florentine minting in the republican era.

This official monetary register may have been introduced in response to a counterfeit coin. In 1316, the so-called bargellino was illegally coined by Lando da Gubbio, Bargello of Florence. Although its face value was 6 *denari*, its intrinsic value was much lower. As Villani records: "They struck a false coin in Florence, made almost entirely of copper, plated with silver on the outside. These coins, called bargellini, were reckoned at the value of six *danari*, while they were really not worth four" (Villani [*ante* 1348], ed. Moutier 1823, IV, book IX, p. 74). No examples of this coin have survived, although Orsini describes a piece which was probably a kind of picciolo (Orsini 1760, pp. 23–4). The bargellini in fact had quickly been requisitioned by the Republic and melted down.

Beatrice Paolozzi Strozzi

Bibliography: Bernocchi 1975, no. 51; Bernocchi 1976, p. 172, Pl. LIII; Paolozzi Strozzi 1984, pp. 28–9, no. 20; Toderi, Vannel 2005, p. 4, no. 20.

1.7
Picciolo, worth one denaro
first semester 1323
Obverse: "+ (six-pointed star) FLORENTIA (six-pointed star)"
The Florentine lily without flowers; beaded rim
Reverse: "SIOAN NESB"
St. John the Baptist viewed knee-length, with beaded halo, hair shirt and mantle fastened at the breast. His right hand is raised in blessing; in his left he holds a rod with a cross, leaning against his shoulder; rimless. Beside the inscription, a conch shell, symbol of the Mint Master for Alloy Stefano di Cambio
silver; Ø 1.5 cm; weight 0.52 g
Florence, Museo Nazionale del Bargello, inv. 839 (Gift Ginori Conti)

This picciolo is very worn and almost illegible, like almost all of the widely circulating low-alloy coins used in Florence at that time, but nevertheless retains a curiosity value as an example of what was actually in use. First issued in 1315, they were all made of the same alloy, 1 troy ounce of silver and 11 of copper.

The picciolo or *denaro* is in fact the smallest unit (hence its name, which means "little") in the Florentine coinage. It was sometimes called fiorino picciolo (little florin) or fiorino picciolo nero (little black florin). It is mentioned by the latter name in the *Libro della Zecca* in a 1321 provision authorizing a new issue. At the time, "black" was the common term for all coins having a high percentage of copper or bronze (that is, *mistura*), just as those with a high percentage of silver were called grosso (large). From 1325 a white picciolo was also coined. It was silver-plated on the surface, but made of the same alloy (see 1.12). Bernocchi comments, "As for the use of whitened money, in many issues of piccioli and quattrini the signs of a light coating of silver can still be seen, ordered by the Florentine Republic to make minor coins more acceptable to people. Other mints also had recourse to this inexpensive but short-lived stratagem to mask the high percentage of copper in their coins" (Bernocchi 1976, p. 174).

The example shown here comes from the series of piccioli coined from the first half of 1323 to the first half of 1326. It dates from the first issue, since it displays the symbol of the Mint Master in office that half year.

Beatrice Paolozzi Strozzi

Bibliography: Bernocchi 1975, no. 1297; Bernocchi 1976, Pl. XLVIII; Paolozzi Strozzi 1984, pp. 30–1, no. 24; Toder, Vannel 2005, p. 37, no. 408.

1.8
Gold florin
second semester 1375 (XI series)
Obverse: "+ FLOR ENTIA"
The Florentine lily as in the previous example, but with flowers opened wider
Reverse: "·S·IOHA NNES·B·"
St. John the Baptist standing, full-figure, and blessing as in the preceding examples, but with a mantle fringed at top and bottom, and a finer-cut minting. A swallow beside a "P", symbol of the Mint Master for Gold Paolo Rondinelli
gold; Ø 1.95 cm; weight 3.44 g
Florence, Museo Nazionale del Bargello, inv. 253 Monete

In addition to the progressive formal refinement in the engraving of minting dies, the florins struck in the second half of the 14th century were now personalized with the Mint Masters' symbols. They usually consisted of the family coat of arms (or, as in this case, its most salient feature), flanked by the initial of the Mint Master's name. Commenting on the evolution of these symbols recorded in the *Libro della Zecca*, Vettori noted: "Up to the year MCCCLXXII, the signs imprinted on the coins were recorded, and afterwards only the names of the Mint Masters. Perhaps they did not continue to describe them because it was just at that time that the Mint Masters, who came from the city's most prominent families, began to have their family coat of arms imprinted on the coins, rather than simply signs and symbols as before" (Vettori 1738, p. 42).

Beatrice Paolozzi Strozzi

Bibliography: Bernocchi 1975, no. 1876; Bernocchi 1976, Pl. XI; Paolozzi Strozzi 1984, p. 32, no. 29; Toderi, Vannel 2005, p. 57, no. 617.

1.9
Grosso Guelfo, worth five soldi *six* denari
first semester 1402–second semester 1406
Obverse: "DE TIBI FLORERE XPS FLORENTIA VERE"
The Florentine lily, with two budding flowers
Reverse: "·S·IOHANNES·B ATISTA"
St. John the Baptist seated on a throne, with hair shirt and mantle fastened at the breast. In his left hand he bears a rod with a cross, leaning against his shoulder; his right hand is raised in blessing. Escutcheon with three bands, surmounted by a cross, symbol of the Mint Master for Silver (unknown)
silver; Ø 2.34 cm; weight 2.50 g
Florence, Museo Nazionale del Bargello, inv. 38 Monete

In 1369 the mint decided to modify the grosso guelfo (worth 5 *soldi*, six *denari*), because it was of higher alloy than other foreign coins of the same face value. As a result, it was regularly filed down, or even melted and recoined elsewhere. The new coin was lower in weight, with some slight changes in the minting die (see Bernocchi 1976, pp. 203–4). This operation was repeated in 1402 when once the 5-*soldi* 6 *denari* grosso was "lightened" still further; it was fate of all Florentine silver coins originally minted in the second half of the 14th century. As compared to the earlier grossi, those struck between 1402 and 1406—like the one shown here—are distinguished by the different shape of the saint's throne, with an arched backrest.

Beatrice Paolozzi Strozzi

Bibliography: Bernocchi 1975, no. 872; Bernocchi 1976, Pl. LXX; Paolozzi Strozzi 1984, p. 37, no. 45; Toderi, Vannel 2005, p. 24, no. 263.

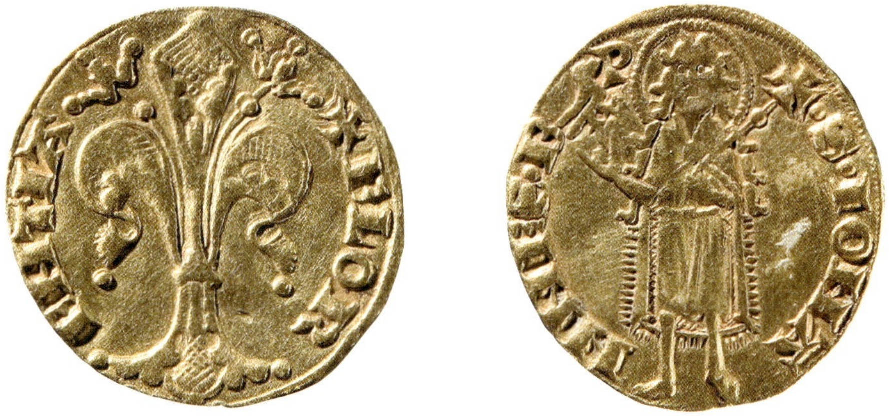

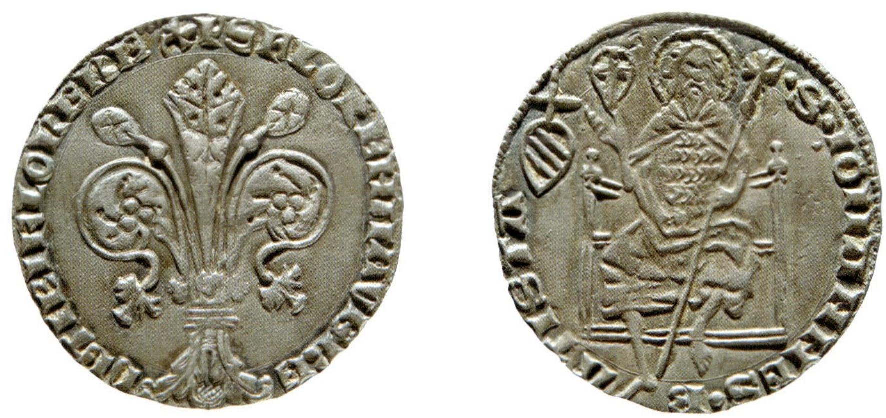

1.10
Gold florin
second semester 1422 (XXI series)
Obverse: "+ FLOR ENTIA"
The Florentine lily as before, but the two flowers are smaller and very close to the stem; the letters in the inscription are taller and slenderer
Reverse: "·S·IOHA NNES·B"
St. John the Baptist standing and bestowing blessings, as in the previous examples, but with a mantle smooth at the sides and below; the orb of the cross on the rod and the button on the mantle are full; the letters of the inscription are taller and slenderer; a coral branch, symbol of the Mint Master for Gold Marcello di Strozza Strozzi
gold; Ø 2.04 cm; weight 3.47 g
Florence, Museo Nazionale del Bargello, inv. 275 Monete

In response to increasingly fierce competition from the Venetian ducat, especially in Eastern markets, on May 6, 1422 the Florence Signoria ordered the minting of a "wide florin," giving Michelozzo di Bartolomeo, "tool-cutter," the task of making the appropriate die.

The "wide florin"—which continued to be struck until 1533—was slightly larger in diameter than the traditional florin, and a little heavier (0.415%), to make it fully equivalent to the Venetian ducat. Although this was chiefly a protectionist measure, it was not without practical implications, since, as noted by Bernocchi, "trimming (that is, filing a coin to remove powdered gold), up to this point widely practiced, now became very difficult. The thickness of the original Florin had, in fact, made it difficult to see if it had been vertically filed" (Bernocchi 1976, pp. 64–5). The "wide florin", which also differed from the earlier coin for its greater formal refinement, is sometimes referred to in the documents as the "fiorino novissimo e di galea." From 1442, although retaining its greater diameter, it returned to its traditional weight.

Beatrice Paolozzi Strozzi

Bibliography: Bernocchi 1975, no. 2366; Bernocchi 1976, Pl. XX; Paolozzi Strozzi 1984, pp. 38–9, no. 49; Toderi, Vannel 2005, p. 74, no. 792.

1.11
Soldino, worth twelve denari
first semester 1465
Obverse: "+ ·DE · FLOR ENTIA·"
The Florentine lily with two flowers; beaded rim
Reverse: "·S·IOHA NNES·B"
St. John the Baptist standing, full-figure, with beaded halo and hair shirt; in his right hand he holds a ribbon, in his left a rod with a cross. The figure extends beyond the beaded rim; Serristori coat of arms surmounted by a "G", symbol of the Mint Master for Silver and Low-alloy coins Giovanni Serristori
silver; Ø 1.51 cm weight 0.52 g
Florence, Museo Nazionale del Bargello, inv. 93 Monete

To satisfy people's everyday needs, the Signoria issued this new coin, through a provision dated April 13, 1462, which established the appearance of the *soldino* and its particular alloy (six troy ounces of silver and six of copper), used for the first time in Florentine coinage (see Bernocchi 1976, p. 217). The soldino, retaining these characteristics, was struck from the second semester of 1462 through to the first of 1496. An example dating from 1465, one of the many in the Bargello's numismatics collection, is shown here. Unlike the fifteenth-century gold florin (see 1.10), clearly influenced by Renaissance refinement although remaining true to the traditional iconographic themes, this "vernacular" coin appears rather crude and old fashioned.

Beatrice Paolozzi Strozzi

Bibliography: Bernocchi 1975, no. 2898; Bernocchi 1976, Pl. LXXXII; Paolozzi Strozzi 1984, p. 41, no. 63; Toderi, Vannel 2005, p. 93, no. 968

1.12
White quattrino, *worth four* denari
first semester 1493
Obverse: "· + · FLOR ENTIA · +"
The Florentine lily with two flowers; rimless
Reverse: "·S·IOAN NES·B·"
The young St. John the Baptist standing, full-length, his head turned slightly to the left. He has a plain halo and is wrapped in a cloth mantle that partially covers his hair shirt. His right hand is raised in blessing, his left holds a long rod with a cross; rimless. A capon surmounted by a dot, symbol of the Mint Master for Silver and Alloy Mico Capponi
silver; Ø 1.83 cm; weight 0.72 g
Florence, Museo Nazionale del Bargello, inv. 830 Monete

In a provision dated June 30, 1490, the Signoria authorized the issuing of a new series of quattrini, called "white" due to their greater silver content (two troy ounces of silver and ten of copper) as compared to the earlier "black" quattrini, which were thus devalued, three "white" quattrini being equivalent to four "black" ones.
The new quattrini also used a new minting die, with St. John the Baptist shown full-figure, like the image on the grossi worth six *soldi*.
Through this new issue of small change, the mint attempted to meet the needs of retail businesses, drive low-quality foreign coins out of circulation and replace old, worn coins which were now collected and melted down by the mint.

Beatrice Paolozzi Strozzi

Bibliography: Bernocchi 1975, no. 3410; Bernocchi 1976, Pl. LXXXV; Paolozzi Strozzi 1984, pp. 42–3, no. 67; Toderi, Vannel 2005, p. 111, no. 1167.

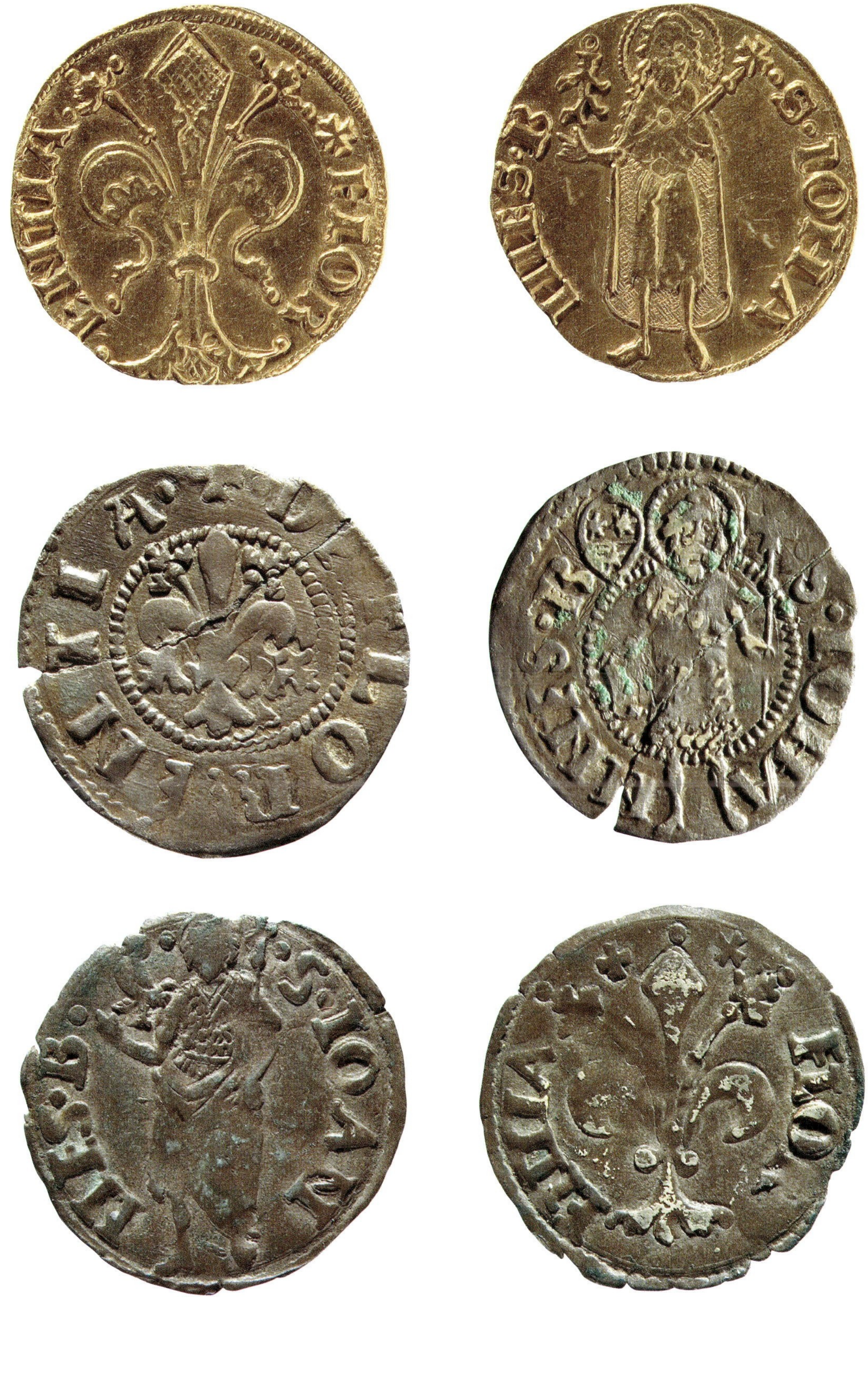

1.13
Jacopo di Cione (Florence, doc. 1365–98), Niccolò di Tommaso (Florence, doc. 1346–76), Simone di Lapo (Florence, doc. 1371–2)
Coronation of the Virgin, with St. John the Baptist, St. Catherine of Alexandria, St. Anne, St. Matthew, St. Victor the Pope (left), *St. Zanobius, St. Barnabas, St. Anthony the Abbot, St. Reparata, St. John the Evangelist* (right); *the Prophets Isaiah and Ezekiel* (above); *Coats of arms of the Florentine mint* (on the predella)
1372–3
panel painting
350 x 190 cm
Florence, Galleria dell'Accademia, 1890 inv. no. 456

The painting, restored by Lucia Biondi for this exhibition, is known as the *Mint Coronation* because it was commissioned by the officials of the Florentine magistrature that supervised minting. The documentation on this imposing panel, dating from 1372–3, states that three painters worked on it together: Niccolò, identified as Niccolò di Tommaso, Jacopo Cini, that is, Jacopo di Cione, and Simone, probably Simone di Lapo, an artist whose stylistic traits are still unknown (documents transcripted by G. Poggi in Sirén 1908, pp. 101–2, no. III; Offner, Steinweg 1965; A. Labriola in *Cataloghi* 2003). It was thus produced by three artists working in collaboration, although the composition and formal characteristics seem most typical of Jacopo di Cione.

The documents show that the painting was done for the Mint Masters' residence, situated near the Palazzo dei Priori. The stonecutter Giovanni di Ambrogio was commissioned to provide an ornate frame carved with the coats of arms of the Commune of Florence and the Calimala and Cambio Guilds (A. Labriola in *Cataloghi* 2003). The painting remained at the mint until 1863, when it was moved to the Galleria degli Uffizi, and later to the Galleria dell'Accademia.

The civic destination of this painting explains the choice of saints represented. They include the Patron Saints of Florence, John the Baptist, Reparata, and Anne (holding a miniature model of the city) and the first Bishop of Florence, Zanobius; Barnabas and Victor, saints honoured in Florence after the victory of the Ghibellines in the Battle of Campaldino on June 11, 1289, the Feast Day of St. Barnabas, and against the Pisans at Cascina on July 28, 1364, the Feast Day of St. Victor. The Patron Saints of the Cambio and Calimala Guilds—Matthew the Evangelist and John the Baptist again—also appear in honour of the members of these two guilds then serving as officials of the mint.

Even the gradine of the altarpiece, whose end pieces adorned by two shields bearing the mint's heraldic arms are probably not original, celebrates the civic and political life of Guelph Florence, displaying (from left) the arms of the Alberti family, those of the Calimala Guild, the lily of Florence, the Angevin coat of arms, the Seal of Florence, the emblems of the Angevins of Durazzo, the Parte Guelfa, the Arte del Cambio and the Davanzati family. The Alberti and Davanzati armorial bearings refer to the members of the Calimala and Cambio Guilds holding office when the picture was painted, Bartolomeo di Caroccio Alberti and Davanzato di Giovanni Davanzati (Labriola in Boskovits, Tartuferi 2003).

The devotional, but also civil and political, significance of the painting is perfectly consonant with its destination, comparable in meaning to the religious images that often decorated public buildings (see Camelliti 2010). The theme, the *Coronation of the Virgin*, was a common iconographic tradition in 14th-century Florence (see Solberg 2002, p. 218).

Daniela Parenti

Bibliography: Offner, Steinweg 1965, pp. 85–93; A. Labriola in *Cataloghi* 2003, pp. 127–35.

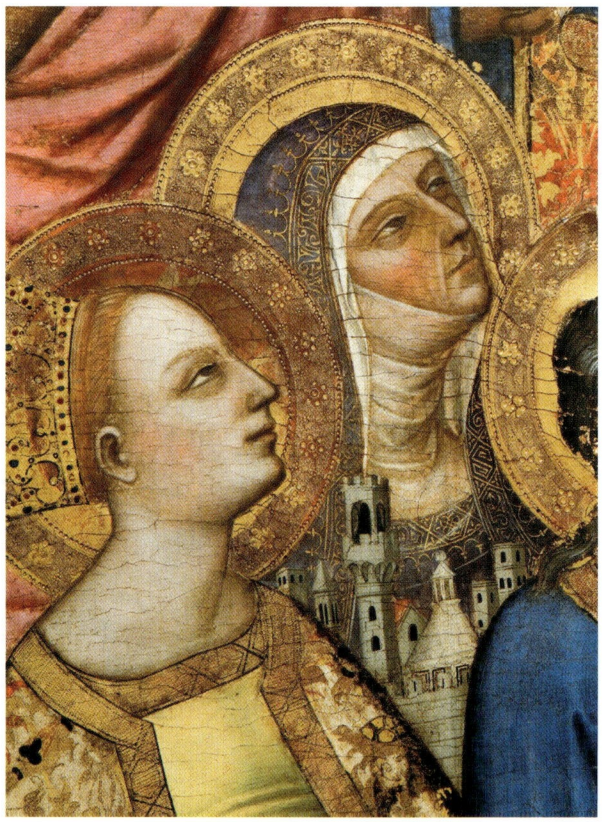

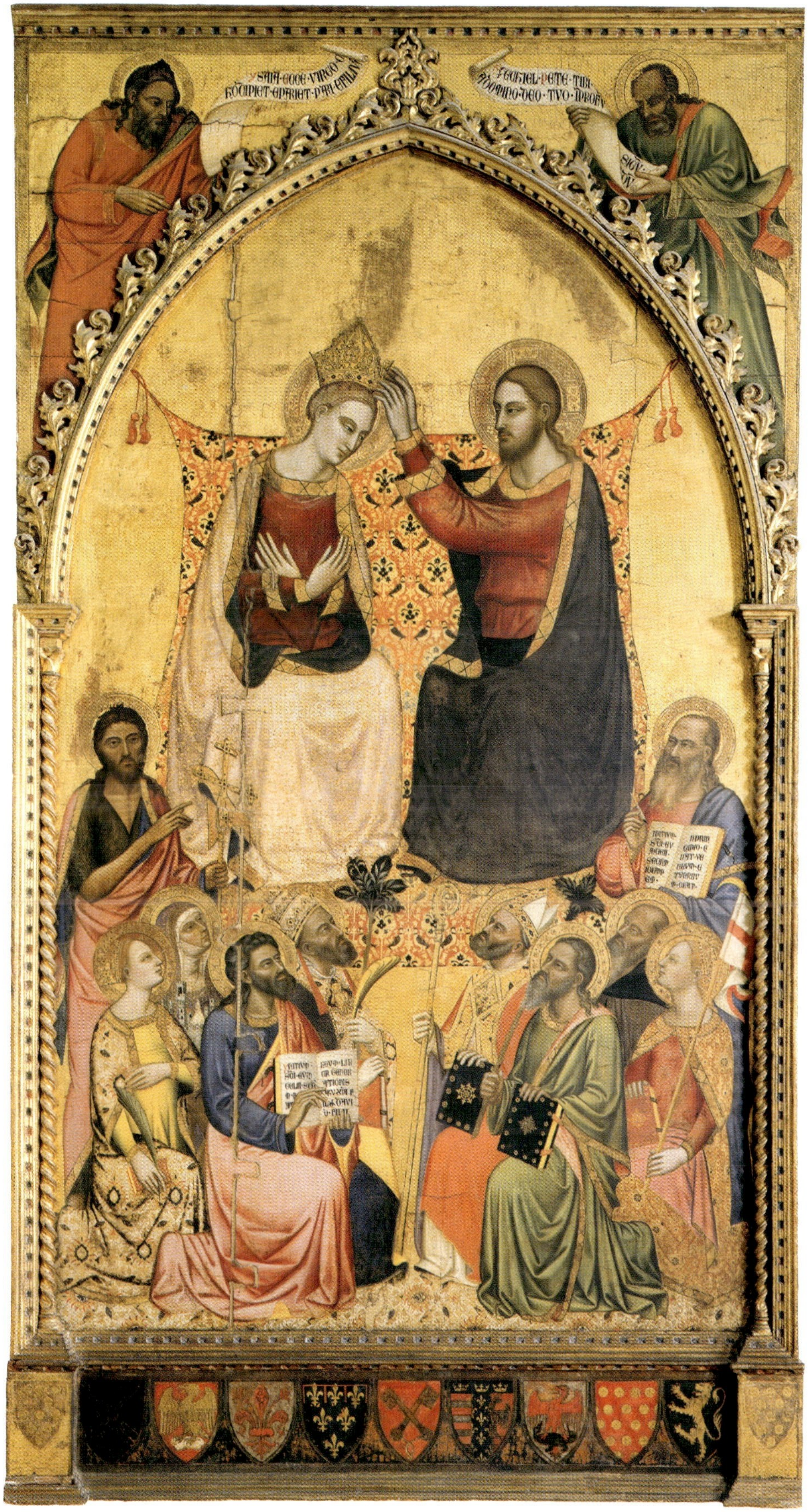

Section 2
Everything has its Price

However pleased the Florentines may have been with the success of their Florin, there is always something scandalous about money. Here is a little poem written in the first half of the 14th century:

> Money makes the man,
> Money makes the stupid pass for smart,
> Money buys the treasury of sins,
> Money shows;
> Money buys the pleasure-giving women,
> Money keeps the soul in bliss,
> Money puts the common man in high estate,
> Money brings your enemies down.
> And every man seems down without it,
> The world and fortune being ruled by it,
> It even opens, if you want, the doors of paradise.
> So wise he seems to me who piles up
> What more than any other virtue
> Conquers gloom and leavens the whole spirit.[1]

It's disgraceful of course; all the same, we can feel the poet's horrified fascination. With money you can change your social position, you can buy women *and* a place in heaven. We must condemn this outrage, but actually we are thriving on it. Nothing is clearer, reading the letters and diaries of the merchants and bankers of the time, than their obsession with money, how to make it and how to spend it. The one hundred and forty thousand letters left by Francesco Datini, the so-called merchant of Prato, are testimony to a psychology absolutely in thrall to moneymaking with all its exciting risks and accounting complexities: letters enquiring prices—of a bale of wool, a shipment of currants, a mule, a slave—letters worrying about insurance, protesting about taxation, haggling over transportation costs, import duties. Even when ordering devotional paintings, the price is paramount: "Let there be in the centre Our Lord on the cross, or Our Lady, whichever you find—I do not care, so long as the figures are handsome and large, the best and finest you can buy and the cost no more than five and a half or six and a half florins."[2] Everywhere in these letters you feel the tension of a determination to be wise and thrifty running up against an irrepressible zest for show and luxury. "One moment you're counting every lamp wick," complained Datini's wife, "and the next you let a whole torch blaze when there's no need."[3]

Behind this tension lay the conundrum of a religion that had begun by calling the Christian out of the evil world to live a life of honest poverty while waiting for the imminent Second Coming, but then later, when the Second Coming was inexplicably and interminably delayed, became the religion of the establishment and the rich, of people entirely in and of the world, a religion that put a money price on prayers and allowed you to spend your way out of Purgatory, whose bishops and cardinals were a banker's biggest clients and whose Popes bestowed lavish gifts on their illegitimate children. "Never," remarked Cosimo de' Medici, having spent vast sums to restore and decorate churches, "shall I be able to give God enough to set him down in my books as a debtor."[4] All the same, one can't help thinking that that was the relationship Cosimo would have preferred.

Throughout the 14th and 15th centuries Florentine bankers explored the limits of what money can buy. They bought consensus in Church and government (money was always well spent that was bestowed on judges, remarks Datini, for "gifts blind the eyes of the wise and alter the words of the just"[5]), they financed mercenary armies and expeditions of discovery, acquired country houses that they could escape to when the plague struck, bought exotic animals and pretty slave girls (some of whom shared their beds); they built libraries and paid to have them filled with beautifully copied and illuminated books, they paid for their children to be expensively educated and again for them to acquire expensive aristocratic wives, they built and restored churches filling them with colourful images that suggested the Holy Family had worn their own expensive clothes and lived in their own magnificently built *palazzi*.

And at the end of their lives they planned impressive funerals and prepared wills that they hoped would smooth the path to heaven. Money couldn't buy immortality on this earth but might be persuasive in paradise. Datini left his entire fortune to a foundation for the poor, that bore his name: Casa del ceppo dei poveri di Francesco di Marco. Cosimo de' Medici left a large endowment to the Dominicans who in return were to say prayers for his soul three hundred and sixty-five days a year until the end of time. Whether this investment brought a decent return we cannot know.

Tim Parks

1. Niccolò de' Rossi, *Denari fano l'omo comparere* in *Rimatori* 1969, pp. 689–90.
2. Origo 1957, p. 15.
3. Ibid., p. 220.
4. Machiavelli 1532, ed. Montevecchi 2007, VII, cap. 6.
5. Origo 1957, p. 89.

2.1
Tommaso di Pietro Trombetto
(Prato *c.* 1464–*post* 1529)
Portrait of Francesco di Marco Datini
1491–2
oil on wood
131 x 69 cm
Prato, Palazzo Datini

The full-length portrait of the merchant Francesco Datini, commissioned by the charity institution called Ceppo dei Poveri di Cristo for the Commune of Prato, can be interpreted according to chironomy, the science of gestures. The right hand index finger is raised in blessing (the classic oratory pose of the "speaking hand") as a *post mortem* consecration of Datini's role as worthy citizen (the coats of arms of both Datini and the Ceppo were added later at the bottom). In its hieratic calm, the portrait resembles the life-like wax figures (or *boti*) that were hung in sanctuaries. Trombetto, regularly employed by the church of the Carceri, was a real specialist in this genre.

It is interesting to note the epigraph (or *titulo*) below the painting: "FRANCESCHO IO SON DI MARCHO CHE LASCIAI DI MIE SUSTANZE HEREDE I MIEI PRATESI PERCHE' LA PATRIA MIA PIU' CH'ALTRO AMAI" ("I am Francesco di Marco, who left my property to my fellow townsmen of Prato because I loved my native city above all else"), which amounts to an expression of his deterministic thought, typical of the new merchant class.

In heraldic symbolism, the purplish red of his gown (along with the colour black) symbolizes the wearer's nobility of heart and high rank in society. Moreover, the sleeves and hem of his long gown are trimmed in ermine, the prerogative of nobility. In his other hand Dantini elegantly holds up a fold of his gown, like Filippo Lippi in his self-portrait (1469) frescoed in the apsidal vault of the Spoleto Cathedral.

In the late 15th century the Commune of Prato decided to honour eleven worthy citizens by placing their portraits in the enormous council hall of the Palazzo Comunale. Among the first to be painted were Michele Dagomari, who brought back the Virgin's Girdle from the Holy Land, and Datini. Their portraits, distinguished by written dedications, were entrusted to the same artist, also chosen as collaborator by Filippino Lippi for the *Udienza Altarpiece* in 1504. This was Tommaso di Piero, a native of Prato, nicknamed "Trombetto" because he worked for the Commune as town crier and trumpeter. On May 31, 1491, the Ceppi paid twelve lire for the painting (Morselli 1987, p. 32 and Fantappiè 1986, II, no. 86). In a later modification, a damasked headboard was added. It was painted over later, only to re-emerge in the recent restoration as a sort of *drappo d'onore*; resembling the one in its companion piece, the portrait with the *Monte Pugliesi* (C. Gnoni Mavarelli in *L'immagine ritrovata* 2010, pp. 56–9).

In the abundant iconography honouring Datini through the centuries, his features are almost never altered by the various artists. The merchant is always shown wearing the same cloth *habitus*, distinguished by its symbolic colour, red, first in the "realistic" portrait painted in his lifetime by the Master of the Datini Spouses (attr. Pietro Nelli), then in the *Trinity with his Wife Margherita and his Natural Daughter Ginevra* (Rome, Galleria Capitolina), in the Romita outdoor tabernacle frescoed in 1415 in Prato after his death by Pietro di Miniato, and even in the posthumous portraits where he is always hailed as the man who incarnates the image of the Ceppo institution (Lodovico Buti, *Full-length Portrait of Francesco Datini*, 1588, Prato, Palazzo Comunale).

Maria Pia Mannini

Bibliography: Morselli 1987, pp. 32–3; Fantappiè 1986, II, no. 86; Lapi Ballerini 1986, p. 19; Fantappiè 1987, p. 86; C. Gnoni Mavarelli in *L'immagine ritrovata* 2010, pp. 56–9.

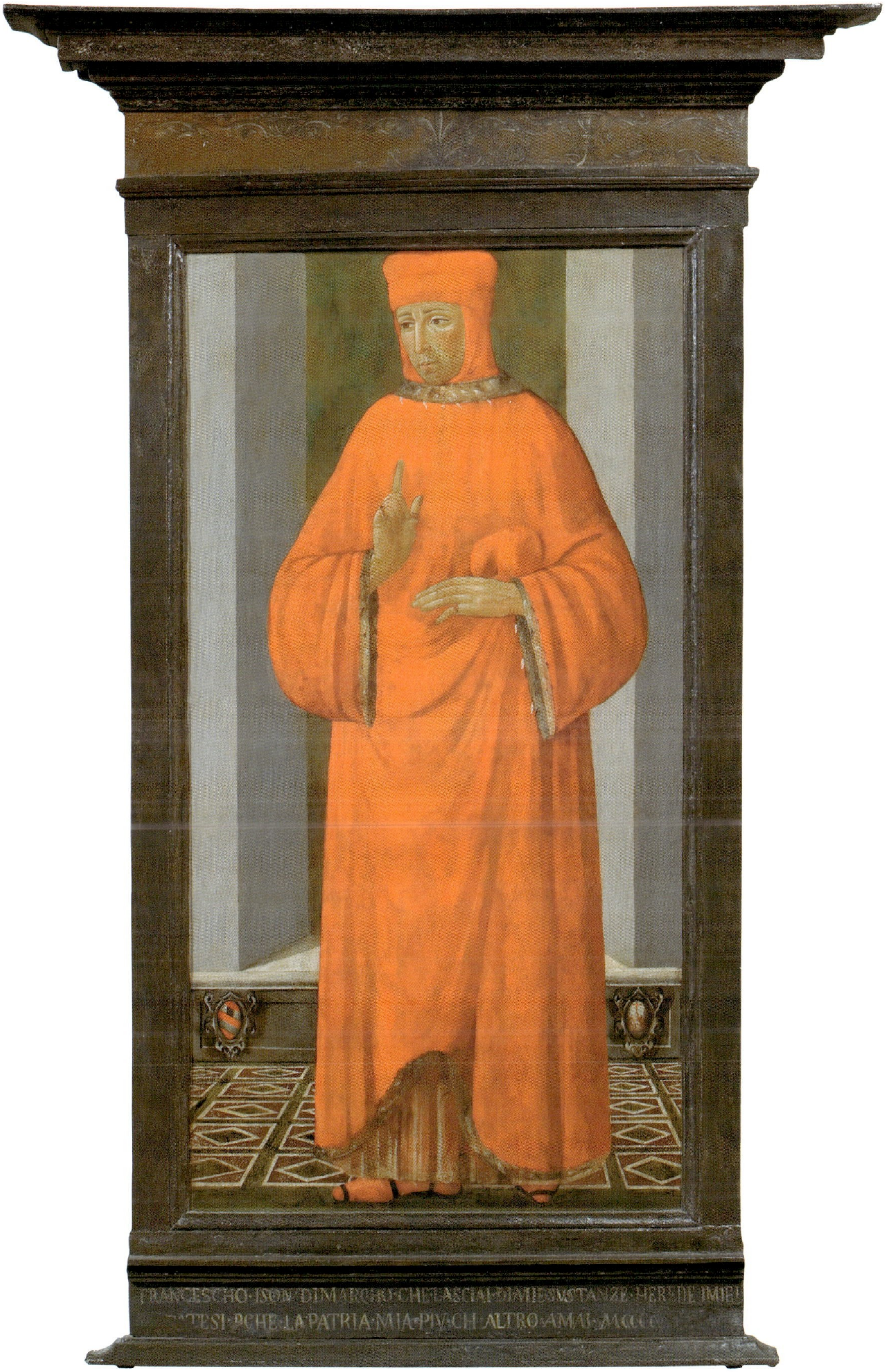
FRANCESCHO·ISON·DIMARCHO·CHE·LASCIAI·DI MIE SUSTANZE·HER·DE I MIEI
TESI·PCHE·LA PATRIA·MIA·PIU·CH ALTRO·AMAI·MCCCC

2.2
Florentine painter
The Miracle of the Bianchi Crucifix
(*The Miracle; Homage to the Crucifix;*
The Procession)
post 1399
tempera on panel
18 x 86.5 cm (*The Miracle, The Procession*)
18 x 103.5 cm (*Homage to the Crucifix*)
Empoli, Museo della Collegiata di Sant'Andrea,
inv. no. 11

These three small panels, originally joined to form a predella, illustrate a miracle that took place in Val di Marina, between Florence and Prato, on August 24, 1399. On that day and in that place, a withered almond tree burst into bloom when a crucifix was leaned against it by a group of pilgrims from Empoli who had stopped to rest. This event is represented in the first scene. The next scene shows the people exulting over the miracle. In the last scene we see the procession approaching Empoli, where news of the miracle has already arrived (Caterina Proto Pisani 2006, pp. 70–2). Antonio Paolucci (1985, pp. 53–5), who recognized a relationship with the Bianchi movement, proposed a different order for the scenes, with the last two inverted; but the scene of the festivities, bordered at the sides by slender gilt columns, longer and more brightly coloured than the other two, probably occupied the central position.

To the cry of "mercy and peace" the Bianchi movement, originating in France, marched through Italy in 1399 on the eve of the Jubilee. Some of the processions were headed for Rome, but many spontaneous groups, not members of established brotherhoods, marched in local pilgrimages lasting nine days. The faithful, dressed in white, followed priests holding Crucifixes. They were obliged to sleep on benches, on the ground or on straw, to fast on Saturday, eat no meat, flog themselves, sing lauds, recite prayers and invoke peace, without ever undressing (on the Bianchi see among others Bornstein 1993).

Although tradition holds that the cross appearing in the predella belonged to the Company of St. Andrew from Empoli, and was carried in pilgrimage by members of the Brotherhood of the Cross, founded in that same year, 1399 (Del Vivo 1776, pp. XII–XIV), it is more probable that this group was formed after the occurrence of the miracle. The pilgrims are not dressed, in fact, in the habit of a brotherhood but in the costume of the Bianchi: an ample white mantle with a red cross on the right shoulder, tightened at the waist by a cord, which covered the head leaving the face and forehead bare. Already by 1417 these three scenes, painted soon after the miracle, formed the predella of the altar of the Brotherhood of the Cross (Paolucci 1985, pp. 54–5).

Painted by a Florentine artist active on the threshold of the 15th century, these images offer interesting testimony of the processions held at the time: a meal eaten seated on the ground in the first panel, adults carrying children dressed in red (perhaps not by chance) joyfully crowding around the cross, and the barefoot pilgrims holding scourges.

Francesco Datini took part in one of these pilgrimages. His journey and even the expenses incurred for himself and a group of twelve friends have been traced (see Byrne 1989; Nigro 1994, pp. 232–7; Cassandro 2010, pp. 27–8). The departure was set for August 28, 1399 when Datini resolved "to go on a pilgrimage, dressed all in white linen, and barefoot, as was the custom in those days," "carrying scourges, flogging themselves, and repenting of their sins to our Lord Jesus Christ."

The expenses were precisely noted. Among other things, "one hundred loaves of baked bread" at a cost of 3 lire, 6 *soldi* and 8 *denari*; a rosary costing 14 *soldi* and 8 *denari*, and a cord belt, 3 *soldi*. Much wine was purchased, along with "cabbages and beans, and salad greens and melons and onions," along with figs and peaches, to follow a meatless diet. At mealtime the group split up, "some staying on the road, some going into the fields," exactly as shown in the Empoli scene.

Ludovica Sebregondi

Bibliography

Del Vivo 1776, pp. XV–XVI; Paolucci 1985, pp. 53–5; L. Sebregondi in *La Chiesa e la Città* 1992, pp. 93–4; Caterina Proto Pisani 2006, pp. 70–2.

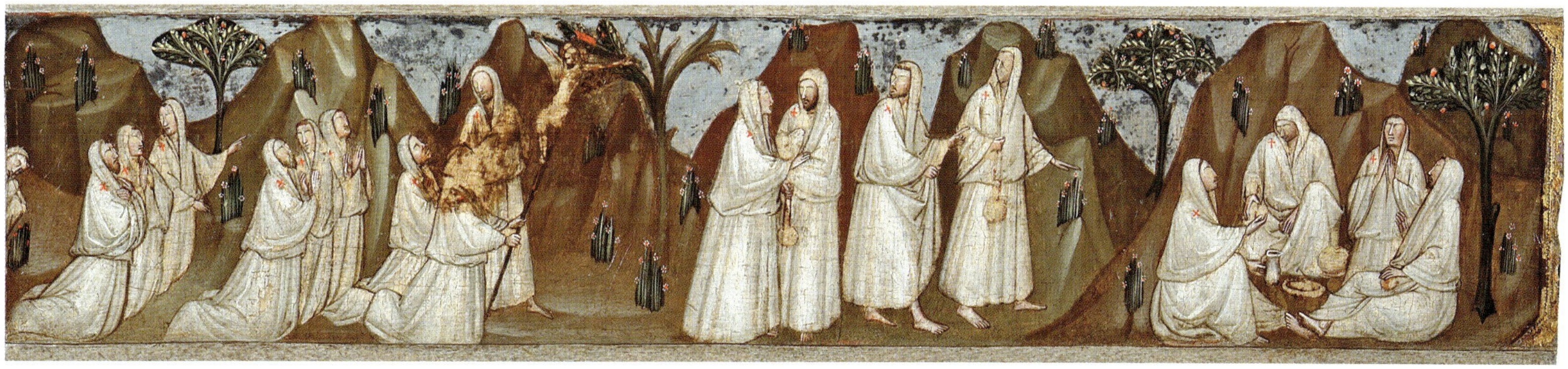

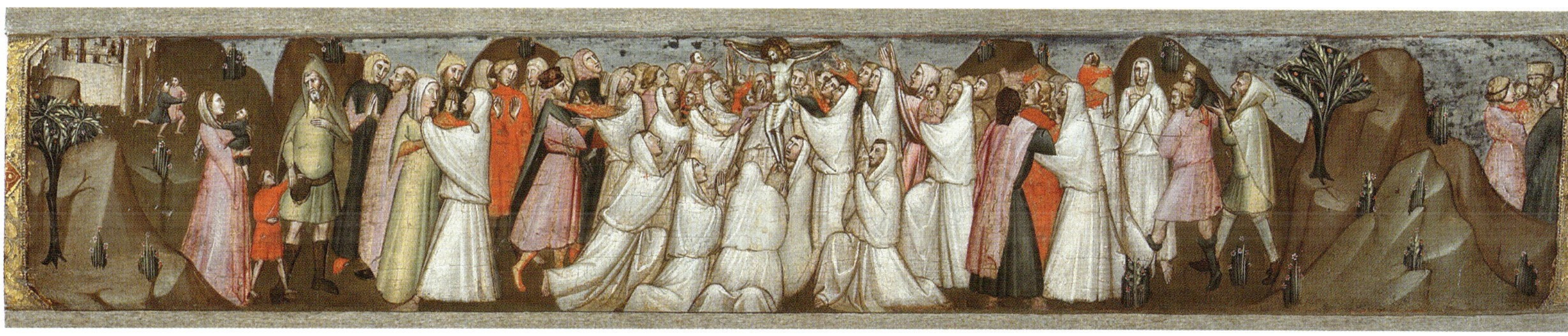

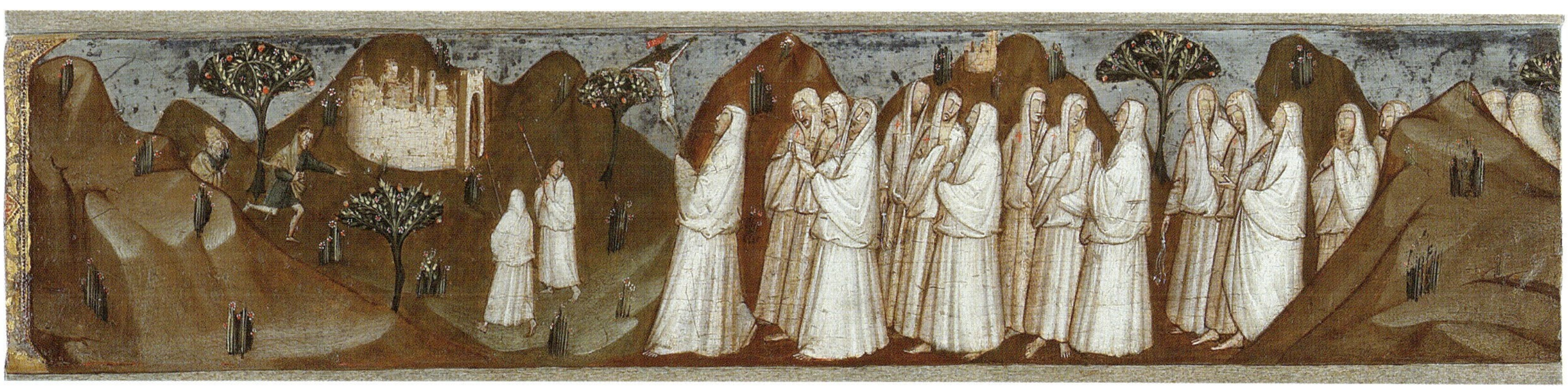

2.3
Fra Angelico (?) (Fra Giovanni da Fiesole, Guido di Pietro; Vicchio *c.* 1395–Rome 1455)
Madonna Enthroned with the Infant Jesus
early 15th century
panel painting
63 x 34 cm
Florence, Mario and Luigi Bellini Collection, inv. no. 1645

This painting, recently exhibited in Korea and China with other works from the Bellini Collection, has been attributed by Giuseppe Fiocco (written communication, May 10, 1942) to the young Fra Angelico, whose early career is still subject to debate. The painting, of refined workmanship, portrays the Madonna and Child against a gold-leaf background in the original curved frame. It is datable to the early 15th century, a time when Florentine art showed the influence of the Late Gothic revival in terms of elegance, brilliant colours, rich material and naturalism, in a scenario dominated by the forceful personalities of Lorenzo Monaco, Gherardo Starnina, and Lorenzo Ghiberti.

Originally the painting must have been the central panel of a small private altar designed for domestic worship. The back of the panel is finely crafted, covered by a well-smoothed gesso priming, evidently to be left in view, while the outer edges of the frame contain housings for the hinges that probably hooked onto side panels. In the 14th and 15th centuries, paintings and sculptures of religious subject occupied an important place in the homes of the Florentine upper classes. Wealthy merchants and bankers invested imposing financial resources in purchasing true works of art (Tomasi 2004; Pons 1992 and 2009). Moreover, domestic devotion was a daily practice recommended by the preachers. Giovanni Dominici, a Dominican of the Strict Observance, in his *Regola del governo di cura familiare* [Rules for family care] (1410) recommended placing religious images in the home, not only as objects of private worship but also to educate the children.

Inventories, record books and old sources in general report various kinds of painted works designed to fulfil this purpose. Widely diffused were tabernacles with side doors "to be closed" (Lydecker 1987, p. 69)—as this one must have been—and rounded plaques (*colmi*), as well as tondos, terracottas, plaster and wooden sculptures; not to mention the objects made of waxed cloth, stucco and papier-mâché purchased by families of modest means.

Particularly recommended by Dominici for display in the home were images of the "Virgin Mary with the Child in her arms or holding a pomegranate. A good image will be Jesus nursing at the breast, Jesus sleeping in his Mother's lap, Jesus appearing courteously before her, Jesus in profile with his Mother gazing at that profile" (Dominici [1410], ed. Salvi 1860, p. 131). Paintings of the Virgin and Child were frequently bought by merchant bankers, to be hung in the bedchamber (for example in Däubler-Hauschke 2003, pp. 126–34) or sold abroad in cities where their banks had branches (Cavaciocchi 2010, p. 219). The painters' workshops offered a more or less mass production of devotional images for the home, selling at a wide range of prices. "Pictures of a Lady" could be found at prices as low as 3 lire (Cavaciocchi 2010, p. 218). In 1383 instead, the wealthy merchant of Prato, Francesco di Marco Datini, could afford to pay three gold florins for a "Picture of a Lady," said to be beautiful, bought in Florence (Piattoli 1929, p. 225). Again in 1390 Datini asked his friend and partner in Florence, Domenico di Cambio, to find a good master from whom to commission two pairs of small panel paintings, "with devout and pious figures" on a gold-leaf background (Piattoli 1929, p. 229). For this commission, various painters were contacted. Their prices ranged from 1 to 3 florins for each painting, depending on the size of the support, the value of the materials and the number of figures to be painted (Piattoli 1929, pp. 228–9). In 1395 then, the renowned Florentine artists Niccolò di Pietro Gerini and his son Lorenzo, commissioned by Datini to fresco his residence in Prato, painted for the merchant of Prato a little gold-leaf triptych dedicated to the Virgin at the price of 4 florins (Piattoli 1930, p. 105).

Elena Capretti

Bibliography: *Bellini Museum Collection* 2005, pp. 100–1; *400 anni di pittura italiana* 2006, pp. 24–5; Bellini 2009, pp. 36–7.

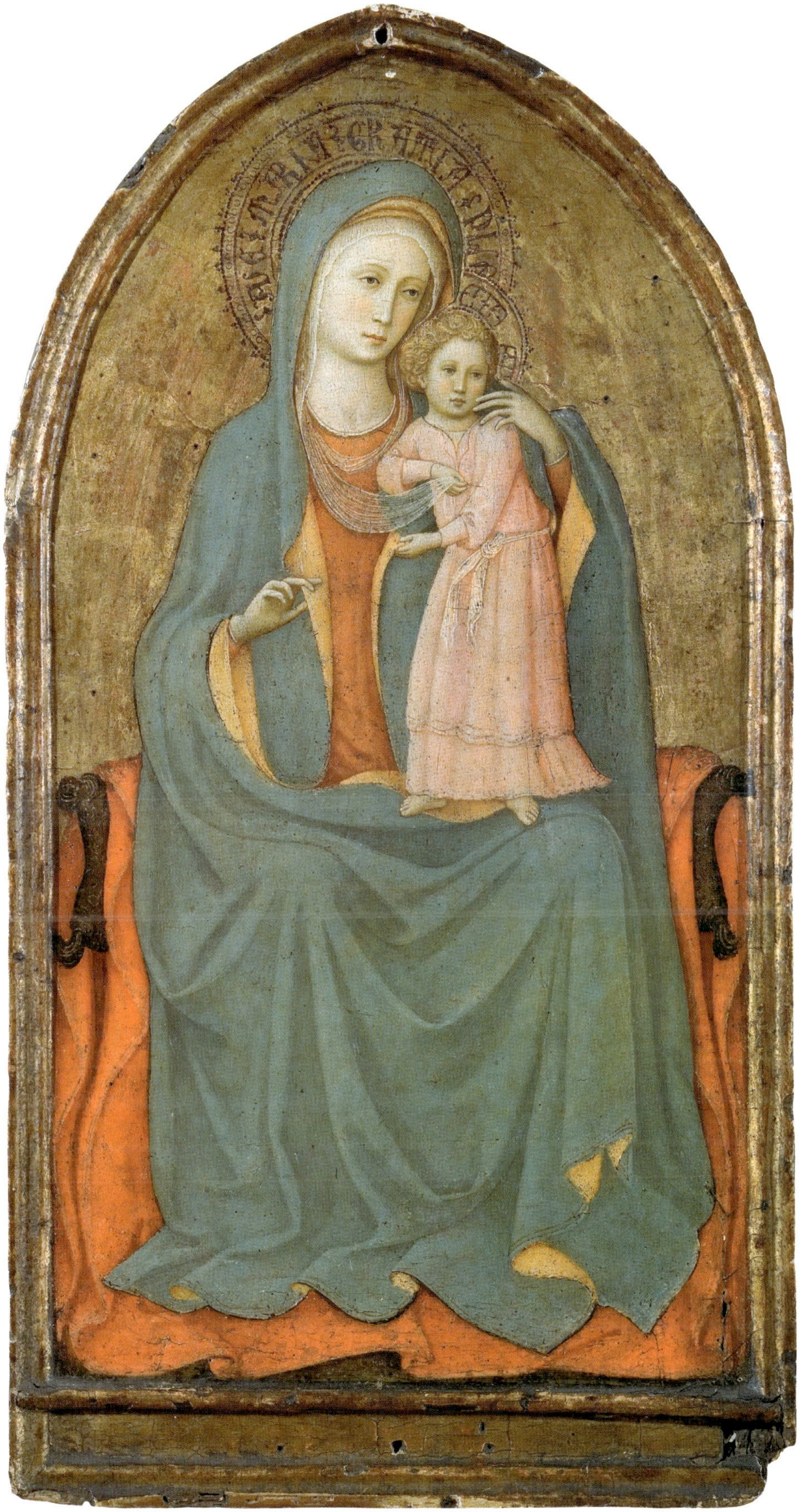

2.4
Tax Register
middle of the 14th century
parchment manuscript, binding restored with panels, leather back; II, 76, II fols.
260 x 190 mm
Florence, Biblioteca Riccardiana, Ricc. 2526

"A kind of monument to the Florentine mercantile spirit" (De Robertis 1968), this manuscript lists the rates paid on goods entering and leaving Florence, reflecting the regulations of the guilds in each of the fourteen sectors. The volume, written by Antonio di Ventura, beautifully crafted on good parchment of substantial size, seems almost a luxury codex, unusual for an item normally limited to functional use where appearance is a secondary concern. Certainly it was made for a merchant who wanted an enduring testimonial to his work, raising it to the level of art and showing commerce to be the backbone of society.

The miniatures, inserted at the beginning of the Revenue column, while the Disbursement column is left blank, illustrate the arts and trades. They provide precious documentation on daily life and customs, vivaciously depicting persons dressed in the fashion of the day with their merchandise spread out before them on benches. The scene opens with a shepherd shearing a sheep, illustrating "*Lanaggio,*" or wool production, followed by representations of the woollen fabrics trade, of the Arte dei Linaioli (linen drapers) and Farsettai (doublet-makers), the goldsmiths and the Arte di Por Santa Maria, a furrier displaying a squirrel's skin, an armour maker, a dyer, a leather goods dealer, a pharmacist with the open and closed books included among his goods, a grocer, an animal dealer, a grain merchant and a herb vendor.

The text is compiled with a precision unusual in manuscripts of this kind. All of its sections are marked by paragraph signs, the first letters are calligraphically traced and touched up with yellow, and the chapters are indicated in filigree letters in the ordinary style. Between the lines of text, the pages are strewn with human profiles, frequently contracted in grotesque grimaces, with brutish men and animals, especially birds and fish but also crickets, butterflies and monstrous creatures, as well as amusing vignettes often showing a man pecked by a bird. Since these are not in the miniator's hand, they may have been done for fun by the owner of the book, who shows himself to be not only witty but cultivated, since he uses an iconographic repertory rather distant in time but well known in illustration, not pictorial alone and not secular alone.

Using a vast number of words to list merchandise, this codex provides a highly interesting linguistic repertory of terms in use in the mid-14th century. The codex is datable to 1360–70 according to Arrigo Castellani, a period consonant with the stylistic traits of the decoration. It is no coincidence that it belonged to Anton Maria Salvini, a renowned member of the Accademia della Crusca, and then went to the Riccardi family when they bought his library.

Giovanna Lazzi

Bibliography: D'Ancona 1914, I, p. 17, II, p. 117; Scuricini Greco 1958, pp. 273–4, no. 288; De Robertis 1968, pp. 3–119; Partsch 1981, pp. 99–100; Frosini 1993, pp. 380–1; *Biblioteche* 1998, p. 84; *Alambicchi* 1999, pp. 161–2; *Firenze* 2004, p. 215; *Ibn Jaldun* 2006, pp. 162–3; *The Splendour* 2008, p. 65.

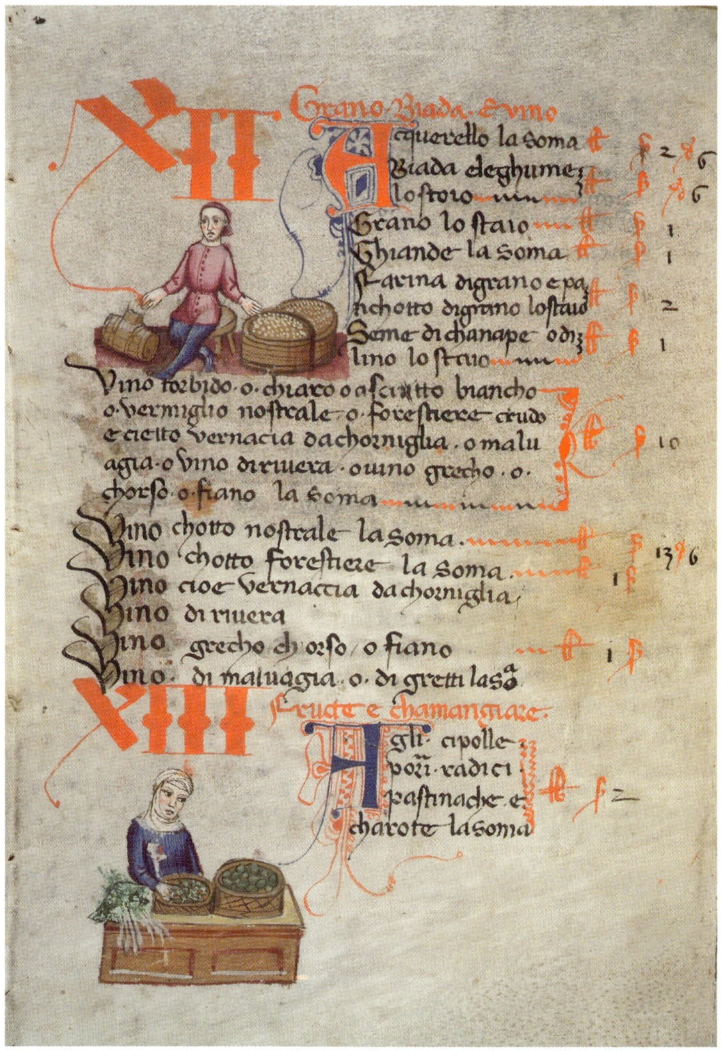

2.5
Theatrum Sanitatis
14th–15th century
miniature on parchment; fols. III. 106
346 x 242 mm
Rome, Biblioteca Casanatense, ms. 4182, fol. 170

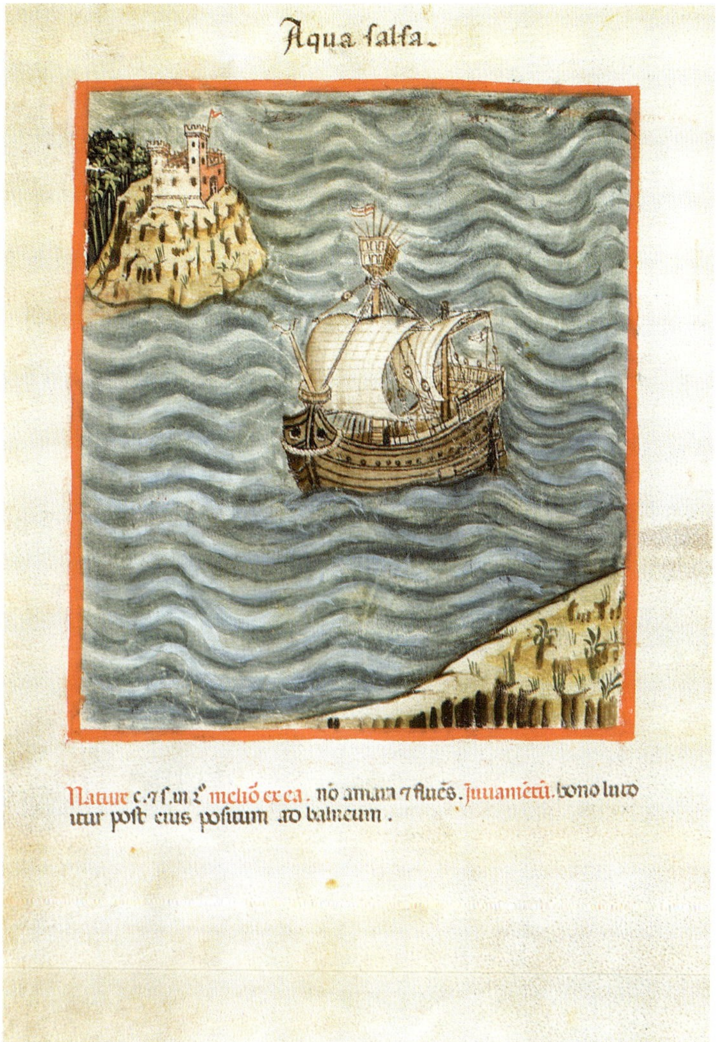

The *Theatrum sanitatis*, attributed to Ububchasym de Baldach, a Christian physician born in Baghdad, was a treatise widely known in the 14th and 15th centuries for the ample range of topics it covered. The text sets forth the principles deemed essential for health by "rational" medicine. Illness was thought to be caused by some alteration in nourishment, the environment, activity and repose, sleep and wakefulness, secretions and excretions, or the motions of the soul. On the subject of nourishment, the properties of various foods, their hot/cold and dry/damp nature, are discussed in relation to the temperaments of man, according to the prescriptions of classic antiquity and the Salerno School.

Splendid decorations accompany a brief but concise text, forming an integral part of it. This elegant, fascinating volume was especially attractive to the wealthy classes able to afford such a luxurious codex, combining prescriptions for health with aesthetic appeal. The original practical function of the book was almost secondary to its ornamental beauty.

Of the three most prized codices of the *Tacuinum sanitatis*, now in Vienna (Österreichische Nationalbibliothek, Vindob. 2644), Paris (Bibliothèque nationale de France, Lat. 9333) and Rome, the Casanatense version has taken the name of *Theatrum sanitatis*. It provides precious visual testimony of day-to-day life in sixty-five pages of exquisite craftsmanship, where miniatures illustrate the precepts, commenting on and supplementing the text, reduced to a few marginal lines. The illustrations, including a few boldly erotic scenes, are narrative in style, showing pictures of life ranging from work in the fields to fishing, from daily occupations in the kitchen to the courtly entertainments of noble youths and ladies moving gracefully in elegant gowns. A world of clearly defined social levels appears, each engaged in its own activities, primarily commerce, transport and shop-keeping. Detailed views of landscapes and interiors heighten the immediacy of the scenes.

Here the medieval interest in herbariums, luminous showcases of nature, is combined with the practical mentality of the middle classes, attentive to health as the indispensable element for active life, and to the refinement of aristocratic taste in decorations.

The illustrations are traditionally attributed to the sphere of Giovannino de' Grassi, after suggestions that the volume may have been produced in Verona, or possibly by the Master Modena Book of Hours. In any case, they are perfectly consonant with the highly refined Lombard Late Gothic style, tinged by French influences, distinguished by elegant lines, refined costumes and vivacious scenes.

Giovanna Lazzi

Bibliography: *Theatrum sanitatis* (sec. XIV), ed. Serra 1940; *Theatrum sanitatis* (sec. XIV), ed. Pazzini *et al.* 1969; *La Biblioteca* 1993; *Theatrum sanitatis* (sec. XIV), facs. ed. 1999.

Section 3
Usury

From Late Antiquity to the present day, usury has been one of the most widespread and hotly debated moral problems arising from economic activity. Given the serious social implications behind the practise, theologians and financial experts have frequently clashed over the issue. What interest rate constitutes usury? At what point does just recompense for a loan become an illicit gain that destroys not only the economic well-being but the very life of those obliged to borrow?
Forbidden by the church, usury indicates financial practices that involve no concrete production or transformation of goods but only the charging of monetary interest on a loan.[1] As St. Ambrose concisely stated, "Usury is taking more than you have given." The Church's condemnation was so vehement that in 1179 the III Lateran Council issued a decree denying Christian burial to known usurers. The practice was deemed wicked and unnatural, and together with simony, stealing, perjury, theft, lying, robbery, violence, harassment, misjudging, deceit and desiring fame, one of the twelve of the fifth Capital Sin, Greed, which the Florentine Bono Giamboni in the mid-13th century summed up in the one word "pestilence."[2]
The usurers in Dante's *Inferno* exemplify all of the money lenders who, over the centuries, have applied exorbitant interest rates, reducing the borrowers to poverty: "Each had a purse hung round his neck/ Adorned with certain colours and a certain device/Which each of them with hungry eyes consumed."[3] In numerous pietistic images, usurers and tax collectors are portrayed with deformed, rapacious features, reflecting their ungodly but lucrative dealings.
There were some exceptions, however, to the Church's strict prohibition of usury. Thomas Aquinas, by introducing the concept of "consequential damage" (the loss suffered by the lender if the debtor defaults) and "loss of profit" (the profit not earned by the lender on money he has lent and so cannot utilize), laid the basis for including interest rates in legitimate contracts. Only in the 15th century, however, with the preaching and writings of Bernardino da Siena, was a distinction made between the usurer, whose activity is immoral, and the banker, whose money-lending allows a broader and faster circulation of wealth.[4] Lending money is, in fact, a way of increasing capital, fundamental to the development of the modern financial system. The merchant-bankers who operated on a Europe-wide level also extended loans to popes, kings and institutions, clearly revealing the ambiguity of a world that condemned these operators but did not hesitate to recur to their services when necessary.
The figure of the usurer was closely linked to that of the Jew. Forbidden to engage in almost all economic activities, Jews were allowed to practice only medicine or money-lending. According to the Old Testament, moreover, it was no sin to lend money to individuals or institutions outside of their community; hence this was one of the activities most frequently pursued by Jews.
As time passed, the Church felt the need to lighten the burden of those obliged to borrow money. The Franciscans, although opposed by the Dominicans and Augustinians, founded the pawnshops called Monti di Pietà (the first was opened in 1462) as anti-usury institutions, providing an alternative to loans extended against pledges by private bankers. These institutions were addressed however to the "well-off poor," who owned something they could leave as a pledge. Operating on a non-profit basis, they charged low interest rates, only enough to cover expenses. The original concept of the Monti di Pietà, still active today, is reflected in a modern initiative: the Grameen Bank, or Village Bank, founded in 1977 by Muhammad Yunus, offers micro-loans without interest and without collateral to women especially, allowing them to set up small businesses.[5]

Ludovica Sebregondi

1. See Le Goff 2007, pp. 11–23.
2. See in Santambrogio 2002, p. 63.
3. *Inferno*, Canto XVII, vv. 55–7.
4. Nigro 2010, pp. 84–5.
5. Santambrogio 2002, p. 87.

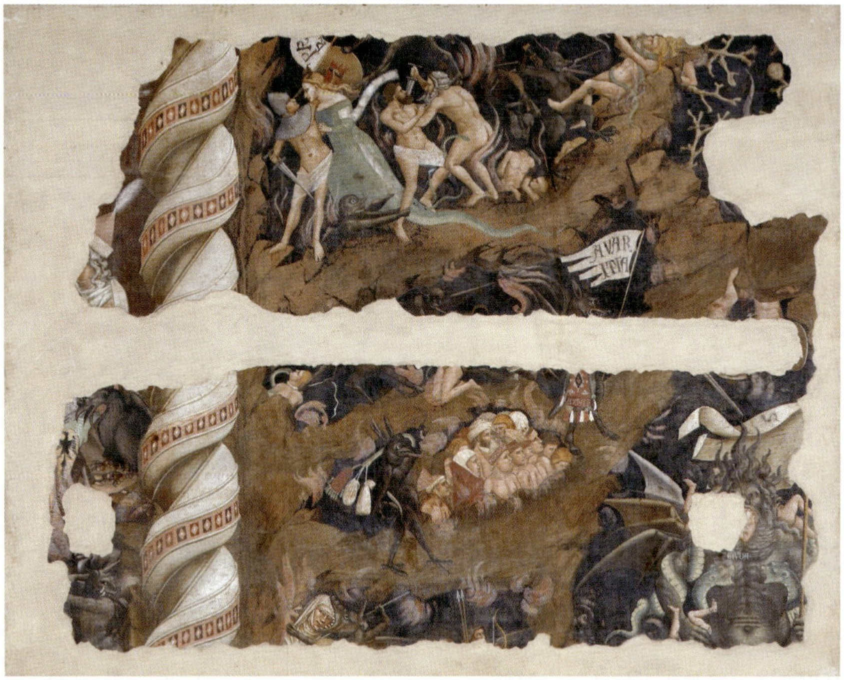

3.1
Andrea Orcagna
(Andrea di Cione; Florence
documented 1346–68)
Punishment of the Misers
c. 1345
detached fresco
246. 2 x 336 cm
Florence, Museo dell'Opera di Santa Croce

This fragment comes from a great wall painting that once decorated the nave of the Franciscan Basilica of Santa Croce in Florence. Only a few fragments of it have survived, but Renaissance documents recall scenes depicting the *Triumph of Death*, the *Last Judgement*, and the *Inferno* (see Offner 1962).

The fresco, nearly 18 metres long and 7 high, was completed by a painted frame including formelle with scenes of the Apocalypse. Destroyed in the 16th century when the Church of Santa Croce was refurbished by Giorgio Vasari, the fresco is known from the citations of 15th-16th century historiographers, who unanimously attributed the work to Orcagna (for a critical analysis, see Offner 1962 and Kreytenberg 2000). This attribution is generally accepted by modern scholars, who date the painting around the middle of the fifth decade of the 14th century (Boskovits 1971; Kreytenberg 2000).

This scene, part of the *Inferno*, portrays sinners condemned for avarice, one of the Seven Deadly Sins listed by Gregory the Great, along with pride, envy, anger, sloth, gluttony and lust (Bonora 1970). Although some of the iconography in Orcagna's mural derives from Dante's *Divine Comedy* (Kreytenberg 1989), his portrayal of the punishment of misers seems to follow a different tradition, where they are not shown beside squanderers, guilty of the opposite sin.

In the fresco a group of souls, nude but wearing headdresses and hairstyles identifying them as a bishop, a cardinal, a pope, a king, a nun and some laymen, are casting fearful glances at the demons surrounding them, one of them carrying an enormous, gorgeously decorated purse and holding a banner inscribed "AVAR/ITIA." Behind them another diabolical creature is about to strike the condemned souls with a whip made of bags and purses stuffed with money, held in a serpent's mouth.

The wealth and social status of this large group of sinners are evinced by a few details in their dress and by their well-fed, well-cared for appearance. As a whole, they illustrate the more complex meaning assigned at the time to avarice, now become synonymous of stinginess. Avarice was condemned above all as the insatiable greed that could take the form of usury or fraudulent possession (Casagrande, Vecchio 2000, pp. 96–123; Mariani 1970). With the development of mercantile society in the late Middle Ages, this vice became so rampant that Dante deemed it one of the chief causes of the fratricidal struggles in Florentine society and the decadence of the city (Bonora 1970). As shown by the members of religious orders standing in the first row of the painting, greed also ran rife among the representatives of the secular Church, in contrast to the mendicant orders with their vow of poverty (Bonora 1970). No friar, in fact, appears in the group of sinners, perhaps as an implicit tribute to the morality of the Franciscans, who had commissioned the fresco.

Daniela Parenti

Bibliography: Offner 1962, pp. 43–58; Boskovits 1971, p. 244; Kreytenberg 1989; Kreytenberg 2000, pp. 39–61.

3.2
Pesellino
(Francesco di Stefano; Florence *c.* 1422–57)
Nativity, Martyrdom of Saints Cosmas and Damian; St. Anthony causes a usurer's heart to be found in a strong-box (predella)
c. 1445
panel
34 x 144 cm
Florence, Galleria degli Uffizi,
1890 inv. no. 8355

The Uffizi panel, along with one in the Louvre portraying *St. Francis receiving the stigmata* and *Saints Cosmas and Damian curing Dean Justin*, originally made up the predella painted by Pesellino for the altarpiece of the *Virgin and Child with Saints Francis, Cosmas, Damian and Anthony of Padua* by Filippo Lippi. Although no commission has been documented, the work must have been done at the request of Cosimo the Elder de' Medici for the Chapel of the Novitiate in Santa Croce, and in fact, its presence there is confirmed in Albertini's *Memorial* (1510, ed. De Boer 2010, p. 98), the first guide to Florence, and in later sources as well. The altarpiece was probably painted in view of the completion of the chapel built around 1445 by Michelozzo for Cosimo, who donated it to the Franciscan Order, owner of the Santa Croce building complex. The client and the beneficiary of the donation are recalled by the saints appearing beside the Virgin and in the narrative scenes on the predella. St. Francis was the founder, St. Anthony an illustrious member of the Franciscan Order, while the martyrs Cosmas and Damian—standing closest to the Virgin, and appearing again in the stained-glass window of the chapel—were chosen as patron saints by Cosimo and the Medici family because of their calling as physicians. Along the trabeation of the architectural structure that serves as setting for the scene runs a frieze adorned with red balls against a gold background, a reference to the bezants on the Medici coat of arms.

Lists of liturgical obligations dating from the 16th century recall that the Chapel of the Novitiate was dedicated expressly to Saints Cosmas and Damian, and that every Saturday the novices had to sing a Mass to the Virgin for the soul of Cosimo the Elder (Ruda 1993, p. 415). Furthermore, Vespasiano da Bisticci, a librarian and close friend of the Medici, recalls in his biography that Cosimo, while successfully engaging in the "temporal affairs of his city," began to fear that sooner or later his good luck would run out, due to that "money not very well acquired" (Vespasiano da Bisticci [*c.* 1480–98], ed. Greco 1970–76, II, 1976, p. 177). Accordingly, "to take this weight off his shoulders" he began to devote himself "to pious things," promoting works—churches, chapels, convents, ecclesiastical robes, altarpieces—destined to religious orders and institutions. In the *Altarpiece of the Novitiate*, the concern of Cosimo, hoping to save his soul as a money changer and usurer, is obvious in the predella panel depicting a miracle of St. Anthony imbued with moral significance (Kent 2000, ed. 2005). In this episode Anthony, while preaching at the funeral of a famous usurer, declared that the body did not deserve to be buried in consecrated land, recalling a passage from the *Gospel of St. Luke* (12:34): "Because where your treasure is, there also will be your heart." The surgeons then opened the usurer's chest, to find that his heart was missing; it was hidden in his strongbox along with the money he had amassed.

Elena Capretti

Bibliography: Ruda 1993, pp. 413–6 no. 32; Kent 2000, ed. 2005, pp. 197–9.

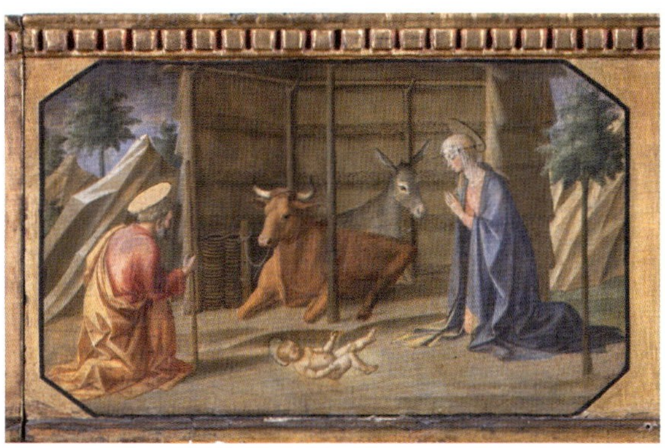

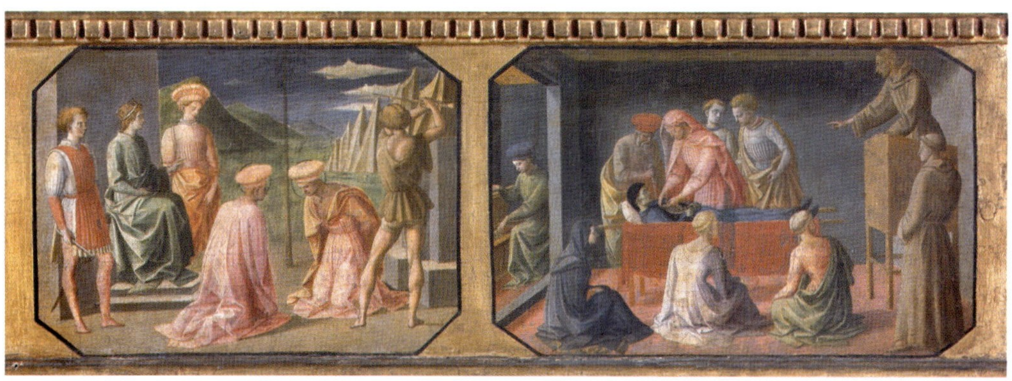

3.3
Jan Provoost (Mons 1462–Bruges 1529)
Death and the Miser
1505–10
oil on panel
119.7 x 78.5 cm
119.8 x 78.8 cm
Bruges, Groeningemuseum,
inv. no. 0000.GR00217.I-0218.I

These two panels originally decorated the reverse sides of the two lateral panels in a triptych, whose fronts are also in the Groeningenmuseum in Bruges. The front and back of the side panels were separated prior to 1861 by cutting the wooden support lengthwise. The central panel has been lost.

On the front of the side panels appear the two donors kneeling, each accompanied by a patron saint: St. Nicholas of Bari on the left and St. Godelieve on the right. The donor is represented again on the back of the side panels, which formed a single painted scene when closed. From this scene we can guess that he must have been a money changer, a tax collector or a banker, portrayed in his shop seated at a table, with bags of money and strips of paper covered with writing in the foreground. The man, dressed in a warm red overgarment trimmed with fur, marks his place in an account book with one hand, while holding out a sheet of paper to Death, personified by a skeleton robed in white. Death puts his own money on the table, arranging the coins to be counted, while he looks at the sheet of paper. Behind the skeleton a frowning youth wearing a black hat looks on, pointing at something, perhaps the sheet of paper, with his finger. The writing on the sheet is fragmentary and obscure in meaning, like the rest of the scene. The inscription begins with "Ic Ian Lanckart...," which may be the name of the man on the left. Since he is probably the client who commissioned the work, it is unlikely that the scene express a negative judgement on him. It would thus seem that Death has arrived to pay a debt left unsettled by the young man behind him, now dead (and thus not a self-portrait of the artist as has sometimes been thought), while the money lender checks the amount in his account book and returns the promissory note. On the whole, the composition appears to illustrate the popular proverb, "Death pays the debts and the purges the soul of them."

Since medieval times the Church had openly condemned usury, viewed by canon law as "any amount, large or small, demanded in addition to the capital in a mutuum, the legal term used to indicate the loan of money proper" (De Roover 1963, ed. 1970, pp. 12–3). The theologians even deemed it heresy to declare that usury was not a sin. In reality, bankers devised clever stratagems to mask certain transactions as legal. For example, interest could be entered in the account books as a donation. But the preferred method for gaining profit from money was the letter of exchange, used in exchanging money or buying and selling foreign currency (De Roover 1963, ed. 1970, p. 14). This instrument of credit, introduced by the great Italian merchants as early as the 13th century, spread through the trade centres of Europe, Flanders in particular (Stabel 2002; Galoppini 2009). The advantages of the letter of exchange were clear. It avoided the problem of having to transport money and precious metals with the inevitable risk and expense incurred, importantly, it could be used to evade the Church's ban on usury.

In fact, a loan with interest could be made to seem an exchange of money in another currency, making use of a network of banks situated in different countries.

Elena Capretti

Bibliography: Friedländer 1972–3, II, 1973, p. 112, no. 133; Huvenne 1997, p. 163; *Les marchands* 2002, p. 120; A. van Oostrewijk in *Van Eyck bis Dürer* 2010, pp. 204, 524, no. 66.

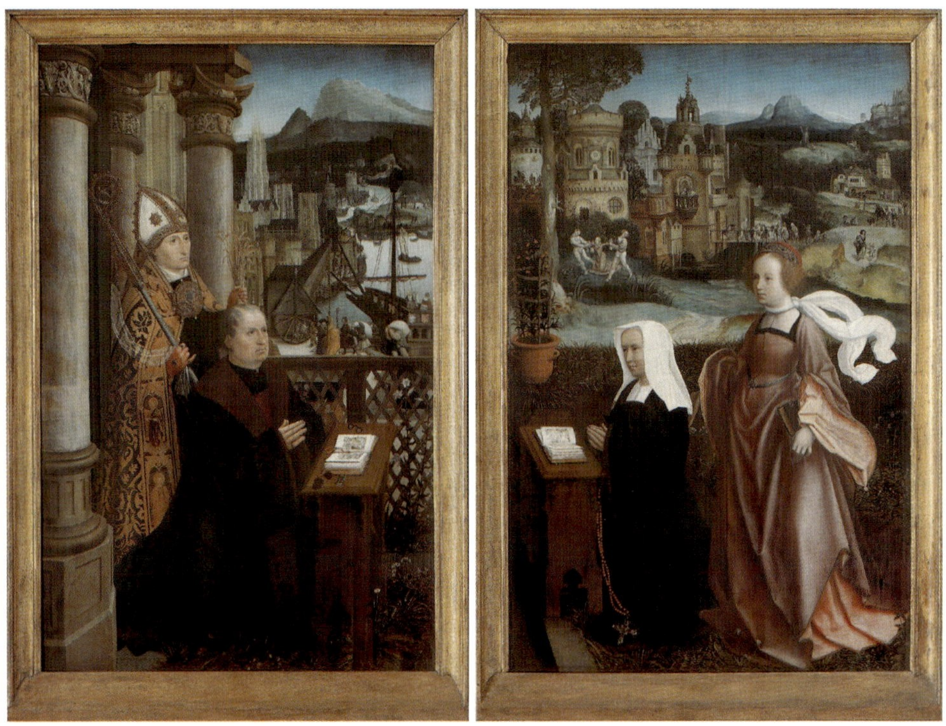

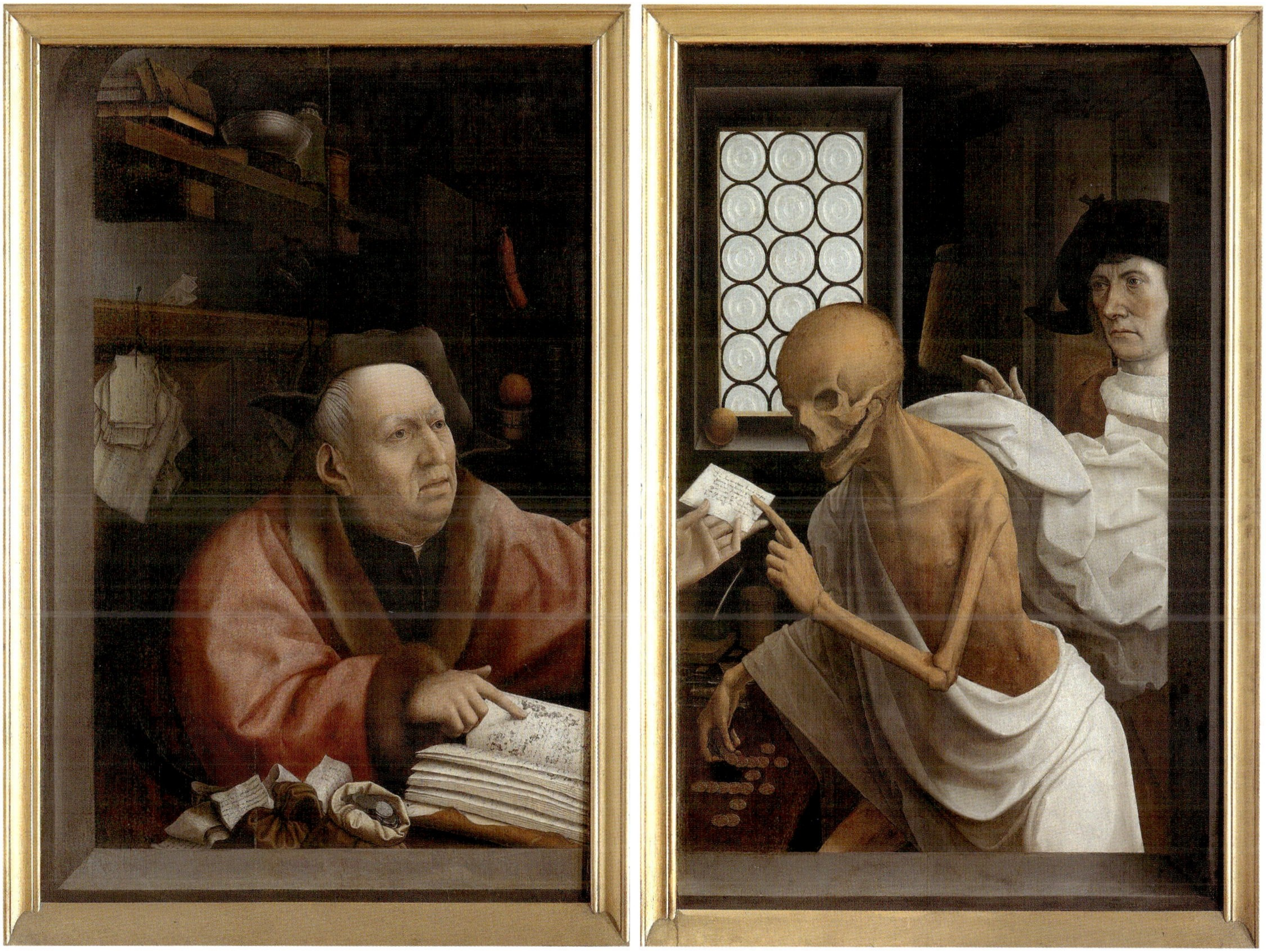

3.4
after Marinus van Reymerswaele (Reymerswaele *c.* 1490–Middleburg, documented until 1567)
The Usurers
c. 1540
oil on panel
100 x 76 cm
Florence, Museo Stibbert, inv. no. 4080

From the mid-15th century on, the mercantile class, fully aware of its social status, did not hesitate to propose itself as subject of the works of art it commissioned. Inevitably, however, this class aroused resentment, due to the unscrupulous practices that often lay behind success and wealth. This painting, depicting two avaricious individuals intent on counting their riches, clearly demonstrates the prejudice against not only the mercantile class, but all those whose businesses involved money, whether bankers, money changers, usurers or tax collectors.

To these professional categories, so numerous in industrious Flanders, are dedicated a series of paintings, vivacious and ironical, illustrating their most detestable traits. Among these, the subject of usurers was enormously popular. For decades it inspired replicas by artists of varying talent. The scholars have endeavoured to find an archetype for these paintings, which exist in many variations, all apparently based on a lost original by Jan van Eyck, painted for the Lampognano merchants of Milan and known only by a verbal description. It was the source of inspiration for at least two of the most famous works: *The Money Changer and his Wife* by Quentin Metsys, copied also by Marinus van Reymerswaele, and *The Usurers*—variously called in the different collections *The Misers*, *The Usurers*, *The Money Lenders*, *The Tax Collectors*—showing two men of rapacious aspect, the second especially hideous, intent on recording transactions in an account book. They are surrounded by the symbols of their trade: coins, jewels, moneybags, accounting papers, candles and scissors. In later versions of the painting, the scissors are sometimes replaced by a little parrot perched on a shelf. Their clothing openly proclaims prosperity, with jewels and fur pieces bearing witness to the wealth they have amassed by trading in money. Their ostentatious hoods, typical of Italian and Flemish fashion in the 15th century, appear somewhat archaic in the mid-16th, as if to accentuate the symbolism of the two figures, subject to ethical censure for their greed. Although the two are presumably checking accounts in their book, the writing on the page before them contains only the edifying message, "L'avaricieux n'est jamais rempli d'argent. Etc. N'ayez point s[ouci] des richesses [in]justes, car elles ne vous proufyteront [rien] au jour de la visitation et de vangeance. Souyes doncq sans avarice." ("The miser is never satiated with money, etc. Do not covet unjust riches, since they will be of no aid to you on the day of the Coming [of Christ] and the Last Judgement. And so be free of greed").

Simona Di Marco

Bibliography: *Il Museo Stibbert* 1974, p. 55, no. 364; Campbell 1985, p. 116, fig. 40; Sotheby's London 2008, no. 8.

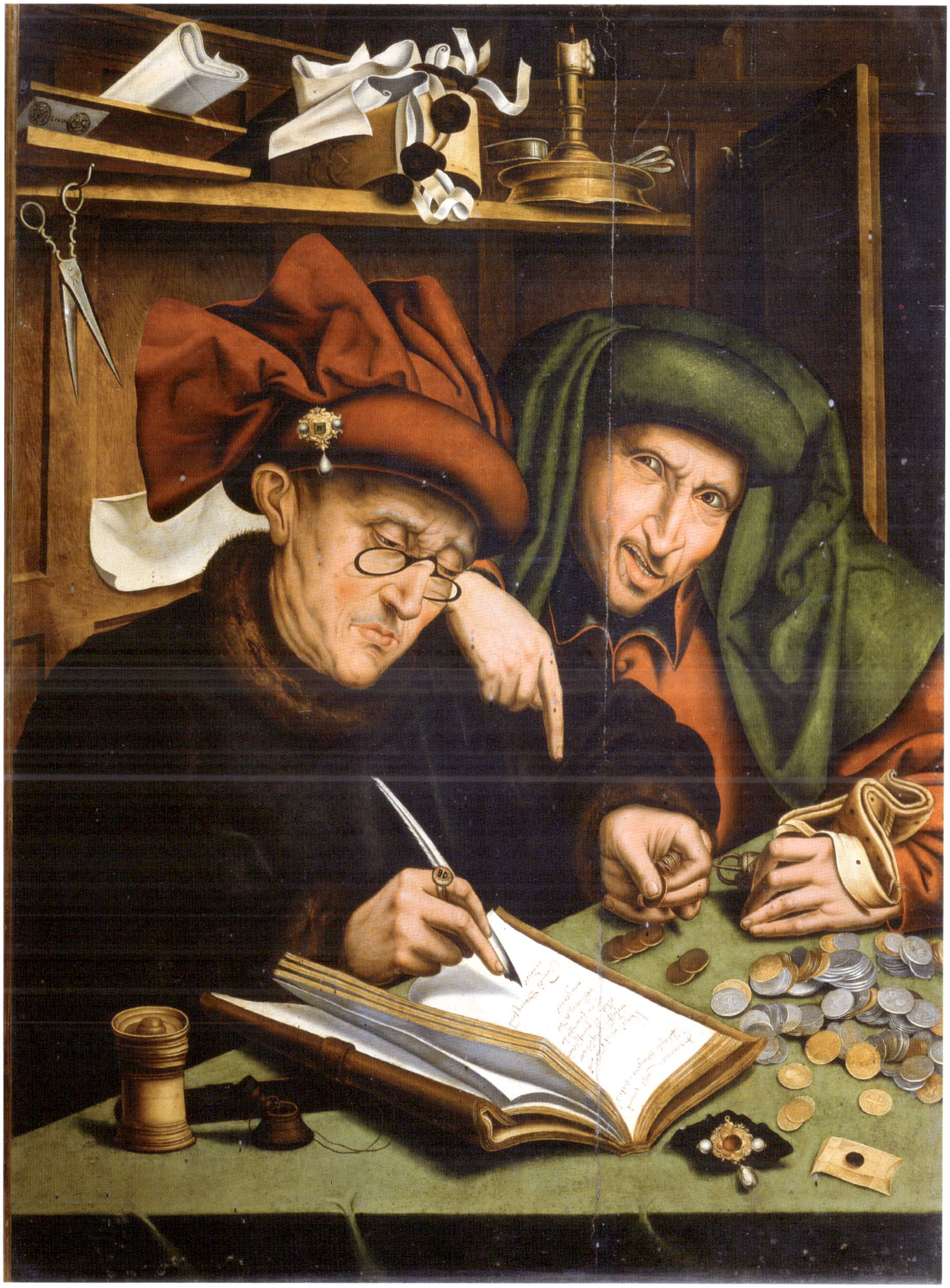

3.5 - work not on display
Quentin Metsys (Louvain 1466–Antwerp 1530)
The Usurers
c. 1515–20
oil on panel
73 x 95 cm
Rome, Galleria Doria Pamphilj, inv. no. 307

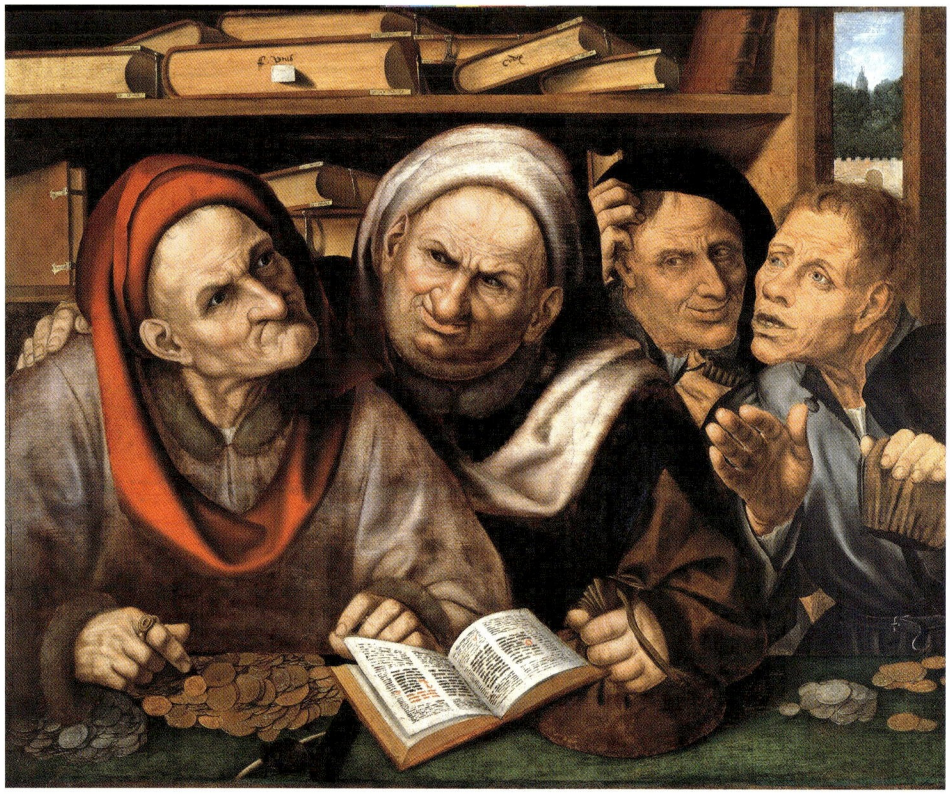

Two usurers stand before a table with a heap of coins and an account book on it. Their faces are caricatures of duplicity and cruelty. The man on the left, immediately noticeable for his bright red turban and the big ring on his index finger, casts a grudging, bullying look at the poor debtor on the far right who, his desperate face furrowed with wrinkles, his beret clutched in his hand, is imploring understanding and pity. The other usurer, fleshy and corpulent, his face contorted in a cruel grimace, throws his right arm over his partner's shoulders in sign of approval, while grasping his moneybag in the left. Behind him a man with a mocking smile looks on complacently. The figures are crowded together in the foreground in the narrow space between the table and the shelves behind them, where a few books lie in disorderly array. In the background to the right, a landscape can be glimpsed.

This composition is one of a group of paintings of secular subject accomplished in the second and third decade of the 16th century by Quentin Metsys, founder and master of the Antwerp school. The subjects portrayed are for the most part money changers, tax collectors, notaries, and debt collectors. Inaugurating the series is the famous *The Money Changer and his Wife* from 1514 (Paris, Louvre; fig. p. 18), where, in a scene of limpid clarity pervaded by a serene sense of order, the personages appear quietly engaged in their industrious activity. The setting is depicted precisely but surprisingly, as if each tiny detail had a meaning that transcends material reality to become a symbol and moral paradigm (Moffitt 2008). After this masterpiece, Metsys painted *The Usurers*, now in the Galleria Doria Pamphilj and other pictures of the same bitingly satirical tone, such as the *A Grotesque Old Woman* (London, The National Gallery), the *Odd Couple* (Washington, The National Gallery of Art), *The Contract* (Berlin, Gemäldegalerie) and *The Hypocrites* (also in the Galleria Doria Pamphilj).

Echoing the grotesque, caricatured faces of Leonardo's drawings, they show a moralizing purpose; that of revealing, in a detached, amused manner, the vile souls of men who incarnate the typical vices of the Netherland's mercantile and banking society, already proto-capitalistic. Antwerp in particular—where the artist from Louvain moved in 1491—was enjoying a prodigious boom which, while it brought wealth, led to the pursuit of easy profits and the debasement of customs. The works of Metsys, created within this context, inaugurated a genre that was to encounter great success in 16th-century Netherlands (Moxey 1985).

For his paintings Metsys drew inspiration from the humanists his contemporaries, most notably Erasmus of Rotterdam and Pierre Gillis, friends whose portraits he painted (Rome, Palazzo Barberini; Salisbury, Longford Castle). According to northern intellectuals, a citizen should practice Christian ethics within the context of an active professional life, reconciling virtue with profit to build his fortune with a businessman's intelligence and experience, far from any meanness or ineptitude. Such theories paved the way for Calvinism, which, unlike Lutheranism, was to look favourably on usury and the amassing of wealth.

Elena Capretti

Bibliography: Limentani Virdis 1974; Bosque 1975, p. 195; Huvenne 1997, pp. 172–3.

3.6
Tuscan sculptor (assistant of Agnolo di Polo?)
Bust of St. Antoninus Pierozzi
late 15th–first decades of 16th century
polychrome terracotta
58 x 60 x 32 cm
Florence, Basilica di Santa Maria Novella

There are numerous portraits of St. Antoninus, all quite similar, apparently derived from his death mask, which was probably made during the week following his decease on May 2, 1459. Pohl lists six other portraits in addition to this one, and a seventh was donated on June 20, 1716 by the noblewoman Maria Rosa Niccolini to the Compagnia di Sant'Antonino, adjacent to the Church of Santa Maria a Carraia near Calenzano (F. Cerboni, entry OA, SBAS, no. 09/00159019, March 3, 1982). Paul Westheim believes the Santa Maria Novella portrait to be a 19th-century copy, by Giovanni Bastianini. However, as compared to the busts of the saint surely dating from the 19th century, like the one in the Church of San Domenico at Fiesole (*La civiltà del cotto* 1980, pp. 143–4), the portrait in the exhibition appears undeniably much older and based on the death mask, used by the sculptor to model a realistic image of the saint at a time when his features were no longer clearly recalled but memories of him were still vivid. The popular cult of the Florentine bishop was intensified, in fact, at the time of Savonarola, Antoninus's successor as director of the Monastery of San Marco, who proclaimed his populist and anti-Medicean positions even more vehemently. The Dominicans' efforts to have Antoninus canonized, crowned by success in 1523, may have favoured the dissemination of copies of the prototype bust, made for that occasion in the years immediately prior to it by a sculptor similar in style to Agnolo di Polo, the author of numerous devotional busts of similar modelling and expressive intensity (Lorenzi 1998).

St. Antoninus was greatly beloved, even decades after his death, thanks to his commitment to the propaganda of the Dominican Observance and his active participation in the city's political life in defence of the legal rights of the poor, in opposition to the abuses attempted by the government of Cosimo the Elder. Already in February 1442, in calling together the twelve Florentine citizens who joined him in founding the Provveditori de' Poveri Vergognosi (known later as the Buonomini di San Martino), Antoninus urged the citizens to attend to the needs of those Florentines who, once members of the upper class, had been deprived of their wealth by political struggles. In the *Summa Moralis*, written between 1440 and 1459, he denounced the widespread practice of usury, at the base of the wealth amassed by bankers, re-echoing, albeit with greater intellectual clarity and less severity, the preaching of St. Bernardino of Siena, his counterpart Observant in the Franciscan Order. In the second part of the *Summa*, Antoninus condemns the practice of charging interest on loans, but admits a distinction between a loan constituting usury and other contracts resembling it. Furthermore, he recognizes the legitimacy of interest on loans extended to navigators or merchants who run special risks, or in the case of a debtor who delays repayment of the contractually stipulated amount. He shows perplexity over the five percent interest acknowledged to guardians who administer their wards' property, but is favourable to partnership contracts where all of the participants are equal. He takes a stance on the subject of exchange transactions, which do not guarantee the same value to money in different cities, and unconditionally condemns the papal court's practice of sending bulls of benefice only after the payment of a fixed sum, thus providing the banker with interest in addition to the profit already ensured by the exchange (Morçay 1914, pp. 366–76).

The *Summa* is a valid ensemble of observations and a real treatise on the science of economy, compiled by a wise, judicious moralist. As a good Florentine, Antoninus Pierozzi recognized the importance of commerce, which, by ensuring prosperity, favours peace and friendship among the different peoples. In a vision of social equality traditionally linked to the thought of St. Thomas Aquinas, he calls for attention to the needs of the weak, at a critical time for Florence, whose centuries-long democratic traditions were then under threat.

Francesca Petrucci

Bibliography: Fabriczy 1895, p. 155; Westheim 1930, p. 193; Pohl 1938, p. 51; Schuyler 1972, p. 144 and ff.; Pope-Hennessy, *The Forging* 1974, p. 261.

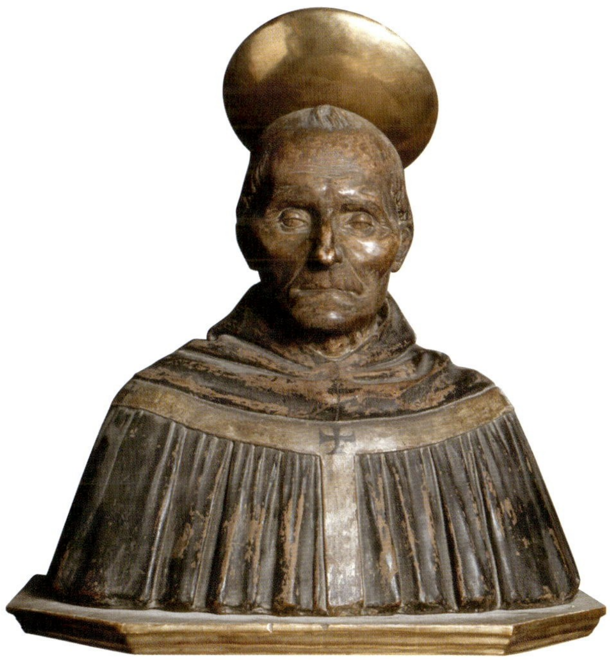

3.7
Vicino da Ferrara (Ferrara 1432–1509)
Bernardino da Feltre
post 1494
tempera on canvas
172 x 70 cm
Ferrara, Pinacoteca Nazionale, inv. no. 67

The painting portrays Bernardino da Feltre, born Martino Tomitano in 1439, of a wealthy family, in the Veneto town whose name he then took as his own. He studied law and grammar at Padua before entering the Order of the Observant Friars Minor in 1456. Ordained a priest in 1463, he became a famous preacher. In the painting, probably done soon after his death in 1494, his head is surrounded by rays of light, showing the veneration accorded him even before his beatification in 1654. In his right hand he holds a three-tier rock formation covered by a grassy mantle—with a pennant bearing the name "MONS PIETATIS"—on which are scattered coins. At the top rises a banner with the image of Christ as the Man of sorrows surrounded by the letters "YHS," the name of Jesus in the formula popularized by Bernardino da Siena, he too a Franciscan and, for Bernardino, a model to be emulated. In his left hand he grasps another pennant with the inscription *Nolite dilegere mundum*, a reference to the *Gospel of St. John*, "Do not love the world nor the things that are in the world. If a man love the world, the love of the Father is not in him" (*John* 1:15.17).

The institution of the Monte di Pietà was not invented by Bernardino, although he was one its most fervent advocates. The Monti had been established as institutes of credit that lent money without interest, a means of combating usury and safeguarding the poor against "debts with interest." Lending money at high interest rates, although condemned by the Church, was practiced on a vast scale. The term "Lombardi" was, like "Caorsini," linked to the banking profession, since the Lombards had founded Cahors, the first banking centre in the medieval world. In 16th-century Florence, it was an important financial institution, with bankers operating throughout the known world. The Jews too worked in finance, one of the few professions allowed them in Christian lands. Against them Bernardino da Feltre hurled bitter arrows in his struggle to promote the Monti di Pietà, aligning himself with others who brought persecution and death to the Italian Jewish community of the time. In 1487 the civil authorities, fearing riots, forbade the Franciscan friar to preach in the city during Lent.

The first Monte di Pietà was founded in 1465 in Perugia. Bernardino da Feltre helped to found others, in Mantua in 1484, in Padua in 1491, at Crema and Pavia in 1493, at Montagnana and Monselice in 1494. As shown in this painting, while preaching he bore a standard depicting Christ as the "Man of Sorrows," or *imago pietatis*, employing an figure that had been well known in Northern Italy for over a century. This powerful image, insisting on the sacrifice of Christ, aroused compassion in the spectators. The *imago pietatis* was often used later as emblem or insignia even by the Monti di Pietà that had not been founded by Bernardino.

It is probable that his painting, which hung in the Church of the Monte di Pietà in Ferrara in the 18th century, originally decorated the oratory annexed to the more ancient seat, and was painted expressly for the institution, founded in 1507. The format suggests that it was used only not only as an altarpiece but also as a processional standard. The painting is attributed to Vicino da Ferrara, a little-known artist.

Philine Helas

Bibliography: *La Pinacoteca Nazionale* 1992, pp. 79–81; Meneghin 1967, pp. 28–9; Muzzarelli 2001, p. 137; Puglisi, Barcham 2008, p. 58.

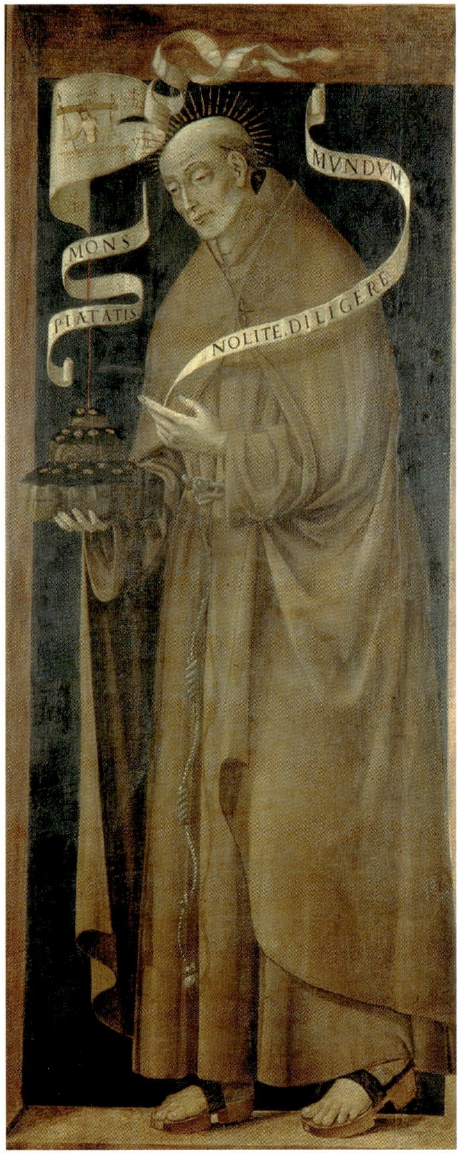

3.8
Anonymous engraver
The figure of Eternal Life
in Marco da Montegallo,
Libro delli comandamenti di Dio del testamento vecchio et nuovo e sacri canoni
Florence, for Antonio Miscomini, 1494
woodcut
210 x 138 mm
Florence, Biblioteca Nazionale Centrale,
Palat. E.6.3.99, fol. 1v

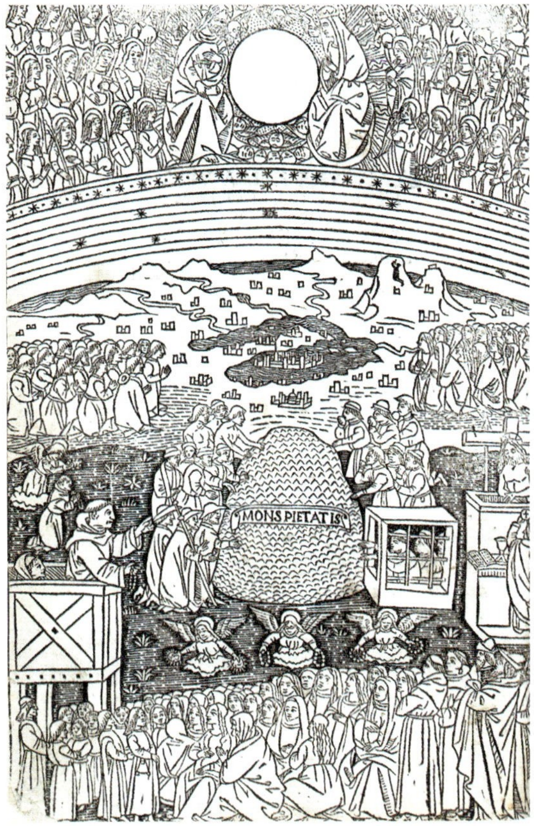

Fra' Marco da Montegallo, who was born in 1425, practiced medicine at Ascoli in 1448 before entering the Franciscan Observance in 1452. Like Bernardino da Feltre, he was a famous preacher who was instrumental in founding the Monti di Pietà, the central theme of this woodcut, where he appears preaching before a symbolic image of the *Mons pietatis*. The friar wrote three treatises. The first, the *Libro intitulato de la divina lege*, is an explanation of the Ten Commandments, printed in Venice in 1486 and expanded under the title *Libro delli comandamenti di Dio* in 1494 in Siena and Florence. The second, the *Tabula della salute* [Table of health] printed in 1486 in Venice and 1494 in Florence, is linked by its title to the other treatise, since *tavola* means "table of the law". *Salute* refers to both spiritual and corporal health, since it deals with religious themes as well as advice on health. The Florentine edition alone has four chapters on the Monte di Pietà. The last of Montegallo's writings, *La corona della Vergine* [The Virgin's Crown], probably printed in Venice in 1486, was inspired by the friar's commitment to found a brotherhood of "Raccomandati alla Vergine." This is illustrated in the woodcut where, at left, the friar is shown kneeling in prayer with a rosary while being crowned by an angel (Lomastro Tognato 1996; *Marco da Montegallo* 1999).

Both the *Libro delli comandamenti di Dio* and the *Tabula della salute* published in Florence in 1494 were preceded by the woodcut called *La figura della vita eterna o vero del paradiso & delli modi & vie di pervenire a quello* [The figure of eternal life, that is, of paradise and the manner and ways to arrive there] in which the *Mons pietatis* appears surrounded by six groups of persons representing the six works of charity according to the *Gospel of St. Matthew* (25:34-46). Behind the "Monte" the landscape opens out into a kind of world map with Paradise and its host of angels above it. In two pages, perhaps printed separately, "THE MEANING AND EXPLANATION OF ALL OF THIS PICTURE" is made clear. This shows the friar's active role in inventing the image, insisting on his authorship "as we have had it depicted in our painting of eternal life."

The model for the woodcut was an engraving of the same subject in a larger format (490 x 354 mm), done in much greater detail and accompanied by inscriptions. The map-like landscape shows the Mediterranean area in minute detail, with the Italian peninsula and its major cities at the centre. To the left appears Mount Sinai, where Moses is receiving the Ten Commandments. The author of the woodcut had no cartographic knowledge, since he represents the view in reverse, and Moses is barely recognizable on the mountain appearing here to the right.

The image tries to convey the idea that supporting the Monte di Pieta financially can take the place of works of charity. In addition to the anti-Jewish movement, there also appears a tendency to organize aid to the needy in a more controlled form, through institutions that took the place of spontaneous, individual charity. On the symbolic level the Monte di Pietà is the counterpart of Mount Sinai, showing the transition from the *sub lege* to the *sub gratia* era. It is the centre of an ideal Christian *communitas* in the name of the Eucharistic body of Christ, evoked in the woodcut (at right) by the pious image of St. Gregory's Mass, during which St. Gregory the Great saw the real presence of Christ in the bread and wine.

Philine Helas

Bibliography: *Marco da Montegallo* 1999, pp. 158–78; Helas 2004, pp. 105–44.

Section 4
The Art and Mystery of Exchange

They belonged to a trade guild known as the Arte del Cambio, the Art of Exchange, and what they did was stand behind tables in the porticoes around Orsanmichele changing silver money into gold and vice versa. Some bought and sold jewels. But they would not have become fabulously wealthy doing just that.

They could not underwrite contracts offering interest-bearing loans, since that would be manifest usury, and though manifest usurers did exist, they were mainly Jews, were not allowed to join the Arte del Cambio and for the most part dealt in modest loans to ordinary citizens who needed help to make ends meet.

Instead, the larger bankers changed money on international markets. Imagine a Florentine merchant is buying sugar, spices and currants from Barcelona. He needs to make a payment to his supplier there but does not wish to move coin between the cities. So he goes to a banker in the Mercato Nuovo, gives him the money and receives a letter of exchange which is then sent to his supplier in Barcelona who takes it to the bank's agency there and receives the money in the local currency. If the bank didn't have an agency in Barcelona, they might deal through an associate bank who did, perhaps in another town. Triangulation was common; hence it was a point of strength for the Florentines that the city had so many banks, many of which had agencies in different towns in Italy and abroad. Team effort was important.

But again, beyond charging a small percentage for their services, the banks could hardly have become major financial institutions in this way. It was when the letter of exchange became an instrument of credit that serious money started to be made.

How? It was "a delicate invention" and "a most subtle activity,"[1] wrote Benedetto Cotrugli, attempting to explain the question in his *Book of the Art of Commerce*. Essentially, it depended on the fact that the bank did not hold foreign currencies in Florence, so that an exchange deal would require a trip to a foreign centre which, in those days, would take a certain time. Imagine now that instead of the Florentine bank receiving money to be paid out abroad, it gives a thousand florins to a merchant planning to sell spices and alum in England, asking him to repay in pounds in London. This time it is officially the bank requiring an exchange deal, although it has no particular reason for wanting sterling. A letter of exchange is written out:

> In the year of our Lord 1417 June 15,
> in Florence,
> 1000 Florins.
> Pay *as is the custom* 1000 florins at 40 pence to the florin to whoever is appointed by Giovanni de' Medici and partners in London. May Christ protect you.

Here the expression "as is the custom" refers to the time officially taken to travel from Florence to London. Such times were stipulated by the Arte del Cambio, thus:
Florence to Bruges 60 days.
Florence to Avignon 30 days.
Florence to Barcelona 60 days.
Florence to London 90 days

Of course it didn't take anything like 90 days to get to London on horseback, but that was about the time it would take a laden galley to sail across the Mediterranean, round the Bay of Biscay, up the west coast of France, and through the English Channel to the Thames.

In London, then, on the appointed day the bank's agency receives 1000 x 40 pence = 40,000 pence = £166 13s. 4d. Good, but where is the gain? Well, in London the exchange rate between sterling and florins is more favourable to the English currency by four pence to the florin, so that if the bank now gets involved in a similar deal, giving the same money to another merchant, or perhaps even the same one, to be paid back in florins three months hence, it will get an exchange rate of 36 pence to the florin and hence 1111 florins, a gain of 11% in just six months.

Exchange rates were fixed daily and in such a way that each currency was worth a small percentage more in the country of issue than abroad, and it was in the country of issue, of course, that the exchange rate of a deal was fixed, even though the money was then received abroad, in the other currency, that was now worth more...

Of course there was always the danger that some sudden, radical shift in rates might lead to a banker's losing on the transaction, and it was this risk that made the practise legitimate in the eyes of theologians. But the truth is that there was very little danger involved. Out of sixty-seven exchange deals between London, Bruges and Venice of which the Medici left records, only one resulted in a loss, while the remaining 66 yielded gains ranging from 7.7 to 28.8%.

Who needed interest rates?

Tim Parks

1. Goldthwaite 2009, p. 221.

4.1
Anonymous Florentine engraver
De mercatanti et cambiatori
in Jacopo da Cessole,
Libro di giuocho di scacchi
Florence, for Antonio Miscomini
March 1, 1493–4
woodcut
205 x 141 mm
Florence, Biblioteca Nazionale Centrale, P. 5.4.

The treatise *De ludo scachorum or Libellus de moribus hominum et officiis nobilium ac popularium super ludo scachorum* was written in Latin by the Dominican monk Jacopo da Cessole (1250–1322). The text, one of the first on the game of chess, was translated into many languages and printed in various countries over the course of the 15th century. The volume published in Florence by Master Antonio Miscomini in 1493 is the first edition in Italian.

The book explains the rules of the game but, more importantly, describes it as an allegory of society, where each individual—from the king to the peasant—has his own role to play and his own duties (Jacopo da Cessole [c. 1300], ed. Boyle 1988; Plessow 2007). The idea that people had rights as well as obligations explains its considerable success. The third book, *Delle forme degli Scacchi popolari* is dedicated to "the people," considered as "pawns," shown in eight chapters engaged in the various arts and trades. In the incunabulum, each chapter is headed by a woodcut representing the trade described. These illustrations refer to older images found in manuscripts, such as the 14th-century codices in the Biblioteca Nazionale Centrale of Florence (Magl. XIX, 91) and the Biblioteca Estense of Modena (ms. a G. 6.5 = It. 197.) The figures follow the text they illustrate, furnishing a model for the illustrators. In the fourth chapter, "merchants and money changers" are represented by the image of a man who "holds a balance with a weight in his right hand & in his left a rod, that is, a braccio-stick. At his belt he has a bag with money counted out to lend to those requesting it." Here the incunabulum updates the text of Jacopo da Cessole, who calls it a "canna da misurare" (measuring rod) while the printed text reads "*canna ovvero il braccio*" ("rod, that is a braccio-stick"). The man is, in fact, shown inside a shop or a bank. The measuring rod was the tool used by cloth merchants, while the bag is the attribute of the money changer. "All of them must flee avarice; stay out of debt; bear witness to and keep promises; and give back entirely the money that has been entrusted to them." The author develops the theme of avarice, or greed, through different examples, but does not discuss dealing in money as such, and the profession of merchant-banker is not one of those automatically deemed sinful. The figure of the man, however, evokes a subject well known at the time, the *Calling of St. Matthew*. The tax collector who followed Christ is often represented in the act of leaving his bench, as in the 14th-century painting for the pillar of the Arte del Cambio in the Florentine church of Orsanmichele (fig. p. 39).

Philine Helas

Bibliography: Jacopo da Cessole (c. 1300), ed. Marocco 1829, p. 85.

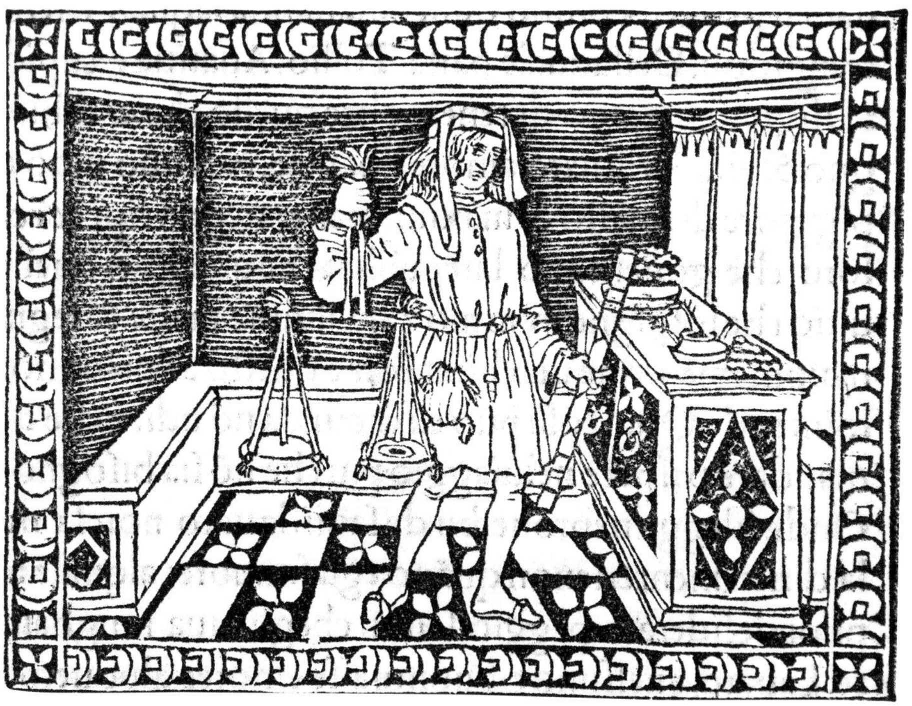

4.2
Anonymous Florentine engraver
Bankers at Work in the Libro di Mercatantie et usanze de paesi
Florence [Bartoleomeo de' Libri], for Piero Pacini da Pescia
c. 1490
woodcut
154 x 104 mm
Florence, Biblioteca Nazionale Centrale, Palat. E.6.4.95, fol. 1r

Beginning with the words, "this is a book on commerce and the customs of countries," the text is one of a genre called *Pratiche di mercanzia* [Merchant handbooks] that became popular in medieval times in the Italian trade centres, Florence, Genoa and Venice in particular. These texts were manuals compiled by merchants as guides for commercial purposes, describing the European and Middle Eastern markets and their economies, such as the currency in use, the other currencies accepted, the system of measurement employed and its corresponding values, the products available and their quality. The most famous Florentine treatise is the *Pratica della mercatura* by Francesco Balducci Pegolotti, who was born in 1310 and died in 1347 (Balducci Pegolotti [c. 1335–43], ed. Evans 1936).

Three manuscripts of "mercatantie et usanze de paesi" have survived. The oldest is the Panciatichiano 72 in the Biblioteca Nazionale di Firenze (BNCF) dated 1458; then there is a 15th-century codex in the Paris BNF (ms. Ital. 911) and another copy in the BNCF (Magliabechiano 203, class XXIX) bearing the date 1483. This manuscript, which belonged to Francesco del Pugliese, contains a medallion with a miniature portrait, accompanied by the name "Giorgio di lo Chiarini." On this basis, the authorship of the treatise has been attributed to Giorgio Chiarini. It should however be considered a collective work, which was used also by Pegolotti, a compendium of knowledge on business and commerce. Such information had previously been transmitted through the shops or families of merchants and bankers, but this treatise was soon printed in several editions, the first book of its kind to become a best-seller (*El libro* [c. 1458], ed. Borlandi 1936). The earliest printed edition dates from 1481, when the text appeared as part of Luca Pacioli's *Summa de arithmetica* (*Distinctio* IX, *Tractatus* XII), which was published in many editions, ensuring vast circulation of the merchants' handbook as well. The second edition, not dated, was printed by Bartolomeo de' Libri, probably in 1490; the third was printed in Parma in 1498.

The woodcut shows the interior of a shop, introducing us to the world of merchants and bankers. The little volume, in reduced format, was designed to be used as a handbook, brought along on voyages and utilized not only in strictly commercial negotiations but also by the traveller curious to know "tucti e cho[s]tumi, cambi, monete pesi, misure et usanze di lectere di cambi et termini di decte lectere che ne' paesi si chostuma et in diverse terre" ("all of the customs, currency exchange rates, coins, weights, measurements and methods of reading exchange rates and terms of such reading in use in the different lands and countries") .

Philine Helas

Bibliography: *El libro* (c. 1458), ed. Borlandi 1936.

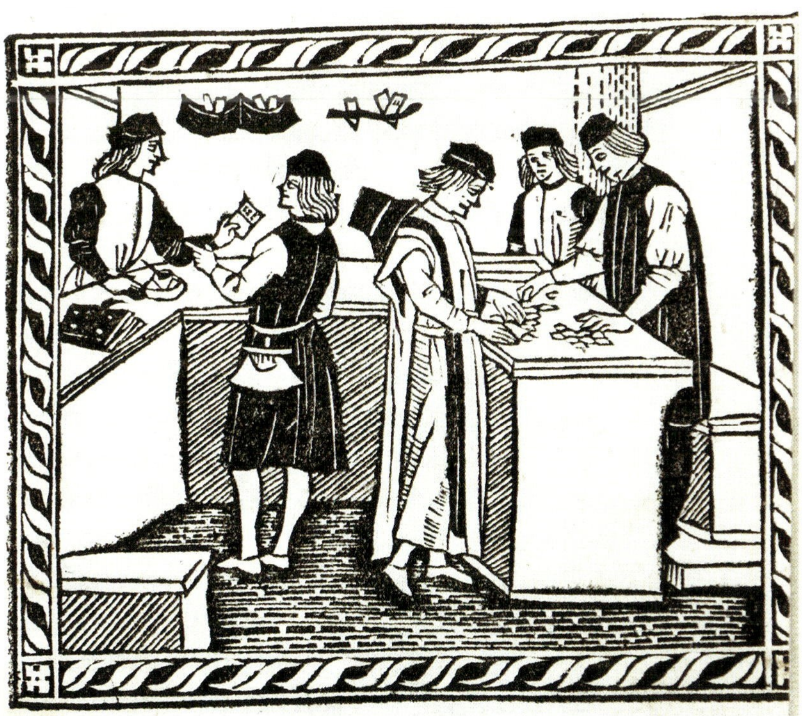

4.3
Filippo Calandri
Treatise on Arithmetic
late 15th century
manuscript on parchment; binding restored (2000) in blue velvet on panels; fols. XII, 110
170 x 110 mm
Florence, Biblioteca Riccardiana, Ricc. 2669

The text of this little abacus book has been attributed to Filippo Calandri, based on an incunabulum printed in Florence in 1491 dedicated to Giuliano, the future Duke of Nemours, born in 1479 (Calandri). The exquisitely crafted manuscript, probably very similar to the printed edition, shows how the practice of commerce, source of the Medici wealth, was deemed fundamental to the education of a young son of the family destined to occupy a prominent position in society.

The pagination of the little codex is finely done, and the abundant references to heraldry show that economic and political power had become closely interwoven. The pages are filled with emblems, coats of arms, and heraldic devices: first among them the burning bough entwined with roses, alluding to Lorenzo and Clarice Orsini, the parents of the young man for whom the book was made; then the diamond-tipped ring with the falcon and three plumes, emblems of Cosimo the Elder, and other Laurentian devices subtly alluding to the struggle and triumph of knowledge over ignorance, a theme most appropriate to education.

Preceding the text is an image of Pythagoras at work in his study, appearing in the typical iconography of the humanist man of letters, again with the aim of glorifying the erudite patron of the arts, direct heir to the virtues and knowledge of antiquity. Even culture could serve as political propaganda, and its importance was acknowledged as the indispensable point of departure for a future ruler.

The illustrations consist mainly of "trading" scenes, vivacious, realistic sketches filled with images of fabrics, bales of goods and merchant's benches, visual documentation of the fervent activity carried out in the city, aware that its power and wealth were based on manufacturing and trade.

From the splendid first pages containing the tables, similar in imagery to the liturgical tables in evangelisteries, the tone becomes pleasantly discursive, but never stylistically remarkable, in the many little scenes illustrating the text, intended to present studies perhaps found boring in a more entertaining light. In the last folios, the presence of the Dell'Antella coat of arms in one of the pendentives of the loggia suggests close ties with a family always linked to the Medici. The two families had children of the same age, and may have been brought into daily contact by their friendship (Giovanni dell'Antella was born in 1475). A hypothetical attribution to Boccardino the Elder should perhaps be changed to one or more of his assistants, familiar with his style but also with Attavante's work, interpreting the scenes with that pleasant, discursive air reminiscent of certain cycles of Florentine frescoes.

Giovanna Lazzi

Bibliography: D'Ancona 1914, I, pp. 839–40, no. 1637; Scuricini Greco 1958, pp. 277–80, no. 296; Calandri (*ante* 1491), ed. Arrighi 1969; *Lorenzo Ghiberti* 1978, p. 308; Van Egmond 1981, p. 159; *Testimonianze medicee* 1997, pp. 33–6, no. 6; *Immaginare l'autore* 1998, pp. 61–2, no. 4; *Le Biblioteche* 1998, pp. 132–4; *Il Rinascimento in Italia* 2001, pp. 82–3; Calandri (*ante* 1491), facs. ed. 2002; Lazzi, Salavaert, Ciardi Duprè Dal Poggetto 2002; *Firenze* 2004, pp. 167–9; *The Splendour* 2008, p. 59.

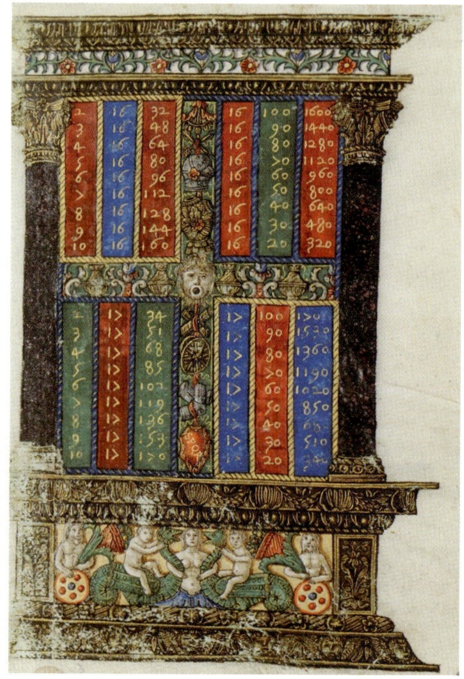

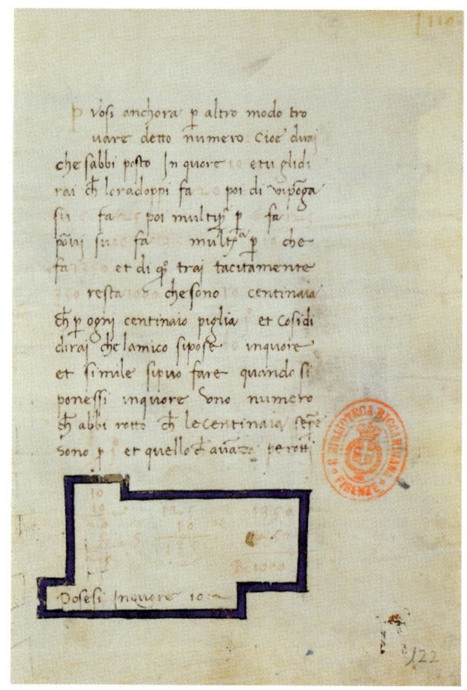

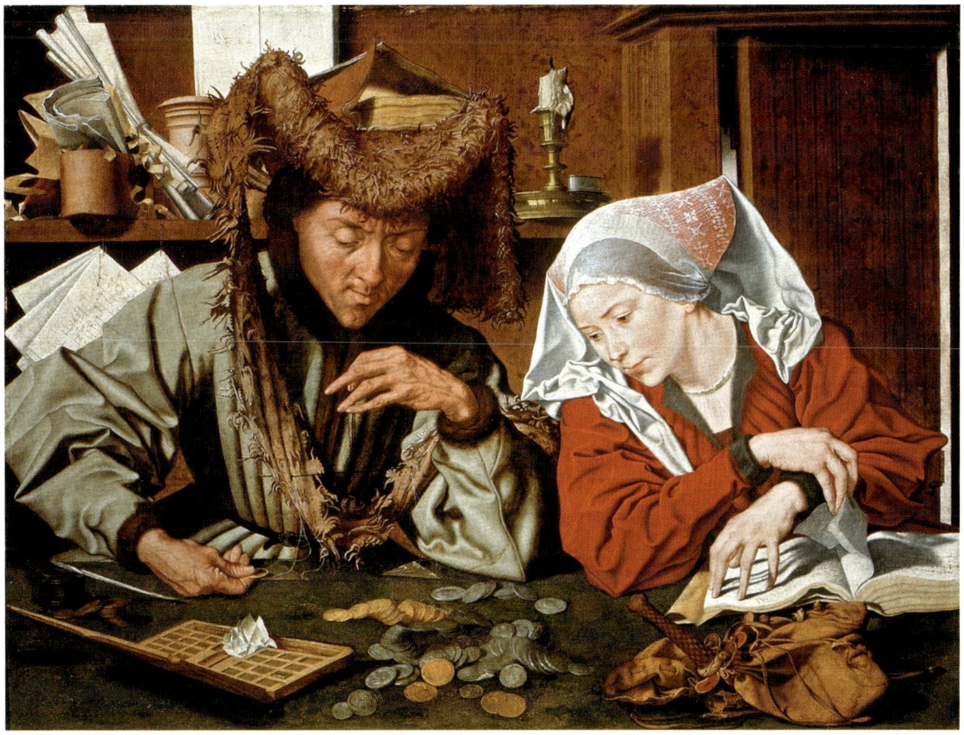

4.4
Marinus van Reymerswaele (Reymerswaele *c.* 1490–Middelburg, documented up to 1567)
The Money Changer and his Wife
1540
oil on panel
84 x 114 cm
Florence, Museo Nazionale del Bargello, Carrand Legacy, inv. 2058 C

Signed and dated 1540, as appears on the scroll hanging on the back wall, this painting—which arrived at the Bargello in 1889 with the entire collection of Louis Carrand—owes its fascination to a setting rendered in minute detail, offering a palpably real, almost "live" perception of the scene represented. Starting in the mid-1530s, Marinus van Reymerswaele, one of the most vivacious figures in Flemish art, painted numerous replicas of this subject, distinguished by a few variants, found today in the world's most important museums. The artist was inspired by a painting of the same subject done by Quentin Metsys in 1514, now at the Louvre (cf. p. 18), which derived in turn from a lost prototype by Jan van Eyck, as can be seen by the style of the clothing and headdresses, no longer fashionable in the mid-15th century but dating instead from nearly a hundred years earlier. As stated in the title, the subject of the painting is a money changer, a leading figure in medieval and renaissance mercantile society, with his young wife. Comparable in many ways to bankers, money changers played a major role in international trade, exchanging foreign money for the local currency for the merchants who flocked to the great European fairs.

Portrayed with the minute, realistic detail of Flemish tradition, the husband and wife appear intent on counting, with subtle greed, the coins spread out on the table in the foreground. Special attention is focused on the symbolic significance of their hands: marked by the years, those of the man, who is weighing a coin on a little balance; softer and whiter, but almost rapacious, those of his wife, who is holding the account book. On the shelf behind them, splendid "still life" touches appear in the disorderly array of letters, sheets of paper and objects of daily use. The extinguished candle, eloquently symbolic, is placed to the right but positioned, not by chance, between the husband and wife, alluding to the brevity of life. The composition is in fact based on a recurrent theme of Flemish painting from the first half of the 16th century, the representation of merchants, bankers and usurers, surrounded by the tools of their trade or by their wealth but also by objects that allegorically symbolize the vanity of human existence. These are not mere traditional portraits, but expressions of a moralistic line of painting that, in keeping with the more radical currents of Lutheran thought, visualized the condemnation of commerce, deemed a vehicle of greed leading to immoral consequences.

Ilaria Ciseri

Bibliography: S. Castri in *Arti del Medio Evo* 1989, pp. 384–5; E. Carrara in *La storia del Bargello* 2004, pp. 296–7.

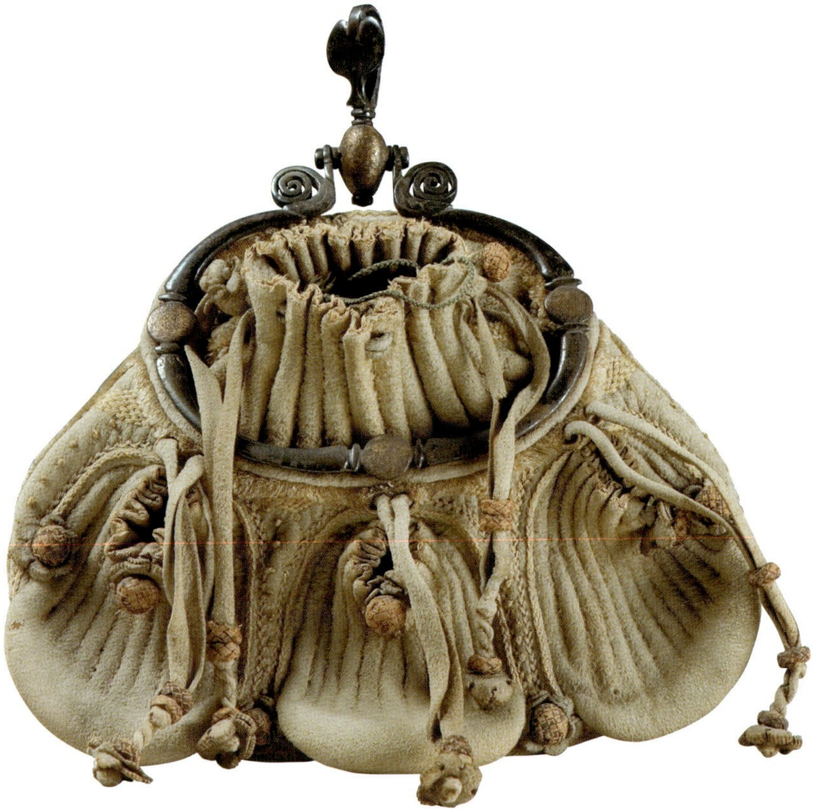

4.5
Flemish or French art
Chamois leather money-bag with eight pockets
16th century
embroidered leather; forged, burnished
and gilt metal
28 x 26 cm
Firenze, Museo Nazionale del Bargello,
inv. no. 1810 C

Among the rare "Works in leather and parchment" donated by Louis Carrand to the Museo Nazionale del Bargello in 1889 is this singular leather purse, dating from the 16th century. Few such purses have survived to our own day. As objects used in everyday life, they were subject to severe wear and deterioration. Moreover, being made of inexpensive materials, they were not deemed worthy of any special attention, and were not preserved. In the past, the term *scarsella* indicated a purse used mainly by merchants and travellers. It is described in the dictionary compiled by the Accademia della Crusca, already in its first edition of 1612, as follows: "A kind of leather pocket, or bag, sewn to an opening made of iron or other metal, used to carry money." The etymology of the word *scarsella* evokes the Provencal *escarsela*, sometimes thought to derive from the Latin *scarpsus*, "scarce," and hence indicating a bag used to keep small change. The Old German *scherbe*, which meant pocket, is another possible source of derivation.

The Bargello bag is a classic *scarsella*. It consists of an elliptical ring of wrought iron with six pockets hanging from it, three at the back and three at the front, fastened with leather laces ending in tassels shaped like flowers or balls, their contours marked by embroidery. At the centre of the metal ring is a large pocket, containing another smaller one, probably serving to secure more safely the money or valuable objects—sometimes even relics—placed in them.

The most elaborate workmanship is found in the iron element, whose circumference is decorated with three gilt disks. It terminates in two curls, connected to a mechanism consisting of an oval-shaped bulge traversed by a pin, then continues upward to form a ring, embellished on the front by a little heart-shaped plaque. Through this ring passed a belt securing the bag to the traveller's body, or a string hung round his neck. The experts believe this purse to be a French-Flemish production of the 16th century, also based on analogous figurative elements found in the paintings of the time. A very similar bag, from which a money changer has just taken the coins to be weighed in the balance, appears in the right foreground of the painting by Marinus van Reymerswaele displayed in this exhibition (no. 4.4).

Ilaria Ciseri

Bibliography: Supino 1898, p. 267; F. Guidi Bruscoli in *Arti del Medio Evo* 1989, pp. 471–2; *Les marchands* 2002, p. 174, no. 53; H. Derschka in *Bayern-Italien* 2010, p. 114, no. F45.

4.6
German artist (Nuremberg?)
Balance for gold and gemstones owned by Hans II Harsdorf
1497
wooden case covered with painted paper; iron; partially gilded silver; yarn; needlepoint pearl
17.4 x 10.3 x 2.5, height of bipartite rod (without base) 22.8 cm, diameter of scale-pans 2 cm
Nuremberg, Germanisches Nationalmuseum, HG 11 161
property of the Freiherrliche Harsdorfsche Familienstiftung

This measuring instrument, used to weigh gold and gemstones, is in itself an object of great value. Dated on the top of the case "1 · 4 · 9 · 7," it is the earliest surviving example of a dated balance (Rosenberg 1910, pp. 46–7, fig. 40). Commissioned by Hans II Harsdorfer († 1511) and owned later by the Barons of Harsdorf at Fischbach near Nuremberg, it has been displayed at the Germanisches Nationalmuseum since 1962, on loan from the family. The client who commissioned it, owner of a copper foundry at Enzensdorf near Nuremberg and a silver mine in Bohemia, belonged to that elite group of entrepreneurs and bankers who played important roles in the financial administration of the Empire and the imperial city (Reichsstadt) of Nuremberg. Under King Ladislaus II, Harsdorf was also appointed head Mint Master (Oberster Münzmeister) of Bohemia, so that, from 1496 to 1499, he directed not only the mints but also the mines of Bohemia. In 1497 he was appointed head Mint Master for Nuremberg as well, where he settled in 1499.

This balance was thus commissioned at the height of Hans Harsdorf's career, to showcase not only his vast wealth but also his family pride. The painted decoration focuses on heraldic themes. On the top of the case, against a dark green floral-pattern background, two wild men (*Wilde Männer*), bearded and hairy, are fighting with swords. Above the fastener appears the date. Both the men and the floral pattern resemble those in the portrait of the rich merchant Oswald Krell painted by Albrecht Dürer in 1499. In sharp contrast to this duelling scene, two elegantly dressed Lansquenets appear on the inside, against a blue background with gilt floral motifs. They each hold a dagger and a halberd in one hand, in the other a laurel wreath with the Harsdorfer and Nützel heraldic arms (the latter pertaining to Margarete, daughter of the *Sculdascio* Gabriel Nützel and wife of Hans Harsdorf since 1481), crowned with a crest and red and white plumes. On their shirts appear the initials "AT" and "KAG," which have not yet been deciphered.

The inscriptions are especially interesting. On the surface of the silver-gilt base appear the arms of the Harsdorf and Nützel families, hanging from a leather belt inscribed with the initials "·I· ·E· ·F· ·H·." The tongs used for handling the tiny weights bear the inscription: "Jhs + Autem + Transiens + Permedium + Illorum + Ibat" (Luca IV: 30): a formula used in the Middle Ages to seek protection from the dangers of travelling, assault in particular. On the opposite side appears a battle cry: "Xpvs [Christus] Vincit · Xpvs Regnat · Xpvs Imperat." The anonymous artist thus proclaims through images and words not only the wealth of Hans II Harsdorfer but also his prowess in *arma et litterae*.

Nicole Hegener

Bibliography: Kohlhaussen 1968, pp. 280–1, cat. 340; F. Irsigler in *Martin Luther* 1983, p. 28, no. 20; R. Kahsnitz in *Nürnberg* 1986, pp. 218–9, cat. no.+ 77; S. Witt in *Heiliges Römisches Reich* 2006, p. 63, no. I.46.

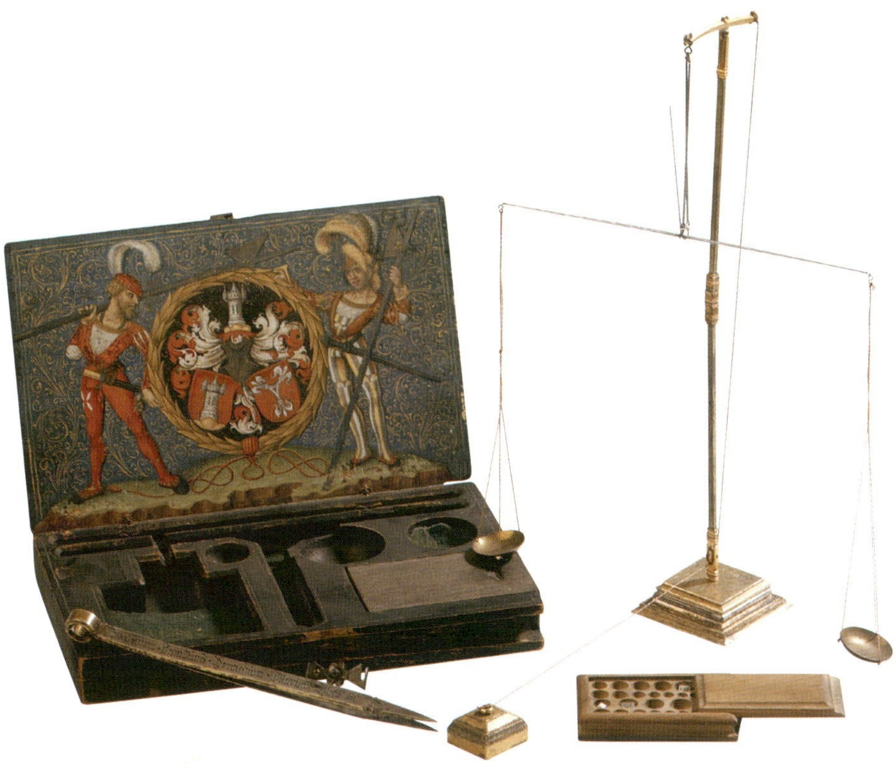

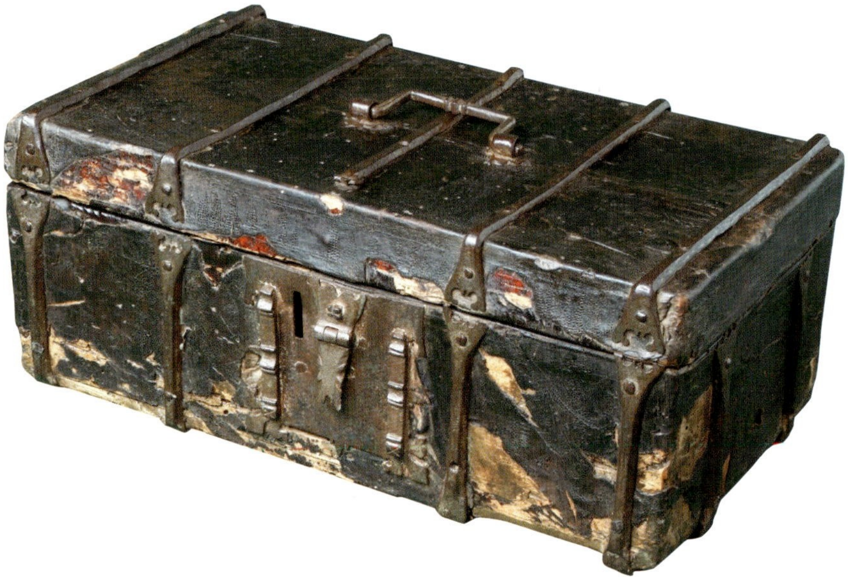

4.7
Casket/strong-box
14th–15th centuries
wood covered in tooled leather
15 x 38 x 22.5 cm
Florence, Museo di Palazzo Davanzati,
inv. no. 22

The casket/strongbox from the Museo di Palazzo Davanzati is made of wood covered in leather reinforced by hinged iron bars. The tooled leather is decorated with tiny floral motifs cut with a punch, or some other sharp instrument such as the tooth of a carnivorous animal. The front of the lid once bore a brief inscription, probably a motto; only a few letters of it remain, barely decipherable. In late medieval Florence, strong-boxes of this type were produced by the Chiavaioli, the locksmiths' independent guild, or the Fibbiai (buckle-makers), a branch of the Fabbri (smiths) with the collaboration of the Cuoiai (leather-workers), who furnished the raw material for the covering. A glance at the numerous inventories and notarized deeds conserved in Tuscan archives shows surprising variety in these containers for money, documents or jewellery, which for their practical function might be thought to differ little from one another.

As shown by the documents, these portable coffers were produced in France, mainly in Lyon, in other countries such as Spain and Flanders, and in Venice. The stylistic and structural features of the Palazzo Davanzati strong-box seem to indicate a Spanish provenance, in comparing it to the coffer (18.4 x 28 x 17.8 cm) sold at auction by Christie's in London on November 5, 2009 (lot 64), differing in the lid but similar in the iron bars, the processing of the leather and the type of decoration. An inventory of the furniture conserved at Lucca, in the Ospedale della Misericordia (A.S.L., Spedale di San Luca, 268), drawn up in 1391, lists "an iron-bound vermillion casket; two vair caskets; a long, narrow iron-bound casket." These were small strong-boxes of different shape, one coloured red while the other two had painted "vair" decoration, which could mean, if understood in the natural sense, white and black; or in the heraldic sense, azure and argent, or azure and white. At a later time, as demonstrated by the examples displayed, objects of this type, often called *cofani*, or coffers, were usually covered in hide or leather. A notarial deed compiled in Lucca in 1572 lists a coffer "of black leather barred in iron" (A.S.L., Archivio dei Notari I, 3845, fol. 91). In the same Lucca Archive there appear, in the second half of the 16th century, coffers of "red dressed leather," "calfskin," "studded red dressed leather," "red leather trimmed with decorative iron," as well as a "small coffer of inlaid bone; a little coffer inlayed with ivory, antique-style." Less clear are the descriptions of an "iron-bound Lyon" coffer; two "black Lyon coffers," and "5 Lyon coffers, one bound in iron, and a Venetian coffer." These were strong-boxes and caskets of various sizes with features characteristic of their places of provenance, whose typical aspects are still unclear. In the inventories and other notarized deeds preserved in the State Archive of Siena, coffers are frequently mentioned—in Latin the object is almost always called *ghoffinus*—but since this term is used for containers of all types, large or small, without further specification, it is hard to understand for what purpose they were used. See for example the *duos ghoffinos* listed in a document dated May 8, 1426 (A.S.Si, Notarile ante-cosimiano 333, cc. 6v-8v).

Romano Silva

Bibliography: *Palazzo Davanzati* 1986, p. 42.

4.8
Florentine workshop
Document box belonging to the Cavalcanti family
third or fourth quarter of the 15th century
wood, cast iron, tooled leather, leather tanned with rock alum
15 x 51.4 x 29 cm
Cerreto Guidi (Firenze), Museo Storico della Caccia e del Territorio, deposit from the Galleria e Museo di Palazzo Mozzi Bardini, inv. Bd. 5822

This object, referred to simply as a box, because of its flattened parallelepiped form, but more properly a case or casket, belonged to the Florentine family of the Cavalcanti. It may have been designed to hold a volume, such as an account book that had to be kept confidential, a likely possibility since it has a compartment that could have held writing materials. On the other hand, it may have been used to keep money, documents and small valuable objects. In the numerous notarial inventories that have survived, terms such as *scrigno* (casket) and *cofano* (coffer) or more generically *cassa* (strongbox), are used indiscriminately to indicate containers that, apart from sturdy locks, had no particular systems to keep out intruders. Moreover, the Latin term *arca* covers all of these meanings. Such objects, in fact, follow a line of continuity from Roman antiquity to the 16th century, when chests with much more sophisticated locking systems came into use, evolving later to become the modern safe. For example, the strong-box found in Villa B at Oplontis, not far from Pompeii, filled with coins and jewellery, is lined with wood on the inside, while the outside, including the lid hinged onto the body, is covered with bronze and iron platelets fastened with rows of bronze-headed nails inserted to form geometric motifs. The lid and front were decorated with bronze *appliqués*. Although sturdiness might seem more important than appearance in these containers, their elegance and beauty increased still further in the Middle Ages. The *scrinium* owned by Cardinal Guala Bicchieri (*c.* 1150–1227), now in the Museo Civico d'Arte Antica of Turin, is exemplary for its exceptionally fine decoration in Limoges enamel. Cardinal Guala's will, dating from 1227, the year of his death, lists three *scrinei* (caskets) and two *cophani* (coffers), apparently quite similar to one another, with some shades of meaning perhaps determined more by size than by structure.

While modern systems for safeguarding money and jewels are based mainly on a robust outer shell, devoid of any decorative element, from classical times up to and throughout the 17th century, a container for precious objects or money devoid of elegance and refined workmanship was unthinkable, showing a relationship between the container and the contents entirely extraneous to the functionalism of modern thought. This "box" too, in the refined elegance of its decoration, appears to favour ornamental beauty over security. In addition to vine tendrils, the decoration includes two candelabra with cherubs and horse-head escutcheons within garlands, with the crosslets pattées characteristic of the Cavalcanti heraldic arms, and is completed by a motto: "VIRTUS/VIVET/ IN ETERNUM IN D[EO]." The borders are made of the so-called boiled leather, produced by heating calfskin in a mixture of wax, rubber, resin and glue to reinforce it, as the Romans did with the leather used for armour. Neither the devotional nature of the inscription nor the presence of the cherubs can be considered as proof that the object belonged to an ecclesiastic.

Romano Silva

Bibliography: Scalini 2005, pp. 44–5.

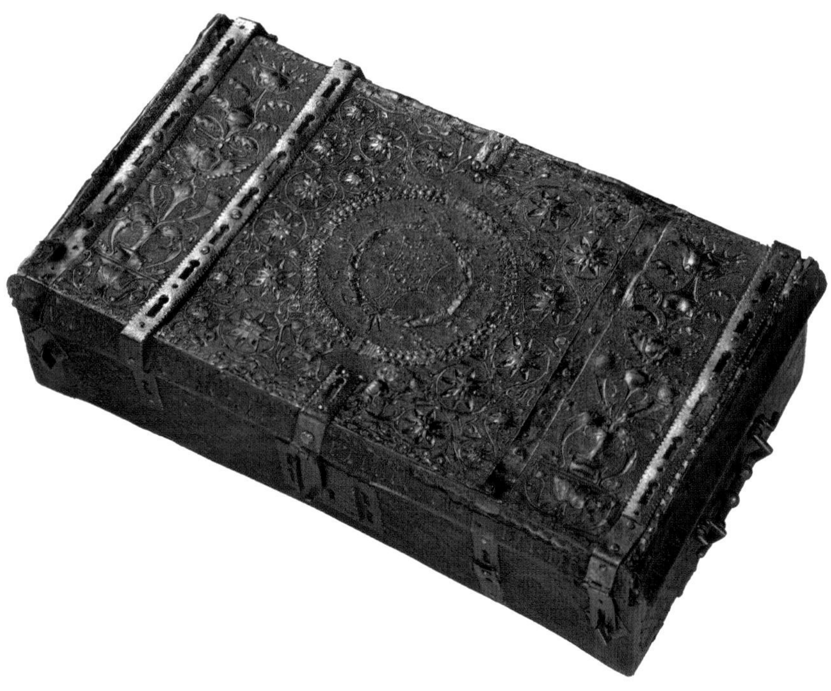

4.9
Safe
16th century
iron, wood
43.5 x 87 x 43 cm
Lucca, Museo di Villa Guinigi, inv. no. 314

In the 16th century strong-boxes, safes and locking methods in general were revolutionized by the introduction of elaborate, innovative locking systems such as the "multiple bolt." This ingenious system, probably invented in Nuremberg, spread to Bavaria when Michael Mann's important workshop moved to Augsburg, and to Brescia, where iron, the necessary raw material, was readily abundant. Some of these strong-boxes had parts made of steel, gilt copper and brass. Of the two wood-and-iron safes in the Museo Nazionale di Villa Guinigi in Lucca, the one shown here originally belonged to the Pia Casa di Beneficienza, and was purchased in 1929. On the outside, thin strips of metal are interwoven to form a pattern of orthogonal lines with an imitation lock at the centre, a trick designed to make anyone trying to rob the safe waste precious time. The real lock, opened by a key, is found instead at the centre of the lid, concealed by a camouflaged iron plaque opened by pressing an inconspicuous little button at a certain distance from the lock. When the key is turned, the bolts locking the lid to the edges of the box at various points slide open. The multiple bolts serve not so much to complicate the opening of the strongbox as to make it very hard to break into.

Although these objects served an eminently practical purpose, they are not devoid of decoration. For example the security elements, such as reinforcing bands and groups of springs and bolts controlled by the key, are often arranged to form decorative patterns. Surprisingly, a picture sometimes appears inside, as is the case with the other safe in the Villa Guinigi Museum, whose provenance is unknown (inv. no. 244). The front of the box, apparently integral with the frame, can instead be lifted, revealing a monochrome painting in red lead depicting a horseman galloping through grapevine and pomegranate tendrils of gigantic size, evocative of Bosch's *Garden of Earthly Delights*. Who was this ingenious, unexpected *divertissement* painted for? Considering that, for obvious reasons, the safe was opened exclusively, with rare and well-motivated exceptions, by its owner, it is curious to think of him placing gold and silver coins and jewellery in the safe while gazing with pleasure at the secret painting.

Romano Silva

Bibliography: *Museo di Villa Guinigi* 1968, p. 188.

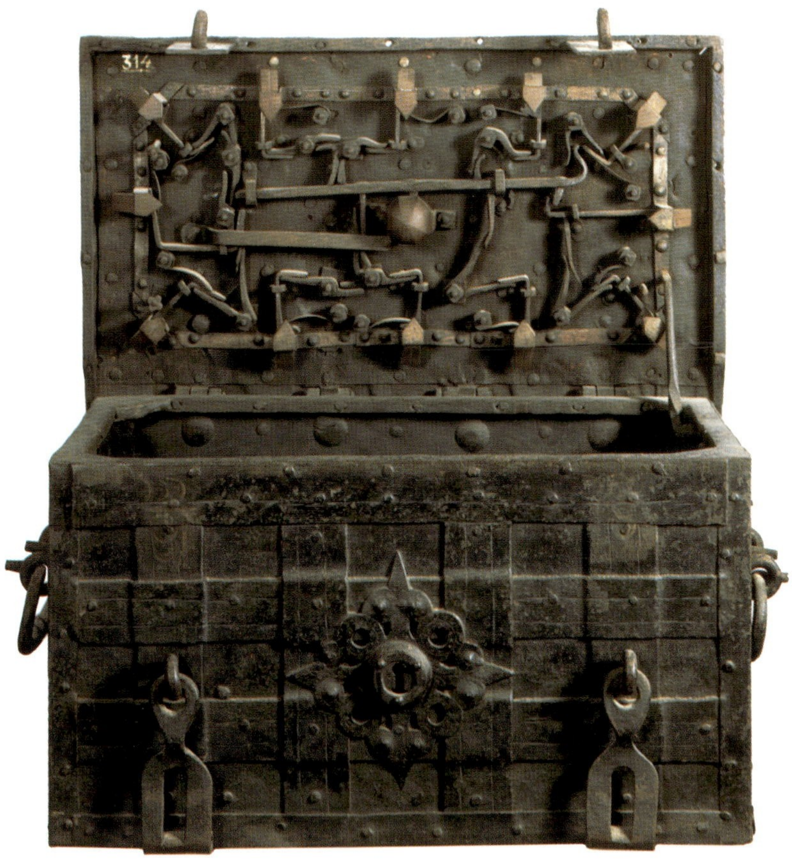

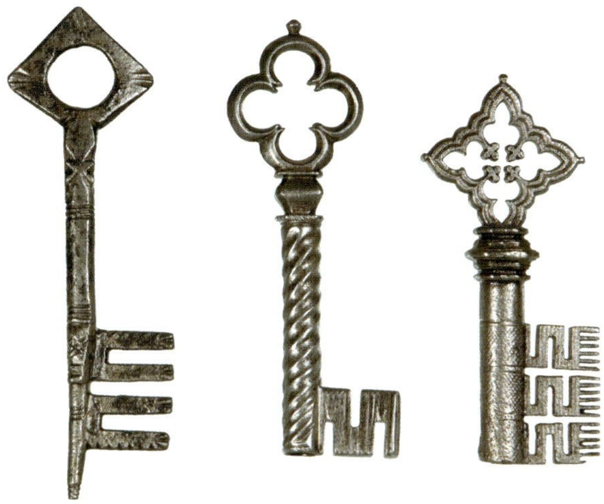

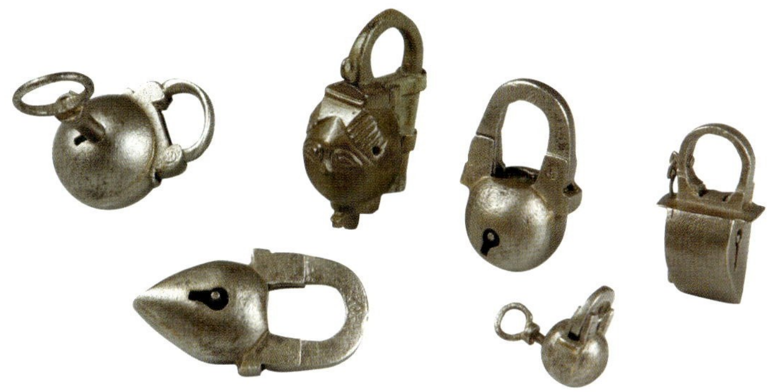

4.10
Italian art
Keys
13th century (a); 14th century (b-c)
iron; 13 cm (a, key-bit 3.2 cm); 11.5 cm (b, key-bit 1.8 cm); 10.2 cm (c, key-bit 3.8 cm)
Florence, Museo Nazionale del Bargello, inv. nos. 1460 C, 1465 C, 1464 C

4.11
French art
Six padlocks
13th century (a); 15th century (b-c-d-e-f)
bronze (a); iron (b-c-d-e-f); 4.5 x 3 cm (a); 2.1 x 16 cm (b); 3.6 x 2.3 cm (c); 3.7 x 2.1 cm (d); 4.2 x 2.5 cm (e); 5 x 2.5 cm (f)
Florence, Museo Nazionale del Bargello, inv. nos. 1449 C, 1450 C, 1451 C, 1452 C, 1453 C, 1454 C

The key is an object that no one, today as yesterday, can do without. At the same time it has a high symbolic value, reaching its apex in the papal emblem of the "keys of St. Peter." The key is in fact a symbol of power, possession, and wealth; and it is for this reason that such an imminently utilitarian object has often been beautifully decorated to underline its importance. The Carrand Collection at the Museo del Bargello contains some thirty keys, including French keys from the 11th and 12th centuries. The keys displayed here represent the evolution of this object from the 14th to the 16th century. The oldest key, made of chased wrought iron, dates from the 14th century but has 13th-century features. Of Italian make, it is simple and elegant with a bow shaped like a flattened lozenge and a bipartite key-bit adorned with indentation. The second key, almost certainly Italian, has a four-foiled haft connected by a prismatic node to a slender rod with spiral grooving. The 15th-century key, also Italian, is more elaborate, being made of forged and wrought iron with a mixtilineal lozenge-shaped ring divided into four trefoil sections and a fretted tripartite key-bit terminating in a comb-like structure. Very different and less elaborate is the short-stem French key from the 16th century (inv. no. 1463 C), whose round bow contains an openwork shield reminiscent of heraldic arms. These four examples clearly reveal the affinity between keys, which constitute an integral part of locks, and the goldsmith's art. In these devices the decorative aspect coexists with functional and mechanical features whose complexity, reflected in the key-bits, seems influenced at times by the science of applied mathematics.

A special type of hanging lock, usually quite small, is the padlock. Six padlocks coming from the Museo del Bargello are displayed here. In eastern countries, the padlock was as finely crafted as a goldsmith's piece, as demonstrated by the one securing the door of the Kaaba at Mecca. In the Western World it was a poor relative, mentioned rather often starting from the 16th century, although Byzantine padlocks have been found in excavating the Palazzo delle Blacherne in Constantinople. They must have been used in the capital of the Eastern Empire for much the same purpose as in Rome, that is, to lock cupboards containing food, a usage also documented in the courts of medieval kings. Padlocks, as can be seen from these examples, existed in a vast range of shapes: round, heart-shaped, triangular, in the form of an escutcheon, an egg, or an acorn; globular, circular, etc. The padlock, limited by its size to a few mechanical components, is easier to open than locks with complex, ingenious mechanisms. For this reason padlocks were used to protect things that were necessary but not highly valuable, such as food, or to conceal from sight objects to be kept private, but unlikely to be stolen.

Romano Silva

Bibliography: *La storia del Bargello* 2004, pp. 208–9.

4.12-4.13
Messenger's dispatch bags
late 15th–early 16th century
leather, velvet
19.5 x 20.5 cm
Florence, Museo Nazionale del Bargello,
inv. nos. 1338 C, 1339 C

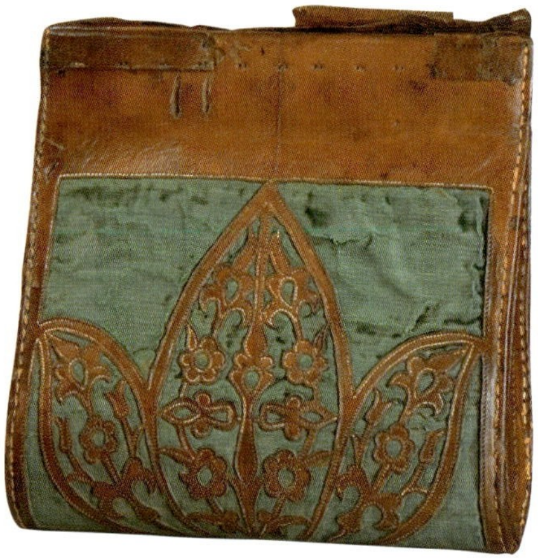

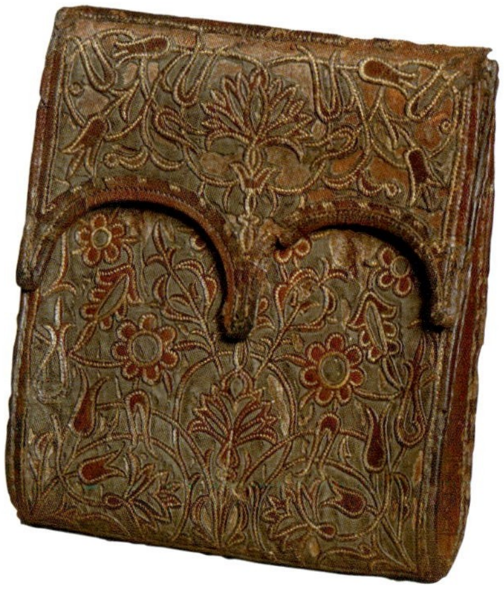

The two messenger's dispatch bags in the Museo Nazionale del Bargello document a type widely used in the 15th–16th century. Few examples of these bags have survived, due to the perishable nature of leather and the relentless dispersion of everyday objects over the course of time. The two bags are in a moderately good state of conservation, although some parts are missing. Specifically, the first bag (4.12) has lost the closure flap, while the other is complete as a whole, but the fabric and leather are severely deteriorated, partially obscuring the refined plant-and-floral motif decoration.

Bags of various types, serving different functions, were a necessary fashion accessory from the 14th century to at least the middle of the 16th, since pockets sewn inside clothing had not yet come into use. Bags, carried mainly by men, became a distinctive element of the upper classes (Levi Pisetzky 1964–9, II, 1964; Wilcox 1999). Messenger's dispatch bags, of rectangular shape and rigid structure, were perfectly suited to carrying documents, letters and papers. The opening at the top, protected by a flap, provided rapid access to the content while ensuring its safe transport. The form of a bag differed according to its use, ranging from almoners, used to carry money, to *scarselle*, soft purses, sometimes having pockets, closed by sliding laces (see for example item 4.5 in this catalogue, and see Goretti 2006).

In the field of commerce, rapidity, security and secrecy in exchanging information were crucial to the success of negotiations, and the time taken up in negotiating severely affected the profit that could be earned on foreign exchange transactions. Messengers' pockets were worn at the belt, hung through loops sewn onto the back, as can still be seen today in the green velvet pocket, while on the other, only the mark of the seam that originally fastened the loops remains today. The position of the pocket, so close to the body, was a further guarantee of safety as compared to bags hung round the neck. Contemporary sources frequently mention the cutpurses who, concealed in the crowd, cut off leather and fabric bags to steal their contents (Levi Pisetzky 1964–9; Wilcox 1999). The shape of these pockets had to comply with practical requisites and the decoration was simpler than that of contemporary "ceremonial" bags or purses used almost as personal embellishment (see for example item 6.4), with a preference for such resistant materials as leather, decorated only on the front. In the case of these two bags, the decoration consisted not of embroidery or precious yarns but of leather punched in a plant or floral motif, applied to a velvet ground. The effect, thanks to the vividly contrasting colours, is striking and elegant, as can be seen in the first bag. In the second bag the decoration, more graphic and minute, now appears somewhat flattened, due to the state of conservation of the fabric.

Both bags may be assumed to date from the late 15th-early 16th century. No specific provenance can be determined, given the wide circulation of these objects (Supino considers them generically as Italian-made). These two bags come from the Louis Carrand collection, which was donated to the Bargello in 1888. The Lyonese collector left no information on the provenance of the works. Despite the vast iconographic testimony on purses and bags, in both paintings and illuminated manuscripts, only a few medieval and renaissance examples exist today. In this context, the Bargello's collection of over twenty works in leather is of great historical interest.

Benedetta Chiesi

Bibliography: Supino 1898, pp. 306–7, nos. 1338, 1339.

4.14
Letter of exchange from Diamante and Altobianco degli Alberti to Francesco di Marco Datini and Luca del Sera
Bruges–Barcelona
September 2, 1398
sheet of paper
73 x 224 mm
Prato, Archivio di Stato, Datini, b. 1145/1, c. 1403803

Transcription (for the exact transcription see the Italian opposite):
"SC) In the name of God. This day of the 11th of September, 1398. Pay for this first letter, as is the custom, to Filipozzo Soldani four hundred and forty scudos, at a rate of ten and a half soldi per scudo, the which 440 scudos at X 1/2 soldi per scudo are in payment for the money here from Riciardo degli Alberti and company. Pay promptly as due and put on the account here of the friend of the Melline. May Christ protect you. Regards from Diamante and Altobiancho degli Alberti in Bruges.
[in another hand] "Accepted, on XXVIII of September."
Transcription of the reverse:
"Franciesco di Marcho and Lucha del Sera and companions in Barcelona. (SM). First"

The letter of exchange is a banking instrument serving both as tool of credit and means of transferring money. Issued in relation to a currency exchange transaction, it allowed funds to be transferred from one place (*piazza*) to another, in our case from Bruges to Barcelona, with no material transfer of money but only through accounting transactions. This movement of money takes place when the merchant who wishes to send a remittance (here the company of Ricciardo Alberti) deposits the sum to be transferred with a trustworthy merchant-banker (here the company of Diamante and Altobianco Alberti). The merchant-banker compiled the letter of exchange in his own hand, according to a special formula and on a standard paper form, issuing it as an order to pay on the merchant-banker with whom he does business (here the Datini company in Barcelona), indicating the amount of the remittance and its currency (440 scudi), the rate of exchange (10 *soldi* and ½ *denaro* of Barcelona lire per scudo) and the beneficiary (here, Filipozzo Soldani). The date of issue (September 2, 1398) and the number of the letter issued are always specified, and repeated again on the "envelope." It was customary to send several copies (up to four) to ensure that at least one of them would arrive at its destination. Only the copy arriving first was validated, as in this case, by the acceptance formula that allowed the bill to be cashed.

In this case the Datini company in Barcelona then debited the transaction to the account of someone specified only as a "friend of the Melline" (Maline textiles) in Bruges, who had a current account with the company of Diamante and Altobianco degli Alberti.

The Datini Archive, with its 150,000 letters, including well over 50+00 letters of exchange, and its 600 accounting entries, is remarkably complete, allowing us, as in this case, to trace the issuing of our letter of exchange in a missive sent from the Diamante and Altobianco Alberti company to the Datini firm in Barcelona, and to identify with certainty the relevant accounting entries.

Chiara Marcheschi

Bibliography: De Roover 1953, pp. 43–50; *Guida* 1972, pp. 52–63; Melis 1972, pp. 87–103, 98–9, 488–91; Melis 1987; Melis 1990; *L'Archivio* 2004, pp. 189–90; Sosnowski 2006, pp. 51–7; Palermo 2008, pp. 34–43; Goldthwaite 2009, pp. 210–21.

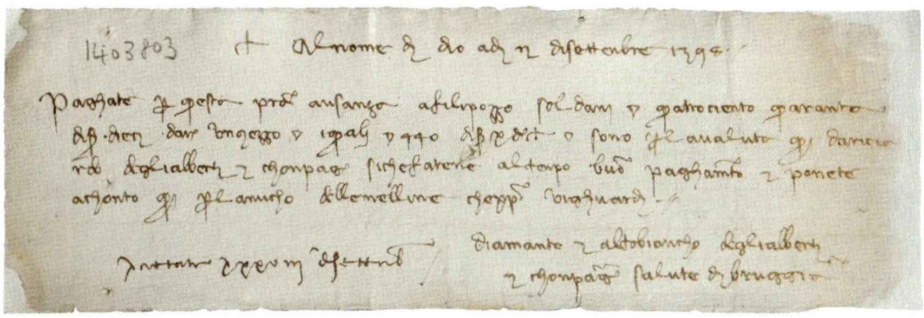

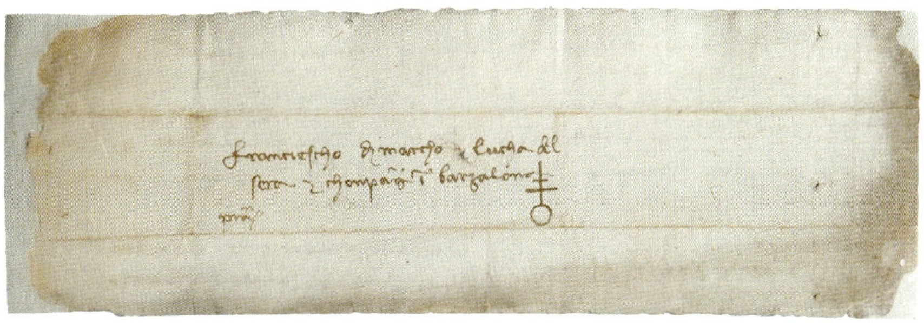

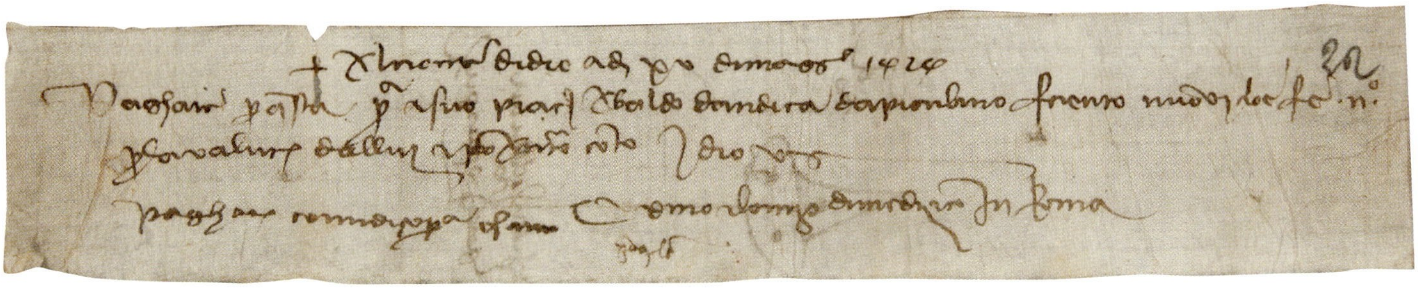

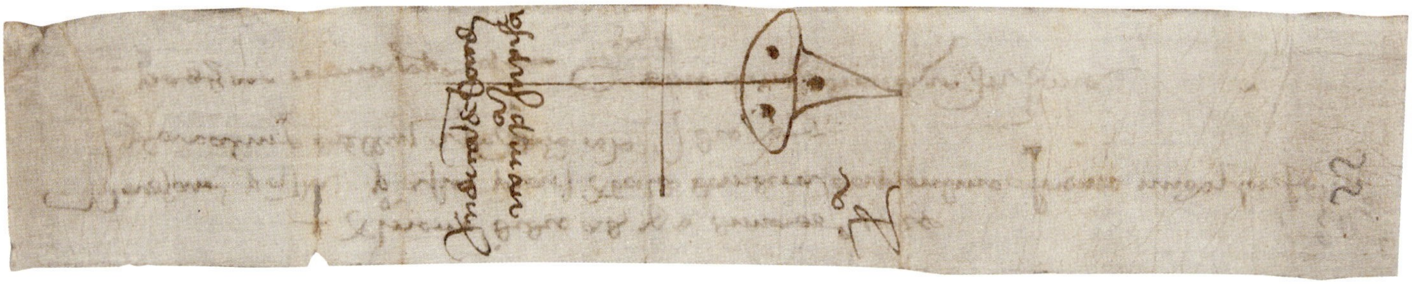

4.15
Letter of exchange from the Medici Bank to Baldo d'Andrea di Piombino
May 15, 1424
sheet of paper; mercantile penmanship; on the back, in addition to the address, the Medici Bank trademark
40 x 225 mm
Florence, Archivio di Stato, Mediceo avanti il Principato 148, no. 22

For the bankers of the Middle Ages and Renaissance, the letter of exchange was the most important tool of work. It could be used to transfer money to another market as well as to extend credit. And by reimbursing a loan in another place and another currency, it was possible to lend money at high interest rates, evading the prohibition of the Church. The letter of exchange, small in format, had a very basic formula, as shown by the example displayed in the exhibition: "Pay for this first order Baldo d'Andrea da Piombino, at his discretion, one hundred new f(lorins) (...) in his currency and charge it to our account," in addition to the conventional heading, "In the name of God, on the 15th day of May 1424," the conventional greeting, "May God keep you" and the signing of the bank's name: "Coximo e Lorenzo de' Medici & C., in Roma." The typical letter of exchange usually involved four persons or firms, but in this case one is missing. Baldo di Andrea da Piombino, in fact, acts as both giver and beneficiary. Furthermore, lacking indication of any different currency in which to effect encashment, this document resembles more a letter of credit, or the modern traveller's cheques, than a letter of exchange strictly speaking.

On the back, in addition to the Medici Bank's trademark, appears the name of the consignee, "Andrea de' Bardi and company in Pisa." It was under this company name in fact, that Averardo di Francesco de' Medici operated. A cousin of Cosimo and Lorenzo, he worked closely with them. In spite of Pisa's commercial importance, Cosimo and Lorenzo did not open their own branch there until 1442, perhaps to avoid competing with their cousin, a trusted collaborator in both politics and finance. Averardo's company in Pisa not only operated as a bank but also traded in wool and other merchandise, issued maritime insurance policies, and so on. Andrea di Lippaccio Bardi, director and junior partner of Averardo's company, was the brother of Benedetto and Ilarione, both general managers of the Medici Bank at different times.

This document is thus an order to pay issued by the Rome branch of the Medici Bank to Averardo's company in Pisa, in favour of Baldo di Andrea da Piombino. It may be seen in relation to another document, conserved in ASF, Diplomatico-Mediceo, May 31, 1425, in which that letter of exchange was protested because the firm Andrea de' Bardi e Compagni had not made the requested payment, and the credit was transferred to the company of Benedetto e Gabriele Borromei, also based in Pisa. Since letters of exchange were written on small strips of paper, they were rather perishable documents, at a time when means of communication were uncertain. Hence it was customary to make a double original; in the case of a second copy, the formula was slightly different from this one, which instead is expressly described as the "first copy."

Vanna Arrighi

Bibliography: *Mostra Medicea* 1939, p. 64; Camerani Marri 1951, p. 40; De Roover 1963, pp. 54–8.

4.16
Account book of Averardo de' Medici's steward
1412–7
register on paper; 212 fols.; contemporary numbering up to fol. 189, other numbers added later; parchment flyleaves; contemporary parchment binding, partially restored; on the front panel, in pen and ink: "Libro del fatore d'Averardo de' Medici. A" [Account Book of Averardo de' Medici's steward]
320 x 250 mm
Florence, Archivio di Stato, Mediceo avanti il Principato 130, fol. 1r

Averardo di Francesco di Averardo, known as Bicci (died 1434) was a cousin of Cosimo the Elder and like him active in commerce and banking, as well as one of the highest tax-payers on land and real estate of 1427. The two cousins, owners of separate enterprises, were however close collaborators in business, and so united in political life that Averardo left Florence to go with his cousins when they were sentenced to exile in 1433. Like them, and as was customary in Florence's mercantile class, he periodically invested some of his earnings in real estate. In his case this consisted mainly of houses, farms and lots in the Mugello area, concentrated around the fortress/villa of Cafaggiolo, near San Piero a Sieve. Described in a report to the land registry in 1427 as "a residence serving as fortress situated in Mugello, in the vicinity of the Pieve di San Giovanni in Petroio, long known as Chafagiuolo, surrounded by a moat," it was grouped with 21 farms, 8 houses and cottages "numerous cultivated fields" as well as "orchards, vineyards, pastures, woods," etc. Most of these holdings operated on the métayage system, where the crops were shared by the landowner and the farmer on an almost equal basis. This kind of farming contract was so widespread in the countryside around Florence that the term *lavoratore* (worker) was perfectly synonymous with *mezzadro* (sharecropper). The owner often had to advance loans to his workers, in money, seeds or other things. In 1430, for example, Averardo de' Medici lent one of his sharecroppers, Jacopo di Tura, who occupied a farm in the area of Santa Maria a Spugnole, 45 florins in cash, 22 bushels of wheat, 4 bushels of other fodder and a pair of oxen (ASF, Catasto 60, fol. 85v). Operating on the métayage system called for the owner's assiduous presence in the background and strict surveillance at the time of sharing the products. The Medici however, deeply engaged in politics, trading and banking, soon took recourse, long before it became customary, to the services of a steward. This was a trustworthy person who administered the farms and recorded in writing the expenses and proceeds, as shown by this account book for the Averardo farms kept by a steward named Jacopo, of whom nothing else is known.

The death of Averardo in 1434 was followed less than two years later by the demise of his son Giuliano, and some eight years later by that of his grandson Francesco. With the death of Francesco, the genealogical line descending from Francesco di Bicci died out, and all of his property, including the fortified villa of Cafaggiolo, was inherited by his cousins Cosimo and Lorenzo di Giovanni.
Vanna Arrighi

Bibliography: Franchetti Pardo, Casali 1978.

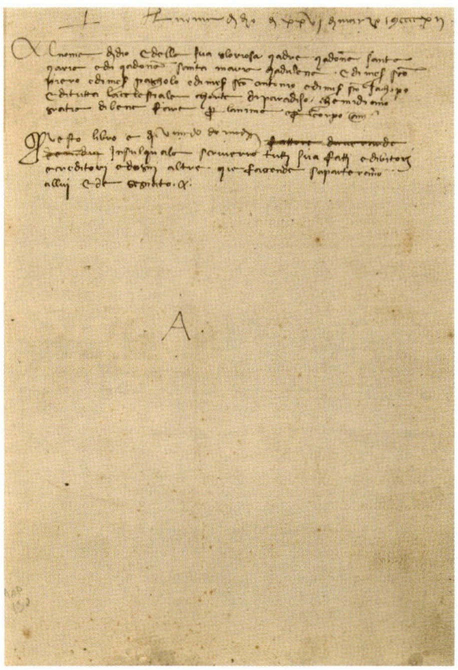

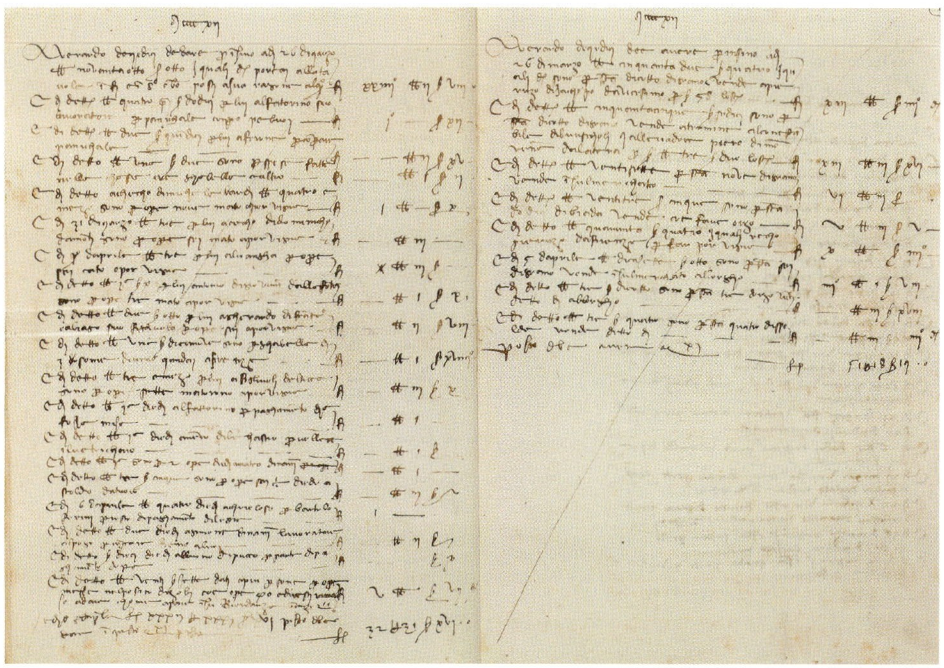

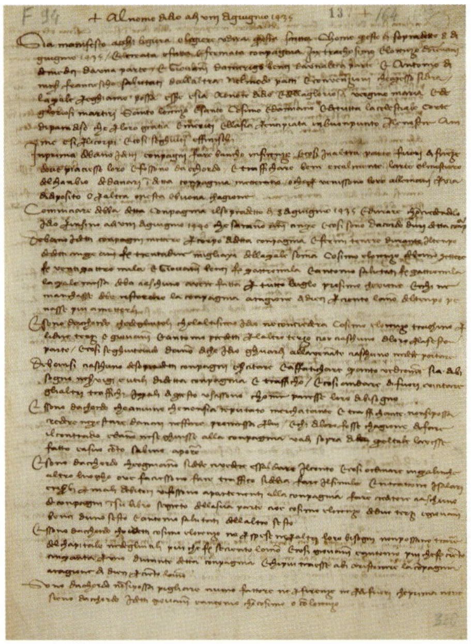

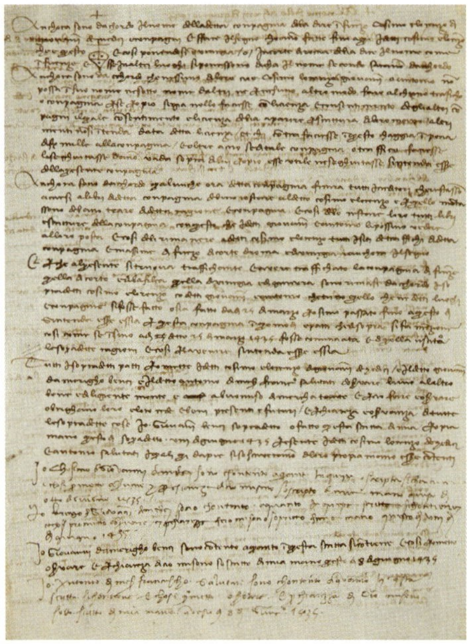

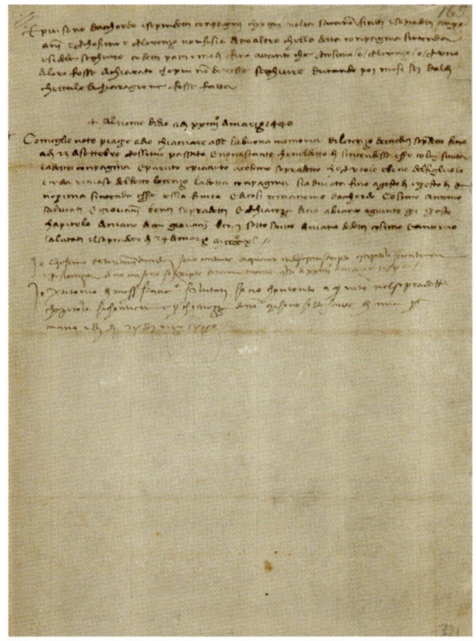

4.17
Contract reorganizing the central "holding" company of the Medici Bank
June 8, 1435
sheet of paper; composed of two sheets numbered in pencil 320-321; mercantile penmanship in the hand of Giovanni Benci
400 x 320 mm
Florence, Archivio di Stato, Mediceo avanti il Principato, 94, 137

This is a private contract authorizing the total reorganization of the Medici Bank, stipulated just after Cosimo the Elder's triumphant return to Florence from exile. On that occasion, all ties with the Bardi family were severed. Although Cosimo was related to them by marriage through his wife Contessina, they had given him no support after his fall from grace in 1433. Close relations with the Bardi had been a hallmark of the Medici Bank during its previous thirty years of life, concretely expressed by the appointment of three successive general managers from this family: Benedetto di Lippaccio (1402–20), Ilarione di Lippaccio (1420–33) and Lippaccio di Benedetto (1433–5). To fill the place left empty by the Bardi, Antonio Salutati and Giovanni Benci were called back to Florence to become general managers of the Rome and Geneva branches, respectively, as well as partners in the parent company. It was the Medici bank's practice, in almost all cases, not to consider their directors mere employees, but to make them partners entitled to a share of the profit, as a stimulus to their active participation and productivity. Accordingly, a new partnership contract was stipulated, with an increase of capital, which rose from 24,000 to 32,000 florins. The majority shareholders, Cosimo and Lorenzo de' Medici, contributed a total of 24,000 florins and the two general managers, minority shareholders, 4000 florins each, equivalent to one-eight of the company capital. However, the profit was not allocated in the same proportions, since each of the two directors was assigned one-sixth of the earnings, their shares including recompense for their managerial duties. All four partners affixed their signatures to the contract, indicating acceptance of all of its clauses. The new company, named "Cosimo e Lorenzo de' Medici e Compagni," kept the same trademark as the bank's old controlling company. The contract was supposed to have a duration of five years and could be tacitly renewed, as in fact happened at the expiration date, June 7, 1440; but one of the majority shareholders, Lorenzo di Giovanni de' Medici, died on September 23, 1440, an event which should have automatically closed down the company. Instead, Cosimo opted for an extension, for "the profit and benefice of said Lorenzo's remaining son and heir," but the company was finally liquidated on March 24, 1441 and a new one was founded under a different name.

Salutati died in 1443, while for Benci that partnership contract marked the beginning of a long and profitable collaboration in the capacity of general manager, a period coinciding with the height of success of the Medici Bank.

Vanna Arrighi

Bibliography: De Roover 1963, pp. 547–50.

4.18
Secret account book of the Medici Bank kept by Giovanni Benci
1440–50
parchment register; 100 fols; old style page numbering, inserted in a file with modern parchment binding and containing two more parchment notebooks relevant to the Medici Bank; mercantile penmanship in the hand of Giovanni Benci
360 x 265 mm
Florence, Archivio di Stato, Mediceo avanti il Principato, 153, c. 1

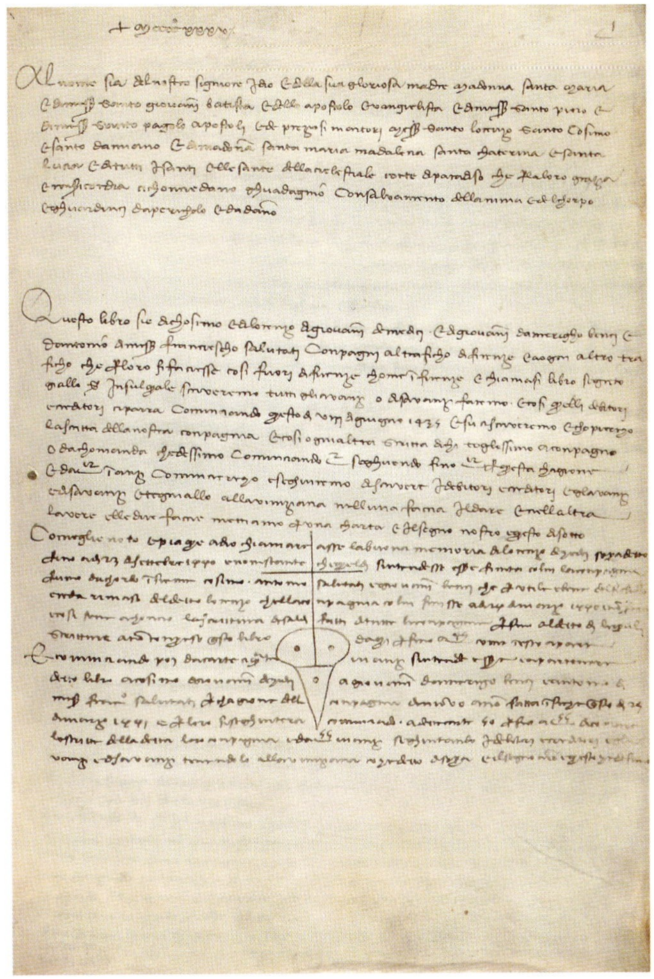

The so-called Medici Bank was actually made up of many different enterprises (with the Medici family as majority shareholders), consisting of banks and production workshops, all controlled by a mother company in which the proprietary family was assisted by general managers *pro tempore*, who were made minority shareholders, as an incentive to diligence and hard work.

Giovanni Benci (1394–1455) entered the service of the Medici at the age of fifteen, as a simple employee. Later he became director of the Geneva branch, which, thanks to him, was so profitable as to quadruple its initial capital in ten years. In the wake of this success, when the company was reorganized in 1435, he became one of the key directors of the bank, as well as a partner. At first he shared this responsibility with Antonio Salutati, but remained the sole general manager after Salutati's death in 1443. Benci remained at the top level of the Medici Bank for the rest of his life. This was the time of maximum prosperity for the Bank, due largely to Benci's managerial skill and to his perfect accord with Cosimo the Elder, who, while intensely engaged in political life, never neglected to exert control over his financial empire. Benci, from a much more modest background, also managed to acquire personal wealth through the profit earned by his partnership share, equivalent to one-eighth.

Unlike ordinary account books, compiled on paper and kept by stewards and employees, the "secret book," on parchment, was written by the general manager in person, since it was used to record financial transactions of confidential nature, most notably the apportioning of profit among the partners and investors. The book displayed here covers almost all of Benci's term of office at the head of the Medici holding company. On the date of September 23, 1440, it was divided into two parts, in coincidence with the death of Lorenzo di Giovanni de' Medici, Cosimo's brother and one of the "seniors." Each of the two sections begins with a copy of the agreements stipulated in the periods 1435–9 and 1441–6 respectively, and continues with a brief summary of the accounting records of the various branch offices, compiled under the form of "debtors and creditors." At the peak of its expansion the Medici holding company included the "Florence bench" plus three other branch offices in Italy, in Rome, Venice and Pisa; four foreign branches, in Geneva (moved to Lyon in 1464), Bruges, London and Avignon; as well as two wool-worker's shops and one silk manufactory in Florence. The budget drawn up on March 24, 1451, at the closure of the "secret book," shows that the capital of the general company, on which depended all of the branches, had risen to 90,000 florins, 72,000 of which owned by the Medici and 18,000 by Benci.

When Benci died in 1455, no one could be found to take his place. To compensate for this loss, the Medici Bank had to be reorganized again.

Vanna Arrighi

Bibliography: De Roover 1948, pp. 83–5.

4.19
Francesco Sassetti's personal secret account book
1462–9
parchment register bound in leather; 66 fols.; Venetian old style numbering from 1 to 71; fols. 42–7 are missing, having been torn out; fols. 41 and 48 left blank; the first side of the first page, containing the title of the register, is not numbered; mercantile penmanship in the hand of Francesco Sassetti
28 x 21.5 mm
Florence, Archivio di Stato, Carte Strozziane, II series, 20, fol. 1r

Francesco di Tommaso Sassetti (1421–90) began his career as an agent, or simple employee. Later he became vice-director and then director of the Geneva branch office, in whose management company, called "Francesco Sassetti e Compagni," he was also a partner. In 1458 he was summoned to Florence by Cosimo de' Medici to assist his son Giovanni in managing the family holding company. When Giovanni died in 1463, Sassetti became the sole general manager. His power grew still further under Lorenzo the Magnificent who, much more interested in politics than in the family businesses, put Sassetti in charge of everything. Under Sassetti's management, however, due to his lesser managerial skill and to adverse economic conditions, progressive decline became inevitable. During the latter years of his life, spent almost entirely in Florence, Sassetti also held public office, becoming a member of the Ufficiali del Monte in 1467 and the Ufficiali dello Studio in 1485.

This book, containing Sassetti's private accounts during the period of greatest prosperity, was used by its owner to record "valuable and secret things." Begun on November 1, 1462, it was divided into two parts. Recorded in the second, which comprises the last two folios, are the "secret records" of the profit deriving from his share of the Medici Bank. Profits were not allocated in direct proportion to the quota of company capital owned. Sassetti, who held a one-eighth share, was allocated one-sixth of the profit, as additional recompense for his productive management of the bank. In addition to his share of capital, Sassetti also invested in the Medici Bank by depositing funds, at times under another name. This situation gave rise to extremely complicated accounting. The first part of the book, written on the first 70 folios and organized according to "Debtors and creditors," records mainly the investments made by Sassetti in real estate and luxury articles during the years 1462–72. Sassetti in fact, was not only a businessman but also a refined collector of books and art objects, as can be seen by the entries recording purchases of "jewels," "wearing apparel," "books in Latin," "books in the vernacular" and, as on the page displayed here, "*argienti in vassella*," that is, silver plate. In the 1480s however, he was obliged to sell most of his collections in an attempt to compensate for the bank's losses.

Vanna Arrighi

Bibliography: De Roover 1948, pp. 67–72; De Roover 1963, pp. 452–555 and 526–8; Edler de Roover 1943, pp. 65–80; De La Mare 1976, pp. 160–201.

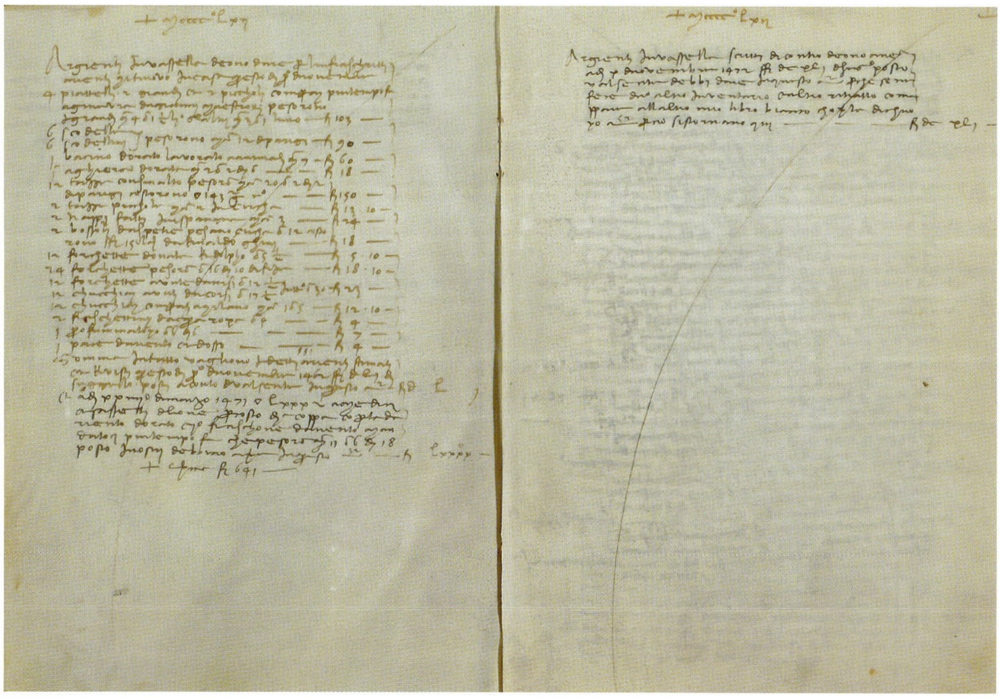

4.20
Secret code used by Lorenzo de' Medici
1470
sheet of paper; not numbered, found in a paper envelope bound in cardboard containing 97 documents without numbers. On the back, in the hand of Giovanni Lanfredini: "Cifra con Lorenzo de' Medici"
290 x 215 mm
Florence, Archivio di Stato, Manuscripts, 727, doc. 7

This folio contains the code used during a particular period in the letters sent by Giovanni Lanfredini (1437–90) to Lorenzo de' Medici. In 1469–70 Lanfredini was in Venice with his brother Jacopo, supervising the entrepreneurial activity of the family, when the Venetian branch of the Medici Bank was liquidated and he was delegated to recover its credits. He was so successful at this endeavour that the branch was re-opened some years later. Lanfredini became its general manager and was allowed to participate as partner in its management company. Later however a new crisis led to the definitive closure of the Venice branch and even to Lanfredini's imprisonment for a brief period in 1480. Returning to Florence, he continued however to collaborate with the Medici Bank and with Lorenzo the Magnificent, becoming one of his trusted advisers. At this time he began to participate intensely in Florentine political life, holding various public offices and ambassadorial posts. The code was used during Lanfredini's first stay in Venice, when his work for the Medici family was strictly private and confidential, meriting the greatest reserve. As we know, employees of the Medici family on any level, in addition to carrying out the tasks of banking proper, constituted a crucial information network for the family, a kind of diplomatic corps parallel to and alternative to the official ambassadors of the Florentine Republic. Through the Medici employees arrived first-hand news of the solvency of companies and individuals, but also of troop movements, palace intrigues and popular discontent. In communications of this type, secret codes were often employed, as in this case. In the code system documented here, each letter in the alphabet is represented by one or more symbols. For the safest possible coding of a text, each of the most commonly used alphabetical letters was represented by several symbols, called homophonies, which were alternated at random. Some particular signs indicate the doubling of a consonant. In thirty-seven cases then, a particular symbol or number corresponds to an entire word or the name of a person. It is in fact the presence of a symbol for the name Otto Niccolini, later scratched out and flanked by the word "dead," that allowed this code book to dated to 1470, the year of Niccolini's death. Subsequent research then led to identifying Lanfredini as the consignee and user of the code system and, consequently, to specifying its precise period of utilization, from the months of July through September in the year 1470.
Vanna Arrighi

Bibliography: R. Fuda in *Consorterie* 1992, pp. 137-138 no. 5.11.

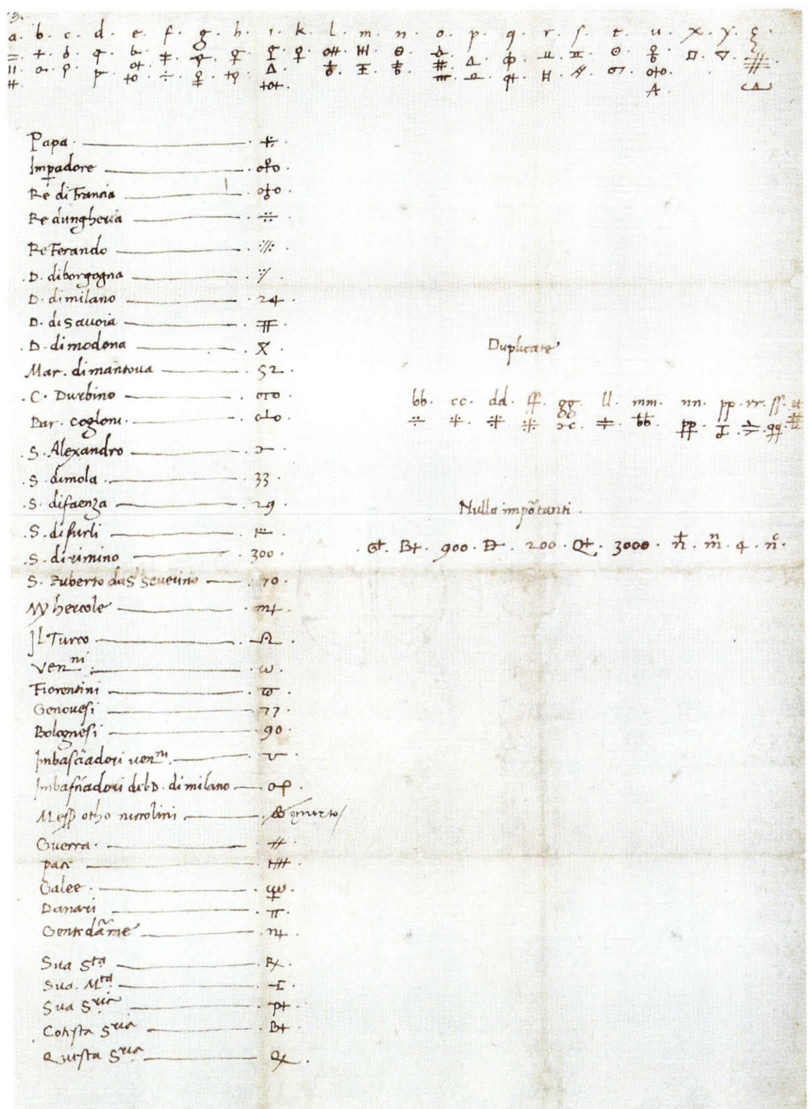

4.21
Memorandum of Lorenzo de' Medici detailing losses incurred by Tommaso Portinari in the management of the London and Bruges branches of the Medici Bank
1478
sheet of paper; mercantile penmanship
295 x 220 mm
Florence, Archivio di Stato, Mediceo avanti il Principato, 84, 21

This folio, presumably dictated by Lorenzo the Magnificent, since it is headed by the words "Parrla Lorenzo" ("Lorenzo speaks") instead of a title, contains a brief survey of the losses incurred by the London and Bruges branches of the Medici Bank. It is basically an act of accusation against the management of Tommaso Portinari (1428–1501). Portinari, the son and brother of directors of the Medici Bank, had been sent to Bruges as a young man to work as simple employee. He then went on to pursue a brilliant career that led him to become director and partner of the branch office in 1465. Highly ambitious, Portinari devoted more energy to courtly life under Charles I the Bold, who appointed him his councillor, than to the affairs of the Medici Bank, which he brought to ruin. He ventured the company's capital in risky investments, such as becoming the tax-farmer for the Gravelines tolls (abolished shortly thereafter), or constructing two galley ships. Another loss and expenditure for prestige alone was the purchase in 1466 of the Hotel Bladelin, one of the most imposing buildings in Bruges, bought however by the Medici family and not for the Bank, which had to pay rent for occupying it.

In 1473 disaster arrived, with exorbitant loans extended to Charles the Bold, amounting to more than double the entire capital of the Bruges branch. Moreover, through an agreement stipulated between Portinari and Francesco Sassetti, the Bruges bank took over the debts of the London branch, it too in deep trouble for the loans granted to King Edward IV. Furthermore, Portinari had, it seems, financed a Portuguese expedition to Guinea for which, having no liquidity at that time, he had taken out a loan to be repaid with interest. Even worse, he had founded a separate company for the only still profitable business managed by the Medici Bank in Bruges: the wool trade. In this new company Portinari had a 45% share of the profit, while for his partnership in the Bruges branch it was 27.5%. Accordingly, most of the profit went to him, while most of the bank's losses were incurred by the Medici. Finally, at the expiry of the last partnership contract in March 1478, Lorenzo the Magnificent realized the extent of the overall losses of the two branches, amounting to over 70,000 ducats. With restrained sarcasm, he commented, "And these are the great profits that have been consigned us by the management of Tommaxo Portinari." In 1480 Lorenzo sent Rinieri da Ricasoli to Bruges to liquidate the bank. He forced Portinari to assume personal responsibility for at least part of the debt and to suffer the consequences of his errors. After having spent and squandered, Tommaso Portinari died in poverty in 1501. His heirs were obliged to refuse their inheritance, judging it more financially burdensome that profitable.

Vanna Arrighi

Bibliography: De Roover 1948, pp. 565–7.

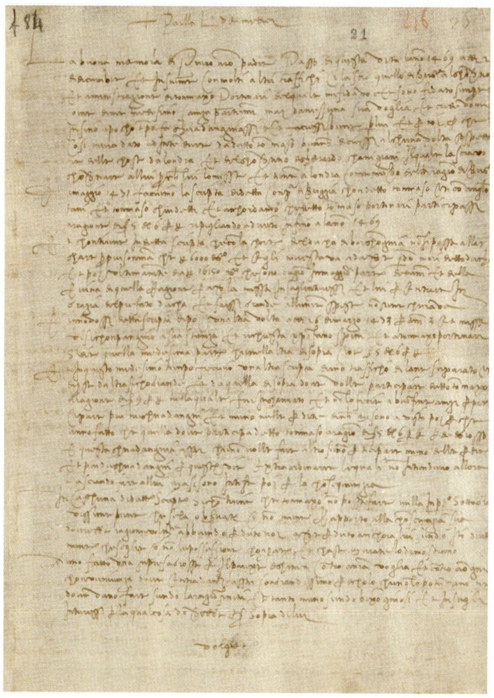

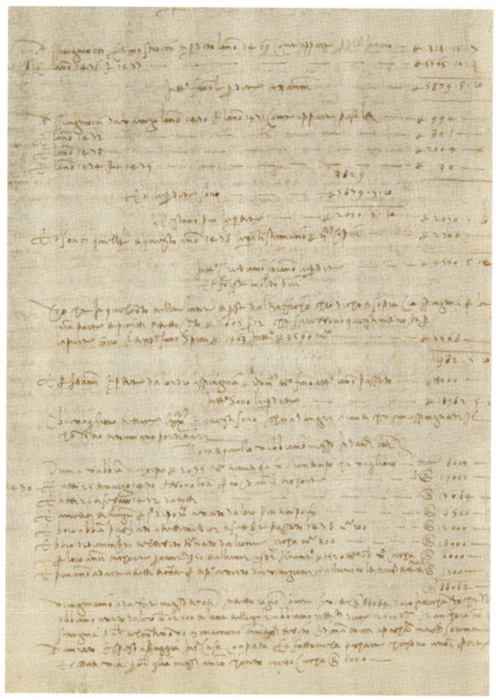

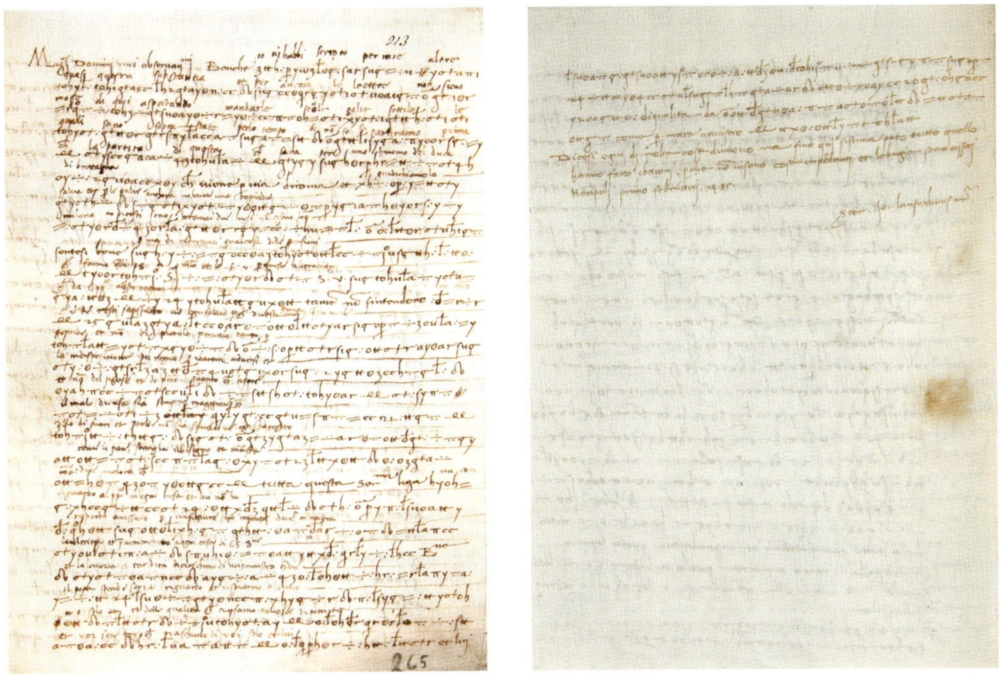

4.22

Coded letter from Ambassador Giovanni Lanfredini to the Dieci di Balia

Naples, February 1, 1486 (ordinary style)
paper file bound in parchment; 613 fols.; modern binding. Original autograph, in code, deciphered between the lines; on the back the address: "[Magnifi]cis dominis Decem [Bali]e inclite civitatis [Flo]rentie, dominis meis observandissimis. Florentie" 2 chancellery note: "1485. Johannis de Lanfredinis, primo ianuarii[sic]. Ricevuta VIII Martii d VIII Martii."
330 x 300 x 80 mm
Florence, Archivio di Stato, Dieci di Balia, Responsive 33, fols. 265–268

Giovanni Lanfredini (1437–90), director of and partner in the Venetian branch of the Medici bank from 1476 to 1480, was one of Lorenzo de' Medici's most trusted collaborators. Although he had been appointed envooy at Naples in 1484 by the Dieci di Balia, there is no doubt that the choice was suggested, if not actually imposed, by the Magnificent. The Dieci di Balia was the magistrature responsible for the foreign relations of the Florentine Republic in times of war. In this case, war had broken out in the summer of 1485 when the barons in the Kingdom of Naples rebelled against their sovereign, Ferrante of Aragon, accused of violating their traditional rights. Pope Innocent VIII had immediately sided with the rebels, triggering troop movements near the borders and putting the Kingdom of Naples in difficulty, undermined within by domestic revolt and threatened without by invasion. The king then asked his allies, Florence and Milan, through their ambassadors, to send help as quickly as possible. Florence, though acknowledging its duties as ally, responded slowly and cautiously to the king's appeal, afraid that Florentine Merchants in the Papal States would be exposed to retaliations..

In this delicate situation, it was crucially important to ensure maximum speed and secrecy to correspondence. Postal couriers were sometimes stopped at the boundary with the Papal States, where their letters were confiscated. Lanfredini's letter, in addition to informing the Dieci of the latest developments, discusses at length the problems involved in safely delivering diplomatic dispatches. Not only was it indispensable to recur to codes, but also necessary to make several copies of the same letter and send them along different routes, entrusting them to merchants or persons extraneous to the warring parties, and sometimes having them hide the letters in the most improbable places. In the episode narrated in this letter, a Milanese envoy had sent a dispatch to his government through a servant, ordering him to hide it in the sole of his shoe. In the case of this letter, Lanfredini intended to entrust it to a "man faithful to the Duke of Brittany" and was confident that it would arrive successfully, but for greater certainty he planned to send a duplicate by way of the galley ships about to set sail from Naples. The deciphering of the letter, written between the lines, was done in Florence by one of the secretaries in the chancellery of the Dieci.

Vanna Arrighi

Bibliography: R. Fuda in *Consorterie* 1992, pp. 137–8, no. 5.11; Lanfredini (1485–rte de1486), ed. Scarton 2002, pp. 488–91.

Section 5
International Trade, Merchants and Merchandise

There was no clear distinction between the worlds of the banker and the merchant. Involved as they constantly were with letters of exchange that required a network of agencies throughout the major cities of Europe, bankers were naturally drawn into trade, as merchants often found themselves extending credit to customers. In the absence of roads fit for heavy overland haulage, trade meant sea travel: storms, pirates, mutinies, anxious delays. To insure or not to insure was always a pressing question. So while their financial dealings provoked criticism and on occasion even public anger, the risks that merchant bankers ran when they committed their wealth and sometimes even their lives to the sea redeemed them in the collective imagination. Ships could sink, especially the newer, faster ships, which carried so much sail. "May God and fortune be our aid," implored the shipping documents.

Main trading destinations for the Florentines were Naples, Rome, Venice, Barcelona, Avignon, Geneva, Lyons, Paris, Bruges and London. The main products moving back and forth were, from south to north: silks, spices, alum, almonds and citrus fruits; and from north to south: raw wool, linen, tapestries, horses. Throughout the 14th and 15th centuries there was a problem with the trade balance, in that the demand in northern Europe for goods purchased from or through Italy was greater than the return supply of wool and sundries. Florentine bankers would find their northern agencies flush with cash from products sold and letters of exchange honoured but without an easy means of getting the wealth back to Florence. The situation deteriorated when the English sought to work their wool themselves rather than sell it raw to the Florentines. Export duties were set at prohibitive rates. Bankers offered substantial loans to the English king in return for waiving these export duties, thus attracting the hostility of the English wool merchants, and running the risk that they might never see their capital again. But one way or another, something had to be loaded into the ships that had arrived from Italy, since they could not safely make the voyage home empty.

Elaborate triangular operations were invented. Excess money in Bruges might buy cloth which was sent to Barcelona where accumulated incomes could be drawn on by Florentine merchants who paid into their local bank to purchase raw Spanish wool and saffron. The accounting became complicated. A steady flow of reliable information about exchange rates and going market prices was crucial. Regular courier services were run. "If your letters arrive bundled up with letters for other merchants," remarks Paolo da Certaldo in his *Libro di buoni costumi*, "make sure to read your own first; if they suggest you buy or sell something at once to make a profit, do it and only then give the others their letters, otherwise the service you do to them could prove a loss to yourself."[1] "It's hard to get rich without some trickery,"[2] another commentator remarks.

The trickery might start when merchants bid at auction for the cargo space in Florence's state-owned galleys which operated out of the port of Pisa. The auction lasted an hour and ended with the chiming of the clock on the tower of the Palazzo della Signoria, audible, but not visible, from the auction room. Without watches of their own, the merchants couldn't know exactly when it would sound. The official clock-minder was put under armed guard for the duration, in case the hour should shrink or expand. Packed with a wide range of goods, to spread the commercial risk, the galleys set out in spring when the weather permitted. Since the delay between departure and arrival was considerable, commodity prices could shift drastically before your cargo arrived, particularly if another ship came in before yours. In the 1470s the Medici+ hoped to resolve their financial problems by securing sole rights to trade in alum mined in Papal territory. Alum was a key mineral, essential for wool dyeing. But when Genoese and Venetian ships defied a papal ban and continued to import Turkish alum, a glut in the market led to a collapse in prices and considerable losses. The impression we get from letters at the time is of men living under constant stress. Certainly the need to be ready for all eventualities, to seize an opportunity on the spur of the moment, to deal astutely with princes and politicians, tax collectors and sea captains, made them a special breed. The perfect merchant was a "most universal man" contemporary Benedetto Cotrugli tells us "whose hard work is glorious" since "it intensifies and increases his intelligence."[3]

Perhaps it was this mental alertness of the merchant bankers that gave them an appetite for art and a certain affinity with the artists whose work they commissioned. In 1472 Agnolo Tani, a manager for the Medici in Bruges, commissioned a magnificent *Last Judgement* from the Flemish painter Hans Memling. Alas, the galley it travelled on was waylaid by Polish pirates and the painting (see pp. 74–5) remains to this day in Danzig.

Tim Parks

1. Braunstein, Franceschi 2007, pp. 663–4.
2. Ivi, p. 670.
3. Ivi, p. 657.

5.1
Material from a sunken riverboat at Empoli

In the early 1980s, after weeks of drought with the consequent lowering of the water level, there emerged at Empoli, on the banks of the Arno, the remains of a riverboat used for transporting merchandise. Built of oak wood, it was approximately 13 m long and 3.10 m wide, with one side missing. Based on the ceramic materials found in it, the boat has been dated to the second quarter of the 14th century. It presumably sank while moored to the wharf, during the great flood of 1333 that destroyed the first belt of walls around Empoli. The craft, emerging halfway out of the sand, was not salvaged but was explored and documented. The following objects were found in it:

Jug
c. 1290-1330
archaic majolica (early tin-glazed ware)
13.8 cm, max Ø 7.8 cm; Ø foot 5.9 cm
Florence, Museo Archeologico Nazionale,
inv. no. 260757

The jug, whose upper part is missing, has a trefoil mouth, ovoid body, high flared foot, and rod handle. The body is decorated in "stripes," simple vertical undulating bars in manganese brown and verdigris. A double horizontal edging, also brown, marks the beginning of the foot and forms horizontal bars on the handle. The interior, glazed, shows evident turning marks.

The type of decoration and the shape are reminiscent of similar objects found at Puntazza, near Montelupo, produced there and datable between 1290 and 1330.

Fragment of steelyard
c. 1290–1330
brass, iron, wood
length 9.3 cm; sides 3.3 x 2.8 cm;
riders h. 8 cm; hooks h. 9.5 cm
Florence, Museo Archeologico Nazionale,
inv. no. 260758

Only the end of the wooden rod, covered in punched brass sheet, and the three iron hooks remain.

The steelyard, in the form that has lasted from Roman times to our own day, was used to take progressive measurements marked on the sides of the graduated rod, along which slid the counter-weight, called *romano*, keeping the hook for goods to be weighed fixed at one end and varying the suspension hook by tipping the instrument. In our case the weighing capacity, calculated as approximately a hundredweight, could be linked to the salt trade. Salt, arriving from Pisa by riverboat, was unloaded and stored here, before continuing its journey overland on the Via Salaiola.

"Double-Tee" shaped dagger (basilarda)
c. 1290–1330
steel, iron, lead, wood
length 44 cm; length of blade 30.5 cm;
width of blade at root 3.5 cm
Florence, Museo Archeologico Nazionale,
inv. no. 260759

Steel blade with lozenge-shaped section and "forte" marked by concave grooves, formed of a single piece with a straight handle having an inner duct, bounded at the bottom by the crosspiece and terminating in a pommel with ends curving upward. The "double Tee-shaped" hilt is made of ironclad wooden plaques, fastened with rivets to components

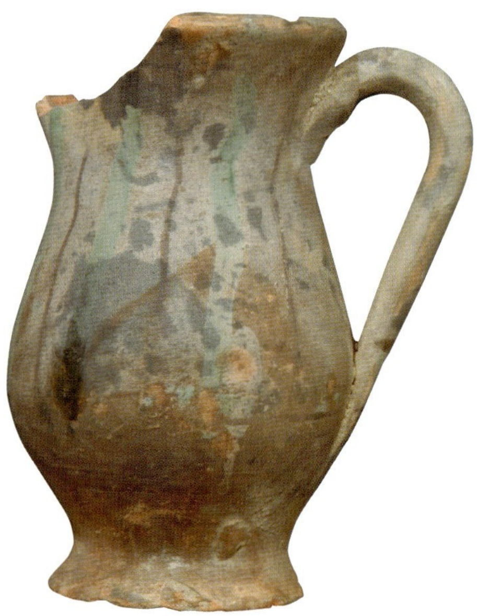

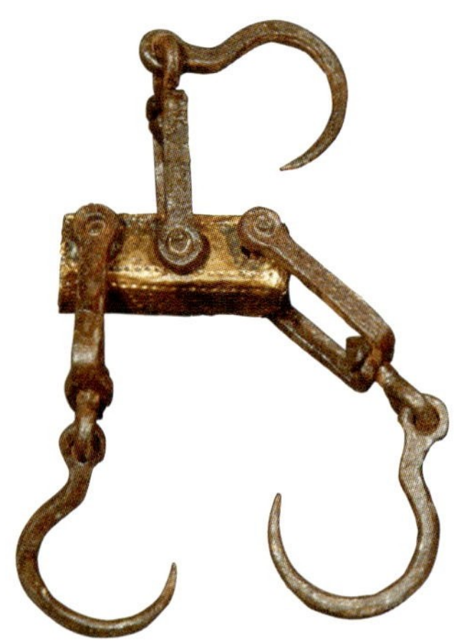

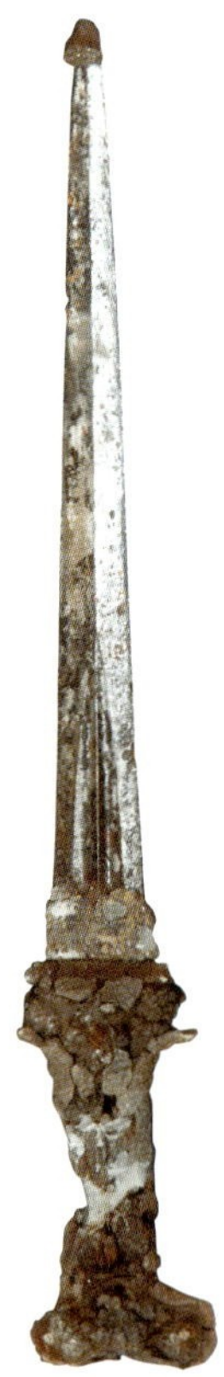

made of lead. On the blade remain traces of the wooden sheath, it too decorated with iron sheeting.

The dagger resembles two others coming from the sandbars in the river near Signa, and two found, along with other weapons such as lances and daggers, at the river port of Puntazza, near Montelupo, where a forge driven by a water mill probably existed. The dating to the late 13th and 14th centuries, based on numerous iconographic and material sources, could be more precisely established in relation to the chronology of the Puntazza archaeological site, and the image on the tombstone of Gherarduccio dei Gherardini (died 1331) in the Pieve di Sant'Appiano.

Although rightly pertaining to the individual arms of a knight, daggers were commonly used by traders for personal defence.

Bucket
c. 1290–1330
iron
h. 9 cm; Ø rim 14.5 cm; bottom 16.6 cm
Florence, Museo Archeologico Nazionale,
inv. no. 260760

Probably contained pitch used for caulking; made of iron sheeting bent and fastened with rivets. The handle, also made of iron, has been repaired with a nail at the lower point of attachment.

Boats were caulked by inserting tow, using a mallet or chisel, into the cracks in the planking, then pouring tar over them. This operation had to be repeated periodically to keep the hull waterproof. Although the specialists in this operation, called caulkers, had to serve eight years of apprenticeship to learn their trade, all boatmen were sufficiently skilled to carry out this maintenance procedure.

Barrel-maker's axe
c. 1290–1330
iron, wood
length 18 cm; width at edge 9.4 cm; at heel 3.1 cm
Florence, Museo Archeologico Nazionale,
inv. no. 260761

The iron blade and parts of the wooden handle have survived. This was a tool used by carpenters and boatmen to build furnishings for boats.

Fragments of a chain
c. 1290–1330
forged iron
length of elements 12.5; maximum length 115 cm
Florence, Museo Archeologico Nazionale,
inv. no. 260762

Composed of figure-8 shaped links, the chain was probably used for mooring. At the time when it was found, a long section had remained in place, connected to the anchor deeply buried in the sand, near the wharf. Although the Arno was susceptible to considerable changes in water level, the flat bottoms of these boats, built especially for fluvial navigation at Limite sull'Arno, allowed them to navigate up the river with their cargo as far as Porto di Mezzo (Signa) even during times of drought.

Lorella Alderighi

Bibliography: G. de Marinis, P.R. Del Francia in *Capolavori* 1986, pp. 197–8, no. 3.A; Cibecchini, Gambogi 2003, pp. 251–60.

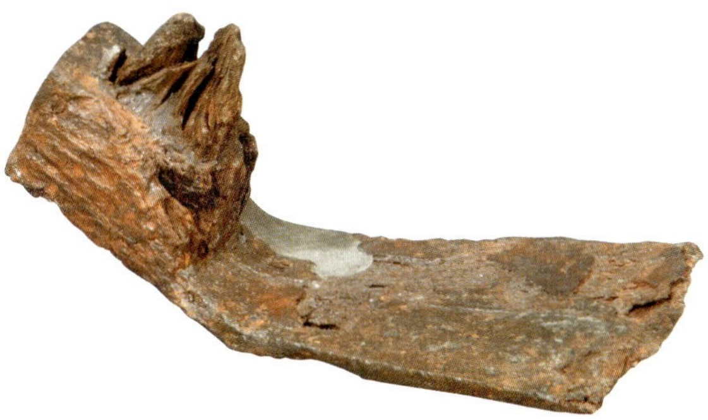

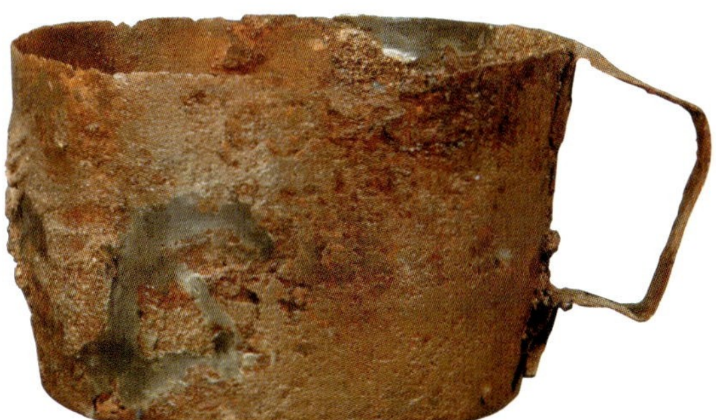

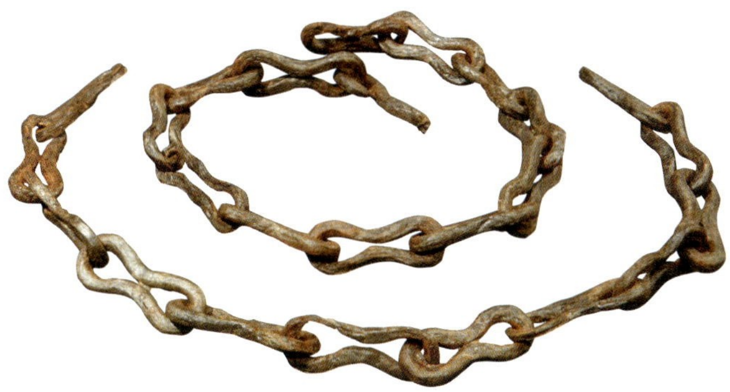

5.2
Francesco de Cesanis (active *c.* 1420)
Nautical Map
1421
watercolour and ink on parchment
580 x 966 mm
Venice, Fondazione Musei Civici di Venezia, Museo Correr, *Portolano* no. 13, Emanuele Cicogna Legacy 3451

The growth of commerce in the late Middle Ages indubitably depended on the vast increase in Mediterranean shipping. A parallel development was the production of nautical maps, used not only by navigators but also by merchants and pilgrims. Venice, having a port that traded with the entire Mediterranean basin and beyond, was a major centre for the production of nautical maps. In the late Middle Ages and early Renaissance, a nautical map was frequently called a *portolano* a term deriving from the Latin *portus* (port). The portolano, however contained the written instructions for navigators that accompanied nautical maps, and described the coastlines with their ports and other features. The map and text together furnished a maximum of information on such things as the anchorage, the port and the political situation of a city. Nautical maps were used not only in conjunction with the *portolano*, but also with such important instruments as the compass.

The oldest nautical map of the Mediterranean Sea is the one made in Pisa (dating from the late 13th century) now in the Bibliothèque nationale de France in Paris. The first *portolano* accompanied by nautical maps is *De Spieghel der Zeevaerdt* (1583–4) by the Dutchman Lucas Janszoon Waghenaer, which was translated into French, English and German. Produced at a time when atlases and globes did not yet exist, maps such as that of Francesco de Cesanis would not meet any modern standards, but were sufficient for the needs of the time. They lack, in fact, any description of the sea bed, of the underwater mountains, or information on obstacles to navigation, which were entrusted to the *portolani*. For greater legibility however, islands, promontories and the mouths of rivers are shown enlarged.

The De Cesanis map comes from the small but precious collection of nautical maps and *portolani* owned by the Museo Correr (over forty). Like many medieval and renaissance charts, it is drawn on a parchment skin. The neck of the animal (a calf or goat) is recognizable in the part usually found on the left (on the right here). There are descriptions of the Mediterranean, the Black Sea (represented a little higher up due to lack of space), the Sea of Azov, part of the Atlantic coastline of Europe and Africa, and to the North, small portions of England and Denmark. At first glance the map seems poorly designed, but in looking at it from the neck down, it becomes clear that it was constructed in an orderly system of lozenges, with a central wind rose of sixteen winds (the eight main winds are shown in black and yellow, the eight half-winds in green or blue and the sixteen quarter-winds in red) and another sixteen wind roses along the edges. With this entirely empirical reference grid, a navigator could stay on course even when sailing by night, and at times in the open sea (Tonini 2009).

Various colours are used to facilitate the reading of the map. The islands stand out in red, blue and gold; the topographical indications along the coasts appear in red and black. The major ports are marked with flags bearing ensigns of different size to indicate their importance. Venice is marked with a big flag, and the lion of St. Mark's is the most noticeable figure on the map. The flag of Zara in nearby Dalmatia is also large. Red ink is used to indicate the main trading centres, black ink the smaller ones. The ports of call along the Venetian routes can be seen in the dense succession of place names along the Adriatic coasts and the Aegean archipelago.

This map is still rooted in 14th-century cartographic tradition, based on more ancient archetypes such as the atlas of Pietro Vesconte (Campbell 1987) from 1318 and that of Angelino Dalorto from 1330 (Gerola 1934). The taking of Ceuta by the Portuguese in 1415, for instance, is lacking, and it is marked by the old flag with two keys against a red field (*Carte da navigar* 1990). It is still unclear whether these maps were used aboard ship or on land in preparation for a voyage. Obviously, however, this one was very much in use, as demonstrated by the torn edges and the holes in the parchment. The artist, not without pride, has placed his signature on the neck at the centre of the frame running around the map, indicating his name, his Venetian origin and the year: "+ Franciscus de cesanis de Veneciis fecit in anno Domini MCCCCXXI."

Nicole Hegener

Bibliography: Gerola 1935, pp. 101–23; Campbell 1987; *Carte da navigar* 1990, pp. 46–7; Biadene, Tonini 2000, pp. 2–31; T. Kennedy in *Venice* 2007, p. 310; Pujades i Battaller 2007; Tonini 2009, pp. 26–7; *Weltbilder* 2009.

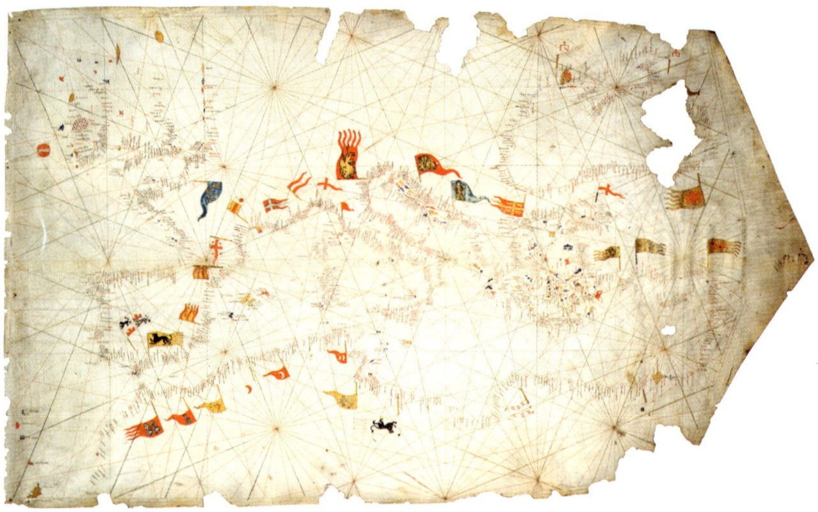

5.3
Fra Angelico (Fra Giovanni da Fiesole, Guido di Pietro; Vicchio *c.* 1395–Rome 1455)
St. Nicholas with the Emperor's Envoy and *The Miraculous Rescue of a Sailing Vessel*
between 1437 and 1449
tempera and gold on panel
34 x 63.5 cm
Vatican City, Musei Vaticani, inv. 40252

The episodes of St. Nicholas meeting an envoy from the emperor and miraculously saving a sailing vessel perfectly reflect not only the wealth of the client—whose name is unknown—but also the refinement of his taste, considering that he chose Fra Angelico to paint one of the most important altarpieces of the early 15th century. Beneath the painting of the *Virgin and Child*, this was the central panel in the predella of the so-called *Perugia Poliptych*, painted for the Chapel of San Nicola in San Domenico. Moved to the sacristy in 1706, it was taken to Paris during the Napoleonic campaign. Upon its return to Italy, two of the three predella panels were purchased by the Vatican.

On the left, St. Nicholas discusses with a messenger and a merchant—all elegantly clad in gold-embroidered fabrics—the merchandise that has arrived at its destination thanks to his miraculous aid. On the right appears the great ship in a storm, its sails swollen with wind, its crew imploring help from Nicholas, patron saint of navigators. The saint, his golden halo standing out against the dark sky, answers their prayers. In the central scene, the vessel sails on to take refuge in the port. A tongue of rock divides, like a watershed, the scene of the perilous journey over the sea from the safe harbour. The three episodes are linked by the sailing vessel. In the scene of the miracle, it appears in the foreground with sails billowing above the poop deck, then in port it is seen from the bow with the sail being hauled down after lowering two anchors.

Despite its importance, some aspects of the *Perugia Poliptych* remain unclear. The uncertainty of its date, ranging between 1437 and 1447, has raised doubts as to a possible collaborator (the Master of the Orange Tree Cloister or Benozzo Gozzoli) and the identity of the client. It is uncertain whether the client may have been Benedetto Guidalotti (1388–1429), the Archbishop of Recanati buried in the chapel of the altar, or Niccolò V Parentucelli who, elected Pope in 1447, took the name of the patron saint of mariners. It is intriguing to think that Fra Angelico may have given the central figure of St. Nicholas the features of this pope, his friend and client in the last years of his life.

With the *Perugia Poliptych*, Fra Angelico attempted to surpass a work commissioned by a powerful Florentine: the famous *Quaratesi Poliptych* painted by Gentile da Fabriano in 1425 for the chapel of Bernardo Quaratesi in San Niccolò Oltrarno. Now in the Pinacoteca Vaticana, it too represents the scene of the *Miracle of St. Nicholas*, showing the same type of 15th-century rounded vessel, which also appears in the *Ideal City*, now in Berlin. Unlike Gentile, Fra Angelico does not dramatize the danger of shipwreck and, by painting the same ship three times, hails it as a means of transport and symbol of profitable trade. The rounded shape of the vessel is emphasized to show its capacity. The powerful mast, supporting the crow's nest, conveys the impression of sturdiness in the presence of danger. Ships like this carried such riches that the clients could afford to commission paintings of priceless value and beauty. The opulent use of gold in the frame and the enamelled colours reflected the wealth of the clients. And in fact, the grain poured on land from the ship's great bins into rough sacks to be brought to the city, seems pure gold.

Nicole Hegener

Bibliography: De Marchi 1985, pp. 53–7; Spike 1996, pp.164–9 and pp. 243–4, no. 94; Bonsanti 1998, pp. 139–41, no. 59; Ahl 2008, pp. 187–93; G. Cornini in *Beato Angelico* 2009, pp. 202–3, no. 24.

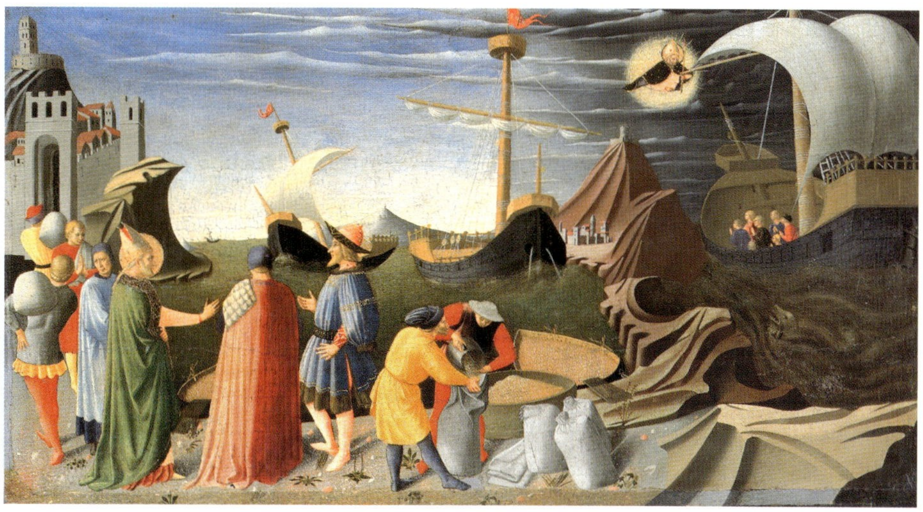

5.4
Model of a merchant ship of about 1450
First half of the 20th century
wood and cotton
104 x 119 x 58.1 cm
Antwerpen, MAS - Museum Aan de Stroom, AS 1946.005.005

Until the 19th century, the waters of the Low Countries varied in character—treacherous shallows kicked up steep choppy seas, and leeward coasts and strong tides were a constant danger. To deal with these difficulties, very different types of vessels emerged. Viking ships such as the knarr evolved during the 13th century into the "cog" or "cogge," the main seagoing merchant ship in the northern seas. Although they were only about 20 metres long, they carried cargoes for the Hanseatic towns from the Baltic to Northern France. The square-rigged cogge was a single masted, clinker-build vessel, with a relatively low freight capacity. In the early 15th century, a different type of ship developed in the Mediterranean began to influence the design. These vessels, the "nau" or "nao"—a form of "carrack"—were carvel-built, which allowed for a smoother upward and downward sweep. This in turn provided more loading capacity. Carracks from Genoa to Florence, exporting dyes, called at English ports for the cloth trade. New types of vessels appeared, with a mix of cogge and carrack features in hull and rigging type.

The model on display belongs to the family of the "pleyt" or "pleitscip." It is a clinker built coaster with little sheer and low freeboard. On first impression, the lower hull form has a flat appearance ("*pleyt*" means "flat" in Middle Dutch). This construction allowed for the use of oars when entering or leaving ports in adverse winds or tides, or when crossing breaking surf. Because the vessel had an almost level bottom it could be unloaded on tidal flats or beaches without entering port. Features like the forecastle gave some protection against the waves, and served as a platform for archers or gunners; political turmoil and piracy were problems then as now. The upper beams, protruding from the ships' hull, are a typical cog feature, used here to support the castles. The rudder is operated by a tiller on the aftcastle. The model is square-rigged at the foremast and mainmast, and lateen-rigged on the mizzen. The mainmast is topped with a crows' nest. This type of rigging shows the influence of Mediterranean shipbuilding styles.

The heraldry represents Flanders and different regions of the Netherlands. The Scheldt and Rhine delta, a plethora of islands and inlets which offered protection, was the perfect setting for ports to emerge. In the mid 15th century Bruges, Ghent and Antwerp all became important trading towns. The region was the richest in Northern Europe at the time and the increasing population density fuelled the economy. Transfer of goods between ships and boats provided work, and taxes could be levied. The tax on hops, for example, was an important revenue for the towns of Zeeland. In Bruges, cargo and shipping were insured by Florentine agents. The trade in beer, wine, fur, dye, raw wool, as well as Florentine cloth and other luxury textiles created wealth and hence a demand for art: tapestries, painting, music…

This type of ship disappeared at the end of the 15th century, but its name was carried into the early 20th century, when it applied to a form of barge with a sprit or gaff sail and a mizzen.

Geert Geysen and Willy Durinx

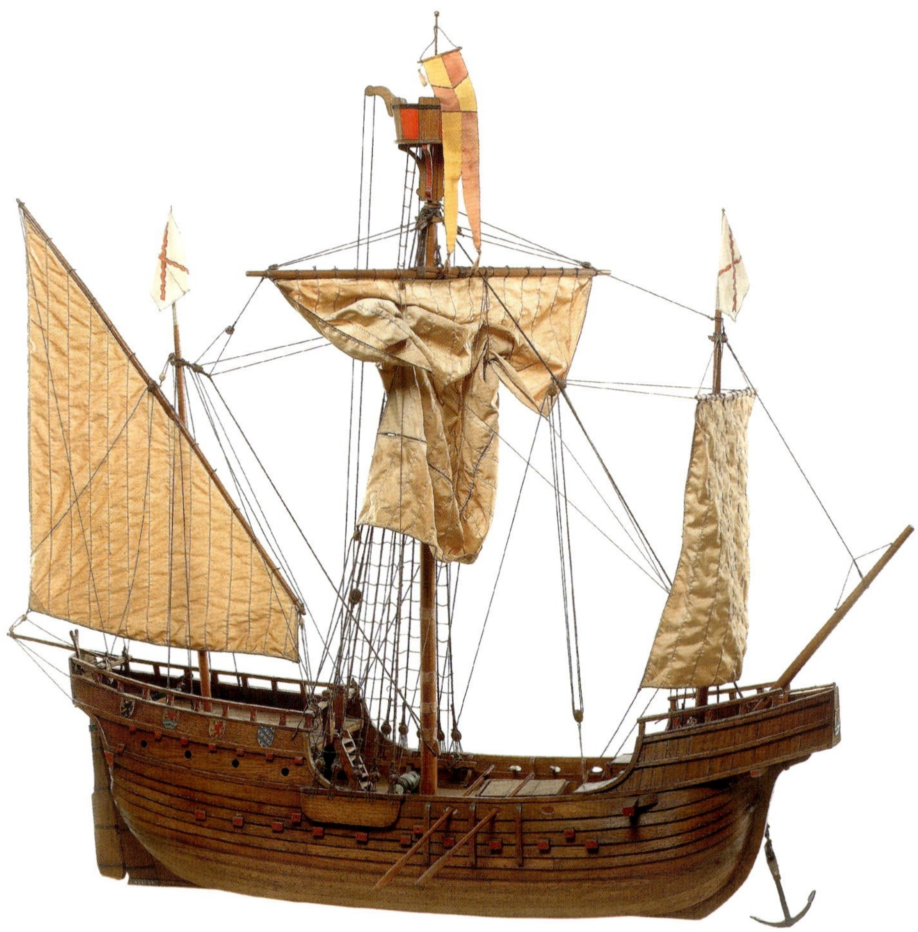

5.5
Master of Charles III Durazzo
(active *c.* 1370–*c.* 1420)
Stories of Saladin and Torello di Strà
early 15th century
fragment of chest, painted wood and gilt plaster
45.5 x 121.5 cm
Florence, Museo Stibbert, inv. no. 16202

Very few wedding chests have remained intact through the centuries, but often the front, decorated with edifying stories or scenes evoking the feminine virtues, have survived. This is the case of our chest front which, at the time of Frederick Stibbert, was completed with 19th-century integrations and later disassembled, retaining only the original part, decorated in three formelle narrating the beginning of the story of Messer Torello and Saladin, told by Boccaccio in the *Decameron* (X, 9). In keeping with the matrimonial customs of the time, there was a second matching chest, depicting the last three episodes of this popular tale that has been found decorating several strong-boxes, some of them, recognized by the scholars, now in various collections (see Miziolek 1996, pp. 19, 48; Baskins 2005, pp. 81–99; Miziolek 2010, p. 70).

In painted formelle with rich frames of gilt pastille, the chests tells how the merchant Torello di Strà from Pavia meets Saladin, who is travelling incognito in the guise of a merchant with his entourage. Torello, showing great generosity, welcomes the unknown guest and his wife into his home, showering him with gifts at his departure. In the third episode, Torello departs for the Crusades, leaving his wife at home alone. She has promised to wait for him a year, a month and a day, after which she will be free to marry again. In the continuation of the story, represented on the chest that once formed a pair with this one, Messer Torello, taken prisoner by the Saracens, is freed by Saladin himself, who recognizes him and helps him by magic arts to return quickly to Pavia, where his wife, having heard nothing from him and urged on by relatives, is about to marry again.

The choice of this novella has a dual value for a wedding. It celebrates conjugal fidelity, which overcomes all adversity, essential to the ethics of marriage., while simultaneously hailing the vitality of the mercantile role, which leads men to voyage through unknown lands, confronting adversities of all kinds, certain of the mutual aid guaranteed by the common nature of all men, stronger than any difference in religion. The mutual esteem felt by Torello and Saladin is based on respect for shared values deriving from the practice of trade: generosity, recognition, and consideration for the intrinsic value of the individual based on nobility of spirit. It is no coincidence that the clothing chosen to represent the personages faithfully reflects the mercantile fashion of the day.

The differences appear in the accessories: the long curved sabre of Islam identifies Saladin, who is dressed in a rich gown decorated with a Kufic inscription on the hem, but wears a merchant's headdress, like Torello. Adalieta, Torello's wife, wears a long-sleeved tunic, a garment typical of the second half of the 14th century, also called *cipriana*, adorned with little buttons on the front and on the tight sleeves, enriched by ermine trimming, bearing witness to the rich lifestyle she enjoys thanks to her husband the merchant.

Simona Di Marco

Bibliography: *Il Museo Stibbert* 1974, p. 42, no. 164.

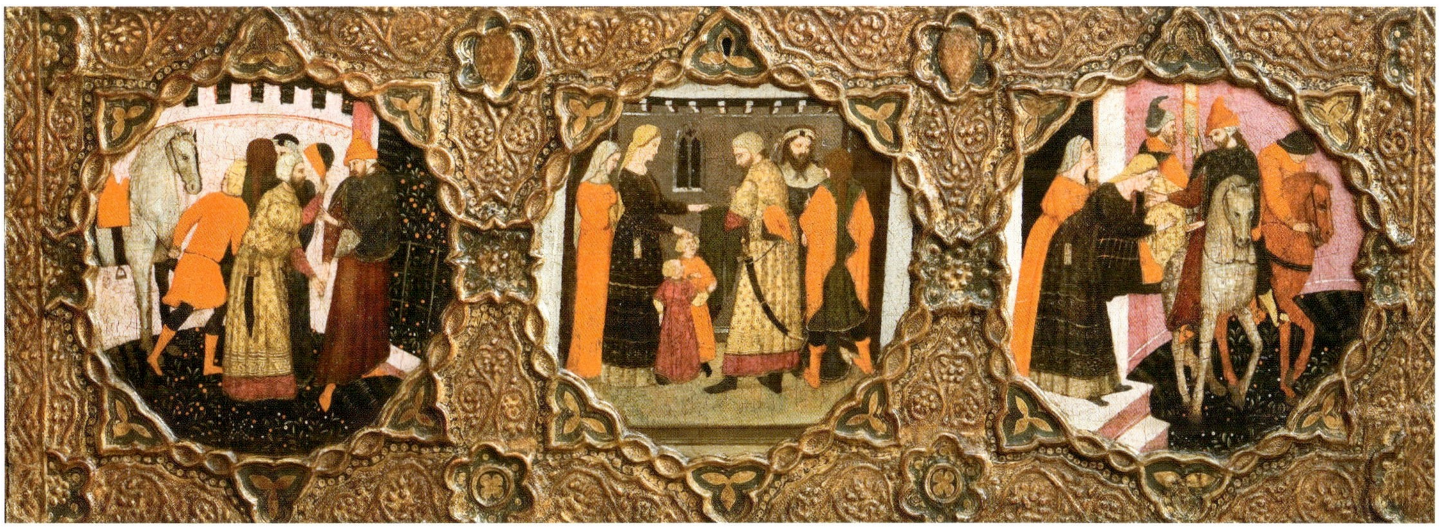

5.6
Francesco Botticini (Florence 1446–97)
The Archangel Raphael and Tobias with a Young Devotee
c. 1485
tempera on panel
156 x 89 cm
Florence, Soprintendenza Speciale per il Polo Museale, 1890 inv. no. 8676

In this painting, the clients are identified by their heraldic emblems. On the left is the coat of arms of the Doni family (although the colours differ from those specified in the Ceramelli Papiani papers, "Azure, with a lion d'or, and at the bend gules, charged with three silver crescent moons, turned toward the piece," ASF, Fascicolo 1794). The Doni were wealthy wool merchants and dyers whose residences and businesses were situated in the San Giovanni quarter. On the right appears the *palato*, emblem of the Badia Fiorentina. Both of these devices may have been added when the painting was moved to the church from its original domestic ambiance. Destined to private devotion, it may have been painted in connection with the departure of a young man for a distant, perilous place, perhaps that city in the North, overlooking a lake or the sea, surrounded by high mountains, glimpsed in the distance. Paintings of "Tobiolo" (as the young Tobias of the Biblical story was called in Tuscany) with his faithful little dog, accompanied by the Archangel Raphael, were very popular in 13th–and 14th–century Florence. The sons of merchant-bankers, at the age of only eleven or twelve, often undertook dangerous voyages to reach the branch offices in Naples, Geneva, Lyon and London.

On such occasions the protection of a powerful intercessor was invoked by means of a devotional painting. The most suitable subject was Tobias, led safely by Raphael through dangerous, unknown lands. In transposing the Biblical story into Florentine reality, Tobias became an adolescent of the times (see Schaeffer 1904, pp. 80–4; Gombrich 1972, pp. 26–7).

It has been suggested that the painting was commissioned by Agnolo Doni's father (Cecchi 1987, pp. 430–1), but the kneeling boy is more likely Raffaello, son of Attaviano Doni, who was born around 1473 and died while still an adolescent in 1487, the year when he was buried in the Badia. It may have been decided, after this grievous event, to move the painting from the family's home to the Benedictine church. Significantly, Attaviano was acquainted with the painter Francesco Botticini, since both were members of the Brotherhood of the Archangel Raphael, known as "del Raffa," headquartered in Via Maffia, and both had named their firstborn sons for the brotherhood's patron saint (Venturini 2004, pp. 79–80). Botticini headed an important art workshop in 15th–century Florence, one of those flourishing businesses whose trade was handed down from one generation to another, often from father to son.

The kneeling worshipper is dressed austerely, and yet in the fashion of the times. His gown is long and high-necked, as prescribed by the moralists, but from his fine belt hangs a moneybag similar to the one displayed in the exhibition (cat. 6.4) and his hair is cut *alla franciosa*—two fashions that were to be stigmatized by Savonarola years later.

Ludovica Sebregondi

Bibliography: Cecchi 1987, p. 431; L. Venturini in *Maestri e botteghe* 1992, pp. 123–4; Venturini 1994, pp. 79–80, 121–2, no. 61; M. Tamassia in *Pulchritudo, Amor, Voluptas* 2001, pp. 124–5.

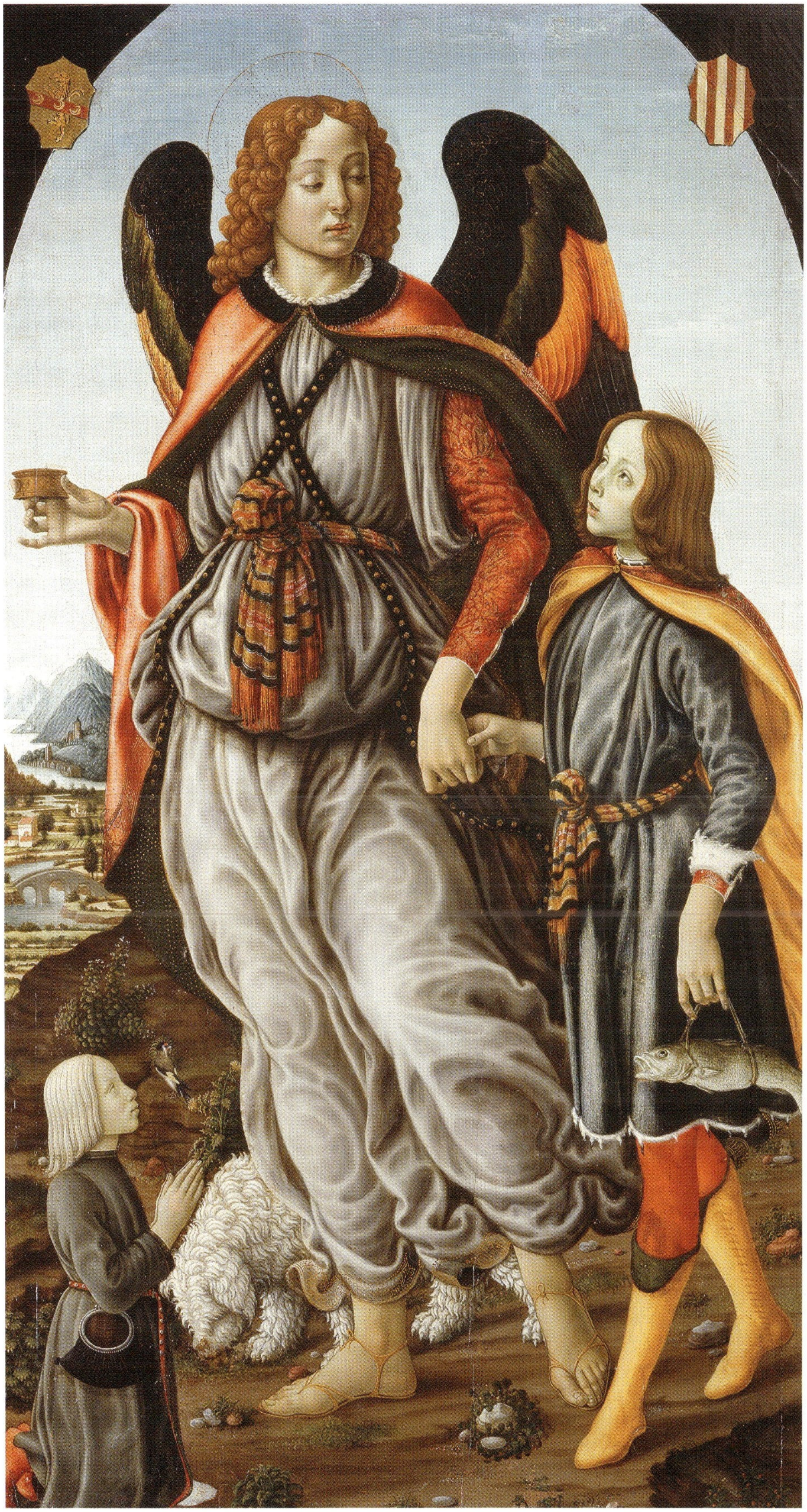

Section 6
The Sumptuary Laws

In the late 13th century, with the increased circulation of wealth, new demands and new lifestyles spread through the city. A growing number of people could now afford to wear costly gowns and ornaments, something that threatened to undermine the hitherto insuperable barrier between the social classes, and ran contrary to the Church's emphasis on penitence. Preachers abhorred shameless ostentation which they saw as a dangerous combination of vanity and excess.
Modesty was also linked to morality, as when Dante speaks with regret of an older Florence "peaceful, sober and modest" where women wore "No golden chain… nor coronal/That caught the eye more than did the person."[1]
The city government, however, had to accommodate contradictory imperatives: to support the city's commerce and the circulation of wealth; but also to counter a growing confusion between social classes caused by the spread of wealth.
The sumptuary laws, which regulated not only clothing and ornaments but also banquets, weddings, christenings and funerals, were issued to restrain the exhibition of wealth, limiting imports and spending and defending traditional values of austerity.
The laws attempted to control the morality of women and young people in particular, even to the detriment of the new opportunities opening up to commerce. In the 14th century, two major innovations appeared in the sumptuary laws. Previously addressed to the whole population, the laws now exempted *cavalieri, dottori*, physicians, judges and their womenfolk. To keep the pyramidal structure of society intact, lawmakers forbade anyone to wear clothing appropriate only to a social class other than his or her own. Another innovation made it possible to evade regulations by paying fines, with different fines being specified for different transgressions.
In this instance, the moral basis for the sumptuary laws was overlooked to fill the city's coffers. In still another development, newly forbidden garments already in the possession of the wearer could be authorized by having them "marked."[2]
The sumptuary laws represented an unattainable ideal. The fact that the regulations were constantly revised while moralists continued to denounce fashions displayed in the city's streets suggests that evasion was the norm. Despite the frequent renewal of these laws, in her first letter to her son Filippo Strozzi, exiled to Naples, Alessandra Macinghi describes the gowns and accessories given by her son-in-law Marco Parenti to her daughter in 1447: "When she goes out, she will be wearing over four hundred florins on her back;" including "a garland of feathers with pearls, worth eighty florins." Headdresses of this sort, obviously banned, appear in numerous paintings.
The dual scope of enforcing morality and curbing ostentation appears evident in a law issued in 1497, under the government of Francesco Valori, a follower of Savonarola, regulating the apparel worn by boys. Appealing to citizens to lead a sober, decent, moral life, the law banned boys under fourteen from wearing gold, silver, silk or embroidery work. Boys were also forbidden to wear hoods (the elaborate head coverings that surrounded the face as well), while outer clothing, including stockings, could be neither pink nor red, colours which were permitted only for "under garments," visible in the privacy of the home. In the event of children not observing the law, their parents would be held responsible.[3]

Ludovica Sebregondi

1 *Paradise*, Canto XV, vv. 97–9
2 See in the catalogue the article by Dora Liscia Bemporad and entries 6.1, 6.2.
3 See Sebregondi 2002.

6.1
L'Ufficiale delle donne, degli ornamenti e delle vesti [Regulations for women, ornaments and clothing]
1343–4
parchment codex with parchment cover, 21 fols., modern page numbers in pencil, 350 x 255 mm
Florence, Archivio di Stato, Giudice degli appelli e nullità, 119, ins. 16

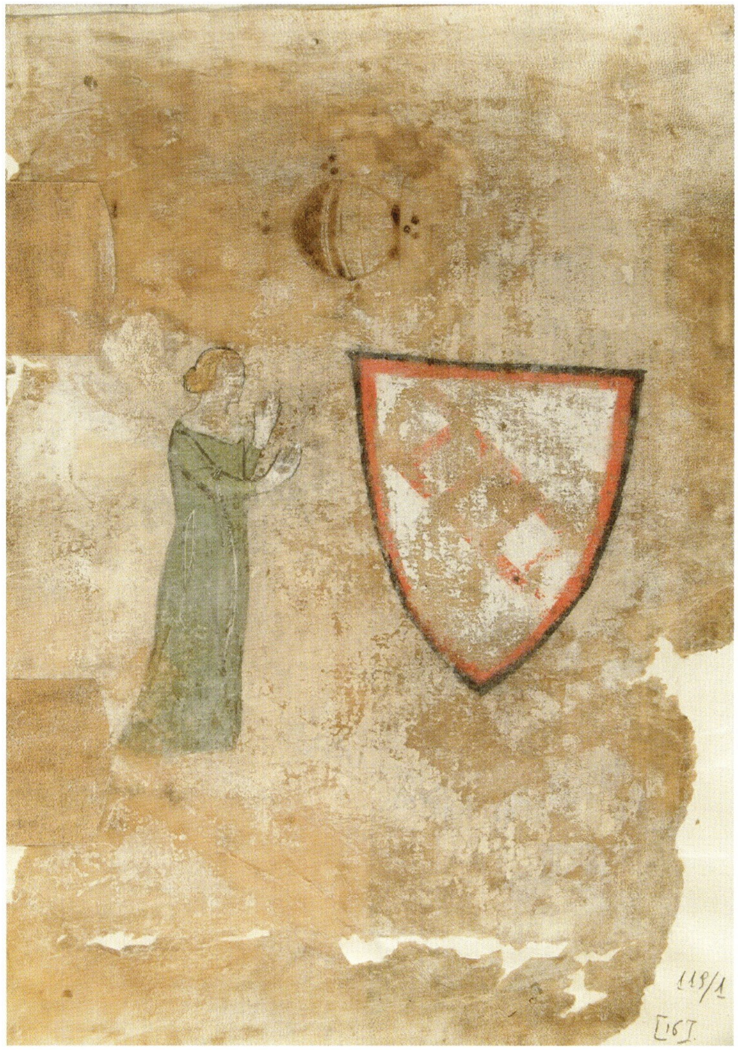

A provision issued by the Council on March 26,1330 instructed a commission of six Florentine citizens, including Messer Bartolomeo da Castelfiorentino and Masino di Maso dell'Antella, to elect a non-Florentine official to be responsible for enforcing the laws regulating spending on luxury goods. The same commission had already been ordered to draw up dispositions harmonizing all of the laws issued up to then concerning clothing and ornaments worn by men and women and excessive spending on baptisms, weddings and funerals. The official elected for a term of six months was Ser Matteo Bochacerie da Gubbio and on April 18 of that same year he was sworn in together with a notary and six policemen who were to assist him. The decree issued in March had also established that, on expiry of the mandate of the first *Ufficiale delle donne degli ornamenti e delle vesti*, as he was then called, a new official would be elected every six months by the Priors, the Gonfalonier of Justice and the Council of Twelve Good Men. This was done up to the rule of the Duke of Athens, under whose government no such official seems to have been elected. After the Duke's expulsion from Florence however, these magistrates held office again, at least up to 1345.

In 1345, the Executor of Judiciary Provisions was made responsible for enforcing the sumptuary laws, though he was succeeded in 1356 by the Judge of Appeals and Nullity. In the following years, jurisdiction ceased to be held by a single magistrate, and was assigned to the five "foreign" magistrates of the Florentine Commune. In the 1415 statutes, in fact, the section containing the sumptuary laws specifies that all of the magistrates having civil, criminal and financial jurisdiction were empowered to deal with infractions of the sumptuary laws. These bodies included the Podestà, the Captain of the People, the Executor of Judiciary Provisions, the Judge of Appeals and Nullity and the Official of Justice of the Commune.

On the cover of the register are two miniatures in colour. On the right, the coat of arms of the judge: "d'argento, bordato di rosso, alla scala posta in banda dello stesso;" and on the left, a woman seen in profile wearing a long, elegant green gown. Both of these images were damaged in the flood of 1966. The codex contains the sentences handed down by the Official Ser Cecco di Severino da San Severino and entered in the records by the notaries Ser Giovanni di Cecco da Sanseverino and Ser Andrea Porcellini da Montecchio from November 17, 1343 to April 1344.

How effective, or rather ineffective, the sumptuary laws were in curbing extravagance is well illustrated in Sacchetti's novella CXXXVI.

Giuseppe Biscione

Bibliography: Biscione forthcoming.

6.2
Sumptuary provisions inserted in the Florentine Statutes
1415
parchment codex, bound in the 19th century, bound in cardboard and all leather, with two clasps and seven brass plates at the corners; 314 fols., modern page numbers in pencil, 453 x 330 mm
Florence, Archivio di Stato, Statuti del Comune di Firenze, 24, fols. 280v-281r

The Florentines passed a great deal of legislation to limit spending on luxury, and from as early as the 13th century up to 1532, when the Florentine Republic ceased to exist, hundreds of sumptuary provisions were issued. This will seem strange in a city whose economic power was based on manufacturing, processing and trading wool, silk and linen, precious metals and luxury goods in general.

Most of these provisions, however, are unknown to us, since the manuscripts they were written on have been lost or destroyed. The provisions were deliberated in the city Councils, or by a commission specially appointed by the Signoria. They dealt with men's and women's clothing, its nature, style, quality and quantity; with the ornaments and embellishments worn with this clothing, of whatsoever kind or material; and lastly, with the jewels used to adorn them. In the same spirit, they governed weddings, baptisms and funerals.

Since the many sumptuary provisions, issued in rapid, insistent succession, were often dispersed in various collections of laws, the most important ones were then periodically inserted in the *corpus* of statutes. In fact, the four main editions of the Florentine statutes contain a core group of these laws which, beginning in the mid-14th century, were at least partly written in the vernacular. So the 1415 edition of the statutes has a section regulating spending on luxury goods, weddings, baptisms and funerals.

The section contains a total of forty-three chapters or indexes. The first is introductory, specifying the kind of clothing and ornaments forbidden to women. The next twelve contain regulations on weddings and betrothals, followed by another fourteen dealing with funerals and a further two on baptisms. The section concludes with fourteen chapters of procedural regulations.

The first chapter (whose opening page is displayed here), containing general regulations, specifies how many and what kind of gowns a woman could have; which styles and fabrics were permissible for these gowns; what and how many decorations, patterns, fabrics (velvet, silk, ribbons, fur) could be worn; which ornaments, with their size and weight, precious or otherwise (gold, silver, enamel, buttons, buckles) were allowed and which were banned.

The following paragraph is a perfect example: "Item, no woman can presume to wear silver weighing over a pound, either in garlands or buttons, or in any other way, worn either on the head or elsewhere [...] except that, in addition to said pound of silver, she can wear a silver belt weighing, with its stone, fifteen ounces and no more, including the buckle; and the silver may be gilt as long as it does not exceed the said weight." How changeable these provisions were is clearly demonstrated in the folio displayed. It was, in fact, rewritten over erasures because by the time new statutes were issued, the sumptuary provisions had already changed.

Giuseppe Biscione

Bibliography: Biscione 2009, pp. 714–8.

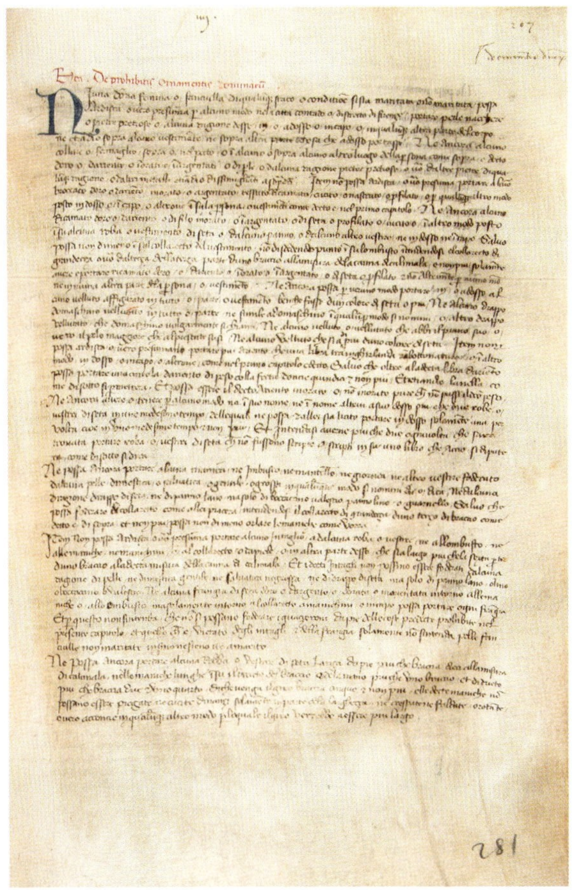

6.3
Florentine workshop
Belt
c. 1470
red taffeta brocaded and shot with gold thread wound around a yellow silk core; silver-gilt, cast, chased, fretwork; translucent enamel with drowned threads; niello-work
6.8 x 154.5 cm
London, Victoria and Albert Museum, inv. no. 4278-1857

The edges of the band of red fabric brocaded in gold are decorated with a motif of opposed crescent moons alternating with fleshy leaves. The frame simulates flat ribbing. The borders are voided, leaving the profile of the design to emerge. The buckle, enamelled on the tip with an acanthus leaf motif formed by threads drowned in blue enamel, is decorated with fretted, crumpled leaves crowned by a palmette. On one side of the tongue is inserted, within a horse-head shield, a coat of arms with a radiant sun above it, a full moon below. Within round niellos, two of which are missing, are the inscriptions: "VIRTUS VINO ; AMOR. E. VOL; SPERA. IN. DIO." The band, designed for a man's belt, was purposely woven on a small loom, as shown by the ribbing forming the border around the band. Silk shops specialized in this field of production worked for innumerable goldsmiths' shops, where the belts were assembled with their buckles and ferrules. Extra-sturdy fabric, reinforced by rich brocading in metal threads, was always used. Similar belts have been taken as reference point for the dating of the one displayed here, although agreement on this point is not unanimous. All of these belts were splendid gifts donated by Pope Julius II to the eminent personages of his time: to King James IV in 1507 (Edinburgh, Crown Treasure, see Fingerlin 1971, pp. 341–2, no. 73); to Wladislaus II of Hungary in 1509 (Budapest, Magyar Nemzeti Múzeum, inv. no. 55.5235, ivi, p. 327, no. 56); and to the Swiss Confederates in 1511 (Zurich, Landesmuseum, inv. no. Dep. 853, ivi, p. 479, no. 550).

The belt now in London at Victoria and Albert Museum, where it arrived in 1857 (p. 402) has similar features and has thus been dated to the same period by Fingerlin. Marion Campbell instead (2009, fig. 72, p. 71) dates it as early as 1450. Erich Steingräber (1963, pp. 311–2) and Lorenz Selig (1991, pp. 94–5) collocate the belt, whose heraldic arms are unrecognizable, in the Florentine area, produced around the same time as the binding of two of the three *Books of Hours* (of one, only the original cover has survived). These volumes were commissioned by Lorenzo the Magnificent for the weddings of his daughters, Lucrezia, Maddalena and Luisa, who all planned to marry in 1488. Luisa, however, died prematurely before marrying Giovanni de' Medici, and Lorenzo probably kept the precious illuminated manuscript for himself. The buckle on the belt can be compared both with the binding of the Florence codex (Biblioteca Medicea Laurenziana, ms. Ashburnham 1874), and that of the codex now in Munich (Bayerische Staatsbibliothek, cod. Wittelsbach Clm 23639). With the former it has in common the leaves, full-blown, fretted and crumpled, as well as the rich decoration of twisted threads; with the latter, the palmette motif. Such decorations were, moreover, common to all of the book bindings produced at that time, as can be seen for example in the *Mare Magnum* (Florence, Convento della Santissima Annunziata) made by Antonio di Salvi and company in 1488, and in the *Dante* with commentary by Cristoforo Landino (Florence, Biblioteca Nazionale Centrale, B.R. 341) made by Baccio Baldini and donated to the Florentine Republic in 1481 (Liscia Bemporad 2005, pp. 234–5). Another term of comparison consists of one of the most important Florentine decorative schemes, found in the *Reliquiario del Libretto* done in 1500 by Paolo di Giovanni Sogliani, who uses the crumpled, fretted leaves as well as the twisted threads to flank the frames of enamelled medallions depicting the Evangelists. Sogliani had probably been to Rome with Antonio del Pollaiolo, with whom he worked until the latter's death in 1498. Although he returned to Florence, it seems that one of his sons remained in Rome, and probably continued to utilize his father's designs and stylistic traits, which would explain the persistence of certain decorative schemes even in later years, when they had fallen out of fashion elsewhere. Despite the indubitable similarity of the belts donated by Julius II to the one in London, we can recognize in ours a Florentine matrix, based on the use of niello, as well as the plant volutes created by threads drowned in translucent blue enamel.

Dora Liscia Bemporad

Bibliography: Steingräber 1964, pp. 303–13; Fingerlin 1971, p. 402; Seelig 1991, pp. 77–166; Campbell 2009, pp. 71, 97, fig.72.

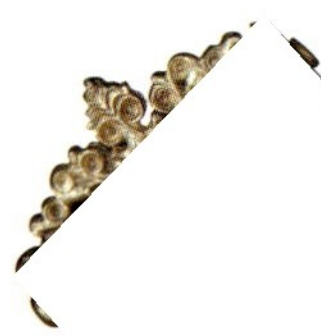

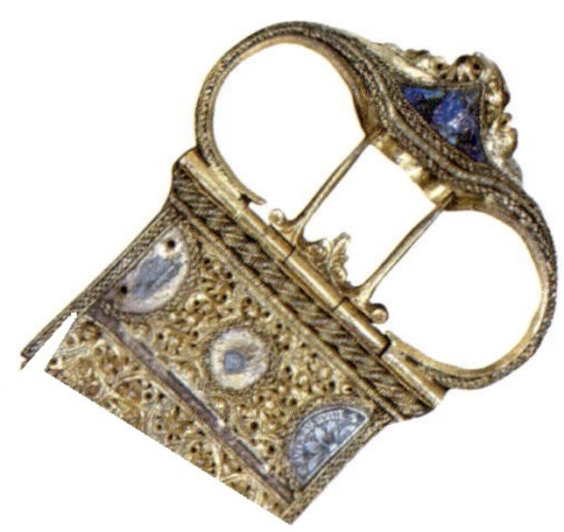

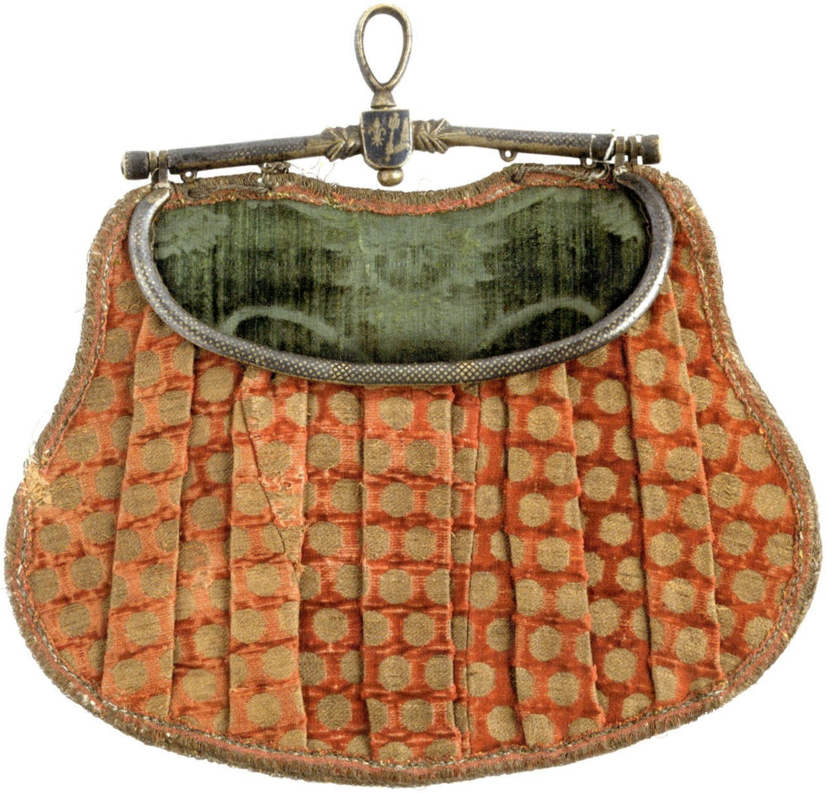

6.4
Florentine workshop
Money-bag
last quarter of the 15th century
silk and gold metal thread; leather;
cast bronze, scraped with graving tool,
chased and nielloed. Monochromatic
cut voided velvet with brocading weft;
monochromatic cut voided velvet
30.5 x 32 cm
Prato, Museo del Tessuto, Collezione Comune–Cariprato, inv. no. 81.01.182

This bag, with shaped profile and box pleats, is formed of two pockets: the first is decorated with gold coin motifs in chequered parallel rows brocaded on a red velvet ground; the second in green trellis velvet, probably in ogival network. The bag is reinforced with leather. Sewn to the mouth is a semicircular element in niellated bronze decorated with small chequered motifs appearing also on the support hinged to this element, formed of two opposing serpents' heads, their open mouths swallowing the two circular segments. At the centre is a drop-shaped eyelet above a shield with a ball at the top. It has been identified as the family crest of the Bracci, a Florentine mercantile family ("azure with a right arm grasping a metal mace;" Bonito Fanelli 1988, pp. 332–3). The lily beside the symbol, normally absent, could allude to the family's friendship with the Medici and to their role as bankers (De Roover 1963). Moreover, the red velvet motif seems to evoke, as Sangiorgi has suggested (1926, pp. 116–7) for fabrics of similar type, the heraldic arms of the Cambiatori, or Money Changers' Guild, with shields and gold coins scattered over a red field.

For this one-of-a-kind object, two different hypotheses have been advanced by the experts. On the one hand, it has even been suspected of being a 19th-century fake; on the other, it is thought to have belonged to the Florentine Canon Antonio Bracci, a friend of Cardinal Ludovico Strozzi, who was a cousin of Caterina de' Medici, wife of Henry II of Valois (Bonito Fanelli 1988, pp. 332–3; D. Degl'Innocenti in *Arti a Firenze* 2009, pp. 220–1). In fact, bags of this kind have been amply documented in France, and its style is consonant with that of Northern Europe. Other evidence, however, could collocate the bag in the Florentine sphere, as for instance Baccio Baldini's engravings of the *Matto* or *Bagatto*, a Tarocchi figure, done around 1464. This figure, dressed as the Jester, wears a bag hanging from his belt, where the stamps on the fabric make this hypothesis more credible. Since Baccio Baldini was one of the greatest niellator artists of his day, it may even be presumed that such a valuable bag could have come from his workshop. Any suggestion, however, risks being contradicted, since as of now we have no other object of this kind.

Dora Liscia Bemporad

Bibliography: *La Città degli Uffizi* 1982, p. 72; Bonito Fanelli 1988, pp. 331–6; D. Degl'Innocenti in *Il Museo del Tessuto* 1999, pp. 38–9; *Misteriosi scrigni* 2001, pp. 211–2; Desrosiers 2004, pp. 318–20; Goretti 2006, pp. 577–603; D. Degl'Innocenti in *Arti a Firenze* 2009, pp. 220–1, no. 76.

6.5
Maso Finiguerra (Florence 1426–64),
attributed to
Woman Wearing Peacock Feather Headdress
c. 1460
pen and brown ink, traces of stylus;
white lined paper
197 x 100 mm
Inscriptions: "2" (on verso); "1748-Ignoto del sec. XV°" (Ferri) (on verso of the controfondo)
Florence, Gabinetto Disegni e Stampe degli Uffizi, inv. no. 59 F.

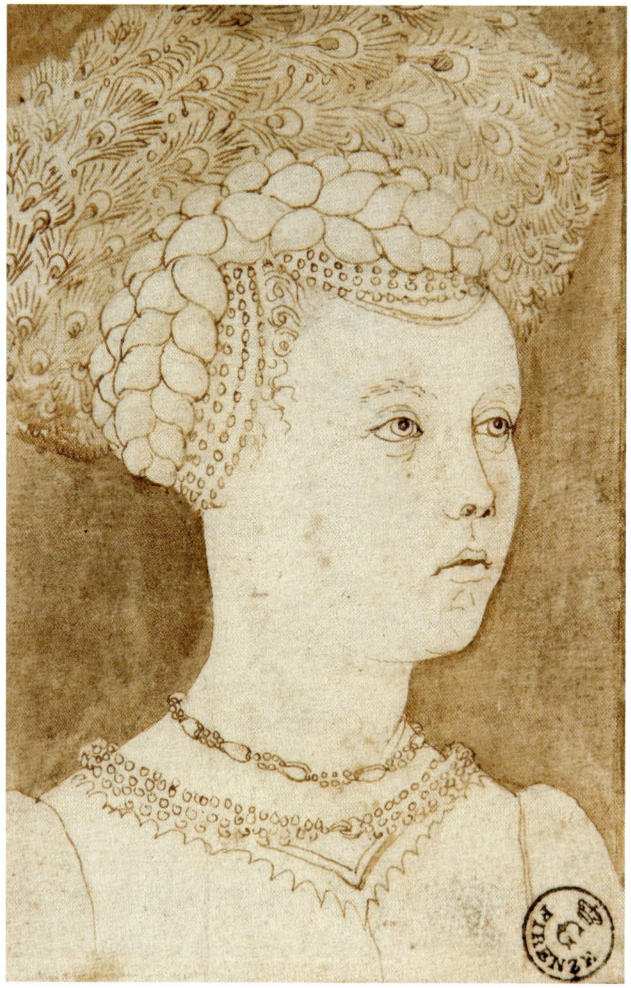

This drawing depicts a woman wearing a peacock feather headdress that highlights the thick braid of hair around her head. The rest of her hair is held back by a headband adorned with three rows of pearls, like those bordering the neckline of her dress. She wears a necklace formed of a series of two segments of pearls alternating with teardrop pearls.

The drawing, which belonged to Leopoldo de' Medici, has been variously attributed: to the School of Pollaiolo, under whose name were grouped most of the drawings later attributed to Maso Finiguerra; or to Finiguerra himself, whose artistic personality has emerged more clearly in recent studies. Finiguerra is thought to have left books in which he bound the many drawings he and his assistants produced. Since they probably served as models for his pupils as well as for other artists, it is very hard to attribute them definitively to one or the other (Elen 1995, pp. 26–9). Some technical traits, such as emphasizing profiles with the stylus, have made the attribution to Finiguerra even more plausible. His shop in Via Vacchereccia produced not only goldwork but also copper sulphate etchings, niellos and plates, creating numerous models that spread to places far from Florence (*Oreficeria sacra* 1990, p. 38). Lorenza Melli hypothesizes that this drawing may represent a mannequin "used to display the necklaces and headdresses created in the goldsmith's shop" (1995, p. 36). The sumptuary provisions often dealt with ornaments for the head, which represented, in addition to the natural crowning of the wearer's apparel, a distinctive sign of wealth and nobility, since the head was the symbol of intelligence and many other virtues, not physical alone. It was forbidden to wear on the head more than "6 ounces of pearls on a twig or anything else used to adorn said head." Obviously, the strings of pearls worn by the girl in the picture weighed more than this. It was also forbidden to wear more than one necklace at a time (*Due provvisioni* [1464–72], ed. Mazzi 1908, p. 5). Alessandra Macinghi Strozzi, in a letter written in 1447 to Filippo Strozzi, in Naples at the time, describes a similar headdress worn by her daughter Caterina on her engagement day: "It was a garland of feathers with pearls, which cost eighty florins; and the hair below was dressed with two strings of braided pearls, which cost sixty or more florins" (Macinghi Strozzi [1447–70], ed. Bianchini 1987, pp. 62–3). Marco Parenti's *Libro di Ricordi* [Memoirs] mentions "a garland of peacock feathers adorned with silver and pearls" (ivi, p. 51). Peacock feathers bore a dual meaning, symbolizing on the one hand vanity, on the other, in Christian iconology, the resurrection and the life as well as the perfect knowledge of God.

Dora Liscia Bemporad

Bibliography: Ferri 1890, p. 191; Giglioli 1933, p. 380; Degenhart, Schmitt 1968, I-2, fig. 859; Kubiak 1974; Collobi Ragghianti 1974, p. 55; Angelini 1986, no. 126, fig. 150; Petrioli Tofani 1991, p. 29; Elen 1995, cat. 25; Melli 1995, p. 36 and 73, no. 38.

6.6
Lo Scheggia (Giovanni di ser Giovanni;
San Giovanni Valdarno 1406-Florence 1486)
Virgin and Child,
in the cusp *God the Father and the Holy Spirit*
c. 1470–80
tempera on panel
150 x 84 cm
Arezzo, Museo Statale d'Arte Medievale
e Moderna, inv. no. 28

At the centre of an imposing tabernacle, the painting shows the Virgin in adoration of the Child held in her lap. Behind her two angels are playing a lute and a viola da braccio beside a marble niche; above, trees stand out against a wedge of sky. Mary, seated on a cushion of precious fabric, wears a red gown with gilt decorations, and over it a blue mantle with a star on the left shoulder. The Child is wrapped in a strip of red cloth, above white swathing bands garnished in gold. A lavish wealth of materials appears in the use of gold, vermillion and blue, the decorative punching of the halos, and the bronze-like column capitals. The scene is bounded by two columns; along the architrave runs a festoon alternating with a shell motif, and in the cusp appears God the Father bestowing blessings, accompanied by the dove of the Holy Spirit and by cherubim. On the gradine, the inscription "AVE-GRATIA-PLENA-DOMINUS-TECUM-BENEDITA/ TU-IMMUGLIERIBUS-E-BENEDITUS VEN" is flanked by two coats of arms, identified by Mario Salmi (1921, pp. 28–9) as the emblems of the Chiari, a Florentine family, but which could instead belong to the Bardelli ("Azure, with three gold wheels, 2.1, topped by two discussated keys of silver, or gold, bound with red," see ASF, Archivio Ceramelli Papiani, insert 388).

The tabernacle is an example, quite rare insofar as original in every part, of those *colmi da camera*, frequently mentioned in documents, used for private worship. They consisted not only of paintings but also of sculptures, carved in marble or modelled in terracotta. The bedchambers of the upper classes were in fact decorated by paintings and reliefs, usually of religious subject. The Dominican moralist Giovanni Dominici advised the head of a house "to have paintings in the home of saints and youths or young virgins, in which your child, while still in swathing bands, will delight and from which he will draw inspiration" (Pons 1992, p. 226; see also Musacchio 2008, pp. 198–202, 209–16).

The panel displayed here has been attributed to the Master of the Adimari Chest, identified later as Giovanni di ser Giovanni, known as lo Scheggia, Masaccio's brother. From the 1440s to the 1460s, he headed one of Florence's most active shops in the sector of painting chests and furnishings (see L. Cavazzini in *Il fratello di Masaccio* 1999, p. 62). The work can be dated precisely based on its musical iconography. As noted by Gabriele Rossi Rognoni, the angel playing the lute is plucking the chords with his fingers and not with a plectrum. Since the transition from the plectrum (usually made of a quill) to the fingers took place in the second half of the 15th century, and both techniques were still in use in 1489, the date can be hypothesized as around 1470–80.

The luxurious clothing depicted here was prohibited for the population in general by the sanctuary laws, being allowed only to "knights, doctors of both civil and canon law, physicians, and foreign men and their women," who could wear "whatever they wished" (*Due provvisioni* [1464–72], ed. Mazzi 1908, p. 7).

Ludovica Sebregondi

Bibliography: Salmi 1921, pp. 28–9; L. Cavazzini in *Il fratello di Masaccio* 1999, pp. 62–3.

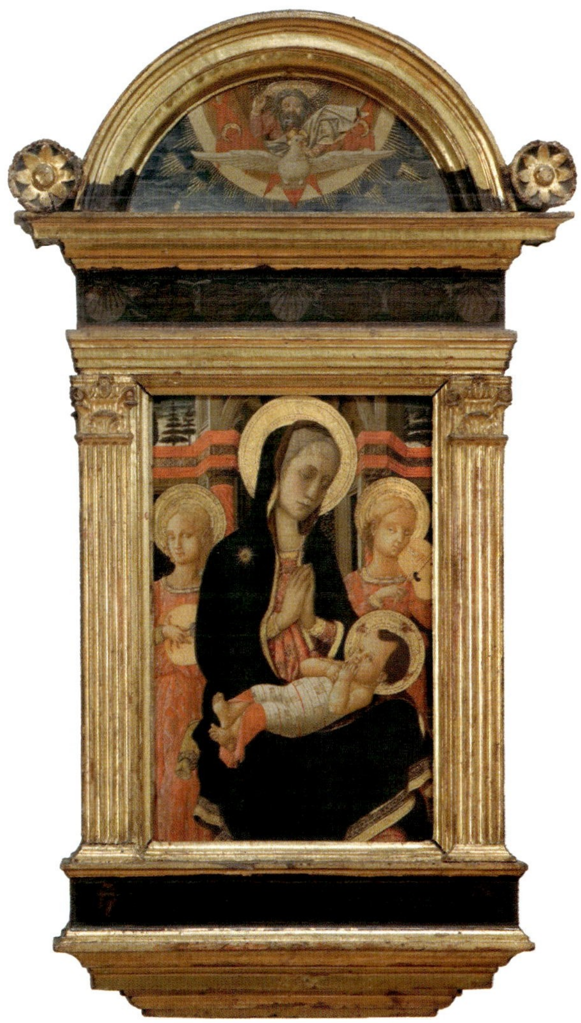

6.7
Jacopo del Sellaio (Florence 1442–93)
The Banquet of Ahasuerus
c. 1485
panel painting
44.5 x 62 cm
Florence, Galleria degli Uffizi,
1890 inv. no. 491

This is one of five panels now divided among Florence (the Uffizi), Paris (the Louvre) and Budapest (the Szépmüvészeti Múzeum). They narrate the story of Esther, the Biblical heroine who lived in Susa at the court of King Ahasuerus the Great, better known as Xerxes I (485-465 B.C.). After Queen Vasti had been banished, Esther, wise and obedient, became the king's second wife. In the Uffizi panel, the first in the series, Ahasuerus, wearing sumptuous garments and a crown, is seated at a banquet table laid with precious plate and surrounded by splendid decorations in the garden of his royal palace (*Book of Esther*, 16: 1. 8). At this moment Ahasuerus is informed that his wife Vasti, defying her husband's orders, refuses to greet his guests because she is attending another banquet. On the right, the king appears in the same scene, consulting with his advisers on how to punish his wife's disobedience; he finally decides to banish her.

Sellaio's panels must have formed part of a *spalliere*, consisting of wooden panels of various sizes, intaglioed, inlaid or painted, used to line the walls of a room in an interior decoration scheme fashionable in 15th–century Florence (Pons 2009). The clients for the series painted by Sellaio are unknown. He probably painted the panels in anticipation of a wedding, since on those occasions entire "supplies" of furniture for the nuptial chamber were often prepared (Pons 2008).

The Uffizi *Banquet of Ahasuerus* seems to take place in the flowery garden of an elegant 15th-century residence, similar in some ways to the garden of the Medici's "old house", enclosed on four sides by high embattled walls and divided into a flagstone courtyard and a "little orchard"(Carl 1990, pp. 42–3). In Sellaio's painting the table, under a grapevine pergola, is covered by a refined tablecloth, perhaps made of Rheims linen, and is laid with gilt and bronze plate: goblets, dishes, knives and two-tined forks (very rare at the time) in addition to salt-cellars and cutting boards for slicing food. As the courses are served, the guests are entertained with music. Behind the banqueters, luxurious drapes divide the dining room from the area behind it, where imposing pavilions made of elegant brocade and velvet fabric gleam with refined decorations, mainly plant and floral motifs. Expensive fabrics, like elegant tableware and choice dishes, contributed to the opulence of banquets (Liscia Bemporad 1994, pp. 74–5). The gowns, hairstyles and headdresses of the guests, however, do not reflect Florentine fashion of the times, but rather the eastern style (*alla grecanica*), in keeping with the iconographic model brought to Florence in 1439 by the participants in the great Ecumenical Council (see Lazzi 1994).

The banquet depicted by Sellaio reflects some of the true characteristics of banquets of the time, held in the courtyards, loggias and gardens of palaces for important festivities such as weddings. Famous in this regard, thanks to the descriptions left by contemporaries, are the wedding of Bernardo Rucellai and Nannina de' Medici in 1466 and that of Lorenzo the Magnificent and Clarice Orsini in June 1469 (Sebregondi 1994, pp. 53–8). The luxury flaunted in such events persisted even after 1472, when the sumptuary laws issued by the 1415 Statutes came back into force. Special derogations to these laws were granted to families whose wealth was commensurate to such vast expenditure and so were not at risk of squandering their entire fortunes.

Elena Capretti

Bibliography: N. Pons in *Virtù d'Amore* 2010, pp. 170–5, no. 4a.

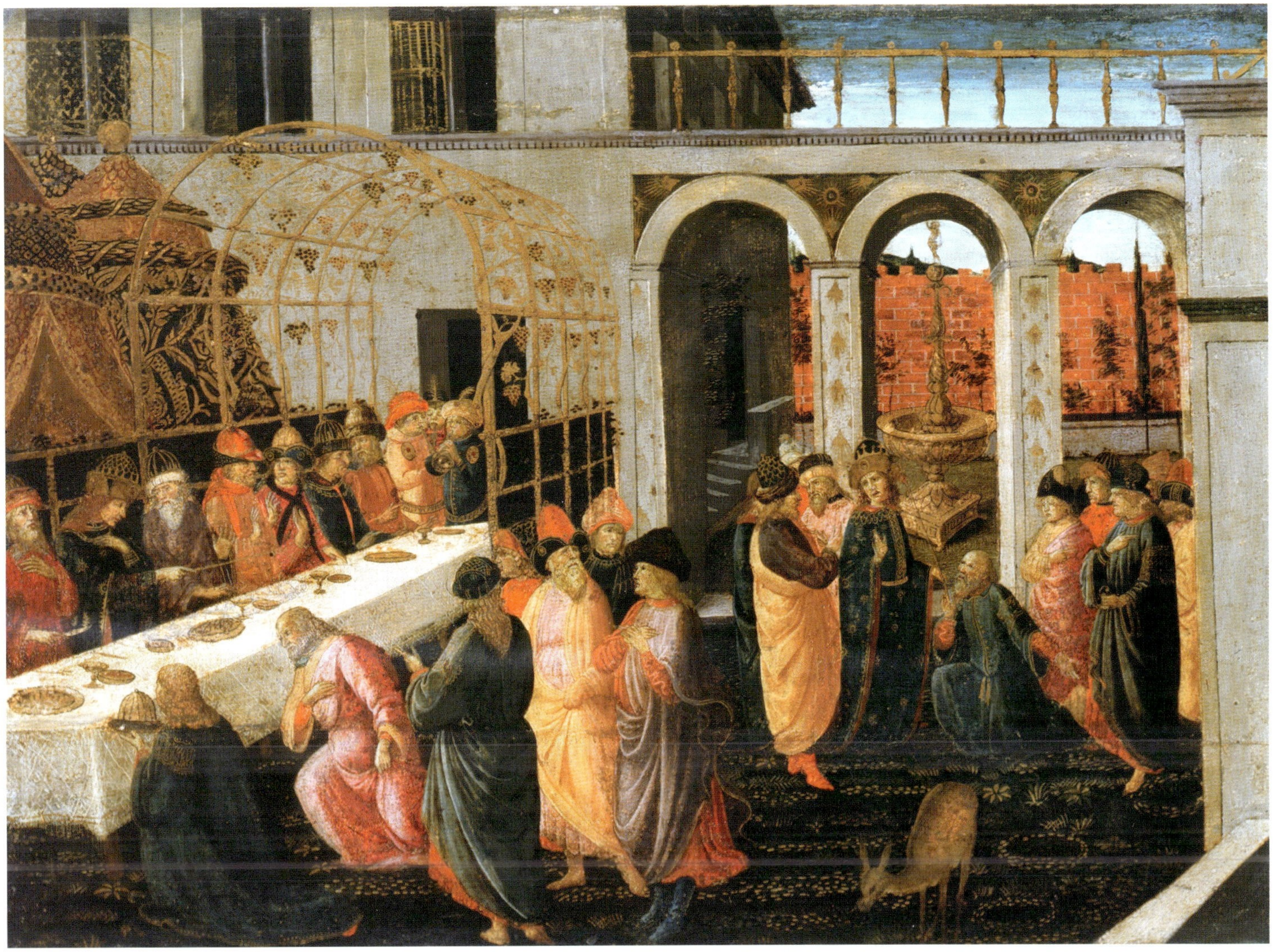

6.8
Niccolò di Pietro Gerini
(Florence, information from 1368–1415)
Funeral of a Brother in the Company of Gesù Pellegrino (predella)
1404–8
tempera on panel
81 x 156 cm
Florence, Galleria dell'Accademia,
1890 inv. no. 5066

The predella forms the lower part of a *tavola da morti* that belonged to the Flagellant Company of Gesù Pellegrino, which had its home at Santa Maria Novella. Typical of the production of Niccolò di Pietro Gerini, an artist who trained in Orcagna's workshop, it depicts the funeral of a member of the society. Twenty brothers are kneeling around the body of the deceased, which has been dressed in the white robes of the group and laid upon the ground in preparation for burial. The corpse lies before a crucifix held up by one of the brothers. The sleeves of his gown are wide enough to cover his hands as he lifts the cross, in keeping with the eastern usage of not touching sacred objects with one's bare hands. The other brothers hold scourges (or "disciplines") used for flagellation, formed of sticks with knotted cords hanging from them. One of the brothers is pulling the edges of his hood together, to keep his identity secret. The *buffa* (as the hood was called) was used in charitable associations to keep those who practiced philanthropy from being recognized, in obedience to the Gospel precept "charity must be done in secret." The image complies with the prescriptions laid down by the Chapters of the Company of Gesù Pellegrino. At news of the death of a brother it was prescribed that two members would bring to the home of the deceased "the disciplinary gown, in which he had been accustomed to do penitence and to dress him in that." The members of the society gathered in their oratory, wearing hoods "above their other clothes." From there, in a group of sixteen or more, they went out in procession, accompanied by the priest, to the home of the deceased. Eight brothers remained kneeling outside with the empty coffin. The others entered the dead man's home, wrapped his body in a shroud and brought it to the church for the funeral and burial (ASF, Capitoli di Compagnie Religiose Soppresse 152, fol. 8v; see Sebregondi 2006, Sebregondi 2009).

This kind of ceremony was popular with members of the upper classes, since it allowed them to evade the sumptuary laws issued to curb ostentation in commemorating death; and with the rest of the population because it offered a respectable funeral and burial in the tomb shared by the members in a church or their own oratory. Arranging for a proper funeral and burial place was a matter of great concern, and the solemnity of the ritual, the number of commemorative masses celebrated, the use of expensive decorations, were incentives that might lead a man to decide to enrol in one or another company. However, a funeral could also be enormously expensive, like that of Francesco Datini, which, notwithstanding the sumptuary laws, cost almost 1000 florins (Cassandro 2010, p. 43).

Ludovica Sebregondi

Bibliography: Arthur 1990, pp. 350–1; Henderson 1994, p. 162; *Galleria dell'Accademia* 1999, p. 110; Sebregondi 2006, p. 105; Sebregondi 2009, p. 351.

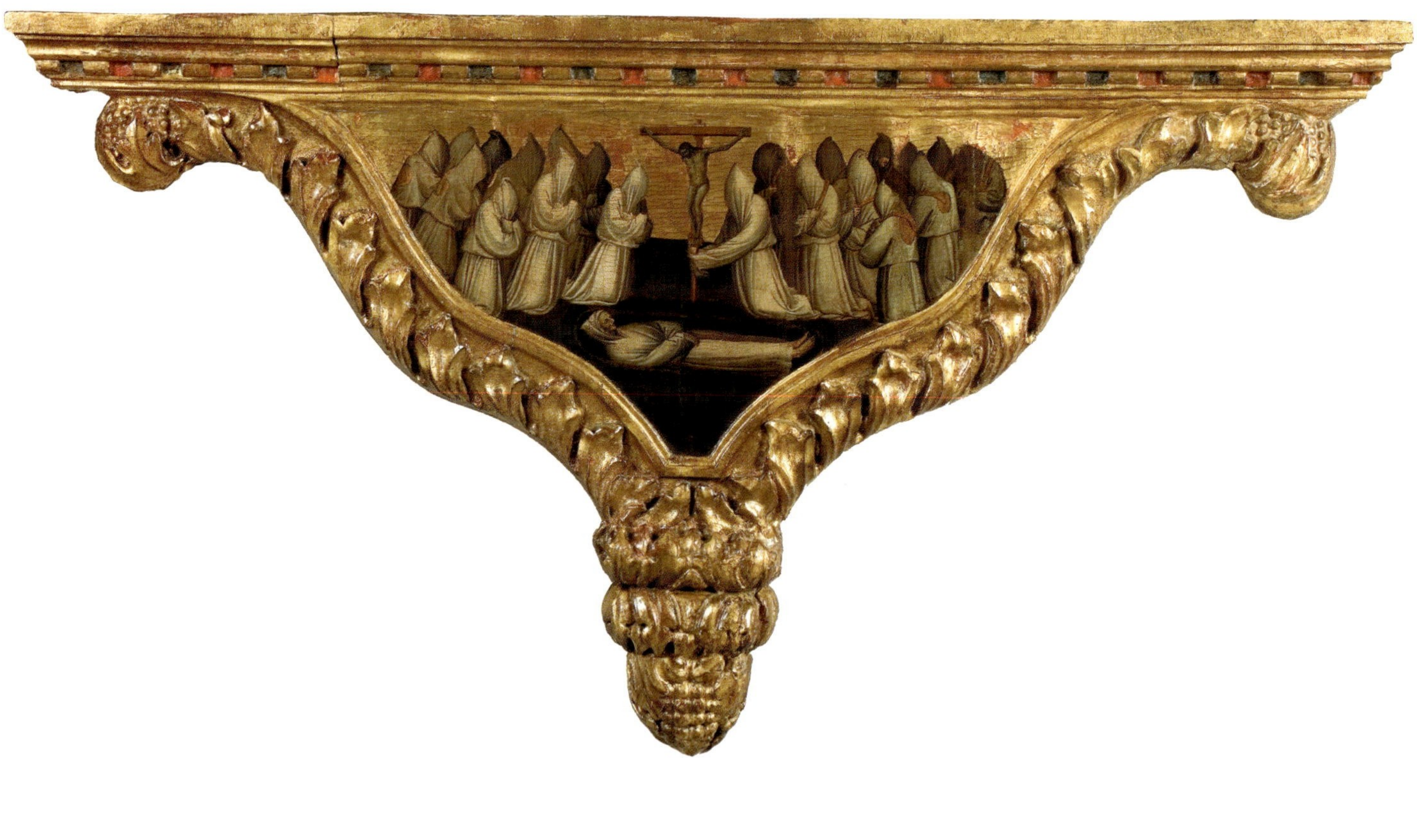

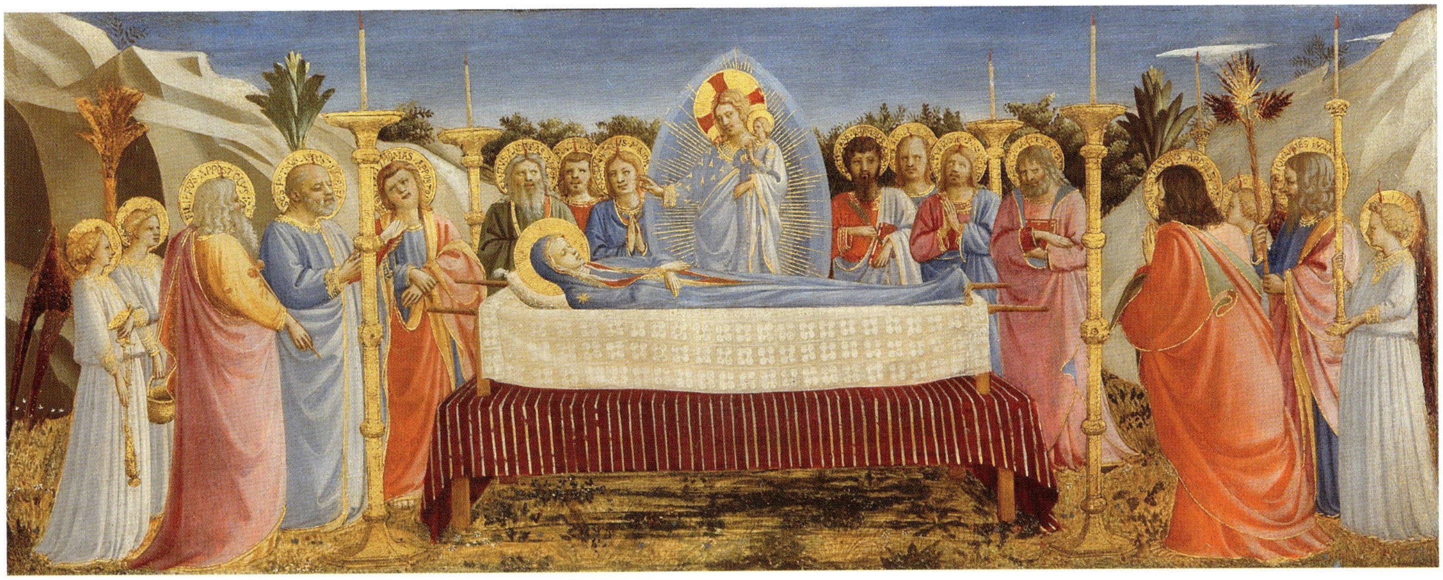

6.9
Fra Angelico
(Fra Giovanni da Fiesole, Guido di Pietro;
Vicchio *c.* 1395–Rome 1455)
Funeral of the Virgin (predella)
1432–5
tempera on panel
19 x 51.5 cm
Florence, Museo di San Marco,
1890 inv. no. 1493

This panel with its companion piece depicting the *Marriage of the Virgin* (no. 6.10) very probably composed the predella of another picture painted by Fra Angelico, the *Coronation of the Virgin*, now in the Uffizi, dating from around 1432–5. The altarpiece originally adorned an altar standing beside the altar screen in the Church of Sant'Egidio, which belonged to the hospital of Santa Maria Nuova.

In the *Funeral*, according to apocryphal tradition, Christ, descended from Heaven and surrounded by a mandorla, stands beside the body of his Mother and welcomes her *animula*. At the head of the corpse Peter assumes the role of celebrant, reading from the liturgical book, while behind him two angels are holding thuribles and holy-water sprinklers. The Virgin lies on a litter draped in embroidered white fabric, resting on a catafalque draped in a red-and-gold cloth. For funerals, the sumptuary laws prohibited costly gold-and-silver fabrics. Furthermore, only two candles or torches were allowed, for a total of thirty pounds of wax at most. Around the Virgin's body instead stand four monumental gilt candle-holders, while two more candelabra, lighter in weight but equally costly, are borne by two angels on the right. The Apostles, looking on, are praying. They are not dressed in mourning, which was reserved by law to only a few of the closest relatives, and was at the expense of the heirs (on this subject, see Klapisch-Zuber 1988, pp. 285–303; Strocchia 1992). The colours of the fabrics, dear to the style of Fra Angelico, are for the most part red, sky-blue and white, delicate and glowing. In 15th-century funerals, instead, black and brown were customary for gowns and dark blue for mantles (Levi Pisetzky 1964–9, II, 1964, p. 461).

For funerals, just as for banquets and weddings, the sumptuary laws tried to curb needless expenditure, especially for families that could ill afford it. And yet we have records of remarkably sumptuous funerals, such as the one held by Giovanni di Bicci de' Medici in honour of Cardinal Bartolomeo Coscia, who was buried in the Baptistery. The coffin was surrounded by a great number of burning candles while the relatives and friends who sat around it bore lighted torches. They were joined by forty-four "poor men dressed in white [...] holding lighted candles" (Bartolomeo del Corazza [1405–39], ed. Gentile 1991, p. 267). Strikingly lugubrious, instead, was the funeral of Piero di Cosimo de' Medici, held on December 3, 1469. Laid in a coffin lined with simple black cloth, the body was escorted by his closest kinsmen wearing black clothes roughly basted together—so that the fabric would not be ruined and could be used later for some other purpose—and by other members of the family wearing black hoods and mantles (Levi Pisetzky 1964–9, II, 1964, pp. 461–8).

Elena Capretti

Bibliography: A. Cecchi in *Miniatura* 2003, pp. 121–3 no. I.23 (with bibliography).

6.10
Fra Angelico
(Fra Giovanni da Fiesole,
Guido di Pietro; Vicchio *c.* 1395–Rome 1455)
Marriage of the Virgin (predella panel)
1432–5
tempera on panel
19 x 51.5 cm
Florence, Museo di San Marco, 1890 inv. no. 1493

The *Marriage of the Virgin* is based on the *Golden Legend* written by Jacopo da Varagine in the mid-13th century, recounting an ancient tradition based on the Apocryphal Gospels (Klapisch-Zuber 1988, pp. 131–47). Before the temple, the High Priest summons all of the unmarried male descendents of the house of Judah, so that a miraculous sign can indicate which of them is worthy to become Mary's husband. Each man carries a rod. A white dove flies down and lights on the rod carried by the older man Joseph, causing it to burst into bloom as a sign of the Divine will. The High Priest then celebrates the wedding of Mary and Joseph. Since the time when Giotto painted this subject in the Scrovegni Chapel in Padua, the wedding of the Virgin had been interpreted by artists in modern terms. In keeping with the traditional iconography, Fra Angelico's composition fixes the moment when the rings are exchanged (*immissio anuli*), after both bride and groom have expressed their consent, recorded by the notary, and before the priest gives his blessing in the wedding ceremony.

In the 15th-century ritual, which took place in front of or inside the bride's home in the presence of friends and kinsmen, the notary, or the father of the bride, took the girl's right hand in his left and placed it in the hands of the groom. The groom then placed the ring on the bride's index or ring finger (which is not known), then received his own ring and put it on his finger. During the wedding, it was customary for the bridegroom's friends to strike him on the shoulders with open hands or closed fists, in a gesture indicating his abandonment of celibacy. This gesture frequently appears in Tuscan scenes depicting the *Marriage of the Virgin*, together with the gesture of Mary's rejected suitors, who break the staffs that had failed to blossom (Sebregondi 2010, p. 38). Music enlivened the various stages of the ceremony, from the wedding proper, represented in Fra Angelico's painting, to the moment when the bride left her home for that of her husband.

In the Uffizi painting the bride, who was the chief target of the sumptuary laws governing marriage, is bareheaded and displays no complicated hairstyle. She wears a simple dress, unadorned by expensive buttons, luxurious belts, fur lining or a long train, all ornaments condemned by the laws designed to curb the ostentation, splendour and lavish expenditure customary to these occasions (Gagliardi 2010, p. 32). On the whole, Mary's wedding dress is far removed from certain excesses such as the outfit worn by the daughter of the wealthy Prato merchant Francesco Datini on her wedding day in 1407: a gown of silk velvet dyed in the costly colour crimson, with a train over nineteen metres long, "at the exorbitant cost of 118 florins, equivalent at the time to six months of wages for a good builder" (Lurati 2010, p. 45).

Elena Capretti

Bibliography: M. Scudieri in *Rinascimento* 2001, p. 56 no. I.12; A. Cecchi in *Miniatura* 2003, pp. 121–3, no. I.23; M. Scalini in *Specchio del tempo* 2006, pp. 288–9.

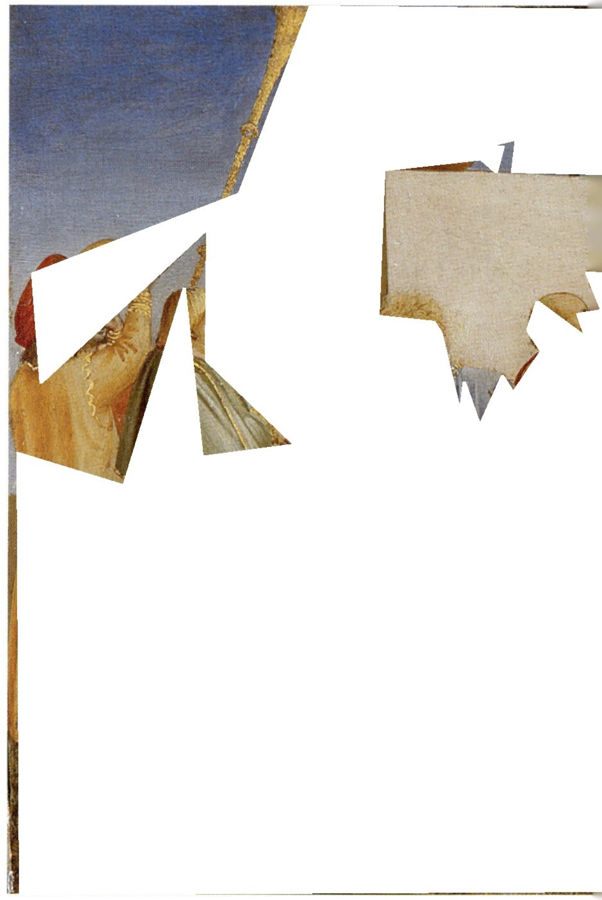

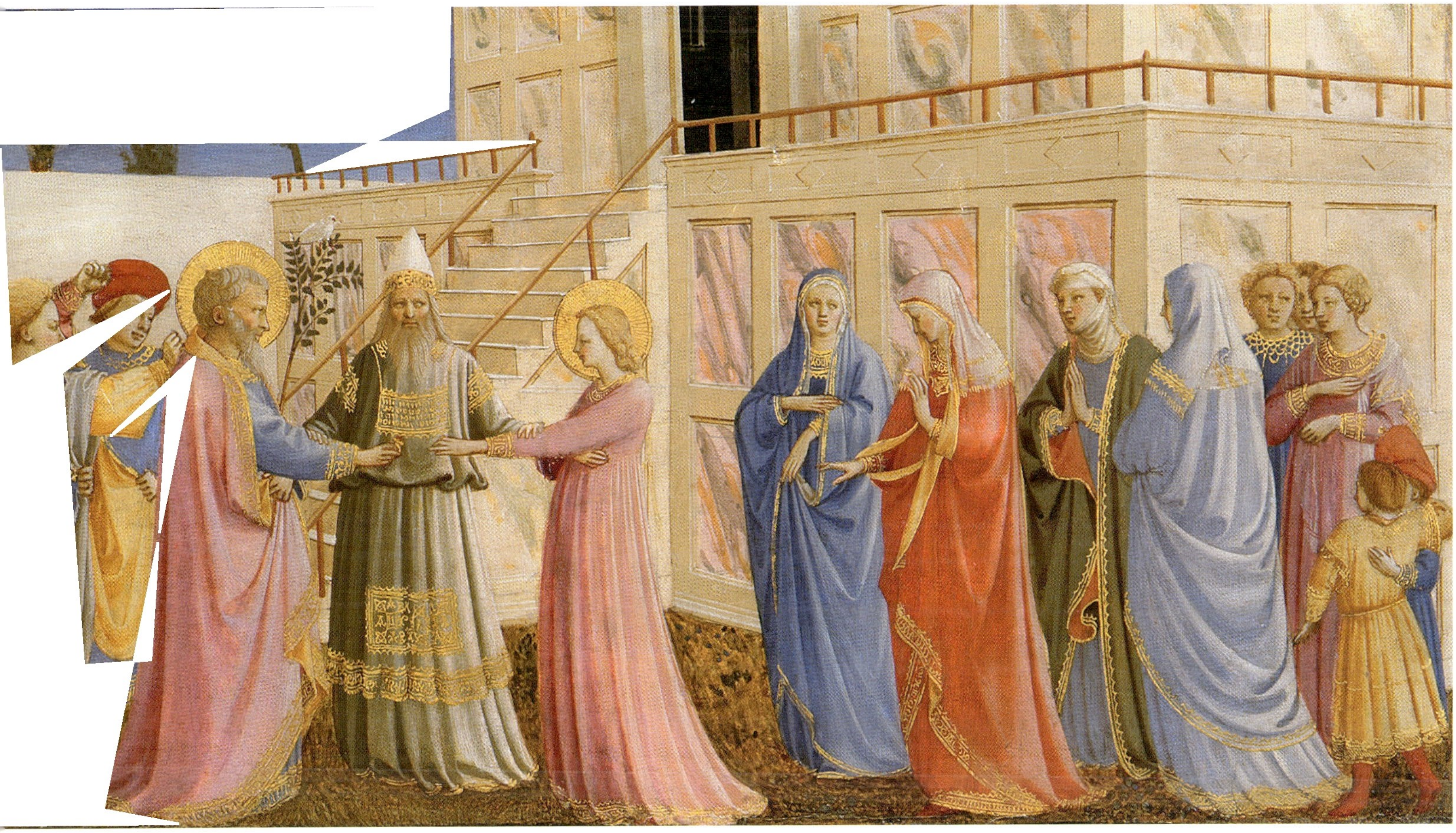

Section 7
Bankers and Artists

Although a boom in art commissions requires considerable financial resources, money alone cannot explain the phenomenon. Beginning in the 1300s through to the early 16th century, Florence saw a gradual shift in values and a relaxation of those moral inhibitions that had barred conspicuous consumption and the flaunting of wealth. Remembering that both Aristotle and Thomas Aquinas had spoken of the proper use of financial means as a virtue, people began to accept that to live in a manner appropriate to his social rank a wealthy man could and should spend on building and display.
In Renaissance Florence, moreover, the open, mobile structure of the ruling classes favoured patronage of the arts, reflecting the behaviour and values of the powerful families that governed the town.[1]
Patronage is the link that brings art and the economy together. Well aware of the difference between productive and non-productive investment, merchants and entrepreneurs, were nevertheless well disposed toward non-profitable expenditure.[2] Commissioning works of art may thus be analyzed as a form of social behaviour among the Florentine upper class, made up for the most part of merchant-bankers. While in the first four decades of the 15th century the great artistic achievements (the Loggia of the Innocenti, the dome of the Duomo, the decoration of the niches at Orsanmichele) were all public works celebrating the city as a whole, in the following years the main commissions were private, with magnificent buildings decorated with artworks intended for personal and private enjoyment. The homes of the upper classes experienced a transformation in this period which was to be important in this regard. In the 14th century the typical residence and workplace of the leading merchants, a house with courtyard, differed little from other homes, except in size. Integrated in the urban grid, its structure was adapted to whatever irregular space was left free by the adjacent buildings. The ground floor was used as a shop, business and private life being kept in close proximity. But starting with Cosimo the Elder, a new type of residence designed to house the leading families of the oligarchy began to appear. The construction of Palazzo Medici (1444) and then the palaces of the Pitti, Rucellai (1446), Pazzi (1465), Antinori (1465), Strozzi (1489) and Gondi (1490) families changed the face of the city. Their clearly defined perimeters, achieved by demolishing entire city blocks, stand out boldly even today. Symbolizing magnificence, these buildings enclosed a central courtyard surrounded by columns while outside a masonry bench running along the external wall formed the *seggetta da via*, a seat for passers-by.
The merchant-banker dynasties of Florence were also celebrated in complex cycles of frescoes. At different epochs the chapels of the Bardi, Peruzzi and Castellani families in Santa Croce, the Sassetti in Santa Trinita, the Tornabuoni and Strozzi in Santa Maria Novella, to mention only a few, served to display the social status and prestige of the clients who commissioned them.
Refined works of art and precious collectors' items were imported from afar, arriving after arduous and perilous journeys in a Florence eager to possess these unique status symbols. The banks, the Medici Bank in particular with its agents belonging to the most prominent families, offered connections with distant countries. From Flanders in particular came paintings, tapestries, illuminated manuscripts, and gold jewellery bearing witness to the financial success of the Portinari, Baroncelli and Tani families in Bruges.[3] The merchant-bankers surrounded themselves with Beauty and enhanced it with cultural references: objects of daily use might be made of a rare material like ivory but this would be decorated with allusive Biblical stories; musical texts would be illuminated linking a mastery of music with knowledge of the classical world, literature and philosophy, in a fusion of harmony and erudition.
The same positive synthesis pervades the work of Sandro Botticelli, whose long career, beginning in a style close to his master Filippo Lippi's, passing through a period of idealized Neo-Platonist Beauty (the famous mythological paintings), to close with tormented expressions of intense religious faith, made him the most sensitive representative of the figurative side of the Florentine Renaissance. In this fascinating world, Money and Beauty were at the service of one another, allowing the creation of immortal masterpieces that have indelibly marked one of the most important epochs in the history of mankind.

Ludovica Sebregondi

1. Lydecker 1987, pp. 211–3.
2. Esch 2002, p. 25.
3. Mejer 2008.

7.1
Hans Memling (Seligenstadt *c.* 1435–94)
Portrait of Benedetto Portinari
(on the back, *Oak Stump with Banderole*)
St. Benedict
1487
oil on panel
54.4 x 34.5 cm each
Florence, Galleria degli Uffizi,

1890 inv. nos. 1090 and 1100

These two panels originally formed part of a triptych with a central panel portraying the *Virgin and Child*, now at the Gemäldegalerie in Berlin (inv. no. 528B), the only work of its kind by Memling all of whose parts have survived to our own day.

The triptych, which had been commissioned by Benedetto di Pigello Portinari, was moved to the Uffizi from the Hospital of Santa Maria Nuova in 1825. Based on that provenance, it was possible to identify the personage represented (Warburg 1932), after the original structure of the work had been traced by Kämmerer in 1899.

Benedetto, born in 1466 and thus a little over twenty when he commissioned this portrait from the illustrious Flemish painter, was the nephew of that Tommaso Portinari whose financial and personal vicissitudes were so closely associated with Flanders and the city of Bruges, and the son of Pigello Portinari, director of the Milan branch of the Medici Bank. Tommaso arrived in Bruges while still very young. Although occupying a subordinate position in that branch of the Medici Bank for years, he became expert in the local financial sector and made a brilliant entrance into society. He was an important client for works of art, among them the famous *Portinari Triptych* by Hugo van der Goes now in the Uffizi.

In commissioning a triptych from one of the greatest masters of Flemish art, Benedetto was probably following the example of his uncle, who had ordered a work of this kind from the same artist around 1470, with a *Virgin and Child* at the centre and portraits of himself and his wife Maria Baroncelli on the side panels. This hypothesis seems confirmed by the rarity of the triptych commissioned by the bachelor Benedetto, where the portrait of the client is accompanied by the image of his name saint.

In the painting done for Benedetto, stylistically more refined than the earlier work, the figures stand out against a broad landscape rather than a flat, dark background. A wealth of detail clearly demonstrates the social rank attained by the client and his international taste in art. The elegance of Benedetto Portinari's attire, the precious binding of his prayer book, and the marble columns supporting the arch behind him are all details expressing the status of this still youthful man. The pastoral of St. Benedict, displaying the images of Samson and the lion and St. John with the poisoned chalice, and the devotional print hanging from the saint's shoulders, allude to the triumph of Christ over death. On the back of the panel, as if to contrast the secular with the sacred, a scroll bearing the motto "DE BONO IN MELIUS" winds round the stump of an oak tree, from which new branches are budding, probably expressing a hope for genealogical regeneration after the untimely death of the client's father.

Silvia Mascalchi

Bibliography: Kämmerer 1899, pp. 120–2; Warburg 1932, p. 210; J. Bogers in *Firenze e gli antichi Paesi Bassi* 2008, pp. 182–5; *Il Potere e la Grazia* 2009, p. 207.

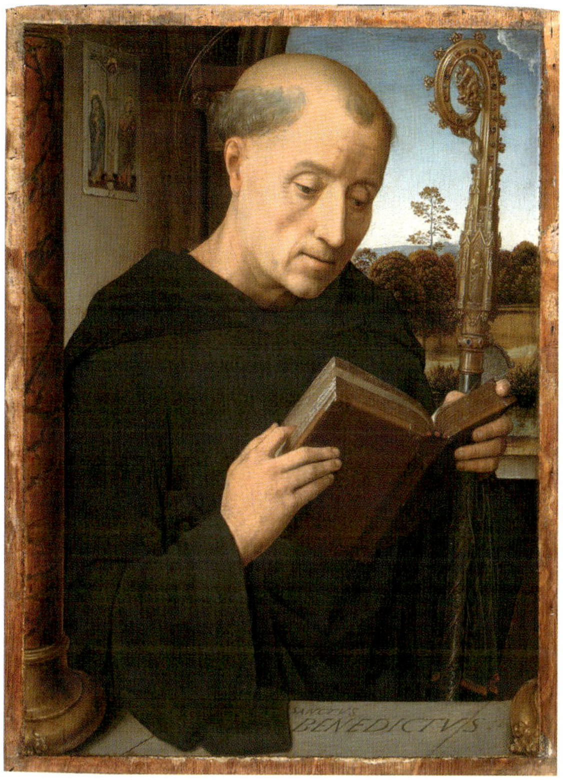
BENEDICTVS

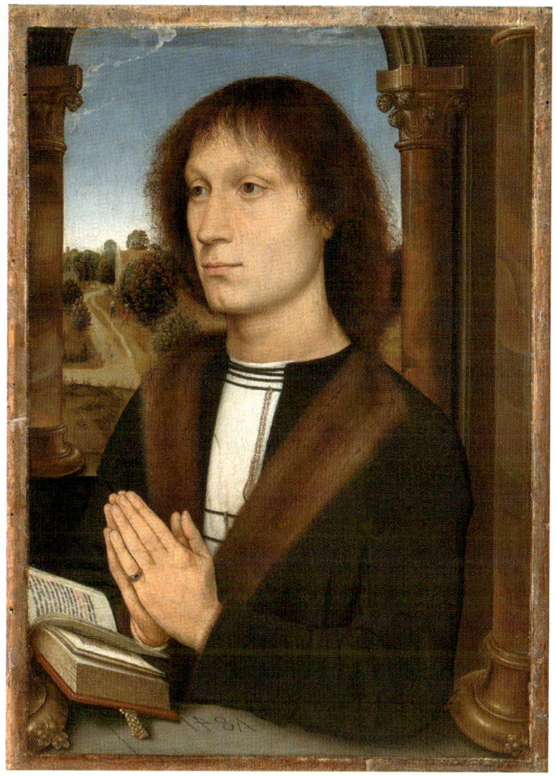

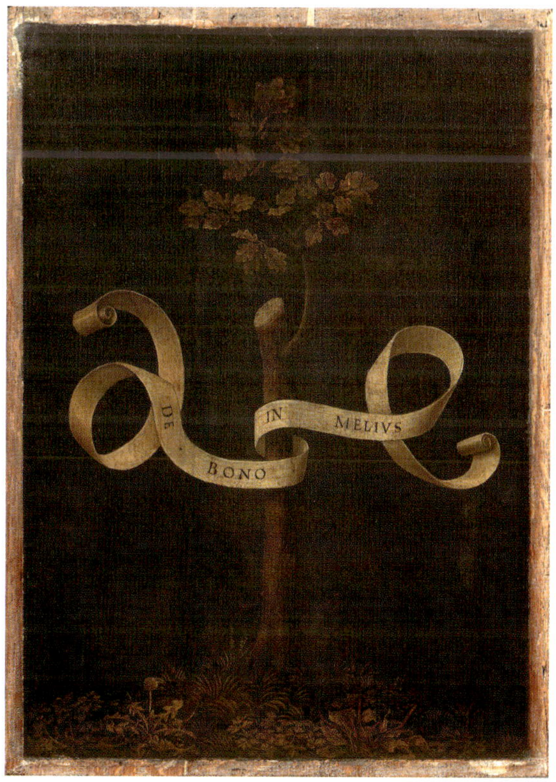
DE
BONO
IN
MELIVS

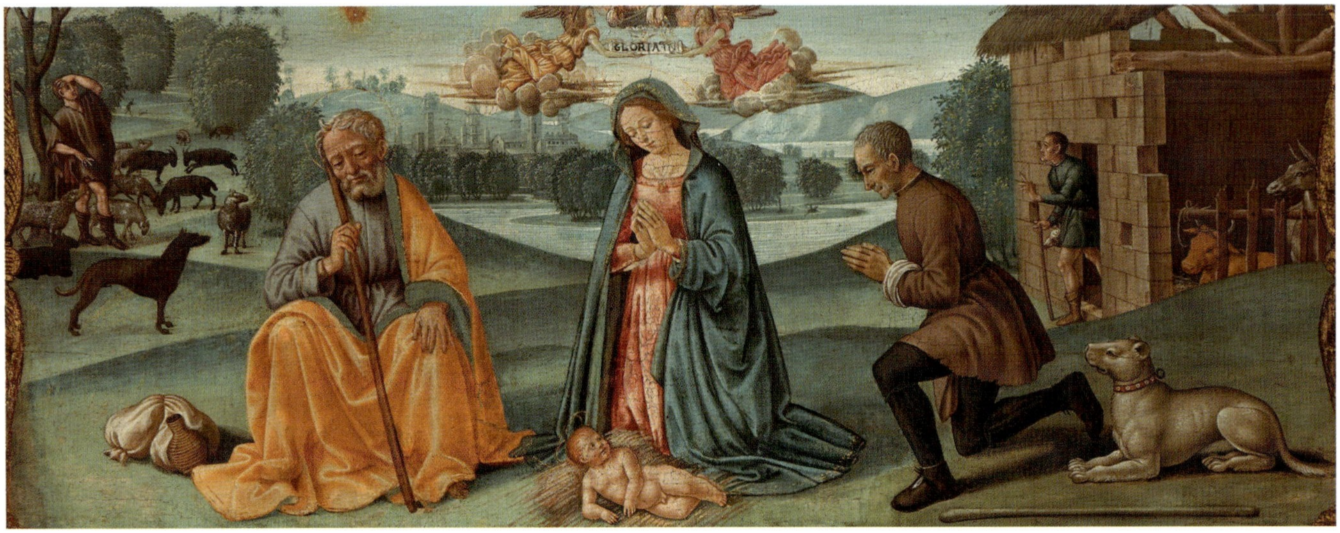

7.2
Domenico Ghirlandaio Workshop
Adoration of the Shepherds with Filippo Strozzi
(predella of the *Lecceto Altarpiece*)
1487–8
panel painting
27 x 65.5 cm
Rotterdam, Museum Boijmans Van Beuningen, inv. no. 2553

Originally, the little picture representing the *Adoration of the Shepherds* was probably the central panel in the predella of an altarpiece—now lost—commissioned by Filippo Strozzi from Domenico Ghirlandaio for the high altar in the church of Santa Maria a Lecceto, at Malmantile, near Lastra a Signa. The main part of the altarpiece, painted by Ghirlandaio and his assistants in 1487–8, represented the Virgin and Child with "St. John and St. Philip," as stated in the Carte Strozziane (Borsook 1970, pp. 5 and 17, nos. 34-35). Hence the predella may have included the stories of these two saints as well, in addition to the *Adoration of the Magi* formerly in the Vitetti Collection in Rome (Zeri 1971).

Identification of the Rotterdam panel as part of the gradine of the *Lecceto Altarpiece*, hypothesized by Eve Borsook (1970) and generally accepted by art historians, finds confirmation in the personage shown praying, dressed in shepherd's clothing, in the right foreground. His features clearly identify him as Filippo Strozzi, based on comparison with the terracotta portrait bust in the Berlin museum and the marble one in the Louvre, both sculpted by Benedetto da Maiano.

Filippo Strozzi (Florence, July 4, 1428–May 1, 1491) grew up in the hardship and uncertainty of exile, imposed on his father Matteo, an enemy of Cosimo the Elder de' Medici, in 1434. Filippo's family steered him toward the career of merchant, and he completed his professional training in Naples, settling there in 1446. He soon became a highly esteemed businessman, merchant and banker, well deserving of the favour bestowed on him by King Ferdinando I. Through his professional capability, Filippo managed to settle the quarrel with the Medici and establish profitable relations with the Medici Bank, becoming its representative in Naples.

In 1466, under pressure from the Florentines, Piero de' Medici revoked the ban, allowing Filippo to return to his native city, where he prudently avoided any conspicuous presence on the political and cultural scene. At first he invested his money in commissioning works of singular beauty for himself and his influential friends, such as the famous *lettuccio* made by Giuliano da Maiano for Ferdinando of Aragon. Then, starting in the mid-1490s, he turned his patronage to the countryside around Florence, concentrating mainly on architectural works. His intention was to "make something to be remembered," but also to show himself "recognizant" to God who had granted him so many "temporal goods" (Borsook 1970, pp. 14–5, nos. 16 and 18). This is the case of the Lecceto church with its hermitage, founded by the Observant Dominicans of San Marco in Florence and brought to completion through funds donated by Filippo Strozzi, who became its patron in 1477. In the last years of his life, Filippo devoted himself to great works in the city, designed to publicly sanction his definitive social and economic status: the funerary chapel in Santa Maria Novella decorated with the frescoes of Filippino Lippi, the marble sculptures of Benedetto da Maiano, and the construction of the great palace (see also entry 2.6), the most beautiful yet built in Florence, which he did not live to see completed. When Filippo Strozzi died in 1491, his extraordinary wealth amounted to over 116,000 "wide" florins (Goldthwaite 1968, pp. 60, 63).

Elena Capretti

Bibliography: Borsook 1970, pp. 5, 11 note 50, 17; Zeri 1971, pp. 56–8; L. Venturini in *Maestri e botteghe* 1992, pp. 143-–4, n. 4.7 (with bibliography); Cadogan 2000, p. 286, no. 63; Romagnoli 2005, pp. 103–4.

7.3

An Astrologer's advice to Filippo Strozzi on laying the first stone of his palace

[*Filippo Strozzi's register of debtors and creditors*]

1484–91

register on paper bound in leather with envelope-type cover, hot-printed decorations, parchment flyleaves, 240 fols., contemporary numbering in Roman numerals, fols. 117-149 and fols. 181-240 left blank, initial alphabetical rubric in slim register

355 x 265 x 70 mm

Florence, Archivio di Stato, Carte Strozziane, Quinta serie, 41, fol. 172

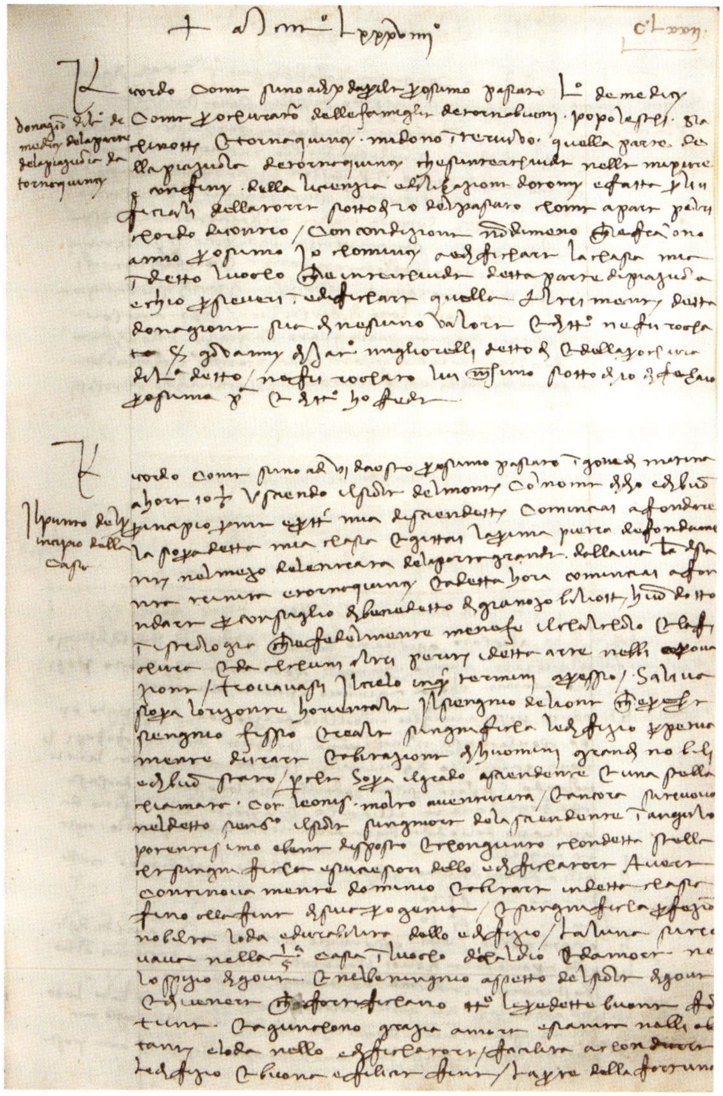

The register, written entirely in the hand of Filippo Strozzi (1428–91), the wealthiest man of his time (according to the historian Bernardo Segni), was begun on March 25, 1484. It is divided into two sections, the first containing records of Debtors and Creditors on folios 1-116, the second, reserved to memoirs, on fols. 150–80. Both sections remained unfinished at the death of Strozzi on May 14, 1491. The register is important insofar as it records the preparations for and first stages of building Palazzo Strozzi, which Filippo planned to make the most grandiose building of the time, to symbolize the power of his family. The preparations were very complicated, due not only to the monumental scale of the construction project, but also to the fact that it would profoundly change the surrounding urban grid. Filippo Strozzi, as head of the family, was responsible for organizing the project, as well as for conducting time-consuming preliminary negotiations with his relations, some of them co-owners of the building, with the bordering property owners, in a situation of uncertain rights of ownership and utilization, and even with the officials of the city government, since the new building would invade the space of the public square it faced on. When all appeared to be going well and the first supplies of material and some of the labour force had arrived, the construction site was opened and the first stone laid, but the date—and even the hour—for this ceremony was not left to chance. As recorded on this page, at the advice of the astrologer Benedetto di Giannozzo Biliotti, who had performed complicated astral calculations, the date of August 6, 1489, and the time of 10 and 1/6 hours were chosen, because just at that moment, "There rose over the horizon the sign of the lion, which, being a fixed and regal sign, signified that the building would last perpetually and would be the habitation of men who are great, noble and of good state, because above the ascending degree is a highly adventurous star called *Cor leonis*, and even more, we find in this sign the sun, lord of the ascendant, in a most powerful and fortunate angle and conjoined with said star, which means that the successors to the builder of this house will have continuous dominion and will live in said house as long as his line shall last." The prediction did not come true and, despite all the precautions taken, the undertaking came to no good end. No sooner had Strozzi died than bitter quarrels broke out among his three sons, while the palace remained unfinished.

Vanna Arrighi

Bibliography: Strozzi (*ante* 1549), ed. Bini, Bigazzi 1851, pp. 70–1; Pampaloni 1963, pp. 87–8; Gareffi 1991, pp. 130–1; Bigazzi 2005, p. 25.

7.4
Lo Scheggia (Giovanni di ser Giovanni;
San Giovanni Valdarno 1406–Florence 1486)
Game of the "Civettino" (front)
Two Children Wrestling (reverse)
c. 1450
tempera on panel
Ø 59 cm
Florence, Museo di Palazzo Davanzati,
1890 inv. no. 488

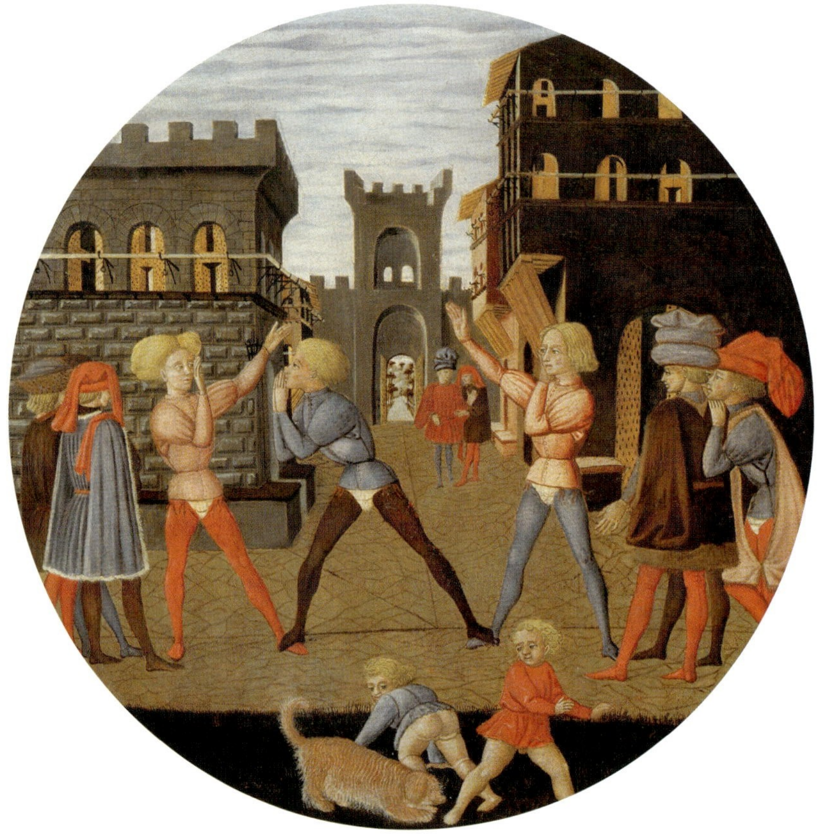

This work, along with many others once grouped under the fictitious name of Master of the Adimari Chest, or Master of Fucecchio, has been attributed to Giovanni di ser Giovanni, known as Lo Scheggia, by Luciano Bellosi (in *Mostra d'arte* 1969, pp. 56–7, no. 42). Giovanni, Masaccio's younger brother, was known chiefly for large-scale works—such as altarpieces and frescoes—in Valdarno where he was born. He was appreciated in Florence instead, where he had a workshop, as a painter of domestic furnishings, "works in which the attractive story narrated in costume, the erudite gratification of the subject, often classical, the rich display of gold, lacquer and bright colours frequently prevailed over the need for original innovation and, at times, even over the more properly stylistic, qualitative features" (Cavazzini 1999, p. 11). The artist probably had to make his peace with the comparison, as burdensome as it was inevitable, with the great talent of his brother Masaccio, who although dying young in 1428, had left an indelible mark on Italian art. As a compensation of sorts, Giovanni was skilled at interpreting the direction taken by the art market, where private commissions sharply increased in the 1440s. Accordingly, he specialized in paintings for chests, strongboxes, interior furnishings, birth trays and works of private devotion, produced for the residences of the Florentine nobles, among them Palazzo Medici. His nickname, lo Scheggia (the Splinter), alluded not only to the painter's slim figure but also—and above all—to his close ties to woodworkers and inlayers.

The tondo from Palazzo Davanzati is also a work of domestic art. Painted on both sides, it is a *desco da parto*, or birth tray. These objects, frequently exchanged as gifts at weddings and childbirths, were used to bring food to a mother who had just given birth. The scenes represented on both sides are games. On the front, in a perspective view of an urban scenario, three youths wearing shirts and hose with shoe-soles are playing the game of *civettino* or *civetta*. The boy in the middle must strike the other two, whose feet are held down by other boys, without letting them hit him back. Around them, young men are strolling in pairs, elegantly dressed in tunics and caps, while in the foreground two children are playing with a dog on the grass. On the back are two more small children, this time entirely nude, grabbing at each other's penises, one of them holding the other by the hair. This playful subject may be seen as a good-luck token, wishing a newly married couple male heirs and fertility in general (C. Paolini in *Mythologica et erotica* 2005, p. 322). A coat of arms hangs from each of the two trees at the sides. Only the one on the right is clearly legible. It represents a salient silver stag on an azure field. This could be, in my opinion, the heraldic arms of the Corbinelli family, rich Florentine merchants who resided in Via Maggio, in the Santo Spirito quarter. They were the patrons of four chapels in the left transept of the Santo Spirito church, for which they commissioned paintings still in place today, bearing the same coat of arms (Capretti 1996, pp. 243–8).

The other *desco da parto* attributed to Scheggia is the extraordinary work portraying the *Triumph of Fame*, now in the Metropolitan Museum of New York, painted in 1449 for the birth of Lorenzo the Magnificent, son of Piero il Gottoso de' Medici and Lucrezia Tornabuoni.

Elena Capretti

Bibliography: S. Francolini in *Il fratello di Masaccio* 1999, pp. 72–4, no. 19; C. Filippini in *In the Light of Apollo* 2004, pp. 176–7, no. I.64 a-b; C. Paolini in *Mythologica et Erotica* 2005, p. 322, no. 201; M. Bietti in *The Splendour* 2008, p. 89, no. 33.

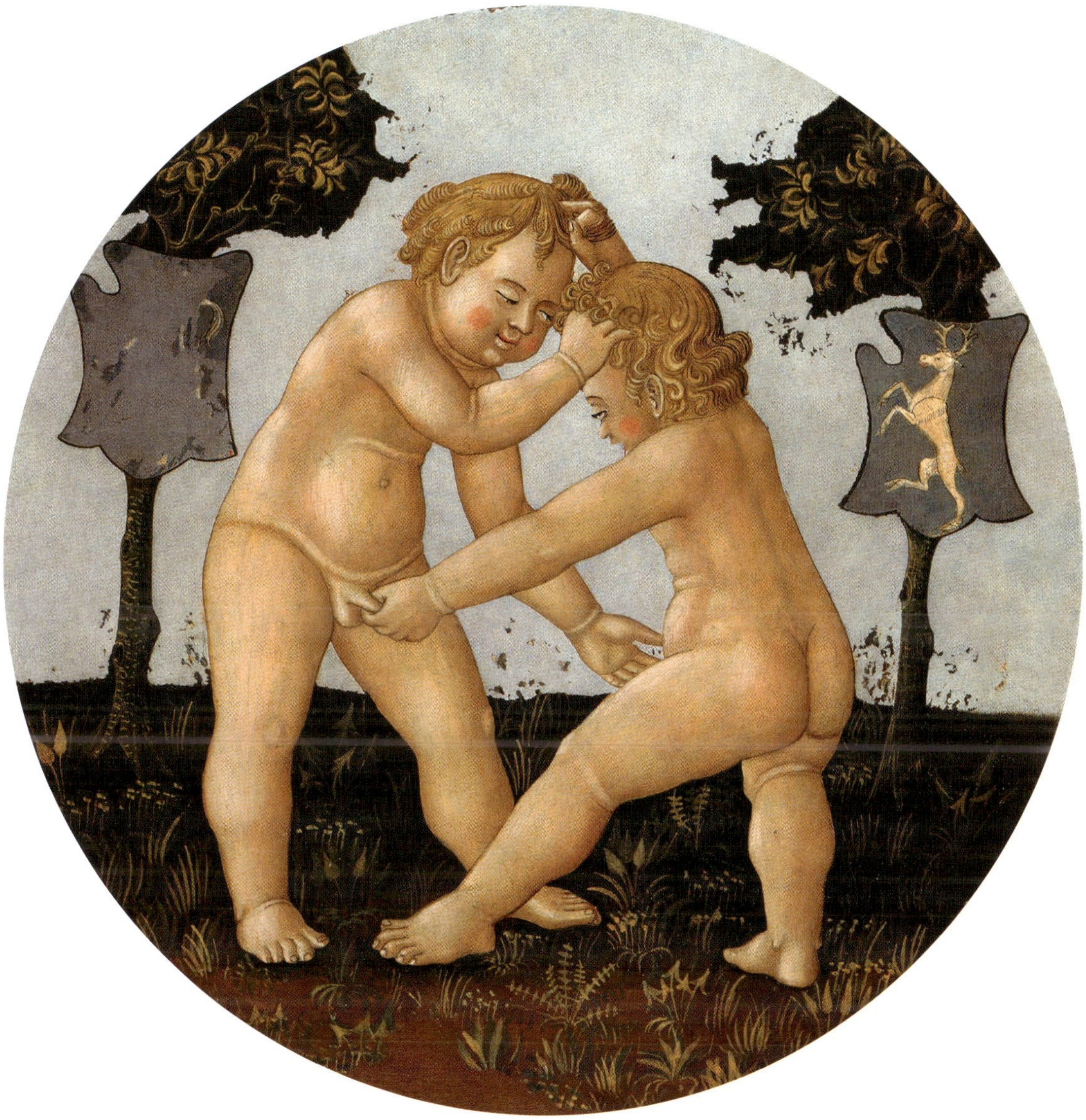

7.5
"Stories of Susannah" Workshop,
Northern Italy
Wall mirror
second quarter of the 15th century
bone, horn and wood, parts dyed in green and orange
51.5 x 28.2 cm
Florence, Museo Nazionale del Bargello, inv. no. 125 C

The octagonal wooden mirror frame is decorated *alla certosina*, with inlaid geometric motifs of variously coloured bone and wood, to which are applied bone plaquettes carved in bas-relief. The relief carvings on the frame depict couples formed of girls and nude, winged sprites, flying against a background of rose leaves with serrated edges. At the centre of the tympanum, composed of three bone plaquettes, is another nude sprite (the God of Love?) flanked by two youths in an attitude of prayer.

Objects of this kind, highly fashionable in the 15th century, must have been popular with the upper-middle classes especially, as shown by the numerous surviving examples similar to the Bargello piece (for instance, two octagonal mirrors in the Museo Civico di Bologna, one in the Walters Art Museum in Baltimore, and fragments of plaquettes between the Museo Duca di Martina in Naples and the Museo Civico in Turin; see P. Giusti in *Medioevo* 1981, pp. 138–9, no. II, 25 bis; Pincelli 1959, pp. 53–4, no. 125; Randall 1985, p. 236, no. 354).

With such relatively inexpensive raw materials as wood and bone, instead of costly ivory, fine pieces could be produced, strikingly effective in domestic furnishings but of limited cost. Such mirror frames, like the jewel caskets produced by the Embriachi and other Italian workshops of the time and later, including the "Stories of Susannah Workshop" (Tomasi 2001), were frequently offered as wedding or engagement gifts. They could be found ready-made in shops, where they were personalized upon request with the insignia of the two families. On the Bargello mirror, in fact, are two triangular shields that must have once borne the devices of the bride and groom who were given the mirror. This decoration is almost entirely lost today, only faint traces of colour remaining.

Wall mirrors became fashionable in the 15th century, as shown by the splendid iconographic testimony of the famous *Arnolfini Painting* by Jan van Eyck (1434).

The reflecting plate now inserted in the Bargello frame is modern but, like the one in the Van Eyck painting, it must have been convex originally too. The first portable mirrors were made of polished sheets of metal (usually tin or steel, but also silver and gold), or a pane of glass with metal foil applied to the back, but by the 15th century hemispheric glass mirrors had appeared, especially in Germany. In Italy they were echoed in the research on optics and the refraction of light conducted by Luca Pacioli and by Leonardo (Lagabrielle 2000, pp. 112–9; Musacchio 2008, pp. 166–8). Originally, the mirror proper must have been much more expensive than the decorated frame around it, offering its owner the entirely private luxury of seeing himself reflected in his own home, itself a confirmation of the financial and social status he had attained.

Benedetta Chiesi

Bibliography: Supino 1898, p. 237, no. 125; Tomasi 2001, pp. 28–31, no. 5.

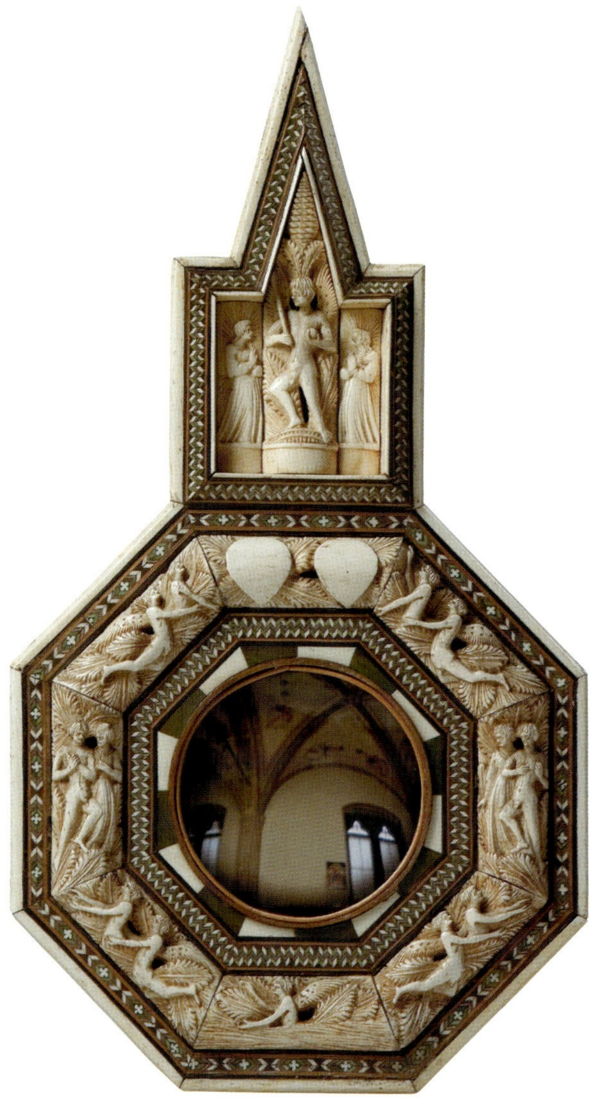

7.6
Mino da Fiesole (Poppi 1429–Florence 1484)
Mirror frame
c. 1460–70
carved, painted and gilt marble
50 x 33.5 cm
Paris, Bibliothèque nationale de France,
inv. no. 57-244

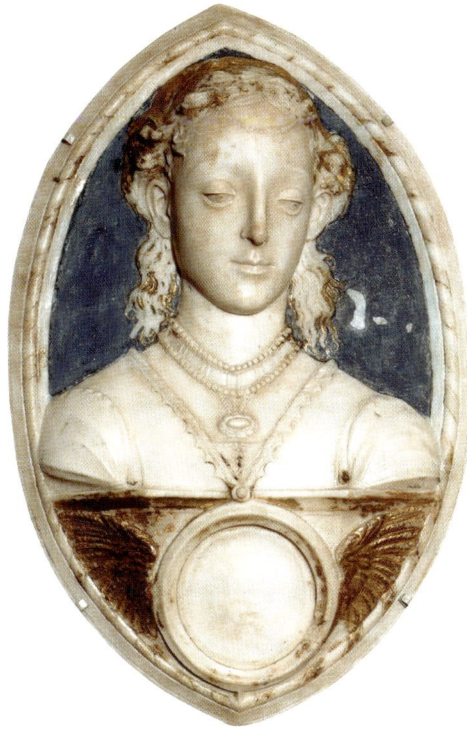

Describing this polished high-relief carving of noble marble, embellished by splendid colours and the lavish use of gold as a mere "mirror frame" seems inadequate. It should more properly be called a sculpture that, to fully communicate its meaning, contains a reflecting element. The relief carving, in the form of a mandorla, portrays the bust of an elegantly dressed young woman wearing a necklace made of a double string of pearls and a pendant set with a gemstone. Another string of pearls adorns her hair, interwoven with the wavy locks and curving like a festoon over her high forehead. From a ribbon that apparently becomes a braid along the neckline of her gown hangs a round medallion, in which a little mirror decorated by side wings was placed. This Platonic image suggests that the girl with her regular features should be interpreted symbolically. Gazing modestly downward in a pose evocative of True Beauty, she seems to invite all those who see her reflection in the mortal world to put on "Platonic wings" and soar upward, escaping the limitations of the body to arrive at the contemplation of perfect visions in pure light, as proposed by Plato in the *Phaedus* (XXX) and the *Symposium* (XXVIII). If the sculpture was intended as a Platonic admonition not to remain imprisoned by the bonds of matter, the mirror becomes important as the first moment of reflection suggested by Socrates to his disciples (*Know Thyself*), to know their own limitations, which are to be exceeded through the spiritual yearning of love toward the absolute.

The relief appears to be an expression of Ficino's thought, which pervaded the Medici sphere in the second half of the 15th century. The client must have been uncommonly rich and erudite, as the extreme rarity of the object also suggests. It is already exceptional to find a Florentine mirror at a date when they were being produced mainly in Germany and in Venice, thanks to the invention of "crystal" by Angelo Barovier, but the insertion of a mirror in a marble sculpture is truly unique. That it was made by Mino da Fiesole is proven by the proud signature "OPUS MINI" on the back, written in capital letters as on the tomb of Bernardo Giugni and that of Bishop Salutati at Fiesole. Moreover, the superb quality of the workmanship seems to confirm the attribution and the dating, ranging between 1460 and 1470, as had previously been hypothesized. The relief apparently arrived at the Bibliothèque nationale de France near the end of the 18th century, brought from the Abbey of Sainte-Genevieve, with no trace of its original provenance, to be collocated in the Florentine sphere at the beginning of the second half of the 15th century. At that time Mino was working for the Medici family (*Portrait of Piero* and *Portrait of Giovanni*, now in the Bargello, and *Portrait of Lucrezia*, Piero's wife, recalled by Vasari in the *Life of Mino*) and members of their circle, the Giugni and in particular the Neroni, for whom he made the altar frontal planned for San Lorenzo (but which remained instead at the Badia Fiorentina) and the bust of Diotisalvi, a close friend of Cosimo the Elder.

At the request of a client who shared the cultural interest in Ficino's Neo-Platonic philosophy, Mino may have produced this work as a secular furnishing of most unusual type. The few existing parallels are all of lower artistic and material quality, such as the painted stucco frame depicting Mars and Venus with cupids attributed to the workshop of Antonio Pollaiolo (London, Victoria and Albert Museum) or, in the same museum, the papier-mâché frame from Neroccio de' Landi's workshop, depicting a woman who alludes to Beauty, like Mino's lady, but without the Platonic attributes. The esteem enjoyed by Mino's sculpture is also declared by the painted terracotta copy made in Montelupo, now in the Cluny Museum (Giacomotti 1974, pp. 74–5, no. 294), modelled by hand and thus an individual artefact, unlike the series of mirrors decorated with the *Isoretta galante*, whose moulds have been found in excavations conducted in this Tuscan town, then as now famous for its ceramics (Alinari 1989, pp. 263–8).

Francesca Petrucci

Bibliography: Foville 1911, I, pp. 149–56; Sciolla 1970, pp. 83–4; Zuraw 1993, II pp. 813–6; Musacchio 2008, p. 167.

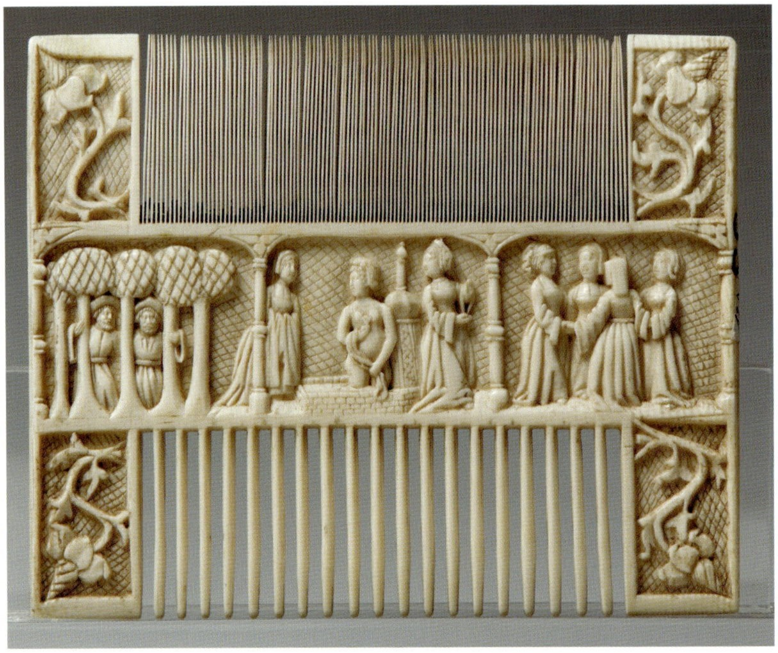

7.7
Northern French or Flemish
Comb decorated with stories of Susannah
late 15th–early 16th century
ivory
12 x 14.8 cm
Florence, Museo Nazionale del Bargello, inv. no. 12A

In the *Miroir de Mariage*, a French text from the late 14th century, combs are explicitly mentioned, along with ivory mirrors, as objects necessary to the beauty care of wealthy women of the time.

The shape and structure of combs remained unchanged in the 15th and 16th centuries, with a row of wide-spaced teeth to dress the hair and a row of close-spaced teeth to remove parasites from hair and beards. Designed mainly for women, these combs were also used by men. Combs were sold individually, in leather cases, or as part of a set containing mirrors and hair-parters. Combs made of wood, metal and bone were found on the market, but the use of ivory marks this Florentine comb as a luxury product, an expensive gift to be displayed rather than used daily, as indicated by the perfect state of conservation of its teeth, still intact.

The value of the raw material, making it unfeasible for daily use, shows it to be an object demonstrative of its owner's wealth, like a modern status symbol. Since rich families owned more than one of these articles, it is unsurprising to find in the inventory drawn up at the death of Lorenzo the Magnificent no less than twelve ivory combs in his bed chamber. This comb too has a Medicean provenance, but its stylistic traits date it at a time later than that of Lorenzo's collection (Campani 1884). Based on the typology of the decoration and the style of the relief, the Bargello comb can be dated to the last decade of the 15th century, if not already the early years of the 16th. Scratching the ivory background is common to ivory sculpting in the second half of the 15th century, and the candelabra-shaped columns that divide the scenes, as well as the costumes of the figures, confirm the hypothesized dating. A second ivory comb, now in a British private collection, undoubtedly comes from the same workshop, having identical decoration and architectural ornamentation. It too has been attributed to French art of the early 16th century (Courtauld Institute of Art - Gothic Ivories Project, database on line - www.gothicivories.courtauld.ac.uk). The Florentine comb illustrates the story of Susannah, one of the favourite subjects for objects of this type in the 15th and 16th centuries, along with Bathsheba at her Bath, as can be seen in contemporary combs at the Victoria and Albert Museum and the Musée du Louvre (Malgouyres 2010, pp. 182–3). These items gave sculptors the chance to portray nude female figures, caught at their toilette, a ritual for which the object itself was designed. In different narrative contexts, these subjects all evoke the power of feminine beauty. They were especially suited to adorn objects destined to women, frequently offered to young brides as wedding gifts (Musacchio 2008, pp. 162–8).

Benedetta Chiesi

Bibliography: Campani 1884, p. 123; Supino 1898, p. 367.

7.8
Maso Finiguerra (Florence 1426–64)
Nude Woman Draped in a Cloth
c.1455–60
pen and brown ink, brown watercolour wash, traces of black pencil, white paper
194 x 100 mm
Florence, Gabinetto Disegni e Stampe degli Uffizi, inv. no. 74 F.

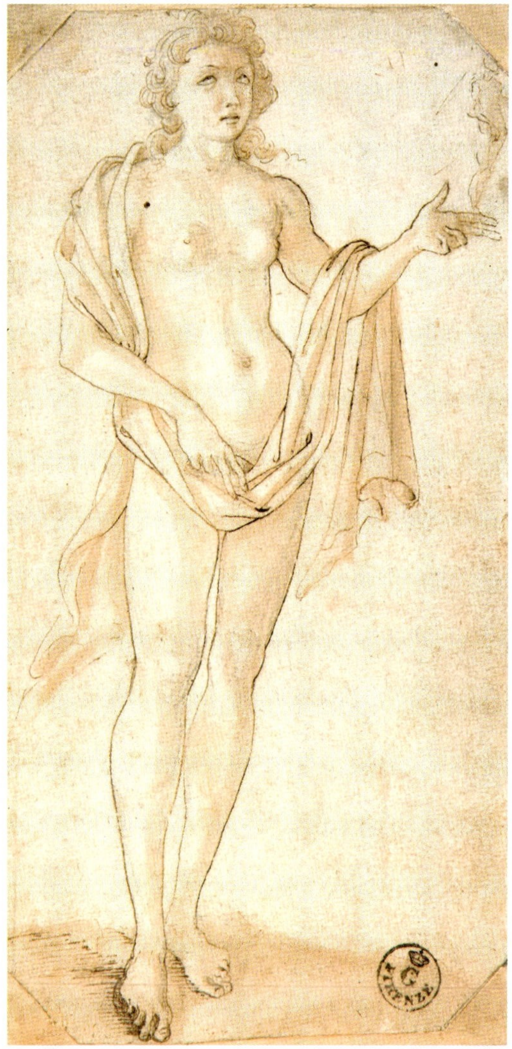

This drawing is one of many, nearly a hundred, in the Medicean Collections traditionally attributed to Maso Finiguerra. After a time when the entire group was generically classified as "School of Pollaiolo" (Ferri 1890), the experts have recently agreed that they come from books of drawings by Finiguerra, the famous Florentine goldsmith active around the middle of the 15th century.

This drawing shows a nude woman, half covered by a cloth falling from her shoulders to her hips. The black pencil marks, erased but still visible at places in the outline, served as guide for the definitive drawing, in pen and brown ink, which describes the shape subtly and decisively. At the upper right is a pen-and-ink sketch of a little human figure, not to be interpreted as a statuette resting on the woman's hand, as has sometimes been suggested (Petrioli Tofani 1991), but as a sketch of the same figure in reduced size and without the cloth, a preliminary study for the final drawing. When the folio is held against the light a detailed study of the figure's left hand can be seen on the *verso* (Melli 1995).

The clear-cut, incisive graphic style is typical of Maso, who used drawn models for his figurative compositions on chased and niellated silver, a process very similar to copperplate engraving, from which it developed. Finiguerra was famous specifically for his niello work, and for his ability to portray a myriad of personages in the restricted space of a plaque, as reports Vasari, and as demonstrated by the pax created for the Florentine Baptistery, which have been conserved to our own day (Museo del Bargello).

In this drawing the subject, emulating the pose of an ancient Venus, especially in the gesture of holding the edge of the cloth over her pudenda, is preparatory to the portrayal of the goddess in the "niello trial" depicting the *Judgement of Paris* at the Louvre (Angelini 1986). The same model, now fully clothed, was used for the figure of St. Lucia in the pax depicting the *Madonna and Child in a Tempietto* at the British Museum (see Hind 1936, fig. 1).

Maso's drawings, preparatory studies for his niello works, show that fine line of transition from using existing models of medieval origin to drawing from life, based on the cautious observation of reality. Maso represents one of the fundamental stages in this process. The figure shown here mingles 1) a standard anatomical typology used by the artist, 2) a vague emulation of antiquity, and 3) the anatomical precision derived from a growing tendency to observe reality. In this slow process, lasting throughout the century, Finiguerra was an important figure in the transition toward drawing from life, preliminary to the experience of Pollaiolo and Verrocchio (see next entry 7.9).

Lorenza Melli

Bibliography: Ferri 1890, p. 112; Degenhart, Schmitt 1968, I-2, fig. 858; Kubiak 1974, p. 184; Angelini 1986, no. 94, fig. 112; Petrioli Tofani 1991, p. 35; Elen 1995, cat. 25; Melli 1995, pp. 65–6, p. 79, no. 62, fig. 76.

7.9
Piero del Pollaiolo (Florence 1441–Rome 1496)
Nude Male Figure in Semi-reclining Pose
1465–70
pen and brown ink, brown watercolour wash, white watermarked paper
("three hills surmounted by a cross")
210 x 248 mm
Florence, Gabinetto Disegni e Stampe degli Uffizi, inv. no. 100 F.

This study of a *Nude Male Figure* clearly reveals the nascent interest in representing the human body realistically that emerged in Florence in the second half of the 15th century, around the artistic personalities of Antonio del Pollaiolo and Andrea del Verrocchio. In the ancient Medicean collections, this folio was recorded under the name Mantegna (Petrioli Tofani 1991) but was attributed to Piero del Pollaiolo by Ferri (1885–1901) and then declassed to School of Pollaiolo following Berenson (1938), who deemed it a copy of a lost original by Antonio.

The graphic style of the drawing speaks a formal language midway between the linear, static drawings of Maso Finiguerra (see entry 7.8) and the more incisive, vibrant ones of Antonio del Pollaiolo. The draughtsman traces the outlines, then builds the muscular structure through strong watercolour wash evincing swells and hollows illuminated by the white background of the paper. The line is a containing but not descriptive element, lacking the sense of motion that pervades every mark made by Antonio. Based on a recent reassessment of Piero del Pollaiolo as painter within the context of the two brother artists' activity (see Galli 2003, 2005 and Tartuferi 2007), the drawing can be attributed to Piero, along with others, as proposed earlier by myself (Melli 2007, pp. 64–7). In addition to the powerful but calm physique, other resemblances appear, in the physiognomy for instance, to the St. Vincent in the *The Cardinal of Portugal's Altarpiece*, painted by Piero in 1466–8.

The figure is drawn from life, as shown by the model's left hand, which, to remain raised without fatigue during the pose, grasps a barely sketched support, the so-called "posing stick." The point of observation, a bold three-quarter view of the body from nearby, is slightly higher than the plane of rest of the figure, reclining nude on a cloth. The pose, inspired by ancient sculptural models (notably the *Dying Gaul*), is well suited to the representation of various iconographies, such as Adam in the *Creation*. A semi-reclining figure with one leg extended, the other flexed, and the raised bust supported by a forearm was used for the First Man at the moment of the Creation in Paolo Uccello's fresco in the Green Cloister at Santa Maria Novella; and was used again, even more famously, by Michelangelo in the Sistine Chapel. In this interpretation of a traditional iconographical theme, Pollaiolo translates the familiar stylistic vein in peaceful, composed terms, inspired by classical canons and by naturalist observation, entirely in keeping with Florentine humanist concepts of the 1470s.

Lorenza Melli

Bibliography: Ferri 1895-1901, fol. 20r; Berenson 1938, II, no. 1933C, p. 269; Petrioli Tofani 1991, p. 46; Melli 2007, pp. 65–6, fig. 13.

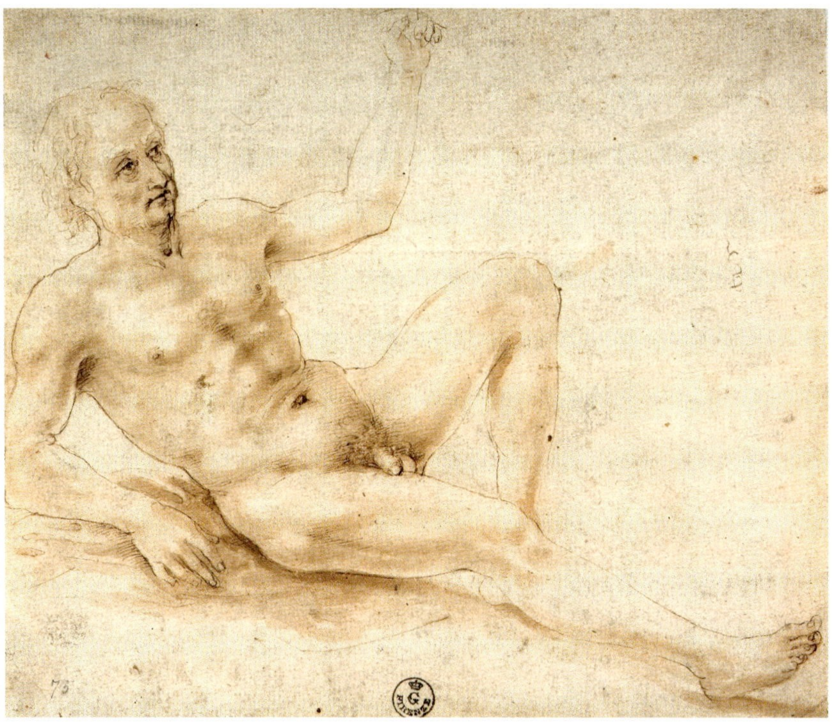

7.10
Sandro Botticelli
(Alessandro Filipepi, Florence 1445–1510)
Virgin and Child with an Angel
c. 1465
tempera on panel
95 x 64 cm
Florence, MUDI - Museo degli Innocenti

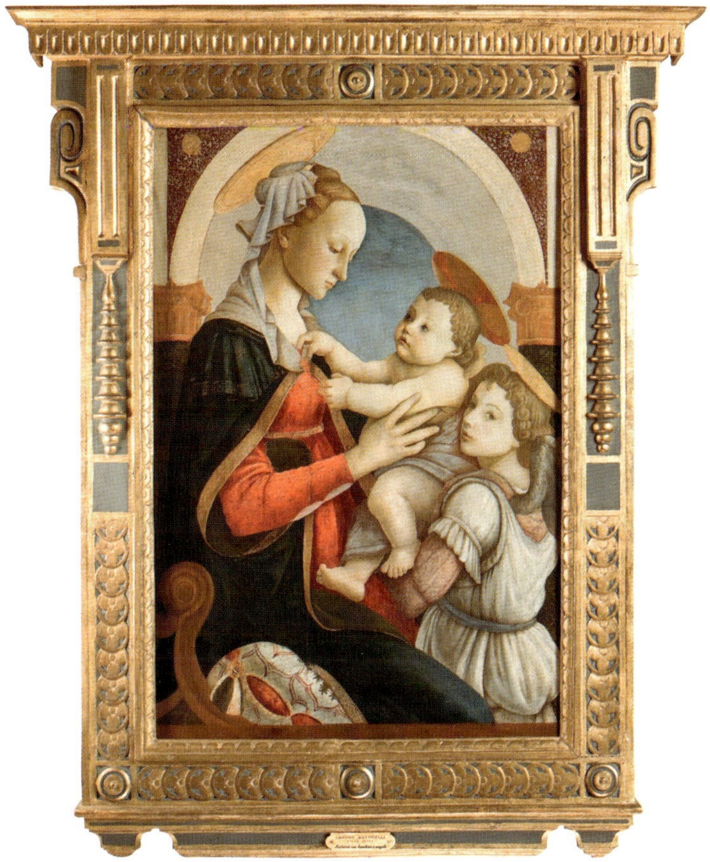

This painting has been recorded in the Spedale degli Innocenti since the mid-19th century, first in the room frescoed by Poccetti with the *Massacre of the Innocents* (AOIF, no. 3629, fol. 3r)—where the most important pieces in the Institution's collection were displayed—then in the Council Assembly Hall, which formed part of today's Brunelleschi Room (AOIF, 3632, c. 1v).

First listed in the inventories as the work of Filippo Lippi or his school, the painting has been attributed to Sandro Botticelli since the end of the 19th century (Ulmann 1893, pp. 24–6). This attribution has received authoritative confirmation, with some disagreement due primarily to the poor state of conservation of the work, whose surface is badly worn. While Bellosi (1977, p. 234 with preceding bibliography), Lightbown (1978, A1, p. 11), and most recently Dombrowski (2010, pp. 41–4) and Pons (1989, p. 54; 2010, p. 110) assign it to the first stage in Botticelli's career, Horne (1987, p. 130) and Cecchi (2005, p. 46) deem possible only a generic reference to the Carmelite friar's entourage.

Undoubtedly, the painting was inspired—along with two others, in the National Gallery of Washington and the Metropolitan Museum of New York—by the iconographic model of Lippi's *Madonna and Child with Two Angels* in the Uffizi, dating from around 1465. Among these variants, differing in interpretation from the prototype—as Boskovits has clearly shown (in *Italian Paintings* 2003, pp. 146–9)—the Innocenti *Madonna* stands out for the high quality of the composition, showing that it cannot be a mere workshop production.

The Virgin, viewed almost in profile, is seen taking the Child into her arms, assisted by an angel, who is gazing out at the spectator. Here we are far from Lippi's image of the Virgin in prayer and the blissful Child. Here Mary has the pensive gaze of one meditating on the destiny of her Son, but He is leaning toward her as if to play with the broach fastening her mantle. The interaction among the three figures is continuous, focussing the spectator's attention on the composition (Dombrowski 2010). Only later does the incongruous background, where the arch is out of line with the columns, become noticeable.

The painting clearly exemplifies the abundant presence, in the houses and palaces of 15th-century Florence, of devotional images portraying the Virgin with the Christ Child, derived from famous models.

The archival documents on the restoration conducted in 1924–5 by the famous restorer Augusto Vermerhen (AOIF, 6693, file 30) have brought to light some interesting aspects; first of all, the fact that the present frame is not the original. It was in fact loaned by the Monuments and Fine Arts Service the year the restoration was completed, as replacement for another "not consonant […] with either the value of the picture or the epoch in which it was painted." Furthermore, it has been confirmed that while the condition of the work was so poor as to make restoration mandatory, not all of the figures were damaged. Photographs taken at the time show that the worst damage involved the angel's face—almost entirely deleted—the Virgin's right hand, the left side of the painting and the background. The faces of the Madonna and Child were instead basically intact, as seems confirmed by recent reflectographic analysis performed during an examination now in course.

Eleonora Mazzocchi

Bibliography: AOIF, no. 3629, c. 3; AOIF, 3632, c. 1v; AOIF, 6693, fasc. 30; Ulmann 1893, pp. 24–6; Bellosi 1977, p. 234; Lightbown 1978, A1, p. 11; Horne 1987, p. 130; Pons 1989, p. 54; M. Boskovits in *Italian Paintings* 2003, pp. 146–9; Cecchi 2005, p. 46; Dombrowski 2010, pp. 41–4; N. Pons in *Il mercante* 2010, p. 110.

7.11
Sandro Botticelli
(Alessandro Filipepi, Florence 1445–1510)
Madonna and Child, Two Angels
and the Young St. John
1468
tempera on panel
85 x 62 cm
Florence, Galleria dell'Accademia,
1890 inv. no. 3166

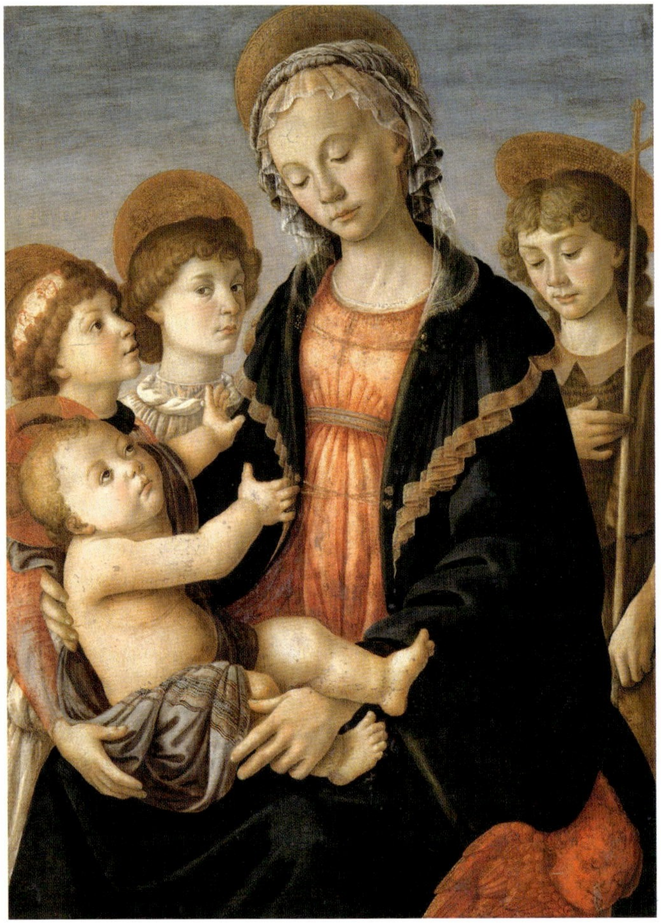

This painting, which hung in the Hospital of Santa Maria Nuova until 1900, was brought first to the Galleria degli Uffizi, and then in 1919 to the Galleria dell'Accademia. It was attributed to Sandro Botticelli for the first time in 1893 by Wilhelm von Bode and Hermann Ullmann, in separate studies. The attribution as well the early dating at around 1468, proposed by Roberto Salvini in 1968, are now generally accepted. In its stylistic traits the painting shows the influence of both Filippo Lippi and Verrocchio, as was typical of the stage in which Botticelli was developing a style of his own. Here the young painter seems intent on producing his own version of one of Filippo Lippi's favourite themes: the Virgin taking into her arms the Child held out to her by one or two angels. Images of the *Madonna and Child* were frequently found in the upper-class homes of the Renaissance. They indicated not only a family's piety but also its social and economic status, as works of art increasingly came to represent wealth. For an artist just starting out, the popularity of these devotional images was an excellent chance to attract clients.

Botticelli's version of this theme is distinguished by its precise description of the Virgin's clothing, inspired by models currently fashionable in Florence, and by the well-balanced spacing of the figures. Moreover, he adapts the iconographic model, skilfully combining mystical and secular aspects in an interpretation he was to use again in the Uffizi *Madonna of the Magnificat* as well as the *Madonna of the Book* in the Museo Poldi Pezzoli.

The presentation of the Son to the Virgin takes place in the present, and this is what our eyes see, drawn by the gaze of the second angel on the left. But in pausing to meditate before the picture, a deeper meaning emerges. On the lower right, the purple-gowned cherub beside the Virgin's chair probably alludes to the celestial throne she will occupy after her assumption into heaven. It is this symbolic reference, projecting the temporal sphere of the image into the future, that has caught the gaze of the Child, fixed well above his Mother's face. It is the image in which both Mary and John, with lowered eyes, are absorbed in meditation.

The ability to combine in the same representation the gentle love of a young mother and an elevated concept of Christian devotion was a further attraction for works of art that increasingly served the function, for the wealthy Florentine mercantile society, of communicating the client's financial, social and cultural status.

Silvia Mascalchi

Bibliography: Zöllner, *Sandro Botticelli* 2009, p. 185 (with preceding bibliography); Dombrowski 2010, pp. 48–51.

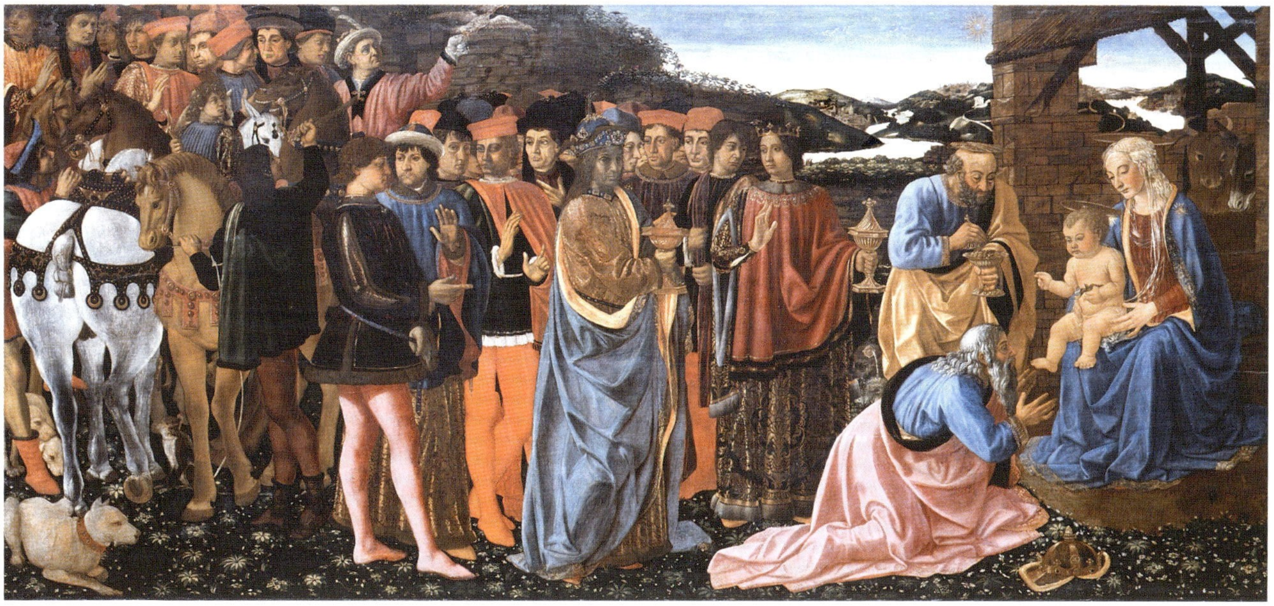

7.12
Cosimo Rosselli (Florence 1439–1507)
Adoration of the Magi
c. 1470
tempera grassa on panel
101 x 217 cm
Florence, Galleria degli Uffizi, 1890 inv. no. 494

For this painting, Padoa Rizzo (1987) has hypothesized a provenance from the Company of the Magi, headquartered first at the Monastery of San Marco, then in the Sacristy and later in the Chapter Room (Hatfield, 'The Compagnia' 1970, pp. 107–61; Castelli 1991, pp. 59–62).

Originating as a gonfalone company, the association became a disciplinary company, with stricter penitential practices, in 1475. On the 6th January—at first every three years, and after 1447 every five—a *cavalcade* of the Magi wound its way through the city to arrive at Piazza San Marco, with great splendour, solemnity and theatrical pageantry. It was just this splendour that contributed to "draw it at last into the Medici sphere of influence, to the point of qualifying it *in toto* as a projection of their power. Starting with Cosimo the Elder's re-entry into Florence in 1434 [...] the company that organized the procession became a meeting place for the Medicean political clique" (P. Ventrone in *Le tems revient* 1992, p. 139). Lorenzo, like his father and grandfather before him, was the leader of this brotherhood (Chastel 1964, p. 250). In Rosselli's painting the Medicean element appears in the device with the diamond and two feathers, the emblems of Cosimo the Elder and Piero, adorning the gilt trappings of the horse in the left foreground (C. Morandi in *Le tems revient* 1992, p. 145), an element that appears to indicate Medicean patronage.

The Medici may have commissioned this work for the oratory of the brotherhood, as suggested by the unusual shape of the painting, horizontal and elongated. Its dimensions are, in fact, those of Leonardo's *Annunciation*, which may originally have been inserted in the wooden panelling of a monastery room (Natali 2002, pp. 53–4). In the same way, Rosselli's painting may have decorated a room in the premises occupied by the Company of the Magi.

The painting seems inspired by a "Medicean" work, Benozzo Gozzoli's *Cavalcade of the Magi* in the Medici Riccardi Palace Chapel, especially in the rows of portraits juxtaposed one above another. In the group on the left, the man appearing in profile in the top row, wearing a headdress ("*tocco*"), may be a portrait of Cosimo the Elder; and the profile of the young man in the foreground, who also appears in Benozzo's *Cavalcade* (C. Morandi in *Le tems revient* 1992, p. 145), is thought to represent Sigismondo Pandolfo Malatesta. Moreover, Cristina Acidini believes that "the three-quarter view of an elderly man with an imposing nose over whose grey head wave the three Medicean feathers [...] whose identity remains for the moment mysterious" (Acidini Luchinat, 'L'immagine medicea' 1991, p. 126) appearing in Gozzoli's *Cavalcade* may be recognized among Rosselli's portraits as well, which, although harder to identity, all have highly individual features. And we may recall with Chastel that "the Magi are not kings, but priests and philosophers, in a certain sense 'Platonists'" (Chastel 1964, p. 251).

Nicoletta Pons

Bibliography: Padoa Rizzo 1987, p.11; Acidini Luchinat, 'L'immagine medicea' 1991, p. 126; C. Morandi in *Le tems revient* 1992, pp. 144–6; Padoa Rizzo 2001, p. 62; Gabrielli 2007, pp. 155–7 (with preceding bibliography); E. Gabrielli in *Il Potere e la Grazia* 2009, pp. 222; N. Pons in *Benozzo Gozzoli e Cosimo Rosselli* 2011, pp. 156–7.

7.13 - work not on display
Sandro Botticelli
(Alessandro Filipepi, Florence 1445–1510)
Portrait of a Young Man
1470–3
tempera on panel
51 x 33.5 cm
Florence, Galleria Palatina di Palazzo Pitti, Palatina inv. no. 372 (1912 inv.)

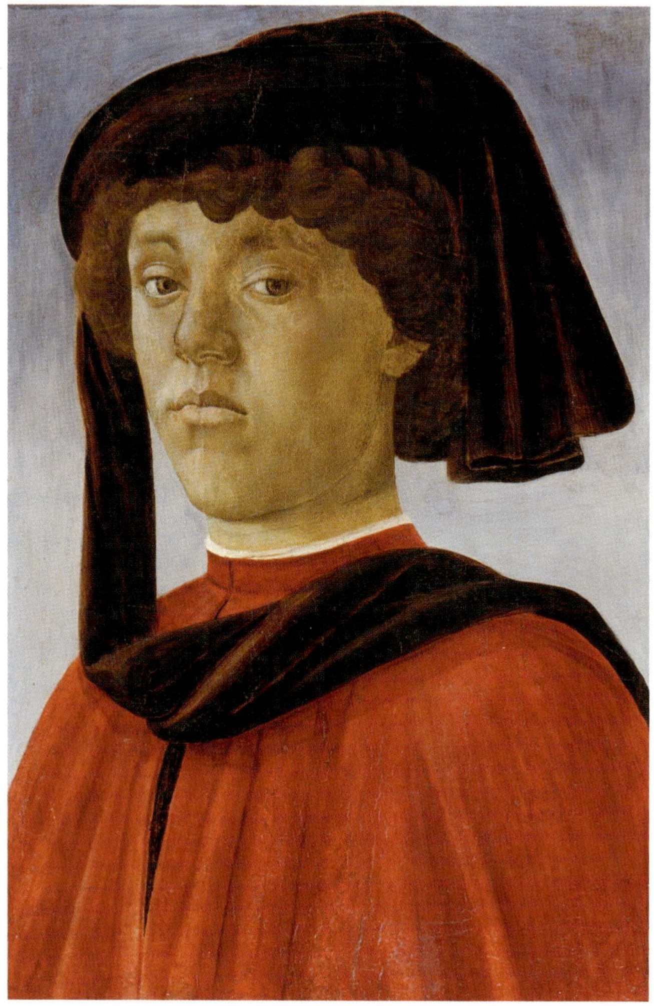

The Pitti Palace *Portrait of a Young Man*, usually dated around 1470, is probably the earliest extant example of Sandro Botticelli's vast portraiture production (Zöllner, 'Botticelli portraitiste' 2009). Conserved in the Palatine Gallery and thought to be by Andrea del Castagno, the painting was attributed to Botticelli for the first time by Adolfo Venturi in 1891, but this hypothesis was generally accepted only after it had been restored in 1935.

The identity of the young man depicted is unknown, but based on how he chose to be portrayed, some interesting deductions can be made. He wears a red tunic, the typical garment of Florentine citizens, over a white shirt barely showing at the neck. His curly hair is covered by a *mazzocchio* lined in dark purple felt or velvet, its brim falling to his shoulder as if to frame his face. The colour scheme, a significant element in this simple but intense image, appears carefully chosen. The brilliant red sharply contrasts with the line of luminous white at the neck; in a more sober effect, the dark purple contrasts with the blue background. The three-quarter pose, the slight foreshortening from below and the austere elegance of his attire confirm that the young man is of noble birth, and that he has assumed a public role despite his youth. His gaze, still a little boyish, looks outward, seeking confirmation of the admiration he hopes to arouse.

Even at this early date, the subject is painted in a three-quarter pose. It was in the 1470s, in fact, that Florentine painters began to adopt this Flemish innovation, which gradually supplanted the portrait in profile. It may be reasonably assumed that the prototype for Botticelli's portrait was Andrea del Castagno's *Portrait of a Man*, now in the National Gallery, Washington.

The Pitti portrait may be seen in relation to a lost portrait previously attributed to Botticelli, which was kept in the Museo Filangieri in Naples up to World War II. Although of little stylistic interest, the Neapolitan work arouses our curiosity for an amorous inscription at the bottom of the painting, indicated by the subject with a gesture of his hand, "NE TIMEAS TIBI FIDUS ERO TUUS USQUE MANEBUS." Although there is no evidence that the Florentine portrait was painted as a pledge of love, it may be that the young man in question commissioned Botticelli to commemorate a significant moment in his life, the delicate watershed that divides boyhood from manhood.

Silvia Mascalchi

Bibliography: Venturi 1891, p. 4; Zöllner, *Sandro Botticelli* 2009, pp. 196–7 (with preceding bibliography); Zöllner, 'Botticelli portraitiste' 2009, pp. 249–69.

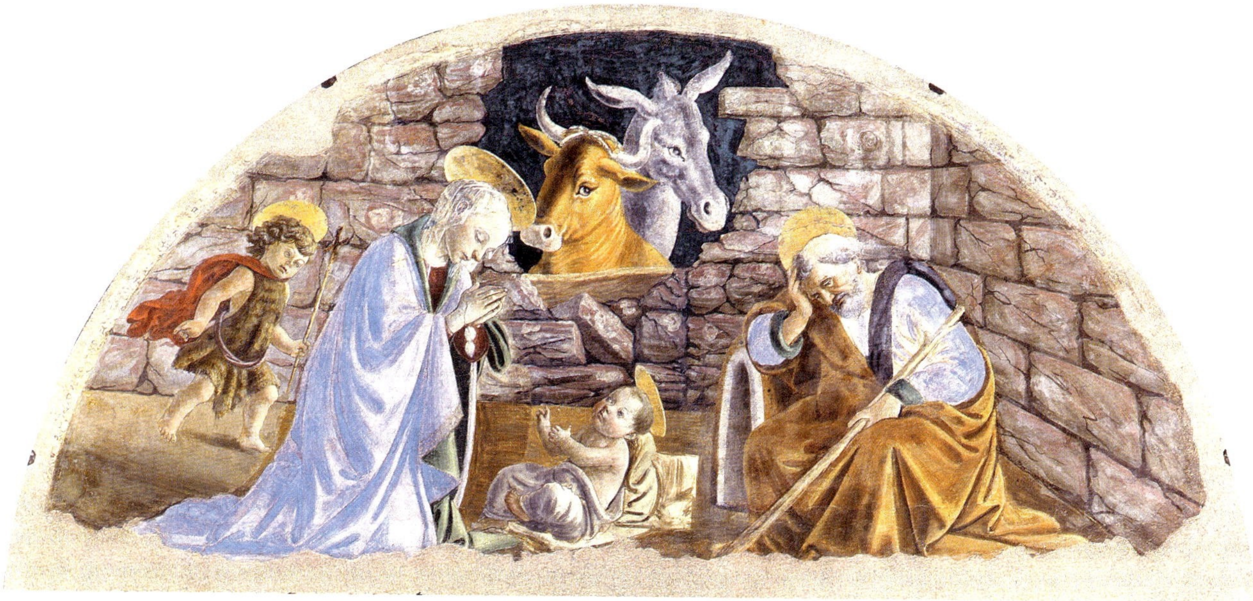

7.14
Sandro Botticelli
(Alessandro Filipepi, Florence 1445–1510)
Nativity
1472–4
detached fresco
117 x 226 cm
Florence, Basilica di Santa Maria Novella, inner façade

This frescoed lunette adorned the upper register of the altar of Guasparre di Zanobi del Lama (Florence, 1411–81) in Santa Maria Novella (Gamba 1931–2), which stood between the two doors in the church's inner façade before being destroyed by Vasari in 1569 (Hatfield 1976; Cecchi 2005, p. 136). The client, a Medici supporter, was a sensale de' cambi, or stockbroker, for the Arte del Cambio, the bankers' guild (Parks 2006, pp. 29–56). Dedicated to the Magi, the altar, lavishly decorated in marble and gilt intaglio, was still being built in 1469 (Hatfield 1976; Cecchi 2005, p. 136) and was later to include Botticelli's panel painting depicting the *Adoration of the Magi*, now at the Uffizi (111 x 134 cm), which was smaller than the lunette above it. The difference in size would not have been incongruous, considering that the painting had an imposing marble frame that must have been quite thick. Scholars have noted a gap in time between the frescoed *Nativity*, datable to the early 1470s, and the painting, dating from around 1475 and in any case prior to 1476, the year when Del Lama was condemned for dishonest conduct by the Arte del Cambio (Hatfield 1976; Cecchi 2005, p. 136). After that date it is unlikely that he could have commissioned such an important work. Guasparre, who bears the name of one of the Magi, is portrayed among the group of onlookers to the left as an elderly man (he was about sixty-five at the time) with white hair, looking out toward the spectator and pointing at himself. Not far from him, Botticelli has painted his own self-portrait. The Three Kings instead, as recalled by Vasari (1568, ed. Milanesi 1878–81, III, 1878, pp. 135–6), are portraits of the Medici. The patriarch Cosimo can be identified as the old man kneeling before the Virgin, Piero as the King in a red mantle turning toward the younger Magus (Giovanni), who is kneeling beside the man with black hair seen in profile, recognizable as Lorenzo the Magnificent.
In addition to being a sort of captatio benevolentiae addressed to the most prominent family in Florence, the painting refers to the Company of the Magi, headquartered in San Marco, of which the Medici were patrons and illustrious members (see entry 7.12).

Interestingly enough, the notary for the Arte del Cambio was at the time Nastagio Vespucci, a neighbour of the Filipepi family and client of the painter, who may have recommended Sandro to Del Lama for the project of decorating the chapel in Santa Maria Novella (Hatfield 1976, p. 15 note 18). Moreover, Sandro's brother, Giovanni di Mariano Filipepi, was also a stockbroker (Goldthwaite 2009, p. 414).

Around 1470 Botticelli painted a moulded panel depicting the *Virgin and Child in Glory with Cherubim* (now in the Galleria degli Uffizi, 1890 inv. no. 504) for the seat of the Arte del Cambio in Piazza Signoria, as has been recognized by Cecchi and more recently by Waldmann (2009, p. 106), based on the original frame's decoration of gold coins against a red field, alluding to the Guild's armorial bearings (Cecchi 2005, p. 102).

Nicoletta Pons

Bibliography: Hatfield 1976; Cecchi 2005, pp. 136–42; Goldthwaite 2009, p. 384; N. Pons in *Filippino Lippi* forthcoming.

7.15
Sandro Botticelli
(Alessandro Filipepi, Florence 1445–1510): design
Florentine manufacture: embroidery
Hood of a liturgical cope showing the Coronation of the Virgin
1490–5
silk, gold and linen
46.4 x 46.5 cm
Milan, Museo Poldi Pezzoli, inv. no. 444/155

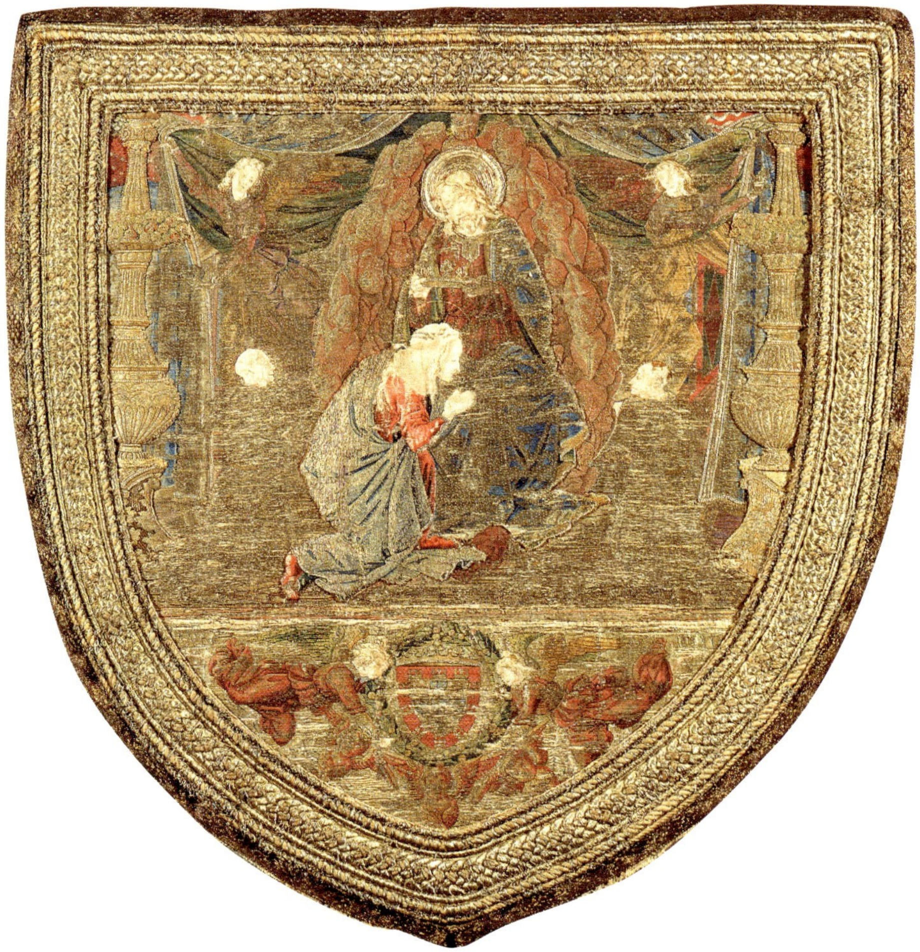

The upper part of this hood is decorated with a scene of the *Coronation of the Virgin*, framed at the sides by two candelabra. Christ, surrounded by a mandorla of seraphim, appears crowning the Virgin, who kneels before him with hands clasped in worship. The scene takes place in a pavilion, held open by two angels. Mary is flanked by two worshippers, also kneeling, wearing monk's habits, their heads adorned with the luminous haloes of the Blessed. Below, in another scene at the tip of the hood, two angels in flight bear a laurel wreath enclosing an escutcheon surmounted by a crown. This is the heraldic emblem of the Aviz dynasty, rulers of Portugal from 1385 to 1580, in the form it assumed—with lateral inescutcheons pendants and the absence of the cross-flory of Aviz—in 1485, during the reign of John II (Mendes Atanasio 1963, p. 234).

This splendid work of embroidery, superbly crafted *à or nué* (for a detailed description of the technique, see Mottola Molfino 1984, pp. 340–1, cat. no. 142; Carmignani 1989; Pertegato 1989, pp. 46-51; M. Carmignani, in *Botticelli* 2003, pp. 172–4 cat. 25; M. Rizzini, in *Botticelli* 2010, pp. 70–3 cat. 5), was bought in 1889 at the price of 200 lire by Giuseppe Bertini, the first director of the Museo Poldi Pezzoli, from the Milanese antiquarian Giuseppe Goldberg. After some initial doubts, art historians have unanimously attributing the preparatory drawing to Sandro Botticelli, who furnished drawings for other textile works as well (Vasari 1550 and 1568, ed. Bettarini-Barocchi 1966–97, III, 1971, p. 520).

Based on the presence of the Portuguese coat of arms, the cope has also been recognized as one of the liturgical vestments prepared for the Cardinal of Portugal's Chapel in the Florentine Church of San Miniato al Monte; but on this point some doubt is legitimate. In the chapel itself and the works designed for it appear, in fact, the armorial bearings of Cardinal Jacopo of Lusitania, and not those of his relation. Moreover, the documentation on the building of the chapel reports that the vestments designed for it, bearing the Cardinal's emblem, were made between 1468 and 1472 (Mendes Atanasio 1963); it seems highly unlikely, then, that new ones would be made for it only a few years later.

In the restoration conducted by Francesco Pertegato from 1986 to 1988, it was also found that the embroidered scene at the top depicting the *Coronation of the Virgin* and the one at the bottom, with the coat of arms held up by two angels—which perfectly fits into the tip of the cope and must have been designed for it from the beginning—although contemporary, were originally made for different robes. They were assembled together only later, soon after being completed (Pertegato 1989, pp. 51–5), as confirmed by some distortions in the workmanship of the seraphim and the dimensions of the angels. During restoration, the two kneeling Blessed Ones were photographed from the back, where the silk threads are best preserved (Pertegato 1989, pp. 65, 70–1 figs. 28, 36). These clearer images show that they are not, as had been thought, dressed in the habit of the Olivetan order, which directed the Basilica of San Miniato al Monte from 1373 to 1553, but are wearing instead the white habit gathered at the waist by a leather belt of the Jesuates, with the hood resting on the right shoulder.

It is very likely that the embroidered scene at the top was originally made for San Giusto alle Mura, the church of the Florentine Jesuate monastery, for which both Pietro Perugino and Domenico Ghirlandaio painted important works in the last two decades of the 15th century. In this scene the Blessed Ones appear without tonsures, since throughout the 15th century the Jesuate Order was a free association of laymen. They can probably be identified as Giovanni Colombini, founder of the congregation, and Antonio Bettini (or in alternative, Antonio Tavelli da Tossignano). The cope decorated at the tip with the coat of arms was instead commissioned by John II Aviz, probably for a Portuguese destination. This may have been his own funerary chapel, which, commissioned of Andrea Sansovino, was never finished due to the Portuguese sovereign's untimely death in 1495, at the age of only forty (letter from Sebastiano Resta to Giuseppe Ghezzi, in Bottari 1754–73, III, 1759, pp. 333-334, no. CCV; Höfler 1992; Moreira 2001). The liturgical robes that were to be decorated by the embroidered works—made between 1490 and 1495, as confirmed by stylistic analysis (Lightbown 1978, I, p. 152; Cecchi 2005, p. 272)—were probably never completed, and the two fragments were then assembled to make a finished work. King John II Aviz commissioned this splendid cope within the context of the intense cultural, commercial and financial exchange inaugurated in the 15th century between Portugal and Florence, monopolized and coordinated by the Cambini company. From Portugal, Florence received raw materials (coral, fish, leather, silk, grain, cork and sugar), sending back in turn luxury products: paintings, goldwork, illuminated manuscripts, geographical maps, fabrics and fine embroidery, plate, Della Robbia ware and decorated chests (Melis 1970; Spallanzani 1997, pp. 8–19; Tognetti 1999; De la Mare 2000; Tognetti 2002, pp. 121–37). In the 15th century, moreover, members of the Portuguese royal house invested heavily in Florentine financial institutions—such as the Monte Comune, that is, the public debt (Martelli [1433–83], ed. Pezzarossa 1989, p. 207; Ciappelli 2006, pp. 60–1), and the Medici Bank (G. Corti in Kennedy 1964, p. 41 note 18; De Roover 1963, ed. 1970, p. 339 note 47)—which yielded high profits and were among the most efficient, functional and advanced of the time. Contacts with Florentine humanists, merchants, ecclesiastics and political figures were also frequent and fertile (Battelli 1936; Battelli 1939; Lavagnino 1940, pp. 7–27; Mendes Atanasio 1963; Cecchi 2005, pp. 272, 283 note 189; Höfler 1992; Lowe 1999; Moreira 2001).

Bibliography: *Catalogo* 1902, p. 21; Sant'Ambrogio 1903; Mendes Atanasio 1963; Mandel 1967, p. 117; Garzelli 1973, pp. 25–7, 45 notes 46-47; Natale 1982, pp. 154–5, cat. no. 190; Mottola Molfino 1984, pp. 340–1, cat. no. 142; Horne 1908, ed. it. 1986, pp. 452–3; Carmignani 1989; Pertegato 1989; M. Carmignani, in *Botticelli* 2003, pp. 172–4, cat. no. 25; Cecchi 2005, pp. 272–6, 283 note 183; M. Rizzini, in *Botticelli* 2010, pp. 70–3, cat. no. 5.

7.16
Sassanian (body); Andrea del Verrocchio
(Florence 1437–88) (setting), attributed to
Ewer
11th century, 1469–77
sardonyx (hardstone); embossed, chased,
engraved and gilded silver; cast and chased
(setting)
42 cm
Florence, Museo degli Argenti,
1921 inv. no. 777

The ewer, with the inscription "LAV·R·MED" running round it, has a bombé body and moulding at the neck; the semicircular handle is shaped like a dragon. The setting involves only the base, the spout, the lid with its crown and the joint with the handle. This piece, one of the most beautiful in the Laurentian collection, was formed by mounting a ewer made of dark sardonyx, veined and mottled, attributed to the Sassanid epoch, in a 15th-century silver-gilt setting. Various hypotheses have been advanced for the dating of the sardonyx body, ranging from Late Antiquity to the 10th-11th century, and for its provenance, either Byzantium or Persia, although these two areas were subject, as we know, to profound, continuous contaminations (see D. Heikamp in *Il Tesoro* 1973–4, II, 1974, pp. 108–11, no. 11).

The setting involves even more complex problems, since it enters into the debate over the distribution of the pieces collected in the lifetimes of Piero di Cosimo and Lorenzo the Magnificent. Ample, detailed discussion has arisen over the presence at the top of the embricated lid of a ball surrounded by three rings, one of the most common Medicean emblems, on which are enamelled the red balls of their armorial bearings, in the form used before Louis XI granted Piero di Cosimo the right to use the blue ball charged by the fleur-de-lis in 1465. This date has thus been indicated as the definitive *terminus* after which the setting could not have been made. However, since the coat of arms appears inside the lid in its later complete form, the date must necessarily be moved forward to a time not long after this honour had been conferred, that is, a brief period when the Medici family continued to use both heraldic forms contemporaneously (Liscia Bemporad 2002, pp. 197–8).

As of now, no mention of the artists who created the Medicean settings has been found in the documents. However, the stamps of the Arte di Por Santa Maria and the goldsmith found on the silver- gilt structure of another ewer made of rock crystal, adapted for use as a reliquary (first for the relics of Saints Cosmas and Damian, then, since 1785, for the arm of St. Anastasia) has begun to clear up the uncertainties surrounding one of the richest treasures of the 15th century, and not Florentine alone (D. Liscia Bemporad in *San Lorenzo* 1993, pp. 159–60, no. 3.7; Liscia Bemporad 2002, pp. 198–9). In any case, based on some stylistic traits of the setting in question, it has been attributed to one of the greatest Florentine sculptors. The name of Andrea del Verrocchio has been advanced on the basis of style, primarily, and on historical facts. After having trained as goldsmith in the workshop of Francesco di Luca Verrocchi (whose name he adapted), Verrocchio had already abandoned this trade by 1457, at the age of twenty-five since, not being enrolled in the Arte di Por Santa Maria, he could not open a workshop of his own cut. In the following decade he became one of the favourite artists of the Medici family, Lorenzo in particular, his patron, who procured him innumerable commissions. Strong in such supporters, he was probably entrusted with the only other goldsmith's piece surviving to our own day, created by his hands, the formella depicting *The Beheading of the Baptist* on the silver altar of St. John. This work has served as basis for attributing the setting of the ewer to Verrocchio. Specifically, the bat's wing joining the lid and the handle, the scales motif, and the curves of the spout precisely match some figures in the formella, and in other works sculpted by Verrocchio.

Dora Liscia Bemporad

Bibliography: D. Heikamp in *Il Tesoro* 1973–4, II, 1974, pp. 108–11, no. 11; Scalini 1997, pp. 29-50; Liscia Bemporad 2002, pp. 189–206.

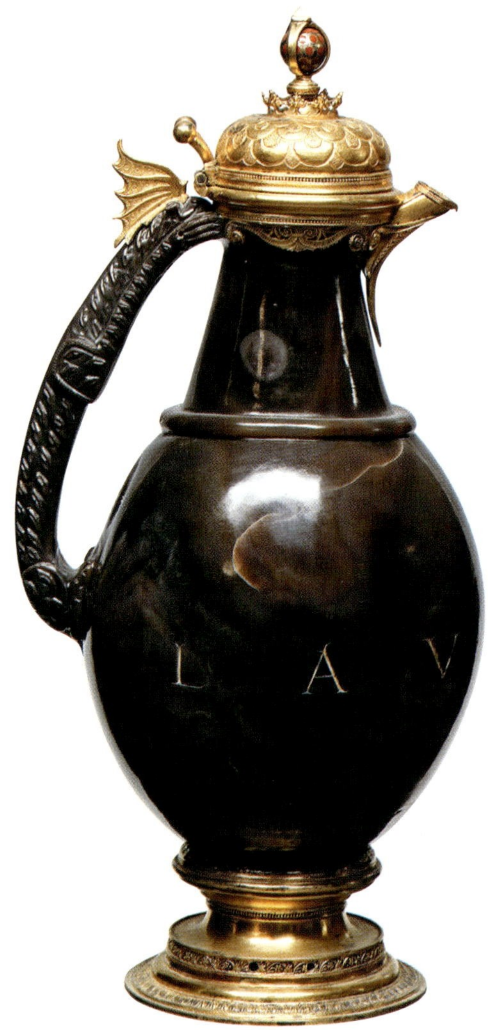

7.17
Domizio Calderini
(Verona 1446–Rome 1478)
Commentary on Juvenal
1471
miniature on parchment; fols. III, 154;
Medicean binding
270 x 180 mm
Florence, Biblioteca Medicea Laurenziana,
Plut. 53.2 fol. 5r

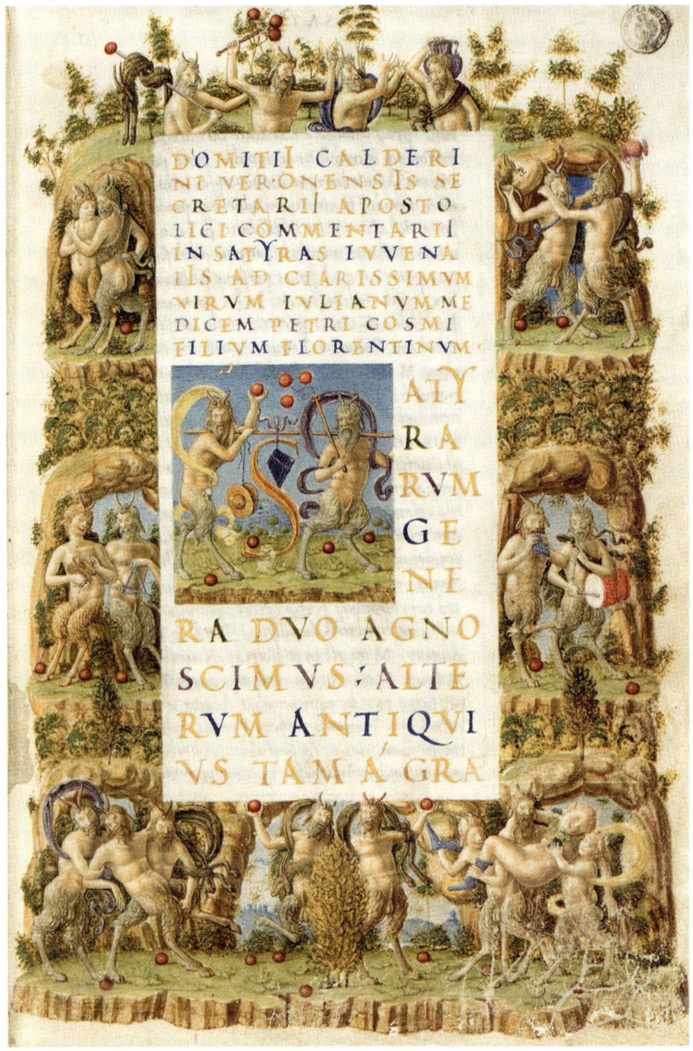

This vivacious page, peremptorily heralding the beginning of a manuscript, is fully worthy of its noble destination. It is in fact the dedicatory codex presented by the author to Giuliano de' Medici, along with another (Plut. 53.33) containing a commentary on Martial that rendered homage to Lorenzo. With the obsequious flattery of a courtier, the author compares the young lord to the great heroes of the ancient world, in keeping with the concept of Florence as heir to Rome expressed in the strictest form of Florentine civil humanism. The elegant penmanship of Bartolommeo Sanvito, one of the most refined copyists of his time, with its classic composure and refined colours, sharply contrasts with the brutal games played by the satyrs who, in erudite citation of the content, become the true protagonists, amidst expressions of violent struggle and open eroticism. Especially striking are the two appearing at the centre of the page, in a sort of plaque, where the culture of the upper classes emerges as a recognizable element. The initial capital "S" of the text (*Satyrarum*) is hanging from a stick held up by two playful satyrs who are juggling the balls of the Medici heraldic arms with amazing dexterity. Allusion to heraldic emblems is not new in visual language, nor is the utilization of elements from the classical world, especially creatures that are part man, part beast. And here there springs to mind one of the tondoes adorning the Palazzo Medici courtyard depicting a beautiful centaur carrying the Medici balls in a basket, an image copied from a splendid engraved gemstone. This play of references between allegory and courtly flattery, between political allusions and references to antiquity (skilfully employed for the purposes of propaganda) show how the family, already openly launched on the road to hegemony, made use of culture, finding in books, and specifically in the relationship between words and images, an unrivalled channel of expression.

Art historians disagree over the attribution of the illuminated decoration, first assigned to Gaspare da Padova and then to Lauro Padovano. The page is, however, a fantastic example of the utilization of ancient-style ciphers in the liveliest of scenes, where gaiety and fantasy imbue a mode of expression profoundly different from the more codified Florentine productions, where the classical influence appears in a sense of measure, rational organization, and clear spatial divisions.

The invention of the illuminated initial letter, much admired in Veneto and then in Rome, is highly interesting, being a real crucible of styles and the meeting point for master craftsmen of all sorts. In Florence too, the experience acquired in other centres of art and culture was assimilated and re-elaborated. The city did not reject innovations and diversity in these fields, but sought, as for its commerce and its economy, to protect and safeguard its sources of wealth, never hesitating to improve them with any external contributions recognized as valid.

Giovanna Lazzi

Bibliography: Dunston 1968, pp. 72, 75–8, 124–7, 139; Bauer-Eberhardt 1989, p. 52; *Lorenzo dopo Lorenzo* 1992, pp. 98–101, 195–8.

7.18
Songs for Three and Four Voices
late 15th century
manuscript on paper and parchment; fols. V, 325; binding restored using original leather cover, embossed and gilt edge
250 x 170 mm
Florence, Biblioteca Nazionale Centrale, Banco rari 229, fols. IIIIv-Vr

This codex contains two-hundred-sixty-eight compositions, nineteen of them attributed to Jannes Martini and no less than twenty-two to Heinrich Isaac, a prominent member of the Medicean court. The sumptuous parchment folios contrast with the paper pages, decorated with initials in the shape of stiff ribbons, at times enlivened with multiform figures showing the influence of the many marginal vignettes found in French-Flemish manuscripts. The first two splendid "tinted pages," rare in Florentine production, resemble precious fabrics or slabs of antique marbles. Against a red and blue background, an erudite reference to luxurious ancient codices and the wall paintings of Pompeii and Rome, the text appears in the illusionist guise of a page within a page. The modern-style portrait, within the classical clypeus, is inserted in a delicate monochrome decoration, whose borders stand out vividly against the dark background. Ciardi Duprè (1994) attributes the decorative insert to Pedro Berruguete who, on his way to Urbino, may have stopped in Florence where he met Gherardo di Giovanni and his assistants, to whom the decoration has traditionally been attributed (see also Ciardi Duprè dal Poggetto 2002, p. 143, correcting the attribution of the portrait to Gherardo).

The coat of arms suggests that the Florentine nobleman Alessandro Braccesi, a political and literary figure, should be identified with the personage previously recognized as Jannes Martini. Portrayed on the facing page is Tubalcain, the mythological inventor of music, shown bearing an anvil as in Andrea Pisano's formella of *Metallurgy* on Giotto's Bell Tower, but also reminiscent of Luca della Robbia's *Astrology*, demonstrating once more how important were the arts to the life of Florence.

The circular canon represents the world, according to Bartolomé Ramos de Pareja, famous for his treatise *Musica practica*. It is the visual translation of a complex idea: the macrocosm and the microcosm are constructed in the same harmonious proportions, and music reflects the laws that govern the universe. Classical culture is evoked in the monochromes, where the cameo depicting the infant Dionysus, with Donatello's variation of Amore Atys, is reproduced (Garzelli 1985, p. 300). It would be interesting to link the Eros-Antheros citation to the Neo-Platonic interpretation of the harmony of the spheres and the cathartic, organizing function of music, considering the frequent association of the Dionysian theme with the erotic impulse viewed as the urge to acquire knowledge.

Florentine society had now become so culturally refined as to appreciate and assimilate distilled suggestions from antiquity, but without forgetting its solid mercantile base, founded on the activities and economic power of the crafts. And it was just this meeting of commercial pragmatism and erudite intellectualism that gave birth to the ruling class's new approach to communication and propaganda.

Giovanna Lazzi

Bibliography: M.A. Bartoli Bacherini in *Lorenzo dopo Lorenzo* 1992, 1.14, pp. 41–4 n. 1.14 (with preceding bibliography); *Pregio e Bellezza* 2010, p. 118, no. 31.

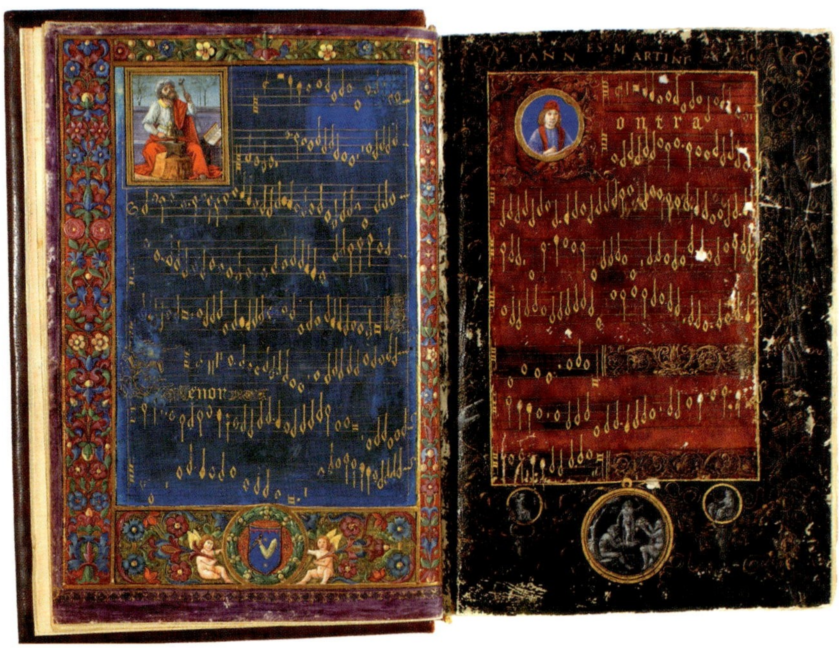

7.19
Florentine textile manufacture
Fragment of fabric composed of six pieces with Medici coat of arms
late 15th century
silk and gold metal thread; polychrome cut voided velvet, brocaded, satin weave ground
37 x 120 cm
Florence, Museo Nazionale del Bargello, Franchetti inv. no. 114

Against a white background, worked in satin weave of 5 ends doublé, the pattern of the damasked velvet emerges as the effect of three warps of "pile"—the first crimson red, the second green and the third blue—forming a pattern of hexagonal stitches forming little flowers with corollas, alternating with inflorescences of similar type but much larger size, marking the connection points of the decorative pattern. Within the stitch, heart-shaped element in crimson damasked velvet compose a great open inflorescence, distinguished by palmette motifs appearing in blue, by elongated leaves, bordered in green, arranged to frame the Medici coat of arms, alluded to, in the central clypeus, by the seven red balls "voided" against the spun gold brocade ground.

For the opulent materials employed and for the technical and aesthetic connotations, differing entirely from the most lavish production of previous centuries, velvet is the textile that became in the Renaissance symbolic of the unrivalled superiority of Italian manufacturers over those of the other Mediterranean countries. The system for creating the "pile" called for the appropriate tools, such as velvet cutters, used only by specific professional figures. When heraldic arms were to be brocaded into the fabric, as on, as on the fragment in question, the textile could be extremely expensive, because the two production processes, for velvet and for brocade, were totally different, the former being worked first from the front and the latter from the back of the fabric. Weavers capable of such craftsmanship were in fact the highest-paid of their profession, and it is hardly surprising that their production capacity was no more than two pieces a year. In the Bargello velvet, a further precious element consists of the polychromy, calling for painstakingly slow, elaborate work that indubitably affected the price of the finished product. An added value then consisted of the use of costly dyes, such as azure blue and crimson red. In speaking of these dyes (also used in this fragment), the anonymous silk worker in the famous treatise *L'Arte della Seta in Firenze* [The Art of Silk in Florence] calls Alexandrine azure "one of the freshest [...] most beautiful colours that can be made" and crimson red "the noblest colour and the most important [that] we have" (Gargiolli 1868, pp. 30, 39). Emblematical, then, of luxury and social status, velvet became in the Renaissance the favourite means of personal celebration for bankers and merchants, the new governing class that, to demonstrate the political role it had attained, did not disdain to display the emblems of its house, specially woven in fabrics created on weaving looms of specific width and mounting.

Donatella Mascalchi

Bibliography: Gargiolli 1868; *Velluti e Moda* 1999; Cardon 2000, pp. 63-73; Boccherini, Marabelli 1995; Edler de Roover 1999; *Seta* 2006.

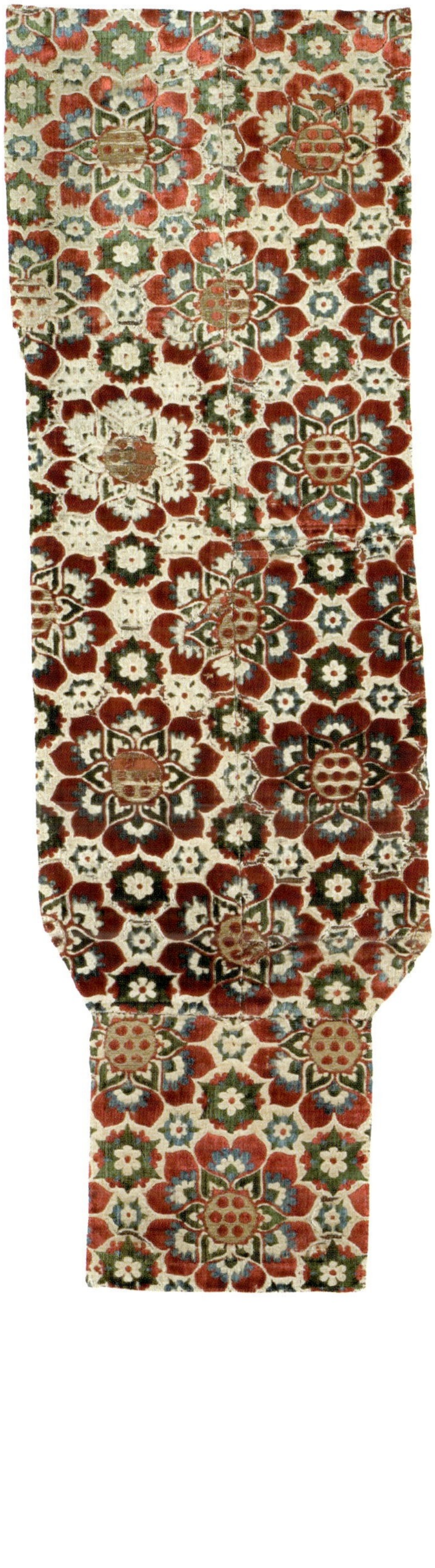

7.20
Sandro Botticelli
(Alessandro Filipepi, Florence 1445–1510)
Workshop
Venus
c. 1482
oil on canvas
174 x 77 cm
Turin, Galleria Sabauda, inv. 172, Cat. no. 656

In one of his *Sermons on Haggeus*, preached during Advent of 1494, Savonarola admonished the Florentines, "O ye whose houses are filled with vanities and images and dishonest things and indecent books, and the Morgante and other poems against the faith, bring them to me to be burned as a sacrifice to God" (Chastel 1964). These words find an echo in Giorgio Vasari, who recalls that Botticelli "in various houses around the city painted tondoes of his own hand with many female nudes;" information confirmed by other sources as well, such as the Anonymous Magliabechiano, which attributes to him "a number of lovely female nudes" and the Libro by Antonio Billi, reporting that he painted "more beautiful female nudes than any other artist."

The sources thus document not only the presence, in the homes of wealthy Florentines, of pictures with subjects taken from classical mythology showing nude women, but also Botticelli's pre-eminence in this production. And in fact, some of his great masterpieces belong to this category, where the nude female figure, either veiled or bare, is rendered with an enchanting flow of outline and learned references to ancient statuary. Unsurprisingly, these pictures, painted in the 1480s at the height of the Laurentian Age, became to the eyes of the Piagnoni intellectuals the manifestation of a secular, hedonistic spirit, opposed to the principles of religious orthodoxy, decency and clarity then being preached by Savonarola and his followers.

The painting exhibited here is one of three Venuses (the other two are in the Gemäldegalerie, Berlin, and a private collection) created in Botticelli's workshop and deriving from the prototype of the Uffizi *Birth of Venus*; the original model is the classical *Venere pudica*, like the statue of the *Medici Venus* now displayed in the Tribune of the Uffizi. The three Botticellian paintings of Venus differ slightly from the prototype in the hairstyles and veiling of the forms. Moreover, the absence of a landscape in the background, by highlighting the nude female figure against a dark background, vividly transposes the memory of antiquity into a pleasure to the eye.

The elongated dimensions of the picture suggest that it may have been used as a *spalliera*, a painted element inserted in the wooden panelling of a refined interior decoration scheme.

Silvia Mascalchi

Bibliography: Chastel 1964, p. 404; Lightbown 1978, II, p. 121 (with preceding bibliography); Pons 1989, p. 72; *Botticelli* 2009, pp. 236–9.

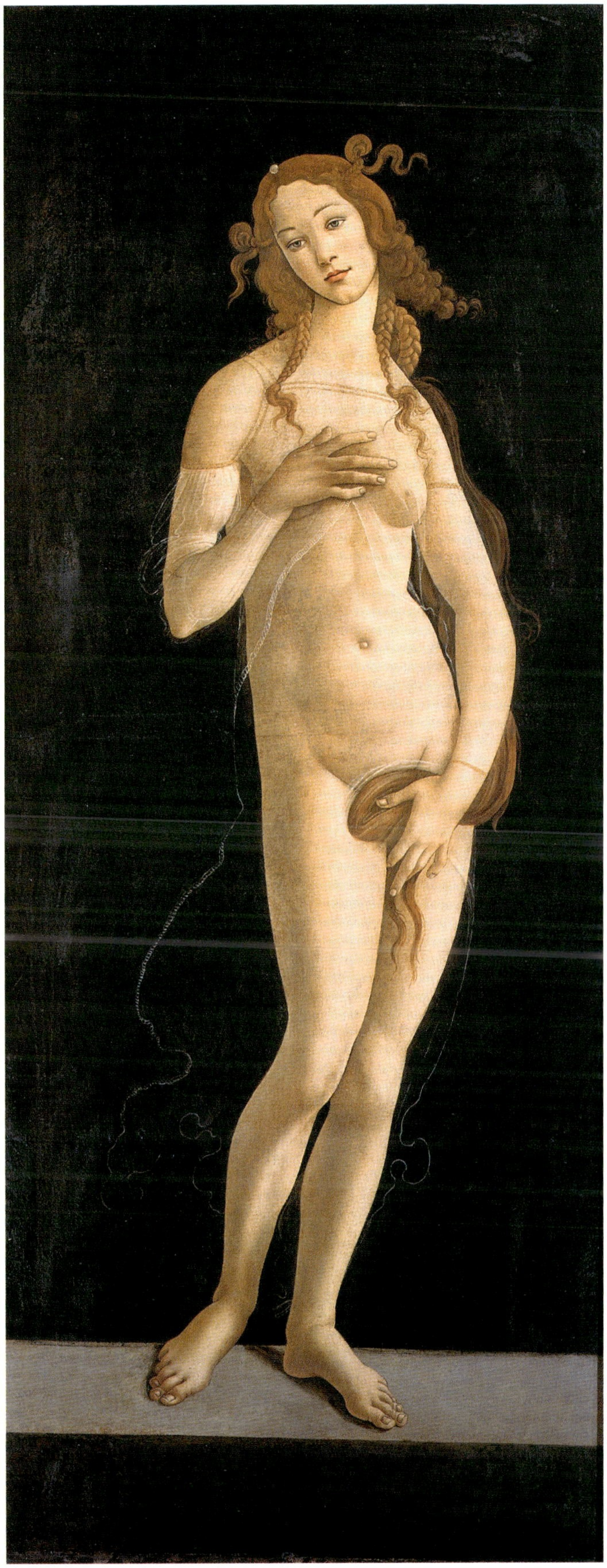

7.21 - work not on display
Sandro Botticelli
(Alessandro Filipepi, Florence 1445–1510)
Pallas and the Centaur
c. 1482
tempera on canvas
207 x 148 cm
Florence, Galleria degli Uffizi,
Depositi inv. no. 29

This canvas has long been identified as the painting described as "Camilla with a Satyr" in the 1498 inventory of the "Substance and Goods of Lorenzo and the heirs of Johanni di Pierfrancesco de Medici" in the Palazzo on Via Larga. Owned by the cadet branch of the Medici family, the painting was recorded as hanging above the door between the bedchamber and antechamber of Lorenzo "Minor," as he was called by Marsilio Ficino. This elevated position, often recorded for paintings and sculptures of the time, would justify "the foreshortening from below, especially evident in the woman's face" (Acidini Luchinat 2001, p. 167).

In the 16th century the painting was moved to the suburban villa at Castello, also owned by the cadet branch. Doubt has been cast on the assumption that it was commissioned by Lorenzo di Pierfrancesco (Florence 1463–1503), due to the insistent presence of the three intertwined diamond-tip rings on the woman's gown, an emblem attributed with certainty by Cecchi (in *Sandro Botticelli* 2000, p. 129) to the descendents of Cosimo alone, and thus to the main branch of the family only. This would presume, according to Cecchi, that Lorenzo the Magnificent himself commissioned the painting, probably as a wedding gift to his cousin, who was his ward, on the occasion of his marriage to Semiramide Appiani in 1482. Some experts, however, continue to explore the possibility that Lorenzo di Pierfrancesco may have commissioned the painting from Botticelli, his favourite artist, from whom he ordered numerous other works. The cadet branch of the family had been plagued with financial problems up to 1485, the year when the Magnificent was obliged to return to his wards the money he had taken from them in his capacity as guardian. Hence the painting would date from after this time, when Lorenzo di Pierfrancesco reacquired the financial means necessary to invest in such an important work of art (in the 1499 inventory it is listed as worth 40 lire) (De Roover 1963, ed. 1970, pp. 532–3; Acidini Luchinat 2001, p. 168).

Portrayed on the canvas are a centaur, with bow and arrows, and a female personage recognized as Minerva-Pallas (Pallas Athena) for the presence of the shield on her back, although her traditional lance is missing, replaced by an unusual halberd. For this reason she has been variously identified as Camilla, the virgin warrior (Deimling 2009, pp. 63–79), a sentinel (Acidini Luchinat 2001, p. 169), or the Venus of Cythera (Smith 1975, pp. 35–7). Among the many interpretations of the subject, the traditional one, recently proposed again by Cecchi, seems convincing. In his opinion, the painting is a Neo-Platonic moral allegory.

The surrender of man's animal instincts (the centaur) to reason (Pallas/Minerva), "symbolizes the supremacy of the mind and reason over the senses and earthly desires, elements that could lead a youth astray from a life of *studia humanitatis*" (A. Cecchi in *Sandro Botticelli* 2000, p. 128): a sort of viaticum for the young Lorenzo di Pierfrancesco, then standing of the threshold of adulthood.

Nicoletta Pons

Bibliography: L. Venturini in *Giovinezza di Michelangelo* 1999, pp. 246–8; A. Cecchi in *Sandro Botticelli* 2000, pp. 127–8; Acidini Luchinat 2001, pp. 166–70; N. Pons in *Botticelli e Filippino* 2004, pp. 238–40; Cecchi 2005, p. 202; Deimling 2009, pp. 63–79; A. Schumacher in *Botticelli* 2009, pp. 214–7.

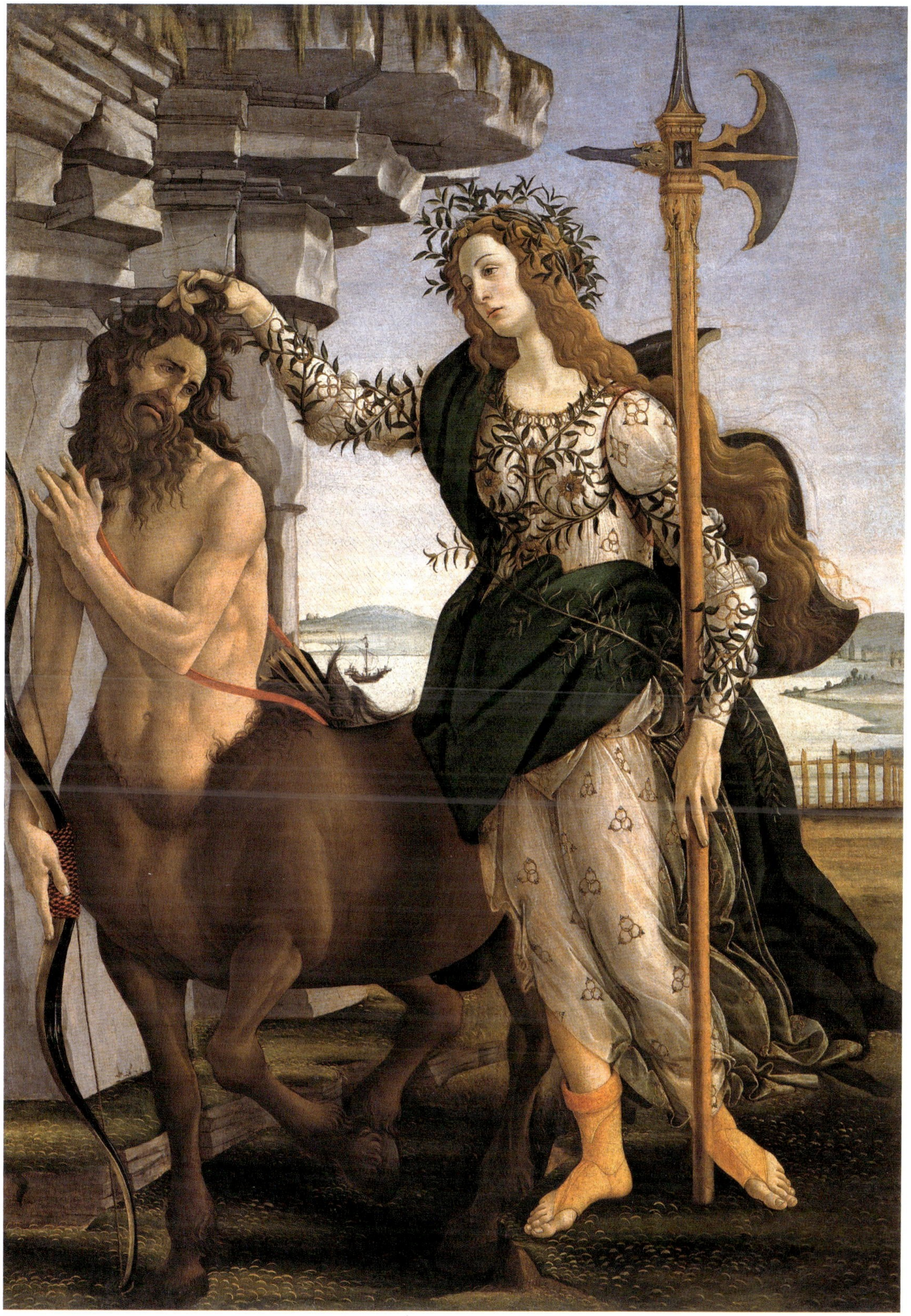

7.22
Sandro Botticelli
(Alessandro Filipepi, Florence 1445–1510)
Portrait of a Woman
c. 1485
tempera on panel
61.3 x 40.5 cm
Florence, Galleria Palatina di Palazzo Pitti, Palatina inv. no. 353 (1912)

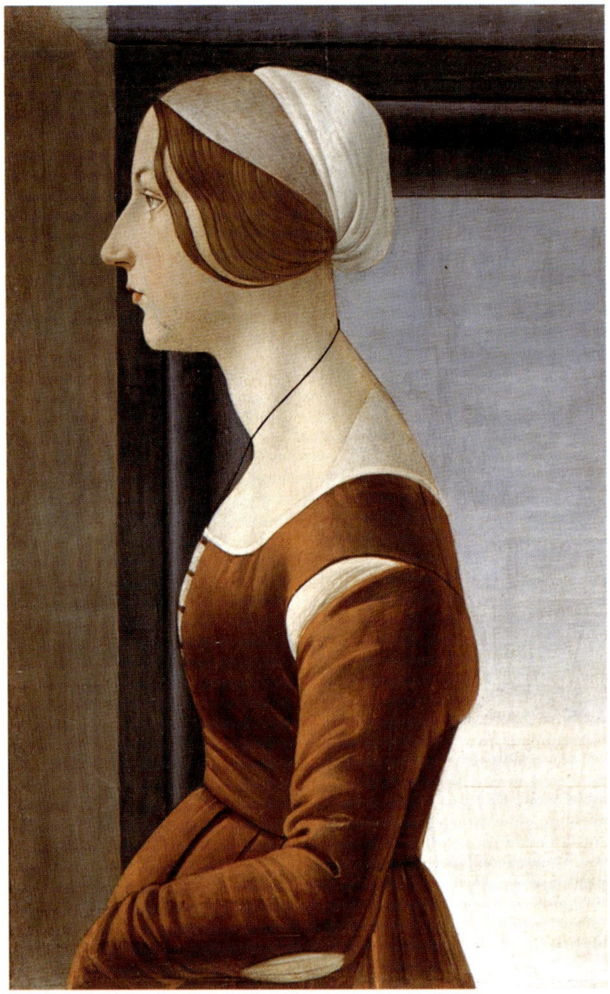

Traditionally called "*Portrait of the Beautiful Simonetta*", this painting in the Palazzo Pitti collection was described for the first time under this name in Inghirami's guide published in 1834. Recognition of the subject as Simonetta Vespucci, the woman beloved by Giuliano de' Medici, is based on Vasari, who mentions having seen two portraits of the women by Botticelli in Duke Cosimo's collections, one of Simonetta Vespucci, the other of Lucrezia Tornabuoni, Lorenzo the Magnificent's mother. Recent criticism has rejected this hypothetical identification, and despite attempts to assign a name to the woman in question, her identity is still unknown.

The attribution of the work is also controversial, but Botticelli's authorship is generally accepted by scholars today.

Like the *Portrait of a Young Man*, also by Botticelli, in the Palazzo Pitti's Galleria Palatina, this portrait depicts a personage whose noble aspect does not depend on any display of material wealth but on the austere, almost modest elegance of a simple gown and an ivory complexion, and on the concentrated flow of the line designing the profile, on the border between domestic space and the light blue clarity of the open air.

The woman is clothed in the everyday attire of Renaissance Florence: a gown bound at the waist, called *camurra* (or *gamurra*), which was worn especially at home, a simple white cap that partially covers the hair and a slender black braided cord ending at the neckline edged with the white of a blouse. Pope-Hennessy has noted the unusual composition chosen by Botticelli, with the woman's profile shifted slightly to the left, so that the facial features stand out against the dark background of the lintel over the door, while the contour of the neck and upper back contrast with the clear, transparent air. All of these elements suggest that this portrait of a woman should be seen as programmatically designed to celebrate the renowned virtues of Florentine women: shrewd management of domestic affairs, discretion in appearance, devotion to the family, along with an elegance of form always kept within the limits imposed by honesty and modesty.

The profile pose, still used for women even when the three-quarter pose of Flemish inspiration had been widely adopted for portraits of men, was inspired by the ancient tradition of medals. Botticelli deemed it best suited to exalt the delicate, intellectual flow of the line that, in its essentiality, admirably describes the delicate features of the woman.

Silvia Mascalchi

Bibliography: N. Pons in *Botticelli e Filippino* 2004, p. 226, no. 36 (with preceding bibliography); Zöllner, *Sandro Botticelli* 2009, p. 278.

7.23
Tuscan sculptor
Young Gentlewoman
last twenty years of the 15th century
marble relief
48 x 38 cm
Florence, Museo Nazionale del Bargello,
Bargello Sculptures inv. no. 226 (1879)

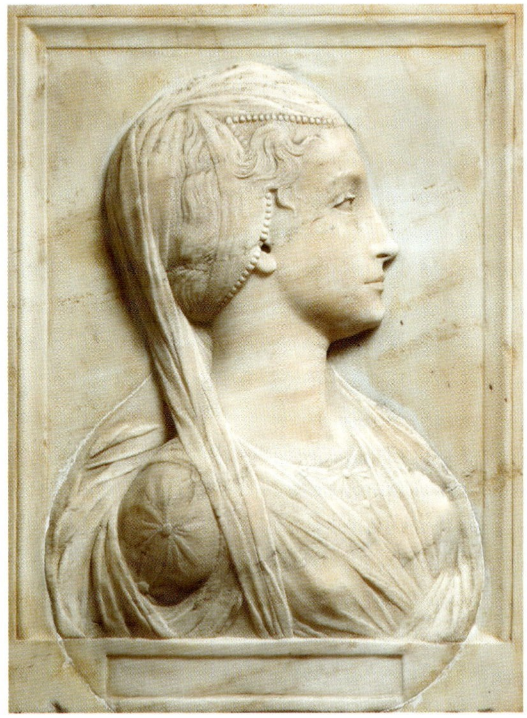

This marble bust portrays a richly attired young woman, her head in profile looking to the right, her bust turned toward the spectator, offering a foreshortened view of her breast, in a pose often used for painted portraits in late 15th-century Florence. The girl's hair is swept back and held in place by a headband consisting of a row of pearls applied to the hem of the veil that covers her head and falls from the nape of the neck onto the right shoulder. Only a lock of hair escapes from this stiff structure, waving in serpentine curls on the temple. She wears a gown with a rounded neckline buttoned over the breast. A mantle is draped over her gown, revealing at the shoulder a portion of the blouse below, made of light fabric fastened with little round buttons, but this part of her clothing is slightly confused, as if the sculptor found it hard to render an all-round sculpture or a detailed painting in the flattened form of a relief carving. On the frame is a groove for the inscription, which has been lost. Although here the costume has an ancient, and more regal tone, the bust evokes the numerous relief sculptures of *condottieri* and rulers who, in emulation of Desiderio da Settignano, were carved later by Mino da Fiesole (F. Caglioti in *Matteo Civitali* 2004, pp. 310–1 e 334–5) and by Gregorio di Lorenzo, recently recognized as the mysterious Master of the marble Madonnas (Bellandi 2010).

This marble relief came to the Bargello from the Florentine Palazzo Salviati da Cepperello, in Via del Corso, which seems to have been built by Jacopo Salviati over the ancient houses of the Portinari family, starting in the 1470s (*Il Palazzo Portinari-Salviati* 1960, pp. 35–6). Francesco Bocchi (1591, pp. 185–8) describes with admiration the palace's splendid array of art, consisting of ancient and modern works, including numerous sculptures of emperors and illustrious men, portraits of family members by Bronzino and Santo di Tito, rooms frescoed by Alessandro Allori and such important pieces as Donatello's relief representing *The Ascension with Christ Giving the Keys to St. Peter*, now at the Victoria and Albert Museum in London.

Purchased in Florence prior to 1859, this marble relief has been identified as the one listed in the inventory of Lorenzo the Magnificent's property at his death in 1492 and probably left to his daughter Lucrezia, the wife of Jacopo Salviati (Pope-Hennessy 1964, I, pp. 70–1). The wedding of Lucrezia de' Medici and Jacopo Salviati had in fact taken place in September 1488. The bride, barely eighteen at the time, was a faithful wife and exemplary mother throughout her long life (Pieraccini 1924–5, I, 1924, I, pp. 240–6). Lucrezia is known to us only from the image carved on her tombstone in the chapel of San Giacomo in Santa Maria sopra Minerva, Rome, where she appears in old age, dressed in a simple nun's tunic gathered by a cord around her waist, her head covered by a veil. At the time of her wedding, however, her name would certainly have evoked the conjugal virtues of chastity and industry symbolized by the Roman Lucretia, wife of Collatinus, depicted in painting since the Middle Ages as a heroine of ancient history, along with Virginia and Clelia (Passalacqua 2004, pp. 205–21).

We may thus hypothesize that our relief portrays the young Lucrezia di Lorenzo de' Medici, adorned with veils and pearls as was fitting to her virginal purity at the time of her wedding. Through her features, it represents the Roman heroine of the same name, icon of conjugal virtue, thus assigning a precise celebratory meaning to the noble pose, like that of an ancient imperial coin, combined with the modern apparel of the girl, whose dress and hairstyle resemble those of the women depicted by Ghirlandaio in the Tornabuoni Chapel in Santa Maria Novella, they too in the dual role of recognizable members of the family and historic personages in Christian life.

Francesca Petrucci

Bibliography: unpublished.

7.24
Lorenzo di Credi (Lorenzo d'Andrea d'Oderigo, Florence, *c.* 1460–1537)
Portrait of a Young Woman
or *Lady with Jasmine Flowers*
1485–90
oil on panel
77.2 x 55.2 x 2.2 cm
Forlì, Musei San Domenico, Pinacoteca civica, inv. no. 119

This painting was donated to the Pinacoteca of Forlì in the mid-19th century, with an attribution to Lorenzo di Credi that has been generally accepted after extensive critical debate, recently resumed by Giordano Viroli. The restoration of 1999, which brought to light the original layer of paint and what has remained of the sfumato and velature after the strong abrasive action of previous restorations, has confirmed the attribution.

The young woman is shown sitting under a loggia, viewed half-length, her body turned three-quarters to the left, her face turned slightly toward the observer. Her long tapered hands rest on a vase filled with jasmine flowers, from which she is picking a blossom. Behind the loggia is a serene, motionless landscape, with a castle on the left surrounded by a broad stretch of water, and hills and rocks in the distance. The volumes of the face, neck and shoulders stand out clearly against the background of red drapery hanging between the columns of the loggia and dividing the landscape into two parts. The vase is placed on a stand covered by a red carpet with dark green horizontal stripes, intensifying the perception of its volume. In contrast to the straight back wall, the oblique shape of the stand underscores the position of the figure (Dalli Regoli 1966, p. 39). The woman's hair, dressed in curls at the sides of the face and gathered on the nape of the neck, and her clothing, typical of Florentine fashions in the 1480s and early 1490s, are amply reflected in the figures of women decorating the Tornabuoni Chapel. The gaze of her large amber-coloured eyes is intense, while the sobriety of her dress and the absence of jewellery accentuate her austere attitude.

The identity of the woman and the occasion for the portrait are still shrouded in mystery. 19th-century historiography and local chroniclers have tried to identify her as Caterina Sforza, the natural daughter of Galeazzo Maria, Duke of Milan and Lord of Forlì, due to the presence of the castle in the background and the vase of jasmine flowers, symbol of purity, but indicative in this case of Caterina's knowledge of herbs. Magdalena Soest has recently (2002) proposed this identification again in the international press, suggesting that this is the same woman painted by Leonardo in the *Mona Lisa* (the attribution to Leonardo has recently been reiterated by Vogt-Lüerssen 2011, pp. 79-80) although no elements exist to confirm this hypothesis (De Vries 2010, p. 259).

In this painting, Lorenzo di Credi seems to look not only to Leonardo, and even more to Ghirlandaio, but also to the Botticelli of the Villa Lemmi frescoes (Viroli 1998, p. 165).

Luciana Prati

Bibliography: Dalli Regoli 1966, p. 39; Viroli 1980, p. 79; Viroli 1998, p. 165; G. Viroli in *I Borgia* 2002, pp. 268–9, no. III.24; G. Viroli in *Dürer* 2007, pp. 134–5, no. I.20; De Vries 2010, p. 259; Vogt-Lüerssen 2011, pp. 79–80.

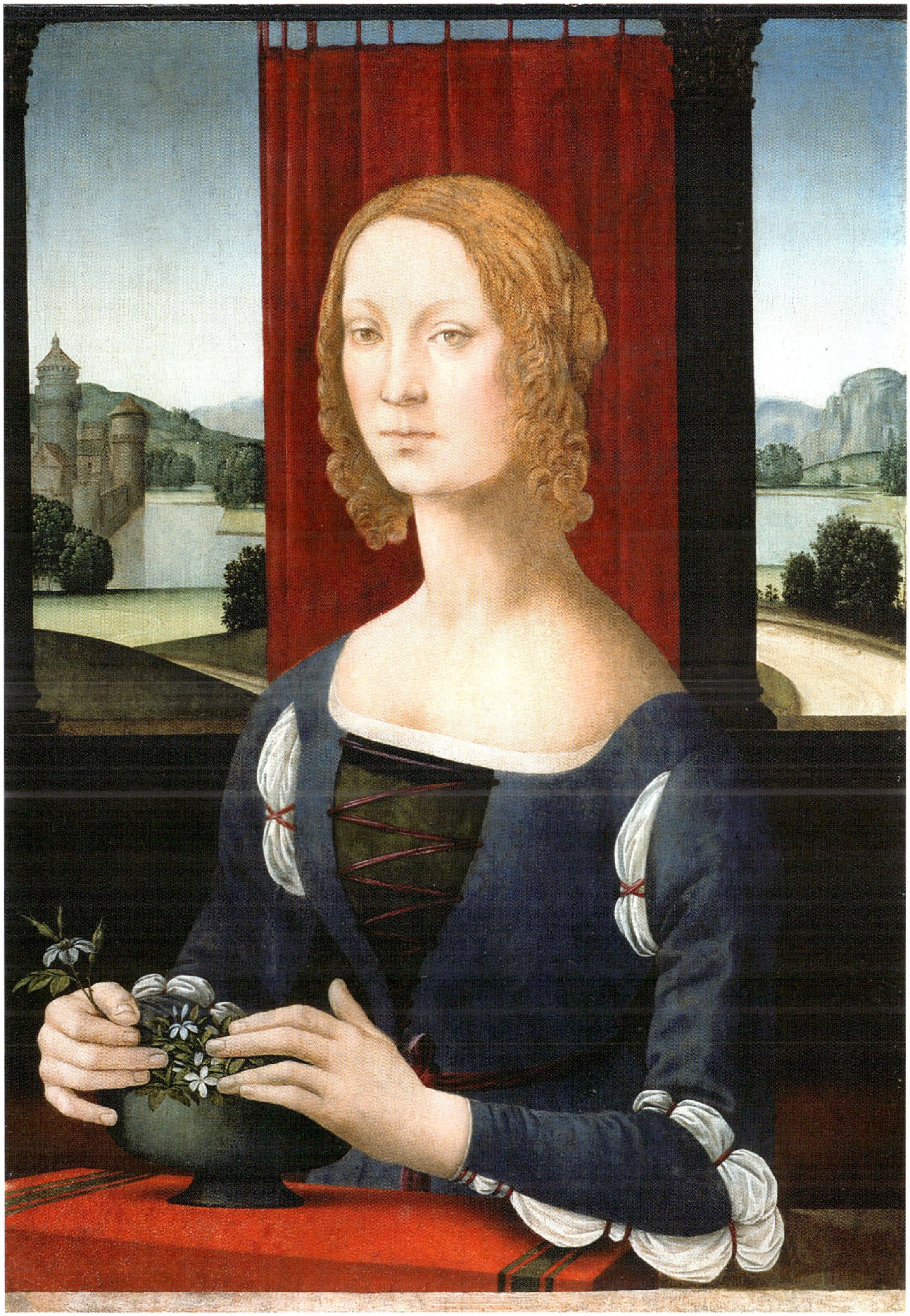

Section 8
Crisis

The crisis in Florentine society at the end of the century is closely linked to the Medici family and their great antagonist, Girolamo Savonarola. The political, moral and cultural struggle that set Lorenzo the Magnificent against the friar from Ferrara left a deep mark on the closing years of the 15th century. In terms of the works he commissioned, Lorenzo did not leave an indelible imprint on the city as his grandfather, Cosimo the Elder, had done. Cosimo, the greatest patron of the 15th century, had financed the building of churches, monasteries, castles and chapels as well as spending heavily on books, paintings and art works of many kinds.[1] Lorenzo the Magnificent lived in a different time and his finances were severely depleted by the decline of the Medici Bank. Hence his patronage was addressed mainly to illuminated manuscripts, paintings and precious objects, the one exception being the building of the Villa di Poggio a Caiano.

Arriving in Florence from Ferrara, Savonarola established a reputation as a provocative and vehement preacher, who wasn't so much opposed to art itself as to its worldly dimension. Not only were his sermons inspiring, but Savonarola was quick to understand and exploit the invention of printing to have them published only days after they had been pronounced from the pulpit.[2] Numerous editions with woodcut illustrations show Savonarola's awareness of the importance of images both as propaganda tools and as works of art, so much so that he took the time to give his advice to the illustrators working on the sermons.

Botticelli's adoption of Savonarola's doctrines came somewhat later after a personal crisis that coincided with the drastic events that were to mark the end of Florence's humanist dreams: the death of Lorenzo the Magnificent on April 8, 1492 (which meant a loss of patronage and commissions for Botticelli), the expulsion of Lorenzo's son, Piero, the invasion of the city by Charles VIII on November 17, 1494 and—on the same day—the death of Pico della Mirandola. It was a crisis emblematically represented by the collapse of the Medici Bank that same year. This moment of transition is captured in Botticelli's the *Calumny*, a last manifestation of the culture of Lorenzo's period and perhaps painted for Antonio Segni, banker to the Papal Curia, who had been an active part of that culture.

"Not by usura was *La Calunnia* painted":[3] declared Ezra Pound in a poem as powerful as it is historically inaccurate. In fact, it had been the banking system and the whole mercantile world (including the practice of money-lending) that made possible the great commissions for works of art. Only after Savonarola's death did Botticelli unconditionally embrace the friar's thinking, as is shown by the works dating from the last period of his life.[4] Hence the artist did not throw his own works onto the bonfire of vanities that destroyed paintings, splendid gowns and even animals, as the century drew to a close. Other artists did, however, casting their achievements into the flames on the two Carnival Tuesdays of 1497 and 1498. Vasari mentions Lorenzo di Credi and Fra Bartolomeo, but among Savonarola's followers were many other artists: Cronaca, Baccio da Montelupo and the Della Robbias, two of whom donned the Dominican habit in San Marco and took up arms to defend Savonarola when the monastery was attacked on April 8, 1498. Their efforts were in vain; Savonarola was taken to prison, subjected to three trials (two before the Signoria, one before the Church), tortured and condemned to death along with two of his brother monks.[5] The execution took place on the morning of May 23, 1498. The three men were hanged in Piazza dei Signori in Florence, their bodies burned and the ashes thrown into the Arno; a bonfire whose ashes still smoulder today.

Ludovica Sebregondi

1. See Reinhardt 2009, pp. 111–28.
2. See Garfagnini 1999, pp. 310, 313–4.
3. Ezra Pound, *Contro l'usura* 1948, in Id. 1985, pp. 444–7.
4. See among others Cecchi 2010, p. 13.
5. *I processi* 2001, pp. LIV–LXXIX.

8.1
Buglioni Workshop
Tondo with Medicean device
first quarter of the 16th century
enamelled terracotta relief
Ø 79 cm
Florence, Galleria degli Uffizi, Donazione Contini Bonacossi, inv. CB 93

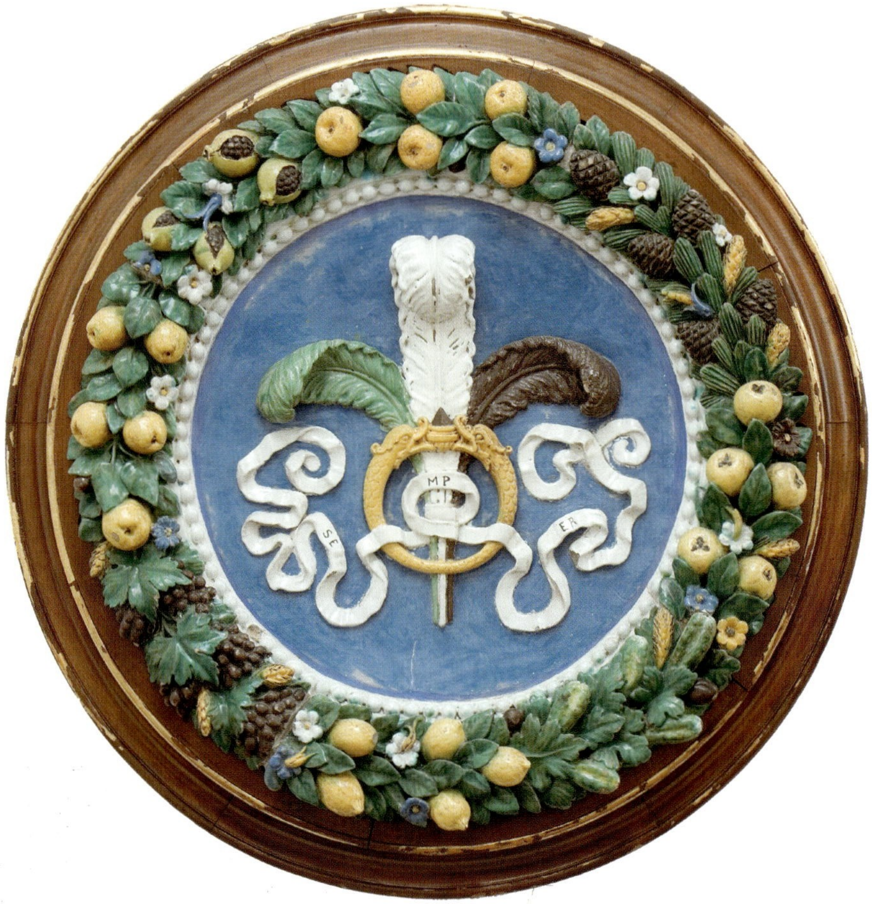

The garland of fruit and foliage runs counter-clockwise around the rim. There is a single group of four pomegranates, while the other seven groups contain five fruits each (bunches of grapes, apples, lemons, pears, cucumbers, pine cones) alternating with scattered ears of grain and flowers of various kinds and colours. At the centre is one of the Medicean devices, adopted as emblem in parallel to the more traditional heraldic arms, sometimes found on architectural elements in churches and palaces, and in widely differing forms of art. The devices of the ostrich feathers and the diamond-tipped ring were first adopted by Cosimo the Elder and then handed down to his son Piero di Cosimo. They became additional heraldic elements, symbolically denoting the dynasty in the same way as the famous "balls."

Cosimo the Elder, son of Giovanni di Bicci, was one of the dominant figures in the Medicean dynasty. Founder of the family's wealth and hailed by his successors as *Pater Patriae*, the father of his country, Cosimo was not only a shrewd businessman but also an intellectual, a lover of ancient literature, a refined collector and patron of the arts.

The three feathers, green, red and white, may refer to the theological virtues or to the Holy Trinity. In combination with the ring and the scroll bearing Piero's motto, "SEMPER," they form one of Lorenzo the Magnificent's most famous devices (see for example Lorenzo's so-called birth tray at the Metropolitan Museum of New York, painted by Giovanni di ser Giovanni, known as Lo Scheggia). The tondoes from the Della Robbia workshop decorated with Medicean devices include interesting examples done by Luca the Younger, dating from the time of Pope Leo X (1513–21). They come from the Roman villa of Cardinal Alessandro de' Medici (six of them are now at the Museo di Roma, one at the Museo di Castel Sant'Angelo). On three of the medallions appears a lion's head within a diamond-tipped ring; on two of them, the yoke and a scroll bearing the word "SUAVE;" and on the remaining two, the three ostrich feathers bound by a fluttering ribbon with the motto "SEMPER." Their distinctive feature is that they are not framed by the usual garland of fruit and foliage but by the ring or the other Medicean device, the laurel branch (*Gaetano Ballardini* 2000, pp. 136–8, no. 132 for the device with feathers and ring).

In the Uffizi Tondo, the device stands out against an azure background, as in the examples found at the Museo di Roma, but the enamel is applied by brush and is bounded by the garland with a circular fillet of spherical elements resembling a pearl necklace. The same motif of the ribbon with spherical elements, used elsewhere only sporadically, appears on the heraldic arms of Cristofano Risaliti on Palazzo Pretorio in Cutigliano (1509, attributed to Benedetto Buglioni's workshop; Domestici 1995, pl. CXVII, p. 254) and in the tondo depicting the *Adoration of the Christ Child*, formerly in a private collection in New York (Marquand 1912, no. 56, pl. 57; also attributed to Benedetto Buglioni).

Marino Marini

Bibliography: Paolucci 1980, no. C35, p. 1112; Gentilini 1992, p. 334; *The Splendour* 2008, p. 52.

8.2
Giovanni della Robbia
(Florence 1469–1529/1530)
Tondo with Pazzi coat of arms
1510–25
enamelled terracotta relief
Ø 121 cm
Florence, Galleria degli Uffizi,
Donazione Contini Bonacossi, inv. CB 92

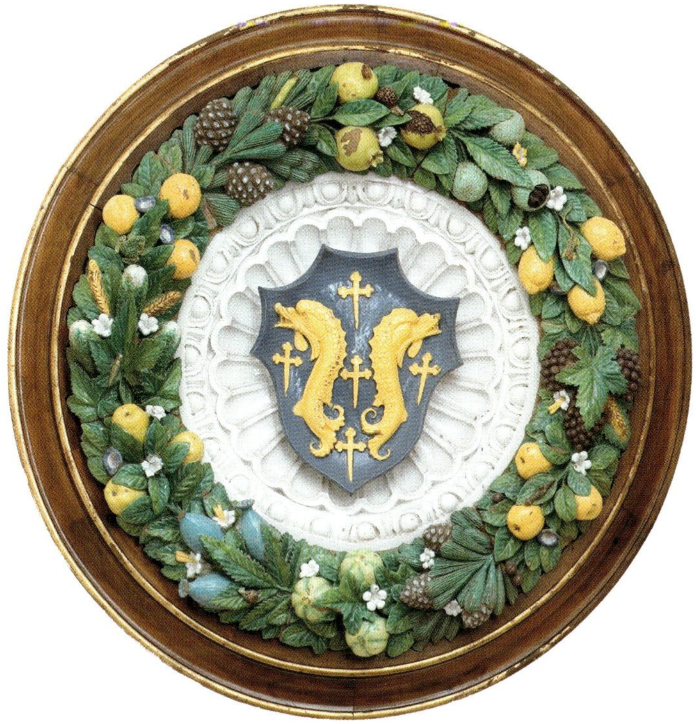

The central tondo containing the Pazzi coat of arms ("azure with two golden dolphins back to back and five small crosses") is modelled as an escallop, in imitation of a cup made of marble or semi-precious stone. The garland, composed of foliage, flowers and fruit, with eleven groups of three fruits each, runs clockwise. Pomegranates, chestnuts in their husks, citrons, lemons, apples, bunches of grapes and melons, as well as pinecones, poppies and cucumbers, can be recognized. This exuberant composition is completed by a few ears of grain, cherries, flowers of various colours, a bean pod and some small insects and reptiles (snails, grasshoppers, a frog and a lizard). The emblem for the Pazzi family created by Luca della Robbia around 1460 at the centre of the cupola in the family chapel in Santa Croce, designed by Filippo Brunelleschi, serves as guide to the vast production of heraldic emblems produced by this workshop, whose clients included secular and religious institutions as well as noble families. In fact, although the form of the escutcheon with heraldic arms changed over the course of time, the surrounding elements remained virtually the same: the garland, the classic egg-and-dart motif of the frame, and the central medallion appearing as a great escalloped cup.

In the 15th century the fortunes of the Pazzi family reached their highest peak, both socially, as shown by the marriage of Guglielmo de' Pazzi to Bianca de' Medici, sister of Lorenzo the Magnificent, in 1469, and in the economic field, being appointed managers of the papal finances by Pope Sixtus IV in 1471.

To display their social status the family not only erected imposing buildings but also commissioned the Della Robbia workshop to create ostentatious emblems in ceramics glazed with the polychrome enamels that have proven so resistant to the wear of time.

A superb example of Della Robbia heraldry, made for the family palace and similar to the one shown here, is the tondo commissioned by Jacopo Pazzi, attributed to Luca but perhaps modelled by Andrea, which serves as companion piece to the tondo of his wife Maddalena Serristori (Marquand 1919, no. 20, pp. 23–4 and figs. 20–1; Gentilini 1992, p. 137, fig. p. 114).

Note that the figures on Jacobo's escutcheon were scratched off, perhaps when the palace was sold (by Cardinal d'Estouteville to Franceschetto Cybo and lastly to Lorenzo Strozzi, between the late 15th century and the second half of the 16th). It is much more likely however, that this sort of *damnatio memoriae* had to do with the thwarted conspiracy against Giuliano and Lorenzo de' Medici in 1478, the culminating point of the bitter enmity between these two powerful families.

It was this episode, in fact, that decided the fate of the wealthy Florentine family, whose property was expropriated and whose leading members were decimated by the ruthless vengeance of the Medici. Every emblem of the Pazzi was deleted from the streets and squares of Florence, and their name was stricken from all official documents.

Only after the death of Lorenzo de' Medici did their forced exile come to an end, and the members of the family who had not joined in the conspiracy could reclaim their property and, in time, return to public life, occupying some important posts.

Another piece commissioned by the Pazzi family of the Della Robbia workshop is the coat of arms in majolica of Niccolò Pazzi, deputy at San Giovanni Valdarno in 1515–6 (Marquand 1919, no. 284, p. 223; Borgia 1986, pp. 146–7, no. 99), where the frogs, lizards and grasshoppers enlivening garlands overflowing with fruit of various kinds are recognizable as distinctive features of Giovanni della Robbia's style.

Marino Marini

Bibliography: Paolucci 1980, no. C34, p. 1111; Gentilini 1992, p. 307; Quinterio 1998, p. 65; *The Splendour* 2008, pp. 100–1.

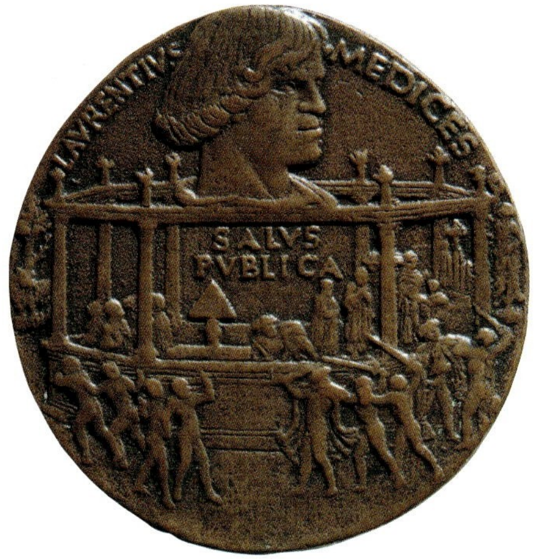

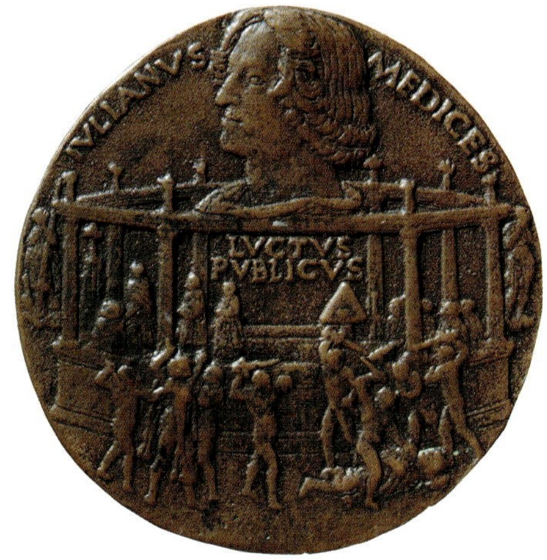

8.3
Bertoldo di Giovanni
(Florence c.1440–Poggio a Caiano 1491)
Medal commemorating the Pazzi Conspiracy
1478
bronze
Ø 64.85 mm; 1.9-4.7 thk.; 70 g
Florence, Museo Nazionale del Bargello, inv. 5956 Medaglie
Lorenzo de' Medici, the Magnificent (1449–92) and Giuliano de' Medici (1453–78)
Front: "LAVRENTIVS MEDICES." Lorenzo's head, in half-profile turned to the right. Below, the choir of the Florence Cathedral, where Mass is being celebrated, and at the centre the inscription, on two lines: "SALVS/PVBLICA."
Back: "IVLIANVS MEDICES." Giuliano's head, in half-profile turned to the left. Below, the choir of the Florence Cathedral, where Mass is being celebrated, and at the centre the inscription, on two lines: "LVCTVS/PVBLICVS."

A merchant and man of letters, Piero di Marco Parenti, born in 1449 to one of the richest families in Florence and the pupil of such humanists as Marsilio Ficino and Demetrio Calcondila, has left us a remarkably detailed account of the Pazzi Conspiracy, which took place on April 26, 1478. Written in the meticulous style of mercantile records, the event is narrated almost "live," beginning with a description of those involved, "Francesco d'Antonio di Messer Andrea de' Pazzi, a man small in person, but great in soul […] aroused the enmity first of Lorenzo de' Medici, and consequently of his brother Giuliano" (Parenti [*ante* 1519], ed. Matucci 1994–2005, I, 1994, p. 12). "Count Girolamo, nephew of Pope Sixtus and governor, so to say, of the Roman court" (ivi, p. 13), his nephew Cardinal Raffaelle Riario, the Archbishop of Pisa, Francesco Salviati, and other enemies of the Magnificent met in the Pazzi Villa at Montughi, on the Florentine hills. A first attempt to assassinate the two brothers at Fiesole having failed, they resolved to try again. Lorenzo was then asked if "he would like to invite the Cardinal to dinner in Florence, because he wished very much to see his house in Florence and its beautiful silver plate and gemstones, medals and other fine things […]; the conspirators planning at this dinner, where they would be all together, to assault the brothers and, having killed them, take possession of their house […], seize the Palace and do as they wished" (ivi, p. 15). The planning and preparations for the assassination attempt, made in the Duomo, during the Mass, are rendered in a crescendo of tension, up to the moment of the stipulated signal, "which was just after the priest had taken communion," when Francesco Pazzi and Bernardo Bandini threw themselves on Giuliano, while Antonio de' Maffei da Volterra assaulted Lorenzo. At this point the merchant's story finds visual confirmation in the medal commissioned by the Magnificent a few weeks later, to commemorate his unfortunate brother in one of his favourite artistic genres, considering that in 1492 the inventory of his property listed no fewer than "one thousand-eight-hundred and forty-four bronze medals" (*Inventario* [1492], ed. Spallanzani, Gaeta Bertelà 1992, p. 53).
Of this medal, which must have been widely diffused, several examples exist today, including one in the Metropolitan Museum of New York (Draper 1992, pp. 86–95). Modelled by the sculptor Bertoldo di Giovanni and cast by Andrea Guazzalotti from Prato, who sent Lorenzo four copies on September 11, 1478, the medal represents the dynamics of the facts in the paratactic narrative style proper to painting, aimed at identifying the characters, action and place with the utmost clarity. The cathedral's ancient choir with the wooden scaffolding mounted by Brunelleschi, at the centre of which Mass is being celebrated, is finely rendered. The triangular shape of the lectern, appearing on the front to the left of the medal's centre, and on the back to the right of it, shows how the scene was reproduced from two opposite points of observation. The Luctus publicus shows on the left, outside of the choir, the first stage in the attack, when Bernardo Bandini "leaps onto Giuliano, and with a knife strikes him in the side" (Parenti [*ante* 1519], ed. Matucci 1994–2005, I, 1994, p. 18); at right, the young man's body lies on the floor, slain by Francesco Pazzi's dagger. On the other side, at right, is Lorenzo surrounded by the conspirators, and at left his providential escape: "into the old sacristy and toward the altar of San Zanobius […], crossing the high altar and fleeing from the choir by the other exit, he leaped into the new sacristy, taking refuge along with many citizens who had fled there out of fear, and thus he escaped" (ibid.).
Ilaria Ciseri

Bibliography: F. Vannel Toderi, G. Toderi in *Eredità del Magnifico* 1992, pp. 62–3, no. 26 (with preceding bibliography); Toderi, Vannel 2003, p. 34; M.G. Vaccari in *Masters of Florence* 2004, p. 75; A. Schumacher in *Botticelli* 2009, pp. 172–3.

8.4
Germany or Austria
Dagger
15th century
chased and gilt bronze, steel
64 x 12 cm
Cerreto Guidi (Florence), Villa Medicea, Museo della caccia e del Territorio, deposit from the Galleria e Museo di Palazzo Mozzi Bardini, inv. Bd. 2445

The dagger, which has been restored by integrating the pommel and the ancient blade, has a gilt bronze hilt attributed to a 15th-century German or Austrian workshop. It is a small arm, easy to conceal, "suited mainly to pointed blows, capable in certain cases of passing through such protective gear as a coat of mail covered with iron platelets" (Salvatici 1999, p. 12). Small arms, such as daggers, knives and dirks, usually have a simple, functional structure, although not without refinement in the decorative parts of the hilt, which is generally sturdy and functional.

Arms of this kind were used in the Pazzi Conspiracy, which took place on April 26, 1478. This tragic event was the direct consequence of an international plot contrived by Pope Sixtus IV, the Duke of Urbino Federico da Montefeltro, and the King of Naples Ferdinando of Aragon, who aimed to overthrow the primacy of the Medici in Florence, then in the hands of Lorenzo and Giuliano, the young sons and heirs of Piero di Cosimo (Simonetta 2008).

A precedent had been set by the assassination of Galeazzo Maria Sforza, Duke of Milan and the Medici's faithful ally, slain by the blows of daggers on 26th December, 1476 in the Milanese church of Santo Stefano. This encouraged the conspirators to adopt the same extreme solution—the assassination of the two Medici brothers—for their coup d'état. The Italian rulers, to pursue their own political designs, skilfully nourished the growing tension and ancient rancour between these families and the Medici. The plotters won the support of the Pazzi and Salviati families, who consolidated the conspiracy with a group of supporters. A perfect occasion seemed to be provided by the festivities in honour of the seventeen-year-old Raffaele Riario Sansoni della Rovere, elected cardinal four months earlier, who was stopping in Florence on his way to Perugia, where he had been appointed Legate.

Jacopo Pazzi and his nephew Francesco, Francesco Salviati the Archbishop of Pisa, with their families and trusted collaborators, and with Giambattista Montesecco, Captain in the Papal army and hired assassin by profession, had originally planned to kill Lorenzo and Giuliano on Saturday, the 25th April. On that day, in fact, they had convinced Lorenzo to hold in honour of Cardinal Riario a banquet for only a few guests in his villa on the slopes of Fiesole, to be followed by a visit to the Badia Fiesolana. There, in a room in the Badia's monastery, the two Medici brothers were to be assassinated. But that morning an stomach upset obliged Giuliano to remain in Florence. The conspirators decided to postpone their plan. They could not wait too long however, because in the meantime the papal troops led by Girolamo Riario, nephew of Sixtus IV, with the complicity of several militias from cities bordering on Tuscany, were ready to move toward Florence. On the next morning, Sunday April 26, 1478, Lorenzo and Giuliano de' Medici with their guests were to attend the Mass celebrated in the Cathedral for Ascension Day, during which the young cardinal would sit beside the officiating priest. Following the Mass, a sumptuous banquet would be held at Palazzo Medici, with the high-ranking prelate as the guest of honour. Giuliano's illness convinced the conspirators to move quickly and and perpetrate the dual assassination in the cathedral during the Mass, rather than in the Medici residence. But the attempted coup failed, since Giuliano alone fell victim to the blows rained down by the conspirators.

Elena Capretti

Bibliography: E. Carrara in *Masters of Florence* 2004, p. 75.

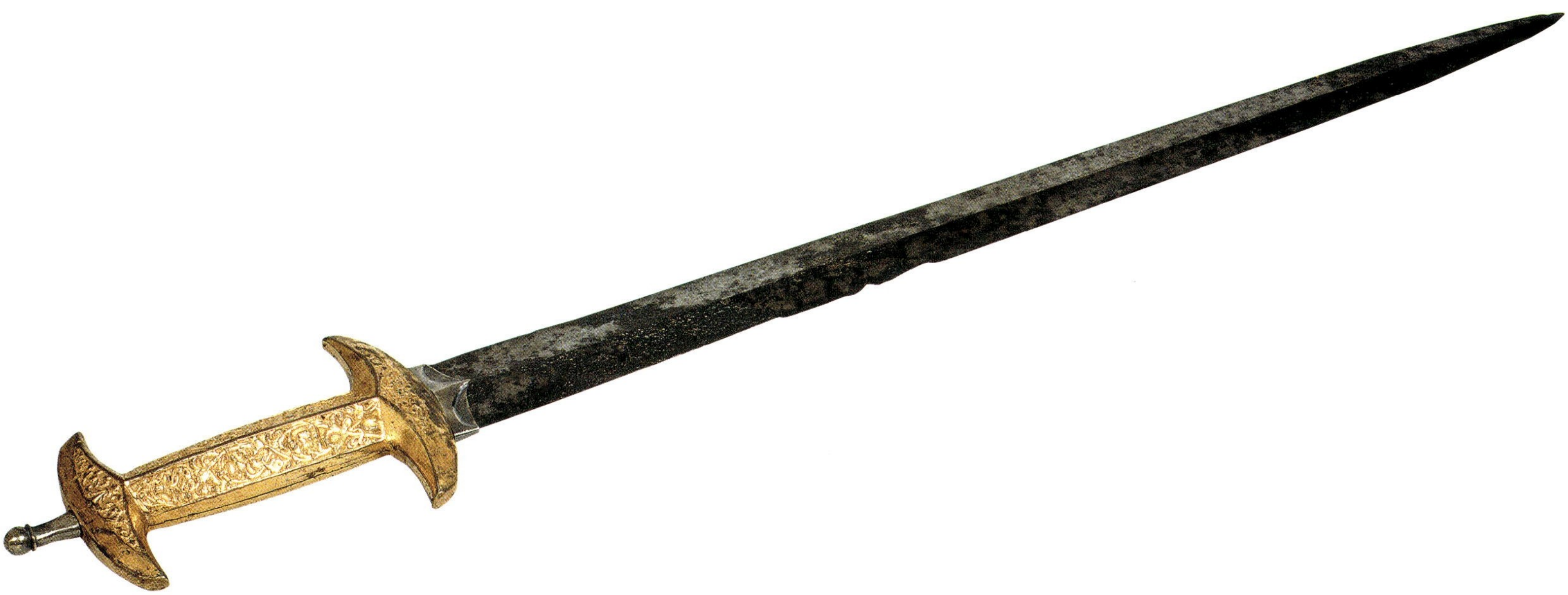

8.5
Fragment of bloodstained shirt
(once thought to be that of Giuliano de' Medici)
15th–16th century
display case: late 19th–early 20th century
fabric; wood and glass display case
display case 23 x 28 x 55 cm
Florence, Provincia di Firenze, depositi,
Provinciale inv. no. 22.118

This fragment of a shirt made of fine pleated cloth, originally white with an embroidered border, bears traces of bloodstains. In 1929 the fragment was displayed at the Medici Museum then being set up on the ground floor of Palazzo Medici Riccardi, owned by the Province of Florence since 1874. As a sort of secular relic, the object was included among the "macabre remains taken from the tomb of Lorenzo and Giuliano during the inspection conducted in 1895," wrote Nello Tarchiani in the guide to the museum published in 1930, "of Lorenzo, teeth and hair; of Giuliano, a piece of his tunic, still rent by the blows of the daggers," loaned by the Museo del Bargello (Id. Mag. R. nos. 90–1) and kept in glass display cases. The inspection of the Medici tombs, authorized in 1895 by the Ministry of Public Education, had identified with certainty the tomb of Lorenzo the Magnificent, who died in 1492, and his brother Giuliano, victim of the Pazzi Conspiracy of 1478, with the sarcophagus in Michelangelo's New Sacristy, standing before the altar surmounted by the *Virgin and Child* and by *Saints Cosmas and Damian*. During the inspection, the skulls of the two brothers were photographed. At the top of Giuliano's skull, clear signs of the wounds inflicted by the conspirators could be seen.

When the Medici Museum was dismantled after the flood of 1966, all trace of the Medici relics was lost, until they were found again in 1988 in the basement of Palazzo Medici Riccardi, and displayed in various exhibitions (*Stanze segrete* 2003; *Masters of Florence* 2004). According to recent studies (Di Domenico, Lippi 2005; Lippi 2006), the traditional identification—although fascinating—of these materials is probably the result of a mistake caused by an error in recording. The teeth and hair may in reality be those of Lorenzo Duke of Urbino, who died in 1519, while the fragment of a shirt may have belonged to Duke Alessandro, he too assassinated by the blows of a dagger in 1537. The remains of both were disinterred in 1875 from the sarcophagus decorated with Michelangelo's marble statues of *Dawn* and *Dusk* in the New Sacristy. The evocative power of this fragment of a bloodstained shirt is undeniable, however, recalling how the history of the Medici family from the 14th through the 16th century often hung in the balance between splendour and vile deeds, between intellectual curiosity and ruthless cruelty. And the crime perpetrated on April 26, 1478 by the Pazzi and Salviati families against Lorenzo and Giuliano de' Medici is one of the most emblematic events (see Simonetta 2008, with bibliography). The murderous plan, enacted in the cathedral near the high altar during celebration of the Mass, was only partially successful, and failed to achieve the conspirators' purpose, that of destroying the political supremacy of the Medici. Although Giuliano died a tragic death under the blows inflicted by the daggers of Francesco Pazzi, Bernardo Bandini and others (no less than nineteen wounds were counted on his body by Agnolo Poliziano), Lorenzo managed to take refuge in the Sagrestia delle Messe behind the bronze doors only recently completed by Luca della Robbia. Furthermore, contrary to their expectations, the conspirators lacked the support of the people, who reacted with rage and vindictive fury against the assassins. Outside of the cathedral the streets and plazas were witness to a real bloodletting, in which the conspirators and their supporters, real or presumed, along with their servants, were slaughtered, their corpses disfigured and hacked to pieces. The occupation of Palazzo Vecchio having failed, the bells of the Arnolfo Tower rang out the call to arms. The citizens responded, crying "balls, balls" and "arms, arms," and hailing the Medici coat of arms as the symbol of a common political association passionately confirmed. Many of the conspirators (including Francesco Pazzi and Archbishop Salviati) were hanged from the windows of Palazzo Vecchio, others thrown from them alive. The corpse of Jacopo Pazzi, repeatedly desecrated and torn, was thrown into the Arno. The vendetta against the Pazzi was ruthless. All of their property was seized, their bank accounts in Florence and elsewhere were frozen, the family memorial stones were town down, their portraits were destroyed and their women deprived of dowries. At last the funeral of Giuliano de' Medici, celebrated on April 30th, with an austere, composed Mass in San Lorenzo, placated the vindictive fury of the crowd.
The same ceremony celebrated the funeral of Francesco Nori, who had sacrificed his life to save his friend Lorenzo. The conspiracy had failed, but its repercussions were not restricted to those bloody days alone.
Elena Capretti

Bibliography: Tarchiani 1930, pp. 43–4; Acidini Luchinat 2003, pp. 21-26; *Stanze segrete* 2003, p. 137; E. Carrara in *Masters of Florence* 2004, p. 75; Di Domenico-Lippi 2005, pp. 23, 49–52; Lippi 2006, pp. 91–3.

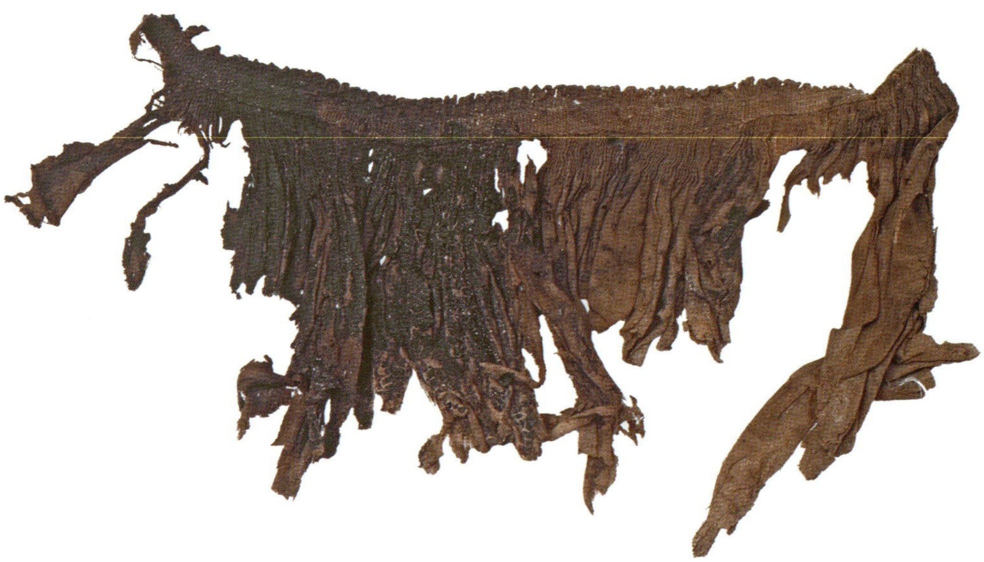

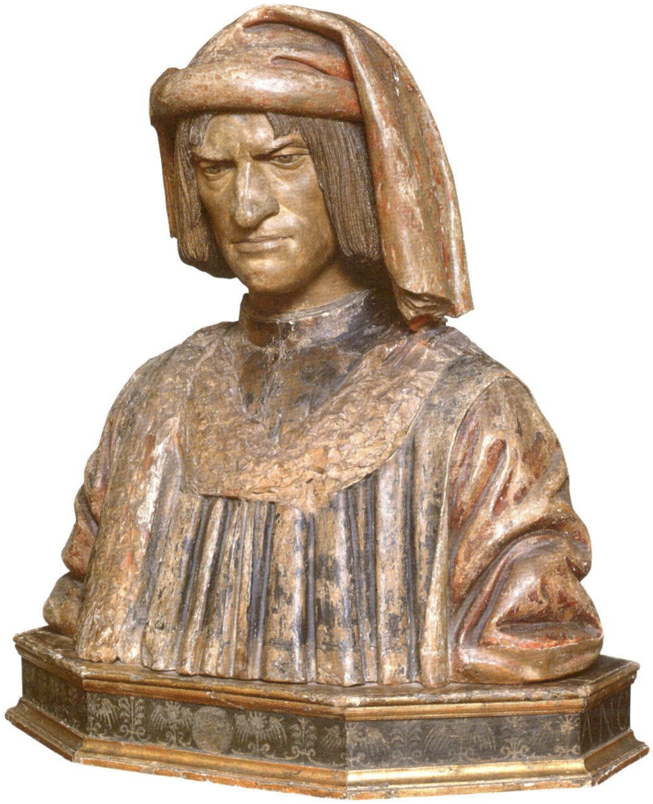

8.6
Pietro Torrigiano (Florence 1472–Seville 1528)
Bust of Lorenzo the Magnificent
1515–20
polychrome terracotta
80 x 80 x 40 cm
Florence, Liana and Carlo Carnevali Collection

The provenance of this bust of Lorenzo the Magnificent is unknown. Published in 1923 by Bode as the work of Andrea del Verrocchio, it belonged at the time to the Florentine antiquarian Elia Volpi. Bode's attribution was accepted by Planiscig, but Venturi instead assigned it to Leonardo da Vinci. The authenticity of the work, called into question by Negri Arnoldi (1970) and Pope-Hennessy ('The Forging' 1974), was then reconfirmed by Middeldorf (1976) who considered it, for the quality of the modelling and precise rendering of the clothing, the most coherent among the known portraits of Lorenzo. Langedijk (1981–7, II, 1983) included it, but with some doubts, among the numerous copies derived from the bust in the Kress Collection (Washington, National Gallery of Art). It is only since 1992, when the bust was displayed during the Laurentian Celebrations (*L'architettura* p. 125), that its superior quality and originality have were unanimously appreciated. This intense portrait of Lorenzo, in showing the lack of beauty in his irregular features—the olive complexion of his grandfather Cosimo, the powerful jawbone and low forehead—highlights his great qualities of energetic will and speculative intelligence, concentrated in a severe expression willingly abstracted from the earthly sphere of politics and mercantile *negotia*. The artist has thus managed to present a realistic picture of the subject's true appearance as well as a penetrating psychological study aimed at recording his moral and intellectual qualities, idealized and enhanced with the intent of mythicizing his memory.

Alessandro Cecchi and Giancarlo Gentilini (G. Utari in *Mugello* 2008) offer convincing reasons for dating the sculpture at the time of Leo X. When the new Pope, elected on March 11, 1513 triumphantly re-entered Florence on November 30, 1515, he promised to commemorate his father Lorenzo in his native city by resuming his public and private initiatives, giving rise to a new, utopian "golden age" of peace and prosperity (A. Cecchi in Cecchi, Natali, Sisi 1996, pp. 32–7).

Equally valid appears the attribution of the bust, by two scholars, to Pietro Torrigiano, who together with Michelangelo Buonarroti had grown up in the shadow of the great patron of the arts, frequenting the Sculpture Garden of San Marco. While the most important projects begun by Leo X—the façade of San Lorenzo, the New Sacristy, the Laurentian Library—were assigned to the greater sculptor and architect, Torrigiano, returning in 1515 from a stay at the Royal Court of England, where he had excelled in portraiture, could reasonably expect to be given the task of portraying Lorenzo in an image that would mingle personal recollections with the public effigies done in his lifetime. Among these were the ex voto portraits, done in wax by Orsino Benintendi after the failure of the Pazzi Conspiracy, recorded also by Vasari, which may have served as inspiration for other terracotta busts (Schuyler 1972, pp. 148–51).

In comparing the *Portrait of Henry VII* painted by Torrigiano during his stay in England (London, Victoria and Albert Museum) with this one of Lorenzo, we find the same expressive force and a notable ability to interpret the charismatic role of these noble personages. Created as an apologetic monument commemorating the moral, cultural and political grandeur of the Magnificent, this sculpture assumes an important place in Florentine history as an early document of that process of mythicizing Lorenzo's patronage of the arts which was to culminate in the grandiose cycle of frescoes decorating the Sala di Giovanni da San Giovanni in Palazzo Pitti.

Francesca Petrucci

Bibliography: Langedijk 1981–7, II, 1983, pp. 1158–62; *L'architettura* 1992, p. 125 (with preceding bibliography); G. Utari in *Mugello* 2008, pp. 237–38 (with preceding bibliography).

8.7
Francesco Granacci
(Villamagna di Volterra 1469–Florence 1543)
Arrival of Charles VIII at Palazzo Medici in Florence
1522–30
tempera on panel
76 x 122 cm
Florence, Galleria degli Uffizi,
1890 inv. no. 3908

This painting records the arrival of Charles VIII of Valois, King of France, at Palazzo Medici, on November 17, 1494. In a delicate historical situation, the French monarch was intent on marching down the peninsula to Naples. Piero de' Medici, the de facto lord of Florence, had been driven out of the city as a result of the concessions he had granted the French sovereign, and the newborn Republic was eager to begin negotiations with the king to deal with the emergency caused by his passage. Charles VIII entered Florence by the San Frediano Gate, passed through Piazza della Signoria and around the Cathedral, from where he entered Via Martelli, arriving at Palazzo Medici from the opposite direction to the one shown in the painting. The palace, abandoned by Piero, was to become the residence of the Valois. For this reason it was lavishly decorated, as recalled by the chronicler Luca Landucci: "Great decorative displays were made for the king in Piero de' Medici's house, and most of all at the door of the Medici Palace" (Landucci [1450-1542], ed. Del Badia 1883, p. 79). A wooden triumphal arch bearing the sovereign's insignia was erected in front of the palace (Perugino was one of the artists who worked on it) while Via Martelli was adorned with yellow lilies and hung with tapestries (Borsook 1961–3, pp. 115, 121–2).

In the picture, the long procession winds on between crowds lining both sides of Via Larga. On the right, a soldier waves a blue banner with the lilies of France. The palace appears as it was originally designed by Michelozzi, before being enlarged by the Riccardi family. Charles VIII is portrayed at the centre, on horseback, wearing armour and a crown, although the chronicles report that he was "dressed in brocade, with a white hat on his head" (Parenti [*ante* 1519], ed. Matucci 1994–2005, I, 1994, p. 133). Granacci's imprecision as to the route taken by the procession, the decorations and the king's attire is explained by the fact that he did not witness the event, and painted this picture some years later. The most convincing hypotheses for its dating link the painting to the Republic of 1527–30 (Holst 1974) or to the conspiracy against the Medici in 1522 (Cecchi 1986, p. 44).

The painting was most probably commissioned by the exiled Francesco Nasi (1498–1571), an enemy of the Medici and advocate of republican views favourable to the arrival of the French king —a traditional ally of the republicans—in the city freed of its long-ruling dynasty. In 1579 his son Luttozzo Nasi donated the painting to Cardinal Ferdinando de' Medici, future Grand Duke of Tuscany (Cecchi 1986). The picture was sent to Rome, where it remained in the prelate's Roman residence at least until 1740. In 1914 it was purchased for the Uffizi by the Galleria Crespi of Milan, and from 1930 to 1973 it was displayed in the Medici Museum, which occupied premises in the very palace depicted in the painting.

Stefano Dall'Aglio

Bibliography: Venturi 1900, pp. 205–9; *Mostra medicea* 1939, p. 68; Holst 1974, pp. 159–60; S. Meloni Trkulja in *Il primato del disegno* 1980, pp. 124–5; Cecchi 1986; Berti 1993, p. 11; S. Blasio in *Firenze e la sua immagine* 1994, pp. 74–5; Acidini Luchinat 1999, p. 2; E. Capretti in *Ghirlandaio* 2010, pp. 130–3, no. 12.

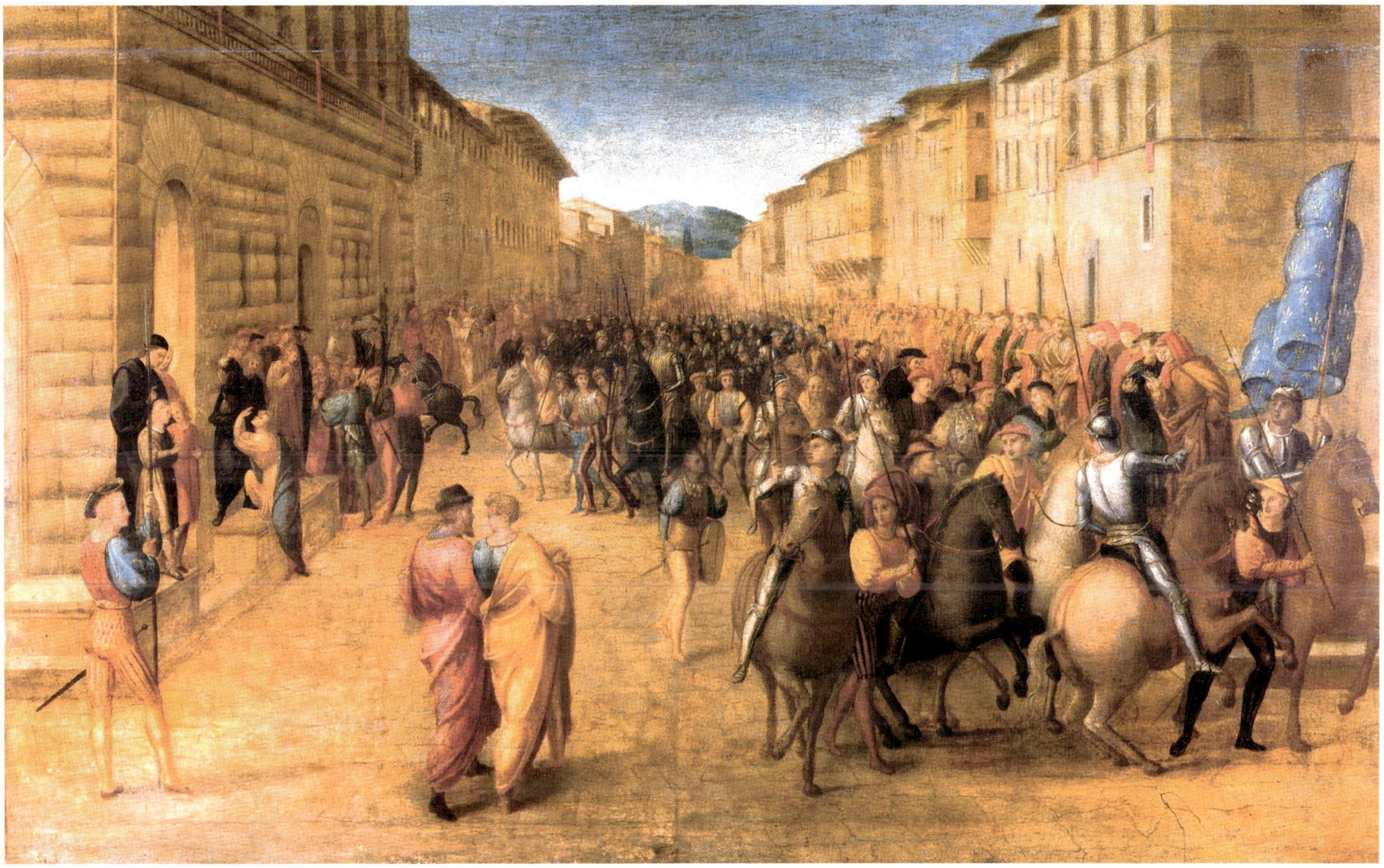

8.8
Sandro Botticelli
(Alessandro Filipepi, Florence 1445–1510)
The Calumny
c. 1497 (?)
tempera on panel
62 x 91 cm
Florence, Galleria degli Uffizi,
1890 inv. no. 1496

According to Vasari, this picture was donated by Botticelli himself to "Antonio Segni his very dear friend," and at the time when he saw it, bore the following inscription, written by his son Fabio Segni: "Indicio quemquam ne falso laedere tentent/Terrarum Reges parva Tabella monet/Huic similem Aegypti Regi donavit Apelles/Rex fuit & dignus munere: Munus eo" (Vasari 1568, ed. Milanesi 1878–81, III, 1878, p. 324). These words refer to a picture described by Lucian, of similar subject, that had been painted by the Greek artist Apelles as a sort of admonishment against accusations based on false evidence.

The scene, set in a porticoed hall filled with statues and relief carvings, should be read from right to left. On the throne King Midas, flanked by bad advisors, Ignorance and Suspicion, is leaning toward Envy, who holds Calumny by the hand. She, with Deception and Fraud arranging her attire, is pulling the victim of slander by his hair. Following them is Penitence, dressed in black, who turns imploringly toward the nude figure of Truth. Agitation and apprehension pervade the scene, expressed through the nervous, frenetic motion of the figures, characteristic of this stage in Botticelli's career (1496–7), far removed from the poetic beauty of the mythological fables painted in the 1480s. After the return to Florence of his brother Simone, a follower of Savonarola, Sandro too seemed influenced by the Friar's sermons, although he did not fully embrace his ideas until the early years of the new century. In the Uffizi painting the statue of Judith, prominently placed behind King Midas, symbolizes justice and alludes to Donatello's Judith, the statue that had stood with menacing sword upraised in Piazza Signoria since 1494 (F. Nicosia in *Sandro Botticelli* 2000, p. 156).

Apelles had painted his picture as response to slanderous accusations made against him by another painter, and Botticelli's painting too has been seen as an act of defence against some such allegation. But to fully understand the message of the painting, subjected to widely varying interpretations, we should start from the words of Vasari. It is probable, in fact, that the victim of calumny was Antonio Segni (Florence 1457–information up to 1502), the friend to whom Botticelli donated the painting, perhaps to defend him against groundless slander, endemic to the atmosphere of denunciation and suspicion prevailing in Savonarola's time. Such accusations might find grounds in the fact that Antonio, unlike his forebears, was never appointed to any public role (Cecchi, Natali 2000, p. 31). It is certain that both Antonio, linked to Sandro and to Leonardo da Vinci, and his son Fabio, possessed the humanist sensitivity and cultural refinement that must have been scorned in the Florence of Savonarola's Republic.

The painting appears in fact to be "the extreme testimony of the Laurentian culture, in which Antonio must have been educated, and the farewell of Sandro, the new Apelles, to a world that disappeared with the death of the Magnificent, under the relentless pressure of Savonarola's reforms" (Cecchi 2005, p. 306).

Nicoletta Pons

Bibliography: Cecchi, Natali 2000, pp. 30–1; F. Nicosia in *Sandro Botticelli* 2000, pp. 156–7 no. 4.13; N. Pons in *Botticelli e Filippino* 2004, pp. 244–6, no. 40; Cecchi 2005, pp. 300–2.

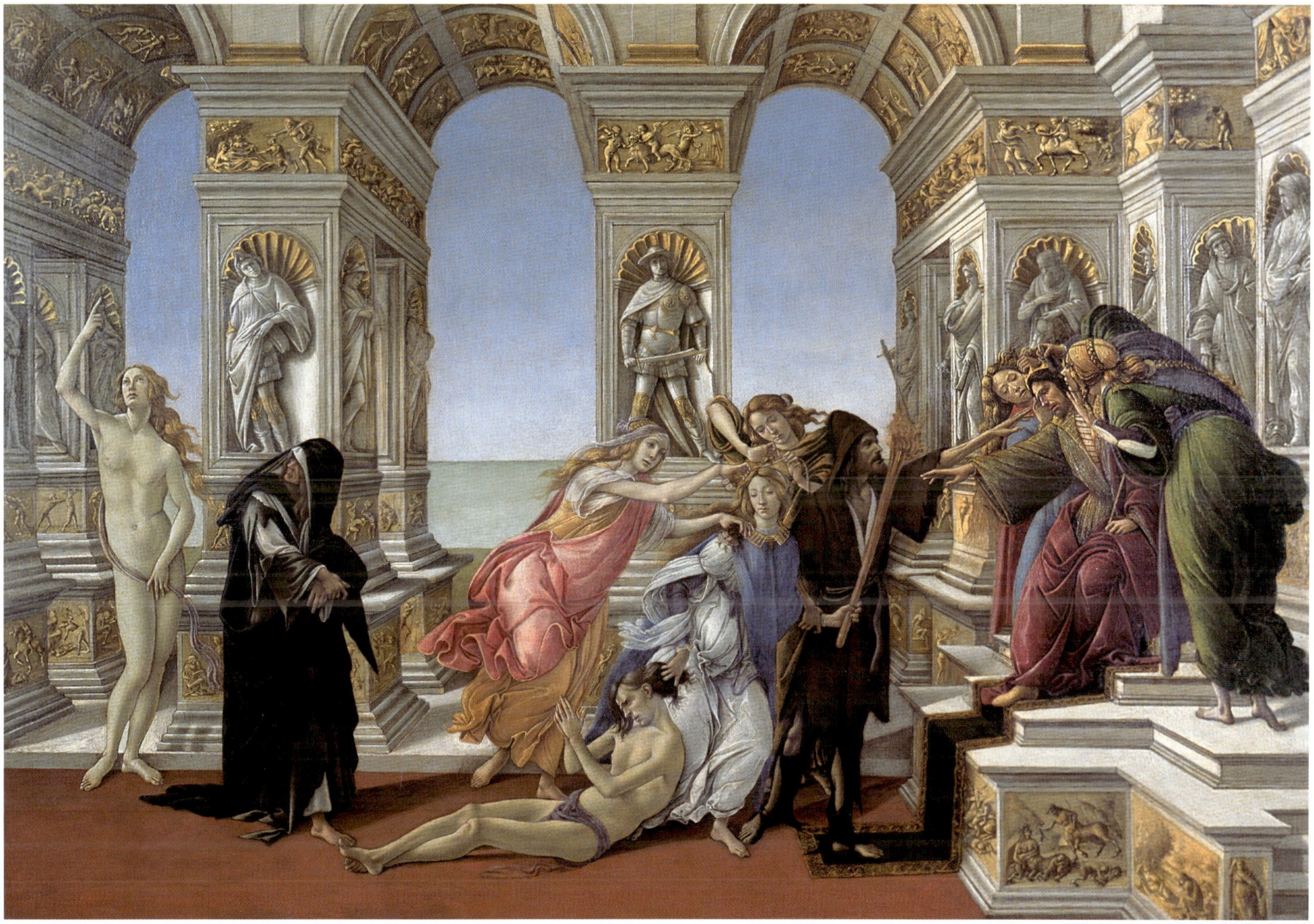

8.9
Ludwig von Langenmantel
(Michaelsberg 1854–Munich 1922)
Savonarola Preaching Against Luxury and Preparing the Bonfire of the Vanities
1881
oil on canvas
193.04 x 312.42 cm
St. Bonaventure, NY, St. Bonaventure University, The Regina A. Quick Center for the Arts

In 1881, the Bavarian artist Ludwig von Langenmantel chose to paint a canvas entitled *Savonarola Preaching against Luxury and Preparing the Bonfire of the Vanities*: an extremely rare subject, considering that—despite the indubitable fascination of the episode—there exist no known representations of objects being collected to be burned in Piazza della Signoria during the Carnivals of 1497 and 1498. At the Porträtsammlung Bildarchiv und Fideikommißbibliothek of the Österreichische Nationalbibliothek in Vienna is an engraving (Pk 400/278, see. L. Sebregondi, in *Savonarola* [1494–98], ed. Viti, Sebregondi 1998, p. 39) accompanied by an explanatory text and a description of the painting: "In a lavishly adorned church, Savonarola, standing on a pedestal like those still today used in Italy during Lent, pronounces a fiery sermon against luxury before a large audience, which includes the noblest names of the time. N. Macchiavelli, A. Pollaiolo, Picus de Mirandula, Fra Bartolommeo, S. Botticelli, G. dei Becchi, Andrea della Robbia, Filippino Lippi and a host of noble ladies are solemnly listening to the orator's admonitions, while others are acting out his words, fallen on fertile terrain, and gathering luxurious objects, some heaped at the feet of the preacher, some still in the hands of the almoners charged with collecting them." The friar stands on a high platform in a monumental building. Numerous ladies with "saddle" hairstyles in the northern fashion, are listening to his exhortations, while others are responding to his teachings by heaping precious objects at his feet (amphorae, fabrics, bowls, musical instruments, and a book by "Boccaccio").

The possibilities offered by the subject—taken from the biography of Savonarola written by the school inspector Looff and published in Langensalza by the Bauerschen Buchhandlung—fascinated the artist, who intended to show the richness and opulence of Renaissance art, inserting portraits of famous masters and renowned personages. Thanks to the diagram accompanying the painting, we can recognize on the left Niccolò Machiavelli wearing a red headdress. On the far right are Gentile Becchi, seen in profile, lifting his hand to his cheek, the faces of Botticelli and Antonio del Pollaiolo (the older man in the foreground). Pico della Mirandola, dressed in green, wears a red cap on his curly hair. Fra Bartolomeo is the young man looking out at the spectator, resting his chin on his hand. Higher up, Filippino Lippi looks out from behind a column. Near him, the man with the walking stick has been indicated as Andrea della Robbia, although he looks more like Luca della Robbia in the engraving inserted by Vasari in the 1568 edition of his *Lives*. The features of Fra Bartolomeo also seem to have been taken from Vasari, although Langenmantel has transformed the face in the woodcut—where the painter appears as an old friar—into that of a young man, as Baccio della Porta was at the time of the bonfire of vanities.

The scene is a represented as a theatrical event, while it was instead the so-called "Savonarola boys" who searched through the houses for objects considered instruments of the devil, such as playing cards, cosmetics, paintings and sculptures deemed erotic, and collected them to be destroyed in the bonfire (see among others Bredekamp 1973, pp. 41–64; Ciappelli 1996, pp. 47–59).

This painting, previously displayed at the Munich Kunstverein and then donated to the American University in 1932, was found by myself after extensive research, in preparation for the exhibition.

Ludovica Sebregondi

Bibliography: L. Sebregondi, in Savonarola (1494–8), ed. Viti, Sebregondi 1998, p. 39; Sebregondi 2000, pp. 116–7; Sebregondi 2004, p. 230.

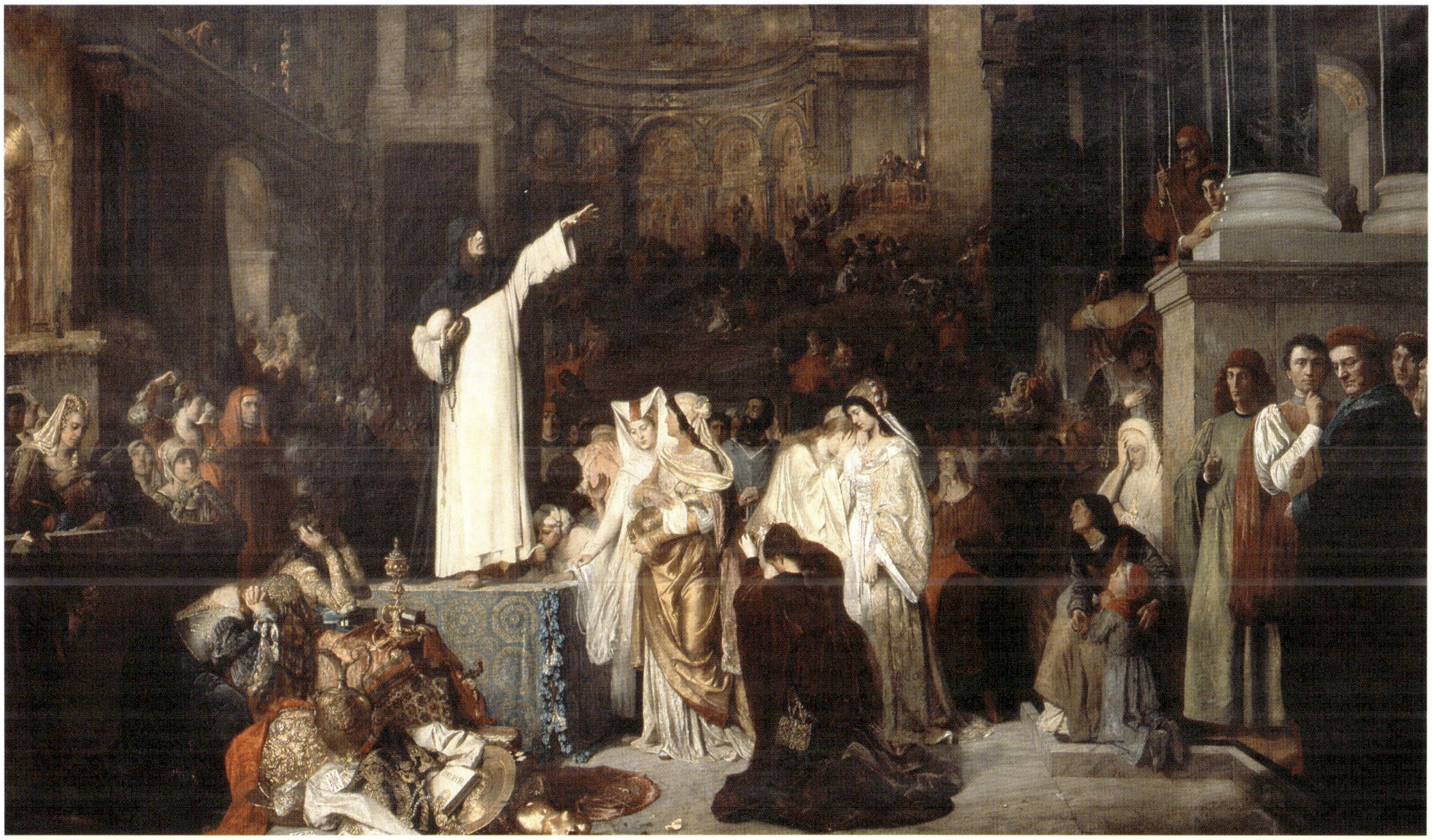

8.10
Filippo Dolciati (Florence 1443–1519)
attributed to
Execution of Girolamo Savonarola
1498
tempera on panel
38 x 58 cm
Florence, Museo di San Marco,
1915 inv. no. 479

This small panel in vernacular style illustrates the last stages in the lives of Savonarola and his followers, who were sentenced to be hanged and then burnt in Piazza della Signoria in Florence. Among the many pictures narrating the events of that dramatic spring, this is the most important, and probably the oldest extant today. The inscription "*morì il sopra/detto Padre il dì/23 maggio*" (the aforesaid Father died on May 23) makes the image a kind of live news report—or an ex voto—as seen by a follower intent on recording the memory immediately after its tragic conclusion. Other details appear to confirm that the picture was painted very soon after the event it depicts.

This painting is the only one to illustrate—in the image at lower left—what happened on the evening of April 8th, when Fra Girolamo Savonarola and Fra Domenico Buonvicini were brought in chains to Palazzo Vecchio after the assault on the monastery of San Marco. In the picture, Fra Silvestro Maruffi, who had in fact hidden, is missing. The path of the marching guards escorting the prisoners through the crowd is lit by torches, since they were transferred by night (for a detailed description, see Villari, ed. 1898, II, p. 174). The words used by Ser Lorenzo Violi to describe the episode are perfectly consonant with the scene: "And so these Companions in that night were led away, taken cum fustibus et lanternis, amid such cries and shrieks of the populace as would seem to dwell in hell [...] some striking them with fists, others kicking them" (Violi [*c.* 1545], ed. Garfagnini 1986, p. 91). For the versions showing a broader view of the city, see entry 8.13.

The painting has been attributed to an artist close to Cosimo Rosselli or Domenico Ghirlandaio (M. Scudieri in *Savonarola e le sue 'reliquie'* 1998, p. 85), or to an illuminator from the Monte di Giovanni circle (Acidini Luchinat 1999, p. 2; *Eadem* 2001 p. 89). It is very similar, however, to the panel painting narrating *The Story of Antonio Rinaldeschi*, dating from around 1501 and now unanimously attributed to Filippo Dolciati (Connell, Constable 2006; see entry 8.14).

The original collocation of the painting, purchased in 1915 from private owners (M. Scudieri in *Savonarola e le sue 'reliquie'* 1998, p. 84), is unknown. However, the presence at upper left of a luminous mandorla with God the Father bestowing blessings and the three executed men (Fra Girolamo at the centre in a frontal view, Fra Domenico and Fra Silvestro shown in profile) holding the martyr's palm leaves and wearing crowns, indicates the painting's commemorative purpose, as well as the fact that it was destined to private devotion, since its subject (see Sebregondi 2004, p. 89) could not be displayed in public.

Ludovica Sebregondi

Bibliography: Sebregondi 1996, p. 157; M. Scudieri in *Savonarola e le sue 'reliquie'* 1998, pp. 84–5; Acidini Luchinat 1999, p. 2 (ed. 2001, p. 89); Sebregondi 2004, pp. 14–23.

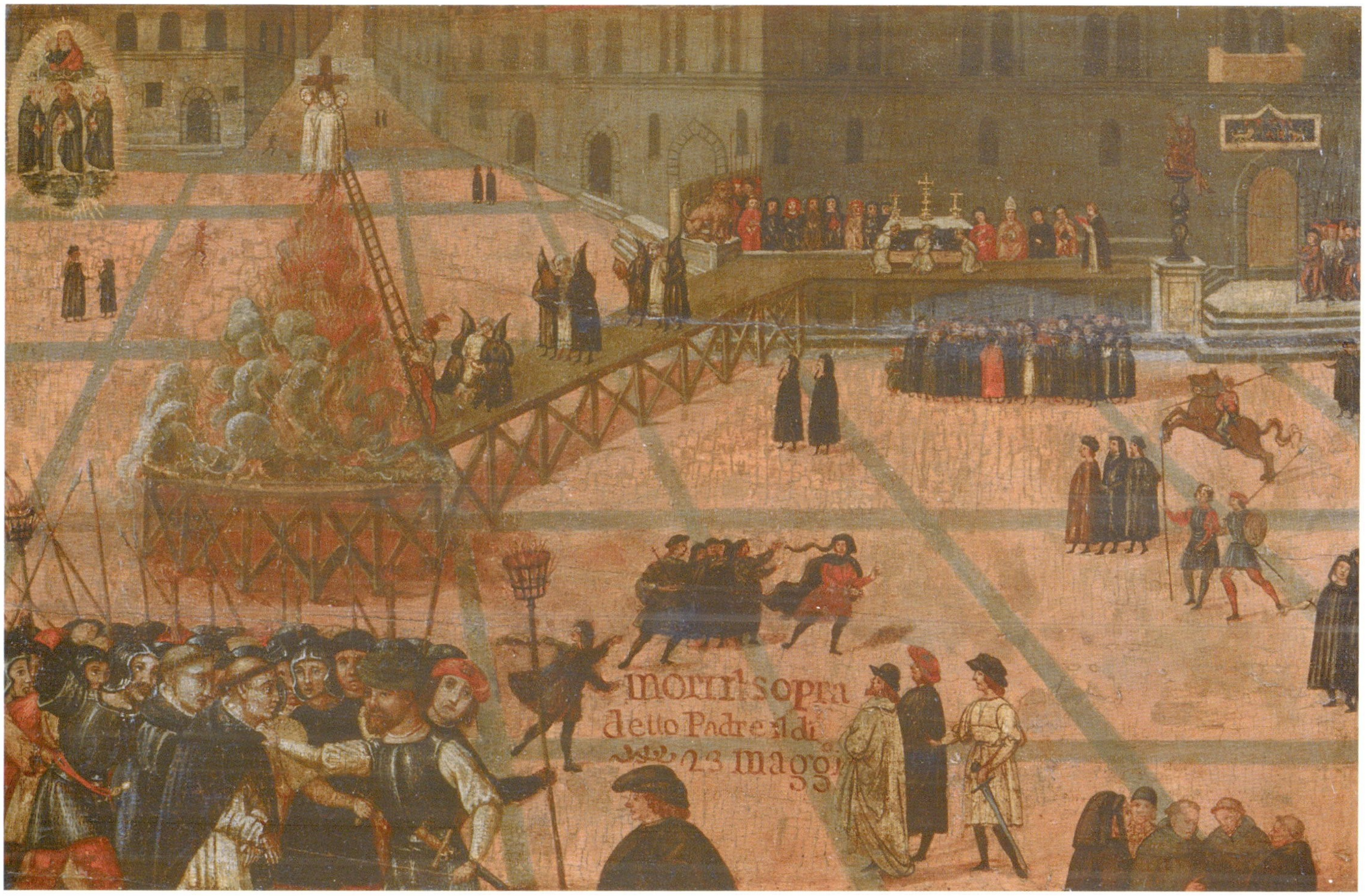

251

8.11
Veneto wood engraver
Sic transit Gloria mundi in *Processo de fra Hieronymo Savonarola da Ferrara*
[The trial of Fra Girolamo Savonarola of Ferrara]
[Venice, Simone Bevilacqua, *post* May 23,1498]
frontispiece
1498
woodcut
210 x 160 mm
Florence, Biblioteche della Cassa di Risparmio di Firenze, Fondo Ridolfi 261A/210

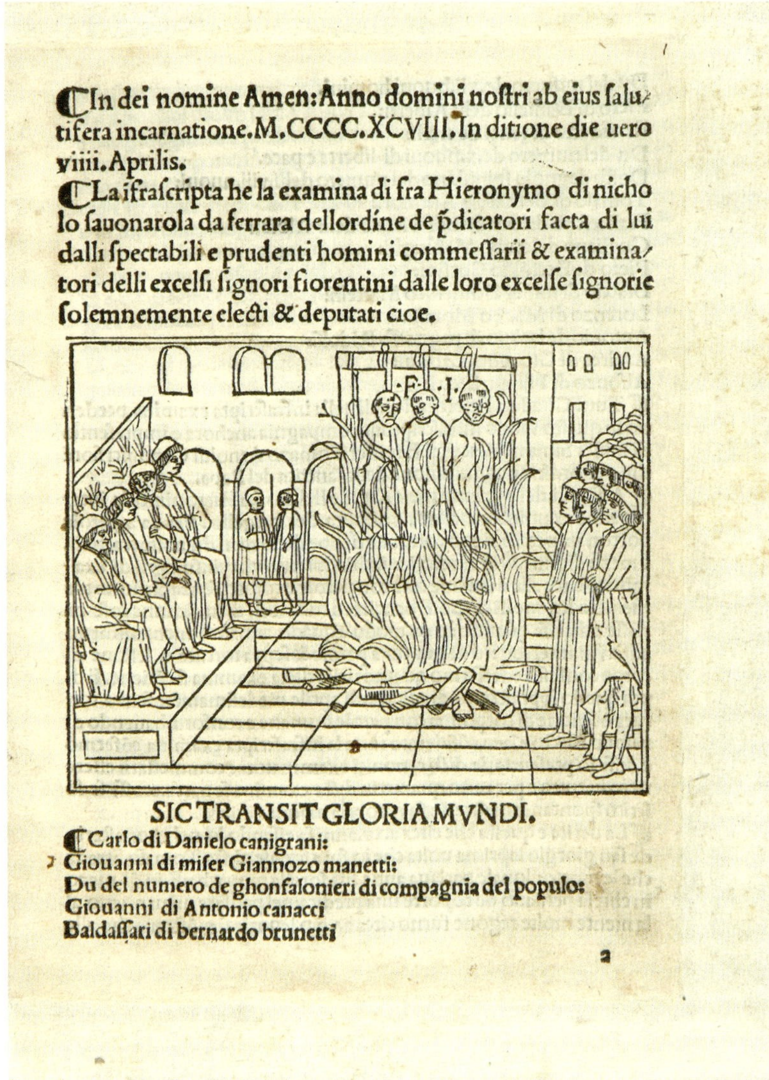
In dei nomine Amen: Anno domini nostri ab eius salutifera incarnatione. M.CCCC.XCVIII. In ditione die uero viiii. Aprilis.
La ifrascripta he la examina di fra Hieronymo di nicholo sauonarola da ferrara dellordine de p̄dicatori facta di lui dalli spectabili e prudenti homini commessarii & examinatori delli excelsi signori fiorentini dalle loro excelse signorie solemnemente electi & deputati cioe.

SIC TRANSIT GLORIA MVNDI.
Carlo di Danielo canigrani:
Giouanni di miser Giannozo manetti:
Du del numero de ghonfalonieri di compagnia del populo:
Giouanni di Antonio canacci
Baldassari di bernardo brunetti
a

Girolamo Savonarola was hanged and his body burned on the bonfire in Piazza della Signoria on May 23, 1498. His two brother monks Domenico Buonvicini from Pescia and Silvestro Maruffi from Florence were executed with him. In this woodcut, the bodies of the three monks enveloped by flames on a crude scaffold occupy the centre of the scene. To their right, four magistrates are sitting in a little stand. To their left, a group of citizens stands to witness the execution. In the background, further away, are two men, perhaps guards. The initials "F.I." beside the head of one of the three friars clearly identify Savonarola (F[rater] I[eronimus]). Furthermore, as noted by Ludovica Sebregondi (2004) the friar furthest to the right could be Domenico; he is significantly taller and heavier than the other two, and we know from chronicles of the time that Buonvicini was a man "of large stature."

This image was published in the Venetian edition of the so-called *First Trial of Savonarola*, reporting the interrogations the friar was subjected to immediately after his arrest, from April 9 to 19, 1498. Before his execution, two more interrogations were conducted, in April and May, the second of them in the presence of two ecclesiastical commissioners sent by Pope Alexander VI. The woodcut preceded the names of the members of the commission appointed by the Florentine Signoria to examine Savonarola on that occasion. In another edition of the trial, also printed in Venice, a different version of the same image appears, with ecclesiastics instead of citizens, and the three friars depicted as having the same body structure.

The image is accompanied by the inscription "SIC TRANSIT GLORIA MUNDI," a phrase that derives from the ceremony of crowning the pope, and was made famous by Thomas à Kempis in his *Imitation of Christ* (*I processi* 2001, pp. 52–3). As noted by Paolo Viti, that inscription probably served to underscore the failure of Savonarola's presumed aspirations to glory on earth (Viti 1999, p. 252), a question repeatedly raised by his interrogators. In the subsequent printed edition of the trial, published in Florence, the image is omitted but the words remain, probably by mistake, since without the image the inscription lost its original meaning, appearing as an awkward insertion in the text (Ridolfi 1945, pp. 15–7).

Stefano Dall'Aglio

Bibliography: Gruyer 1879, p. 175 note 1; Ridolfi 1945, pp. 15–7; Giovannozzi 1953, p. 132 note 271; Klein 1960, p. 377; Sebregondi 1996, p. 157; Sebregondi, 'La fortuna' 1998, pp. 8, 227; Acidini Luchinat 1999, p. 2; Viti 1999, p. 252; *I processi* 2001, pp. 52–3; Barbieri 2001, p. 226; Sebregondi 2004, pp. 54–5, 398.

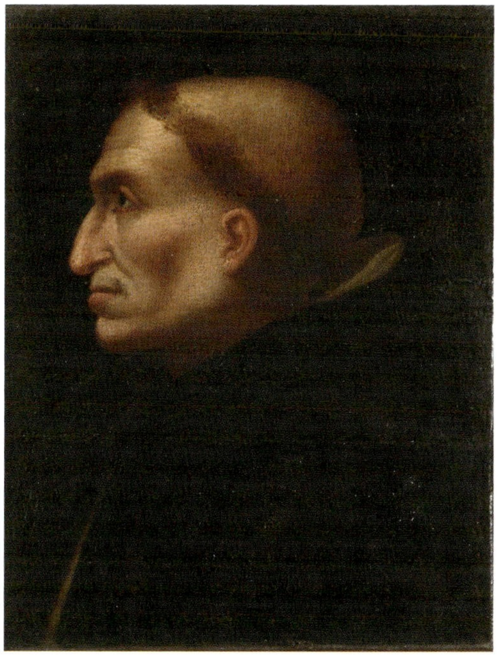

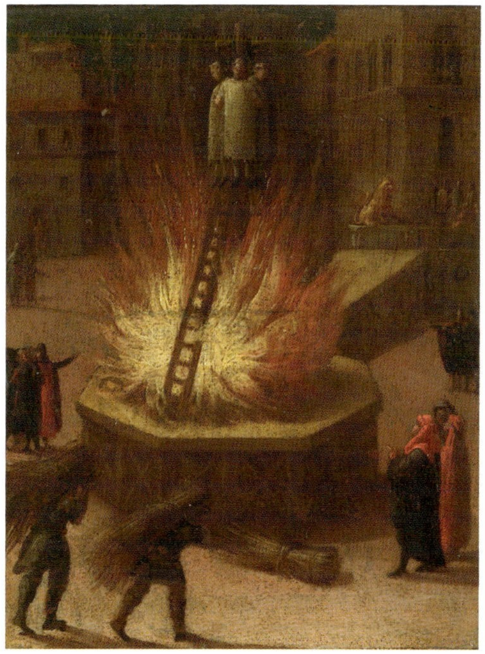

8.12
Florentine painter
Portrait of Girolamo Savonarola (front)
Execution of Girolamo Savonarola (reverse)
ante 1520
oil on panel
21.2 x 16.5 cm
London, The National Gallery, gift of Dr. William Radford, 1890, inv. no. NG1301

This small panel constitutes a little-known testimonial. On the front the portrait of Savonarola in profile, bareheaded, looking to the left, stands out against a dark background. On the reverse appears the scene of his death, with the bodies of the three friars burned in the square before Palazzo Vecchio.

For the portrait of Savonarola, the painter probably drew inspiration from an original unknown to us, since it differs from the famous image by Fra Bartolomeo, now in the Museo di San Marco, not only in the bared head but also for its attempt to portray with less abstraction and greater veracity the deep-cut features, resembling a painted terracotta medal in the Wicar Collection at Lille (see Sebregondi 2004, pp. 52–3).

According to Pasquale Villari, the portraits of Savonarola usually show him hooded, except for the second painting by Fra Bartolomeo at San Marco, where he has been transformed into the St. Peter Martyr and where "a slight deformity can be seen in the skull near the top: the reason why, it is said, he always kept his head covered" (1898, I, p. 19 note 1). Giuseppe Portigliotti, author of a psychiatric study of Savonarola, in observing two portraits of the friar with bare head, noted "an important cranial anomaly," in which "the upper line sinks toward the top" (Portigliotti 1902, pp. 17–8; see also Sebregondi 2004, p. LXXV).

The painting on the front is a copy of the central part of the *Execution*, differing from it in the absence of the three condemned friars advancing on the scaffold. The view is narrower, showing neither the Friar's comforters from the company of the Neri nor the executioner, but only the hanged men with the ladder on the side opposite the customary one.

The painting, which may have belonged to the Tornaquinci family, was given to Robert Southey by Walter Savage Landor in 1839 and donated to the National Gallery by William Radford in 1890 (Baker, Henry 1995, p. 342). In the past generically attributed to the Florentine sphere and dated between 1500 and 1540 (Ibidem), it has been compared by Serena Padovani to 253
the three small panels depicting the *Stories of St. Antoninus* attributed with some doubt to Fra Bartolomeo, and then classified as "School of San Marco, no later than the second decade of the 16th century" (in *Fra' Bartolomeo* 1996, p. 137).

According to Angelica Dülberg (1990, p. 165) this unusual portrait was commissioned by an unknown follower of the Friar who wanted a historic document combining a portrait of Savonarola with the representation of his dramatic end. This interpretation too suggests a dating no later than the second decade of the 16th century, when the memory of Fra Girolamo's preaching and his death was still alive. In this connection, it should be recalled that the bodies were burned and their ashes thrown into the Arno in a futile attempt to repress Savonarola's cult and keep his followers from procuring relics.

Ludovica Sebregondi

Bibliography: Dülberg 1990, p. 165; Baker, Henry 1995, p. 342; S. Padovani in *Fra' Bartolomeo* 1996, pp. 135, 137; Sebregondi 2004, p. 25 (with preceding bibliography).

8.13
Anonymous painter
Execution of Girolamo Savonarola
17th century
tempera on canvas
94 x 120 cm
Perugia, Galleria Nazionale dell'Umbria, Deposito Superiore, inv. no. 187

The various stages in the execution of Fra Girolamo Savonarola, Fra Domenico Buonvicini and Fra Silvestro Maruffi in Piazza della Signoria are represented contemporaneously. The three Dominicans first appear kneeling at an altar on the railing before the palace, then proceeding along the raised platform leading to the gallows, escorted by comforters, and lastly hanged from a rod, with flames licking upward at their bodies. The square paved in terracotta tiles striped with grey stone, the Loggia della Signoria, the Church of San Pier Scheraggio to the right and that of San Romolo to the left, are precisely represented. In the background appears the unfinished façade of Santa Croce, with, shifted to the left, the tower of the Bargello, the Badia bell tower, and behind them the domed cathedral.

254

In the foreground, two Franciscans and two Dominicans are engaged in discussion. In the upper register, two angels are pointing at the scene with one hand. With the other, they are holding the ends of a long scroll bearing the inscription "ECCE•QVOMODO•MORITVR•IVSTUS• /ET•VIRI•SANCTI•DE•TERRA•TOLLVNTUR" ("See how the just die and how saints are removed from the earth," words taken from a text by Savonarola). The emotional impact of the little devotional panel (entry 8.10) is missing here, as the painter is clearly more interested in representing topographical features. The real subject of the painting is in fact the city, as shown by the falsified perspective that places the cathedral with its dome on the left, when it is actually not visible from this viewing point.

This Perugian version, coming from a Dominican monastery, is the earliest of the surviving paintings bearing the inscription on the scroll, often omitted (in at least thirteen versions of the subject—whose prototype, attributed to Francesco Rosselli, is now in the Museo di San Marco—see Sebregondi 2004, pp. 13–31).

The painting faithfully reflects contemporary accounts of the event, with a priest standing at the far right near the entrance to the Palace, from which the condemned prisoners have come out into the plaza, and the Bishop of Vaison seated with the papal commissioners (Gioacchino Torriani and Francisco Remolins) at another altar. The three friars, dressed only in white tunics, are kneeling before this altar after having been stripped of their dark Dominican habits. The Tribunal of the Eight, with its red-robed magistrates, appears next to the statue of the Marzocco. The painting also concords with the texts as regards the platform (which covers the railing, and the scaffolding, a little above head level, starting at the Marzocco statue and extending into the square) along which the three condemned men proceed. It differs instead in the length of the raised platform—which has many more than three supports and a size greater than the approximately 11 and a half metres reported—and in the absence of a drawbridge, undoubtedly a precaution taken to keep the fire from spreading up to the railing.

In the painting, each of the Dominicans is flanked by two comforters from the Compagnia dei Neri, recognizable by their dark gowns with lowered hoods and by the "pax panel" that was brought to the condemned men for a last act of devotion. The ladder climbed by the three Dominicans on their way to the gallows, and the iron collars and chains that bound the bodies to keep them from falling, are also shown.

Ludovica Sebregondi

Bibliography: Sebregondi 1996, p. 154; Acidini Luchinat 2001, p. 87, note 1; Sebregondi 2004, pp. 28–9 (with preceding bibliography).

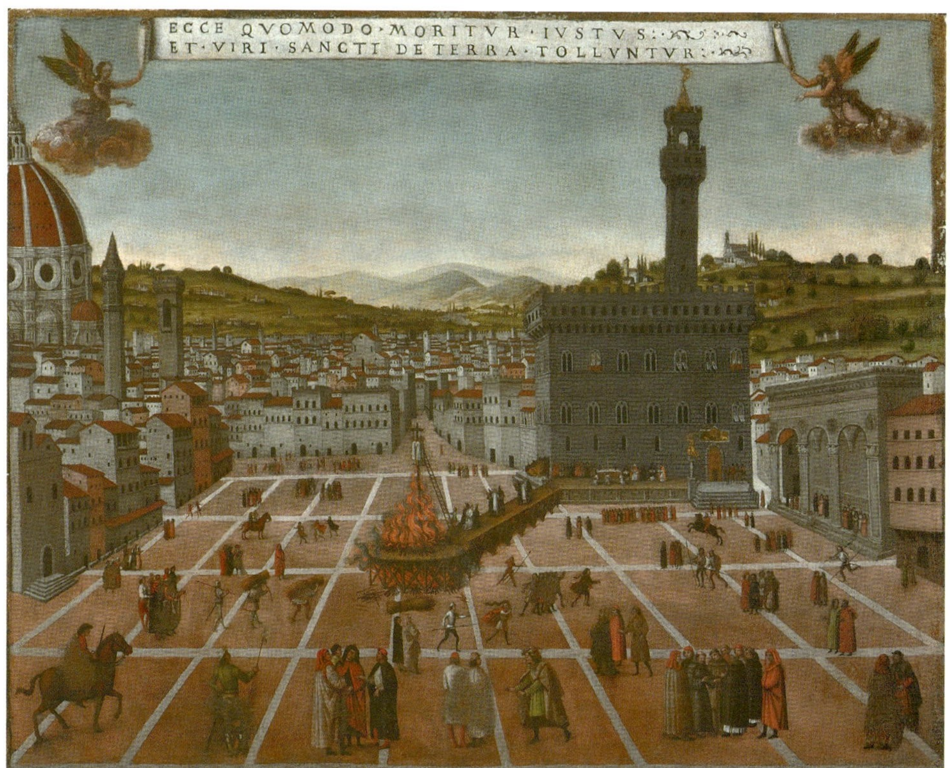

8.14
Filippo Dolciati (Florence 1443–1519)
Story of Antonio Rinaldeschi
1501
oil on canvas and wood
102 x 115.5 cm
Florence, Museo Stibbert, inv. no. 16719

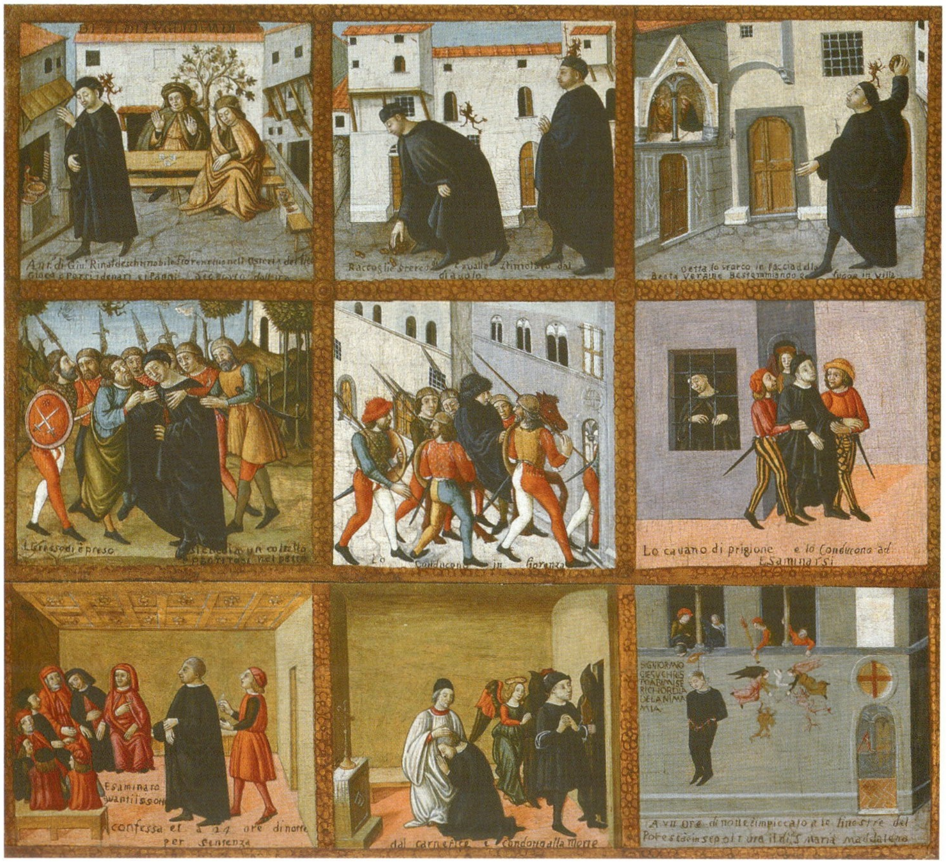

This painting narrates the sad story of Antonio Rinaldeschi, a Florentine who committed sacrilege in 1501 by offending the image of the Madonna, as described in the chronicles of the time. This event is illustrated vividly and realistically in nine sections: the game of dice at the Osteria del Fico, where Rinaldeschi, dressed in black, loses and becomes enraged; his profanation of the Tabernacle of the Madonna de' Ricci at the instigation of the devil; Rinaldeschi's flight through the countryside to avoid capture; his arrest by the guards of the Podestà; his transfer to the Bargello and detention there; his trial before the the Tribunal of Eight; Rinaldeschi's condemnation, confession of his sin and lastly, his execution by hanging from the window of the Bargello courtyard, before angels and devils contending for his soul.

The painting was probably commissioned as a *memento* of the event, which had shocked the whole city. After the profanation, the holy image is said to have acquired miraculous powers, and a popular cult soon grew up around the small 14th-century tabernacle displayed in the Piazza di Santa Maria degli Alberighi, on a corner known as "Canto de' Ricci." The tabernacle was moved later to an oratory specially built to house it, enlarged later to become the church of Santa Maria de' Ricci nel Corso, where the image is still to be seen today on the high altar.

This work is most interesting for its faithful documentation of life in Florence in the late 15th and early the 16th centuries, immediately after the time of Savonarola. The urban views, perfectly recognizable today, enlivened by remarkably realistic figures and activities, the architecture true in every detail, and the clothing depicted with photographic precision, display the life of Florence in the vivacious tone of popular narrative.

The institutions too are faithfully represented. The guards conducting Rinaldeschi to the Bargello, at the time seat of the Podestà and first detention centre, bear on their shields the emblems (two spades crossed on a red field) of Messer Monaldo de' Fascioli from Orvieto, who held office from April to October 1501. The Tribunal of Eight, the magistrates who administered justice, are shown in their authoritative red mantles, and the condemned man is accompanied to the execution place by the brothers of the Compagnia dei Neri.

An artist called Filippo di Lorenzo Dolciati, a workshop assistant whose family lived in the area, was paid for this painting. His name appears only in the documents, and no other works by him are known.

The painting, restored in 2004, has a very strange structure. The first six sections are painted on canvas, then applied to a larger panel that includes the three lower sections, painted directly on the wooden support. The inscriptions, added later, probably date from the 18th century, except for the one in the last episode, beside the figure of the hanged man: "SIGNIOR MIO GIESV CHRISTO ABI MISERICHORDIA DE L'ANIMA MIA" ("O Lord Jesus Christ, have mercy on my soul").

Simona Di Marco

Bibliography: *Il Museo Stibbert* 1976, p. 32, no. 16; N. Pons in *Firenze* 2004, pp. 90–1; Connell, Constable 2006.

8.15
Sandro Botticelli
(Alessandro Filipepi; Florence 1445–1510)
Christ Crucified
post 1496
tempera on moulded panel
157.5 x 98.8 cm
Prato, Diocesi di Prato - Musei Diocesani
MOp35

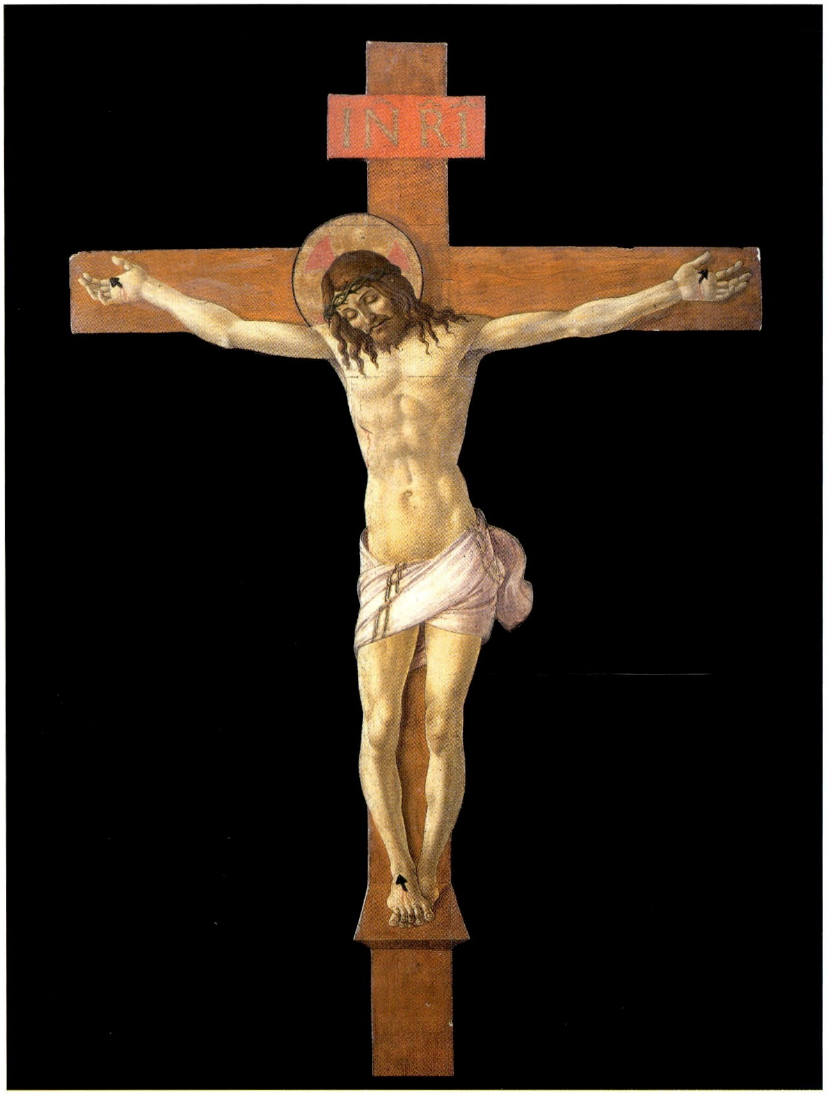

From the Dominican Monastery of San Vincenzo in Prato, nerve centre of Savonarola's cult, comes this evocative *Christ Crucified*, moulded and painted in the loincloth on both sides in imitation of processional Crucifixes, according to a penitential model very common in Florentine painting of the 14th and 15th centuries. The Crucifix, depicted with attentive care in the vibrant anatomical rendering of the body and the sinuous waving loincloth, fully accords with the dictates of Savonarola, who praised the representation of Christ's suffering body in painting and sculpture; a tender, delicate Christ, so that "any tiny wound was most painful to him," states the *Tractato dello amore di Jesù Cristo* [Treatise on the love of Jesus Christ].

For its exceptionally high quality, Alessandro Cecchi (2005, p. 335) has attributed this painting to Botticelli, as an important work commissioned by the Friars of San Domenico in Prato, for whom Savonarola had preached a highly acclaimed sermon against the corruption of the clergy on April 17, 1496. Dating from early 1492 are two fundamental texts, the *Tractato divoto e utile della umiltà* [Devout and useful treatise on humility] and the *Tractato dello amore di Jesù Cristo* [Treatise on the love of Jesus Christ], along with a condemnation of all those who preferred the works of Aristotle, Ovid, Cicero, Virgil, Dante and Petrarch to the Gospels. The living Christ thus wrought a profound change in the life of Botticelli, leading to his painful "conversion" and consequent rejection of the Renaissance ideals.

The painted crucifix was moved later to the nearby convent of San Vincenzo, when the Dominican monastery became the centre of Savonarola's cult with his relics (originally, the portrait of Savonarola "from life," painted by Fra Bartolomeo and then acquired by the Museo di San Marco).

According to Federico Zeri (1985, p. 138), no other artist has left a school production as ample and numerous as Sandro Botticelli's. Zeri suspects that Botticelli's models, notebooks, and paintings that had for various reasons remained unfinished may have been utilized by the very active workshop he had headed in his lifetime, which probably continued to produce even after 1510 (see Zeri 1985, pp. 135–9).

A very similar example, although with a repainted face, apparently coming from the same workshop, is found in the Galleria dello Spedale di Santa Maria Nuova in Florence (Brasioli, Ciuccetti 1989, no. 44 p. 61). But in the refined, almost extenuated linearity of the body it differs from the more deeply felt, more spiritual interpretation of Filippino Lippi, in the small panel painting *Christ Crucified*, a preparatory study for the *Valori Altarpiece*, dating from 1498–1500 (recently acquired by the Prato Civic collections from the Denver Museum).

Maria Pia Mannini

Bibliography: C. Cerretelli in *I Tesori della Città* 1998, no. 51; M.P. Mannini in *Filippino Lippi* 2004, p. 46, no. 7; Cecchi 2005 p. 335; M.P. Mannini in *Filippo e Filippino* 2009, p. 162, no. 28.

8.16
Sandro Botticelli
(Alessandro Filipepi, Florence 1445–1510)
and workshop
Coronation of the Virgin
last decade of the 15th century
oil on panel
279 x 191 cm
Florence, Villa La Quiete, Pini inv. no. 5 (1862)

This panel painting, which originally decorated the high altar in the church of San Francesco, known as San Lodovico, at Montevarchi, was moved in 1596 to the left arm of the transept over the Mini family altar, as shown by the documents (Del Vita 1993). It is presumably the work mentioned by Vasari in stating that Botticelli "painted the panel for the high altar in San Francesco at Montevarchi."

The general layout derives from a work of similar subject painted by Botticelli for the church of San Marco, now in the Uffizi. It is distinguished by a sharp separation between the spheres of heaven and earth, an iconography adopted in Florentine painting already from the ninth decade of the century but expressed by the painter of the *San Marco Altarpiece* in a more fervent, monumental mode, in keeping with the anxious atmosphere that pervaded Florence near the end of the 15th century (Caneva 1990, pp. 34, 45).

In the Villa della Quiete painting, gold serves as background, as in the spherical vault of an apse, to the scene of the *Coronation*, where the Virgin, her hands crossed over her breast, kneels before God the Father, who wears a papal tiara, in the act of crowning her. Musical angels celebrate the solemn event to the sound of trumpets and a great number of chamber music instruments: at left a portative organ, a lute, a plucked psaltery, a lira da braccio, at right a recorder, tambourines, a medieval harp, and a rim with disk bells, only partially visible. Since this part of the picture shows the refined touches characteristic of Botticelli, we may hypothesize that it was painted by the master himself, based on its similarity to his *Coronation of the Virgin* drawing at Göttinger, generally linked to the *San Marco Altarpiece*; but even more on the musical angels at left, more closely resembling that panel, probably a different version of the earlier work that had remained in the workshop. The presence of a large group of saints in the lower part of the painting—obviously painted by the master's assistants, in a generic emulation of his style—is unusual. Since the church at Montevarchi was owned by the Minorites, the Franciscans appear in the foreground: St. Anthony of Padua and St. Ludwig of Toulouse on the left, St. Francis and St. Bernardino on the right. As of now, we have no information on the commissioner of this painting of ample scope, which may date from the early years of the 16th century. It is however legitimate to hypothesize that here, more than elsewhere, the Virgin taken up into Heaven and crowned alludes specifically to the entire "Ecclesia" of Rome at the moment of its triumph, upheld by members of the militant Church, present in great number. This hypothesis is supported by the sumptuous, ceremonial nature of the altarpiece and the figure of St. Peter holding the keys placed in the central position, behind the cross of St. John the Baptist, which is aligned with the dove of the Holy Spirit. Moreover, this theme seems even more pertinent during a historical period of tension in the Franciscan Order and a Florentine context pervaded by mystical, prophetic tones. The painting, moved during the Napoleonic suppressions to the church of San Jacopo di Ripoli in Via della Scala and presumably trimmed at the edges on that occasion, arrived at Villa della Quiete, seat of the Montalve Conservatory, in 1886.

Mirella Branca

Bibliography: N. Pons in *Maestri e botteghe* 1992, p. 140; L. Venturini in *Villa La Quiete* 1997, pp. 180–2 (with bibliography); Cecchi 2005, pp. 86–7, note 93; L. Melli in *Botticelli* 2009, p. 338; Branca 2010, p. 52.

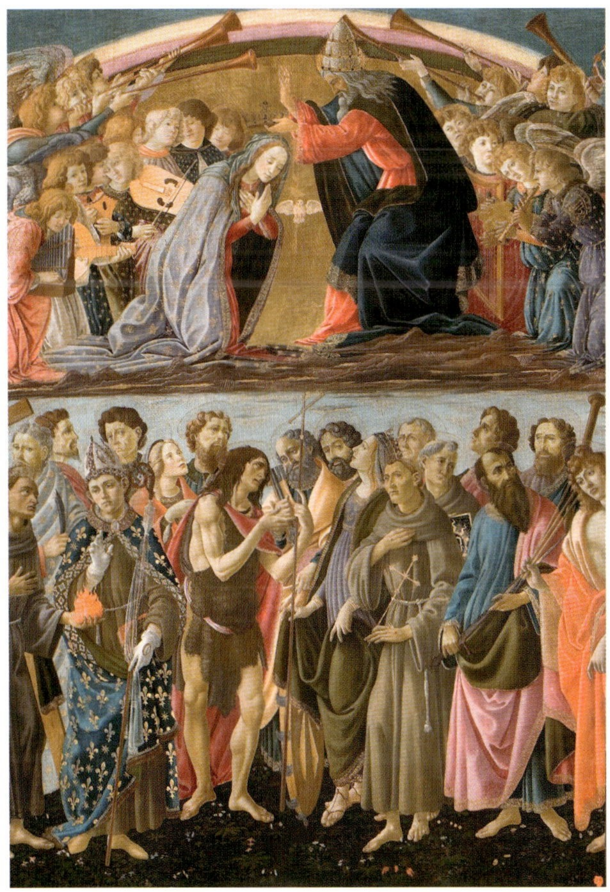

8.17
Sandro Botticelli
(Alessandro Filipepi, Florence 1445–1510)
Madonna and Child with the Young St. John
c. 1500
panel painting
134 x 92 cm
Florence, Galleria Palatina,
Palatina inv. no. 357 (1912)

This painting, for its subject and its size, was certainly destined to private devotion. The monumental Madonna, who seems too large for the format of the picture, bends with the Child as he leans to embrace the young St. John. The surface of the painting is entirely filled by these three figures. This sense of constricted space, along with the "hierarchical" elongation of the Virgin, date the work to a late stage of Botticelli's career, when his style had changed under the influence of Savonarola's preaching. In 1499, Sandro's workshop was, according to the *Cronica* of his brother Giovanni, a place of open debate "on the case of [Fra] Girolamo." Even one of the Friar's persecutors, Doffo Spini, joined in these discussions.

During this stage Botticelli purposely chose unnatural poses, heedless of spatial laws and the rules of perspective. The same lack of proportion observed in the Palatina *Madonna* appears in the grief-stricken Mary of the contemporary *Pietà* at the Poldi Pezzoli (1499-1500), known to have been commissioned by a Piagnone, and in the figures depicted in the Birmingham *Pentecost*, also attributable to Botticelli's late stage, as has now been confirmed by a document dating it to 1505. The document also shows that the *Pentecost* was commissioned by the Brotherhood of the Spirito Santo at Montelupo, a town near Florence (Waldman 2009, pp. 291–5), which undoubtedly appreciated Botticelli's new devout, pious, style. The same archaic rendering of space distinguishes the *Mystic Nativity* in London, dated 1501, which may be considered the manifesto of Botticelli's artistic maturity for its return to the canons of 14th-century art, as recommended by Savonarola, "because 'archaic' art was good and even saintly" (Verdon 1999, p. 11).

The loving embrace of the two children also alludes to Christ's acceptance of the Passion, symbolized by the cross of reeds that the little Jesus is pulling to himself, away from St. John. This symbolism has led Joannides (1995, p. 170) to see the painting as Botticelli's reflection on the drawing of the *Virgin and Child with St. Anne and St. John the Baptist*, displayed by Leonardo at the Basilica of Santissima Annunziata after his return to Florence, where it was acclaimed by crowds of people, among them many ordinary citizens and labourers. Moreover, Blume (1995, p. 35) sees in the contemporary *Pietà* at the Poldi Pezzoli a confrontation with Leonardo's pyramidal experiments, perhaps showing a desire to assimilate the innovations of the great artist.

Although Botticelli continued to receive some commissions from the Piagnone and the brotherhoods, in the late 15th-early 16th century his fame was overshadowed by the competition of other painters such as Perugino and Filippino. In 1502 in fact, as appears from a famous letter sent by her agent to Isabella d'Este, Botticelli was the only painter available to lend his talents to the Lady of Mantua, the other two being so overloaded with work as to have no time for her.

Nicoletta Pons

Bibliography: Joannides 1995, pp. 170 and 176; N. Pons in *Botticelli e Filippino* 2004, pp. 216–7; Cecchi 2005, p. 86; B. Eclercy in *Botticelli* 2009, pp. 332–4.

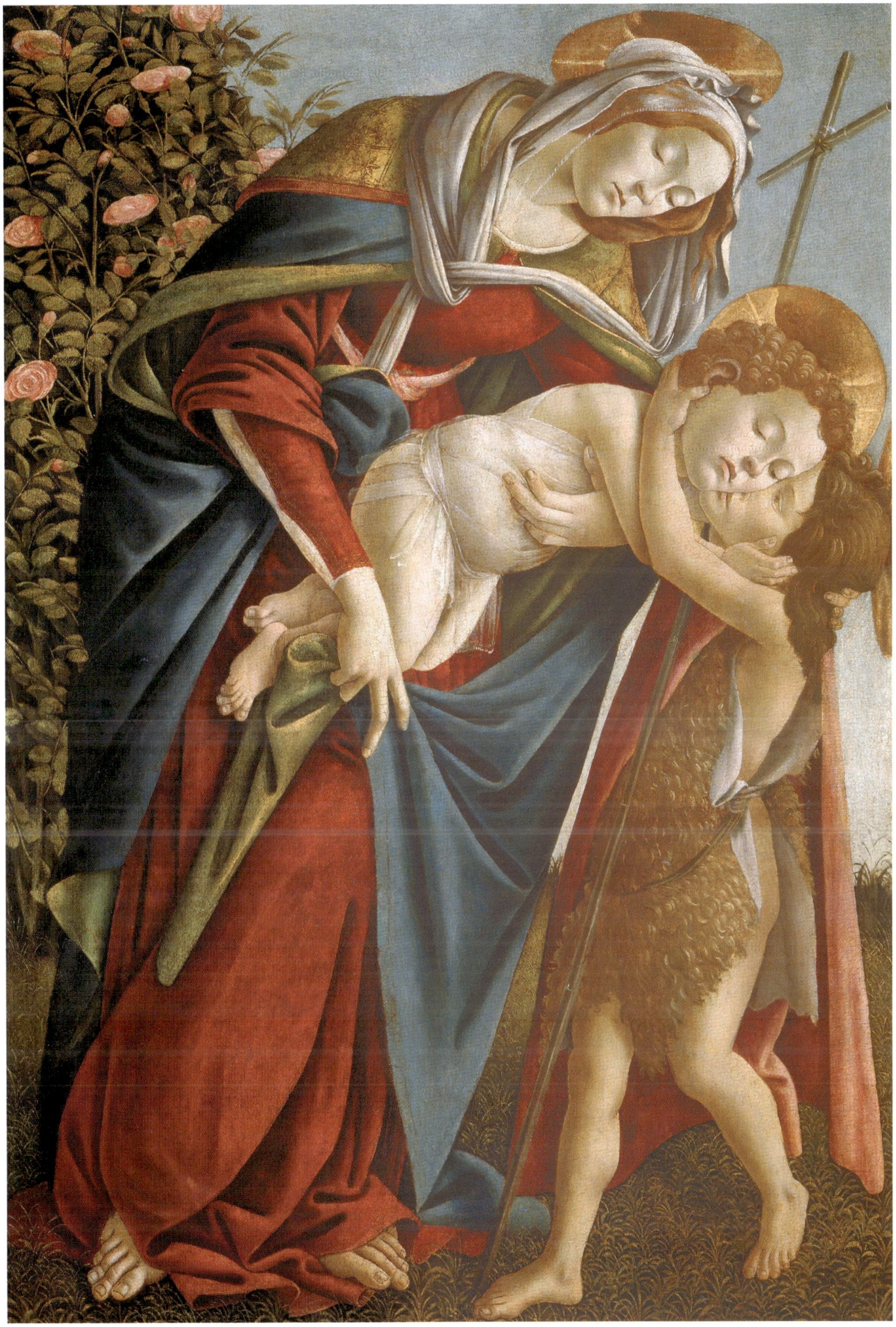

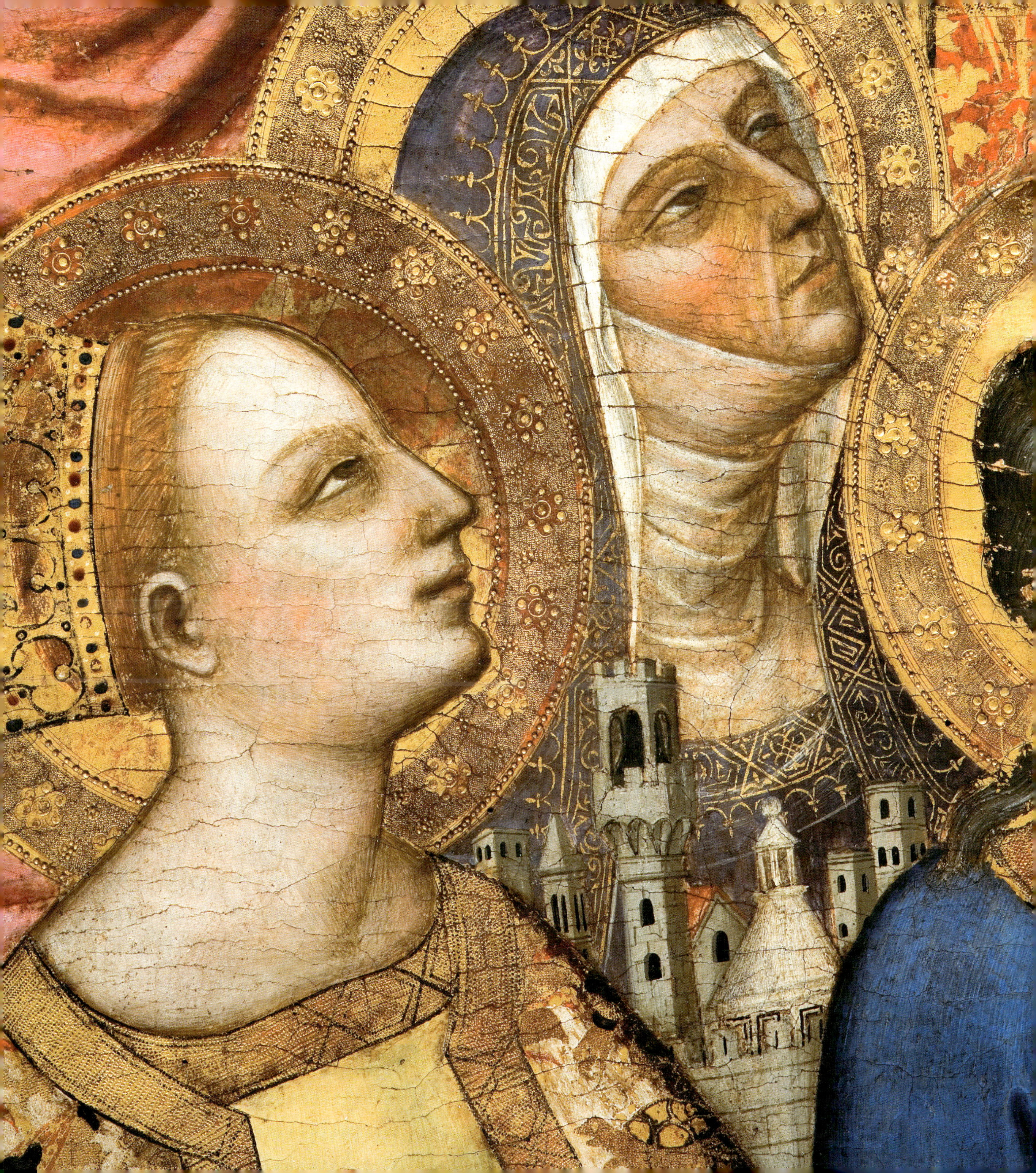

Appendix

Bibliographical references

edited by Elena Capretti

Acidini Luchinat, 'L'immagine medicea' 1991 = Cristina Acidini Luchinat, 'L'immagine medicea: i ritratti, i patroni, l'araldica e le divise', in *Per bellezza* 1991, pp. 125–42.

Acidini Luchinat, 'La "santa antichità"' 1991 = Cristina Acidini Luchinat, 'La "santa antichità," la scuola, il giardino', in *Per bellezza* 1991, pp. 143–60.

Acidini Luchinat, 'La Cappella dei Magi' 1993 = Cristina Acidini Luchinat, 'La Cappella dei Magi', in *Benozzo Gozzoli* 1993, pp. 7–24.

Acidini Luchinat, 'Library' 1993 = Cristina Acidini Luchinat, 'Library', in *Renaissance Florence. The Age of Lorenzo de' Medici, 1449–1492*, exhibition catalogue (London, Accademia Italiana delle Arti e delle Arti Applicate, 14 October 1993–23 January 1994) edited by Cristina Acidini Luchinat, Milan, 1993, pp. 119–21.

Acidini Luchinat 1999 = Cristina Acidini Luchinat, 'Dal fuoco all'acqua: il "Supplizio del Savonarola" nella storia di Piazza della Signoria', in *Girolamo Savonarola. Storia* 1999, pp. 1–7; then under the title 'Dal fuoco all'acqua: il "Supplizio del Savonarola" nello sviluppo di Piazza della Signoria', in *Una città e il suo profeta. Firenze di fronte al Savonarola*, proceedings of the symposium (Florence, 10–13 December 1998) edited by Gian Carlo Garfagnini, Florence, 2001, pp. 87–94.

Acidini Luchinat 2001 = Cristina Acidini Luchinat, *Botticelli. Allegorie mitologiche*, Milan, 2001.

Acidini Luchinat 2003 = Cristina Acidini Luchinat, 'Il genio del luogo... Vicende del Museo Mediceo', in *Stanze segrete* 2003, pp. 1–39, 149–75.

Ahl 1996 = Diane C. Ahl, *Benozzo Gozzoli*, New Haven & London, 1996.

Ahl 2008 = Diane C. Ahl, *Fra Angelico*, London, 2008.

Alambicchi 1999 = *Alambicchi di parole: il Ricettario fiorentino e dintorni*, exhibition catalogue (Florence, Biblioteca Riccardiana, 18 October 1999–15 January 2000) edited by Giovanna Lazzi, Florence, 1999.

Albertini 1510, ed. De Boer 2010 = Francesco Albertini, 'Memoriale di molte statue et picture sono nella inclyta cipta di Florentia', [Florence 1510]; critical edition annotated by Waldemar H. de Boer, in *Memoriale di molte statue et picture sono nella inclyta cipta di Florentia di Francesco Albertini (1510). Un volumetto dedicato all'arte fiorentina*, edited by Michael W. Kwakkelstein, Florence, 2010.

Alinari 1989 = Alessandro Alinari, 'Specchiere rinascimentali in maiolica da Montelupo', in *Atti. XIX Convegno Internazionale della Ceramica. "La ceramica graffita"* (Albisola, Villa Faraggiana, 30 May–4 June 1986), Albisola 1989, pp. 263–8.

Ames-Lewis 1984 = Francis Ames-Lewis, *The Library and Manuscripts of Piero di Cosimo de' Medici*, New York, 1984.

Angelini 1986 = Alessandro Angelini, *Disegni italiani del tempo di Donatello*, exhibition catalogue (Florence, Gabinetto Disegni e Stampe, 1986), Florence, 1986.

Angelo Polizianos Tagebuch 1929 = *Angelo Polizianos Tagebuch (1477–1479), mit Vierhundert Schwänken und Schnurren aus den Tagen Lorenzos des Grossmächtigen und seiner Vorfahren*, edited by Albert Wesselski, Jena, 1929.

L'architettura 1992 = *L'architettura di Lorenzo il Magnifico*, exhibition catalogue (Florence, 8 April–26 July 1992) edited by Gabriele Morolli, Cristina Acidini Luchinat, Luciano Marchetti, Cinisello Balsamo, 1992.

L'Archivio 2004 = *L'Archivio di Francesco di Marco Datini. Fondaco di Avignone*, edited by Elena Cecchi Aste, Rome, 2004.

Arthur 1990 = Kathleen G. Arthur, 'Cult Objects and Artistic Patronage of the Fourteenth-century Flagellant Confraternity of Gesù Pellegrino', in *Christianity and the Renaissance. Image and Religious Imagination in the Quattrocento*, edited by Timothy Verdon and John Henderson, Syracuse-New York, 1990, pp. 336–60.

Arti a Firenze 2009 = *Arti a Firenze tra Gotico e Rinascimento*, exhibition catalogue (Aosta, Museo Archeologico, 27 June–1 November 2009) edited by Giovanna Damiani, [Italian/French], Florence, 2009.

Arti del Medio Evo 1989 = *Arti del Medio Evo e del Rinascimento. Omaggio ai Carrand 1889–1989*, exhibition catalogue (Florence, Museo Nazionale del Bargello, 20 March–25 June 1989) edited by Giovanna Gaeta Bertelà and Beatrice Paolozzi Strozzi, Florence, 1989.

Arti fiorentine 1998–2003 = *Arti fiorentine. La grande storia dell'artigianato*, Florence, 1998–2003, 6 vols.

Aspetti 1985 = *Aspetti della vita economica medievale*, proceedings of the symposium held on the 10th anniversary of the death of Federigo Melis (Firenze-Pisa-Prato, 10–14 March 1984), Florence, 1985.

Assonitis, 'Art and Savonarolan Reform' 2003 = Alessio Assonitis, 'Art and Savonarolan Reform at San Silvestro a Monte Cavallo in Rome (1507–1540)', in *Archivum Fratrum Praedicatorum*, 73, 2003, pp. 205–88.

Assonitis, *Art and Savonarolism* 2003 = Alessio Assonitis, *Art and Savonarolism in Florence and Rome*, Ph.D. Diss., New York, Columbia University, 2003.

Averlino, Antonio see Filarete.

Báez 2007 = Fernando Báez, *Storia universale della distruzione dei libri. Dalle tavolette sumere alla guerra in Iraq*, presentation by Marino Sinibaldi, Rome, 2007.

Bagemihl 1993 = Rolf Bagemihl, 'The Trevisan Collection', in *The Burlington Magazine*, 135, 1993, pp. 559–63.

Baker, Henry 1995 = Christopher Baker, Tom Henry, *The National Gallery. Complete Illustrated Catalogue*, London, 1995.

Baldini 1986 = Umberto Baldini, *Beato Angelico*, Florence, 1986.

Balducci Pegolotti (*c.*1335–43), ed. Evans 1936 = Francesco Balducci Pegolotti, *La pratica della mercatura* (*c.*1335–43), edited by Allan Evans, Cambridge, Mass., 1936.

Banchi pubblici 1991 = *Banchi pubblici, banchi privati e monti di pietà nell'Europa preindustriale. Amministrazione, tecniche operative e ruoli economici*, proceedings of the symposium (Genoa, 1–6 October 1990), Genoa 1991, 2 vols. (*Atti della Società Ligure di Storia Patria*, new series, 31 (105), 1991, pp. 1–2).

Barbieri 1963 = Gino Barbieri, *Il pensiero economico dall'Antichità al Rinascimento*, Bari, 1963.

Barbieri 2001 = Edoardo Barbieri, 'Episodi della fortuna editoriale di Girolamo Savonarola (secc. XV–XVI)', in *Girolamo Savonarola da Ferrara all'Europa*, proceedings of international symposium (Ferrara, 30 March–3 April, 1998) edited by Gigliola Fragnito and Mario Miegge, Florence, 2001, pp. 195–237.

Barletti, Boddi 1998 = Emanuele Barletti, Vito Donatello Boddi, 'Appunti di viaggio tra Oriente ed Occidente sulla via di Damasco e una testimonianza inedita di Fra' Mariano da Firenze su Cosimo il Vecchio per tacere di Michelozzo', in *Michelozzo* 1998, pp. 303–7.

Barlucchi 1997 = Andrea Barlucchi, 'I signori del denaro', in *Medioevo*, 1, 1997, 2, pp. 69–71.

Baron 1988 = Hans Baron, *In Search of Florentine Civic Humanism. Essays on the Transition from Medieval to Modern Thought*, Princeton, N.J., 1988.

Bartolomeo del Corazza (1405–39), ed. Gentile 1991 = Bartolomeo del

Corazza, *Diario fiorentino (1405–1439)*, edited by Roberta Gentile, Anzio, 1991

Baskins 2005 = Cristelle L. Baskins, 'Scenes from a Marriage: Hospitality and Commerce in Boccaccio's Tale of Saladin and Torello', in *The Medieval Marriage Scene: Prudence, Passion, Policy*, edited by Sherry Roush and Cristelle L. Baskins, Tempe, Ariz., 2005, pp. 81–99.

Battelli 1936 = Guido Battelli, *Andrea Sansovino e l'arte italiana della Rinascenza in Portogallo*, Florence, 1936.

Battelli 1939 = Guido Battelli, 'La corrispondenza del Poliziano col re Don Giovanni II di Portogallo', in *Rinascita*, 2, 1939, pp. 280–98.

Bauer-Eberhardt 1989 = Ulrike Bauer-Eberhardt, 'Lauro Padovano und Leonardo Bellini als Maler, Miniatoren und Zeichner', in *Pantheon*, 47, 1989, pp. 49–82.

Bayern-Italien 2010 = *Bayern-Italien. Die Geschichte einer intensiven Beziehung*, exhibition catalogue (Füssen, Ehemaliges Kloster Sankt Mang; Augsburg, Maximilianmuseum; Augsburg, Staatliches Textil- und Industriemuseum; 21 May–10 October 2010) edited by Rainhard Riepertinger *et al.*, Augsburg, 2010.

Beato Angelico 2009 = *Beato Angelico. L'alba del Rinascimento*, exhibition catalogue (Rome, Musei Capitolini, 8 April–5 July 2009) edited by Alessandro Zuccari, Giovanni Morello, Gerardo de Simone, Geneva-Milan, 2009.

Bellandi 2010 = Alfredo Bellandi, *Gregorio di Lorenzo. Il Maestro delle Madonne di Marmo*, Morbio Inferiore 2010.

Bellini 2009 = Luigi Bellini, *Galleria Bellini. Museo Bellini dal 1756*, [Italian/English], Florence, 2009.

Bellini Museum Collection 2005 = *Bellini Museum Collection. Renaissance. Great Family and Art*, exhibition catalogue (Seoul, Asia Museum, 2005), [text in Korean], Florence-Seoul 2005.

Bellodi Casanova 1957 = Lucia Bellodi Casanova, 'Inventario dei Portolani e delle Carte Nautiche del Museo Correr', in *Bollettino dei Musei Civici Veneziani*, 2, 1957, pp. 3–4, 17–36.

Bellosi 1977 = Luciano Bellosi, *Il Museo dello Spedale degli Innocenti*, Milan, 1977.

Benozzo Gozzoli 1993 = *Benozzo Gozzoli. La Cappella dei Magi*, edited by Cristina Acidini Luchinat, Milan, 1993.

Benozzo Gozzoli e Cosimo Rosselli 2011 = *Benozzo Gozzoli e Cosimo Rosselli nelle terre di Castelfiorentino. Pittura devozionale in Valdelsa*, exhibition catalogue (Castelfiorentino, Museo Be.Go., 1 May–31 July 2011) edited by Serena Nocentini and Anna Padoa Rizzo, Florence, 2011

Berchet 1866 = Guglielmo Berchet, *Portolani esistenti nelle principali biblioteche di Venezia*, Venice, 1866.

Berenson 1932 = Bernard Berenson, *Italian Pictures of the Renaissance. A List of the Principal Artists and Their Works*, Oxford, 1932.

Berenson 1938 = Bernard Berenson, *The Drawings of Florentine Painters*, edition augmented, Chicago 1938, 3 vols (I ed. London 1903, 2 vols.).

Bernardino da Feltre (1493), 1940 ed. = *Sermoni del B. Bernardino da Feltre, nella redazione di Fr. Bernardino Bulgarino da Brescia, Min. Oss.. Il Quaresimale di Pavia del 1493*, edited by f. Carlo Varischi da Milano, Milan, 1940.

Bernocchi 1974 = Mario Bernocchi, *Le monete della Repubblica fiorentina*, I, *Il Libro della Zecca*, revised text, notes and introduction by Renzo Fantappiè, Florence 1974.

Bernocchi 1975 = Mario Bernocchi, *Le monete della Repubblica Fiorentina*, II, *Corpus Nummorum Florentinorum*, Florence, 1975.

Bernocchi 1976 = Mario Bernocchi, *Le monete della Repubblica Fiorentina*, III, *Documentazione*, Florence, 1976.

Berti 1967 = Luciano Berti, *Angelico*, Florence, 1967.

Berti 1993 = Luciano Berti, *Pontormo e il suo tempo*, Florence, 1993.

Biadene, Tonini 2000 = Susanna Biadene, Camillo Tonini, 'Viaggio attraverso le pianure liquide. La collezione di portolani e carte nautiche del Museo Correr di Venezia', in *Raggi di venti sul mare*, edited by Evangelos Livieratos, Thessalonica, 2000, pp. 25–31.

Biagi 1925 = Guido Biagi, *Fiorenza fior che sempre rinnovella: quadri e figure*, with preface by Isidoro Del Lungo, Florence, 1925.

La Biblioteca 1993 = *La Biblioteca Casanatense*, edited by Angela Adriana Cavarra, concept and presentation by Carlo Pietrangeli, Florence, 1993.

La biblioteca di Michelozzo 2000 = *La biblioteca di Michelozzo a San Marco: tra recupero e scoperta*, exhibition catalogue (Florence, Museo di San Marco, 30 September–30 December 2000) edited by Magnolia Scudieri and Giovanna Rasario, Florence, 2000.

Biblioteche 1998 = *Biblioteche Riccardiana e Moreniana in Palazzo Medici Riccardi*, Fiesole, 1998.

Bigazzi 2005 = Isabella Bigazzi, 'Palazzo Strozzi. L'architettura, la situazione urbanistica, i restauri', in *Palazzo Strozzi. Cinque secoli di arte e cultura*, edited by Giorgio Bonsanti, Florence, 2005, pp. 14–51.

Biscione 2009 = Giuseppe Biscione, *Statuti del Comune di Firenze nell'Archivio di Stato: tradizione archivistica e ordinamenti*, Florence, 2009.

Biscione forthcoming = Giuseppe Biscione, 'L'Ufficiale delle donne, degli ornamenti e delle vesti. Profilo istituzionale e vicende archivistiche', in *Cervi bianchi e cani vermigli. "La Prammatica" sulle vesti delle donne fiorentine (1343)*, transcription edited by Laurence Gérard-Marchant, Florence, forthcoming.

Blume 1996 = Andrew C. Blume, *Studies in the Religious Paintings of Sandro Botticelli*, Ann Arbor, Mich., 1996 (Ph.D. Diss., Cambridge, Mass., Harvard University, 1995).

Boccherini, Marabelli 1995 = Tamara Boccherini, Paola Marabelli, *Atlante di storia del tessuto. Itinerario nell'arte tessile dall'antichità al Déco*, Florence, 1995.

Bocchi 1591 = Francesco Bocchi, *Le bellezze della città di Fiorenza, dove à pieno di pittura, di scultura, di sacri tempij, di palazzi i più notabili artifizij, & più preziosi si contengono*, Fiorenza, 1591.

Bonito Fanelli 1988 = Rosalia Bonito Fanelli, 'A Renaissance Purse. A Case Study in Attribution', in *Il Costume nell'età del Rinascimento*, edited by Dora Liscia Bemporad, Florence, 1988, pp. 331–6.

Bonora 1970 = Ettore Bonora, 'Avarizia', in *Enciclopedia Dantesca*, I, Rome, 1970, pp. 463–4.

Bonsanti 1998 = Giorgio Bonsanti, *Beato Angelico. Catalogo completo*, Florence, 1998.

Borghini 1585, ed. 1755 = Vincenzo Borghini, 'Della moneta fiorentina', in *Discorsi, recati à luce da' deputati per suo testamento*, in Fiorenza 1584–85, 2 vols., II, 1585; in edition with the title *Discorsi di Monsignore D. Vincenzio Borghini*, with annotations, Florence, 1755, 2 vols. II, pp. 133–250.

Borgia 1986 = Luigi Borgia, *Gli stemmi del Palazzo d'Arnolfo di San Giovanni Valdarno*, with an article by Augusto Antoniella, Florence, 1986.

I Borgia 2002 = *I Borgia*, exhibition catalogue (Rome, Palazzo Ruspoli, Fondazione Memmo, 3 October 2002–23 February 2003) edited by Carla Alfano, Felipe V. Garin Llombart, Milan, 2002.

Bornstein 1993 = Daniel E. Bornstein, *The Bianchi of 1399. Popular Devotion in Late Medieval Italy*, Ithaca-London, 1993.

Borsook 1961–63 = Eve Borsook, 'Decor in Florence for the Entry of Charles VIII of France', in *Mitteilungen des Kunsthistorischen Institutes in Florenz*, 10, 1961–63, pp. 106–22, 217.

Borsook 1970 = Eve Borsook, 'Documenti relativi alle Cappelle di Lecceto e delle Selve di Filippo Strozzi', in *Antichità viva*, 9, 1970, 3, pp. 3–20.

Boskovits 1971 = Miklós Boskovits, 'Orcagna in 1357-and in Other Times', in *The Burlington Magazine*, 113, 1971, pp. 239–51.

Bosque 1975 = Andrée de Bosque, *Quentin Metsys*, Brussels, 1975.

Bottari 1754–73 = Giovanni Gaetano Bottari, *Raccolta di lettere sulla pittura scultura ed architettura*, Rome, 1754–73, 7 vols.

Botticelli 1989 = *Botticelli e il ricamo del Museo Poldi Pezzoli. Storia di un restauro*, Cinisello Balsamo, 1989.

Botticelli 2003 = *Botticelli. De Laurent le Magnifique à Savonarole*, exhibition catalogue (Paris, Musée du Luxembourg, 1 October 2003–22 February 2004) edited by Daniel Arasse and Pierluigi de Vecchi, Milan, 2003.

Botticelli 2009 = *Botticelli: Bildnis, Mythos, Andacht*, exhibition catalogue (Frankfurt, Städelsches Kunstinstitut, 13 November 2009–28 February 2010) edited by Andreas Schumacher, Frankfurt-Ostfildern, 2009; English ed. with the title *Botticelli: Likeness, Myth, Devotion*, Frankfurt-Ostfildern, 2009.

Botticelli 2010 = *Botticelli nelle collezioni lombarde*, exhibition catalogue (Milan, Museo Poldi Pezzoli, 12 November 2010–28 February 2011) edited by Andrea Di Lorenzo, Cinisello Balsamo, 2010.

Botticelli e Filippino 2004 = *Botticelli e Filippino. L'inquietudine e la grazia nella pittura fiorentina del Quattrocento*, exhibition catalogue (Florence, Palazzo Strozzi, 11 March–11 July 2004) edited by Daniel Arasse, Pierluigi de Vecchi and Jonathan K. Nelson, Milan, 2004.

Branca 2010 = Mirella Branca, 'Il patrimonio artistico di Villa la Quiete', in *Ville e giardini nei dintorni di Firenze. Da Fiesole ad Artimino*, edited by Stefano Casciu and Mariachiara Pozzana, Florence, 2010, pp. 50–55.

Brasioli, Ciuccetti 1989 = Francesca Brasioli, Laura Ciuccetti, *Santa Maria Nuova. Il tesoro dell'arte nell'antico ospedale fiorentino*, presentation by Fabrizio Bini, coordination and introduction by Sergio Ardinghi, Florence, 1989.

Braunstein, Franceschi 2007 = Philippe Braunstein, Franco Franceschi, '"Saperssi governar." Pratica mercantile e arte di vivere', in *Il Rinascimento italiano e l'Europa*, IV, *Commercio e cultura mercantile*, edited by Franco Franceschi, Richard Goldthwaite, Reinhold Mueller, Vicenza, 2007, pp. 663–4.

Bredekamp 1973 = Horst Bredekamp, 'Renaissancekultur als "Hölle": Savonarolas Verbrennungen der Eitelkeiten', in *Bildersturm. Die Zerstörung des Kunstwerks*, edited by Martin Warnke, Munich, 1973, pp. 41–64.

Bulgarelli, Ceriana 2009 = Massimo Bulgarelli, Matteo Ceriana, 'L'architettura e i Della Robbia', in *I Della Robbia* 2009, pp. 137–43.

Burke 1972 = Peter Burke, *Culture and Society in Renaissance Italy, 1420–1540*, Batsford, 1972.

Burke 2000 = Jill Burke, 'Patronage and Identity in Renaissance Florence: the Case of S. Maria a Lecceto', in *Fashioning Identities in Renaissance Art*, edited by Mary Rogers, Aldershot, 2000, pp. 51–61.

Byrne 1989 = Joseph P. Byrne, 'The Merchant as Penitent: Francesco di Marco and the Bianchi Movement of 1399', in *Viator*, 20, 1989, pp. 219–31.

Cadogan 2000 = Jean K. Cadogan, *Domenico Ghirlandaio Artist and Artisan*, New Haven-London, 2000.

Calandri (*ante* 1491), ed. Arrighi 1969 = Filippo Calandri, *Aritmetica. Secondo la lezione del codice 2669 (sec. XV) della Biblioteca Riccardiana di Firenze*, edited by Gino Arrighi, Florence, 1969.

Calandri (*ante* 1491), facs. ed. 2002 = [Filippo Calandri], *Tratado de aritmética de Lorenzo el Magnífico* (*ante* 1491), facsimile of ms. Ricc. 2669 in the Biblioteca Riccardiana di Firenze, with commentary in Lazzi, Salavaert, Ciardi Dupré Dal Poggetto 2002, Valencia, 2002.

Camelliti 2010 = Vittoria Camelliti, 'Patroni "celesti" e patroni "terreni": dedica e dedizione della città nel rituale e nell'immagine', in *Städtische Kulte im Mittelalter*, proceedings of the symposium (Regensburg, 12–14 November 2009) edited by Susanne Ehrich, Jörg Oberste, Regensburg 2010, 97–121.

Camerani Marri 1951 = Giulia Camerani Marri, *I documenti commerciali del fondo diplomatico mediceo nell'Archivio di Stato di Firenze*, Florence, 1951.

Campani 1884 = Annibale Campani, *Guida per il visitatore del R. Museo Nazionale nell'antico Palazzo del Potestà in Firenze*, Florence, 1884.

Campbell 1985 = Lorne Campbell, *The Early Flemish Pictures in the Collection of Her Majesty The Queen*, Cambridge, 1985.

Campbell 1987 = Tony Campbell, 'Portolan Charts from the Late Thirteenth Century to 1500', in *The History of Cartography*, I, *Cartography in Prehistoric, Ancient and Medieval Europe and the Mediterranean*, edited by John Brian Harley, David Woodward, Chicago-London, 1987, pp. 371–463.

Campbell 2009 = Marian Campbell, *Medieval Jewellery in Europe 1100–1500*, London, 2009.

Caneva 1990 = Caterina Caneva, 'L'Incoronazione ritrovata', in *L'Incoronazione della Vergine del Botticelli. Restauro e ricerche*, exhibition catalogue (Florence, Galleria degli Uffizi, 1990) edited by Marco Ciatti, Florence, 1990, pp. 33–50.

Canzona (1497), ed. 1864 = *Canzona d'un piagnone pel bruciamento delle vanità nel Carnevale del 1498 aggiuntavi la descrizione del bruciamento fatta da Girolamo Benivieni* (1497), Florence, 1864.

Capolavori 1986 = *Capolavori & Restauri*, exhibition catalogue (Florence, Palazzo Vecchio, 14 December 1986–26 April 1987), Florence, 1986.

Cappi Bentivegna 1962 = Ferruccia Cappi Bentivegna, *Abbigliamento e costume nella pittura italiana. Rinascimento*, Rome, 1962.

Capretti 1996 = Elena Capretti, 'La pinacoteca sacra', in *La chiesa e il convento di Santo Spirito a Firenze*, edited by Cristina Acidini Luchinat with Elena Capretti, Florence, 1996, pp. 239–303.

Cardon 2000 = Dominique Cardon 'Du "verme cremexe" au "veluto chremesino": Une filière vénitienne du cramoisi au XV° siècle', in *La seta in Italia dal Medioevo al Seicento. Dal baco al drappo*, edited by Luca Molà, Reinhold C. Mueller, Claudio Zanier, Venice, 2000, pp. 63–73.

Careri 2001 = Flavia Careri, 'Il "Presto ai Quattro Pavoni": dal libro-giornale di Isacco da San Miniato (1473–75)', in *Archivio storico italiano*, 159, 2001, pp. 395–421.

Carl 1990 = Doris Carl, 'La casa vecchia dei Medici e il suo giardino', in *Il Palazzo Medici Riccardi di Firenze*, edited by Giovanni Cherubini and Giovanni Fanelli, Florence 1990, pp. 38–43.

Carmignani 1989 = Marina Carmignani, 'Un cartone di Sandro Botticelli.

I monaci Olivetani di San Miniato al Monte. Il Principe Giovanni del Portogallo e i ricamatori fiorentini', in *Botticelli* 1989, pp. 18–39.

Carnesecchi 1902 = Carlo Carnesecchi, *Cosimo I e la sua legge suntuaria del 1562*, Florence, 1902.

Carte da navigar 1990 = *Carte da navigar. Portolani e carte nautiche del Museo Correr 1318–1732*, exhibition catalogue (Venice, Museo Correr, 29 September–9 December 1990) edited by Susanna Biadene, Venice, 1990.

Casagrande, Vecchio 2000 = Carla Casagrande, Silvana Vecchio, *I sette vizi capitali. Storia del peccato nel medioevo*, with an article by Jérôme Baschet, Turin, 2000.

Casolini 1939 = Fausta Casolini, *Bernardino da Feltre. Il martello degli usurai*, Milan, 1939.

Cassandro 1976 = Michele Cassandro, *Il Libro giallo di Ginevra della compagnia fiorentina di Antonio della Casa e Simone Guadagni, 1453–1454*, Prato, 1976.

Cassandro 1977 = Michele Cassandro, 'Per la storia delle comunità ebraiche in Toscana nei secoli XV–XVII', in *Economia e storia*, 24, 1977, 4, pp. 425–49.

Cassandro 1979 = Michele Cassandro, *Gli ebrei e il prestito ebraico a Siena nel Cinquecento*, Milan, 1979.

Cassandro 1990 = Michele Cassandro, 'Interazioni economiche tra la Svizzera e il mondo mediterraneo nel basso Medioevo: il ruolo delle fiere e la strategia dei mercanti banchieri', in *Die Schweiz in der Weltwirtschaft*, edited by Paul Bairoch and Martin H. Körner, Geneva, 1990, pp. 19–35.

Cassandro 1991 = Michele Cassandro, 'Commercio, manifatture e industria', in *Prato: storia di una città*, I/1, *Ascesa e declino di un centro cittadino (dal Mille al 1494)*, edited by Giovanni Cherubini, Florence, 1991, pp. 395–477.

Cassandro 2008 = Michele Cassandro, *Intolleranza e accettazione. Gli ebrei in Italia nei secoli XIV–XVIII. Lineamenti di una storia economica e sociale*, Turin, 2008 (1st ed., Turin, 1996).

Cassandro 2010 = Michele Cassandro, 'Aspetti della vita dell'uomo e del personaggio', in *Francesco di Marco Datini* 2010, pp. 3–55.

Cassuto 1918. = Umberto Cassuto, *Gli ebrei a Firenze nell'età del Rinascimento*, Florence, 1918 (xerographic reprint Florence, 1965).

Castelli 1991 = Patrizia Castelli, 'Motivi astrologici ed ermetici nel governo laurenziano', in *Per bellezza* 1991, pp. 55–78.

Cataloghi 2003 = *Cataloghi della Galleria dell'Accademia di Firenze. Dipinti*, I, *Dal Duecento a Giovanni da Milano*, edited by Miklós Boskovits and Angelo Tartuferi, Florence, 2003.

Catalogo 1902 = *Catalogo del Museo Artistico Poldi Pezzoli*, Milan 1902.

Catarino 1548 = Ambrogio Catarino Politi, *Discorso contra la dottrina et le profetie di fra Girolamo Savonarola*, Venice, 1548.

Caterina Proto Pisani 2006 = Rosanna Caterina Proto Pisani, *Il Museo della Collegiata di Sant'Andrea a Empoli*, Florence, 2006.

Cavaciocchi 2010 = Simonetta Cavaciocchi, 'Francesco Datini e i pittori', in *Francesco di Marco Datini* 2010, pp. 217–31.

Cavalcaselle, Crowe 1883–1908 = Joseph A. Crowe, Giovan Battista Cavalcaselle, *Storia della Pittura in Italia dal secolo II al secolo XVI*, Florence, 1883–1908, 11 vols.

Cavazzini 1999 = Laura Cavazzini, 'Il fratello di Masaccio tra i palazzi di Firenze e le chiese del Valdarno', in *Il fratello di Masaccio* 1999, pp. 9–24.

Cecchi 1986 = Alessandro Cecchi, 'L'ingresso di Carlo VIII in Firenze del Granacci: nuovi documenti e ipotesi sulla committenza', in *Paragone*, 37, 1986, 439, pp. 41–8.

Cecchi 1987 = Alessandro Cecchi, 'Agnolo e Maddalena Doni committenti di Raffaello', in *Studi su Raffaello*, proceedings of international symposium (Urbino-Florence, 6–14 April 1984) edited by Micaela Sambucco Hamond and Maria Letizia Strocchi, Urbino 1987, pp. 429–39.

Cecchi 2005 = Alessandro Cecchi, *Botticelli*, Milan, 2005.

Cecchi 2010 = Alessandro Cecchi, 'La bottega di Botticelli nella Via Nuova di Ognissanti', in *Botticelli* 2010, pp. 13–25.

Cecchi, Natali 2000 = Alessandro Cecchi, Antonio Natali, 'Viatico romano per Botticelli illustratore', in *Sandro Botticelli* 2000, I, pp. 26–32.

Cecchi, Natali, Sisi 1996 = Alessandro Cecchi, Antonio Natali, Carlo Sisi, 'L'officina della maniera', in *L'officina della maniera* 1996, pp. 7–69.

Cella 2009 = Roberta Cella, *La documentazione Gallerani-Fini nell'Archivio di Stato di Gent (1304–1309)*, Florence, 2009.

Chastel 1964 = André Chastel, *Arte e umanesimo a Firenze al tempo di Lorenzo il Magnifico*, Turin, 1964 (title of original edition *Art et Humanisme à Florence au temps de Laurent le Magnifique. Etudes sur la Renaissance et l'Humanisme Platonicien*, Paris, 1959).

La Chiesa e la Città 1992 = *La Chiesa e la Città a Firenze nel XV secolo*, exhibition catalogue (Florence, Sotterranei di San Lorenzo, 6 June–6 September 1992) edited by Gianfranco Rolfi, Ludovica Sebregondi, Paolo Viti, Cinisello Balsamo, 1992.

Ciappelli 1996 = Giovanni Ciappelli, 'Il carnevale del Savonarola', in *Studi savonaroliani* 1996, pp. 47–59; then in Id., *Carnevale e Quaresima: comportamenti sociali e cultura a Firenze nel Rinascimento*, Rome 1997, pp. 213–33.

Ciappelli 1997 = Giovanni Ciappelli, 'I bruciamenti delle vanità e la transizione verso un nuovo ordine carnevalesco', in *Savonarole* 1997, pp. 133–47.

Ciappelli 1999 = Giovanni Ciappelli, 'Il rogo della cultura: i bruciamenti delle vanità', in *Girolamo Savonarola. L'uomo* 1999, pp. 261–95.

Ciappelli 2006 = Giovanni Ciappelli, 'Carte geografiche e politica nei rapporti tra Firenze e il Portogallo nel Quattrocento', in *Annali dell'Istituto storico italo-germanico in Trento/Jahrbuch des italienisch-deutschen historischen Instituts in Trient*, 32, 2006 (2007), pp. 47–70.

Ciappelli 2009 = Giovanni Ciappelli, *Fisco e società a Firenze nel Rinascimento*, Rome, 2009.

Ciardi Duprè Dal Poggetto 1994 = Maria Grazia Ciardi Duprè Dal Poggetto, 'Un'ipotesi su Pedro Berruguete in Italia e sulla sua attività quale miniatore' in *Studi di Storia dell'Arte in onore di Mina Gregori*, Milan, 1994, pp. 158–63.

Ciardi Duprè Dal Poggetto 2002 = Maria Grazia Ciardi Duprè Dal Poggetto, 'Nota storico-critica al Riccardiano 2669', in Lazzi, Salvaert, Ciardi Duprè Dal Poggetto 2002, pp. 139–45.

Ciardini 1907 = Marino Ciardini, *I banchieri ebrei in Firenze nel secolo XV e il Monte di Pietà fondato da Girolamo Savonarola. Appunti di storia economica con appendice di documenti*, Borgo San Lorenzo 1907 (anastatic reprint, Florence, 1970).

Cibecchini, Gambogi 2003 = Franca Cibecchini, Pamela Gambogi, 'Frammenti di archeologia fluviale in Toscana: da Florentia a Empoli lungo il corso dell'Arno', in *Puertos fluviales antiguos: ciudad, desarrollo e infraestructuras*, proceedings of the *IV Jornadas de Arqueología Subacuática* (València, 2001) edited by

Guillermo Pascual Berlanga, José Pérez Ballester, València 2003, pp. 251–60.

Cinozzi (*ante* 1503), ed. Villari, Casanova 1898 = Placido Cinozzi, 'Estratto d'una epistola de vita et moribus Reverendi Patris fratris Hieronimi Savonarole de Ferraria' (ante 1503), in *Scelta di prediche e scritti di Fra Girolamo Savonarola*, edited by Pasquale Villari and Eugenio Casanova, Florence, 1898, pp. 3–28.

Cipolla 1982 = Carlo Maria Cipolla, *Il fiorino e il quattrino. La politica monetaria a Firenze nel 1300*, Bologna, 1982.

La Città degli Uffizi 1982 = *La Città degli Uffizi. I musei del futuro*, exhibition catalogue (Florence, Palazzo Vecchio, 23 June 1982–6 January 1983), Florence, 1982.

La civiltà del cotto 1980 = *La civiltà del cotto. Arte della terracotta nell'area fiorentina dal XV al XX secolo*, exhibition catalogue (Impruneta, May-October 1980) edited by Antonio Paolucci, Impruneta, 1980.

Collobi Ragghianti 1974 = Licia Collobi Ragghianti, *Il libro de' disegni del Vasari*, Florence 1974, 2 vols.

Connell, Constable 2006 = William J. Connell, Giles Constable, *Sacrilegio e redenzione nella Firenze rinascimentale. Il caso di Antonio Rinaldeschi*, Florence 2006 (original edition with title *Sacrilege and Redemption in Renaissance Florence. The Case of Antonio Rinaldeschi*, Toronto, 2005).

Consorterie 1992 = *Consorterie politiche e mutamenti istituzionali in età laurenziana*, exhibition catalogue (Florence, Archivio di Stato, 4 May–30 July 1992) edited by Maria Augusta Morelli Timpanaro, Rosalia Manno Tolu, Paolo Viti, Florence, 1992.

Constitutum (1314–1407), ed. Ginori Conti 1939 = *Constitutum Artis Monetariorum Civitatis Florentie* (1314–1407), edited by Piero Ginori Conti, Florence, 1939.

Conti 1983 = Alessandro Conti, *I dintorni di Firenze*, Florence, 1983.

Conti 1984 = Elio Conti, *L'imposta diretta a Firenze nel Quattrocento (1427–1494)*, Rome 1984.

Cordero 2009 = Franco Cordero, *Savonarola*, Turin, 2009, 4 vols. (1st ed. Rome-Bari 1986–8).

Cotrugli (*ante* 1469), ed. Tucci 1990 = Benedetto Cotrugli, *Il libro dell'arte di mercatura* (*ante* 1469), edited by Ugo Tucci, Venice, 1990 (1st ed. with title *Della Mercatura e del Mercante perfetto*, Venice, 1563).

Cox-Rearick 1984 = Janet Cox-Rearick, *Dynasty and Destiny in Medici Art. Pontormo, Leo X, and the Two Cosimos*, Princeton, N.J., 1984.

Crowe, Cavalcaselle 1864–66 = Joseph A. Crowe, Giovan Battista Cavalcaselle, *A New History of Painting in Italy from Second to Sixteenth Century*, London 1864–66, 2 vols.

Cultural Links 2000 = *Cultural Links between Portugal and Italy in the Renaissance*, edited by Kate J.P. Lowe, Oxford, 2000.

D'Ancona 1906 = Paolo D'Ancona, *Le vesti delle donne fiorentine nel secolo XIV*, Perugia, 1906 (abstract from the Ferrari-Tonioli Wedding Miscellany).

D'Ancona 1914 = Paolo D'Ancona, *La miniatura fiorentina (Secoli XI–XVI)*, Florence, 1914, 2 vols.

Dalla testa ai piedi 2006 = *Dalla testa ai piedi. Costume e moda in età gotica*, proceedings of the symposium (Trento, 7–8 October 2002) edited by Laura Dal Prà and Paolo Peri, Trento, 2006.

Dalli Regoli 1966 = Gigetta Dalli Regoli, *Lorenzo di Credi*, Pisa, 1966.

Däuble-Hauschke 2003 = Claudia Däuble-Hauschke, *Geburt und 'Memoria'. Zum italienischen Bildtyp der 'deschi da parto'*, Munich-Berlin, 2003.

Davanzati (1581), ed. 1988 = Bernardo Davanzati, 'Notizia de' Cambj' (1581), ed. in Id., *Lezione delle Monete e Notizia de' Cambj*, with preface by Sergio Ricossa, Turin, 1988.

De La Mare 1976 = Albinia C. de La Mare, *The Library of Francesco Sassetti*, in *Cultural Aspects of the Italian Renaissance. Essays in Honour of Paul Oskar Kristeller*, edited by Cecil H. Clough, Manchester, 1976, pp. 160–201.

De La Mare 2000 = Albinia C. de La Mare, 'Notes on Portuguese Patrons of the Florentine Book Trade in the Fifteenth Century', in *Cultural Links* 2000, pp. 167–81.

De Marchi 1985 = Andrea de Marchi, 'Per la cronologia dell'Angelico: il Trittico di Perugia', in *Prospettiva*, 42, 1985, pp. 53–7.

De Robertis 1968 = Domenico de Robertis, 'Una proposta per Burchiello', in *Rinascimento*, 11, 1968, pp. 3–119.

De Roover 1948 = Raymond R. de Roover, *The Medici Bank: its Organization, Management, Operations and Decline*, New York, 1948.

De Roover 1953 = Raymond R. de Roover, *L'evolution de la lettre de change, XIV–XVIII siècles*, Paris 1953.

De Roover 1963 = Raymond R. de Roover, *The Rise and Decline of the Medici Bank (1397–1494)*, Cambridge, Mass., 1963; Italian edition with the title *Il banco Medici dalle origini al declino (1397–1494)*, translated by Gino Corti, Florence 1970 (anastatic reprint) Scandicci, 1988.

De Vries 2010 = Joyce de Vries, *Caterina Sforza and the Art of Appearances. Gender, Art and Culture in Early Modern Italy*, Farnham-Surrey, 2010.

Debby 2001 = Nirit Ben-Aryeh Debby, *Renaissance Florence in the Rhetoric of Two Popular Preachers. Giovanni Dominici (1356–1419) and Bernardino da Siena (1380–1444)*, Turnhout, 2001.

Degenhart, Schmitt 1968 = Bernard Degenhart, Annegrit Schmitt, *Corpus der Italienischen Zeichnungen, 1300–1450. Teil I. Süd und Mittelitalien*, Berlin, 1968, 4 vols.

Deimling 2009 = Barbara Deimling, 'Who Tames the Centaur? The Identification of Botticelli's Heroine', in *Sandro Botticelli* 2009, pp. 63–103.

Del Bravo 1985 = Carlo Del Bravo, 'Luca della Robbia', in id., *Le risposte dell'arte*, Florence 1985, pp. 29–51 (original edition with the title 'L'Umanesimo di Luca Della Robbia', in *Paragone*, 24, 1973, 285, pp. 3–34).

Del Lungo 1926 = Isidoro Del Lungo, *La donna fiorentina del buon tempo antico*, Florence, 1926 (1st ed. Florence, 1906).

Del Treppo 1968 = Mario Del Treppo, *I mercanti catalani e l'espansione della corona aragonese nel secolo XV*, Naples, 1968; 2nd edition with the title *I mercanti catalani e l'espansione della corona d'Aragona nel secolo XV*, Naples, 1972.

Del Treppo 1985 = Mario Del Treppo, 'Aspetti dell'attività bancaria a Napoli nel '400', in *Aspetti* 1985, pp. 557–601.

Del Treppo 1986 = Mario Del Treppo, 'Il re e il banchiere. Strumenti e processi di razionalizzazione dello stato aragonese di Napoli', in *Spazio, società, potere nell'Italia dei Comuni*, edited by Gabriella Rossetti, Naples, 1986, pp. 228–304.

Del Vita 1993 = Silvano Del Vita, 'Un dipinto botticelliano ritrovato: l'Incoronazione di Maria della chiesa di San Lodovico a Montevarchi', in *Atti e memorie dell'Accademia Petrarca di Lettere, Arti e Scienze*, 55, 1993 (1994), pp. 231–44.

Del Vivo 1776 = Biagio Costante Del Vivo, *Breve ragionamento intorno all'antica e miracolosa immagine del Santissimo Crocifisso detto volgarmente delle Grazie, posta nell'insigne Collegiata e prepositura di S. Andrea di Empoli*, Florence, 1776.

Deliberazione (1439), ed. Morelli 1881 = *Deliberazione Suntuaria del Comune di Fire-*

nze del XIII aprile 1439, Stefanini-Morelli wedding, edited by Giovanni Morelli, Florence, 1881.

I Della Robbia 2009 = *I Della Robbia. Il dialogo tra le arti nel Rinascimento*, exhibition catalogue (Arezzo, Museo Statale d'Arte Medioevale e Moderna, 2 February–7 June, 2009) edited by Giancarlo Gentilini in collaboration with Liletta Fornasari, Milan, 2009.

Desrosiers 2004 = Sophie Desrosiers, *Soierie et autres textiles de l'Antiquité au XVIe siècle*, Paris, 2004.

Di Domenico, Lippi 2005 = Cristina Di Domenico, Donatella Lippi, *I Medici: una dinastia ai raggi X*, Siena, 2005.

Dini 1982 = Bruno Dini, 'Lo sviluppo delle tecniche amministrative e bancarie', in *Storia della società italiana*, VII, *La crisi del sistema comunale*, Milan, 1982, pp. 99–109.

Dini, *L'economia* 1995 = Bruno Dini, 'L'economia fiorentina dal 1450 al 1530', in Dini, *Saggi* 1995, pp. 187–214 (1st ed. in *La Toscana al tempo di Lorenzo il Magnifico. Politica, economia, cultura, arte*, proceedings of the symposium (Florence, Pisa and Siena, 5–8 November,1992), Pisa, 1996, 3 vols., III, pp. 799–824).

Dini, *L'industria* 1995 = Bruno Dini, 'L'industria serica in Italia. Secc. XIII–XV', in Dini, *Saggi* 1995, pp. 51–85 (1st ed. in *La seta in Europa sec. XIII–XX*, proceedings of the *Ventiquattresima Settimana di Studi* (Prato, 4–9 May 1992) edited by Simonetta Cavaciocchi, Florence, 1993, pp. 91–124).

Dini, *Saggi* 1995 = Bruno Dini, *Saggi su un'economia-mondo: Firenze e l'Italia fra Mediterraneo ed Europa (secc. XIII–XVI)*, Pisa, 1995.

Dini, *Manifattura* 2001 = Bruno Dini, *Manifattura commercio e banca nella Firenze medievale*, Florence, 2001.

Dini, *Mercati* 2001 = Bruno Dini, 'Mercati e piazze bancarie nel mediterraneo e in Europa nei secoli XIV–XVI: presenze e strategie degli operatori economici fiorentini', in Dini, *Manifattura* 2001, pp. 103–24 (1st ed. in *Gli insediamenti economici e le loro logiche*, edited by Vincenzo Giura, Pisa, 1999, pp. 15–42).

Dini, *La ricchezza* 2001 = Bruno Dini, 'La ricchezza documentaria per l'arte della seta e l'economia fiorentina nel Quattrocento', in Dini, *Manifattura* 2001, pp. 9–44 (1st ed. in *Gli Innocenti e Firenze nei secoli. Un ospedale, un archivio, una città*, edited by Lucia Sandri, Florence, 1996, pp. 153–78).

Dini 2006 = Bruno Dini, 'I mercanti-banchieri italiani e le fiere di Ginevra e Lione (XV secolo–inizi XVI sec.)', in *L'Italia alla fine del Medioevo. I caratteri originali nel quadro europeo*, edited by Francesco Cengarle and Federica Salvestrini, Florence, 2006, 2 vols., I, pp. 433–56.

Dombrowski 2010 = Damian Dombrowski, *Die religiösen Gemälde Sandro Botticellis: Malerei als 'pia philosophia'*, Berlin, 2010.

Domestici 1995 = Fiamma Domestici, *I Della Robbia a Pistoia*, Florence, 1995.

Dominici (1410), ed. Salvi 1860 = Giovanni Dominici, *Regola del governo di cura familiare* (1410), edited by Donato Salvi, Florence, 1860.

Draper 1992 = James D. Draper, *Bertoldo di Giovanni: Sculptor of the Medici Household. Critical Reappraisal and Catalogue Raisonné*, Columbia, Mo., 1992.

Due provvisioni (1464–72), ed. Mazzi 1908 = *Due provvisioni suntuarie fiorentine, 29 novembre 1464, 29 febbraio 1471 [1472]*, Olschki-Finzi wedding, edited by Curzio Mazzi, Florence, 1908.

Dülberg 1990 = Angelica Dülberg, *Privatporträts. Geschichte und Ikonologie einer Gattung im 15. und 16. Jahrhundert*, Berlin, 1990.

Dürer 2007 = *Dürer e l'Italia*, exhibition catalogue (Rome, Palazzo del Quirinale, Scuderie Papali, 10 March–10 June 2007) edited by Kristina Herrmann Fiore, Milan, 2007.

Dunston 1968 = John Dunston, 'Studies in Domizio Calderini', in *Italia medioevale e umanistica*, 11, 1968, pp. 71–150.

Eco 2009 = Umberto Eco, *Vertigine della lista*, Milan, 2009.

Edler de Roover 1943 = Florence Edler de Roover, 'F. Sassetti and the Downfall of the Medici Banking House', in *Bulletin of the Business Historical Society*, 18, 1943, pp. 65–80.

Edler de Roover 1999 = Florence Edler de Roover, *L'arte della seta a Firenze nei secoli XIV e XV*, edited by Sergio Tognetti, Florence, 1999.

Elen 1995 = Albert Jan Elen, *Italian Late Medieval and Renaissance Drawing-Books, From Giovannino de' Grassi to Palma Giovane. A Codicological Approach*, Leiden, 1995 (Ph.D. Diss., Leiden, Rijksuniversiteit, 1995).

Eredità del Magnifico 1992 = *Eredità del Magnifico 1492–1992*, exhibition catalogue (Florence, Museo Nazionale del Bargello, 19 June–30 December, 1992) edited by Giovanna Gaeta Bertelà, Beatrice Paolozzi Strozzi, Marco Spallanzani, Florence, 1992.

Esch 1981 = Arnold Esch, 'Le importazioni nella Roma del primo Rinascimento (il loro volume secondo i registri doganali romani degli anni 1452–1462)', in *Aspetti della vita economica e culturale a Roma nel Quattrocento*, Rome, 1981, pp. 9–79.

Esch 2002 = Arnold Esch, 'Prolusione. Economia ed arte: la dinamica del rapporto nella prospettiva dello storico', in *Economia e arte secc. XIII–XVIII*, proceedings of the *Trentatreesima Settimana di Studi* (Prato, 30 April–4 May 2000) edited by Simonetta Cavaciocchi, Florence, 2002, pp. 21–49.

Et coquatur ponendo 1996 = *Et coquatur ponendo... Cultura della cucina e della tavola in Europa tra Medioevo ed età moderna*, exhibition catalogue (Prato, Istituto Internazionale di Storia Economica F. Datini, 1996), Prato, 1996.

Fabriczy 1895 = Cornelio de Fabriczy, 'Andrea del Verrocchio ai servizi de' Medici', in *Archivio storico dell'arte*, series 2a, I, 1895, pp. 163–76.

Fantappiè 1986 = Renzo Fantappiè, *Il bel Prato*, Prato, 1986, 2 vols.

Fantappiè 1987 = Renzo Fantappiè, 'Artisti e artigiani a Prato tra il XV e il XVI secolo', in *Archivio storico pratese*, 63, 1987, pp. 5–254.

Fantozzi 1842 = Federigo Fantozzi, *Nuova guida ovvero Descrizione storico-artistico-critica della città e contorni di Firenze*, Florence, 1842.

Ferri 1890 = Pasquale Nerino Ferri, *Catalogo riassuntivo della Raccolta di disegni antichi e moderni posseduti dalla R. Galleria degli Uffizi*, Florence, 1890.

Ferri 1895–1901 = Pasquale Nerino Ferri, *Catalogo dei disegni, cartoni e bozzetti esposti al pubblico nella R. Galleria degli Uffizi*, Florence, 1895–1901.

Feuillet 2010 = Michel Feuillet, *Botticelli et Savonarole. L'Humanisme à l'épreuve du feu*, Paris, 2010.

Filarete (*c.* 1464), ed. Finoli, Grassi 1972 = Antonio Averlino, known as Filarete, *Trattato di architettura* (*c.*1464), edited by Anna Maria Finoli and Liliana Grassi, Milan, 1972, 2 vols.

Filippino Lippi 2004 = *Filippino Lippi: un bellissimo ingegno. Origini ed eredità nel territorio pratese*, exhibition catalogue (Prato, Antiche Stanze di Santa Caterina, 8 May–25 July 2004) edited by Maria Pia Mannini, Florence, 2004.

Filippino Lippi forthcoming = *Filippino Lippi nella Firenze di Lorenzo de' Medici e Botticelli*, exhibition catalogue (Rome, Palazzo del Quirinale, Scuderie Papali) edited by Alessandro Cecchi, forthcoming.

Filippo e Filippino 2009 = *Filippo e Filippino. La Renaissance à Prato*, exhibition catalogue (Paris, Museé du Luxembourg, 25 March–2 August 2009) edited by Maria Pia Mannini and Cristina Gnoni Mavarelli, Cinisello Balsamo, 2009.

Fingerlin 1971 = Ilse Fingerlin, *Gürtel des hohen und späten Mittelalters*, Munich, 1971.

Firenze 2004 = *Firenze. Alle origini dello 'stile fiorentino'*, exhibition catalogue (Tokyo, Metropolitan Art Museum, 23 October–19 December 2004; Kyoto, Kyoto City Museum, 29 January–10 April 2005) edited by Maria Sframeli in collaboration with Michiaki Koshikawa, [titles and texts in Japanese/Italian; catalogue in Japanese], Tokyo, 2004.

Firenze e gli antichi Paesi Bassi 2008 = *Firenze e gli antichi Paesi Bassi 1430–1530. Dialoghi tra artisti: da Jan van Eyck a Ghirlandaio, da Memling a Raffaello...*, exhibition catalogue (Florence, Palazzo Pitti, Galleria Palatina, 20 June–26 October 2008) edited by Bert W. Meijer, Livorno, 2008.

Firenze e la sua immagine 1994 = *Firenze e la sua immagine. Cinque secoli di vedutismo*, exhibition catalogue (Florence, Forte Belvedere, 29 June–30 September 1994) edited by Marco Chiarini and Alessandro Marabottini, Venice, 1994.

Foville 1911 = Jean de Foville, 'Le Mino da Fiesole de la Bibliothèque Nationale', in *Gazette des Beaux-Arts*, series 4a, 5 (53/1), 1911, pp. 149–56.

Fra' Bartolomeo 1996 = *L'età di Savonarola. Fra' Bartolomeo e la Scuola di San Marco*, exhibition catalogue (Florence, Palazzo Pitti, Galleria Palatina-Museo di San Marco, 25 April–28 July 1996) edited by Serena Padovani in collaboration with Magnolia Scudieri and Giovanna Damiani, Venice, 1996.

Franceschi 1993 = Franco Franceschi, *Oltre il "Tumulto." I lavoratori fiorentini dell'Arte della Lana fra Tre e Quattrocento*, Florence, 1993.

Franceschi 1994 = Franco Franceschi, 'Istituzioni e attività economica a Firenze. Considerazioni sul governo del settore industriale (1350–1450)', in *Istituzioni e società in Toscana nell'età moderna*, proceedings of the symposium on Giuseppe Pansini (Florence, 4–5 December 1992), Rome, 1994, 2 vols., I, pp. 76–117.

Franceschi 2004 = Franco Franceschi, 'The Economy: Work and Wealth', in *Italy in the Age of the Renaissance*, edited by John M. Najemy, Oxford, 2004 (*Short Oxford History of Italy*, 3) (reprint Oxford 2005), pp. 124–44 and 277–80.

Francesco di Marco Datini 2010 = *Francesco di Marco Datini. L'uomo il mercante*, edited by Giampiero Nigro, Florence, 2010.

Franchetti Pardo, Casali 1978 = Vittorio Franchetti Pardo, Giovanna Casali, *I Medici nel contado fiorentino. Ville e possedimenti agricoli tra Quattrocento e Cinquecento*, Florence, 1978.

Il fratello di Masaccio 1999 = *Il fratello di Masaccio. Giovanni di Ser Giovanni detto lo Scheggia*, exhibition catalogue (San Giovanni Valdarno, Casa Masaccio, 14 February–16 May 1999) edited by Laura Cavazzini, Florence 1999.

Fremantle 1992 = Richard Fremantle, *God and Money. Florence and the Medici in the Renaissance, Including Cosimo I's Uffizi and its Collections*, Florence 1992; Italian edition with the title *Dio e denaro: Firenze e i Medici nel Rinascimento, transizione e riforma*, Florence, 2008.

Frick 2002 = Carol C. Frick, *Dressing Renaissance Florence. Families, Fortunes, and Fine Clothing*, Baltimore-London, 2002.

Friedländer 1972–3 = Max J. Friedländer, *Early Netherlandish Painting*, IX, *Joos van Cleve, Jan Provost, Joachim Patenier*, commentary and notes by Henri Pauwels assisted by Monique Gierts, translation by Heinz Norden, Leiden 1972–3, 2 parts.

Frosini 1993 = Giovanna Frosini, *Il cibo e i Signori. La mensa dei Priori di Florence nel quinto decennio del sec. XIV*, Florence, 1993.

Fusco, Corti 2006 = Laurie Fusco, Gino Corti, *Lorenzo de' Medici Collector and Antiquarian*, Cambridge, 2006.

Gabrielli 2007 = Edith Gabrielli, *Cosimo Rosselli. Catalogo ragionato*, Turin, 2007.

Gaetano Ballardini 2000 = *Gaetano Ballardini e la ceramica a Roma. Le maioliche del Museo Artistico Industriale*, exhibition catalogue (Faenza, Museo Internazionale delle Ceramiche-Deruta, Museo delle Maioliche, 15 October–31 December 2000), edited by Gian Carlo Bojani, Florence, 2000.

Gagliardi 2010 = Isabella Gagliardi, 'Il matrimonio in epoca medievale e rinascimentale', in *Virtù d'amore* 2010, pp. 25–33.

Galleria dell'Accademia 1999 = *Galleria dell'Accademia. Guida ufficiale. Tutte le opere*, Florence, 1999.

Galli 2003 = Aldo Galli, 'Risarcimento di Piero del Pollaiolo', in *Prospettiva*, 109, 2003 (2004), pp. 27–58.

Galli 2005 = Aldo Galli, *I Pollaiolo*, Milan, 2005.

Galoppini 2009 = Laura Galoppini, *Mercanti toscani e Bruges nel tardo Medioevo*, Pisa, 2009.

Gamba 1931–2 = Carlo Gamba, 'Opere giovanili del Botticelli', in *Bollettino d'arte*, 3rd series 3, 25, 1931–2, pp. 493–504.

Gareffi 1991 = Andrea Gareffi, *La scrittura e la festa*, Bologna, 1991.

Garfagnini 1999 = Gian Carlo Garfagnini, 'Savonarola e l'uso della stampa', in *Girolamo Savonarola. L'uomo* 1999, pp. 307–30.

Gargiolli 1868 = Girolamo Gargiolli, *L'Arte della Seta in Firenze. Trattato del secolo XV pubblicato per la prima volta, e Dialoghi*, Florence 1868 (anastatic reprint with facsimile of ms. Plut. 89 Cod. 117 of the Biblioteca Laurenziana di Firenze, Florence, 1980, 2 vols.).

Garzelli 1973 = Annarosa Garzelli, *Il ricamo nell'attività artistica di Pollaiolo, Botticelli, Bartolomeo di Giovanni*, Florence, 1973.

Garzelli 1985 = Annarosa Garzelli, 'Le immagini, gli autori, i destinatari', in *Miniatura fiorentina* 1985, I, pp. 5–391.

Gaye 1839–40 = Giovanni Gaye, *Carteggio inedito d'artisti dei secoli XIV, XV, XVI*, Florence 1839–40, 3 vols.

Gennaioli 2010 = Riccardo Gennaioli, 'La collezione di gemme dei Medici nel XV secolo', in *Pregio e bellezza* 2010, pp. 22–7.

Gentilini 1992 = Giancarlo Gentilini, *I Della Robbia. La scultura invetriata nel Rinascimento*, Florence, 1992.

Gentilini 2009 = Giancarlo Gentilini, 'La pittura "eterna" nel "parentado Della Robbia"', in *I Della Robbia* 2009, pp. 153–61.

Gerard-Marchant 1995 = Laurence Gerard-Marchant, 'Compter et nommer l'étoffe à Florence au Trecento (1343)', in *Medievales. Langue, textes, histoire*, 14, 1995, 29 (*L'étoffe et le vêtement*), pp. 87–104.

Gerola 1935 = Giuseppe Gerola, 'Le carte nautiche di Pietro Visconti dal punto di vista araldico', in *Atti del secondo Congresso di studi coloniali* (Naples, 1–5 October 1934), II, *Sezione: naturalistica-geografica*, Florence, 1935, pp. 101–23.

Ghirlandaio 2010 = *Ghirlandaio. Una famiglia di pittori del Rinascimento tra Firenze e Scandicci*, exhibition catalogue (Scandicci, Castello dell'Acciaiolo, 21 November 2010–1 May 2011) edited by Annamaria Bernacchioni, Florence, 2010.

Giacomotti 1974 = Jeanne Giacomotti, *Catalogue des majoliques des Musées Na-*

tionaux. Musées du Louvre et de Cluny, Musée National de Céramique à Sèvres, Musée Adrien-Dubouché à Limoges, Paris, 1974.

Giglioli 1933 = Orazio Hillyer Giglioli, 'Maso Finiguerra', in *Miscellanea di Storia dell'Arte in onore di Igino Benvenuto Supino*, edited by *Rivista d'Arte*, Florence, 1933, pp. 375–95.

Giovannozzi 1953 = Lucia Giovannozzi, *Contributo alla bibliografia delle opere del Savonarola: edizioni dei secc. XV e XVI*, Florence, 1953.

Giovinezza di Michelangelo 1999 = *Giovinezza di Michelangelo*, exhibition catalogue (Florence, Palazzo Vecchio, Sala d'Arme-Museo di Casa Buonarroti, 6 October 1999–9 January 2000) edited by Kathleen Weil-Garris Brandt, Cristina Acidini Luchinat, James David Draper, Nicholas Penny, Florence-Milan, 1999.

Girolamo Savonarola. L'uomo 1999 = *Girolamo Savonarola. L'uomo e il frate*, proceedings of international historical symposium (Todi, 11–14 October 1998), Spoleto, 1999.

Girolamo Savonarola. Storia 1999 = *Girolamo Savonarola. Storia, fede, arte*, edited by Giovanna Uzzani, Florence, 1999.

Gnocchi 1988 = Lorenzo Gnocchi, 'Le preferenze artistiche di Piero di Cosimo de' Medici', in *Artibus et Historiae*, 9, 1988, 18, pp. 41–78.

Goldthwaite 1968 = Richard A. Goldthwaite, *Private Wealth in Renaissance Florence. A Study of Four Families*, Princeton, N.J., 1968.

Goldthwaite 1980 = Richard A. Goldthwaite, *The Building of Renaissance Florence. An Economic and Social History*, Baltimore 1980; Italian edition with the title *La costruzione della Firenze rinascimentale. Una storia economica e sociale*, Bologna, 1984.

Goldthwaite 1985 = Richard A. Goldthwaite, 'Local Banking in Renaissance Florence', in *The Journal of European Economic History*, 14, 1985, pp. 5–55.

Goldthwaite 1987 = Richard A. Goldthwaite, 'The Medici Bank and the World of Florentine Capitalism', in *Past and Present*, 114, 1987, pp. 5–31.

Goldthwaite 1996 = Richard A. Goldthwaite, 'Lorenzo Morelli, Ufficiale del Monte, 1484–88: interessi privati e cariche pubbliche nella Firenze laurenziana', in *Archivio storico italiano*, 154, 1996, pp. 605–33.

Goldthwaite 2009 = Richard A. Goldthwaite, *The Economy of Renaissance Florence*, Baltimore, 2009.

Goldthwaite, Mandich 1994 = Richard A. Goldthwaite, Giulio Mandich, *Studi sulla moneta fiorentina*, Florence, 1994

Gombrich 1972 = Ernst H. Gombrich, *Symbolic Images. Studies in the Art of the Renaissance*, London-New York 1972 (original edition with the title 'Icones Symbolicae. The Visual Image in Neo-Platonic Thought', in *Journal of the Warburg and Courtauld Institutes*, 11, 1948, pp. 163–92); Italian edition with the title *Immagini simboliche. Studi sull'arte nel Rinascimento*, translation by Renzo Federici, Turin, 1978.

Goretti 2006 = Paola Goretti, 'Pellegrini, gentiluomini, mercanti. Le origini della borsa', in *Dalla testa ai piedi* 2006, pp. 577–603.

Gruyer 1879 = Gustave Gruyer, *Les illustrations des écrits de Jérome Savonarole publiées en Italie au XVe et XVIe siècles et les paroles de Savonarole sur l'art*, Paris, 1879.

Guida 1972 = *Guida alla Mostra internazionale di storia della Banca, secoli XIII–XVI. Nell'occasione del V centenario del Monte dei Paschi di Siena*, exhibition catalogue (Siena, Palazzo Salimbeni, 17 September–10 December 1972) edited by Federigo Melis, Siena, 1972.

Guidi Bruscoli 2007 = Francesco Guidi Bruscoli, 'Le tecniche bancarie', in *Il Rinascimento italiano e l'Europa*, IV, *Commercio e cultura mercantile*, edited by Franco Franceschi, Richard A. Goldthwaite, Reinhold C. Mueller, Vicenza, 2007, pp. 543–66.

Guidi Bruscoli 2011 = Francesco Guidi Bruscoli, 'Circolazione di notizie e andamento dei mercati nel basso Medioevo', in *Fama e publica vox nel Medioevo*, proceedings of international symposium (Ascoli Piceno, 4–5 December 2009) edited by Antonio Rigon, Rome, 2011.

Guidotti 1984 = Alessandro Guidotti, 'Gli smalti in documenti fiorentini fra XIV e XV secolo', in *Annali della Scuola Normale Superiore di Pisa. Classe di Lettere e Filosofia*, 3rd series, 14, 1984, 2, pp. 621–68.

Guimbard 1992 = Catherine Guimbard, 'Appunti sulla legislazione suntuaria a Firenze dal 1281 al 1384', in *Archivio storico italiano* 150, 1992, pp. 57–81.

Hatfield, 'The Compagnia' 1970 = Rab Hatfield, 'The Compagnia de' Magi', in *Journal of the Warburg and Courtauld Institutes*, 33, 1970, pp. 107–61.

Hatfield, 'Some Unknown Descriptions' 1970 = Rab Hatfield, 'Some Unknown Descriptions of the Medici Palace in 1459', in *The Art Bulletin*, 52, 1970, pp. 232–49.

Hatfield 1976 = Rab Hatfield. *Botticelli's Uffizi* Adoration. *A Study in Pictorial Content*, Princeton, N.J., 1976.

Heers 1984 = Jacques Heers, *Genova nel Quattrocento. Civiltà mediterranea, grande capitalismo e capitalismo popolare*, translated by Piero Mastrorosa, Milan, 1984 (original edition with the title *Genês au XV siècle*, Paris, 1971).

Heiliges Römisches Reich 2006 = *Heiliges Römisches Reich Deutscher Nation 962 bis 1806. Altes Reich und neue Staaten 1495 bis 1806. Katalog*, exhibition catalogue (Berlin, Deutschen Historischen Museums, 28 August–10 Decembere 2006) edited by Hans Ottomeyer, Jutta Götzmann, Ansgar Reiss, Dresden, 2006.

Helas 2004 = Philine Helas, 'Die Predigt in der Weltenlandschaft. Zur Agitation von Fra Marco da Montegallo für den Monte di Pietà in einem Stich von Francesco Rosselli (ca. 1485)', in *Marburger Jahrbuch für Kunstwissenschaft*, 31, 2004, pp. 105–44.

Henderson 1994 = John Henderson, *Piety and Charity in Late Medieval Florence*, Oxford, 1994.

Herald 1981 = Jacqueline Herald, *Renaissance Dress in Italy 1400–1500*, London, 1981.

Hind 1936 = Arthur Mayger Hind, *Nielli Chiefly Italian of the XV Century. Plates, Sulphur Casts and Prints Preserved in the British Museum*, London, 1936.

Höfler 1992 = Janez Höfler, 'New Light on Andrea Sansovino's Journey to Portugal', in *The Burlington Magazine*, 134, 1992, pp. 234–38.

Holst 1974 = Christian von Holst, *Francesco Granacci*, Munich, 1974.

Horne 1908 = Herbert Percy Horne, *Alessandro Filipepi commonly called Sandro Botticelli painter of Florence*, London 1908; edited by Caterina Caneva, with anastatic reproduction, Italian translation by Caterina Caneva and Serena Gavioli, *Addenda* by Caterina Caneva and Giovanna Giusti, [English/Italian], Florence, 1986, 2 vols.

Horne 1987 = Herbert Percy Horne, *Appendice III. Catalogo delle opere di Sandro Botticelli e dei suoi allievi e imitatori, con note relative alle opere erroneamente attribuitegli nelle collezioni pubbliche e private d'Europa e d'America*, unpublished Appendix to the 1908 monograph, edited by Caterina Caneva, [Italian/English], Florence, 1987, 2 vols.

Horowitz 2003 = Maryanne Cline Horowitz, 'Humanist Horticulture.

Twelve Agricultural Months and Twelve Categories of Books in Piero de' Medici's "Studiolo"', in *Viator*, 34, 2003, pp. 272–307.

Hoshino 1980 = Hidetoshi Hoshino, *L'Arte della Lana in Firenze nel basso Medioevo. Il commercio della lana e il mercato dei panni fiorentini nei secoli XIII–XV*, Florence, 1980.

Hoshino 1988 = Hidetoshi Hoshino, *I rapporti economici tra l'Abruzzo aquilano e Firenze nel basso Medioevo*, L'Aquila, 1988.

Hoshino, 'Il commercio' 2001 = Hidetoshi Hoshino, 'Il commercio fiorentino nell'Impero ottomano: costi e profitti negli anni 1484–1488', in Hoshino, *Industria* 2001, pp. 113–23 (1st ed. in *Aspetti* 1985, pp. 81–90).

Hoshino, *Industria* 2001 = Hidetoshi Hoshino, *Industria tessile e commercio internazionale nella Florence del tardo Medioevo*, edited by Franco Franceschi and Sergio Tognetti, Florence, 2001.

Hughes 2002 = Diane O. Hughes, 'Sumptuary Laws and Social Relations in Renaissance Italy', in *The Italian Renaissance. The Essential Readings*, edited by Paula Findlen, Malden, Ma., 2002, pp. 124–50.

Hunt 1994 = Edwin S. Hunt, *The Medieval Super-Companies. A Study of the Peruzzi Company of Florence*, Cambridge, 1994.

Huvenne 1997 = Paul Huvenne, 'Il Cinquecento e lo "stile nuovo"', in *La pittura nei Paesi Bassi*, edited by Bert W. Meijer, Milan, 1997, 3 vols., I, pp. 147–278.

Ibn Jaldún 2006 = *Ibn Jaldún. El Mediterraneo en el siglo 14. Auge y declive de los Imperios*, exhibition catalogue (Seville, Real Alcázar, 19 May–30 September 2006), Seville, 2006, 2 vols. ([I], *Catálogo de piezas*; [II], *Estudios*).

Immaginare l'autore 1998 = *Immaginare l'autore. Il ritratto del letterato nella cultura umanistica. Ritratti riccardiani*, exhibition catalogue (Florence, Biblioteca Riccardiana, 26 March–27 June 1998) edited by Giovanna Lazzi, Florence, 1998.

L'immagine ritrovata 2010 = *L'immagine ritrovata. La Trinità dei coniugi Datini*, exhibition catalogue (Prato, Palazzo Datini, Museo Casa Francesco Datini, 2 October 2010–9 January 2011) [edited by Maria Pia Mannini and Cristina Gnoni Mavarelli], Prato-Florence, 2010.

In the Light of Apollo 2004 = *In the Light of Apollo. Italian Renaissance and Greece*, exhibition catalogue (Athens, Ethnikē Pinakothēkē kai Museio Alexandru Sutzu, 22 December 2003–31 March 2004) edited by Mina Gregori, Cinisello Balsamo, 2003–2004, 2 vols., I, 2004.

Indice 1943–81 = *Indice generale degli incunaboli delle biblioteche d'Italia*, edited by the Centro Nazionale d'Informazioni Bibliografiche, Rome, 1943–81, 6 vols.

Inventario (1492), ed. Spallanzani, Gaeta Bertelà 1992 = *Libro d'inventario dei beni di Lorenzo il Magnifico* (1492), edited by Marco Spallanzani and Giovanna Gaeta Bertelà, Florence, 1992.

Italian Paintings 2003 = *Italian Paintings of the Fifteenth Century. National Gallery of Art, Washington*, edited by Miklós Boskovits and David Alan Brown, New York, 2003.

Itinerari 1994 = *Itinerari nella casa fiorentina del Rinascimento*, edited by Elisabetta Nardinocchi, Florence, 1994

Jacopo da Cessole (*c.*1300), ed. Boyle 1988 = [Jacopo da Cessole], *Das Schachbuch des Jacobus de Cessolis, Codex Palatinus Latinus 961, entstanden 1458* (*c.*1300), edited by Leonardus E. Boyle, Zurich, 1988.

Jacopo da Cessole (*c.*1300), ed. Marocco 1829 = Jacopo da Cessole, *Volgarizzamento del libro de' costumi e degli offizii de' nobili sopra il giuoco degli scacchi. Tratto nuovamente da un codice magliabechiano* (*c.*1300), [edited by Pietro Marocco], Milan, 1829.

Joannides 1995 = Paul Joannides, 'Late Botticelli: Archaism and Ideology', in *Arte cristiana*, new series, 83, 1995, pp. 163–78.

Kämmerer 1899 = Ludwig Kämmerer, *Memling*, Bielefeld-Leipzig, 1899.

Kennedy 1964 = Clarence Kennedy, 'The Cardinal James of Portugal', in Frederick Hartt, Gino Corti, Clarence Kennedy, *The Chapel of the Cardinal of Portugal 1433–1459*, Philadelphia, 1964, pp. 27–46.

Kent 2000 = Dale V. Kent, *Cosimo de' Medici and the Florentine Renaissance. The Patron's Oeuvre*, New Haven-London 2000; it. edition: *Il committente e le arti: Cosimo de' Medici e il Rinascimento fiorentino*, transl. by Marina Peri, Milan 2005

King 1991 = Margaret King, *Women of the Renaissance*, Chicago, 1991.

Klapisch-Zuber 1988 = Christiane Klapisch-Zuber, *La famiglia e le donne nel Rinascimento a Firenze*, Rome, 1988.

Klein 1960 = Robert Klein, *Il processo di Girolamo Savonarola*, Italian edition edited by Giuseppe Guglielmi, Bologna 1960 (original edition with the title *Le Procès de Savonarole*, with an introduction by Augustin Renaudet, Paris, 1957).

Kluckert 1974 = Ehrenfried Kluckert, 'Die Simultanbilder Memlings, ihre Wurzeln und Wirkungen', in *Das Münster*, 27, 1974, pp. 284–95.

Koch 2010 = Linda A. Koch, 'Power, Prophecy, and Dynastic Succession in Early Medici Florence: the Falcon Impresa of Piero di Cosimo de' Medici', in *Zeitschrift für Kunstgeschichte*, 73, 2010, 4, pp. 507–38.

Kohlhaussen 1968 = Heinrich Kohlhaussen, *Nürnberger Goldschmiedekunst des Mittelalters und der Dürerzeit 1240 bis 1540*, Berlin, 1968.

Kramer 1995 = Karl-Sigmund Kramer, *Bauern, Handwerker und Bürger im Schachzabelbuch. Mittelalterliche Ständegliederung nach Jacobus de Cessolis*, Munich, 1995.

Kretschmer 1909 = Konrad Kretschmer, *Die italienischen Portolane des Mittelalters. Ein Beitrag zur Geschichte der Kartographie und Nautik*, Berlin 1909 (anastatic reprint, Hildesheim, 1962).

Kreytenberg 1989 = Gert Kreytenberg, 'L'Enfer d'Orcagna. La première peinture monumentale d'après les Chants de Dante', in *Gazette des Beaux-Arts*," 6th series, 114, 1989, pp. 243–62.

Kreytenberg 2000 = Gert Kreytenberg, *Orcagna, Andrea di Cione. Ein universeller Künstler der Gotik in Florenz*, Mainz am Rhein, 2000.

Kubiak 1974 = Richard J. Kubiak, *Maso Finiguerra*, Ann Arbor, Mich., 1974 (Ph.D. Diss., Charlottesville, Va., Virginia University, [s.a.]).

La Roncière, Mollat du Jourdin 1984 = Monique de La Roncière, Michel Mollat du Jourdin, *Portulane. Seekarten vom 13. bis zum 17. Jahrhundert*, Munich, 1984 (original edition in French with the title *Les Portulans. Cartes marines du XIIIe au XVIIe siècle*, Paris, 1984).

Lagabrielle 2000 = Sophie Lagabrielle, 'Miroirs et "faiseurs" e miroirs au Moyen Âge et à la Renaissance', in *Miroirs. Jeux et reflets depuis l'Antiquité*, exhibition catalogue (Rouen, Musée Départemental des Antiquités de la Seine-Maritime; Dieppe, Musée; Bernay, Musée Municipal des Beaux-Arts; 28 October 2000–9 January 2001) edited by Geneviève Sennequier, Paris, 2000, pp. 112–19.

Landucci (1450-1542), ed. Del Badia 1883 = Luca Landucci, *Diario Fiorentino dal 1450 al 1516*, continued by anonymous author up to 1542, published in the codices of the Siena Comunale Siena and of the Marucelliana, edited by Iodoco Del Badia, Florence, 1883.

Lanfredini (1485–6), ed. Scarton 2002 = *Corrispondenza degli ambasciatori fiorentini a Napoli*, II, *Giovanni Lanfredini (maggio 1485–ottobre 1486)*, edited by Elisabetta Scarton, Naples, 2002.

Langedijk 1981–7 = Karla Langedijk, *The Portraits of the Medici, 15th–18th Centuries*, Florence 1981–7, 3 vols.

Lapi Ballerini 1986 = Isabella Lapi Ballerini, 'Alcune aggiunte al pratese Tommaso di Piero Trombetto', in *Antichità Viva*, 25, 1986, 4, pp. 18–32.

Lastri 1821 = [Marco Lastri], 'Canto al Diamante, e lusso delle donne', in [Marco Lastri], *L'Osservatore Fiorentino sugli edifizi della sua Patria*, 3rd ed. with addition of various notes by Professor Giuseppe Del Rosso, Florence, 1821, 8 tomes, VI, pp. 83–94.

Lastri 1831 = [Marco Lastri], 'Botteghe d'Orefici, Argentieri, Gioillieri [sic], e Incisioni in Gemme sul Ponte Vecchio', in [Marco Lastri], *L'Osservatore Fiorentino sugli edifizi della sua Patria*, 4th ed. with addenda and corrections by Sig. Cav. Prof. Giuseppe Del Rosso, Florence, 1831, 16 tomes, VI, pp. 57–63.

272

Lavagnino 1940 = Emilio Lavagnino, *Gli artisti italiani in Portogallo*, Rome, 1940.

Lazzi 1994 = Giovanna Lazzi, 'Novità e persistenze nelle tipologie vestimentarie al tempo del concilio: dalla moda "alla franciosa" a quella "all'orientale"', in *Firenze e il Concilio del 1439*, proceedings of symposium (Florence, 29 November–2 December 1989) edited by Paolo Viti, Florence, 1994, pp. 389–405.

Lazzi, Salvaert, Ciardi Duprè Dal Poggetto 2002 = Giovanna Lazzi, Vicente L. Salavaert, Maria Grazia Ciardi Dupré Dal Poggetto, 'Tratado de aritmética de Lorenzo el Magnífico: ilustrado por Pedro Berruguete', commentary to the facsimile of ms. Ricc. 2669 at the Biblioteca Riccardiana di Firenze, [text in Spanish, English and Italian], Valencia [2002], pp. 139–45.

Le Goff 2007 = Jacques Le Goff, *La borsa e la vita. Dall'usuraio al banchiere*, translation by Sabina Addamiano, Rome-Bari 2007 (original edition with the title *La bourse et la vie. Economie et religion au Moyen Age*, Paris, 1986).

Legge suntuaria (1355), ed. Fanfani 1851 = *Legge suntuaria fatta dal Comune di Firenze l'anno 1355 e volgarizzata nel 1556 da Ser Andrea Lancia*, edited by Pietro Fanfani, Florence, 1851.

Legge suntuaria (1456), ed. Pellegrini 1898 = *Legge suntuaria fiorentina del febbraio 1455 (1456)*, Mancini-D'Achiardi wedding, edited by Francesco Carlo Pellegrini, Livorno, 1898.

Lethaby 1906 = W.R. [*sic*] Lethaby, 'Majolica Roundels of the Month of the Year at the Victoria and Albert Museum', in *The Burlington Magazine*, 9, 1906, pp. 404–7.

Levi Pisetzky 1964–69 = Rosita Levi Pisetzky, *Storia del costume in Italia*, Milan, 1964–69, 5 vols.

Levi Pisetzky 1978 = Rosita Levi Pisetzky, *Il costume e la moda nella società italiana*, Turin, 1978.

The Libelle (1436), ed. Warner 1926 = *The Libelle of Englyshe Polycye. A Poem on the Use of Sea-Power, 1436*, edited by George Warner, Oxford, 1926.

El libro (*c.*1458), ed. Borlandi 1936 = *El libro di mercatantie et usanze de' paesi* (*c.*1458), [edited by] Franco Borlandi, Turin, 1936.

Liebenwein 1988 = Wolfgang Liebenwein, *Studiolo. Storia e tipologia di uno spazio culturale*. Modena, 1988 (original edition with the title *Studiolo. Die Entstehung eines Raumtyps und seine Entwicklung bis um 1600*, Berlin, 1977).

Liebenwein 1993 = Wolfgang Liebenwein, 'Die "Privatisierung" des Wunders: Piero de' Medici in SS. Annunziata und San Miniato', in *Piero de' Medici* 1993, pp. 251–90.

Lightbown 1978 = Ronald W. Lightbown, *Sandro Botticelli*, London. 1978, 2 vols. (I, *Life and Work*; II, *Complete Catalogue*).

Lightbown 1992 = Ronald W. Lightbown, *Medieval European Jewellery*, London, 1992.

Limentani Virdis 1974 = Caterina Limentani Virdis, 'Moralismo e satira nella tarda produzione di Quentin Metsys', in *Storia dell'arte*, 20, 1974, pp. 19–24.

Lippi 2006 = Donatella Lippi, *Illacrimate sepolture. Curiosità e ricerca scientifica nella storia delle riesumazioni dei Medici*, Florence, 2006.

Liscia Bemporad 1994 = Dora Liscia Bemporad, 'Suppellettili preziose nella casa fiorentina del Quattrocento', in *Itinerari* 1994, pp. 65–77.

Liscia Bemporad 2002 = Dora Liscia Bemporad, 'Per Andrea del Verrocchio orafo', in *Medioevo e Rinascimento*, new series, 13 (16), 2002, pp. 189–206.

Liscia Bemporad 2005 = Dora Liscia Bemporad, 'La legatura del Libro d'Ore di Lorenzo il Magnifico', in *Il Libro d'Ore di Lorenzo il Magnifico*, edited by Franca Arduini, Modena, 2005, pp. 225–37.

Lomastro Tognato 1996 = Francesca Lomastro Tognato, *Legge di Dio e Monti di Pietà. Marco da Montegallo 1425–1496*, Vicenza, 1996.

Lorenzi 1998 = Lorenzo Lorenzi, *Agnolo di Polo. La scultura in terracotta dipinta nella Firenze di fine Quattrocento*, Ferrara, 1998.

Lorenzo dopo Lorenzo 1992 = *Lorenzo dopo Lorenzo. La fortuna storica di Lorenzo il Magnifico*, exhibition catalogue (Florence, Biblioteca Nazionale Centrale, 4 May–30 June 1992) edited by Paola Pirolo, Cinisello Balsamo, 1992.

Lorenzo Ghiberti 1978 = *Lorenzo Ghiberti: 'materia e ragionamenti'*, exhibition catalogue (Florence, Galleria dell'Accademia and Museo di San Marco, 18 October 1978–31 January 1979) edited by Luciano Bellosi, Florence, 1978.

Lowe 2000 = Kate J.P. Lowe, 'Rainha D. Leonor of Portugal's Patronage in Renaissance Florence and Cultural Exchange', in *Cultural Links* 2000, pp. 225–48.

Lurati 2010 = Patricia Lurati, 'Vesti nuziali nella Firenze rinascimentale', in *Virtù d'amore* 2010, pp. 45–9.

Luschino (1523), ed. Dall'Aglio 2002 = Benedetto Luschino, *Vulnera diligentis* (1523), edited by Stefano Dall'Aglio, Florence, 2002.

Luzzati, Galasso 1996 = Michele Luzzati, Cristina Galasso, 'Primi appunti su Girolamo Savonarola e gli ebrei dello stato fiorentino', in *Studi savonaroliani* 1996, pp. 35–40.

Lydecker 1987 = John K. Lydecker, 'Il patriziato fiorentino e la committenza artistica per la casa', in *I ceti dirigenti nella Toscana del Quattrocento*, proceedings of symposium (Florence, 10–11 December 1982; 2–3 December 1983), Monte Oriolo, 1987, pp. 211–21.

Lydecker 1989 = John K. Lydecker, *The Domestic Setting of the Arts in Renaissance Florence*, Ann Arbor, Mich., 1989 (Ph.D. Diss., Baltimore, Md., John Hopkins University, 1987).

Machiavelli (1497–1513), ed. Gaeta 1961 = Niccolò Machiavelli, *Lettere* (1497–1513), edited by Franco Gaeta, Milan, 1961.

Machiavelli 1532, ed. Mansfield 1988 = Niccolò Macchiavelli, *Istorie fiorentine*, Florence, 1532; edition with the title *Florentine Histories*, English translation by Laura F. Banfield and Harvey C. Mansfield, Jr., introduction by Harvey C. Mansfield, Jr., Princeton, N.J., 1988.

Machiavelli 1532, ed. Montevecchi 2007 = Niccolò Macchiavelli, 'Istorie fiorentine', Florence 1532; published in Id, *Istorie fiorentine e altre opere storiche e politiche*, edited by Alessandro Montevecchi, Turin, 2007.

Macinghi Strozzi (1447–70), ed. Bianchini 1987 = Alessandra Macinghi Strozzi, *Tempo di affetti e di mercanti. Lettere ai figli esuli* (1447–1470), edited by Angela Bianchini, Milan, 1987.

Maestri e botteghe 1992 = *Maestri e botteghe. Pittura a Firenze alla fine del Quattrocento*, exhibition catalogue (Florence, Palazzo Strozzi, 16 October 1992–10 January 1993) edited by Mina Gregori, Antonio Paolucci, Cristina Acidini Luchinat, Cinisello Balsamo, 1992.

Malgouyres 2010 = Philippe Malgouyres, *Ivoires de la Renaissance et des Temps modernes. La collection du Musée du Louvre*, Paris, 2010.

Mallett 1967 = Michael E. Mallett, *The Florentine Galleys in the Fifteenth Century, with the Diary of Luca degli Albizzi, 142-1430*, Oxford 1967.

Mandel 1967 = Gabriele Mandel, *L'opera completa del Botticelli*, presentation by Carlo Bo, Milan, 1967.

Le marchands 2002 = *Les marchands de la Hanse et la banque des Médicis: Bruges, marché d'échanges culturels en Europe*, exhibition catalogue (Bruges, Palais Provincial, 24 May–8 September 2002) edited by André Vandewalle, Bruges, 2002.

Marco da Montegallo 1999 = *Marco da Montegallo (1425–1496). Il tempo, la vita, le opere*, proceedings of the symposium (Ascoli Piceno, 12 October 1996; Montegallo, 23 August 1997) edited by Silvano Bracci, Padua, 1999.

Mariani 1970 = Andrea Mariani, 'Avaro', entry in *Enciclopedia Dantesca*, I, Rome, 1970, pp. 464–5.

Marquand 1912 = Allan Marquand, *Della Robbias in America*, Princenton, 1912.

Marquand 1919 = Allan Marquand, *Robbia Heraldry*, Princenton 1919.

Martelli (1433–1483), ed. Pezzarossa 1989 = Ugolino di Niccolò Martelli, *Ricordanze dal 1433 al 1483*, edited by Fulvio Pezzarossa, Rome, 1989.

Martin Luther 1983 = *Martin Luther und die Reformation in Deutschland*, exhibition catalogue (Nürnberg, Germanisches Nationalmuseum, 25 June–25 September 1983) edited by Gerhard Bott, Frankfurt am Main, 1983.

Martines 2008 = Lauro Martines, *Savonarola. Moralità e politica a Firenze nel Quattrocento*, Milan, 2008 (original ed. with the title *Savonarola and the Struggle for Renaissance Florence*, Oxford-New York, 2006).

Masters of Florence 2004 = *Masters of Florence. Glory & Genius of the Court of the Medici*, exhibition catalogue (Memphis, The Pyramid, 23 April–3 October 2004) edited by Annamaria Giusti with Cristina Acidini Luchinat, Memphis, 2004.

Matteo Civitali 2004 = *Matteo Civitali e il suo tempo. Pittori, scultori e orafi a Lucca nel tardo Quattrocento*, exhibition catalogue (Lucca, Museo Nazionale di Villa Guinigi, 3 April–11 July 2004), Milan, 2004.

Mazzi 1991 = Maria Serena Mazzi, *Prostitute e lenoni nella Firenze del Quattrocento*, Milan, 1991.

Medioevo 1981 = *Medioevo e produzione artistica di serie. Smalti di Limoges e avori gotici in Campania*, exhibition catalogue (Naples, Museo Duca di Martina, October 1981–April 1982) edited by Paola Giusti, Pierluigi Leone de Castris, Florence, 1981.

Mejer 2008 = Bert W. Mejer, 'Firenze e gli antichi Paesi Bassi: una stagione di contiguità culturale del tutto particolare', in *Firenze e gli antichi Paesi Bassi* 2008, pp. 16–21.

Melis 1962 = Federigo Melis, *Aspetti della vita economica medievale (Studi nell'Archivio Datini di Prato)*, Siena, 1962.

Melis 1970 = Federigo Melis, 'Di alcune figure di operatori economici fiorentini attivi nel Portogallo del XV secolo', in *Fremde Kaufleute auf der Iberischen Halbinsel*, proceedings of international conference (Köln, 16–19 April 1967) edited by Hermann Kellenbenz, Köln 1970 (*Kölner Kolloquien zur internationalen Sozial- und Wirtschaftgeschichte*' 1), pp. 56–73; then in Id., *I mercanti italiani nell'Europa medievale e rinascimentale*, edited by Luciana Frangioni, introduction by Hermann Kellenbenz, Florence, 1990, pp. 1–18.

Melis 1972 = Federigo Melis, *Documenti per la storia economica dei secoli XIII–XVI*, with a note on commercial palaeography by Elena Cecchi, Florence, 1972.

Melis 1975 = Federigo Melis, *Origini e sviluppi delle assicurazioni in Italia (secoli XIV–XVI)*, I, *Le fonti*, introduction by Bruno Dini, Rome, 1975.

Melis, 'Industria' 1984 = Federigo Melis, 'Industria commercio credito (secoli XIV–XVI)', in Id., *L'economia fiorentina del Rinascimento*, with introduction by and edited by Bruno Dini, Florence 1984, pp. 31–185 (original edition with title 'Industria commercio e credito', in *Un'altra Firenze: l'epoca di Cosimo il Vecchio. Riscontri tra cultura e società nella storia fiorentina*, Florence, 1971, pp. 141–280).

Melis, 'I trasporti' 1984 = Federigo Melis, *I trasporti e le comunicazioni nel Medioevo*, edited by Luciana Frangioni, Florence, 1984.

Melis 1987 = Federigo Melis, 'Sulla non-astratezza dei titoli di credito del Basso Medioevo', in Federigo Melis, *La banca pisana e le origini della banca moderna*, edited by Marco Spallanzani, Florence, 1987

Melis 1990 = Federigo Melis, *I mercanti italiani nell'Europa medievale e rinascimentale*, edited by Luciana Frangioni, Florence, 1990

Melis 1991 = Federigo Melis, *L'azienda nel Medioevo*, edited by Marco Spallanzani, Florence, 1991.

Melli 1995 = Lorenza Melli, *Maso Finiguerra. I disegni*, Florence, 1995.

Melli 2007 = Lorenza Melli, 'I disegni dei Pollaiolo agli Uffizi', in *La stanza dei Pollaiolo. I restauri, una mostra, un nuovo ordinamento*, edited by Antonio Natali and Angelo Tartuferi, Florence, 2007 (*Gli Uffizi. Studi e Ricerche*, 16), pp. 55–72.

Mendes Atanázio 1963 = Manuel Cardoso Mendes Atanasio [Atanázio], 'Il cappuccio di piviale al Museo Poldi Pezzoli e altri paramenti della Cappella del Cardinale del Portogallo', in *Commentari*, 14, 1963, pp. 227–45.

Meneghin 1967 = Vittorino Meneghin, *Iconografia del B. Bernardino Tomitano da Feltre*,Venice, 1967.

Menning 1992 = Carol B. Menning, 'The Monte's "Monte": the Early Supporters of Florence's Monte di Pietà', in *The Sixteenth Century Journal*, 23, 1992, pp. 661–76.

Il mercante 2010 = *Il mercante, l'ospedale, i fanciulli. Francesco di Marco Datini, Santa Maria Nuova e la fondazione degli Innocenti*, exhibition catalogue (Florence, Spedale degli Innocenti, 27 November 2010–1 May 2011, edited by Stefano Filipponi, Eleonora Mazzocchi and Ludovica Sebregondi, Florence, 2010.

Michelozzo 1998 = *Michelozzo, scultore e architetto (1396–1472)*, proceedings of the symposium *Michelozzo, scultore e architetto nel suo tempo (1396–1472)* (Florence-San Piero a Sieve-Castello del Trebbio, 2–5 October 1996) edited by Gabriele Morolli, Florence, 1998.

Middeldorf 1976 = Ulrich Middeldorf, *Sculptures from the Samuel H. Kress Collection: european schools XIV-XIX century*, London 1976.

Mignani Galli 1977 = Daniela Mignani Galli, *La chiesa di San Jacopo di Ripoli*, Florence 1977.

Miniatura 2003 = *Miniatura del '400 a San Marco. Dalle suggestioni avignonesi all'ambiente dell'Angelico*, exhibition catalogue (Florence, Museo di San Marco, 1 April–30 June 2003) edited by Magnolia Scudieri and Giovanna Rasario, Florence, 2003.

Miniatura fiorentina 1985 = *Miniatura fiorentina del Rinascimento, 1440–1525: un primo censimento*, edited by Annarosa Garzelli, Florence, 1985, 2 vols.

Misteriosi scrigni 2001 = *Misteriosi scrigni. Borse della collezione Cristina Giorgetti dal XVII al XX secolo*, exhibition catalogue (Prato, Museo del Tessuto, 8 December–2 February 2002), Florence, 2001.

Miziolek 1996 = Jerzy Miziolek, *Soggetti classici sui cassoni fiorentini alla vigilia del Rinascimento*, Warsaw, 1996.

Miziolek 2010 = Jerzy Miziolek, 'I decori e le storie dipinte sui cassoni', in *Virtù d'Amore* 2010, pp. 69–77.

Moffitt 2008 = John F. Moffitt, 'Quentin Metsys's *The Money Changer and His Wife* (1514) and the Christological "Speculum humanae salvationis"', in *Arte cristiana*, 96, 2008, 848, pp. 359–64.

Molho 1971 = Anthony Molho, *Florentine Public Finances in the Early Renaissance, 1400–1433*, Cambridge, Mass., 1971.

Molho 2006 = Anthony Molho, 'Tre città-stato e i loro debiti pubblici. Quesiti e ipotesi sulla storia di Firenze, Genova e Venezia', in Id., *Firenze nel Quattrocento*, I, *Politica e fiscalità*, Rome, 2006, pp. 71–95.

Morçay 1914 = Raoul Morçay, *Saint Antonin, fondateur du Couvent de Saint-Marc, archevêque de Florence, 1389–1459*, Tours, 1914.

Moreira 2001 = Rafael Moreira, 'Andrea Sansovino au Portugal (1492–1501)', in *Revue de l'art*, 133, 2001, pp. 33–8.

Morolli 1998 = Gabriele Morolli, '"Sacella." I tempietti marmorei di Piero de' Medici: Michelozzo o Alberti?', in *Michelozzo* 1998, pp. 131–70.

Morolli 2006 = Gabriele Morolli, 'I sacelli e l'ornato', in *L'uomo del Rinascimento* 2006, pp. 295–8.

Morselli 1987 = Piero Morselli, *Tommaso di Piero Trombetto. Aspetti della pittura pratese, 1483–1530*, Prato, 1987.

Mostra d'arte 1969 = *Mostra d'arte sacra della Diocesi di San Miniato, 1969*, exhibition catalogue (San Miniato, Accademia degli Euteleti-Seminario Diocesano, 1969) edited by Luciano Bellosi, Dilvo Lotti, Anna Matteoli, San Miniato, 1969.

Mostra dei tesori 1960 =*Mostra dei tesori segreti delle case fiorentine*, exhibition catalogue (Florence, Circolo Borghese e della Stampa, 11 June–11 July 1960) edited by Mina Gregori in collaboration with Mina Bacci and Carlo Donzelli, Florence, 1960.

Mostra medicea 1939 = *Mostra medicea. Palazzo Medici Firenze*, exhibition catalogue (Florence, Palazzo Medici Riccardi, 1939), Florence, 1939.

Mottola Molfino 1984 = Alessandra Mottola Molfino, 'Ricami', in *Museo Poldi Pezzoli. Arazzi. Tappeti. Tessuti copti. Pizzi. Ricami. Ventagli*, Milan, 1984, pp. 321–408.

Mottola Molfino 1987 = Alessandra Mottola Molfino, 'Tessuti', in *Museo Poldi Pezzoli. Tessuti. Sculture. Metalli islamici*, Milan, 1987, pp. 13–188.

Mottola Molfino 1989 = Alessandra Mottola Molfino, 'Restaurare per conoscere', in *Botticelli* 1989, pp. 13–16.

Moxey 1985 = Keith P.F. Moxey, 'The Criticism of Avarice in Sixteenth-Century Netherlandish Painting', in *Netherlandish Mannerism*, proceedings of the symposium (Stockholm, 21–22 September 1984) edited by Görel Cavalli-Björkman, Stockholm, 1985, pp. 21–34.

Mueller 1997 = Reinhold C. Mueller, *The Venetian Money Market: Banks, Panics, and the Public Debt, 1200–1500*, Baltimore, 1997.

Mugello 2008 = *Mugello culla del Rinascimento: Giotto, Beato Angelico, Donatello e i Medici*, exhibition catalogue (Vicchio, Museo d'Arte Sacra e Religiosità Popolare Beato Angelico; Lucignano, San Piero a Sieve, Convento di San Bonaventura di Bosco ai Frati; Borgo San Lorenzo, Museo della Manifattura Chini; Scarperia, Palazzo dei Vicari: 29 May–30 November 2008) edited by Barbara Tosti, [Italian/English], Florence, 2008.

Municchi 1909 = Alfredo Municchi, *Una provvisione suntuaria della Repubblica Fiorentina*, Florence, 1909.

Munro 1982 = John Munro, 'Il bullionismo e la cambiale in Inghilterra, 1272–1663: politica monetaria e pregiudizio popolare', in *L'alba della banca. Le origini del sistema bancario tra Medioevo ed età moderna*, Bari, 1982, pp. 193–269.

Musacchio 2006 = Jaqueline M. Musacchio, 'Conception and Birth', in *At Home in Renaissance Italy*, exhibition catalogue (London, Victoria and Albert Museum, 5 October 2006–14 January 2007) edited by Marta Ajmar-Wollheim and Flora Dennis, London, 2006, pp. 124–35.

Musacchio 2008 = Jaqueline M. Musacchio, *Art, Marriage, and Family in the Florentine Renaissance Palace*, New Haven-London, 2008.

Il Museo del Tessuto 1999 = *Il Museo del Tessuto di Prato*, edited by Tamara Boccherini in collaboration with Patrizia Bogani de Liguori, Daniela Degl'Innocenti, Milan, 1999.

Museo di Villa Guinigi 1968 = *Museo di Villa Guinigi Lucca. La villa e le collezioni*, edited by Licia Bertolini Campetti and Silvia Meloni Trkulja, Lucca, 1968.

Il Museo Stibbert 1974 = *Il Museo Stibbert a Firenze. Volume secondo: catalogo*, edited by Giuseppe Cantelli, Milan, 1974, 2 tomes.

Il Museo Stibbert 1976 = *Il Museo Stibbert a Firenze. Volume quarto: i depositi e l'archivio*, edited by Lionello Boccia, Giuseppe Cantelli, Fosco Maraini, Milan, 1976, 2 tomes.

Muzzarelli 1978 = Maria Giuseppina Muzzarelli, 'Appunti per un'analisi della struttura dei "Sermones" di Bernardino da Feltre', in *Rivista di storia della Chiesa*, 32, 1978, pp. 153–80.

Muzzarelli 2001 = Maria Giuseppina Muzzarelli, *Il denaro e la salvezza. L'invenzione del Monte di Pietà*, Bologna, 2001.

Muzzarelli 2007 = Maria Giuseppina Muzzarelli, 'Il corpo spogliato. Multe, scomuniche e stratagemmi per il rispetto delle leggi suntuarie', in 'Le corps et sa parure', *Micrologus*, 15, 2007, pp. 399–423.

Mythologica et Erotica 2005 = *Mythologica et Erotica. Arte e cultura dall'antichità al XVIII secolo*, exhibition catalogue (Florence, Museo degli Argenti, 1 October 2005–15 January 2006) edited by Ornella Casazza and Riccardo Gennaioli, Livorno, 2005.

Nardi (*ante* 1563), ed. Gelli 1858 = Iacopo Nardi, *Istorie della città di Firenze* (*ante* 1563), edited by Agenore Gelli, Florence, 1858, 2 vols.

Natale 1982 = Mauro Natale, 'Dipinti', in *Museo Poldi Pezzoli. Dipinti*, Milan, 1982, pp. 63–488.

Natali 2002 = Antonio Natali, *Leonardo: il giardino delle delizie*, Cinisello Balsamo, 2002.

Navigare e descrivere 2001 = *Navigare e descrivere. Isolari e portolani del Museo Correr di Venezia XV–XVIII secolo*, exhibition catalogue (Venice, Museo Correr, 1 December 2001–1 April 2002) edited by Camillo Tonini and Piero Lucchi, Venice, 2001.

Negri Arnoldi 1970 = Francesco Negri Arnoldi, 'Scultura italiana al Victoria and Albert Museum', 2, in *Commentari*, 21, 1970, pp. 201–18.

Nelson 1949 = Benjamin Nelson, *The idea of Usury. From Tribal Brotherhood to Universal Otherhood*, 2nd edition augmented, II Chicago-London, 1969 (1st ed. Princeton 1949; Italian edition with title *Usura e cristianesimo. Per una storia della genesi dell'etica moderna*, Florence, 1967).

Niccoli 1997 = Ottavia Niccoli, 'I "fanciulli" del Savonarola: usi religiosi e politici dell'infanzia nell'Italia del Rinascimento', in *Savonarole* 1997, pp. 105–20.

Nigro 1994 = Giampiero Nigro, *Il tempo liberato. Festa e svago nella città di Francesco Datini*, Prato, 1994.

Nigro 2010 = Giampiero Nigro, 'Il mercante e la sua ricchezza', in *Francesco di Marco Datini* 2010, pp. 81–104.

Noonan 1957 = John T. Noonan, *The Scholastic Analysis of Usury*, Cambridge, Mass., 1957.

Nürnberg 1986 = *Nürnberg 1300–1550. Kunst der Gotik und der Renaissance*, exhibition catalogue (New York, Metropolitan Museum, 8 April–22 June 1986; Nürnberg, Germanisches Nationalmuseum, 25 July–28 September 1986) edited by Gerhard Bott and Philippe de Montebello, Munich, 1986.

L'officina della maniera 1996 = *L'officina della maniera. Varietà e fierezza nell'arte fiorentina del Cinquecento fra le due repubbliche 1494–1530*, exhibition catalogue (Florence, Galleria degli Uffizi, 28 September 1996–6 January 1997) edited by Alessandro Cecchi and Antonio Natali, Venice, 1996.

Offner 1962 = Richard Offner, *A Critical and Historical Corpus of Florentine Painting*, IV/1, *Tendencies of Gothic in Florence. Andrea di Cione*, New York, 1962.

Offner, Steinweg 1965 = Richard Offner with Klara Steinweg, *A Critical and Historical Corpus of Florentine Painting*, IV/3, *Tendencies of Gothic in Florence. Jacopo di Cione*, New York, 1965.

Oreficeria Sacra 1990 = *Oreficeria Sacra Italiana. Museo Nazionale del Bargello*, edited by Marco Collareta and Antonella Capitanio, Florence, 1990.

Origo 1957 = Iris Origo, *The Merchant of Prato Francesco di Marco Datini*, London, 1957.

Orsini 1760 = Ignazio Orsini, *Storia delle monete della Repubblica Fiorentina*, Florence, 1760.

Owen-Hughes 1986 = Diane Owen-Hughes, *Sumptuary Law and Social Relations in Renaissance Italy*, in *Disputes and Settlements. Law and Human Relations in the West*, edited by John Bossy, Cambridge, 1986, pp. 69–87.

Paatz 1940–54 = Walter Paatz, Elisabeth Paatz, *Die Kirchner von Florenz*, Frankfurt am Main 1940–54, 6 vols.

Padoa Rizzo 1987 = Anna Padoa Rizzo, 'La Cappella della Compagnia di Santa Barbara della "Nazione Tedesca" alla SS. Annunziata di Firenze nel XV secolo. Cosimo Rosselli e la sua "impresa" artistica', in *Antichità Viva*, 26, 1987, 3, pp. 3–18.

Padoa Rizzo 1993 = Anna Padoa Rizzo, 'La Cappella dei Magi nell'attività di Benozzo Gozzoli', in *Benozzo Gozzoli* 1993, Milan, 1993, pp. 357–62.

Padoa Rizzo 2001 = Anna Padoa Rizzo, 'Cosimo and Bernardo Rosselli's Work for Lay Confraternities', in *Cosimo Rosselli Painter of the Sistine Chapel*, exhibition catalogue (Winter Park, Fla., George D. and Harriet W. Cornell Fine Arts Museum, 9 February–22 April 2001) edited by Arthur R. Blumenthal, Winter Park, 2001, pp. 61–73.

Palazzo Davanzati 1986 = *Palazzo Davanzati*, edited by Maria Fossi Todorow, 2nd ed., Florence, 1986.

Il Palazzo Portinari-Salviati 1960 = *Il Palazzo Portinari-Salviati, oggi proprietà della Banca Toscana*, edited by Guido Pampaloni, Florence, 1960.

Palermo 2000 = Luciano Palermo, 'La finanza pontificia e il banchiere "depositario" nel primo Quattrocento', in *Studi in onore di Ciro Manca*, edited by Donatella Strangio, Padua, 2000, pp. 349–78.

Palermo 2008 = Luciano Palermo, *La banca e il credito nel Medioevo*, Milan, 2008.

Pampaloni 1963 = Guido Pampaloni, *Palazzo Strozzi*, Rome, 1963.

Panella 1909 = Antonio Panella, 'Una sentenza di Niccolò Porcinari, potestà di Firenze e una minaccia di rappresaglie degli aquilani contro i fiorentini', in *Rivista abruzzese di scienze, lettere e arti*, 24, 1909, 337–67.

Paoletti 1994 = John T. Paoletti, 'The Banco Mediceo in Milan. Urban Politics and Family Power', in *The Journal of Medieval and Renaissance Studies*, 24, 1994, pp. 199–238.

Paolozzi Strozzi 1984 = Beatrice Paolozzi Strozzi, *Monete fiorentine dalla Repubblica ai Medici*, exhibition catalogue (Florence, Museo Nazionale del Bargello, 7 April–15 June 1984), Florence, 1984.

Paolucci 1980 = Antonio Paolucci, 'Le ceramiche', in *Gli Uffizi. Catalogo generale*, Florence, 1980, pp. 1107–13.

Paolucci 1985 = Antonio Paolucci, *Il Museo della Collegiata di S. Andrea in Empoli*, Florence, 1985.

Parenti (1464–67), ed. Doni Garfagnini 2001 = Marco Parenti, *Ricordi storici, 1464–1467*, edited by Manuela Doni Garfagnini, Rome, 2001

.

Parenti (*ante* 1519), ed. Matucci 1994–2005 = Piero di Marco Parenti, *Storia fiorentina* (*ante* 1519), edited by Andrea Matucci, Florence 1994–2005, 2 vols. (I, *1476–1478, 1492–1496*; II, *1496–1502*).

Parks 2006 = Tim Parks, *La fortuna dei Medici. Finanza, teologia e arte nella Firenze del Quattrocento*, translated by Silvia Artoni, Milan, 2006 (original edition with the title *Medici Money. Banking, Metaphysics, and Art in Fifteenth-Century Florence*, New York, 2005).

Partsch 1981 = Susanna Partsch, *Profane Buchmalerei der Bürgerlichen Gesellschaft in Spätmittelalterlichen Florenz. Der Specchio Umano des Getreidehändlers Domenico Lenzi*, Worms, 1981.

Passalacqua 2004 = Silvia Passalacqua, 'La storia di Lucrezia fra Medioevo e Rinascimento', in *Ritratto e biografia. Arte e cultura dal Rinascimento al Barocco*, proceedings of the symposium *Biografia e ritratto paradigmatico nell'arte italiana ed europea dal Rinascimento al Barocco* (Siena, 8–9 October 2003) edited by Roberto Guerrini, Maddalena Sanfilippo, Paolo Torriti, Sarzana 2004, pp. 205–21.

Patetta 1998 = Luciano Patetta, 'Il caso di Michelozzo a Milano', in *Michelozzo* 1998, pp. 237–48.

Per bellezza 1991 = *'Per bellezza, per studio, per piacere'. Lorenzo il Magnifico e gli spazi dell'arte*, edited by Franco Borsi, Florence, 1991

Peri 2006 = Paolo Peri, 'Le leggi suntuarie pistoiesi del XIV e XV secolo e le testimonianze figurative', in *Dalla testa ai piedi* 2006, pp. 367–434.

Pertegato 1989 = Francesco Pertegato, 'Tecniche di realizzazione del ricamo e procedimenti di restauro', in *Botticelli* 1989, pp. 41–84.

Petrioli Tofani 1991 = Annamaria Petrioli Tofani, *Gabinetto disegni e stampe degli Uffizi. Inventario. Disegni di Figura*, Florence, 1991–2005, 2 vols.

Petrocchi 1995 = Stefano Petrocchi, 'Per un'iconografia del denaro nella pittura europea', in *I Gonzaga. Moneta Arte Storia*, exhibition catalogue (Mantua, Galleria Civica di Palazzo Te, 9 September–10 December 1995) edited by Silvana Baldi de Caro, Milan, 1995, pp. 483–94.

Piattoli 1929 = Renato Piattoli, 'Un mercante del Trecento e gli artisti del tempo suo', in *Rivista d'arte*, 11, 1929, pp. 221–53, 396–437, 537–79.

Piattoli 1930 = Renato Piattoli, 'Un mercante del Trecento e gli artisti del tempo suo', in *Rivista d'arte*, 12, 1930, pp. 97–150.

Pico (*c.*1530), ed. Castagnola 1998 = Giovanfrancesco Pico della Mirandola, *Vita di Hieronimo Savonarola (volgarizzamento anonimo)* (*c.*1530) edited by Raffaella Castagnola, Florence, 1998.

Pieper 2011 = Jan Pieper, 'The Ships on the Berlin Città Ideale. Some Observations on their Naval Typology, Structural Characteristics and Rigging Details', in *From the Anchor to the Crow's Nest. Naval Imagery from the Renaissance to the Age of Photography*, edited by Lars U. Scholl and Nicole Hegener, Bremerhaven, 2011, pp. 35–48.

Pieraccini 1924–5 = Gaetano Pieraccini, *La stirpe de' Medici di Cafaggiolo. Saggio di ricerche sulla trasmissione ereditaria dei caratteri biologici*, Florence, 1924–25, 3 vols.

Piero de' Medici 1993 = *Piero de' Medici 'il Gottoso' (1416–1469)*, edited by Andreas Beyer and Bruce Boucher, Berlin, 1993.

La Pinacoteca Nazionale 1992 = *La Pinacoteca Nazionale di Ferrara. Catalogo generale*, edited by Jadranka Bentini, Bologna, 1992.

Pincelli 1959 = Rosanna Pincelli, *Lavori in osso e avorio dalla preistoria al rococò*, Bologna, 1959.

Pini ms.1862 = Carlo Pini, *Inventario degli oggetti d'arte*, ms., 1862, Florence, Soprintendenza Speciale P.S.A.E. and Polo Museale della città di Firenze, Ufficio Catalogo.

Plessow 2007 = Oliver Plessow, *Mittelalterliche Schachzabelbücher zwischen Spielsymbolik und Wertevermittlung-Der Schachtraktat des Jacobus de Cessolis im Kontext seiner spätmittelalterlichen Rezeption*, Münster, 2007.

Pohl 1938 = Joseph Pohl, *Die Verwendung des Naturabgusses in der italienischen Porträtplastik der Renaissance*, Würzburg, 1938 (Diss., Bonn, Universität, 1938).

Polidori Calamandrei 1924 = Egidia Polidori Calamandrei, *Le Vesti delle donne fiorentine nel Quattrocento*, Florence, 1924.

Politi, Lancellotto see Catarino

Polizzotto 1994 = Lorenzo Polizzotto, *The Elect Nation. The Savonarolan Movement in Florence (1494–1545)*, Oxford, 1994.

Polizzotto 1998 = Lorenzo Polizzotto, 'Fanciulli e giovani nella riforma savonaroliana', in *Savonarola. Quaderni del quinto centenario (1498–1998)*, Bologna 1997–98, 8 vols., VIII, 1998, pp. 19–41.

Polizzotto 2009 = Lorenzo Polizzotto, 'L'eredità dell'osservanza domenicana in Savonarola e nei savonaroliani', in *Memorie Domenicane*, new series, 40, 2009.

Pons 1989 = Nicoletta Pons, *Botticelli. Catalogo completo*, Milan, 1989.

Pons 1992 = Nicoletta Pons, 'Il "Tempio in casa": immagini, allegorie, mobili "storiati." Arredi domestici e oggetti di devozione privata', in *Maestri e botteghe* 1992, pp. 219–29.

Pons 2009 = Nicoletta Pons, 'Domestic Art in Renaissance Florence', in *Two Centuries of Italian Masterpieces*, exhibition catalogue (Budapest, Szépmüvészeti Múzeum, 28 October 2009–14 February 2010) edited by Dóra Sallay, Vilmos Tátrai, Axel Vécsey, Budapest, 2009, pp. 98–111.

Pontano 1498, ed. Tateo 1999 = Ioannis Ioviani Pontano [Giovanni Pontano], *De liberalitate. De beneficentia. De magnificentia. De splendore. De conviventia*, Naples, 1498; published in Giovanni Pontano, *I libri delle virtù sociali*, edited by Francesco Tateo, Rome, 1999.

Pope-Hennessy 1964 = John Pope-Hennessy, *Catalogue of Italian Sculpture in the Victoria and Albert Museum*, London, 1964, 3 vols.

Pope-Hennessy, *Fra Angelico* 1974 = John Pope-Hennessy, *Fra Angelico*, London, 1974.

Pope-Hennessy, 'The Forging' 1974 = John Pope-Hennessy, 'The Forging of Italian Renaissance Sculpture', in *Apollo*, 99, 1974, pp. 242–67.

Portigliotti 1902 = Giuseppe Portigliotti, *Un grande monomane Fra' Girolamo Savonarola*, Turin, 1902.

Pound 1985 = Ezra Pound, *I Cantos*, edited by Mary de Rachewiltz, Milan, 1985.

Pound 1996 = Ezra Pound, *The Cantos*, New York, 1996

Il Potere e la Grazia 2009 = *Il Potere e la Grazia. I Santi Patroni d'Europa*, exhibition catalogue (Rome, Museo Nazionale di Palazzo Venezia, 7 October 2009–10 January 2010) edited by Alessio Geretti and Serenella Castri in collaboration with Carlo Corsato, Geneva-Milan, 2009.

Pregio e Bellezza 2010 = *Pregio e Bellezza. Cammei e intagli dei Medici*, exhibition catalogue (Florence, Museo degli Argenti, 25 March–27 June 2010) edited by Riccardo Gennaioli, Livorno, 2010.

Il primato del disegno 1980 = *Firenze e la Toscana dei Medici nell'Europa del Cinquecento. Il primato del disegno*, exhibition catalogue (Florence, Palazzo Strozzi, 1980), Milan-Florence, 1980.

I processi 2001 = *I processi di Girolamo Savonarola (1498)*, edited by Ida Giovanna Rao, Paolo Viti, Raffaella Maria Zaccaria, Florence 2001.

Prosperi 2009 = Adriano Prosperi, 'Savonarola dal falò delle vanità al rogo', in *Gli anni di Firenze*, Rome-Bari, 2009, pp. 59–87.

Puglisi, Barcham 2008 = Catherine R. Puglisi, William L. Barcham, 'Bernardino da Feltre, the Monte di Pietà and the Man of Sorrows. Activist, Microcredit and Logo', in *Artibus et Historiae*, 29, 2008, 8, pp. 35–63.

Pujades i Battaller 2007 = Ramon J. Pujades i Battaller, *Les cartes portolanes. La rapresentació medieval d'una mar solcada*, Barcelona 2007.

Pulchritudo, Amor, Voluptas 2001 = *Pulchritudo, Amor, Voluptas. Pico della Mirandola alla corte del Magnifico*, exhibition catalogue (Mirandola, Centro Culturale Polivalente, 15 December 2001–17 February 2002) edited by Mario Scalini, Florence, 2001.

400 anni di pittura 2006 = *400 anni di pittura italiana. Mostra delle collezioni di Galleria Bellini*, exhibition catalogue (China, various venues, 2006), [Chinese/Italian], Florence-Shangai, 2006.

Quinterio 1998 = Francesco Quinterio, 'Natura e architettura nella bottega robbiana', in *I Della Robbia e l'"arte nuova" della scultura invetriata*, exhibition catalogue (Fiesole, Sant'Alessandro, 29 May–1 November 1998) edited by

Giancarlo Gentilini, Florence, 1998, pp. 57–85.

Rainey 1991 = Ronald E. Rainey, 'Dressing Down the Dressed-Up: Reproving Feminine Attire in Renaissance Florence', in *Renaissance Society and Culture. Essays in Honor Eugene F. Rice, Jr*, edited by John Monfasani and Ronald G. Musto, New York, 1991, pp. 217–37.

Rainey 1996 = Ronald E. Rainey, *Sumptuary Legislation in Renaissance Florence*, Ann Arbor, Mich., 1996 (Ph.D. Diss., New York, Columbia University, 1985).

Randall 1985 = Richard H. Randall, Jr., *Masterpieces of Ivory from the Walters Art Gallery*, New York, 1985.

Reinhardt 2009 = Volker Reinhardt, 'Tyranny or Golden Age? Florence in Botticelli's Day', in *Botticelli* 2009, pp. 111–28.

Renouard 1965 = Yves Renouard, 'Acquisti e pagamenti di drappi fiamminghi da parte dei primi papi avignonesi', in *Studi salentini*, 19, 1965, pp. 88–121.

Ricciardi 2001 = Lucia Ricciardi, 'Simboli medicei: "palle" e imprese nel Quattrocento', in Franco Cardini, *I re Magi di Benozzo a Palazzo Medici*, edition revised and augmented, with an article by Lucia Ricciardi, Florence, 2001, pp. 64–93.

Ridolfi 1945 = Roberto Ridolfi, 'I processi del Savonarola', in *La Bibliofilia*, 46, 1944, pp. 3–41.

Ridolfi 1997 = Roberto Ridolfi, *Vita di Girolamo Savonarola*, Florence, 1997 (1st ed. Rome, 1952).

Rimatori 1969 = *Rimatori del Trecento*, edited by Giuseppe Corsi, Turin, 1969.

Rinascimento 2001 = *Rinascimento: capolavori dei musei italiani. Tokyo-Roma 2001*, exhibition catalogue (Rome, Palazzo del Quirinale, Scuderie Papali, 15 September 2001–6 January 2002; Tōkyō, Kokuritsu-Seiyō-Bijutsukan, 19 March–8 July 2001) edited by Antonio Paolucci, Geneva, 2001.

Il Rinascimento in Italia 2001 = *Il Rinascimento in Italia. La civiltà delle corti*, exhibition catalogue (Tōkyō, Kokuritsu-Seiyō-Bijutsukan, 20 March–8 July 2001) edited by Antonio Paolucci, Tokyo, 2001.

Rodocanachi 1907 = Emmanuel Pierre Rodocanachi, *La femme italienne à l'époque de la Renaissance, sa vie privée et mondaine, son influence sociale*, Paris, 1907.

Romagnoli 2005 = Gioia Romagnoli, *Selve e Lecceto. Due conventi a Lastra a Signa ed un grande mecenate, Filippo Strozzi. Arte e Storia*, Florence, 2005.

Romano 2003 = Giovanni Romano, 'Vincenzo Foppa, gli anni della formazione', in *Vincenzo Foppa* 2003, pp. 25–37.

Rosenberg 1910 = Marc Rosenberg, *Geschichte der Goldschmiedekunst auf technischer Grundlage*, [I], *Einführung*, Frankfurt am Main, 1910.

Rossi 1991 = Adriana Rossi, 'I nomi delle vesti in Toscana durante il Medioevo', in *Studi di lessicografia italiana*, edited by the Accademia della Crusca (Florence), 11, 1991, pp. 5–124.

Ruda 1993 = Jeffrey Ruda, *Fra Filippo Lippi. Life and Work with a Complete Catalogue*, London, 1993.

Salmi 1921 = Mario Salmi, *Catalogo della Pinacoteca Comunale di Arezzo*, Città di Castello, 1921.

Salter 1936 = F.R.[*sic*] Salter, 'The Jews in Fifteenth-Century Florence and Savonarola's Establishment of a *Mons Pietatis*', in *Cambridge Historical Journal*, 5, 1936, pp. 193–211.

Salvatici 1999 = Luciano Salvatici, 'Introduzione', in *Posate, Pugnali, Coltelli da caccia*, exhibition catalogue (Florence, Museo Nazionale del Bargello, 1999) edited by Luciano Salvatici, Florence, 1999, pp. 9–17.

San Lorenzo 1993 = *San Lorenzo: i documenti e i tesori nascosti*, exhibition catalogue (Florence, Complesso di San Lorenzo, 25 September–12 December 1993), Venice, 1993.

Sandro Botticelli 2000 = *Sandro Botticelli. Pittore della Divina Commedia*, exhibition catalogue (Rome, Palazzo del Quirinale, Scuderie Papali, 20 September–3 December 2000), Milan, 2000, 2 vols.

Sandro Botticelli 2009 = *Sandro Botticelli and Herbert Horne. New Research*, proceedings of the symposium (Florence, 8–10 October 2008) edited by Rab Hatfield, Florence, 2009.

Sanesi 1893 = Giuseppe Sanesi, *Le ultime leggi suntuarie della Repubblica Fiorentina*, Pistoia, 1893.

Sangiorgi 1926 = Giorgio Sangiorgi, *Contributi allo studio dell'arte tessile*, Milan, 1926.

Sant'Ambrogio 1903 = Diego Sant'Ambrogio, 'Il prezioso cappuccio di piviale del Museo Poldi-Pezzoli', in *Rassegna d'arte*, 3, 1903, pp. 184–6.

Santambrogio 2002 = Giovanni Santambrogio, *Il colore dei soldi*, presentation by Eugenio Borgna, Milan, 2002.

Sapori 1955–67 = Armando Sapori, *Studi di storia economica (Secoli XIII–XIV–XV)*, Florence, 1955–67, 3 vols.

Savonarola (1475–98), ed. Ridolfi *et al.* 1984 = Girolamo Savonarola, *Lettere e scritti apologetici* (1475–98), edited by Roberto Ridolfi, Vincenzo Romano, Armando F. Verde, Rome, 1984.

Savonarola (1494), ed. Firpo 1965 = Girolamo Savonarola, *Prediche sopra Aggeo, con il Trattato circa il reggimento e governo della città di Firenze* (1494), edited by Luigi Firpo, Rome, 1965.

Savonarola (1494–8), ed. Viti, Sebregondi 1998 = Girolamo Savonarola, *'Se tu non hai carità, tu non sei vero cristiano'. Tre prediche* (1494–1498), edited by Paolo Viti, iconographic research and commentary by Ludovica Sebregondi, Florence, 1998.

Savonarola (1495), ed. Crucitti 1974 = Girolamo Savonarola, *Compendio di rivelazioni e Dialogo de veritate prophetica* (1495), edited by Angela Crucitti, Rome, 1974.

Savonarola (1495), ed. Romano 1969–74 = Girolamo Savonarola, *Prediche sopra i salmi* (1495), edited by Vincenzo Romano, Rome, 1969–74, 2 vols.

Savonarola (1496), ed. Ghiglieri 1971 = Girolamo Savonarola, *Prediche sopra Amos e Zaccaria* (1496), edited by Paolo Ghiglieri, Rome 1971, 3 vols.

Savonarola (1496), ed. Ricci 1959 = Girolamo Savonarola, *De simplicitate christianae vitae* (1496), edited by Giorgio Ricci, Rome, 1959.

Savonarola (1496), ed. Romano 1962 = Girolamo Savonarola, *Prediche sopra Ruth e Michea* (1496), edited by Vincenzo Romano, Rome, 1962, 2 vols.

Savonarola (1496–97), ed. Ridolfi 1955 = Girolamo Savonarola, *Prediche sopra Ezechiele* (1496–97), edited by Roberto Ridolfi, Rome, 1955, 2 vols.

Savonarola e le sue 'reliquie' 1998 = *Savonarola e le sue 'reliquie' a San Marco. Itinerario per un percorso savonaroliano nel Museo*, edited by Magnolia Scudieri and Giovanna Rasario, Florence, 1998.

Savonarole 1997 = *Savonarole. Enjeux, débats, questions*, proceedings of international symposium (Paris, 25–27 January 1996) edited by Anna Fontes-Jean Louis Fournel, Michel Plaisance, Paris, 1997.

Scalini 1997 = Mario Scalini, 'La formazione del tesoro quattrocentesco, la sua dispersione e il ritorno a Firenze dei preziosi medicei', in *Tesori dalle collezioni medicee*, edited by Cristina Acidini Luchinat, Florence, 1997, pp. 29–50.

Scalini 2005 = Mario Scalini, *I tesori d'arte antica a Cerreto Guidi. Museo Storico della Caccia e del Territorio: un'esposizione permanente*, Livorno, 2005.

Schaeffer 1904 = Emil Schaeffer, *Das Florentiner Bildnis*, Munich,1904.

Schiaparelli 1908 = Attilio Schiaparelli, *La casa fiorentina e i suoi arredi nei secoli XIV e XV*, Florence 1908; edited by Maria Sframeli and Laura Pagnotta, presentation by Mina Gregori, Florence, 1983, 2 vols.

Schnitzer 1931 = Giuseppe Schnitzer, *Savonarola*, translated by Ernesto Rutili, Milan, 1931, 2 vols. (original edition with title *Savonarola. Ein Kulturbild aus der Zeit der Renaissance*, Munich, 1924, 2 vols.).

Schuyler 1975 = Jane Schuyler, *Studies of Florentine Quattrocento Portrait Busts*, Ann Arbor, Mich., 1975 (Ph.D. Diss., New York, Columbia University, 1972).

Sciolla 1970 = Gianni Carlo Sciolla, *La scultura di Mino da Fiesole*, Turin, 1970.

La scultura 2010 = *La scultura al Museo d'Arte Antica del Castello Sforzesco di Milano*, edited by Maria Teresa Fiorio and Graziano Alfredo Vergani, Milan, 2010.

Scuricini Greco 1958 = Maria Luisa Scuricini Greco, *Miniature riccardiane*, Florence, 1958.

Sebregondi 1994 = Ludovica Sebregondi, 'La tavola: desinari, feste e conviti nel Rinascimento fiorentino', in *Itinerari* 1994, pp. 47–63.

Sebregondi 1996 = Ludovica Sebregondi, 'Iconografia savonaroliana: prime indagini su ritratti veri, presunti, idealizzati', in *Studi savonaroliani* 1996.

Sebregondi, 'La fortuna' 1998 = Ludovica Sebregondi, 'La fortuna iconografica di Girolamo Savonarola', in *Savonarola rivisitato (1498–1998)*, edited by Massimiliano G. Rosito, Florence, 1998, pp. 201–16, 227–9.

Sebregondi, 'L'immagine' 1998 = Ludovica Sebregondi, 'L'immagine come memoria', in *Savonarola*, ed. Viti-Sebregondi 1998, pp. 65–8.

Sebregondi 2000 = Ludovica Sebregondi, 'Ritratti umanistici e rivisitazioni successive', in *Immaginare l'autore* 2000, pp. 113–20.

Sebregondi 2002 = Ludovica Sebregondi, 'Clothes and Teenagers: What Young Men Wore in Fifteenth-Century Florence', in the proceedings of the symposium *The Premodern Teenager* (Toronto, 8–9 October 1999), Toronto, 2002, pp. 27–50.

Sebregondi 2004 = Ludovica Sebregondi, *Iconografia di Girolamo Savonarola, 1495–1998*, Florence, 2004.

Sebregondi 2006 = Ludovica Sebregondi, 'Carità palese e carità occulta: le vesti confraternali nell'esercizio delle opere di misericordia', in *Armut und Armenfürsorge in der italienischen Stadtkultur zwischen 13. und 16. Jahrhundert. Bilder, Texte und soziale Praktiken*, proceedings of the symposium (Florence, November 2004) edited by Philine Helas and Gerhard Wolf, Frankfurt am Main, 2006, pp. 97–112.

Sebregondi 2009 = Ludovica Sebregondi, *Arte confraternale* in *Studi confraternali: orientamenti, problemi, testimonianze*, edited by Marina Gazzini, Florence, 2009, pp. 337–67.

Sebregondi 2010 = Ludovica Sebregondi, 'Rituali di nozze nella Firenze rinascimentale', in *Virtù d'amore* 2010, pp. 35–43.

Seelig 1991 = Lorenz Seelig, 'Der Einband des Medici-Gebertbuchs. Der Weg der Handschrift in die Bayerische Staatsbibliothek', in *Das Gebetbuch Lorenzos De' Medici 1485. Handschrift Clm 23639 der Bayerischen Staatsbibliothek München. Kommentar*, Frankfurt am Main-Stuttgart, 1991, pp. 77–166.

Sennett 2006 = Richard Sennett, *Il declino dell'uomo pubblico*, Milan, 2006 (original edition with the title *The Fall of Public Man*, New York, 1977).

Seta 2006 = *Seta. Potere e glamour. Tessuti e abiti dal Rinascimento al XX secolo*, exhibition catalogue (Caraglio, Filatoio, 28 October 2006–25 February 2007) edited by Roberta Orsi Landini, Milan, 2006.

Simonetta 2008 = Marcello Simonetta, *L'enigma Montefeltro*, Milan, 2008.

Simonsohn 1972 = Shlomo Simonsohn, 'I banchieri da Rieti in Toscana', in *La Rassegna mensile di Israel*, 38, 1972, 9, pp. 406–23; 10, pp. 487–99.

Sirén 1908 = Osvald Sirén, *Giottino und seine Stellung in der gleichzeitigen florentinischen Malerei*, Leipzig, 1908.

Smith 1975 = Webster Smith, 'On the Original Location of the "Primavera"', in *The Art Bulletin*, 57, 1975, pp. 31–40.

Solberg 2002 = Gail E. Solberg, 'Altarpiece Types and Regional Adaptations in the Work of Taddeo di Bartolo', in *Italian Panel Paintings of the Duecento and Trecento*, proceedings of the symposium (Florence, 5–6 June 1998; Washington, D.C., 16 October 1998) edited by Victor M. Schmidt, New Haven–London 2002 (*Studies in the History of Art*, 61; *Center for Advanced Study in the Visual Arts. Symposium Papers*, 38), pp. 199–227.

Sosnowski 2006 = Roman Sosnowski, *Origini della lingua dell'economia in Italia. Dal XIII al XVI secolo*, Milan, 2006.

Sotheby's London 2008 = Sotheby's, *Old Master Paintings. Evening Sale*, auction, London, 1–9 July 2008.

Spallanzani 1997 = Marco Spallanzani, *Mercanti fiorentini nell'Asia portoghese (1500–1525)*, Florence, 1997.

Specchio del tempo 2006 = *Specchio del tempo. L'uomo e il suo mondo in sei secoli d'arte italiana*, exhibition catalogue (Beijing, The Beijng World Art Museum, 20 January–23 April 2006) edited by Mario Scalini [Chinese/Italian], Beijing, 2006.

Spike 1996 = John T. Spike, *Angelico*, Milan, 1996.

The Splendour 2008 = *The Splendour of the Medici. Art and Life in Renaissance Florence*, exhibition catalogue (Budapest, Szépmüvészeti Múzeum, 24 January–18 May 2008) edited by Monica Bietti and Annamaria Giusti in collaboration with Maria Sframeli, Budapest, 2008.

Spufford 2005 = Peter Spufford, *Il mercante nel Medioevo. Potere e profitto*, Rome 2005 (original edition in English with the title *Power and Profit. The Merchant in Medieval Europe*, New York, 2002).

Stabel 2002 = Peter Stabel, 'La lettre de change: un moyen de paiement international', in *Les marchands* 2002, p. 121.

Stammerjohann, Seymer 2007 = Harro Stammerjohann, Gesine Seymer, 'L'italiano in Europa: italianismo in francese, inglese e tedesco', in *Firenze e la lingua italiana fra nazione ed Europa*, proceedings of the symposium (Florence, 27–28 May 2004) edited by Nicoletta Maraschio, Florence, 2007, pp. 41–78.

Stanze segrete 2003 = *Stanze segrete, stanze scomparse. Frammenti di una residenza-museo*, exhibition catalogue (Florence, Palazzo Medici Riccardi, 25 March–28 September 2003) edited by Cristina Giannini, [Italian/English], Florence, 2003.

Statuta (1415), ed. 1778 = *Statuta Populi et Communis Florentiae. Publica auctoritate collecta, castigata et praeposita anno salutis MCCCCXV*, Frieburg 1778, 3 vols.

Statuti 2009 = *Statuti del Comune di Firenze nell'Archivio di Stato: tradizione archivistica e ordinamenti. Saggio archivistico e inventario*; edited by Giuseppe Biscione, Rome, 2009.

Steinberg 1977 – Ronald M. Steinberg, *Fra Girolamo Savonarola, Florentine Art, and Renaissance Historiography*, Athens, 1977.

Steingräber 1964 = Erich Steingräber, 'Zwei "Libri d'ore" des Lorenzo Magnifico de' Medici', in *Studien zur Toskanischen Kunst. Festschrift für Ludwig Heinrich Heydenreich zum 23 März 1963*, edited by Wolfgang Lotz and Lise Lotte Möller, Munich, 1964, 3 pp. 3–13.

La storia del Bargello 2004 = *La storia del Bargello. 100 capolavori da scoprire*, edited by Beatrice Paolozzi Strozzi, Florence, 2004.

Strocchia 1992 = Sharon T. Strocchia, *Death and ritual in Renaissance Florence*, Baltimore, 1992.

Strozzi (*ante* 1549), ed. Bini, Bigazzi 1851 = Lorenzo Strozzi, *Vita di Filippo Strozzi il Vecchio* (*ante* 1549), edited by Giuseppe Bini and Pietro Bigazzi, Florence, 1851.

Studi savonaroliani 1996 = *Studi savonaroliani. Verso il V centenario 1498–1998*, proceedings of the first seminar (Florence, 14–15 Janaury 1995) edited by Gian Carlo Garfagnini, Florence, 1996.

Supino 1898 = Igino Benvenuto Supino, *Catalogo del R. Museo Nazionale di Firenze (Palazzo del Potestà)*, Rome 1898.

Tangheroni 1996 = Marco Tangheroni, *Commercio e navigazione nel Medioevo*, Rome-Bari, 1996.

Tarchiani 1930 = Nello Tarchiani, *Il Palazzo Medici Riccardi e il Museo Mediceo*, Florence 1930.

Tartuferi 2007 = Angelo Tartuferi, 'I Pollaiolo agli Uffizi e oltre: osservazioni e proposte', in *La stanza dei Pollaiolo. I restauri, una mostra, un nuovo ordinamento*, edited by Antonio Natali and Angelo Tartuferi, Florence, 2007 (*Gli Uffizi. Studi e Ricerche*, 16), pp. 19–40.

Le tems revient 1992 = *Le tems revient, 'l tempo si rinuova. Feste e spettacoli nella Firenze di Lorenzo il Magnifico*, exhibition catalogue (Florence, Palazzo Medici Riccardi, 8 April–30 June 1992) edited by Paola Ventrone, Cinisello Balsamo, 1992.

Terreaux-Scotto 1997 = Cécile Terreaux-Scotto, 'La place des enfants dans la réforme savonarolienne de la cité', in *Savonarole* 1997, pp. 81–103.

I Tesori della Città 1998 = *I Tesori della Città. Pittura del Tre-Quattrocento a Prato*, exhibition catalogue (Prato, Convento di San Domenico, Museo di Pittura Murale, 1998) edited by Claudio Cerretelli in collaboration with Alessandro Pasquini and Maria Pia Mannini, Prato, 1998.

Il Tesoro 1973–4 = *Il Tesoro di Lorenzo il Magnifico*, exhibition catalogue (Florence, Palazzo Medici Riccardi, 1972), Florence, 1973–74 (1975), 2 vols. (I, *Le gemme* edited by Nicole Dacos, Antonio Giuliano, Ulrico Pannuti, II, *I vasi*, edited by Detlef Heikamp).

Testimonianze medicee 1997 = *Testimonianze medicee a confronto*, exhibition catalogue (Florence, Biblioteca Riccardiana, 8 May–5 July 1997) edited by Giovanna Lazzi, Florence, 1997.

Theatrum sanitatis (sec. XIV), ed. Serra 1940 = *Theatrum sanitatis. Codice 4182 della R. Biblioteca Casanatense* (sec. XIV), with introduction by Luigi Serra, Rome, 1940, 2 vols.

Theatrum sanitatis (sec. XIV), ed. Pazzini *et al.* 1969 = *Theatrum sanitatis di Ububchasym de Baldach. Codice 4182 della Biblioteca Casanatense di Roma* (sec. XIV), edited by Adalberto Pazzini, Emma Coen Pirani and Mario Salmi, Parma, 1969.

Theatrum sanitatis (sec. XIV), facs. ed. 1999 = *Theatrum sanitatis* (sec. XIV), facsimile of ms. 4182 in the Biblioteca Casanatense di Roma, commentary by Mónica Miró, translation by Anne Barton de Mayor, [Spanish/English], Barcelona, 1999.

Toderi, Vannel 2003 = Giuseppe Toderi, Fiorenza Vannel, *Medaglie Italiane del Museo Nazionale del Bargello di Firenze*, I, *Secoli XV–XVI*, Florence, 2003.

Toderi, Vannel 2005 = Giuseppe Toderi, Fiorenza Vannel, *Monete Italiane del Museo Nazionale del Bargello*, II, *Firenze: Repubblica*, Florence, 2005.

Tognetti 1997 = Sergio Tognetti, 'L'attività di banca locale di una grande compagnia fiorentina del XV secolo', in *Archivio storico italiano*, 155, 1997, pp. 595–647.

Tognetti 1999 = Sergio Tognetti, *Il banco Cambini. Affari e mercati di una compagnia mercantile-bancaria nella Firenze del XV secolo*, Florence, 1999.

Tognetti 2001 = Sergio Tognetti, 'Attività industriali e commercio di manufatti nelle città toscane del tardo Medioevo (1250 ca.–1530 ca.)', in *Archivio storico italiano*, 159, 2001, pp. 423–79.

Tognetti 2002 = Sergio Tognetti, *Un'industria di lusso al servizio del grande commercio. Il mercato dei drappi serici e della seta nella Firenze del Quattrocento*, Florence, 2002.

Tognetti 2003 = Sergio Tognetti, *Da Figline a Firenze. Ascesa economica e politica della famiglia Serristori (secoli XIV–XVI)*, Florence, 2003.

Tognetti 2005 = Sergio Tognetti, 'The Trade in Black African Slaves in Fifteenth Century Florence', in *Black Africans in Renaissance Europe*, edited by T.F. [*sic*] Earle and Kate J.P. Lowe, Cambridge, 2005, pp. 213–24.

Tognetti 2010 = Sergio Tognetti, 'Pisa, Firenze e il mare (metà XI–fine XV sec.)', in *Firenze e Pisa dopo il 1406. La creazione di un nuovo spazio regionale*, proceedings of symposium (Florence, 27–28 September 2008) edited by Sergio Tognetti, Florence, 2010, pp. 151–76.

Tomasi 2001 = Michele Tomasi, *La bottega degli Embriachi. Museo Nazionale del Bargello*, Florence, 2001.

Tomasi 2004 = Michele Tomasi, 'L'arredo della casa', in *Storia delle arti in Toscana. Il Trecento*, edited by Max Seidel, Florence, 2004, pp. 251–74.

Tonini 2009 = Camillo Tonini, 'Sulla rotta dei pellegrini: carte nautiche, portolani e isolari dalle collezioni del Museo Correr', in *La Dalmazia nelle relazioni di viaggiatori e pellegrini da Venezia tra Quattro e Seicento*, proceedings of symposium (Rome, Accademia Nazionale dei Lincei, 22–23 May 2007) edited by Sante Graciotti, Rome, 2009.

Ulmann 1893 = Hermann Ulmann, *Sandro Botticelli*, Munich, 1893.

L'uomo del Rinascimento 2006 = *L'uomo del Rinascimento. Leon Battista Alberti e le arti a Firenze tra ragione e bellezza*, exhibition catalogue (Florence, Palazzo Strozzi, 11 March–23 July 2006) edited by Cristina Acidini and Gabriele Morolli, Florence, 2006.

Uzielli, Amat di San Filippo 1882 = Gustavo Uzielli, Pietro Amat di San Filippo, 'Mappamondi, carte nautiche, portolani ed altri monumenti cartografici specialmente italiani dei secoli XIII–XVIII', 2nd ed. in *Studi biografici e bibliografici sulla storia della geografia in Italia pubblicati in occasione del III° Congresso geografico internazionale*, Rome, 1882–84, 2 vols., II, 1882 (anastatic reprint, Staten Island, NY, [s.a.]).

Valeri 2010 = Elena Valeri, 'Savonarola e il falò delle vanità', in *Atlante della letteratura italiana*, edited by Sergio Luzzatto and Gabriele Pedullà, I, *Dalle origini al Rinascimento*, edited by Amedeo de Vincentiis, Turin, 2010, pp. 621–27.

Van Egmond 1981 = Warren Van Egmond, *Practical Mathematics in the Italian Renaissance. A Catalogue of Italian Abbacus Manuscripts and Printed Books to 1600*, Florence 1981 (Istituto e Museo di Storia della Scienza. *Monografie*, 4; supplement to *Annali dell'Istituto e Museo di Storia della Scienza*, 1980, 1).

Van Eyck bis Dürer 2010 = *Van Eyck bis Dürer. Altniederländische Meister und die Malerei in Mitteleuropa*, exhibition catalogue (Bruges, Musée Communal des Beaux-Arts, 29 October 2010–30 January 2011) edited by Till-Holger Borchert, Stuttgart, 2010.

Vasari 1550, ed. Bellosi, Rossi 1986 = Giorgio Vasari, *Le Vite de' più eccellenti architetti, pittori et scultori italiani, da Cimabue insino a' tempi nostri*, in Fiorenza 1550, 2 vols.; edited by Luciano Bellosi and Aldo Rossi, presentation by Giovanni Previtali, Turin, 1986.

Vasari 1550, ed. Bettarini, Barocchi 1966–97 = Giorgio Vasari, *Le Vite de' più eccellenti architetti, pittori et scultori italiani, da Cimabue insino a' tempi nostri*, Florence, Lorenzo Torrentino, 1550, 2 vols.; ed. in Id., *Le Vite de' più eccellenti pittori, scultori ed architettori*, in the 1550 and 1568 editions, text edited by Rosanna Bettarini, centennial commentary by Paola Barocchi, index edited by Paola Barocchi and Giovanna Gaeta Bertelà, Florence, 1966–1987–1997, 11 vols.

Vasari 1568, ed. Milanesi 1878–81 = Giorgio Vasari, *Le Vite de' più eccellenti pittori, scultori et architettori...*, revised and augmented, Florence, Giunti, 1568, 3 vols.; ed. in Id., *Le opere*, with annotations and comments by Gaetano Milanesi, Florence, 1878–85, 9 vols. (reprint Florence, 1906), I–VII, 1878–81.

Vasari 1568, ed. Bettarini, Barocchi 1966–97 = Giorgio Vasari, *Le Vite de' più eccellenti pittori, scultori et architettori...*, revised and augmented, Florence, Giunti, 1568, 3 vols.; ed. in Id., *Le Vite de' più eccellenti pittori, scultori ed architettori*, in the 1550 and 1568 editions, text edited by Rosanna Bettarini, centennial commentary by Paola Barocchi, Florence, 1966–1997, 11 vols.

Velluti e Moda 1999 = *Velluti e Moda tra XV e XVII secolo*, exhibition catalogue (Milan, Museo Poldi Pezzoli, 7 May–15 September 1999) edited by Annalisa Zanni with Margherita Bellezza Rosina and Margherita Ghirardi, Milan, 1999.

Venice 2007 = *Venice and the Islamic World, 828–1797*, exhibition catalogue (Parigi, Institut du Monde Arabe, 2 October 2006–18 February 2007; New York, Metropolitan Museum of Art, 27 March–8 July 2007; Venice, Palazzo Ducale, 28 July–25 November 2007) edited by Stefano Carboni, New Haven, 2007.

Ventrone 1992 = Paola Ventrone, 'Feste e spettacoli nella Firenze di Lorenzo il Magnifico', in *Le tems revient* 1992, pp. 21–53.

Venturi 1891 = Adolfo Venturi, *La Regia Galleria di Pitti in Firenze*, Dornach, 1891.

Venturi 1900 = Adolfo Venturi, *La Galleria Crespi in Milano. Note e raffronti*, Milan, 1900.

Venturini 1994 = Lisa Venturini, *Francesco Botticini*, Florence, 1994.

Verdon 1999 = Timoty Verdon, 'Girolamo Savonarola e il conservatorismo dell'arte fiorentina della "fin de siècle"', in *Girolamo Savonarola. Storia* 1999, pp. 9–18.

Vespasiano da Bisticci (*c.*1480–98), ed. Greco 1970–76 = Vespasiano da Bisticci, *Le Vite* (*c.*1480–98), ecritical ed. with introduction and comment by Aulo Greco, Florence, 1970–1976, 2 vols.

Vettori 1738 = [Pier Vettori], *Il fiorino d'oro illustrato. Discorso di un Accademico etrusco indirizzato al Sig. Dottore Antonio Francesco Gori*, Florence, 1738.

Villa La Quiete 1997 = *Villa La Quiete. Il patrimonio artistico del Conservatorio delle Montalve*, edited by Cristina De Benedictis, Florence, 1997.

Villani (*ante* 1348), ed. Moutier 1823 = Giovanni Villani, *Cronica*, "a miglior lezione ridotta coll'aiuto de' testi a penna," edited by Ignazio Moutier, Florence, 1823, 8 vols. (1st ed. with title *Croniche di Giovanni Villani dopo la confusione della torre di Babello insino all' a. 1338*, Venice, 1537).

Villari 1898 = Pasquale Villari, *La storia di Girolamo Savonarola e de' suoi tempi*, new ed. augmented and corrected, Florence 1898, 2 vols. (1st ed. with title *La storia di Gerolamo Savonarola e de' suoi tempi narrata con l'aiuto di nuovi documenti*, Florence, 1859–61, 2 vols.).

Villari 1930 = Pasquale Villari, *La storia di Girolamo Savonarola e de' suoi tempi, con l'aiuto di nuovi documenti*, new ed., Florence, 1930, 2 vols. (1st ed. with title *La storia di Gerolamo Savonarola e de' suoi tempi narrata con l'aiuto di nuovi documenti*, Florence, 1859–61, 2 vols.).

Vincenzo Foppa 2003 = *Vincenzo Foppa*, exhibition catalogue *Vincenzo Foppa. Un protagonista del Rinascimento* (Brescia, Museo Civico di Santa Giulia, 3 March–2 June 2002) edited by Giovanni Agosti, Mauro Natale, Giovanni Romano, Milan, 2003.

Violi (*c.*1545), ed. Garfagnini 1986 = Lorenzo Violi, *Le giornate* (*c.*1545), edited by Gian Carlo Garfagnini, Florence, 1986.

Viroli 1980 = Giordano Viroli, *La Pinacoteca Civica di Forlì*, Forlì, 1980.

Viroli 1998 = Giordano Viroli, *Pittura dal Duecento al Quattrocento a Forlì*, Forlì, 1998.

Virtù d'Amore 2010 = *Virtù d'Amore. Pittura nuziale nel Quattrocento fiorentino*, exhibition catalogue (Florence, Galleria dell'Accademia-Museo Horne, 8 June–1 November 2010) edited by Claudio Paolini, Daniela Parenti, Ludovica Sebregondi, Florence, 2010.

La vita (*c.*1527), ed. Ginori Conti 1937 = *La vita del Beato Ieronimo Savonarola scritta da un anonimo del sec. XVI e già attribuita a fra Pacifico Burlamacchi* (*c.*1527), edited by Piero Ginori Conti, Florence, 1937.

Viti 1999 = Paolo Viti, 'La traduzione latina del primo processo di Girolamo Savonarola', in *Girolamo Savonarola. L'uomo* 1999, pp. 247–60.

Vogt-Lüerssen 2011 = Maike Vogt-Lüerssen, 'Caterina Sforza: identificare Caterina Sforza nei dipinti del Rinascimento attraverso il simbolismo', in *Caterina Sforza. 500° anniversario della morte (28 maggio 1509)*, Proceedings of the international symposium and round table (Forlì, 16 May 2009), edited by Silvia Arfelli and Gilberto Giorgetti, Forlì [2011], pp. 77–95

Waldman 2009 = Louis A.Waldman, 'Botticelli and his Patrons. The Arte del Cambio, the Vespucci, and the Compagnia dello Spirito Santo in Montelupo', in *Sandro Botticelli* 2009, pp. 105–35.

Warburg 1932 = Aby Warburg, 'Flandrische und florentinische Kunst im Kreise des Lorenzo Medici um 1480', in Id., *Gesammelte Schriften*, Leipzig-Berlin, 1932, 2 vols., I, *Die Erneuerung der Heidnischen Antike*, pp. 207–16 (orig. ed. in *Sitzungsberichte Kunstgeschichtliche Gesellschaft zu Berlin*, 8, 1901, pp. 8-11).

Waterhouse 1950 = Ellis K. Waterhouse, 'The Fresco by Foppa in the Wallace Collection', in *The Burlington Magazine*, 1950, 177; then in *The Burlington Magazine: a Centenary Anthology*, edited by Michael Levey, New Haven, 2003 (annexed to *The Burlington Magazine*, 145, 2003), pp. 96–7.

Weinstein 1958 = Donald Weinstein, 'Savonarola, Florence, and the Millenarian Tradition', in *Church History*, 27, 1958, pp. 291–305.

Weinstein 1976 = Donald Weinstein, *Savonarola e Firenze. Profezia e patriottismo nel Rinascimento*, Bologna, 1976 (orig. ed. titled *Savonarola and Florence. Prophecy and Patriotism in the Renaissance*, Princeton, 1970).

Weinstein 1998 = Donald Weinstein, 'Savonarola come medico di anime. Il "Manuale per confessori" del Savonarola', in *Memorie domenicane*, new series, 29, 1998, pp. 21–38.

Weinstein forthcoming = Donald Weinstein, *Savonarola. Rise and Fall of a Renaissance Prophet*, New Haven, forthcoming.

Weltbilder 2009 = *Weltbilder im Mittelalter / Perceptions of the World in the Middle Ages*, proceedings of international symposium (Marburg, 9–11 March 2007) edited by Philipp Billion, Nathanael Busch, Dagmar Schlüter, Xenia Stolzenburg, Bonn, 2009.

Westheim 1930 = Paul Westheim, 'Achtung Falschkunst! Fälscher und Kenner', in *Das Kunstblatt*, 14, 1930, pp. 193–204.

Wilcox 1999 = Claire Wilcox, *Bags*, London, 1999.

Winner 1970 = Matthias Winner, 'Cosimo il Vecchio als Cicero: humanistisches in Franciabigio Fresko zu Poggio a Caiano', in *Zeitschrift für Kunstgeschichte*, 33, 1970, pp. 261–97.

Zeri 1971 = Federico Zeri, *Diari di lavoro*, Bergamo, 1971.

Zeri 1985 = Federico Zeri, 'Questioni di bottega del Botticelli', in *Paragone*, 36, 1985, pp. 419–23, 135–39.

Zöllner, 'Botticelli portraitiste' 2009 = Frank Zöllner, 'Botticelli portraitiste: réflexions sur l'histoire du portrait en tant que genre artistique', in *Le portrait individuel: réflexions autour d'une forme de représentation, XIIIe–XVe siècles*, proceedings of symposium (Paris, 6–7 February, 2004) edited by Dominic Olariu, Bern, 2009, pp. 249–69.

Zöllner, *Sandro Botticelli* 2009 = Frank Zöllner, *Sandro Botticelli*, English edition, Munich, 2009.

Zorzi 1999 = Andrea Zorzi, 'Le fonti normative a Firenze nel tardo Medioevo. Un bilancio delle edizioni e degli studi', in *Statuti della Repubblica fiorentina*, edited by Romolo Caggese, new edition edited by Giuliano Pinto, Francesco Salvestrini, Andrea Zorzi, Florence, 1999, 2 vols., I, *Statuto del Capitano del Popolo degli anni 1322–1325*, pp. 53–101.

Zuraw 1993 = Shelley E. Zuraw, *The Sculpture of Mino da Fiesole (1429–1484)*, Ph.D. Diss., New York, New York University, 1993, 3 vols.

Index of names

Photograph credits

Foto: Jörg P. Anders © 2011 Foto Scala, Firenze/BPK, Bildagentur für Kunst, Kultur und Geschichte, Berlin: pp. 43, 82
Archivi Alinari, Firenze: pp. 39a, 107
© Archivi Alinari, Firenze - Per concessione del Ministero per i Beni e le Attività Culturali: p. 83
Archivio Fotografico Soprintendenza per Beni Archeologici per la Toscana: pp. 182-183
Archivio Giunti: pp. 48, 49, 62, 65, 74-75, 92
Archivio Giunti/Stefano Giraldi: p. 72
Archivio Giunti/foto Rabatti & Domingie, Firenze: pp. 80, 100, 105, 113, 135, 218, 231, 232, 245
Archivio Museo del Tessuto - Prato: p. 195
Archivio di Stato di Firenze, su Concessione del Ministero per i Beni e le Attività Culturali. È vietata ogni ulteriore riproduzione con qualsiasi mezzo: pp. 118, 122, 123, 124, 172, 173, 174, 175, 176, 177, 178, 179, 192, 193, 209
Arti Doria Pamphilj srl: p. 154
© Raffaello Bencini/Archivi Alinari, Firenze - Per concessione del Ministero per i Beni e le Attività Culturali: p. 109
Biblioteca Casanatense, Roma - su concessione del Ministero per i Beni e le Attività Culturali: p. 145
Biblioteca Medicea Laurenziana, Firenze. Su concessione del Ministero per i Beni e le Attività Culturali. © vietata ogni ulteriore riproduzione con qualsiasi mezzo: p. 225
Biblioteca Palatina, Parma - su concessione del Ministero per i Beni e le Attività Culturali: p. 50
Biblioteca Riccardiana, Firenze: pp. 70, 144, 162
Cliché Bibliothèque Nationale de France: pp. 63, 213
© Blauel/Gnamm/ARTOTHEK/ distr. Alinari: p. 31
© The Bridgeman Art Library/ Archivi Alinari: p. 68
© British Library Board. All Rights Reserved/The Bridgeman Art Library /Archivi Alinari: p. 46
Fondazione Musei Civici di Venezia - Archivio Fotografico: p. 184
Fototeca Ufficio Beni Culturali, proprietà dell'opera Diocesi di Prato: p. 256
Germanisches Nationalmuseum, Nürnberg/ Foto: Monika Runge: pp. 77, 165
© Foto Giusti Paolo e Claudio: p. 207
Granger Collection/Archivi Alinari: p. 95
Photo: Bart Huysmans & Michel Wuyts - Musea en Erfgoed Antwerpen: p. 186
Toni Lodigiani, Mantova: pp. 52, 53
© Lukas - Art in Flanders VZW. Stedelijke Musea Brugge: p. 151
Simone Martini, Firenze: p. 166
Tommaso Mattina, Torino: copertina, p. 247
© 2011 Image copyright The Metropolitan Museum of Art/Art Resource/Scala, Firenze: p. 41
Su concessione del MiBAC - Archivio fotografico Soprintendenza BSAE Bologna: p. 156
Su concessione del Ministero per i Beni e le Attività Culturali/Biblioteca Nazionale Centrale Firenze. Divieto di ulteriore riproduzione o duplicazione con qualsiasi mezzo: pp. 157, 160, 161, 226
Museum Boijmans Van Beuningen, Rotterdam: p. 208
Musea Brugge © Lukas - Art in Flanders vzw, Photo H Maertens: p. 150
Forlì, Musei San Domenico, Pinacoteca Civica: p. 235
Foto Musei Vaticani: pp. 17, 185
Museo Horne, Firenze: p. 86
Museo Poldi Pezzoli, Milano: p. 222
Museo Stibbert, Firenze: pp. 153, 255
© 2011 Copyright The National Gallery, London/Scala, Firenze: pp. 23, 253
Nicolò Orsi Battaglini, Firenze: p. 251
Antonio Quattrone, Firenze: pp. 34, 84-85, 89, 141, 163, 170b, 201, 202-203, 219, 224, 242, 243
Rabatti & Domingie Photography, Firenze: pp. 39b, 55, 127, 128, 129, 131, 133, 134, 139, 143, 149, 164, 169, 170a, 187, 189, 196, 197, 199, 200, 210, 211, 212, 214, 215, 216, 220, 227, 233, 238, 239, 240, 252, 259, 261
Rabatti & Domingie Photography, Firenze /su concessione del Fondo Edifici di Culto, amministrato dal Ministero dell'Interno - Dipartimento per le Libertà Civili e l'Immigrazione - Direzione Centrale per l'Amministrazione del Fondo Edifici di Culto: p. 148
Rabatti & Domingie Photography, Firenze/ su concessione del Ministero per i Beni e le Attività Culturali - Archivio di Stato di Prato: p. 171
RMN-Gérard Blot -Réunion des Musées Nationaux/ distr. Alinari: p. 18
© 2011 Foto Scala, Firenze: pp. 36, 98, 108
© 2011 Foto Scala, Firenze/BPK, Bildagentur für Kunst, Kultur und Geschichte, Berlin: p. 26
© 2011 foto Scala, Firenze/su concessione del Fondo Edifici di Culto, amministrato dal Ministero dell'Interno - Dipartimento per le Libertà Civili e l'Immigrazione - Direzione Centrale per l'Amministrazione del Fondo Edifici di Culto: p. 221
© 2011 Foto Scala, Firenze/Heritage Images: p. 60
© 2011. Foto Scala, Firenze - su concessione Ministero Beni e Attività Culturali: pp. 58, 71, 229
© 2011 Foto Scala, Firenze/ V&A Images/Victoria and Albert Museum, Londra: p. 194
Soprintendenza per i Beni Architettonici, Paesaggistici, Storico Artistici ed Etnoantropologici per le province di Lucca e Massa Carrara - Archivio Fotografico: p. 168
Soprintendenza Beni Storici Artistici ed Etnoantropologici dell'Umbria - Perugia (Italy): p. 254
Soprintendenza Speciale per il Patrimonio Storico, Artistico ed Etnoantropologico e per il Polo Museale della città di Firenze - Gabinetto Fotografico /su concessione del Fondo Edifici di Culto, amministrato dal Ministero dell'Interno - Dipartimento per le Libertà Civili e l'Immigrazione - Direzione Centrale per l'Amministrazione del Fondo Edifici di Culto: p. 155
St. Bonaventure University, The Regina A. Quick Center for the Arts: p. 249
Cortesia Marilena Tamassia: pp. 167, 241
George Tatge per Istituto degli Innocenti: pp. 76, 217
Per gentile concessione Università degli Studi di Firenze - Foto Rabatti & Domingie: p. 257
© Wallace Collection, London, UK/ The Bridgeman Art Library/Archivi Alinari: p. 102
© 2011 White Images/Scala, Firenze: p. 97

via Bolognese 165 - 50139 Florenze - Italy
via Dante 4 - 20121 Milan - Italy

www.giunti.it

First edition: September 2011

Reprint	Year
5 4 3 2 1 0	2014 2013 2012 2011

Printed by Giunti Industrie Grafiche S.p.A. - Stabilimento di Prato